Lecture Notes in Computer

T0230139

Commenced Publication in 1973
Founding and Former Series Editors:
Gerhard Goos, Juris Hartmanis, and Jan van Leeuwen

Editorial Board

Hongbin Zha   Zhigeng Pan
Hal Thwaites   Alonzo C. Addison
Maurizio Forte (Eds.)

Interactive Technologies and Sociotechnical Systems

12th International Conference, VSMM 2006
Xi'an, China, October 18-20, 2006
Proceedings

 Springer

Volume Editors

Hongbin Zha
Peking University
Beijing, 100871, China
E-mail: zha@pku.edu.cn

Zhigeng Pan
Zhejiang University
Hangzhou, 310027, China
E-mail: zgpan@cad.zju.edu.cn

Hal Thwaites
Multimedia University
Kuala Lumpur, Malaysia
E-mail: hal.thwaites@gmail.com

Alonzo C. Addison
UNESCO World Hertage Center - VHN
Berkeley, USA
E-mail: addison@socrates.Berkeley.edu

Maurizio Forte
IVHN, Italian NRC
Roma, Italy
E-mail: maurizio.forte@itabc.cnr.it

Library of Congress Control Number: 2006933641

CR Subject Classification (1998): H.5, H.4, H.3, I.2-4, J.4-5

LNCS Sublibrary: SL 3 – Information Systems and Application, incl. Internet/Web and HCI

ISSN   0302-9743
ISBN-10   3-540-46304-6 Springer Berlin Heidelberg New York
ISBN-13   978-3-540-46304-7 Springer Berlin Heidelberg New York

Springer is a part of Springer Science+Business Media

springer.com

© Springer-Verlag Berlin Heidelberg 2006

Typesetting: Camera-ready by author, data conversion by Scientific Publishing Services, Chennai, India
Printed on acid-free paper   SPIN: 11890881   06/3142   5 4 3 2 1 0

Preface

We are very pleased to have the opportunity to bring forth the proceedings of the 12th International Conference on Virtual Systems and Multimedia (VSMM), held in Xi'an, China, in October 2006. This was the first time that VSMM was sited in China. This year, the main topic of the conference was new developments and solutions for cultural heritage, healthcare, gaming, robotics and the arts, focusing on the latest advances in the interdisciplinary research among the fields.

We received over 180 submissions of papers from many countries. Finally 59 regular papers were selected for presentation at the conference and inclusion in the proceedings. In order to provide a quality conference and quality proceedings, each paper was reviewed by at least two reviewers. The international program committee and reviewers did an excellent job within a tight schedule and we are proud of the technical program we put together.

Many people contributed to the conference. We first wish to thank the Virtual Systems and Multimedia Society, who provided strong support to the whole process of the preparation of the conference. In particular, we would like to express our thanks to Takeo Ojika, Daniel Pletinckx (VSMM 2006 conference adviser) and Mario Santana Quintero for their organizational work.

We are grateful to Nanning Zheng, Yuehu Liu, and Jianru Xue from Xi'an Jiaotong University for their hard work on the local arrangements. Special thanks to Jiaxing Wang, and Ling Chen from Tsinghua University, and Xiaohong Jiang from Zhejiang University.

Last but not least, we would like to express our gratitude to all the contributors, reviewers, international program committee and organizing committee members, without whom the conference would not have been possible.

October 2006

Nanning Zheng
Conference Chair, VSMM 2006
Hongbin Zha
Program Co-chair, VSMM 2006
Zhigeng Pan
Organizing Co-chair, VSMM 2006
Hal Thwaites
President, Virtual Systems and Multimedia Society

Acknowledgements and Sponsoring Institutions

The success of the international conference on Virtual Systems and Multimedia (VSMM 2006) was assured by the financial, immaterial and pragmatic support of various institutions.

Sponsor

- Virtual Systems and Multimedia Society

Organizer

- Xi'an Jiaotong University, China
- VR Committee, China Society of Image and Graphics

Co-sponsors

- Nature Science Foundation of China
- International Journal of Virtual Reality (IJVR)
- International Journal of Automation and Computer (IJAC)
- Zhejiang University, China
- Peking University, China
- Tsinghua University, China

Committee Listings

Executive Committee

Conference Honorary Chairs:	Qinping Zhao (Beihang University, MOE, China)
	Takeo Ojika (Chubu Gakuin University, Japan)
Conference Chairs:	Nanning Zheng (Xi'an Jiaotong University, China)
	Daniel Thalmann (EPFL, Switzerland)
Program Co-chairs:	Alonzo C. Addison (UNESCO World Heritage Center - Virtual Heritage Network, USA)
	Maurizio Forte (Italian National Research Council, Italy)
	Hongbin Zha (National Lab on Machine Perception, Peking University, China)
Organizing Co-chairs:	Zhigeng Pan (Zhejiang University, China)
	Yuehu Liu (Xi'an Jiaotong University, China)
	Jiaxin Wang (Tsinghua University, China)
Conference Secretariat:	Jianru Xue (Xi'an Jiaotong University, China)
	Xiaohong Jiang (VR Committee, CSIG, China)

Program Committee

Alfredo Andia (USA)
Theodoros Arvanitis (UK)
J-Angelo Beraldin (Canada)
Mark Billinghurst (New Zealand)
Onno Boonstra (Netherlands)
Marijke Brondeel (Belgium)
Tony Brooks (Denmark)
Erik Champion (Australia)
Chu-Song Chen (China)
Ling Chen (China)
Yung-Yu Chuang (China)
Dora Constantinidis (Australia)
Jim Cremer (USA)
Sabry El-Hakim (Canada)
Mercedes Farjas (Spain)
Dieter W. Fellner (Austria)
Marco Gaiani (Italy)

Sanjay Goel (India)
Armin Gruen (Switzerland)
Susan Hazan (Israel)
Pheng Ann Heng (China)
Zhiyong Huang (Singapore)
Yunde Jia (China)
Ian Johnson (Australia)
Charalampos Karagiannidis (Greece)
Takashi Kawai (Japan)
Sarah Kenderdine (Australia)
Tomohiro Kuroda (Japan)
Yong-Moo Kwon (Korea)
José Luis Lerma Garcia (Spain)
Hua Li (China)
Nadia Magnenat-Thalmann (Switzerland)
Katerina Mania (UK)

Table of Contents

Virtual Reality and Computer Graphics

Vision and Image Technology

Geometry Processing

Collaborative Systems and GIS-Related

Digital Heritage and Healthcare

Sensing and Robotics

The Arts and Gaming

A Novel Parameter Learning Method of Virtual Garment

Chen Yujun, Wang Jiaxin, Yang Zehong, and Song Yixu

State Key Laboratory of Intelligent Technology and System,
Computer Science and Technology Department,
Tsinghua University, Beijing, China, 100084

Abstract. In this paper we present a novel parameter learning and identification method of virtual garment. We innovate in the ordinary parameter identification process and introduce the fabric data (Kawabata Evaluation System data) to combine the expert's knowledge with fuzzy system. With our method the parameters of virtual garment can be calculated automatically which are assigned by the animator's experience and hard to tune in the past years. The statistic analysis and machine learning method are used to build the fuzzy system to present the fabric expert's knowledge. With interactively inputting the human subjective variables to our method, the animator who knows little knowledge in physical attributes of fabric material can also create and tune the virtual garment application. The experimental results indicate that this method can be used in practical virtual environments and has the expansibility to other applications.

1 Introduction

Cloth simulation and virtual garment have gained researchers' public concern in the virtual reality area. One of the most essential problems in virtual garment simulation is how to effectively learn and identify the parameters of the cloth in order to make the virtual garment vivid and natural[2,3]. Because the simulations of virtual garment are difficult to tune by the reason that so many parameters need to be adjusted to achieve the look of a particular fabric. At the same time the lack of fabric knowledge also makes the problem a difficult one. Therefore, some researchers carried out some studies about parameter identification of the cloth simulation recently[2,3].

The former parameter learning methods are basically under some specific learning models, such as video of real cloth [2] or theoretic finite element method model[3]. Although these approaches have good results in specific domains, the computational expends of these methods are high and their learning data are synthetic. Moreover, few of the former method are interactive to the animators. How to use fabric experts' knowledge from real data and make the learning method suit for practical application is a great challenge to the researchers both from virtual reality field and from machine learning area.

H. Zha et al. (Eds.): VSMM 2006, LNCS 4270, pp. 1–6, 2006.

In this paper, we focus on the usage of the experts' knowledge and exert our utmost to derive a method which can be used in the practical virtual reality applications. We present a novel method which combines the fabric industry data, experts' knowledge and fuzzy system. We apply our method to the software Maya, one of the most popular virtual garment modelling and animation tool in the world. The fabric industry data adopted in this paper is Kawabata evaluation system (KES), a method wildly used in the fabric industry [1,5]. We also analysis the practical fabric data [1] and develop a fuzzy system [4] to integrate the knowledge in a more general way. Using our method, the parameter of virtual garment in virtual reality application can be identified and learned automatically by only setting some intuitive linguistic variables.

The contribution of paper is that the fuzzy system method in the machine learning area and the Kawabata evaluation system are skilfully combined together for the parameter learning of virtual garment. This novel method also provides reference for the other virtual reality application.

2   Parameter Learning of Virtual Garment System

In this part we will present the detail of our parameter learning system. First we will introduce the structure of our method. Then the details of the method will be discussed in the following parts. The framework of our parameter learning method of virtual garment is shown in figure 1.

Generally speaking, the method can be divided into 3 parts: analysis of the KES data from fabric database [1], construction of the fuzzy system and

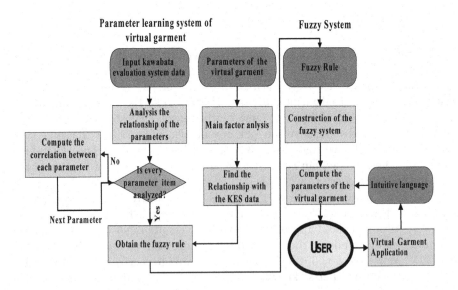

Fig. 1. Structure of parameter learning method

application to the virtual garment application such as Maya. In the following parts these three aspects will be discussed.

The input of the method is the KES data from web database, and then the data are analysis by the statistic analysis module using main factor analysis and other statistic method. After finding the relationship between the fabric data and analyze the expert knowledge of KES data. We obtain the fuzzy rules and build the fuzzy system to represent the relationship between fabric knowledge and actual animation parameters. In the application stage, the users input the subjective linguistic variables to the system and the RBF neural network computes the parameters of the 3D cloth animation and the parameters can reflect the knowledge of fabric industry.

2.1   Analysis of the KES Data

The KES data and analysis method is introduced in this section in order to get the relationship between the KES data and the virtual garment parameter using the experts' knowledge. We take advantage of the correlation analysis and linear regression to find the relation between the fabric data.

Kawabata evaluation system is a standard set of fabric measuring equipments that can measure the bending, shearing and tensile properties of cloth [5]. The equipment measures what force or moment as is required to deform a fabric sample of standard size and shape, and produces plots of force or moment as a function of measured geometric deformation. It can measure 16 parameters that reflect the deformations. First of all, we acquire the data from a fabric database in [1]. We analyze the data using statistic methods, for example, the relativity of the 185 data. The KES parameters illustrate the property of a specific cloth, including the bending property, the shearing property and the stretching property, such as B: the bending rigidity, 2HB: hysteresis of bending moment, and MIU, mean frictional coefficient. The detail of the KES data can be found in [5]. However these parameters of the KES data have some redundancy. The purpose of our analysis is to find the main factor that related to the virtual garment parameter. We use the correlation computation and linear regression analysis to get the relationship between the KES parameters for the purpose of reducing the parameters of the fuzzy system and mapping the expert's knowledge to the practical application.

The linear regression model is a very powerful math analysis tool. Suppose an equation

$$y = \beta_0 + \beta_1 x + \varepsilon \tag{1}$$

where y is the linear function of x and ε, ε is error item. The estimated regression function is $\hat{y} = \hat{\beta}0 + \hat{\beta}1x$. $\hat{y}$ is the estimation of y , $\hat{\beta}_0$ and $\hat{\beta}_1$ are the estimations of the unknown parameters. Using the least squares method, $\hat{\beta}_0$ and $\hat{\beta}_1$ can be calculated as follows:

$$\hat{\beta}_1 = \frac{n \sum_{i=1}^{n} x_i y_i - \sum_{i=1}^{n} x_i \sum_{i=1}^{n} y_i}{n \sum_{i=1}^{n} x_i^2 - (\sum_{i=1}^{n} x_i)^2} \tag{2}$$

$$\hat{\beta}_0 = \bar{y} - \hat{\beta}_1 \bar{x} \tag{3}$$

$$R^2 = \frac{\sum(\hat{y}_i - \bar{y})^2}{\sum(y_i - \bar{y})^2} = [\frac{\sum(x_i - \bar{x})(y_i - \bar{y})}{\sqrt{\sum(x_i - \bar{x})^2} \cdot \sqrt{\sum(y_i - \bar{y})^2}}]^2 \qquad (4)$$

We calculate the linear regression equation between the KES parameters and use the following coefficient of determination R^2 to determine whether the two parameters should be combined. In the equation $\bar{y}$ is the mean value of y, $\bar{x}$ is the mean value of x . If $R^2 > 0.5$ then the two parameters can be linear related and can be combined together. Therefore we can get the main factors for the modelling of the relationship between parameters.

2.2   Construction of the Fuzzy System

We construct a fuzzy system to represent the fabric expert's knowledge which is combined in the human intuitive language called style: *stiffness, smoothness and fullness*. In Kawabata evaluation system, the styles of the fabric are measured and computed by the experts. In order to build the fuzzy system, we project the fabric parameter to the virtual garment parameter by analyzing the relationship between each other, because there are some common properties in KES data, the actual cloth and the virtual garment. The experts have also obtained some experiences and formulas about the cloth measuring. The fuzzy rules are derived from the relationship between cloth simulation data and the subjective variables. The rules are based on the experts knowledge which we analyze and deduce them to the fuzzy rules. Table1 illustrates some example fuzzy rules. We build the fuzzy system based on the theory of the Zadah fuzzy logic. Fuzzy logic includes 3 steps: fuzzifier, fuzzy inference and defuzzifier. In fuzzy inference we use the Mamdani method for calculating the output and use the Gauss function as our membership function. The input of the fuzzy system is the human language by the user interface: *stiffness, smoothness and fullness* with the converted format of fuzzy variables; the output of the fuzzy system is the parameters of the virtual garment for a specific application. The detail of fuzzy system can be found in [4].

Table 1. Sample fuzzy rule of the parameter learning fuzzy system

Input Linguistic	Output Parameter	Rule
Stiffness	bend resistance	if stiffness is hard then bend resistance is high
Stiffness	cloth friction	if stiffness is hard then cloth friction is small
smoothness	cloth friction	if smoothness is hard then cloth friction is small
fullness	cloth friction	if fullness is large then cloth friction is large
fullness	density	if fullness is large then density is large

2.3   Application to the Virtual Garment

After building the fuzzy system, we can apply the fuzzy system to different virtual garment applications. The core idea of the application stage is that our framework use the user interface to identify the human language input, and then the fuzzy system will compute the output parameters. The third step is applying the virtual garment parameters to the cloth model in the related software, such as Maya. The next section will illustrate the Maya results of different inputs.

3 Experimental Results

We testify our framework by giving the human subjective language, computing the parameters of the virtual garment and applying the parameters in a simple sample virtual character. Table 2 shows the example results and Figure2 illustrates the virtual garment application result. The linguistic variables, stiffness, smoothness and fullness, are quantified to $[0\ldots1]$. 0 means it is less stiff, smooth and full, while 1 means it is more stiff, smooth and full. Two different Virtual animations effect of virtual garment with parameters learned in Table2 Example1 and Example3 are showed in Figure2. Both of the animations use the same 3D model in Maya, but they use different parameters. We can observe from the detail that with example1, the virtual garment is smoother, softer than example3, which indicates that our method has excellent ability to learn parameters of the virtual garment.

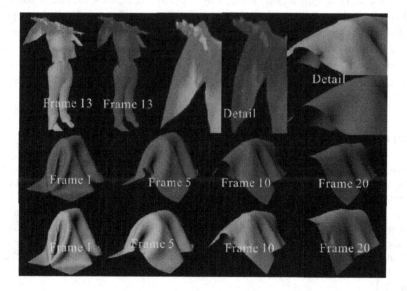

Fig. 2. Cloth simulation comparison result between exmaple1 and exmaple3. Both of the animation use the same 3D physical model in Maya, but they use different parameters derived from the framework of this paper. The graphics in the first line uses exmaple1 parameters which input variables mean the animator wants to make the cloth animation a little softer, smoother and less fullness than exmaple2 parameters in the second line.

Table 2. Sample Results of the fuzzy system parameter identification

Symbol	Input/Output	Example1	Example2	Example3	Example4
Stiffness	input	0.120	0.593	0.837	0.930
Smoothness	input	0.153	0.676	0.859	0.943
Fullness	input	0.257	0.435	0.730	0.796
BendResistance	output	33.0925	52.925	67.2777	76.2751
StrechResistance	output	79.193	116.1286	142.9821	157.8406
ShearResistance	output	77.1645	117.0618	145.2393	159.7052
Density	output	0.0049	0.0055	0.006	0.0065
Friction	output	0.4275	0.3425	0.2752	0.2355
StaticFriction	output	0.5344	0.4378	0.3601	0.3195
DynamicFriction	output	0.5013	0.3854	0.2922	0.2433

4   Conclusion and Discussion

In this paper we present a novel method of parameter learning for virtual garment, which first combines the fabric data with fuzzy system using machine learning and statistic methods. The fuzzy system represents the experts' information in virtual garment simulation which has become an urgent problem in virtual reality applications. From the experiment results we can draw some conclusions: KES data is a potential industry data set for acquiring the experts' knowledge; it is worthful to investigate the method to apply the learning method in more general way and the fuzzy system has the ability to combine the KES knowledge and identify the parameters of virtual garment. Our method can be further applied to invest more human knowledge to make the virtual garment vivid in virtual reality applications.

References

1. Ayse G.: An online fabric database to link fabric drape and end-use properties. Louisiana State University and Agricultural and Mechanical College. Master Thesis, **2004**
2. Bhat K., Twigg C., HodginssJ etc.: Estimating cloth simulation parameters from video. ACM Siggraph/ Eurographics Symposium on Computer Animation. (2003)
3. Bianchi G., Solenthaler B., Harders M.: Simultaneous topology and stiffness identification for mass-spring models based on fem reference deformations. LNCS, Int .Conf. on Medical Image Computing and Computer Assisted Intervention. (2004) 293–301
4. Sun Zeng Qi, Zhang ZaiXing, Deng ZhiDong.: Theory and Technology of Intelligent Control, Beijing. Tsinghua University Publishing Ltd. (1997) 16–24
5. Yu WeiD., Chu CaiY.: Textile Physics, Shanghai. Donghua University Publishing Ltd. (2002) 378–396

Augmented Reality as Perceptual Reality

Jung Yeon Ma and Jong Soo Choi

Graduate School of Imaging Science, Multimedia & Film, Chungang University
156-756, Heukseok-dong 221, Dongjak-gu, Seoul, Korea
dalgurimza@imagelab.cau.ac.kr, jschoi@cau.ac.kr

Abstract. As shown in Paul Milgram et al's Reality-Virtuality Continuum (1994), Augmented Reality occupies a very unique status in the spectrum of Mixed Reality. Unlike Virtual Reality, which is completely made up of the virtual and has been the most important theme for both research and practical applications, theoretical approach for Augmented Reality seems to be not keeping up with the technical development. In this paper, two qualities of Augmented Reality, which are virtuality of Augmented Reality and reality of Augmented Reality, are restated with reference to film and animation studies. In spite of the common and essential factor, computer generated images or virtual images, studies in computer vision appear to be set apart from other fields of studies. The object of this paper is to make an experimental conjunction for Augmented Reality and the concepts of Perceptual Reality, Second-order Reality, and possible world theory. It is expected to be useful particularly for studying artistic potentials and applications of Augmented Reality.

Keywords: Augmented Reality, virtuality, reality, perceptual reality, second-order reality, possible world theory.

1 Introduction

If a philosopher of 17th century, John Locke were alive in this 21st century, how would he categorize Mixed Reality with his terms of Primary qualities and Secondary qualities? He tried to differentiate something objective, mathematical and physical from something subjective and psychological. According to his theory, Primary qualities include solidity, shape, movement or numbers and Secondary qualities include color, sound or taste. Mixed Reality, however, is not so easy to be defined in this way. Especially, among the subdivisions of Mixed Reality, Augmented Reality seems to be the hardest and most complicated concept to be defined. Although Paul Milgram, Haruo Takemura, Akira Utsumi and Fumio Kishino (1994) are definitely credited for the groundbreaking article that has been the milestone of taxonomy of Augmented Reality, the concept of Augmented Reality has hardly been interpreted enough with reference to other academic fields. This fact might restrict artistic potential of Augmented Reality and impede the progress in artistic applications of Augmented Reality. In their Reality-Virtuality Continuum, they place Augmented Reality between real environment and virtual environment, closer to the former. Hence, the Reality of Augmented Reality should be a primary quality and the Virtuality of Augmented Reality should be secondary one. In this paper, these two

H. Zha et al. (Eds.): VSMM 2006, LNCS 4270, pp. 7 – 10, 2006.

qualities of Augmented Reality is restated in terms of Perceptual Reality or Second-order Reality, the two similar terms also called as the 4th reality in the film and animation studies.

2 The Virtuality of Augmented Reality

The concept of Virtual Reality has been coined around mid 1970s, with Myron Krueger's concept of "artificial reality" and "videoplace." Later, the name of Virtual Reality has come to the world by Jaron Lanier in 1989. Michael Heim even used the term "Virtual Realism." Now, it goes without saying that Virtual Reality is an essential part of real life. Lev Manovich pointed out that virtuality has been discussed excessively and now it cannot indicate any specific thing.

Nevertheless, as MS Word system cannot recognize the word virtuality as a grammatically correct word, the meaning of virtuality has not been clearly established in dictionaries. HapperCollins Dictionary explains the word virtual as a word indicates "something is so nearly true that for most purposes it can be regarded as true" or "objects and activities generated by a computer to simulate real objects and activities." In the Far Eastern culture, such as Korea and Japan, Virtuality is translated into a combination of two Chinese Characters of "false" and "idea." However, is Virtual Reality nearly true or false?

Regarding Augmented Reality, it mainly consists of real world and supplemented by virtual factors generated by computer. And it is displayed through either monitor based way or optical see-through way. More importantly, all of the process should be real-time, unlike complete virtual environment processed and created beforehand. Augmented Reality is not only what we are looking at but also what is really happening here and now. Can it be false? Or is it better to say nearly true?

Jacques Derrida[1] mentioned that the Greek word "skepteon", a noun form of a verb which means "to look" in English. The word "skepsis" of which meaning was visual perception, observation and so on changed into "skepticism" of English. Indeed, now is the time when people cannot but be skeptic or may well be skeptic what they are looking at. To see is no longer to believe. According to Derrida's comment, to see might not always have been to believe even long time ago. Moreover, to see does not necessarily mean to believe. It is not important whether we believe it or not. It is because we are already going further into the world of virtuality, or as Richard Allen[2] calls, "sensory deception." Augmented Reality "augments" this kind of complicated questions, or skepticism.

3 The Reality of Augmented Reality

Gottfried Wilhelm von Leibniz is credited for the possible world theory, which bloomed from 1960's by S. Kripke and others. It is about "counterfactuals." It

---

[1] Jacques Derrida, Memories of the Blind; The self-portrait and Other Ruins, History of European Ideas Vol.21, No.4, 618, 1995.

[2] Richard Allen, Projecting Illusion; Film Spectatorship and the Impression of Reality. Cambridge University Press, 1995.

suggests that there is a plentitude of other possible worlds along with the actual world. Warren Buckland notes this theory to explain why Spielberg's dinosaurs catch our eyes and suggests that they are attractive for existing between "science fact" and "science fiction." It is also true in case of *The Host*, a Korean film introduced at Cannes Film Festival in 2006. It attracts spectators with its hypothesis that there might be a genetically mutated creature by pollution in Han River.[3] It is cutting-edge computer graphic technology which makes all these things possible. And the technology can be used for creating Augmented Reality which undermines the distinction between the actual and the possible in real-time.

According to Andre Bazin, in order to be seen realistic just like films and animations, computer generated images need to be ontologically realistic, dramatically realistic and psychologically realistic. Suppose the virtual factors appear to have equal weight and density, are seamlessly blended into, interact with the real environment and seem to occupy the same space with the user, then it is possible to obtain the 4th realism, Stephen Heath's "impression of reality[4]," just like the dinosaurs of *Jurassic Park* do. This mechanism of experience can be applied to explain both spectators' immersion into film and users' immersion into Augmented Reality.

Andrew Darley evokes Super-realism paintings or Radical realism paintings to discuss his "Second-order Reality" in animation. As he comments, Super-realism paintings and animations create images the same with the real but each has different intentions. The former shows perfect mimesis itself is not possible and rather criticizes the photorealistic imitations of the real. On the other hand, the latter intends to simulate images in the most realistic way through computer graphic technologies. However, computer generated or virtual images do not have specific models in the real world. Unlike photography, they are not the proof of existence. Although they look photorealistic, they are not indexical but completely iconic. This is what Darley named Second-order Reality. Stephen Prince suggests that realism is no longer a problem of reference, not it is the problem of perception. As numerous images in films, virtual images are unreal but also perceptually real. These are harmonious with spectators' visual-audio experiences because they are made to be so. This intention is what film makers and computer engineers who create Augmented Reality have in common. However, their works to generate virtual images and coin them into real images have rarely been understood as similar processes. It is needed to approach from a different angle to discuss realism in computer generated images. These views are not rare in the field of film and animation studies but seem to be set apart from studies of Augmented Reality despite their common factor, computer generated images. In addition to the field of film and animation and that of computer vision, artistic experiments will be most benefited by interdisciplinary approaches.

"The owl of Minerva spreads its wings only with the falling of the dusk," G.W.F. Hegel noted. In this century, the owl might flap its wings at dawn fooled by a perceptually realistic scene. Philosophers, along with artists and scientists, seem to expect better what will be coming up next and what they have to do. It is because the world changes a lot faster than before and they can witness later what they have expected, in many cases.

---

[3] Kevin Rafferty of the Orphanage, the visual effect team of *Jurassic Park, Man in Black2, Starwars Episode1*, has supervised the visual effect team of *The Host*.
[4] Stephen Heath, Questions of Cinema. Macmillan, London, 1981.

4 Conclusion

In this paper, two qualities of Augmented Reality, which are Virtuality of Augmented Reality and Reality of Augmented Reality, are restated with reference to film and animation studies. In spite of the common and essential factor, computer generated images or virtual images, studies in computer vision seem to be set apart from other fields of studies. We suggest that Augmented Reality shares impression of reality as well as other realistic qualities of films, because computer generated images are made to be perceptually realistic. They are purely created and do not have any reference in the real world, which presents them Second-order Reality. Augmented Reality and the concepts of Perceptual Reality, Second-order Reality and possible world theory are connected in this paper. The object of this study is to be useful particularly for exploring artistic potential and applications of Augmented Reality.

References

1. Bazin,A, What is Camera? Vol.1, ISBN: 0510000927, University of California Press, Berkeley, CA, (1968)
2. Buckland, W, Between Science Fact and Science Fiction: Spielberg's digital dinosaurs, possible worlds, and the new aesthetic realism, Screen 40:2 summer, (1999)
3. Darley, A, Second-order Realism and Post-modernist Aesthetics in Computer Animation, A Reader in Animation Studies, Chapter 3, (1993)
4. Heim, M, The Metaphysics of Virtual Reality, ISBN: 89-7013-099-3 03110. Oxford University Press Inc, New York, (1993)
5. Milgram, P, Takemura, H, Utsumi, A, Kishino, F, Augmented Reality: A class displays on the reality-virtuality continuum, SPIE Vol.2351, Telemanipulator and Telepresence Technologies, (1994)
6. Prince, S, True Lies: Perceptual realism, digital images and film theory, Film Quarterly, Vol.49, No.3, (1996)

A Multimodal Reference Resolution Approach in Virtual Environment*

Xiaowu Chen and Nan Xu

The Key Laboratory of Virtual Reality Technology, Ministry of Education, China
School of Computer Science and Engineering, Beihang University
Beijing 100083, P.R. China
chen@buaa.edu.cn

Abstract. This paper presents a multimodal reference resolution approach in virtual environment, which is called RRVE. Based on the relationship between cognitive status and reference, RRVE divides the objects into four status hierarchies including pointing, in focus, activated, extinct, and step by step it processes multimodal reference resolution according to current status hierarchy. Also it defines a match function to compute the match probability of referring expression and potential referent, and describes the semantic signification and temporal constraints. Finally, sense shape is used to deal with the pointing ambiguity, which helps the user to interact precisely in immersive virtual environment.

1 Introduction

Multimodal interface provides natural and harmonious human computer interaction through multiple modalities such as speech, gesture and gaze. A key problem in understanding user multimodal inputs is known as reference resolution, which is to identify entities that users refer to in their multimodal inputs. Multimodal language differs linguistically from unimodal language [1]. In fact, it has been demonstrated that multimodal language is briefer, syntactically simpler, and less disfluent than users' unimodal speech [2]. For example, in a scene of QuickSet [3], a user added a boat dock to a map application system by speaking "Place a boat dock on the east, no, west end of Reward Lake." However, when interacting multimodally the user could speak "Add dock'" with a circle by pen. So reference in multimodal interaction has special features which are different from that in natural language.

Three important issues should be considered in multimodal reference resolution: mutual disambiguation, inferring unspecified information and multimodal alignment [4]. There are two kinds of ambiguities in multimodal interaction which is semantic ambiguity and pointing ambiguity. In this paper we will mainly discuss the resolution of

---

* This paper is support by National Natural Science Foundation of China (60503066), Advancing Research Foundation (51*0305*05), Program for New Century Excellent Talents in University, Virtual Environment Aided Design and Manufacture Project (VEADAM), National 863 Program of China, China Next Generation Internet (CNGI) Project (CNGI-04-15-7A), MOE Program for New Century Excellent Talents in University and Beijing Program for New Stars in Research (2004A11).

H. Zha et al. (Eds.): VSMM 2006, LNCS 4270, pp. 11–20, 2006.

pointing ambiguity. Compared to unimodal interaction using mouse, the selection of object is ambiguous in multimodal interaction using natural gesture. Generally, there is more than one object in the pointing region.

Users intend to only provide new information when it is their turn to interact. So there are a lot of phenomena of anaphora in natural language. However, unlike linguistic anaphoric inference in which antecedents for pronouns are selected from a linguistic context, in multimodal interaction, the antecedents are selected from more sources because sometimes integrating individual modalities together still can not provide overall understanding of users' intention. For example, in Fig.1, referring expression "it" does not give enough information on what the user exactly wants. It needs other context such as conversation history to infer unspecified information.

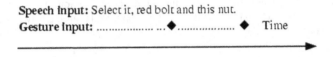

Fig. 1. System architecture of VECA

Figure 1 shows an example of complex multimodal input that involves multiple referring expressions and multiple gestures. In this case, the number of referring expression is not equal to the number of gesture. In order to align multimodal input, the time interval and the order of occurrence should be considered.

This paper introduces a multimodal reference resolution approach in virtual environment which is called RRVE. Based on the relationship between cognitive status and reference, RRVE divides the objects in virtual environment into four status hierarchies which are pointing, in focus, activated and extinct. Then it processes multimodal reference resolution according to the status hierarchy and defines a match function to compute the match probability of referring expression and potential referent. The match function considers semantic and temporal constraints, and a method of SenseShape [5] is used to resolve pointing ambiguity. The remainder of the paper is structured as follows. Section 2 surveys related work in multimodal reference resolution. Section 3 introduces RRVE in detail. Then section 4 briefly describes the implementation of RRVE in VECA [6] which is a virtual environment for collaborative assembly. Section 5 evaluates the effect of RRVE. Finally, section 6 summarizes the paper and suggests future work.

2   Related Work

Multimodal interface which integrates speech and gesture can date back to Bolt's "Put That There" system [7]. It involves many important problems in multimodal domain such as integration strategy and reference resolution. "Put That There" and later "ICONIC" [8] just choose the gesture nearest the relevant word. Now considerable work has been done on studying multimodal reference resolution in 2D or 3D non-immersive environment [9,10,11]. To resolve multimodal reference in 3D immersive environment,

Thies Pfeiffer et al. design a reference resolution engine called RRE [12,13]. In this system, by using fuzzy techniques couples with hierarchical structuring, the interplay of different constraints (temporal and semantic) is modeled down to a very fine-grained level. Alex Olwal et al. present a method of SenseShapes [14] to facilitate selection of objects in virtual or augmented reality environment. SenseShapes are volumetric regions of interest that can be attached to parts of the user's body to provide valuable statistical information about the user's interaction with objects.

Linguistic and cognitive studies indicate that user referring behavior does not occur randomly, but rather follows certain linguistic and cognitive principles. Gundel's Giveness Hierarchy theory [15] explains different referring expressions signal different information about memory and attention state (i.e. cognitive status). As in Fig.2, there are six cognitive statuses corresponding to different kinds of referring expressions. And Gundel et al. explains this division by using Grice's Conversation Implicature theory [16].

Fig. 2. Giveness Hierarchy

However, these theories lack formal, independent conditions for determining the status of a object in a particular conversation circumstance, as well as a way to distinguish between several possible objects that hold the same cognitive status [16]. Kehler [17] codes the cognitive status of the objects as follows: "in focus" which corresponds to selected entities indicated by highlighting, "activated" which corresponds to unselected but visible entities.

3 PRVE

This section introduces RRVE in detail, which includes algorithm description, construction of match function and SenseShape. In the last, a comparison between RRVE and greedy algorithm is presented.

3.1 Algorithm

RRVE has status hierarchy as follows: "gesture" means the entities which are in the pointing domain; "in focus" means the entities which are selected and indicated by highlighting; "activated" means the entities which are visible but unselected; "extinct" means the entities which are not visible and unselected. Based on the Grice's Maxim of Quantity, which can be paraphrased as "Make your contribution as informative as required, but not more so", since user's active gesture input takes a special effort to deliver, the gesture should take priority of context information such as cognitive status. So the priority of the status hierarchy is gesture > in focus > activated > extinct.

The pseudo code of the algorithm is shown as follows. RRVE resolves the referring expressions according to the status hierarchy of the objects in virtual environment:

```
//Get constraints from speech
GetSpeechConstraints();
//Compute Prank by SenseShape
ComputePrank();
//Process the match between referring expressions and pointing objects
ComputePrank();
MatchPointing();
if ( all referring expressions are resolved ) then exit;
else
        //Process the match between referring expressions and objects in focus
        MatchFocus();
if ( all referring expressions are resolved ) then exit;
else
        //Process the match between referring expressions and activated objects
        MatchActivated();
if ( all referring expressions are resolved ) then exit;
else
        //Process the match between referring expressions and activated objects
        MatchExtinct();
```

The relationship of status hierarchy and reference resolution in RRVE can be described by Fig.3. The match between referring expressions and potential referents is processed clockwise. It means that, for each referring expression, unless all entities with the status pointing are not compatible with it, then the match between the entities with lower status hierarchy and the referring expression can be processed later.

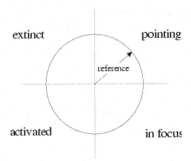

Fig. 3. Status hierarchy and reference resolution

In each match procedure (MatchPointing, MatchFocus, etc.), there is a match matrix in which the row represents referring expression vector r and the column represents object vector o with same status. The value of matrix element is the matching score between a referring expression and an object. The calculation of the matching score will be introduced in the next section. RRVE scans match matrix by row, and then finds the highest matching score in each row. Supposing the highest matching score is element $matrix(i, j)$, RRVE assigns to object o_i to referring expression r_j as referent. Space precludes a detailed introduction of the match procedure which has been described in [18].

3.2   Match Function

RVE uses the following match function which is improved on [18] to calculate the matching score between an object (o) and a referring expression (e).

$$Match(o, e) = \left[\sum_{S \in \{P,F,A,E\}} P(o|S) * P(S|e) \right] * Semantic(o, e) * Temp(o, e)$$

In this formula, S represents the status of an object. It could have four potential values: P (pointing), F (in focus), A (activated) and E (extinct). There are four components in the match function:

- $P(o|S)$ measures the probability of an object to be the referent given a status S. $P(o|S = pointing) = Prank$, which is determined by SenseShape; $P(o|S = infocus) = 1/N$, where N is the total number of objects having the status of in focus; $P(o|S = activated)$ and $P(o|S = extinct)$ have similar definition of $P(o|S = infocus)$.
- The definition of $P(S|e)$ is the same as that in [18]. It measures the likelihood of the status of the potential referent given a particular type of referring expression. Table.1 shows the estimated $P(S|e)$ which is provided by the OZ experiment of Kehler. The referring expressions are divided into six categories. Among them, "full" means full noun phrase such as a proper name. And when the object has the status of extinct, $P(S|e)$ is assigned to 1.

Table 1. Likelihood of status of referents given a type of expression [18]

$P(S|e)$	Empty	Pronoun	Locative	Demonstrative	Definite	Full
Activated	0	0	0	0	0.26	0.37
In focus	0.56	0.85	0.57	0.33	0.07	0.47
Pointing	0.44	0.15	0.43	0.67	0.67	0.16

- $Semantic(o, e)$ measures the semantic compatibility between an object and a referring expression. It is defined as follows:

$$Semantic(o, e) = \sum_k \frac{Attr_k(o, e)}{M}$$

$Attr_k(o, e) = 0$ if both o and e have feature k (e.g. color or type) and the values of the feature k are not equal. Otherwise, $Attr_k(o, e) = 1$. M is the number of the object's features. For example, when a user says "select the red bolt", and a bolt has feature set {color="red", type="bolt", size="small", name="M4-1"}, $Semantic(o, e) = 1 * 2/4 = 0.5$.
- $Temp(o, e)$ measures the temporal compatibility between o and e. For the pointing objects, $Temp(o, e)$ is defined by following segmented function:

When gesture and referring expression occur in one interaction segment:

$$Temp(o, e) = \exp\left(-\left|Time(o) - Time(e)\right|\right)$$

When gesture and referring expression occur in different interaction segments:

$$Temp(o, e) = \exp\left(-\left|OrderIndex(o) - OrderIndex(e)\right|\right)$$

Here the "interaction segment" lies on multimodal integration strategy in RRVE. For example, in Fig.4, a complete selection task is divided into two interaction segments.

Speech input: Select the bolt...l.....and that nut.
Gesture input: ....l..... ◆.......... ◆   Time

Fig. 4. A task, two interaction segments

RVE uses the segmented function to align multimodal input. Usually the referring expression and corresponding gesture have relativity in time, so the interval is an important factor. But if the gesture and the referring expression occur in different interaction segments, the order when the referring expression and the accompanied gesture occur is more suitable than the interval. As the objects in other status, $Temp(o, e) = 1$.

3.3   SenseShape

Virtual reality technology is aimed to help users to get vivid sense of presence as if they are in physical world [18]. Usually, in natural interaction, the gesture is ambiguous and there is more than one object in the pointing region. Due to the limitation of location tracking precision, it is difficult for the user to interact precisely in immersive virtual environment. So RRVE simulates the pointing ambiguity and reduces its influence by SenseShape.

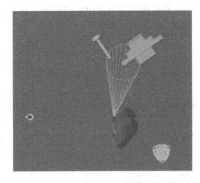

Fig. 5. SenseShape of RRVE

In RRVE, SenseShape is a cone which is attached to index fingertip of virtual hand (Fig.5). It provides valuable statistical rankings about pointing objects through collision detection. Now RRVE provides two types of rankings: time and distance. The time ranking (Trank) of an object is derived from the fraction of time the object spends in the cone over a specified time period: the more time the object is in the cone, the higher the ranking. The distance ranking (Drank) is the fraction of the object's distance from the cone's origin (index fingertip) over the most distance. The closer the object is to the index fingertip, the higher the ranking. The Prank is weighted average of these statistical rankings:

$$P_{rank} = T_{rank} * \lambda + D_{rank} * (1 - \lambda), \quad 0 \leq \lambda \leq 1$$

3.4 Comparison

Compared to Joyce's greedy algorithm, RRVE has following characters:

- RRVE uses SenseShape to reduce pointing ambiguity in virtual environment. Greedy algorithm is applied to an 2D application based speech and pen. This method is not suitable for virtual environment based speech and 3D gesture. SenseShape simulates ambiguity of 3D gesture and reduces its influence via statistical rankings in time and space.
- RRVE considers the influence of speech recognition error. Recognition error is inevitable in current situation. Greedy algorithm measures the semantic compatibility by "multiplication".
- RRVE aligns multimodal input by combining the interval and the order. Greedy algorithm only uses the order to assist multimodal alignment. Compared to combination of speech and pen, speech and 3D gesture have more relativity in time.

4 Implementation

VECA is a collaborative virtual assembly system which allows geographical dispersed engineers to perform an assembly task together. It builds multimodal interface which supports interaction by microphone and CyberGlove. VECA adopts a task-oriented and hierarchical multimodal integration model [19]. In this model, each task slot is composed of three components: action, object and parameters. As shown in Fig.6, RRVE,

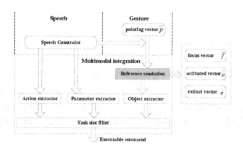

Fig. 6. Reference resolution and multimodal integration

as a multimodal reference resolution approach, is used for object extraction. It gets the referents to fill object slot by accessing speech constraints and status vectors. When the task slot is fulfilled, a command is sent to the module of command execution.

5 Evaluation

We conduct an experiment to evaluate RRVE and greedy algorithm. Twenty users are required to accomplish five tasks twice, one uses RRVE to resolve reference, another uses greedy algorithm. Here SenseShape is used to compute the selection probability $P(o|S)$ in greedy algorithm instead of the ratio of area.

Table 2. Performance comparison

	Total		Recognition error	
	Number of interactions	Number of successful resolutions / success ratio	Number of interactions	Number of successful resolutions / success ratio
Greedy	162	111/67%	33	7/21%
RRVE	146	107/73%	32	14/44%

Table.2 shows the performance comparison between RRVE and greedy algorithm. Greedy algorithm achieves 67% accuracy, and RRVE achieves 73% accuracy. Especially in situation of recognition error, RRVE has better performance. It is because RRVE reduces the influence of speech recognition error.

Table 3. Cognition charge comparison

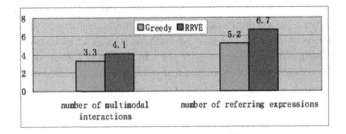

We use number of multimodal interactions and referring expressions per human to measure the cognition charge. Here, "referring expression" means non full name reference. The more a user uses multimodal interactions or referring expressions, the fewer cognition charges. Table.3 shows that, compared to greedy algorithm, RRVE relieves users' cognition charge.

Experiment results show that RRVE has more efficiency than greedy algorithm in virtual environment.

6 Conclusion

The paper introduces a multimodal reference resolution approach in virtual environment which is called RRVE. Based on the relationship between cognitive status and reference, RRVE divides the objects in virtual environment into four status hierarchies which are pointing, in focus, activated and extinct. Then it processes multimodal reference resolution according to the status hierarchy and defines a match function to compute the match probability of referring expression and potential referent. The match function utilizes semantic and temporal constraints, and a method of SenseShape is used to resolve pointing ambiguities. Experiment results show that, compared to greedy algorithm which has approved efficiency in 2D map application, RRVE is more suitable for virtual environment The match function is an experiential formula, and future work will farther explore the influence degree of different factors. In fact, weights of these components differ from each other as following formula shows. It needs to combine more linguistic, cognitive even ergonomic knowledge.

$$Match(o, e) = \left[\alpha \sum_{S \in \{P, F, A, E\}} P(o|S)P(S|e) \right] \left[\beta Semantic(o, e) \right] \left[\delta Temp(o, e) \right]$$

RRVE can deal with egocentric reference which is based the user's view. However, because VECA is collaborative virtual environment, RRVE should have ability to process intrinsic or extrinsic [12] reference which is based on certain object features or a partner's view.

References

1. Oviatt, S.: Ten myths of multimodal interaction. Ten Myths of Multimodal Interaction **42**(11) (1999) 74–81
2. Oviatt, S.: Multimodal interactive maps: Designing for human performance. Human-Computer Interaction **12** (1997) 93–129
3. Cohen, P.R., Johnston, M., McGee, D., Oviatt, S.L., Pittman, J., I.Smith, Chen, L., Clow, J.: Quickset: Multimodal interaction for distributed applications. In: 5th ACM Int. Multimedia Conf. (1997) 31–40
4. Chai, J.: Semantics-based representation for multimodal interpretation in conversational systems(coling-2002). In: The 19th International Conference on Computational Linguistics. (2002) 141–147
5. Olwal, A., Benko, H., Feiner, S.: Senseshapes: Using statistical geometry for object selection in a multimodal augmented reality. In: The Second IEEE and ACM International Symposium on Mixed and Augmented Reality. (2003) 300–301
6. Chen, X., Xu, N., Li, Y.: A virtual environment for collaborative assembly. In: Second International Conference on Embedded Software and Systems (ICESS'2005), Xi'an, China, IEEE CS Press (2005) 414–421
7. Bolt, R.A.: "put-that-there": Voice and gesture at the graphics interface. Computer Graphics **14**(3) (1980) 262–270
8. Koons, D.B., Sparrell, C.J., Thorisson, K.R. In: Integrating simultaneous input from speech, gaze, and hand gestures. American Association for Artificial Intelligence (1993) 257–276

 9. Pineda, L., Garza, G.: A model for multimodal reference resolution. Computational Linguistics **26**(2) (2000) 139–193
10. M., J., S., B.: Finite-state multimodal parsing and understanding. In: Proceedings of the 18th conference on Computational linguistics, Baldonado (2000) 369–375
11. Chai, J.Y., Hong, P., Zhou, M.X.: A probabilistic approach to reference resolution in multimodal user interfaces. In: Proceedings of the 2004 International Conference on Intelligent User Interfaces (IUI-2004), Madeira, Portugal, ACM (2004) 70–77
12. Pfeiffer, T., Latoschik, M.E.: Resolving object references in multimodal dialogues for immersive virtual environments. In: Proceedings of the IEEE Virtual Reality 2004 (VR'04), Chicago, USA (2004) 35–42
13. Latoschik, M.E.: A user interface framework for multimodal vr interactions. In: Proceedings of the 7th international conference on Multimodal interfaces (ICMI'05), Trento, Italy (2005) 76–83
14. Kaiser, E., Olwal, A., McGee, D., Benko, H., Corradini, A., Li, X., Cohen, P., Feiner, S.: Mutual disambiguation of 3d multimodal interaction in augmented and virtual reality. In: Proceedings of the 5th international conference on Multimodal interfaces (ICMI03). (2003) 12–19
15. Gundel, J.K., Hedberg, N., Zacharski, R.: Cognitive status and the form of referring expressions in discourse. Language, **69**(2) (1993) 274–307
16. P, G.H. In: Logic and conversation. Academic Press, New York (1975) 41–58
17. Kehler, A.: Cognitive status and form of reference in multimodal human-computer interaction. In: Proceedings of the Seventeenth National Conference on Artificial Intelligence and Twelfth Conference on Innovative Applications of Artificial Intelligence. (2000) 685–690
18. Chai, J.Y., Prasov, Z., Blaim, J., Jin, R.: Linguistic theories in efficient multimodal reference resolution: an empirical investigation. In: Proceedings of the 10th international conference on Intelligent user interfaces, California, USA (2005) 43–50
19. Pu, J., Dong, S.: A task-oriented and hierarchical multimodal integration model a task-oriented and hierarchical multimodal integration model and its corresponding algorithm. Journal of Computer Research and Development (in Chinese) **38**(8) (2001) 966–971
20. Chai, J.Y., Prasov, Z., Blaim, J., Jin, R.: The reality of virtual reality. In: The Reality of Virtual Reality. Proceedings of Seventh International Conference on Virtual Systems and Multimedia (VSMM01). (2001) 43–50

SC: Prototypes for Interactive Architecture

Henriette Bier[1], Kathleen de Bodt[2], and Jerry Galle[3]

[1] Delft University of Technology, Berlageweg 1, 2628 CR, Delft, The Netherlands
[2] Institute of Architectural Sciences, Mutsaardstraat 31, 2000, Antwerp, Belgium
[3] Royal Academy of Fine Arts, Academiestraat 2, 9000 Ghent, Belgium

Abstract. This paper describes an ongoing research, SpaceCustomiser
: InterActive, [SC : IA] which deals with development of digital design strategies based on non-Euclidean geometries, whereas the body
in movement generates interactively architectural SPACE. The input –
movement – is being electronically processed in such a way that the output represents a continuous, real-time modification of the space. For this
purpose an on-site-built InterFace employing sensor/actuator technology
enables translation of the recorded movement into spatial configurations.
The InterAction between the body and the architectural space gives insight into, how the human body shapes space.

1 Background

At the time being large scale architectural projects incorporate interactive systems focusing on light. Kunsthaus in Graz, for instance, has a light installation
incorporating a matrix of fluorescent lamps integrated into the acrylic glass faade
enabling display of movies and animations.

However, small scale installations seem to target more complex configurations
such as dynamic, interactive systems. R. Glynn's project Reciprocal Space, for
instance, is a room where the walls change shape in response to inhabitant's
movements.

Fig. 1. Reciprocal Space by R. Glynn

Similarly, J. Poenisch's Dynamic Terrain is an interactive surface, which
changes shape in correspondence to spatial and/or bodily requirements in real
time. Other projects such as Decoi's Aegis Hyposurface work with triangulated

H. Zha et al. (Eds.): VSMM 2006, LNCS 4270, pp. 21–28, 2006.

surfaces in a similar way. However, Hyperbody Research Group's MuscleTower adds the third dimension to the movement allowing rotation and torsion of the structure.

All these projects work with input, processing and output tools, such as sensors, camera tracking systems, projectors, speakers, and software such as Macromedia Shockwave, Max/MSP, Virtools. SpaceCustomiser : InterActive uses Max/MSP, camera tracking, and projection to study and implement double-curved space generation by following the movement of the body in space.

Fig. 2. SC: Projection and interactive set-up

In opposition to the horizontal and vertical surfaces employed in the previously mentioned examples, SpaceCustomiser : InterActive employs a three dimensional double-curved cylindrical space surrounding the body in movement.

2   Implementation

The interactive processes in the SpaceCustomiser : InterActive project are controlled with software developed by K. de Bodt and J. Galle in Max/MSP, which is a graphical programming environment to create software using a visual toolkit of objects. The basic environment that includes MIDI, control, user interface, and timing objects is called Max. On top of Max are built object sets such as: MSP, which is a set of audio processing objects that enable interactive filter design, hard disk recording, and Jitter, a set of matrix data processing objects optimised for video and 3D graphics.

The interactive environment has been developed for transcribing the movement of the body into 3D-space based on SpaceCustomiser [1], which has been developed by H. Bier in 2005: SpaceCustomiser and can be seen as the Modulor [2] of the Digital Age, since it establishes relationships between the human body and the architectural space. As a system of proportions Modulor uses measures of the human body in architecture by partitioning it in modules according to the golden section and two Fibonacci Series. It puts, basically, man as measure of architectural spaces, which SpaceCustomiser does as well in a more drastic manner, since it generates 3D space by following the movement of the body in space based on ergonomic principles.

Fig. 3. Deformation of the ellipsoidal cylinder

While Modulor applies a 2D proportioning system, SpaceCustomiser employs a 3D, dynamic, space-generating system. If in this context can be talked about a paradigm shift based on the influence of digital technologies, than this shift can be described in the methodology: In opposition to modular, repetitive architecture developed by using grids and proportions based on functional and formal rules, curvilinear architecture is being developed by generating space through following the movement of the body in space.

The initial space is an ellipsoidal cylinder, which represents the minimum space a standing person needs. This space has been divided in five segments, while the ellipse itself in divided in eight sectors. Each of the eight sectors is being activated, when movement in this area is detected. This means the movement of the arm to left/up triggers a deformation in the corresponding sector. The movement is being tracked by using a colour/movement tracking technique, which involves several steps: A camera captures the movements, while specific data is being extracted from the image sequence, for instance, an arm is tracked, while moving in space. This movement activates the spatial deformation in a direct way: A movement induces a proportional deformation of space. The space enlarges to accommodate the body in movement.

Geometrically speaking, the movement tracking is based on the conversion of the Cartesian coordinates of the tracked point into polar coordinates, while the deformation principle is based on NURBS, which is a mathematical model for generating and representing curves and surfaces. Editing NURBS-based curves

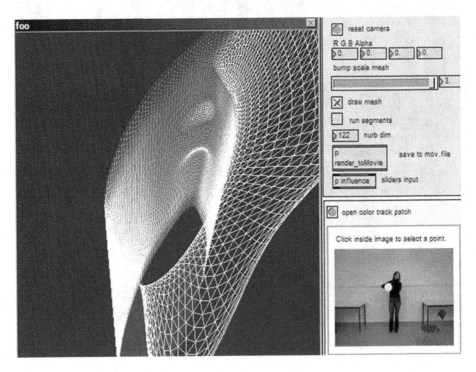

Fig. 4. SpaceCustomiser: InterFace

and surfaces is easy: Control points are connected to the curves and/or surfaces in a way that their pulling or pushing induces a proportional deformation. While it is easy to manipulate NURBS surfaces by puling control points, the question is how to control this manipulation, which rules and design methodologies can be developed to control designs based on NURBS geometries? SpaceCustomiser proposes a NURBS-manipulation based on the movement of the body through space.

The interactive manipulation of space is monitored on two interfaces: One of them is projected on a wall the other one is shown on the computer display. While the projected interface serves as a representation and monitoring device, the interface on the computer screen enables generation and control of spatial deformation. A series of parameters such as mesh resolution, colour, and NURBS dimension can be defined on the computer screen interface.

The computer screen interface has a display window for rendering, one main and several sub-patches, which contain programming packages. The user works mainly on the main patch. By starting the program, the processing of data, which is fed into the system, is initiated, while the NURBS surface is being rendered in the display window.

Interface elements on the main patch are: 1. On/off switch: This is a toggle that sends a trigger signal every 20 milliseconds; 2. RGB alpha: Controls the colour of the NURBS surface. 3. Bump scale mesh: Slider to control the relative amount of the deformation. The input can be chosen for a smaller or larger deformation effect. The default is 1, which represents no scaling, while scaling corresponds to input bigger or smaller then 1; 4. Draw mesh: Switches between shaded and wire mesh rendering; 5. NURB Dim: Slider to reset manually the NURBS mesh density from 0 to 100 or more. The default surface density is set to 48 and the surface order to 3; 6. Video window: 320 x 240 display for the camera image.

3   Programming

Max/MSP is a graphical programming environment for music, audio and multi-media, used to design cross-platform programs and user interfaces. Programming takes place in the Patcher window, where Max/MSP Objects, represented as boxes, are connected with patch cords. The program library includes several Objects to perform a wide range of tasks, from adding two numbers together to waveform editing, etc.

SpaceCustomiser : InterActive consists of three patches: 3.1 3D Shape, 3.2 Deformation, and 3.3 Movement Tracking.

3.1   3D Shape

This patch implements 3D modelling in OpenGL. It is, basically, a rendering patch, enabling NURBS representation in real-time.

The 3D shape itself has been developed by following a more steps procedure: The jit.gl.nurbs object has been used to generate the cylindrical shape, from which the ellipsoidal cylinder has been derived by scaling it down to 1/3 in the y-direction. An 8 x 5 jit.matrix has been mapped onto the control points of the

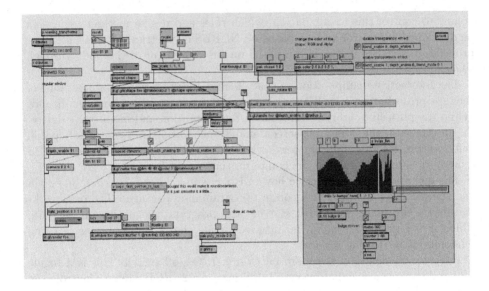

Fig. 5. Programming: 3D Shape & Deformation

NURBS surface, in a way that the cylinder is divided in five sections and each section is subdivided into eight sectors. This enables an accurate implementation of shape deformation according to the movement, since every subdivision can be addressed separately. How?

3.2   Deformation

An initial displacement matrix establishes the way the movement is translated into shape deformation: The sections 1-8 of the ellipse are mapped into the displacement matrix in a way that a row represents the eight sections of the ellipse, while the degree of displacement of each section is shown in the corresponding min-max columns. For instance, the initial ellipse – I – is represented in the displacement matrix as corresponding to a middle value [4], while the deformed ellipse – II – is shown as an alternation between middle and maximum values of displacement.

The displacement matrix establishes, therefore, how the movement of the body is being translated into spatial deformation, while the deformation of the ellipsoidal cylinder is implemented by movement/colour tracking.

3.3   Colour Tracking

The movement tracking in real-time has been implemented by means of computer vision, which employs colour tracking performed with cv.jit.track, which is an external object for Max. It extracts x, y coordinates from the movement and sends them to the Deformation patch, which in turn executes the shape deformation itself.

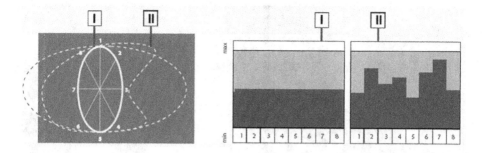

Fig. 6. Diagram of the displacement matrix

The colour to be tracked is being selected by clicking with the mouse in the video frame window, which shows the real-time movements captured with the camera connected to it. The Cartesian coordinates of the tracked colour/point are then converted into polar coordinates, which find their correspondence in the eight ellipsoidal sections.

4   Conclusions

This exercise in interactivity shows that the concept of responsive environments applied to architecture can be implemented in spaces, which dynamically react to the movement of the human body in space.

In this context, emergence and self-organization can be seen as principles on which interactive architectures can be based on, since building components dynamically adjust to their users needs. Space-customisation, as described in this paper, is one of the modes of emergence and self-organisation interactive buildings can be based on.

5   Perspectives

The next step in the development of this interactive prototype is the implementation of movement transcription not only on one segment of the ellipsoidal cylinder but on all five segments. For that, each segment of the ellipsoidal cylinder needs to be connected to push sensors on the floor, so that a forward movement of the body can be applied to the corresponding segment allowing transformation and deformation of space in three dimensions.

Furthermore, the proactive potential of the space has been not yet explored: Following the example of interactive floors, which configure themselves as surfaces to lie and sit on, the interactive building components might follow principles such as *store agenda and move accordingly* and/or might use sensor/actuator technology interacting with the environment according to the principle *sense your proximity and react on it.*

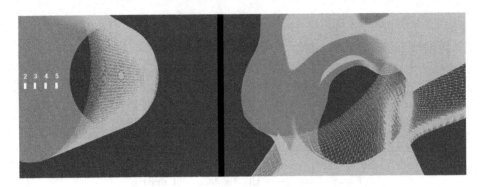

Fig. 7. Five-part segmentation of cylindrical space

In this context, architectural space based on NURBS can be understood as a space, which reconfigures itself according to the principle of swarms: Control points of NURBS can be seen as birds/boids [3] in a swarm, which configure themselves spatially according to preset rules, which accommodate the users' needs.

References

1. Bier, H.: SpaceCustomiser: Towards System Embedded Intelligence in Architecture. Research Portfolio - Architecture 2005-2006, TU Delft, (2005)
2. Le Corbusier: Le Modulor. Birkhaeuser, (2000)
3. Reynolds, C. W.: Flocks, Herds, and Schools: A Distributed Behavioral Model in Computer Graphics. 21/4 SIGGRAPH '87 Conference Proceedings, (1987)

Model-Based Design of Virtual Environment Behavior

Bram Pellens, Frederic Kleinermann, Olga De Troyer, and Wesley Bille

Research Group WISE, Vrije Universiteit Brussel, Pleinlaan 2 - 1050 Brussel, Belgium

Abstract. Designing and building Virtual Environments (VEs) has never been an easy task and it is therefore often performed by experts in the field. This problem arises even more when it comes to the design of behavior. To address this issue, an model-based approach called VR-WISE has been developed. This approach aims at making the design of VEs more accessible to users without or with little background in VE development. This means that the VE is specified by means of high-level models from which the actual VE can be generated. The purpose of this paper is twofold. Firstly, the design environment, supporting the approach, is described. We show how the models can be created in a graphical way. We also discuss the "Verbalizer". This module provides a natural language interface for the models, which enhances the intuitiveness of the specification. Secondly, we explain how behavior models can be specified.

1 Introduction

Today, Virtual Environments (VEs) are used for different purposes. Despite the fact that its use has grown, the design and development of VEs is only performed by a limited number of persons (VR-experts). This is mainly due to the technology being not very accessible to novice users. Although software tools (such as 3D Studio Max [4]) do assist the developer in creating a VE, they require considerable knowledge about VR technology. Authoring tools are most of the time used to create the static part. This static part is then imported in a toolkit where the code of the behavior is added by means of dedicated programming.

We have developed an approach, called VR-WISE, to support the design phase in the development process of a VE. It enables the specification of a VE by means of high-level models. The aim of VR-WISE is to make the design more intuitive, requiring less background and thus making the VR technology available to a broader public.

The approach is supported by a toolbox that allows constructing the models in a graphical way, i.e. by means of diagrams. To model behavior, the diagrams are complemented with a textual language. The diagrams and the textual language are designed in such a way that there is a close relation with natural language. This allows to "read" the diagrams more easily, which increases the understandability and makes them more intuitive. Furthermore, the models are expressed in terms of concepts of the domain of the target application. This helps users to

H. Zha et al. (Eds.): VSMM 2006, LNCS 4270, pp. 29–39, 2006.

bridge the gap between the problem domain and the solution domain. In addition, a graphical notation has a number of well-known advantages. It enhances the communication between designers, programmers and other stakeholders. It is more efficient in its use. Tools can be developed that not only prevent errors, but also provide views on the design from different perspectives and on different levels of abstraction. On the other hand, a textual language can be more expressive and is therefore better to cope with higher complexity. However, the disadvantage of a textual language is that in general, it is more difficult to learn and less intuitive to use. In VR-WISE, we combine the graphical language with small textual scripts. These scripts allow specifying more complex behaviors, while maintaining the intuitiveness of the graphical language.

The approach for modeling behavior is *action-oriented*, i.e. it focuses on the different actions that an object must be able to perform rather than on the states in which an object can be in. Specifying behavior in such a way is more intuitive for non-professionals. To provide additional support for novice users, the toolbox contains the *Verbalizer* module. This module generates a textual formulation of the behavior specifications. Because our approach uses domain terminology and intuitive modeling concepts that have a strong relation with natural language, it is well suited for verbalization. The verbalization reduces the time needed to learn the graphical notation and enhances the communication with non-professionals. Furthermore, this Verbalizer is also useful in the context of iterative design and code documentation, as explained later in the paper.

The paper is structured as follows. In the next section, we give a general introduction of the VR-WISE approach. Section 3 describes the toolbox developed to create the models. Next, section 4 gives an overview of the models used to describe object behavior within the VR-WISE approach. Section 5 discusses related work concerning modeling of object behavior. The paper ends with a conclusion and future work.

2   VR-WISE Approach

The development process in the VR-WISE approach is divided into three (mainly) sequential steps, namely the *Specification step*, the *Mapping step* and the *Generation step*. An elaborated overview of the approach can be found in [6].

The Specification step allows the designer to specify the VE at a high level by means of models. To create the models, domain knowledge together with high-level modeling concepts are used. The models define the objects needed in the VE, the relationships between them, their behaviors, the interactions with other the objects and with the user. Due to the use of domain knowledge and intuitive modeling concepts, there is a strong similarity between how one describes its VE in our approach and how it would be done using natural language. The Mapping step involves specifying the mappings from the conceptual level into the implementation level. The purpose of the mapping is to specify how a particular domain concept described in the Specification step (first step) should be represented in the VE. The Mapping step is needed to be able to transform the models into implementation models and to generate code. This is done in the Generation step.

3   OntoWorld: VR-WISE Toolbox

To support the VR-WISE approach, a toolbox called OntoWorld has been developed. This toolbox enables a designer to build the models that form a complete conceptual specification of the VE, and to specify the mappings. Based on this information OntoWorld will generate a number of code files for the VE.

An important part in our toolbox is the *Visual Designer* (figure 1). This is a graphical diagram editor that allows creating the models in a graphical way. The models describing the static structure of the VE as well as the behavior of its objects can be specified using the Visual Designer. The tool has been implemented using Microsoft Visio. A number of stencils, one for each type of diagram, are built containing the graphical representations of the different modeling concepts available in our approach. Examples of graphical elements can be found on the left side of figure 1. A discussion of the different modeling concepts (and their graphical representation) to specify the static structure of the VE is beyond the scope of this paper. We refer the reader to [2] for more details on this. The modeling concepts available to model the behavior are discussed in the following section. The graphical elements can be dragged from the stencils and dropped onto the canvas and proper connections can be made. Properties can be added, displayed and modified by the designer.

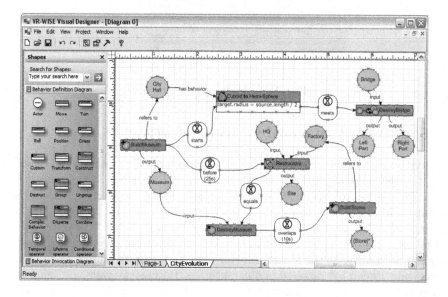

Fig. 1. Screenshot Visual Designer

From the specifications and the mappings, OntoWorld generates VRML/X3D [11] and Java3D [8] (source code which can be compiled and launched either as a local application or on the Web).

An additional interesting tool in the OntoWorld toolbox is the Verbalizer (see figure 2). This module automatically generates a textual formulation for the conceptual specifications. This provides the designer with natural language descriptions of his models and this while making the models. A template-based approach [7] is used to generate the textual formulation. Every semantic representation (e.g., of a behavior) is associated with a (range of) template(s). So, the graphical representation can be converted into a text-like representation. Adding this feature to the design phase has a number of advantages:

- **Interactive Design.** Displaying a natural language-like formulation of the behavior, that has been modeled, provides the designer with a better understanding of what he/she has actually modeled. The automatic generation of textual formulations will allow for an early detection of design errors. The textual formulations will also shorten the learning time.
- **Code Documentation.** After the design process has been completed, the conceptual specifications are used to generate programming code. Generated code is usually not or poorly documented. The code generator can use the formulations generated at design time to document the code, and hereby facilitates the post-modeling phase and possible extensions and customization.

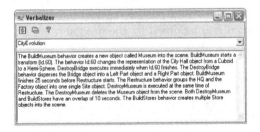

Fig. 2. Screenshot Verbalizer

4   Specifying Behavior by Means of Models

Specifying the behaviors in VR-WISE is done in two separate steps: (1) specifying the *Behavior Definition* and (2) specifying the *Behavior Invocation*.

The first step consists of building *Behavior Definition Models*. A Behavior Definition Model allows the designer to define the different behaviors for an object. The behavior is defined independent of the structure of the object, and independent of how the behavior will be triggered. This improves reusability and enhances flexibility, as the same behavior definition can be reused for different objects and/or can be triggered in different ways. Because we want the definition of a behavior to be separated from the actual definition of the structure of an object, *actors* are used to specify behavior instead of actual object(s). An actor

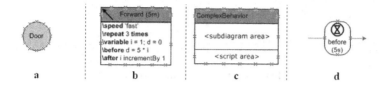

Fig. 3. Actor (a), Behavior (b), Complex Behavior (c), Operator (d)

can be seen as a kind of abstract object and represents an object that is involved in a behavior. An actor is graphically represented by a circle containing the name of the actor (see figure 3a).

We have made a distinction between primitive behavior and complex behavior. A behavior is graphically represented by means of a rectangle. Different types of primitive behaviors are pre-defined. For primitive behavior (see figure 3b), the rectangle carries an icon denoting the type of primitive behavior as well as some additional information (i.e. parameters). For complex behavior, a name is specified and an additional area is used to contain the model that describes the complex behavior (figure 3c).

In order to cope with complex situations, behaviors may have an optional area that holds a (textual) script. The following flags can be specified:

- /**speed** denotes the necessary time for completing a behavior. The possible values for this flag can be *very slow, slow, normal, fast* or *very fast.*
- /**type** sets the type of movement that needs to be made. A movement can be executed in different ways. Possible values here are *smooth, lineair, slow* or *fast.*
- /**condition** states the conditions that need to be satisfied for the action to be executed. An example could be that a door needs to be unlocked before the OpenDoor behavior can be successfully executed.
- /**repeat** denotes the number of times that the behavior (or action) needs to be executed.
- /**variable** specifies custom variables to be used within the action. These variables are in fact placeholders for values. An un-typed system is used so that variables can hold values of any type.
- /**before** allows specifying the expressions that need to be performed before the actual operation is being executed.
- /**after** allows specifying the expressions that need to be performed once the behavior has been fully executed.

In the expressions, either user-defined custom functions (or algorithms) or a number of pre-defined functions can be used. Since the scripts only belong to a single behavior, they will in general be small. For this reason, they are easy to use, even for non-programmers. The scripts can be composed in the Visual Designer through the built-in Script Editor. A large number of predefined functions, constants and operators can be selected and easily used.

To specify complex behavior, behaviors (primitive as well as complex) can be combined by means of the *operators*. There are three types of operators:

Fig. 4. Concept (a), Instance (b), Event (c)

temporal, lifetime and *conditional* operators. The temporal operators allow synchronizing the behaviors (example operators are before, meets, overlaps, starts, ...). Lifetime operators control the lifetime of a behavior (example operators are enable, disable, ...) and the conditional operator controls the flow of a behavior by means of a condition. In the Visual Designer, operators are graphically represented by rounded rectangles (see figure 3d). The icon within the rectangle indicates the type of operator.

The second step in the behavior modeling process consists of creating a *Behavior Invocation Model* for each Behavior Definition Model. This type of diagram allows attaching the behaviors defined in a Behavior Definition Model to actual objects, and to parameterize them according to the needs. Furthermore, these models also specify the events that will trigger the behaviors attached to the objects. The main modeling concepts for these models are *concept* and *instance*, which can be compared to the concepts Class and Object in object-oriented programming languages. They are represented by a rectangle (figure 4a) and an ellipse (figure 4b) respectively.

By assigning an actor to a concept, the behavior is coupled to the concept, i.e. every instance of that concept will obtain all the behaviors defined for the actor. By assigning an actor to an instance, only that particular instance will obtain the behaviors of the actor.

In our approach, behaviors are triggered by means of *events*. Events are graphically represented by a hexagon with an icon denoting the type of the event and possibly some additional information below the icon (see figure 4c). There are four kinds of events: initEvent, timeEvent, userEvent and objectEvent. The initEvent will be invoked at the moment the VE initializes. A timeEvent allows triggering a behavior at a particular time. A userEvent triggers a behavior upon an (inter)action of the user and an objectEvent does this when there is an interaction with other objects. Details on the steps to model behavior as well as the different concepts (to model animations of the objects) can be found in [5]. In the remaining part of this section, we discuss the modeling concepts for modeling object dynamics, i.e. to describe structural changes in the VE (e.g. adding, modifying or deleting objects) rather than just describing the different poses of the objects. Due to space limitations, the Behavior Invocation Models will be discarded in the following examples and only the Behavior Definition Models are given.

4.1   Modeling the Creation and Removal of Objects

A first issue in building dynamic scenes is to cope with new objects. To address this, our approach uses the *construct*-behavior allowing new objects to be

Fig. 5. Creation (a), Removal (b)

added or inserted to the VE at run-time. Similar to the other types of behavior, actors are used in the definition; later on, in the Invocation Models, concepts are associated with the actors. The construct-behavior has at least one output actor, i.e. representing the object that is created. Creating a new object is done by instantiating a concept that has been described in the Domain Model (one of the models created to specify the static structure of the VE). This concept is specified as output actor. The object that is to be created also needs to be positioned and oriented in the VE. This is specified by means of a so-called *Structure Chunk*. This is a small *Structure Model*. Structure Models are used in our approach to specify (at a high level) the structure of the VE. Specifying structure is done by means of spatial relationships and orientation relationships. They are used for placing the objects. Also connection relations can be used for building complex objects. As these relations have been described elsewhere [2], the paper will not discuss their graphical notation in details. For the construct-behavior, the Structure Chunk describes the positioning of the new object (in terms of an actor) at the time of the instantiation. Note that after the creation has been completed, the description given in the Structure Chunk might not be valid anymore, depending on whether the objects involved have performed some other behavior or not. The construct-behavior is graphically represented in a similar way as the other behaviors except that an additional area is used for specifying the Structure Chunk (figure 5a).

To illustrate the construct behavior, an example is provided where a city is expanding with new buildings (see figure 5a). In the Behavior Definition Model, the creation of an actor Museum is defined. This behavior is called BuildMuseum. The Structure Chunk specifies that the newly created object must be north of the City-Hall with a distance of 150 meters and oriented with its right side to the front side of this City-Hall.

Besides creating new objects, building dynamic scenes also includes the removal of objects from the scene. Therefore, the *destruct*-behavior is introduced. Note that destroying an object will not only make the object disappearing from the environment, but it will also delete it from the scene-graph. When the object that needs to be destroyed is part of a connectionless complex object, the relationships in which this object was involved will be deleted too; when it is part of a connected complex object, the connections in which the object is involved will be deleted as well. In figure 5b, the destruct-behavior is defined for a Museum actor, stating that any object that will be associated with this actor could possibly be destroyed.

4.2   Modeling Visual Changes of Objects

An issue that still remains open is the modeling of the visual modifications that an object may undergo. In section 2, it was explained that a concept (or an instance) is given a specific representation in the VE using the mappings. When creating animations stretching over a longer period of time, it could happen that the representation of the concepts should change (during simulation). The first type of modification we considered is the *transformation*-behavior. This type of behavior will change the appearance of an object. Note that the concept itself is not changed; only its representation in the VE is changed.

Figure 6a gives an example of a definition where the actor's representation is changed from a cuboid to a hemi-sphere. Changing the representation of an object may also cause changes of the properties of the representation. These changes can be described by means of transformation rules (specified in the middle area of the graphical representation of the behavior). With a transformation rule, the designer can describe for example, that the length in the original representation (source) is being transformed into the radius of new representation (target) (e.g., radius = length/2). When no rules are given, a standard one-to-one transformation is performed for the corresponding properties when possible; otherwise the defaults of the properties are taken.

To create VEs with a high degree of realism, we also have to consider objects breaking or falling apart. This brings us to the second type of modification supported by our approach, namely the *disperse*-behavior. A disperse-behavior subdivides an object into two (or more) pieces. The disperse-behavior has one input actor and two or more output actors. The input actor represents the object that will be subdivided and the output actors represent the pieces. After such a behavior has been executed, the input object is destroyed and the output objects have been created. Like in the construct-behavior, the new objects that result from such a behavior need to be positioned in the environment. Again, a Structure Chunk is used for relating the newly created objects to each other and for relating them to already existing objects. The positioning of the objects can be done by means of spatial and orientation relations. When no relations are expressed between the newly created objects and already existing objects, then (the bounding box of) the new objects are positioned at the same location as the original (input) object.

In the example in figure 6b the definition for the behavior DestroyBridge is given. It specifies that the complete bridge will disperse in two objects, two smaller pieces of the bridge. The Structure Chunk specifies that one of the pieces (Left Part) is positioned left of the other one (Right Part).

If a disperse-behavior is invoked on a complex object (connected or unconnected), the disperse behavior will remove all the relations that exist between the (parts of the) complex object. This implies that if the user moves one of the objects, the others will not move accordingly since there is no physical connection

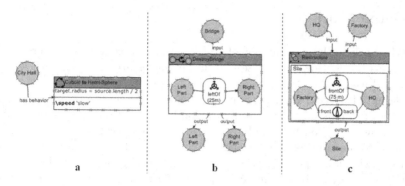

Fig. 6. Transform (a), Disperse (b), Grouping (c)

anymore. In the disperse-behavior, all the information of the original object can be used for the creation of the new objects.

Opposed to objects breaking or falling apart, modeling VEs with dynamic objects also requires having means of joining objects together. In other words, we need to be able to specify that objects can be created by combining objects or assembling objects at runtime hereby creating either complex connected or complex unconnected objects. To support this, we have the *grouping*-behavior. This kind of behavior allows creating spatial relationships or orientation relationships (for unconnected objects) and making connections (for connected objects) at runtime. Such a behavior definition has two (or more) input actors and one output actor. The output actor represents the newly created (complex) object that is built up of the pieces represented by the input actors. Also here, a Structure Chunk is used to describe the structure of the new object, which should be based on the part-objects. Note that in this case, the Structure Chunk is used to express a complex object and therefore the relationships that will be created at run-time will be fixed relationships. This means that after this behavior has been performed for a number of objects, the newly created object will behave as a complex object and therefore if one of its parts or the object itself is moved for example, the relations will ensure that the other parts are moved as well.

In figure 6c, an example is shown on how some objects are grouped to create a new unconnected complex object. The HQ actor and the Factory actor represent the input objects and are being taken together to form a site (represented by the Site actor).

Both the disperse- and the grouping-behavior have counterparts, namely *combine* and *ungrouping* respectively. The combine-behavior will merge a number of objects together in the same way as the grouping but with this difference that the input objects do not exist anymore once the behavior has been performed. The ungrouping-behavior is the reverse of the grouping and removes connections that were made during this grouping. Here, the difference with the disperse-behavior is that the output objects are not created but already exist. We will not give examples for these behaviors, as they are similar to the ones that were already discussed.

5   Related Work

Most of the work on the specification of object behavior is concerned with textual definitions as in [3]. However, these textual languages are not easily accessible by untrained users.

The design of Virtual Environment behavior has also been addressed in [9]. The Flownet formalism is being used as a graphical notation for specifying the behavior. However, even for simple behaviors, the specification becomes large and difficult to read and is therefore not very suitable for non-experts. The VR-WISE approach allows specifying the behavior also through a graphical language but the terminology and modeling concepts used are closely related to how one would describe behavior in natural language.

In [1], an icon-based approach is presented to specify behaviors of objects in VRML. The designer can drag icons, representing VRML nodes, from a palette onto a workspace and create the connections between outputs and inputs of the nodes. Also here, considerable knowledge about the VRML language is required to build a behavior specification.

A commercial development environment that closely relates to our research is Virtools Dev [10]. Also Virtools allows constructing object behavior graphically by combining a number of primitive building blocks (which are pre-made scripts) together. However, the function-based mechanism (where the designer needs to take into account the frame-to-frame basis way of processing the behaviors by the behavior engine) tends to be less comprehensible for novices.

6   Conclusion

In this paper, we have described a model-based approach to specify behavior for VEs. We also introduced the OntoWorld toolbox that supports the approach. The Visual Designer module of the toolbox allows specifying the models by means of diagrams. The Verbalizer module that generates textual explanations for the models was added to improve the understanding of the models and to make documenting of the code possible.

The modeling language for the behavior has evolved to a kind of hybrid mix between a graphical language and a textual scripting language. The behaviors are mainly specified in a graphically way, but a simple scripting language can be used for more complex cases. This way, we offer the advantages of both worlds; the comprehensiveness of the graphical language and the ability to cope with increasing complexity by means of a textual language. The combination of a model-based approach with the use of an intuitive graphical language may seriously reduce the complexity of building dynamic and interactive VEs.

At the time of writing, we are implementing a debugger within the Visual Designer which checks the models for errors. Furthermore, our approach uses a formalization of the different relations and concepts used for modeling behavior. One of the benefits of having a formalization is that errors made by the designer can then be checked at design time. This gives the advantage of accelerating the modeling of behaviors as designers can quickly see where the errors are. This formalization is currently being implemented. The future work will consist of conducting a number of experiments in order to evaluate the modeling power and intuitiveness of the developed tools and the different modeling concepts proposed. Next, we will investigate how we can extend our models with patterns coming from game design research in order to come to a richer set of modeling concepts.

Acknowledgements

This research is carried out in the context of VR-DeMo project, funded by the Institute for the Promotion of Innovation by Science and Technology in Flanders.

References

1. Arjomandy, S. and Smedley, T.J., "Visual Specification of Behaviours in VRML Worlds", In Proceedings of the ninth International Conference on 3D Web Technology, ACM Press, Monterey, California, USA, 2004, pp.127-133
2. Bille, W., De Troyer, O., Pellens, B., Kleinermann, F., "Conceptual Modeling of Articulated Bodies in Virtual Environments", In Proceedings of the 11th International Conference on Virtual Systems and Multimedia, pp. 17-26, Publ. Archaeolingua, Gent, Belgium, 2005
3. M. Kallmann and D. Thalmann, "Modeling Behaviors of Interactive Objects for Virtual Reality Applications", Journal of Visual Languages and Computing, Vol. 13, 2002, pp. 177-195
4. Murdock K.L. 3DS Max 7 Bible. Wiley Publishing Incorporated, 2005
5. Pellens, B., De Troyer, O., Bille, W., Kleinermann, F., Conceptual Modeling of Object Behavior in a Virtual Environment, In Proceedings of Virtual Concept 2005, pp. 93 - 94 + CD-ROM, Publ. Springer-Verlag, Biarritz, France, 2005.
6. Pellens, B., Bille, W., De Troyer, O., Kleinermann, F., VR-WISE: A Conceptual Modelling Approach For Virtual Environments, In Proceedings of the Methods and Tools for Virtual Reality (MeTo-VR'05) workshop, Ghent, Belgium, 2005
7. Reiter, E. and Dale, R. Building applied natural language generation systems. In Journal of Natural Language Engineering, 3:57 - 87, 1997
8. Selman, D., Java3D Programming, Manning Publications, 2002
9. Willans J.S., Integrating behavioural design into the virtual environment development process, Phd thesis, University of York, UK, 2001
10. –, Virtools Dev, http://www.virtools.com/, Accessed August 2, 2006
11. –, X3D, http://www.web3d.org/x3d/specifications/, Accessed May 31, 2006

Beh-VR: Modeling Behavior of Dynamic Virtual Reality Contents

Krzysztof Walczak

Department of Information Technology,
The Poznan University of Economics
Mansfelda 4, 60-854 Poznan
walczak@kti.ae.poznan.pl

Abstract. In this paper, we propose a novel approach to modeling and dynamic creation of behavior-rich interactive 3D contents. The approach, called Beh-VR, enables dynamic generation of virtual scenes from arbitrarily selected sets of specifically designed reusable virtual objects, called VR-Beans. Behavior of the objects is determined by associated scripts encoded in a high-level language called VR-BML. The method significantly simplifies creation of interactive 3D scenes and can be applied to various application domains. Examples discussed in the paper are related to creation of educational and entertainment contents in the cultural heritage domain.

Keywords: Computer Graphics, Virtual Reality, Dynamic Modeling, Programming Languages.

1 Introduction

Virtual reality (VR) technologies have reached the level of maturity that makes possible their use in a diversity of real life applications. Cultural heritage, education, and entertainment are notable examples of application domains that can largely benefit from the use of VR technologies. Widespread use of 3D technologies has been mainly enabled by three factors: significant progress in hardware performance including cheap 3D accelerators available in every contemporary graphics card, increasing availability of automatic 3D modeling tools and consequently also 3D contents [1], and development of standards such as VRML/X3D and MPEG-4, which enable platform-independent representation of interactive 3D scenes. Furthermore, wide availability of 3D computer games and movies based on 3D computer graphics results in increasing familiarity of users with 3D graphics and – at the same time – is raising user expectations. Young generations of people familiar with interactive 3D games and movies based on 3D graphics look for similar experiences in other domains. This may be a good opportunity for many educational and cultural heritage institutions to increase the attractiveness of the employed forms of communicating knowledge.

One of the biggest problems that currently limits wide use of 3D technologies in everyday applications is related to the creation of complex interactive

H. Zha et al. (Eds.): VSMM 2006, LNCS 4270, pp. 40–51, 2006.

behavior-rich contents. A number of solutions exist for *programming* behavior of fixed 3D scenes. However, in most practical applications such predefined scenes are not sufficient. Real-life VR applications require that the contents are created *dynamically*, i.e. instead of fixed programmed scenes, dynamically generated contents are used. Such contents may depend on data provided by a content designer (e.g., a domain expert), end-user's query and privileges, some database contents, current time, system state, etc.

In this paper, we propose a novel approach to modeling and dynamic composition of behavior-rich interactive 3D contents. The approach, called Beh-VR, uses specifically designed objects, called VR-Beans, that can be arbitrarily composed into complex scenes. Behavior of the objects is determined by the use of scripts coded in a high-level language called VR-BML. In this paper we do not present the details of VR-BML syntax. Instead, main aspects of the scene organization, communication between objects and contents design issues are discussed.

The rest of this paper is organized as follows. In Section 2, works related to programming behavior of VR contents are presented. In Section 3, the main elements of the Beh-VR approach are discussed. Section 4 describes the method of dynamic content modeling and generation. In Section 5, examples of interactive scenes based on the Beh-VR approach are shortly presented. Finally, Section 6 concludes the paper and indicates future works.

2   Related Works

Significant research effort has been invested in the development of methods, languages and tools for programming behavior of virtual scenes. These approaches can be classified into three main groups. The first group constitute scripting languages for describing behavior of virtual scenes. An example of a scripting language designed for writing VR interaction scenarios is *MPML-VR* (Multimodal Presentation Markup Language for VR), which enables describing multimodal presentations in 3D virtual spaces [2]. This language is a 3D adaptation of the *MPML* language originally targeted at creating multimodal Web contents, in particular to enable content authors to script rich web-based interaction scenarios featuring life-like characters. Similar solutions, also developed for controlling life-like characters, are *VHML* (Virtual Human Markup Language) [3] for scripting virtual characters' animation and *APML* (Affective Presentation Markup Language) [4] focusing on presenting personality and emotions in agents. Another interesting example is *VEML* (Virtual Environment Markup Language) based on the concept of atomic simulations.

The second group of solutions includes integrated content design frameworks. Such frameworks usually include some complex languages and tools that extend existing standards to provide additional functionality, in particular, enabling specification of virtual scene behavior. A worth mentioning example is *Contigra* [6] together with *Behavior3D* [7]. This approach is based on distributed standardized components that can be assembled into 3D scenes during the design phase. The 3D scene specification is divided into three parts: geometrical, behavioral and aural. A limitation of this approach, is that it uses purely declarative approach of VRML/X3D and standard event processing mechanisms, missing more advanced computational mechanisms. Other works that can be classified into group include [8] and [9].

The common motivation for developing new scripting languages, and content design frameworks, as those described above, is to simplify the process of designing complex VR presentations. However, even most high-level scripts and content description languages become complex when they are used for preparing complicated VR presentations. The third group of solutions try to alleviate this problem by using graphical applications for designing complex VR contents [10][11]. Such applications are often used in connection with the above discussed approaches. Nevertheless, the users still must deal with complex graphic diagrams illustrating how a scenario processes and reacts to user interaction. Such diagrams are usually too difficult to be effectively used by non-programmers.

In addition, numerous works related to behavior modeling have been done in the simulation area. Majority of these works focus on simulation of real environments, physical models and believable interaction between objects (examples include [12] and [13]). These approaches usually require specific execution platforms and target specific application areas and therefore are less related to our work. Nevertheless, some elements can be adapted and reused.

The approaches described above may be successfully used by programmers for preparing fixed predefined VR scenes. This, however, is not sufficient to enable widespread use of virtual reality in real life applications. Such applications require *dynamic contents* that can be created or adapted in response to interactions of end-users. Dynamic composition of contents is also a prerequisite for building high-level domain specific content authoring applications that would enable quick and easy creation of VR contents by domain experts, such as educators or museum curators, even if they do not have profound knowledge in computer science and 3D technologies [14].

3   The Beh-VR Approach

3.1   Beh-VR Overview

The *Beh-VR* approach enables modeling behavior of dynamically created virtual reality contents. Beh-VR scenes can be dynamically composed by selecting sets of virtual objects. The virtual objects, called *VR-Beans*, are constructed according to some specific rules. Each VR-Bean is associated with a scenario that governs its appearance and behavior in a virtual scene. These scenarios specify what actions are performed by objects either at specific points in time or as a result of user actions or interactions with other objects. The Beh-VR approach is based on standard technologies and is fully compatible with X3D/MPEG-4 contents. Therefore, there is no need for special client-side interpretation software.

The Beh-VR approach supports dynamic content composition by clearly identifying high-level independent objects that constitute a virtual scene. Such objects can be easily combined into virtual scenes without the need perform low-level 3D graphics design or programming. Therefore it is possible to build user-friendly authoring tools oriented on domain specific contents. This characteristic of Beh-VR makes it particularly well suited for building VR applications in domains such as education, culture and entertainment, where the contents should be developed by domain experts and not computer graphics specialists.

3.2   VR-Beans

VR-Beans are independent reusable VR objects encoded in a standard content description language (such as VRML/X3D or MPEG-4) but constructed according to some specific patterns. Due to the use of these patterns, VR-Beans can be automatically incorporated in a Beh-VR scene and can communicate with the scene and with each other. VR-Beans are analogous to high-level programming elements or widgets commonly used in modern programming languages.

The main element controlling each VR-Bean is a *scenario script*. Scenario scripts are encoded in *VR-BML* (Virtual Reality Behavior Modeling Language) – a specifically designed high-level XML-based language. Each script contains specification of behavior of a single VR-Bean object. It describes what happens when the object is initialized, what actions are performed by the object and what are responses of the object to external stimuli. Each behavior script may create any number of scene components, which are geometrical or aural manifestation of the VR-Bean in a virtual scene, but there may be also VR-Beans that do not directly manifest themselves.

3.3   VR-BML Scenarios

A scenario script consists of VR-BML *commands*. VR-BML uses a hybrid approach based on both declarative programming for high-level elements (e.g., event actions) and imperative programming for low-level elements (e.g., algorithm details). This hybrid approach enables VR-BML to take best of the two worlds enabling the programmer to concentrate on important elements, and leave the common elements to the Beh-VR framework.

A scenario script may contain three main sections: the *initialize* section, which describes what happens when the object appears in the scene, a number of *action* statements, which describe what actions are performed by the object as a result of changes or events in the scene (time, scene properties, user interactions), and a number of *methods* that can be explicitly called by other objects in the scene.

Scenario scripts can inherit from scenario classes that form inheritance hierarchies. Only single inheritance is allowed. The following rules are respected in the Beh-VR inheritance:

- the initialize section is always inherited implicitly, i.e. initialize section of a super-class is performed before the initialize section of a subclass or scenario;
- methods are inherited normally;
- actions may be inherited or not – depending on the actions' specification in the super-class.

```
<Scenario>
  <Initialize>
    <Load file="model-hr.wrl" comp="statue" position="0,0,0" active="false"/>
    <PlaneSensor comp="statue" active="true" orientation="1,0,0,-1.57"/>
    <Activate comp="statue" active="true"/>
    <Register name="Statue 1" category="objects/cultural"/>
  </Initialize>
  <Action cond="true" time="4000" count="500">
    <RotateTo comp="statue" axis="0,1,0" angle="{2*Pi}" time="1000"/>
  </Action>
  <Method name="position" param="target=0,0,0; time=1000" wait="true">
    <MoveTo comp="statue" target="{@target}" time="{@time}"/>
  </Method>
</Scenario>
```

Fig. 1. Example of a VR-BML scenario script

An example of a simple VR-BML script is presented in Figure 1. The scenario describes behavior of a 3D model of a museum artifact that can be used in virtual exhibitions. The scenario consists of the initialization section, one action specification and one method.

The initialization section loads an VRML/X3D model (a file or a database object) containing the geometry of the museum artifact (a statue) by the use of the *Load* command. The command assigns to the component the name "*statue*" that will enable referring to this component in the future. The component is being initially positioned in the point (0,0,0) in the scene and is not being activated (is loaded to the browser but not activated in the scene). The next command *PlaneSensor* corresponds to the plane sensor nodes in VRML/X3D and MPEG-4 and allows a user to freely move the object in two dimensions on a flat surface. The orientation of the surface is specified as a parameter of the command. Then, the loaded component is activated in the scene – the 3D model is made visible and it can be manipulated by a user. At the end of the initialization process, the VR-Bean is being registered in the scene (*Register* command) in the category "*objects/cultural*" with the name "*Statue 1*". Any VR-Bean in the scene can then discover the registered object. Once the initialization section is completed other sections of the scenario become enabled.

The action command is executed every four seconds (maximum 500 times). The action consists of a full-circle rotation of the *statue* component around the vertical axis. The rotation lasts one second. The rotation allows a user to see the artifact from every direction.

There is also one method specified in the scenario – "*position*". The method causes moving the *statue* component to a new position. By default, the target destination is (0,0,0) but an actual parameter value provided in the method invocation may be different. The second parameter of the *position* method is the animation time (duration).

In real applications, object scenarios are usually more complex than this example, nevertheless they are significantly simpler to write and maintain than corresponding X3D/VRML/MPEG-4 code written with Scripts, ROUTES and Interpolators.

3.4   Identification of VR-Beans

Beh-VR scenes are composed of dynamically selected independent VR-Beans. Therefore, there must be a mechanism to identify VR-Beans that are in the scene and their roles to allow the scene components to communicate. In Beh-VR this is accomplished by the process of *registration* and *discovery*.

Each VR-Bean can register itself in the scene in an arbitrary number of hierarchically organized dynamic categories. In addition, each VR-Bean is automatically assigned to the category "*any*". The tree of categories is built dynamically as the objects assign themselves to the categories. There are no constraints on the structure of the tree, and the tree itself does not define semantics of the categories. Ontology associated with the categories is application dependent. Sample tree of categories used in a virtual museum exhibition is presented in Fig. 2.

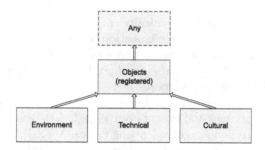

Fig. 2. Example of a simple categorisation tree

For example, a VR-Bean responsible for a presentation scenario in a dynamic virtual reality exhibition may retrieve all objects in the "*objects/cultural*" category, sort them by their age (retrieved from object metadata) and display them sequentially accompanied by an audio description. The object may register itself in another category "*objects/technical*".

3.5   Beh-VR Expressions

VR-BML scripts may use expressions in values of command parameters. Expressions are enclosed in brackets "{ }" and are always evaluated before the command execution. Expressions provide a powerful way of parameterizing commands, verifying complex conditions and calculating values. The Beh-VR built-in expression evaluator provides numerical, geometrical, Boolean and string operators, enables use of variables and provides operations on lists. In our implementation, the evaluator can be easily extended by adding Java classes implementing new operators.

VR-BML expressions enable the use of *variables*, *public values* and *environment properties*. Similarly as in many programming languages, a *variable* is simply a named value. In VR-BML variables are local – they are visible only inside a single VR-Bean. Multiple VR-Bean objects can have variables with the same name and different values. Variables are static (but not constant). One command may set a value of a variable and other commands may read and change this value.

A *public value* is a named expression that is visible by all VR-Beans. Such expression may be a constant value or it may be dynamic and use environment properties, values of variables from the VR-Bean that has published this value, and values of events generated by the content description in the same VR-Bean (e.g., a *translation_changed* event in VRML/X3D).

An *environment property* is a named value that cannot be changed by a script. It may be either a static system value or dynamic value set by the Beh-VR environment. An example of an environment property is *TIME*, which can be used as a variable in expressions and its value is equal to the number of milliseconds passed from the beginning of the current scene's simulation.

3.6   Communication Between VR-Beans

Since the Beh-VR scenes are dynamically composed of independent VR-Bean objects, a crucial element is the communication between the constituting objects. There are three communication mechanisms in the Beh-VR approach: *public values*, *assigned values*, and *method invocation*. Each of these mechanisms may be efficiently used for different purposes.

Public values, as explained in the previous section, are named public expressions that can use variables and events from a single VR-Bean. Communication via public values corresponds to broadcasting values. A VR-Bean executes (once) a *publish* command and the public value remains active until the end of the simulation or until another object publishes a different value with the same name. Since the pool of public values is global, only one object can publish a value of a given name at a given time. The characteristics of public values render them most useful for implementing virtual scene control elements. For example, in a virtual museum, a slider that allows users to "move in time" between centuries publishes a value *"historical_date"*. All cultural objects assigned to this room read this value and appear in the scene or disappear to reflect the periods in time when they were used in the past.

In many cases, public values do not have to be processed by VR-BML scripts, but may be directly assigned to events controlling scene components. To achieve this, the *assigned values* mechanism can be used. Assigned values are expressions assigned to input events of scene components. Again, assignment is performed once by the use of a single command. Since the assignment, whenever the value of the expression changes (e.g., as a result of a changing public value), an event is being sent to the assigned field. Assigned values are convenient when one or more elements have direct influence on selected objects in the scene. Continuing the example of a virtual museum, assigned values can be used to control the scale of cultural objects in a virtual exhibition space. When a user changes the scale factor, the scale is automatically applied to all cultural objects without any additional conditions or processing.

As opposed to the first two methods of communication, the third one – method invocation – is explicit. A VR-Bean script may invoke methods of other

VR-Beans. A method consists of VR-BML commands, which may change the
state of the VR-Bean, alter its representation in the virtual scene, invoke other
methods, etc. A method can be invoked on a single VR-Bean or on a whole list
of VR-Beans. Such list may be retrieved from the pool of registered objects (e.g.,
all objects in a category) or constructed in any other way. Each method may
have any number of parameters. Formal parameters specification is provided in
the method declaration, while actual parameter values are set in the method call
(compare example in Fig. 1). A method invocation may be either synchronous or
asynchronous – depending on the value of the "*wait*" parameter in the method
declaration. Synchronous method invocation blocks the invoking script until the
method finishes execution, asynchronous method invocation does not block the
invoking script. Methods may return values. The name of the result variable may
be provided in method invocation. Fig. 3 provides a summary of the VR-Bean
communication mechanisms supported by Beh-VR.

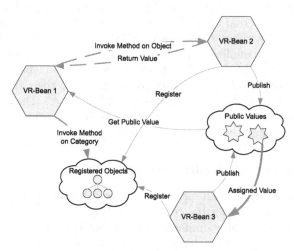

Fig. 3. Communication between VR-Beans

3.7 VR-Beans Implementation

Implementation details of VR-Beans are platform specific (e.g., the content description language and the programming language). Typical implementations
may be based on X3D or MPEG-4 for content description and Java or EC-
MAScript for scenario implementation. In the examples given in this paper, we
use VRML/X3D for content description and Java for script interpretation.

4 Dynamic VR Contents

4.1 Dynamic Content Composition

The basic requirement for the work presented in this paper is dynamic composition of the VR contents. The dynamic composition in our solution is based on the

X-VR approach, which consists of a database model for VR, called X-VRDB [15], and dynamic modeling language, called X-VRML [16] that adds dynamic modeling capabilities to VR content description standards such as VRML/X3D and MPEG-4. The dynamic modeling technique enables the development of dynamic database-driven VR applications by building parameterized models (templates) of virtual scenes that constitute the application, and dynamic generation of instances of virtual scenes based on the models, data retrieved from a database, current values of model parameters, input provided by a user, and user privileges or preferences. The X-VRML language enables parameterization of the virtual scene generation process, permits selection of the scene contents, and provides powerful methods of accessing data stored in databases.

In the presented approach, the X-VRML templates are used to dynamically generate VR contents based on a structure of VR presentations stored in a database. The use of presentation templates enables separation of the process of designing complex virtual scenes and programming object behavior from the process of designing actual contents, allowing the latter to be easily performed by domain experts without extensive knowledge in computer science and 3D technologies. All the visualization and behavior rules necessary to build presentations are encoded in the templates. A content designer can create an interactive presentation by simply collecting content objects, setting their visualization and behavior parameters and creating instances of templates. The process of designing complex interactive VR presentations can be performed by the use of a simple application connected to the content database [17].

4.2   Dynamic Virtual Reality Presentations

The structure of dynamic VR presentations is determined by a hierarchy of presentation spaces stored in the content database (see Fig. 4). The presentation spaces are conceptually similar to folders that may contain three types of elements: *instances of content templates, instances of behavior templates,* and *instances of content objects.*

A template instance is a template supplied with actual values of some of its formal parameters (the non-default values). A single template can have an arbitrary number of instances in different spaces. A content object instance is a content object together with values of object presentation parameters. Again, the same object may have instances in more than one presentation space. The template parameters and content object parameters can be provided by a content designer while setting up a presentation. Different presentations can be achieved by the creation of template instances derived from the same template but supplied with different sets of parameter values. This concerns both the content templates and the behavior templates. In some presentations, parameters that are not fixed by content designer can be changed by an end-user.

Content templates are used to dynamically compose virtual scenes. Simplest templates generate scenes by creating VR-Beans corresponding to content objects. More complex templates may additionally include background elements such as a model of a room (compare examples in Fig. 5). Each of the content objects may include its own VR-BML scenario script. In some cases, however, it is useful to have the same (or similar) behavior shared by a number of objects. To achieve this, an instance of a behavior template, i.e. an X-VRML template of VR-BML scripts, implementing common object behavior may be also included in the presentation space.

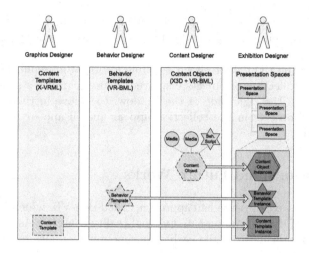

Fig. 4. Database model of dynamic VR presentations

5 Examples

The described approach has been applied in the cultural heritage context in a European Union supported project *ARCO - Augmented Representation of*

Fig. 5. Examples of interactive VR scenes based on the Beh-VR approach

Cultural Objects [18][19]. In Fig. 5, two examples of ARCO interactive VR scenes based on the Beh-VR approach are presented. On the left, there is a simple game. In this game, each cultural object is represented by its geometrical model and a label indicating the object's material (retrieved from metadata). The users' task is to associate each object with appropriate label and then press the 'OK' button. From the content designer perspective, creation of such scenario requires only assigning a group of objects and a behavior template to a presentation space. No programming or 3D designing skills are necessary.

In Fig. 5 on the right, there is an example a virtual museum room (Kornik Castle) with a collection of objects displayed. A user can use a slider, which is always visible on the right side of the window, to "move in time". When the slider is moved objects in the collection appear and disappear reflecting their use in the past.

6   Conclusions and Future Works

In this paper we have presented an approach, called Beh-VR, which enables modeling behavior of dynamically created virtual reality contents. As virtual reality technology is maturing from the early experimentation phase to a deployment phase, the dynamic content composition becomes increasingly important as it enables building real life virtual reality applications in a variety of domains. Modeling of interactivity and behavior are of critical importance in such applications. At the same time these elements are very difficult to program, especially when the contents may be dynamically generated or changed.

Early applications of the proposed approach for building interactive virtual reality exhibitions of museum artifacts demonstrated effectiveness of this approach for programmers and ease of use for content designers.

The examples presented in this paper use simple structure of virtual scenes – scenes consist of flat collections of VR-Bean objects. Future works will concentrate on developing complex objects, i.e. VR-Beans that can be composed of other VR-Beans as spatial, temporal and logical compositions of the constituting objects. This will support development of more complex contents and enable to significantly advance beyond the traditional approach of "programming" virtual reality contents as fixed scenes.

Acknowledgments. This work has been partially funded by the Polish Ministry of Science and Higher Education (grant no 3T11C01428, 2005-2006). Kornik Castle models courtesy of Institute of Micromechanics and Photonics, Faculty of Mechatronics, Warsaw University of Technology. 3D models of cultural objects courtesy of the National Museum of Agriculture in Szreniawa, Poland.

References

1. Sitnik, R., Kujawiska, M., Zaluski, W.: 3DMADMAC system: optical 3D shape, acquisition and processing path for VR applications, Proc. SPIE, Vol. 5857 (2005), 106–117.
2. Okazaki, N., Aya, S., Saeyor, S., and Ishizuka, M.: A Multimodal Presentation Markup Language MPML-VR for a 3D Virtual Space. Workshop Proc. on Virtual Conversational Characters: Applications, Methods, and Research Challenges, (in conj. with HF2002 and OZCHI2002), Melbourne, Australia (2002).
3. Marriott, A., Beard, S., Stallo, J., Huynh, Q.: VHML - Directing a Talking Head. Proc. of the Sixth Int. Computer Science Conf. Active Media Technology, Vol. LNCS 2252. Springer, Hong Kong, 2001, 18–20.
4. De Carolis, B., Carofiglio, V., Bilvi, M., Pelachaud, C.: APML, A Mark-up Language for Believable Behavior Generation. Proc. of AAMAS Workshop Embodied Conversational Agents: Let's Specify and Compare Them!, Bologna, Italy (2002)
5. Boukerche, A., Zarrad, A., Duarte, D., Araujo, R., Andrade, L.: A Novel Solution for the Development of Collaborative Virtual Environment Simulations in Large Scale, 9th IEEE Int. Symp. on Distributed Simulation and Real-Time Applications (2005) 86–96
6. Dachselt, R., Hinz, M., Meissner, K.: Contigra: an XML-based architecture for component-oriented 3D applications, Proc. of the 7th IC on 3D Web Technology, Tempe, AZ, USA (2002) 155–163
7. Dachselt, R., Rukzio, E.: Behavior3D: an XML-based framework for 3D graphics behavior, Proc. of the 8th IC on 3D Web Techn., Saint Malo, France (2003) 101–112
8. Burrows, T., England, D.: YABLE-yet another behaviour language, Proc. of the 10th IC on 3D Web Technology, Bangor, UK (2005) 65–73
9. Mesing, B., Hellmich, C.: Using aspect oriented methods to add behaviour to X3D documents, Proc. of the 11th Int. Conf. on 3D Web Technology, Columbia, MD, USA (2006) 97–107
10. Virtools Solutions, Virtools Dev, http://www.virtools.com/solutions/products/
11. Arjomandy, S., Smedley, T. J.: Visual specification of behaviours in VRML worlds, Proc. of the 9th IC on 3D Web Technology, Monterey, CA, USA (2004) 127–133
12. Devillers, F., Donikian, S.: A scenario language to orchestrate virtual world evolution, Proc. of the 2003 ACM SIGGRAPH/Eurographics symposium on computer animation, San Diego, CA (2003) 265–275
13. Kearney, J., Willemsen, P., Donikian, S., Devillers, F.: Scenario languages for driving simulations. In DSC'99; Paris, France (1999).
14. Walczak, K., Cellary, W.: Building Database Applications of Virtual Reality with X-VRML. Proc. of the 7th IC on 3D Web Techn., Tempe, AZ, USA (2002) 111–120.
15. Walczak, K., Cellary, W.: Modeling Virtual Worlds in Databases, Information Processing Letters, Vol. 88 (2003); Elsevier B.V., 67–72
16. Walczak, K., Cellary, W.: X-VRML for Advanced Virtual Reality Applications. IEEE Computer, IEEE Computer Society Press, Vol. 36, Issue 3 (2003) 89–92.
17. Walczak, K., Wojciechowski, R.: Dynamic Creation of Interactive Mixed Reality Presentations, ACM Symposium on VR Software and Technology - VRST 2005, Monterey, CA, USA, ACM Press 167–176
18. Walczak, K., Cellary, W., White, M.: Virtual Museum Exhibitions, IEEE Computer, IEEE Computer Society Press; Vol. 39, Issue 3 (2006) 93–95
19. ARCO - Augmented Representation of Cultural Objects. http://www.arco-web.org/

N'Files – A Space to React. Communication Between Architecture and Its Users

Christian Fröhlich and Martin Kern

Institute of Architecture and Media, Inffeldgasse 10/II,
A-8010 Graz, Graz University of Technology, Austria

Abstract. This paper describes the concept and the current state of development of "reactive spaces". How can one communicate with architectural spaces, through one's movement or even one's appearance? One goal of the project *N `Files - A Space To React* is it to develop a system which supports the interaction between spatial areas and its users. A space, which is changing with and through the user....which reacts to the user's input. The basis for such experiments was laid in research fields such as Ambient Intelligence (AmI), Ubiquitous Computing or Hybrid Environments. If take these new communication and interaction possibilities some steps further, then it becomes clear that our traditional sense of space will be transformed radically by them.

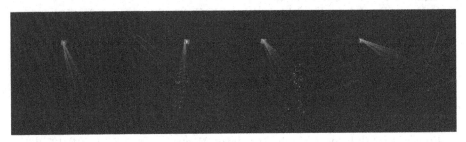

Fig. 1. Fullbody Motion Tracking

One must be accurate, if one daydreams.
If one does not daydream, one can take the liberty liberties.
That is the deadly about academic thinking,
because it thinks always protected and falls therefore into the dust.
If one daydreams, one cannot take that liberty.
(V.Flusser, 2003)

Digital media technology creates the potential for the development of new spaces and new forms of work and exchange. Architecture can become a resource for the development of technology and culture by supplying what is most urgently needed: ideas and insights, which are based on an understanding of technology as an integral component of contemporary culture. What is needed to develop these insights is an architecture laboratory, in which new technologies are developed and tested according to their extended social and societal functions and which could find its definition as an exceptional space of experiments.[1]

---

[1] cp. *Digitale Transformationen, Fleischmann – Reinhard, 2004 – Praxis Reaktorbau, Edler & Edler (S. 216).*

H. Zha et al. (Eds.): VSMM 2006, LNCS 4270, pp. 52–59, 2006.

At the media laboratory no_LAb of the institute for architecture and media recently a high end optical 3D motion tracking system has been installed.[2] Such systems are normally used in the film industry of Hollywood or in medical laboratories for motion analysis. At the institute of architecture and media we use the equipment for experiments, in order to extend architecture beyond its traditional, physical borders (Augmented Architecture). With the assistance of these advanced technical means it is possible to create a fusion of the space of material action and the space of digital data.

One goal of the project N `Files - A Space To React is it to develop a system which supports the interaction between spatial areas and its users. A space, which is changing with and through the user....which reacts to the user's input. The basis for such experiments was laid in research fields such as Ambient Intelligence (AmI)[3], Ubiquitous Computing[4] or Hybrid Environments[5]. If take these new communication and interaction possibilities some steps further, then it becomes clear that our traditional sense of space will be transformed radically by them.

"The architects should finally stop thinking only in materials" - Hans Hollein demanded 1968 in his manifesto "everything is architecture". A demand which nobody tried to put into practice – including Hollein. "Thus if one wants to immaterialize static architecture - i.e. transform it into a dynamic system - architecture became a medium, which always changes, temporal and spatial, a context-steered event world. (...) From the variability of the architectural elements" - door, window, wall, facade, etc. - "from the virtuality of the stored information" - warmth, light, sound, gestures, movements - "a building would arise, which shows life-similar behavior: viability. (...) Architecture, as an intelligent ambiente, which reacts to the inputs of the users and accomplishes intelligently condition changes. Interactivity between users and architecture, both as correlating parts of a dynamic system, which shows life-similar behavior - viable architecture."[6]

The terms virtual and viable architecture - worded by Peter Weibel in 1989 and 1994 - receive a contemporary upgrade in the project N'Files through a practical test row. The challenge in this case is to provide complex technological environments with a certain simplicity and intuition, which one the user requires and expects for a good reason . "We live in an increasingly complex technological world where nothing works like it is supposed to, and at the end of the day makes all of us hunger for simplicity to some degree."[7] The research project follows therefore the question whether an architecture / a space of media can support the user in everyday actions or whether there are actions, which change or simplify by handling media or even actions which will be possible only because of the use of media. Integrated into the two courses, "interdisciplinary media projects" and "innovative methods of design" there is an ongoing workflow between instructors, tutors and students in modules and phases,

---

[2] *The MotionTrackingSystem was financed in the context of the austrian university infrastructure initiative of the advice for research and technology (RFT).*

[3] *Ambient Intelligence (AmI) is an "intelligent environment", which reacts sensitive and adaptive to the presence of humans and objects and supports human everyday life procedures.*

[4] The term "Ubiquitous Computing" (ubiquitous: omnipresent, to find everywhere) was introduced in 1991 by Mark Weiser.

[5] *Hybrid Environments describes the fusion of physical and virtual spaces.*

[6] *Viable and virtual architecture, P. Weibel, 1994.*

[7] Simplicity – the art of complexity, John Maeda, 2006.

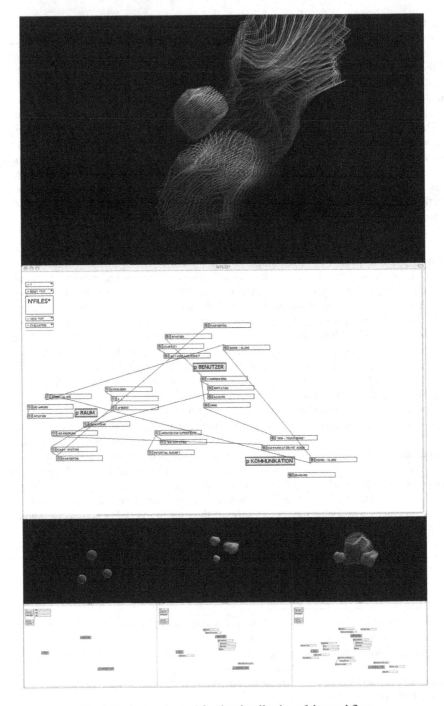

Fig. 2. Brainstormingtool for the visualization of the workflow

which are briefly outlined in the following. In the "research phase" small groups prepared strong researches to the following topic modules:

TechTools: "Built the tools you use and use the tools you built"
Visual programming languages and "data workaround"

Analogies: Learning from metropolis
Inspirations about "space communication" across all disciplines

Space is the place: "The ability of having access to spaces did it to us."
(S. Kracauer)
The space term in the change of times

Media Art: "Do it like an artist, do it deviating." (B. Brock)
Media Art as key phenomena for technological innovation

Devices: Designing tracking target
Integration of tracking objects into everyday life articles

In the "application phase" samples and examples were generated in weekly workshops
and brainstorming , which brought us explanations and skills for the implementation
phase. the "work in progress" is continuously logged and can be seen on our website and
webcams. For the visualization of the workshop results particularly a brainstormingtool
was programmed, which illustrates the development process directly via the room system.

The project N'Files follows the intention to use learned cultural behavior when handling media. Thereby a lot of attention is paid to the senses (seeing, hearing, feeling). At
the centre the touch-less connection of human being – machine - space is located via

Fig. 3. no_LAb__in_feld.. Laboratory for Architecture and Media. TU Graz.

genuine sensual perception. By the immaterial interface (the space is the interface!) and the paradigm of the touch-less a further sense is generated - the non-touch sense.[8] This unusual sensitive experience is starting point for the research of space communication via gestures and movement – one option, how we will use our spaces in the future.

Test section for the project N'Files is the media laboratory no_LAb of the institute of architecture and media at Graz University of Technology, in which the technical facility is given by the optical trackingsystem. For this project the laboratory is transformed into an interactive space volume, which reacts to its visitors and adapts its appearance on these. That means, the space is not steered by computers or classical input devices, but the space is(!) the machine. A machine, which is able "to feel sensory" and to reflect these moods to the users. Architecture as a medium and as intelligent environment, which can react on the inputs of its users - conscious and unconscious - intuitive and "on demand "...

We decided to define these two states - intuitive and on demand - for the "application phase". The intuitive state should be the one where the room plays the keyrole and the user acts like an input-device through his movements and gestures. In this state the space should behave like an independent existence, a space with emotions, which is able to communicate its moods...

Whereas the on-demand-state should transform the space into a smart room, in which the typical objects of the lab - like table, fauteuil, door, wall, etc. - are extended beyond their physical appearance with some kind of intelligence.

This led us directly to the question about the remarkable space elements of the no_LAb - and in the following - what we have made out of it:

Fig. 4. no_LAb Geometry, no_LAb Space Elements, no_LAb Wallpaper (f.l.t.r.)

Dynamic Wallpaper

The main visual output of the room is for sure the projection wall. For the project we installed a double widescreen projection (5m - 2m). It has became something like the image, the branding of the no_LAb. We use it more like a inner facade, a virtual window. The main idea was to install a permanent visual output, which describes the actual state of the room in realtime according to frequency and fluctuation and which shows more than just visualised information. The ideal metaphor for that seemed to be a wallpaper. Because it consists of a strong pattern and because a wallpaper - in its

---

[8] Ohne Schnur, Kwastek, 2004 - Mobile Spaces of Interaction (S.106), Strauss-Fleischmann-Zobel.

appearance - is not part of a wall or not only a layer on a wall, in the right setup it is(!) the wall - in the users perception. To give the wallpaper something like an independent existence, we decided to make it dynamic. That is to say, our wallpaper has the ability to generate a new look, everytime when it is started. If one accepts our wallpaper not as a projection, but as an spatial element a hybrid environment is generated. The idea of immersion is described the best through such magic moments, when a viewer in the cinema is totally absorbed by the aura of the canvas and when he accepts the narrative world as his own. He dives into an artifical world.[9] And no shutter glasses - or whatever - are needed. That is the way how we understand augmented environments...

Fig. 5. Dynamic Wallpaper

Moodboard

We have programmed a patch which translates the room geometry directly into the RGB color spectrum. That is to say, that every room coordinate has its own color. If a visitor

Fig. 6. Moodboard

---

[9] arch plus175 (S.14) Das Immersionsprinzip.

moves through the space the dynamic wallpaper - the projection - reacts with color; from bright red to dark blue...The add-on effect is, that not only the wallpaper appears in RGB but also the entire space, because of the reflections. That's why we have called it "moodboard".

Ambient Objects

There is a table in the no_LAb, which suits best for presentations. The surface of the table is now used as a tangible interface to navigate through presentations. Once again, the main idea was to take an ordinary object - a table - which's function is clear and extend it with a new (intelligent) value. So the challenge is to observe, how would people act with this new object - an ambient object. Will they take the new functions for granted..? A short example introducing the interface: if you want to play a video in your presentation, you have to do the following: On the table there lies a videocassette. If you touch the cassette, the video starts to play. So our goal is an intuitive interaction. That is to say if one moves or points on something, the room system should be able to react.

Space Spirit

Another permanent installation which we designed is the so-called "space spirit" - an audio-ghost which appears just via sound. One of our goals was to pay as much attention to the invisible as to the visible. We have called the invisible: "media furniture", because the invisible media - like audio or infrared tracking-rays - occupies the space as well as the furniture - just in a different way.

A further audio application called "social radar" is dealing with sociological affairs. What happens is a sonification of human behavior concerning nearness and distance. If people come closer to each other the volume of the sound is increasing and the sound-color will be transformed. Audio is a powerful medium to demonstrate the relationship between room and user, between reactive spaces and people in movement, because - as we known - the sense of hearing is even more direct than the sense of seeing.

For all installationparts we used the optical trackingsystem – a six camera setup with a tracking area which is about 5 to 5 to 3 meters. The cameras work with ANSI Infrared at a frequency up to 250 Hz – normally we use 120 Hz. The targets are mainly integrated in normal shoes – we use retroreflexive markers – or in special designed wearables for the visitors. Furthermore we operate with a 16-sensor, wireless UDP interface, LCD projectors and a multi-channel audio system. Next step will be the integration of a light bus system. For Programming we use Max/MSP/Jitter[10], PureData (pd~)[11] and Processing[12]. Communication between these environments and the optical trackingsystem is enabled via Ethernet using the infinitely reconfigurable OSC protocol.[13]

---

[10] http://www.cycling74.com/
[11] http://puredata.info/
[12] http://www.processing.org/
[13] http://www.cnmat.berkeley.edu/OpenSoundControl/

With similar tasks of motion analysis in (architectural) spaces completely different institutions are concerned - e.g. computer science, computer graphics, electronic music, medicine, etc. The project N'Files tries to use offering synergies in this context. It is to be marked at all that the topic "Motion Tracking" could be seen as a transdisciplinary research field and - particularly for the range of architectural research - as a big chance for various cooperations…it' s about using these possibilities.

Christian Fröhlich

Links

website   http://iam.tugraz.at/nolab

live-cams   http://129.27.62.192/
                     http://129.27.62.193/
                     http://129.27.62.65/

References

1. Digitale Transformationen, Fleischmann – Reinhard, 2004 – Praxis Reaktorbau, Edler & Edler (S. 216)
2. Viable und virtuelle Architektur, P. Weibel, 1994 - in *Interaktive Architektur* – Ch. Möller (S. 3-5)
3. Simplicity – the art of complexity, John Maeda, 2006 – in preface *Ars Electronica 2006*
4. Ohne Schnur, Kwastek, 2004 - Mobile Spaces of Interaction (S.102-124), Strauss-Fleischmann-Zobel
5. arch plus175, 2005, Zeitschrift für Architektur und Städtebau (S.14), Das Immersionsprinzip – Anh-Linh Ngo

N'Files
Projectteam: Christian Fröhlich, Martin Kern
                          Blümm, Bräuer, Gerstl, Hohner, Jocham,
                          Kettele, Paar, Pilz, Rust, Trajceski, Zirngast
DI Christian Fröhlich
froehlich@tugraz.at
no_LAb__in_feld
Institute of architecture and media
Inffeldgasse 10 / II
A – 8010 Graz

IPML: Extending SMIL for Distributed Multimedia Presentations

Jun Hu and Loe Feijs

Department of Industrial Design
Eindhoven University of Technology
5600MB Eindhoven, The Netherlands

Abstract. This paper addresses issues of distributing multimedia presentations in an ambient intelligent environment, exams the existing technologies and proposes IPML, a markup language that extends SMIL for distributed settings. It uses a powerful metaphor of play, with which the timing and mapping issues in distributed presentations are easily covered in a natural way.

Ambient Intelligence (AmI) is introduced by Philips Research as a new paradigm in how people interact with technology. It envisions digital environments to be sensitive, adaptive, and responsive to the presence of people, and AmI environments will change the way people use multimedia services [1]. The environments, which include many devices, will play interactive multimedia to engage people in a more immersive experience than just watching television shows. People will interact not only with the environment itself, but also with the interactive multimedia through the environment.

For many years, the research and development of multimedia technologies have increasingly focused on models for distributed applications, but the focus was mainly on the distribution of the media sources. Within the context of AmI, not only are the media sources distributed, the presentation of and the interaction with the media will also be distributed across interface devices. This paper focuses on the design of the structure of multimedia content, believing that the user experience of multimedia in a distributed environment can be enriched by structuring both the media content at the production side and the playback system architecture at the user side in a proper way. The structure should enable both the media presentation and the user interaction to be distributed and synchronized over the networked devices in the environment. The presentation and interaction should be adaptive to the profiles and preferences of the users, and the dynamic configurations of the environment. To structure the media content, the following issues need to be addressed:

1. By what means will the authors compose the content for many different environments? The authors have to be able to specify the following with minimized knowledge of the environments: (a) Desired environment configurations; (b) Interactive content specification for this environment.
2. How can the system playback the interactive media with the cooperation of the user(s) in a way that: (a) makes the best use of the physical environment

H. Zha et al. (Eds.): VSMM 2006, LNCS 4270, pp. 60–70, 2006.

to match the desired environment on the fly. (b) enables context dependent presentation and interaction. Here the term "context" means the environment configuration, the application context, the user preferences, and other presentation circumstances. (c) synchronizes the media and interaction in the environment according to the script.

This paper first exams existing open standards for synchronized media and a scripting language called StoryML, then proposes IPML addressing aforementioned issues.

1   When Technologies Meet Requirements

SMIL and MPEG-4 are contemporary technologies in the area of synchronized multimedia [2,3]. SMIL focuses on Internet applications and enables simple authoring of interactive audiovisual presentations, whereas MPEG-4 is a superset of technologies building on the proven success in digital television, interactive graphics applications and also interactive multimedia for the Web. Both were the most versatile open standards available at the moment of time.

But both were challenged by the requirement for distributed interactions. It requires that the technology is first of all able to describe the distribution of the interaction and the media objects over multiple devices. The BIFS in MPEG-4 emphasizes the composition of media objects on one rendering device. It doesn't take multiple devices into account, nor does it have a notation for it.

SMIL 2.0 introduces the MultiWindowLayout module, which contains elements and attributes providing for creation and control of multiple top level windows [4]. This is very promising and comes closer to the requirements of distributed content interaction. Although these top level windows are supposed to be on the same rendering device, they can to some extent, be recognized as software interface components which have the same capability.

To enable multimedia presentations over multiple interface devices, StoryML was proposed [5]. It models the interactive media presentation as an interactive *Story* presented in a desired environment (called a *Theater*). The story consists of several *Storylines* and a definition of possible user *Interaction* during the story. User interaction can result in switching between storylines, or changes within a storyline. *Dialogues* make up the interaction. A dialogue is a linear conversation between the system and the user, which in turn consists of *Feed-forward* objects, and the *Feedback* objects depending on the user's Response. The environment may have several *Interactors*. The *interactors* render the media objects. And finally, the story is rendered in a Theater.

One problem of the StoryML is that it uses a mixed set of terms. "Story" and "storylines" are from narratives, "media objects" are from computer science, whereas *itneractors* are from human computer interaction. Scripting an interactive story requires various types of background knowledge to some extent. It is questionable whether StoryML has succeeded in both keeping the scripting language at a high level and let the script authors only focus on the interactive content. "Movies did not flourish until the engineers lost control to artists – or more precisely, to the communications craftsmen." [6]

StoryML uses storytelling as a metaphor for weaving the interactive media objects together to present the content as an "interactive story". This metaphor made it difficult to apply StoryML to other applications when there are no explicit storylines or narratives. Moreover, StoryML can only deal with linear structure and use only a storyline switching mechanism for interaction.

Instead of StoryML, it is necessary to design a script language that has a more generic metaphor, that supports both linear and nonlinear structures and that can deal with complex synchronization and interaction scenarios.

2   Play

Instead of storytelling, Interactive Play Markup Language (IPML) uses a more powerful metaphor of *play*. A *play* is a common literary form, refering both to the written works of dramatists and to the complete theatrical *performance* of such. Plays are generally performed in a *theater* by *actors*. To better communicate a unified interpretation of the text in question, productions are usually overseen by a *director*, who often puts his or her own unique interpretation on the production, by providing the actors and other stage people with a *script*. A script is a written set of directions that tell each actor what to say (*lines*) or do (*actions*) and when to say or do it (*timing*). If a play is to be performed by the actors without a director and a script from the director, the results would be unpredictable, if not chaotic.

2.1   Timing in a Play

Timing in a play is very important whether it be when an actor delivers a specific line, or when a certain character enters or exits a scene. It is important for the playwright to take all of these into consideration. The following is an example from *Alice in Wonderland* [7, p.14]:

. . .

ALICE Please! Mind what you're doing!

DUCHESS (*tossing ALICE the baby*). Here . . . you may nurse it if you like. I've got to get ready to play croquet with the Queen in the garden. (*She turns at the door.*) Bring in the soup. The house will be going any minute! (*As the DUCHESS speaks, the house starts moving. The COOK snatches up her pot and dashes into the house.*)

COOK (*to the FROG*). Tidy up, and catch us! (*The FROG leaps about, picking up the vegetables, plate, etc.*)

ALICE (*as the FROG works*). She said "in the garden." Will you please tell me –

FROG There's no sort of use asking me. I'm not in the mood to talk about gardens.

ALICE I must ask some one. What sort of people live around here?

. . .

A few roles are involved in this part of the play. Their lines and actions are presented by the playwright in a sequential manner, and these lines and actions are by default to be played in sequence. However, these sequential lines and actions are often not necessarily to happen immediately one after another. For example, it is not clear in the written play how much of time the duchess should take to perform the action *"tossing Alice the baby"* after Alice says *"Mind what your're doing"* and before the duchess says *"Here ... you may nurse it if you like"*. The director must supervise the timing of these lines and actions for the actors to ensure the performance is right in rhythm and pace. Furthermore, things may happen in parallel – For example, the house starts moving as the duchess speaks, and Alice talks as the frog works. Parallel behaviors are often described without precise timing for performing. It is up to the directors to decide the exact timing based on their interpretation of the play. For example, the director may interpret *"As the DUCHESS speaks, the house starts moving"* as *"at the moment of the duchess start saying 'The house will be going in any minute', the house starts moving"*.

2.2   Mapping: Assigning Roles to Actors

Actors play the roles that are described in the script. One of the important task of the director is to define the cast – assign the roles to actors. This is often done by studying the type of a role and the type of an actor, and finding a good match between them. This is also exactly the problem for distributed presentations: determining which device or component to present certain type of media objects. It can be very hard for a computer to carry out this task, unless these types are indicated in some way otherwise.

In some traditional art of play, these types are even formalized so that a play can be easily performed with a different cast. For example, The character roles in Beijing Opera are divided into four main types according to the sex, age, social status, and profession of the character: male roles (Shēng 生 , fig. 1(a)); female roles (Dàn 旦, fig. 1(b)); the roles with painted faces (Jìng 净, fig. 1(c)) who are usually warriors, heroes, statesmen, or even demons; and clown (Chǒu 丑, fig. 1(d)), a comic character that can be recognized at first sight for his special make-up (a patch of white paint on his nose). These types are then divided into more delicate subtypes, for example Dàn is divided into the following subtypes: Qīng Yī(青衣) is a woman with a strict moral code; Huā Dàn (花旦) is a vivacious young woman; Wǔ Dàn (武旦) is a woman with martial skills and Lǎo Dàn (老) is an elderly woman. In a script of Beijing Opera, roles are defined according to these types. An actor of Beijing Opera is often only specialized in very few subtypes. Given the types of the roles and the types of the actors, the task of assigning roles to actors becomes an easy matching game.

2.3   Interactive Play

Plays can be interactive in many ways. The actors may decide their form of speech, gestures and movements according to the responses from the audience. Again with the example of Beijing opera, plays in early days, which sometimes

(a) Sheng(male)   (b) Dan(female)   (c) Jing   (face   (d) Chou(clown)
painted)

Fig. 1. Role types in Beijing opera

can still be been seen today, may be performed in the street (fig. 2) or in a
tea house, where the actors and the audience are mixed – the actors and the
audience share the stage. The movements of the actors must be adapted to the
locations of the audience, and the close distance between the audience and the
actors stimulates the interaction. An example of such interaction is that the
characters often strike a pose on the stage, and the audience is supposed to
cheer with enthusiasm. The time span of such a pose depends on the reactions of
the audience. Although this is often not written in the script, such an interactive
behavior is by default incorporated in every play of Beijing opera.

Other interactive plays allow the audience to
modify the course of actions in the performance
of the play, and even allow the audience to participate in the performance as actors. Thus in
these plays the audience has an active role. However, this does not mean that the reader of a
novel, the member of audience in the theater are
passive: they are quite active, but this activity
remains internal.

The written text of the play is much less than
the event of the play. It contains only the dialog (the words that the characters actually say),
and some stage directions (the actions performed
by the characters). The play as written by the
playwright is merely a scenario which guides the
director and actors. The phenomenon of theater

Fig. 2. 19th century drawing of
Beijing opera

is experienced in real-time. It is alive and ephemeral – unlike reading a play,
experiencing a play in action is of the moment – here today, and gone tomorrow.

To clarify the discussions, the word *performance* is used to refer to the artifact
the audience and the participants experience during the course of performing a
script by preferred *actors*, monitored and instructed by a *director*. The *script* is
the underlying content representation perceived by the authors as a composite

unit, defining the temporal aspects of the performance, and containing the *actions* which are depicted by the *content elements* or the references to these elements. Traditional multimedia systems use a different set of terms which are comparable to the terms above; they are in many cases similar, but should not be confused.

Next the basic structure of the SMIL scripting language [8] is presented. Using the structure of SMIL and taking the extra requirements into account we then propose Interactive Play Markup Language.

3   SMIL

Synchronized Multimedia Integration Language (SMIL) is an XML-based language for writing interactive multimedia presentations [8]. It has easy to use timing modules for synchronizing many different media types in a presentation. SMIL 2.0 has a set of markup modules.

Not attempting to list all the elements in these modules, we show an object-oriented view[1] of some basic elements in Fig. 3(a): Par, and Seq from the timing and synchronization module, Layout, RootLayout, TopLayout and Region from the layout module, Area from the linking module, MediaObject from the media object module, Meta from the metainformation modules and Head, Body from the structure module. Details about the corresponding language elements can be found in SMIL 2.0 specification [8].

The Region element provides the basics for screen placement of visual media objects. The specific region element that refers to the whole presentation is the RootLayout. Common attributes, methods and relations for these two elements are placed in the superclass named the Layout.

SMIL 2.0 introduced a MultiWindowLayout module over SMIL 1.0, with which the top level presentation region can also be declared with the TopLayout element in a manner similar to the SMIL 1.0 root-layout window, except that multiple instances of the TopLayout element may occur within a single Layout element.

Each presentation can have Head and Body elements. In the Head element one can describe common data for the presentation as whole, such as Meta data and Layout. All Region elements are connected to the Head.

The Mediaobject is the basic building block of a presentation. It can have its own intrinsic duration, for example if it is a video clip or an audio fragment. The media element needs not refer to a complete video file, but may be a part of it. The Content, Container, and Synchronization elements are classes introduced solely for a more detail explanation of the semantics of the Par, Seq, Switch and Mediaobject, and their mutual relations.

Par and Seq are synchronization elements for grouping more than one Content. If the synchronization container is Par, it means that direct subelements can be presented simultaneously. If synchronization container is Seq, it means that direct subelements can be presented only in sequence, one at a time. The Body element is also a Seq container.

---

[1] This UML model only provides an overview of the selected elements and it is not intended to replace, nor to be equivalent to, the DTD specification from W3C.

The connection between Content and Container viewed as an aggregation has a different meaning for the Synchronization element and for the Switch element. If the Container element is Switch, that means that only one subelement from a set of alternative elements should be chosen at the presentation time depending on the settings of the player.

With the Area element, a spatial portion of a visual object can be selected to trigger the appearance of the link's destination. The Area element also provides for linking from non-spatial portions of the media object's display. It allows breaking up an object into temporal subparts, using attributes begin and end.

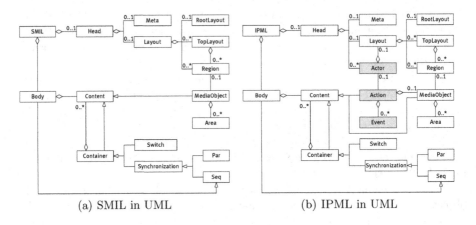

(a) SMIL in UML   (b) IPML in UML

Fig. 3. SMIL and IPML

4   IPML

SMIL seems to have the ingredients for mapping and timing:

- Its timing and synchronization module provides versatile means to describe the time dependencies, which can be directly used in the IPML design without any change.
- The SMIL linking module enables non-linear structures by linking to another part in the same script or to another script. Although the Area element can only be attached to visual objects, this can be easily solved by lifting this concept up to a level that covers all the elements that need to have a linking mechanism.
- The SMIL layout module seems to be very close to the need of distribution and mapping. The concept of separating mapping and timing issues into two different parts, i.e. Head and Body, makes SMIL very flexible for different layouts – if a presentation need to be presented to a different layout setting, only the layout part need to be adapted and the timing relations remain intact, no matter whether this change happens before the presentation in authoring time, or during the presentation in run time.

It is not yet forgotten in section 1, SMIL was considered not directly applicable out of the shelf for the distributed and interactive storytelling: it does not support a notion of multiple devices. However later we also found that we went one step too far – the StoryML does incorporate the concept of multiple actors, but its linear timing model and narrative structure limited its applicability.

What needs to be done is to pick up SMIL again as the basis for the design, extending it with the metaphor of theater play, bringing in the lessons we learnt from StoryML. Fig. 3(b) shows the final IPML extension (marked gray) to SMIL. The Document Type Definition (DTD) of IPML can be found in [9].

Note that in fig. 3(b), if all gray extensions are removed, the remaining structure is exactly the same as the SMIL structure as illustrated in fig. 3(b). This in an intentional design decision: IPML is designed as an extension of SMIL without overriding any original SMIL components and features, so that the compatibility is maximized. Any SMIL script should be able to be presented by a IPML player without any change. An IPML script can also be presented by a SMIL player, although the extended elements will be silently ignored. The compatibility is important, because it can reduce the cost of designing and implementing a new IPML player – the industry may pick up the IPML design and build an IPML player on top of a existing SMIL player so that most of the technologies and implementations in the SMIL player can be reused.

4.1   Actor

The Head part of an IPML script may contain multiple Actor elements which describe the preferred cast of actors. Each Actor has a type attribute which defines the requirements of what this actor should be able to perform. The type attribute has a value of URI, which points to the definition of the actor type. Such a definition can be specified using for example RDF [10] and its extension OWL. RDF is a language for representing information about resources in the World Wide Web. It is particularly intended for representing metadata about Web resources. However, by generalizing the concept of a "Web resource", RDF can also be used to represent information about things that can be identified on the Web, even when they cannot be directly retrieved on the Web. OWL adds more vocabulary for describing properties and classes: among others, relations between classes (e.g. disjointness), cardinality (e.g. "exactly one"), equality, richer typing of properties, characteristics of properties (e.g. symmetry), and enumerated classes. The "thing" we need to describe is the type of the actor.

During the performance time, the real actors present to the theater to form a real cast. Each actor then needs to report to the director about what he can perform, i.e. his actor "type". The "type" of a real actor is defined by the actor manufacturers (well, if an actor can be manufactured). The real actor's type can again be described using an RDF or OWL specification. The director then needs to find out which real actor fits the preferred type best. The mapping game becomes a task of reasoning about these two RDF or OWL described "types". First of all the user's preferences should be considered, even if the user prefers a "naughty boy" to perform a "gentleman". Otherwise, a reasoning process should be conducted by the director, to see whether there is exactly an actor has a type that "equals to" the "gentleman", or to find an "English man" that indeed always "is a" "gentleman", or at least to find a "polite man" that "can be" a "gentleman" and that matches "better than" a "naughty boy", etc. This reasoning process can be supported by a variety of Semantic Web [11] tools, such as Closed World Machine (CWM) [12] and Jena[13] just for example.

4.2   Action

The Action element is similar to the MediaObject element in SMIL. However, Action can be applied to any type of content element which is not explicitly defined using different media objects such as Img, Video and Animation in SMIL. The Action element has an attribute src giving the URI of the content element and its type either implicitly defined by the file name extension in the URI if there is one, or explicitly defined in another attribute type. The type attribute defines the type of a content element as the type attribute of Actor defines the actor type, using a URI referring to a definition.

Action may have an attribute actor to specify the preferred actor to perform it. If it is not specified, the type of the content element may also influence the actor mapping process: the director needs to decide which actor is the best candidate to perform this "type" of action. Again, the user preference should be taken into account first, otherwise a reasoning process should be conducted to find the "gentleman" who can nicely "open the door for the ladies".

In addition, the Action element may have an observe attribute which specifies the interested events. This attribute is designed for an actor to observe the events that are of interest during the the course of performing a specific action. For example, when an actor is performing an action to present a 3D object, it may be interested in the controlling events for rotating the object. This actor can then "observe" these events and react on it. Note that these observed events have no influence on the timing behavior: it will neither start nor stop presenting this 3D object, unless they are included in timing attributes, i.e, begin and end. Events that are not listed will not be passed by the director to the actor during this action, therefore the event propagation overhead can be reduced.

However, some actors may be interested in the events that are not related to certain actions. To accommodate this and not to change the original SMIL structure, we require these Actors to perform an action of the type null, specified using a special URI scheme "null:", which allows events to be "observed" during an action of "doing nothing".

4.3   Event

The third extension of IPML to SMIL is event based linking using the Event element. Event elements in an Action element are similar to Area elements in a visual MediaObject element in SMIL, with the exceptions that it does not require the parent Action element to have a visual content to present, and that the events are not limited to the activation events (clicking on an image, for example) on visual objects. An Event has an attribute enable to include all interested events during an action, including all possible timing events and user interaction events. Once one of the specified event happens, the linking target, specified using the attribute href is triggered. Similar to the Area element, the Event element may also have begin, end and dur attributes to activate the Event only during a specified interval. Event based linking makes IPML very flexible and powerful in constructing non-linear narratives, especially for the situations where the user interaction decides the narrative directions during the performance.

5 Conclude with Alice in Wonderland

To show what a IPML would look like in practice, we again use the example from *Alice in Wonderland* in section 2.1. Since we can't embed multimedia content elements in this printed paper and we only have printed lines and action instructions, we introduce two exotic URI schemes: "say:" for the lines and "do:" for the action instructions, just for the fun of it:

```
<ipml>
<head>
    <actor id="ALICE"    type="http://alice@wonderland.eu/lovelygirl" />
    <actor id="DUCHESS"  type="http://alice@wonderland.eu/seriouswoman" />
    <actor id="COOK"     type="http://alice@wonderland.eu/cook" />
    <actor id="FROG"     type="http://alice@wonderland.eu/frog" />
    <actor id="HOUSE"    type="http://alice@wonderland.eu/woodenhouse" />
</head>
<body>
    <action actor="ALICE" src="say:Please! Mind what you're doing!" />
    <par>
        <action actor="DUCHESS" src="do:tossing Alice the baby"
                id="DuchessTossingBaby"/>
        <action actor="DUCHESS"
                src="say:Here...you may nurse it if you like, I've got to get
                        ready to play croquet with the Queen in the garden." />
        <action actor="ALICE" src="do:receiving the baby"
                begin="DuchessTossingBaby.babytossed"/>
    </par>
    <action actor="DUCHESS" src="do:turns at the door" />
    <action actor="DUCHESS" src="say:Bring in the soup." />
    <par>
        <action actor="HOUSE" src="do:moving" />
        <seq>
            <par>
                <action actor="DUCHESS" src="say:The house will be going any minute!" />
                <action actor="COOK"    src="do:snatches up her pot and dashes into the
                        house" />
            </par>
            <action actor="COOK" src="do:turns to the FROG" />
            <action actor="COOK" src="say:Tidy up, and catch us!" />
            <par>
                <action actor="FROG"  src="do:leaps about" />
                <action actor="FROG"  src="do:picking up the vegetables, plates, etc." />
                <action actor="ALICE" src="say:She said 'in the garden', will you please
                        tell me −" />
            </par>
            <action actor="FROG"  src="say:There's no sort of reason asking me, I'm not
                        in the mood to talk about gardens." />
            <action actor="ALICE" src="say:I must ask some one. What sort of people live
                        around here?" />
        </seq>
    </par>
</body>
</ipml>
```

References

1. Aarts, E.: Ambient intelligence: a multimedia perspective. IEEE Multimedia **11**(1) (2004) 12–19
2. Battista, S., Casalino, F., Lande, C.: MPEG-4: A multimedia standard for the third millennium, part 1. IEEE MultiMedia **6**(4) (1999) 74–83
3. Battista, S., Casalino, F., Lande, C.: MPEG-4: A multimedia standard for the third millennium, part 2. IEEE MultiMedia **7**(1) (2000) 76–84
4. Rutledge, L.: SMIL 2.0: XML for web multimedia. IEEE Internet Computing **5**(5) (2001) 78–84
5. Hu, J.: StoryML: Enabling distributed interfaces for interactive media. In: The Twelfth International World Wide Web Conference, Budapest, Hungary, WWW (2003)
6. Heckel, P. In: The Elements of Friendly Software Design. Sybex (1991) 4
7. Carroll, L., Chorpenning, C.B.: Alice in Wonderland. Dramatic Publishing Co., Woodstock (1958)
8. Ayars, J., Bulterman, D., Cohen, A., Day, K., Hodge, E., Hoschka, P., Hyche, E., Jourdan, M., Kim, M., Kubota, K., Lanphier, R., Layaïda, N., Michel, T., Newman, D., van Ossenbruggen, J., Rutledge, L., Saccocio, B., Schmitz, P., ten Kate, W., Michel, T.: Synchronized multimedia integration language (SMIL 2.0) - [second edition]. W3C recommendation (2005)
9. Hu, J.: Design of a Distributed Architecture for Enriching Media Experience in Home Theaters. Technische Universiteit Eindhoven (2006)
10. McBride, B.: Rdf primer. W3C recommendation (2004)
11. Berners-Lee, T., Fischetti, M.: Weaving the Web: The Original Design and Ultimate Destiny of the World Wide Web by Its Inventor. Harper San Francisco (1999) Foreword By-Michael L. Dertouzos.
12. Berners-Lee, T., Hawke, S., Connolly, D.: Semantic web tutorial using n3. Turorial (2004)
13. McBride, B.: Jena: Implementing the rdf model and syntax specification. In: Semantic Web Workshop, WWW2001. (2001)

The Use of Multi-sensory Feedback to Improve the Usability of a Virtual Assembly Environment

Ying Zhang and Adrian R.L. Travis

Department of Engineering, University of Cambridge, 9 JJ Thomson
Avenue, Cambridge, CB3 0FA, UK
{yz282, arlt1}@cam.ac.uk

Abstract. This paper presents the usability evaluation of our developed multi-sensory Virtual Assembly Environment (VAE). The evaluation is conducted by using its three attributes: 1) efficiency of use; 2) user's satisfaction; and 3) reliability in use. These are addressed by using task completion times (TCTs), questionnaires, and human performance error rates (HPERs), respectively. A peg-in-a-hole and a Sener electronic box assembly tasks have been used as the task cases to perform the experiments, using sixteen participants. The experimental outcomes are analysed and discussed.

Keywords: Usability, Virtual Environment, Assembly Simulation, Multi-sensory Feedback.

1   Introduction

Virtual Environment (VE) technology has the potential for offering a useful method to interactively evaluate assembly-related engineering decisions, and to factor the human elements and considerations into finished products very early in the development cycle, without physical realisation of the products [1][2][3][4][5]. Assembly is an interactive process involving the operator (user) and the handled objects, and hence this requires the assembly simulation environment to be able to react in real time in response to the user's actions. Usability is considered as a multidimensional attribute of software quality and a key concept of human computer interaction, which is concerned with improving the human interaction with computers [6]. Therefore, this research evaluates the usability of a developed VAE, in which the multi-sensory feedback was integrated. The usability is evaluated in its three attributes: 1) efficiency of use; 2) user's satisfaction; and 3) reliability in use. These are addressed by using TCTs, questionnaires, and HPERs, respectively.

2   Experimental Platform

The hardware configuration and software architecture of the developed multi-sensory VAE, on which the evaluation experiment was conducted, can be found in [7].

H. Zha et al. (Eds.): VSMM 2006, LNCS 4270, pp. 71–80, 2006.

3 Experimental Hypotheses

There are three hypotheses: 1) the use of visual feedback can lead to better usability than neutral condition; 2) the use of 3D auditory feedback can lead to better usability than neutral condition; and 3) the use of the integrated feedback (*visual plus auditory*) can lead to better usability than either feedback used in isolation. The usability is evaluated by using its three attributes. The attribute of *efficiency of use* is measured by using TCTs, *user's satisfaction* is assessed by using questionnaires, and *reliability in use* is measured by using HPERs. TCTs and HPERs are expected to decrease by the integration of multi-sensory feedback.

4 Experimental Design

There are two independent variables in this experiment: visual feedback and auditory feedback, which can be present or absent. The variations of the independent variables form the different feedback conditions, namely, neutral condition (*neither* visual *nor* auditory feedback), visual feedback condition, auditory feedback condition, and the integrated feedback condition (visual *plus* auditory feedback). The dependent variables are the TCT and the HPER under each experimental condition, and subjective ratings and preferences.

Task Cases: a peg-in-a-hole and a Sener electronic box assembly task cases are used to evaluate the effectiveness of visual and/or auditory feedback on the usability of VAE. The scenarios of these two task cases can be found in [8].

Experimental Measures: This experiment is a 2×2 (two-factor) within-participants design with the visual feedback (present *vs* absent) along with auditory feedback (present *vs* absent) being the within factors. For the four conditions, the presentation order was counterbalanced across participants and conditions, and determined by a 4×4 Latin Square, providing 16 different orders of feedback presentation. Each participant was randomly assigned to one of the orders. TCTs and HPERs data of the peg-in-a-hole assembly task, and questionnaires data of the Sener electronic box assembly task were recorded in this experiment. Considering the learning effects observed from the pilot study and alleviating the workload of the experiment, although under each condition each participant went through four trials, only data of the assembly TCT from the third and fourth trials were recorded to calculate the average TCT under each condition.

Participants: 16 participants from the students and staff of our research centre were invited to attend this experiment. All of them have normal or corrected normal visual acuity, normal colour vision and normal hearing. They do not have any VE experience, but they may have varying computer experience from basic e-mail and office processing to programming skills. They are healthy without any major cognitive deficits or physical limitations. No participants dropped out in the middle of the experiment, and all of them went through the experiment smoothly.

Experimental Procedures: Participants were randomly assigned to one of the 16 orders of feedback presentation prior to their arrival. Upon arrival, each participant was asked to read and sign a consent form. A questionnaire was then required to complete to assess standard demographic information, including any previous computer and VE experience of the participant. The participants' colour vision and hearing were then tested by simple means. The next step, a brief of the specifics of the two task cases was given, and diagrams of the assembly parts and the processes of the two task cases were shown. The participants were asked to complete the peg-in-a-hole assembly task as quickly as possible, and then were brought to the responsive workbench-based VAE to start the experiment. Each participant was required to complete the peg-in-a-hole task four times and then the Sener electronic box four times respectively under each feedback condition. For the peg-in-a-hole assembly task case, the number of performance failure of each participant under each feedback condition was counted, and the assembly TCT from the third and the fourth trials under each feedback condition were recorded. For the Sener electronic box assembly task case, when the participants completed the task under each feedback condition, they were required to complete the questionnaires described in next paragraph.

Questionnaires: The usability attribute of *user's satisfaction* was evaluated by using the questionnaires including 10-point rating scales of the overall satisfaction, the realism, perceived task difficulty and performance, ease learning, perceived system speed and overall reaction to the received feedback. Additionally, after the participants completed the tasks under all conditions they were required to complete a set of 7-point rating scales and open-ended questions comparing the different feedback cues. The 7-point rating scales asked the participants to compare how well the different feedback cues helped them to complete the task, how they foresaw these cues helpful in a real design application, and which kind of feedback cues they preferred. Preferences were determined by asking participants to rank the four conditions in the order of his/her preference when all trials were completed. Finally, participants were asked to provide general opinions and comments about their experiences. The answers of the participants were recorded and analysed.

5 Experimental Results

TCTs: Both two-way repeated measures ANOVA and post-hoc pair-wise t-test comparisons are conducted, respectively, on the TCTs (see Fig. 1) in order to find the effects of four feedback conditions on the usability. Two-way repeated measures ANOVA on TCTs generate statistically significant results for auditory feedback and visual feedback, respectively. Pair-wise t-test comparisons of TCTs are conducted between neutral condition, visual feedback condition, auditory feedback condition, and the integrated feedback condition. The outcomes (one-tailed tests) are listed in Table 1.

HPERs: The HPERs under the four feedback conditions decrease from $HPER_{neutral-feedback} = 0.44$ under the neutral condition, to $HPER_{visual-feedback}$

Table 1. Pair-wise t-test comparisons of TCTs

t-test comparisons between different feedback conditions	t-value $(t_{(15)})$
neutral vs visual	6.67 $(p < 0.05)$
neutral vs auditory	7.22 $(p < 0.05)$
neutral vs integrated	8.23 $(p < 0.05)$
visual vs integrated	6.23 $(p < 0.05)$
auditory vs integrated	6.51 $(p < 0.05)$
visual vs auditory	0.22 $(p > 0.05)$

$= 0.19$ under visual feedback condition and $HPER_{auditory-feedback} = 0.19$ under auditory feedback condition, and then to $HPER_{integrated-feedback} = 0.03$ under the integrated feedback condition (see Fig. 2). Pair-wise t-test comparisons of HPERs are conducted between the four feedback conditions, respectively. The outcomes (one-tailed tests) are listed in Table 2.

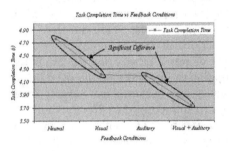

Fig. 1. Mean TCT   **Fig. 2.** HPERs vs Feedback Conditions

Table 2. Pair-wise t-test comparisons of HPERs

t-test comparisons between different feedback conditions	t-value $(t_{(15)})$
neutral vs visual	3.21 $(p < 0.05)$
neutral vs auditory	3.21 $(p < 0.05)$
neutral vs integrated	4.61 $(p < 0.05)$
visual vs integrated	2.40 $(p < 0.05)$
auditory vs integrated	2.40 $(p < 0.05)$

However, there is no statistically significant difference between visual feedback condition and auditory feedback condition, since $HPER_{visual-feedback} = HPER_{auditory-feedback} = 0.19$.

Participants' Preferences and Satisfaction: For the subjective evaluation, Fig. 3 shows the totals for the top preferences of participants. Fig. 4 indicates the helpfulness of the different feedback to the task completion from the results of the 7-point questionnaires. On one hand, it is obvious from the data, the number of participants preferring the integrated feedback is larger than that preferring other feedback types. The number of participants preferring the neutral condition is obviously smaller than that preferring other feedback. On the other hand, there are significant differences between the number of participants preferring the integrated feedback and the number of the participants preferring neutral feedback; between the integrated feedback and either visual or auditory feedback used in isolation; between either visual or auditory feedback used in isolation and the neutral feedback.

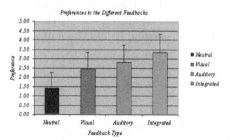

Fig. 3. Preferences to the Different Feedback Conditions

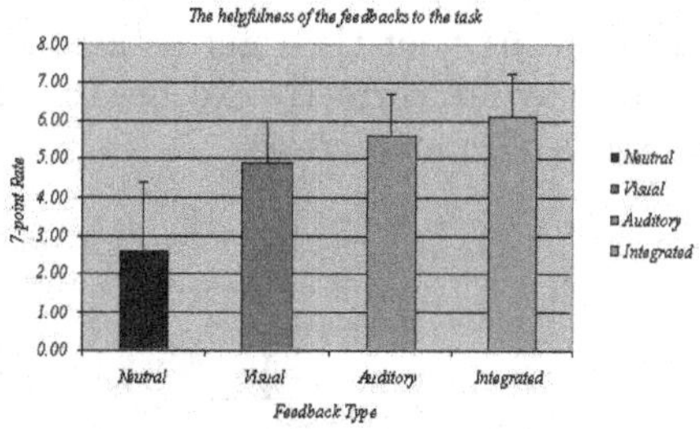

Fig. 4. Helpfulness of the Different Feedback to the Usability

6 Analysis and Discussion

This section uses the experimental data to explain and conclude the hypotheses described in section 3, and then analyses the experimental outcomes from the aspect of HPER.

6.1 Hypotheses Analysis

The two-way repeated measures ANOVA on the TCTs achieved statistically significant results for the visual feedback ($F = 52.98, p < 0.05$) and the auditory feedback ($F = 55.42, p < 0.05$). Furthermore, the pair-wise t-test for TCTs and HPERs described in section 5 also support the three hypotheses. Therefore, the outcomes of the experiment support the hypotheses described in section 3.

In addition, from the participants' general opinions and comments about their task completion experience, the non-realistic or inappropriate feedback had negative effects, and easily made them frustrated. Meanwhile, the participants' frustration was informally observed more frequent when they performed the assembly task under neutral condition than under visual and/or auditory feedback conditions, which is consistent with the subjective experimental data. Therefore, the use of visual and/or auditory feedback could lead to better usability of the developed multi-sensory VAE.

6.2 HPER Analysis

This subsection firstly describes the possible kinds of human errors within the context of information processing, and then analyses the possible reasons behind the above HPER outcomes from two aspects: the prevention of the human errors, and the timely recovery from the human errors. Finally, it concludes that the introduction of visual and/or auditory feedback to the VAE has potential to improve the usability attribute of *reliability in use*.

Prevention of Human Errors. Human may make some errors in the processing of information when interacting with the confronted targets (e.g. world, environment, and various systems). These errors can be classified within a framework shown in Fig. 5. Within the context of information processing, a user may or may not correctly interpret the stimulus evidence which represents the confronted target; given a correct interpretation, the user then may or may not intend to carry out the right action to deal with the situation; finally, the user may or may not correctly execute the intention. According to [9], there are several kinds of human errors:

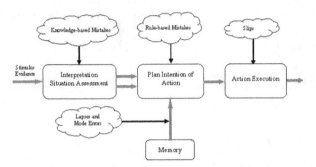

Fig. 5. A Framework of Information Processing Context for Representing Human Errors [9]

a) Mistakes result from misinterpretation, or the wrong choice of intentions, which actually result from the shortcomings of perception, memory, and cognition. The action does occur, but does not succeed in meeting the goal, since either the diagnosis is wrong or the rule for action selection is incorrect. There are two kinds of mistakes discriminated by [10]: 1) *Knowledge-based-mistakes*: this kind of errors is made in decision-making, owing to a failure to understand the situation (i.e. incorrect knowledge) and/or insufficient knowledge or expertise to interpret complex information. Such mistakes can often result from poor information displays (i.e. feedback presentation), either presenting inadequate information or presented in a poor format. Knowledge-based mistakes are more likely to be performed with less certainty of the user. 2) *Rule-based-mistakes*: this kind of errors occurs when the users are somewhat much surer of their ground. They know or they believe they know the situation and therefore they invoke a rule or plan of action to deal with it. Rule-based mistakes are performed with confidence, although in a situation in which the rules do not apply. The probability of making rule-based mistakes is lower than knowledge-based mistakes [10], since there are many more ways in which information acquisition and integration can fail through shortcomings of attention, working memory, logical reasoning, and decision making.

b) Slips occur, where the right intention is incorrectly carried out. The user understands the situation and the goal, and has the correct formulation of the action, but unfortunately performs an incorrect action. There are three possible reasons: 1) the intended action (or action sequence) involves a slight departure from the routine and frequently performed actions; 2) some characteristics of either the stimulus environment or the action sequence itself are closely related to the current inappropriate (but more frequent) action; and 3) the action sequence is relatively automated and therefore not monitored closely by attention [9]. As a result, slips are more likely to occur when attention is directed away from the issues in question.

c) Lapses occur, when the user does not carry out any action at all by the omission or the forgetting of the steps in a procedural sequence, such as maintenance or installation procedures [11].

d) Mode Errors occur, when a particular action, which is highly appropriate in one mode of operation, is performed in a different, inappropriate mode due to that the user has not correctly remembered the appropriate context [12].

The outcomes of HPER are analysed using the aforementioned framework in Fig. 5 as follows: 1) *Mistakes:* Under the neutral condition, without sufficient information the participants can not understand the situation well when performing the assembly task, such as detection of the collisions between the manipulated object (e.g. the peg) and the surrounding objects (e.g. the base with a hole), and the recognition of the motion constraints. This shortcoming of perception (i.e. lack of feedback) causes misinterpretation, and incorrect diagnosis to the situation, therefore, the user has a higher probability of making this kind of errors. With the introduction of the visual or auditory feedback into the VAE, the user can understand the situation better than that with no cues, and consequently, the probability of making this kind of error decreases. Furthermore, under the integrated feedback condition, the developed environment provides the user with adequate feedback in two ways, which may complement each other (e.g. auditory sense can take from any direction and it is transient, visual sense tends to be more continuously available, but can only take from the direction which the user is gazing, and the short-term auditory store is longer than short-term visual store). As a result, the user can better interpret the situation and avoid the wrong choice of intentions, hence the probability of making this kind of errors is lower than either visual or auditory feedback used in isolation. Therefore, the order of the probability of making this kind of human error under these four feedback conditions is: *integrated feedback < visual feedback ≈ auditory feedback < none feedback condition.* 2) *Slips:* The visual and/or auditory feedback can intuitively prompt the user when his/her action (or action sequence) involves a slight departure from the routine and help the user timely amend the departure, so as to avoid this kind of errors. However, this is a double-edged sword, especially under the integrated feedback condition. On one hand, it can assist the user to timely recover from the deviations, on the other hand, it has the risk of distracting the user's attention from the task action (or action sequence) if inappropriately integrated. This research has paid much attention to this issue; the feedback is concomitant with the events, and different feedback modalities are seamlessly integrated. Therefore, the probability of making *'Slips errors'* is the same order as the above one. 3) *Lapses:* Under the neutral condition, without adequate feedback the user frequently forgets or omits some steps in the procedural sequence when performing the assembly task, and sometimes can not even continue the task. S/he frequently tries to pass the step by trial and error. For example, the user tried to align the axis of peg with the axis of the hole in the peg-in-a-hole task case of this research. Another example is that the user forgot to mate the bottom surface of the peg's ear with the top surface of the base, and ended the assembly task incompletely. After the introduction of the visual and/or auditory feedback into the VAE, the feedback indicates the alignment between the axis of peg and the axis of the hole, and prompts the user that the bottom surface of the peg's ear and the top surface of the base have not been mated yet, and need further actions. Certainly, under the integrated feedback condition, the developed environment provides the user with more informative feedback in two complementary ways to reduce the *'Lapses'* errors. Therefore, the probability of making *'Lapses errors'* is the same order as the above one. 4) **Mode Errors:** The visual and/or auditory feedback can reduce this kind of errors. For example, before the user starts the assembly process, s/he needs to use the Wand to point, select and fix the base, and then should change to the assembly mode by pressing a button on the Wand. The user can then start the assembly process by picking up the peg. If the base is not fixed before the user starts assembly process, when the peg collides with the base later, the base would move together with the peg, making it impossible to insert the peg into the hole of the base. Under the neutral condition, owing to the lack of sufficient feedback this kind of mode errors frequently occurs. The visual and/or auditory feedback can prompt the user to change the manipulation to the appropriate mode. The probability of making the *'Mode Errors'* is the same order as the above one.

From the above qualitative analysis of the HPERs, the contribution of the multi-sensory feedback to the prevention of the human errors is in the order: *integrated feedback > visual feedback ≈ auditory feedback > none feedback condition*, which is consistent with the quantitative analysis of human errors by using HPERs. It is thus further concluded that the introduction of auditory and/or visual feedback improves *reliability in use* in one aspect.

Recovery from the Human Errors. The multi-sensory feedback can also decrease the time that the developed VAE takes to recover from errors. Human errors can happen in any phases of task performance and incur the relevant consequences. Therefore, error recovery mechanisms aim to prevent the errors in advance and recover the errors afterwards. Human error recovery should address the following aspects: 1) the information required in human-computer interface to make human errors evident; 2) human-computer interface resources to recover human errors; and 3) time frame in which the recovery procedures are effective [13]. The system design should avoid the errors by introducing feedback or creating recovery functions that make the errors harmless.

Under consideration of these three aspects, the developed VAE uses multi-sensory feedback to convey whether the user's activities are correct or not, which can aid the user to recover from errors, timely. For instance, in the peg-in-a-hole assembly task case, the user grasps the revolute key, moves it towards the base with a hole; the revolute key collides with the base and then stops. Without the aid of intuitive cues, it is quite difficult for the user to judge the mating state between the top planar surface of the base and the bottom surface of the revolute key, and hence the user has high probability of making operational mistakes in this process. The multi-modal interaction metaphor provides visual feedback by changing the colours of the mating surfaces, and auditory feedback by activating a localised sound event, to signal the user whether or not the revolute key has been put and adjusted to the correct position and orientation. If the revolute key has been put to the wrong position and/or orientation, the user is warned of the wrong operation, and then the user can go backward ("undo") and recover from the error. If the revolute key has been put to the precise position and orientation, the collision between the revolute and the base is detected, and the constraint of the revolute key's motion is recognised. The user is then confirmed of the correct operation and prompted to go further. This means that the developed VAE improves the performance of error recovery through providing multi-modal feedback. It is thus further concluded that the introduction of auditory and/or visual feedback improves *reliability in use* in another aspect.

In conclusion, the integration of multi-sensory feedback prevents the human errors to occur, and hence the users make no or less mistakes. Furthermore, it timely and intuitively warns the user of the errors, and hence it takes less time for the user to recover from errors. This explains why the introduction of auditory and/or visual feedback into the VAE decreases HPER, and improves the usability attribute of *reliability in use*.

7   Conclusions

A peg-in-a-hole and a Sener electronic box assembly tasks have been used as task cases to perform the usability evaluation experiments of a developed multi-sensory VAE, using sixteen participants. The outcomes show that the introduction of 3D auditory and/or visual feedback could improve its usability. They also indicated that the integrated feedback offer better usability than either feedback used in isolation. Most participants preferred the integrated feedback to either feedback or no feedback. The possible reasons behind this are that the introduction of visual and/or auditory feedback into VAE provides more cues to collision detection, geometric constraints management involving recognition and deletion, and error indication and recovery. Besides these aspects, it also provides cues to aid the users when they identify and select the next assembly object from a collection of assembly components, identify assembly position, determine the assembly orientation of the object, reason and explore the various assembly options, and alleviate deviations or errors by warning the users timely. Therefore, on one hand, the introduction of intuitive feedback reduces the users' reaction times, response latencies, and mental workload for task complexity reasoning, problem solving and decision making, thus decreasing the TCTs. On the other hand, the intuitive feedback prevents the users' operation errors to occur by warning the users timely and intuitively, and hence the users make no or less mistakes, thus decreasing the HPERs. Furthermore, the integrated feedback provides the users with adequate feedback in two ways, which complement each other when integrated seamlessly. For instance, the auditory sense can take from any direction and is transient; visual sense tends to be more continuously available, but can only take from the direction which s/he is gazing; and the short-term auditory store is longer than short-term visual store in human memory. As a result, the integrated feedback presents assembly task-related information in multiple modes to the users. This mechanism supports the expansion of short-term or working memory and problem solution in spatially-orientated geometry tasks, and reduces the cognitive load of the users. However, the inappropriate integrated feedback distracts the users' attention from the task action (or action sequence), thus having negative impacts on the usability.

References

1. Dai, F. (ed.): Virtual Reality for Industrial Application. Springer Verlag, Berlin, Heidelberg, Germany (1998)
2. Jayaram, S., Jayaram, U., Wang, Y., Tirumali, H., Lyons, K., Hart, P.: VADE: A Virtual Assembly Design Environment. IEEE Computer Graphics & Application, November (1999)
3. Banerjee, P., Zetu, D.: Virtual Manufacturing. John Wiley & Sons Inc, USA (2001)
4. Marcelino, L., Murray, N., Fernando, T.: A Constraint Manager to Support Virtual Maintainability. Computers & Graphics, Vol. 27, No.1, 19-26, (2003)
5. Ong, S. K., Nee, A. Y. C. (Ed.): Virtual and Augmented Reality Applications in Manufacturing. Springer Verlag, London (2004)
6. Folmer, E., Bosch, J.: Architecture for Usability: a Survey. Journal of Systems and Software, Vol. 70, No.1, 61-78, (2002)
7. Zhang, Y., Fernando, T.: 3D Sound Feedback Act as Task Aid in a Virtual Assembly Environment. Proceedings of Theory and Practice of Computer Graphics 2003 (TPCG 2003), IEEE Computer Society Press, 3-5 June, Birmingham, England (2003)
8. Zhang, Y., Fernando, T., Sotudeh, R., Xiao, H.: The Use of Visual and Auditory Feedback for Assembly Task Performance in a Virtual Environment. Proceedings of the 9th International Conference on Information Visualisation (IV'05), IEEE Computer Society Press, 6-8 July, London, England (2005)
9. Wickens, C. D., Hollands, J. G: Engineering Psychology and Human Performance (3rd ed.). Prentice Hall Press (1999)
10. Reason, J.: Human Error. New York: Cambridge University Press (1990)
11. Reason, J.: Managing the Risks of Organisational Accidents. Brookfield, VT: Ashgate (1997)
12. Norman, D.: The Psychology of Everyday Things. New York: Harper & Row (1988)
13. Filgueiras, L.: Human Performance Reliability in the Design-for-Usability Life Cycle for Safety Human-Computer Interfaces. Proceedings of the 18th International Conference on Computer Safety, Reliability and Security, Toulouse, France (1999)

GPU-Based Soft Shadow Rendering Using Non-linear Pre-computed Radiance Transfer Approximation

Lili Wang, Jing Wang, and Qinping Zhao

School of Computer Science and Engineering, Bei Hang University,
Beijing 100083, P.R. China
{lily_w, wangj, zhaoqp}@vrlab.buaa.edu.cn

Abstract. Soft shadow computation plays an important role in generating photo-realistic images. A new method of real-time all-frequency shadow rendering in 3D scenes under dynamic illumination is introduced in this paper. The non-linear wavelet approximation on the pre-computed radiance transfer matrix is used, which can help us to select the main directions sensitive to illumination of each sampling point. This approach efficiently avoids non-linear selection of the light vector in real-time rendering, and the approximation is used only once in the pre-computed phrase. We encode the resulting radiance transfer matrix into a sparse form, and store it as textures in 2D texture buffers. Meanwhile, the light vector is organized into a cube map on GPU to accelerate computation in the run-time process. This approach has been applied to render a variety of 3D scenes with soft shadows, and proved to be able to increase the relighting speed with no image quality reduction.

Keywords: shadow algorithm, pre-computed radiance transfer, relighting.

1 Introduction

Developing techniques for rendering photo-realistic images is one of the most important research areas in computer graphics. Many applications such as visual simulations and games require relighting 3D scenes with natural light sources and describing complicated phenomena of light transfer in order to make users feel more immerged into a 3D world. However, providing a realistic 3D scene with all-frequency shadows at an interactive rate is difficult, and the common problem is that the computation cost only allows crude shadows when an interactive rate is required. Many recent papers suggest using the pre-computed approaches [1,2] to enable detailed shadow generation without heavy computation burden in real-time rendering. But the efficiency of the algorithms suggested still can be improved.

This paper provides a new method for real-time soft shadow rendering in a 3D world. It is based on the pre-computed radiance transfer approximation, but we re-organize the data structure of the resulting radiance transfer matrix and the light vector to make the algorithm adaptive to GPU. Our main contributions can be summarized as below:

H. Zha et al. (Eds.): VSMM 2006, LNCS 4270, pp. 81–92, 2006.

1. Using the pre-computed radiance transfer approximation instead of the approximation of the light vector. This approach avoids non-linear selection of the light vector in the run-time process, and the approximation is used only once in the pre-computed phrase.
2. Encoding the resulting light transfer matrix into the sparse form, storing it as textures in texture buffers, and organizing the light vector into a cube map. The parallel processing ability of GPU is used to accelerate computation in run-time rendering.

The paper develops as follows: Section 2 reviews the existing methods of soft shadow rendering. Section 3 presents the non-linear pre-computed radiance transfer approximation. The run-time soft shadow rendering is detailed in Section 4, the results are discussed in Section 5, and the conclusion is given in Section 6.

2 Previous Work

Rendering shadows in 3D scenes has been a hot topic in computer graphics. The original methods sample a point light source to create the binary mask, which we refer to as "hard shadow" [3]. By contrast, for a light source of a certain shape and size in practice, "soft shadow" will be created. In order to generate shadows at an interactive rate, two basic techniques for computing shadows from a point light source are provided, namely "shadow map" and "shadow volume" [4,5]. Later, they are also extended to soft shadow rendering [6].

A recent technique named Image Based Lighting (IBL) [7] presents new challenges to shadow rendering. It makes shadow computation more complex than ever. A number of IBL-related methods are developed to create soft shadows in virtual environments. Assarsson [6] uses the shadow volume method to construct penumbra wedges, and then looks up into the four-dimensional texture to refill the pixels under the penumbra region. This method cannot deal with area lights directly. Debevec [8] breaks up this limitation, and uses the environment map to re-illuminate convex objects and create the effect of self-shadows. However, this method cannot use in real-time rendering.

Sloan's pre-computed radiance transfer method [1] first computes transfer simulation required by complex transfer functions for given objects. In the run-time process, these transfer functions are applied to actual incident lighting. Ren [2] extends Sloan's method to real-time rendering of objects under all-frequency, time-varying illumination. He chooses a non-linear wavelet approximation to localize small area lights better in space. But a huge amount of storage space is needed to store the light transfer information, and a large sparse matrix multiplication needs to be implemented on CPU during rendering.

In order to accelerate computations, GPU is used to process this multiplication. Much research has been done to explore the non-graphical use of graphics hardware with the broad availability of programmable graphics hardware. GPU's powerful parallel processing ability makes computation more efficient in contrast to CPU[9]. Therefore, redesigning the CPU-based algorithms and refitting them to GPU provides a way to improve the efficiency of the computation.

The fundamental difference between our method and current ones is that we focus on selecting the main directions sensitive to illumination of each sampling point, while other ones deal with approximations on the light map in wavelet basis. We uses the non-linear approximation of the pre-computed radiance transfer matrix only once in pre-computed phrase, and by making use of graphics hardware to accelerate computation, our method performs more efficiently.

3 Non-linear Pre-computed Radiance Transfer Approximation

3.1 Basic Algorithm of Illumination from the Environment Map

Relighting scene with the environment map can be formulated as equation (1)[2]:

$$\mathbf{B}(\mathbf{x}, w_0) = \int \int_\Omega \mathbf{L}(w) S(\mathbf{x}, w) f_r(\mathbf{x}, w \rightarrow w_0)(w * n(\mathbf{x})) dw \tag{1}$$

x represents a sampled vertex in the 3D scene, $\mathbf{w_0}$ is the view direction, w is the direction of the incident, L represents the light source in the environment map, S is a Boolean function of visibility at x from the direction w, $\mathbf{f_r}$ is reflection function at x, and $\mathbf{w_*}$ n(x) is the cosine of the incident angle.

When it is assumed that the reflection in the 3D scene is purely diffuse, $\mathbf{f_r}$ depends only on the position of x. Therefore, we can replace part of equation above with the function T(equation (2)), which contains light transfer information.

$$\mathbf{T}(\mathbf{x}, w) = S(\mathbf{x}, w) f_r(\mathbf{x})(w \cdot n(\mathbf{x})) \tag{2}$$

Then, spatial discretization is done on equation (1), and we get equation (3), which is in the matrix form (4):

$$\mathbf{B}(\mathbf{x}_i) = \sum_j \mathbf{T}(\mathbf{x}_i, w_j) \mathbf{L}(w_j) \tag{3}$$

$$\mathbf{B} = \mathbf{TL} \tag{4}$$

3.2 Non-linear Approximation in Pre-computation

The radiance transfer matrix T is processed in the pre-computation phase. Each row of the matrix represents light transfer conditions of all discrete directions for a single sample. Almost all current lighting models can be applied, and in the case of simple lighting, the elements in the matrix are equal to the binary values of visibility, which later weight with two parameters: one is the reflection function of certain material at the sampling point, and the other is the cosine coefficient of the angle between the normal and the incident direction of light.

In the section below, sampling strategies and non-linear approximation used in T's processing are discussed. We also give an explanation of the resulting matrix storage for the convenience of GPU computation.

3.2.1 Sampling Strategies

The sampling strategies that we adopt to compute matrix **T** in this paper are a little different from those in [2], and prove to be easier to compute and understand.

1. Sampling the vertices of the geometry model. This is a rather simple method because every vertex has its own position in the 3D scene. However, we may need to triangularize the surface before sampling in order to get a more regular mesh.
2. Sampling texels in a texture of the 3D object. Since we cannot get the exact position of each texel of the texture in 3D space because of the distortion introduced by perspective projection, we have to use approximate values as substitutes. Extra space is needed to store this texture even though not all texels are used as sampling points. But this method has its own advantage that it is suitable to be implemented on GPU to accelerate computation.

Both strategies can be applied to a synthetic 3D scene to get radiance, but the type of the object decides one to be chosen.

3.2.2 Non-linear Radiance Transfer Approximation

In order to obtain the main directions that contribute greatly to light transfer for a certain sampling point, wavelet transform is performed in each row of the matrix **T**. First, we choose the 2D Harr wavelet basis function to transform the raw data. Since each row of the matrix **T** is corresponding to the light cube map, the wavelet transform should be conducted on the six 2D faces of the cube map respectively. And then, quantification is executed on the wavelet coefficients.

After this, we rearrange the elements in each row of the transformed matrix, and place the important ones at the head of the rows. In this paper, we rearrange each row according to the area weight, which is the result of multiplying the wavelet coefficient by its area. Therefore, the wavelet coefficients with low frequency are put at the beginning of the sequence, and they play an important role in soft shadow shape rendering. This arrangement can help us to gain more realistic images especially in environments with many low-frequency light sources. To obtain a higher refresh speed, wavelet coefficients in matrix **T** selection are used here in contrast to **L** selection in [2]. We cut off the elements at the rear of the rows in the rearranged radiance transfer matrix, and render a scene only with the radiance in main directions placed at the beginning of each row.

3.2.3 Storage of the Radiance Transfer Matrix

For the convenience of run-time computation on GPU, the radiance transfer matrix **T** should be organized as textures. Fig.1 gives the flow of this data arrangement.

After wavelet transform and quantification, **T** becomes sparse. We compress it into indexed data structure, and discard all zero coefficients. For every non-zero element, an individual data unit is allotted. Table 1 describes the CPU-oriented data structure unit. And then, a table is generated to store the indices and their values according to arranged weight of each sampling point. We select the data from the same rows of the tables, and transform the one-dimensional indices into direction vectors in three-dimensional

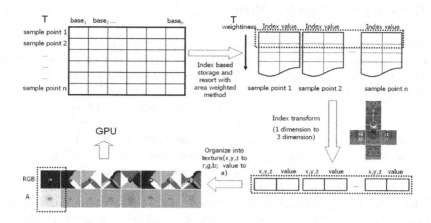

Fig. 1. Flow Chart of Data Arrangement

space based on the cube light map, and another GPU-oriented data structure unit is needed to store the elements (Table 2). The directions with the special weight of all sampling points are stored in a floating point texture including three-colour components that will be treated as x, y and z coordinates. However, the values of wavelet coefficients are placed in a separate channel namely α channel. We extend the 24-bit format to the 32-bit format A8R8G8B8 to accommodate this information. Therefore, each texture is conceptually regarded as a four-dimensional array, and represents the radiance of special directions with given weight of all sampling points.

This GPU-oriented data structure at least has two obvious advantages. One is that the method of storage utilizes 2D texture space adequately; the other is that it also makes the pixel shader fragments process the data at run-time more easily.

Table 1. Data Structure Unit (CPU)

2 bytes	Index
1 byte	Value
1 byte	reserved byte

Table 2. Data Structure Unit (GPU)

3 bytes, RGB channel	3D vector index
1 byte, A channel	value

4   Run-Time Soft Shadow Rendering

We regard every pixel in the original cube light map as the single light source to illumine the 3D scene. At run-time, fast wavelet transform is adopted on the environment map **L** firstly. And then, the multiplication between **T** and **L** is executed, which is the kernel step of relighting rendering.

Because we simulate the scene under dynamic illumination, and the cube light map can be changed arbitrarily in the rendering phrase, wavelet transform on **L** should be performed in the update stage before rendering each frame instead of in the pre-computed phrase. We still choose Harr basis to guarantee orthonormality, and the transform is implemented on the six faces of the cube map respectively.

To render soft shadows under the lighting condition **L**, we multiply the radiance transfer matrix **T** by **L**. **T** becomes sparse because of wavelet transform, quantification and rearrangement, and **L** is a common matrix. We can implement this multiplication both on CPU and GPU, and also can select the fixed length or the changeable length of vectors to process. The method based on fixed length vectors can provide a stable rendering speed, while changeable length vectors do the non-linear approximation dynamically at run-time to get high-quality images.

In order to implement the computation on graphics hardware, we place the original light map **L** in a cube texture buffer, and conduct GPU-based wavelet transform on each face. The FP16 format cube texture is applied to preserve the lighting conditions within the high dynamic range. As the radiance transfer matrix **T** is stored as a group of 2D textures in Section 3.2.3, the processing kernel can be represented with a pixel shader (also called "fragment program"). Texture buffers can be used to save both temporary results and final results.

The pseudo codes of the pixel shader we use in this paper are given below.

```
%%Global Input :

L: cube light map that stores L

C: 2D texture buffer that saves a vertical row of T

%%Single pass rendering

Render(C, R₁ ,R𝒸) :

R₁: 2D texture buffer that saves the temporary result of last
time, and as the input data for next computation

R𝒸: 2D texture buffer that saves the output result

(a_T, P) • Tex(C, u, v)

A_L • TexCube(L, P)

R𝒸(u, v) • A_L × a_T + Tex(R₁, u, v)
```

```
%%Multi-passes rendering

T₁, T₂: 2D texture buffers that save the temporary result

R: 2D texture buffer that saves the final result

Clear (T₁)

Clear (T₂)

P₁ = T₁, Pc = T₂

For every row of T

    Render (row, P₁, Pc)

    Swap (P₁, Pc)

R • P₁
```

At single pass rendering, we refer to the value of the wavelet coefficient as a_T, and the 3D index as direction vector P, and they can be got from one of the 2D texture buffers, which store special weight radiance of all sampling points. Then, the vector A_L containing three components RGB is selected according to P in the input cube map. With that, multiplication can be implemented, and the result will be stored in the texture buffer R_c.

To generate photo realistic images, we execute multi-passes rendering, and sum up the outputs of multiplication between wavelet coefficients with a variety of weight in the matrix **T** and light sources in the cube light map. We use the function Clear () to clear texture buffers as zero, bind two temporary texture buffers T_1, T_2 with the pointers P_l, P_c with the sign "=", and use T_1, T_2 to save the temporary result. At each repetition, the function Render () represents single pass rendering, while Swap () means interchanging the contents of the two buffers. T_1 and T_2 are swapped: one for the rendering target, and the other for accumulation, and the rendering result is saved in R.

We multiply only one texture by **L** in each single pass rendering procedure according to the algorithm above, and it is proved to be a non-optimised version. The current mainstream graphic cards can support eight textures' processing simultaneously. In addition to saving **L** and R_l, we still have six spare texture buffers, which can be used to conduct parallel computation. Thus, a higher rendering speed is obtained with the parallel processing ability of GPU.

5 Results and Discussion

We have experimented with 3D scenes, which include one object model and one base face. We adopt vertex sampling on the object and texel sampling on the base face.

Therefore, the base face can be rendered as two simple triangles rather than meshes with complex structure. The small object is Bunny, which has 8,171 vertices, and the resolution of the texture on its base face is 128*128. The other is Buddha with 32,328 vertices, and the size of its base face texture is 256*256.

Fig.2 shows the scenes rendered as 640×480 pixels, with field-of-view of 90°. The light sources are smooth in RNL map [10], so the shadows in Bunny scene are soft. However, dramatic changes take place on the top, left and right parts of the St. Peter light map, which represents some high-intensity light sources. We see two distinct shadows of Buddha on its base face.

(a) Bunny scene under the RNL
Illumination cube map

(b) Buddha scene under the St. Peter
Illumination cube map

Fig. 2. Rendering Results of Synthetic 3D Scenes

We use a PC with a 3.0 GHz Pentium4 CPU, 1 GB system memory, and an NVidia GeForce 7800 GT with 256MB video memory. The program is developed and run under OS Window XP, DirectX 9.0c API and Shader Model 2.0. Since we focus more on the effect of shadows in the resulting images, only a simple ray tracer with 4*4 super sampling is implemented to get the matrix **T**. The pre-computation of the Bunny scene costs about 12 hours, and that of Buddha about 18 hours.

Space requirement. For Bunny and Buddha scenes, Table 3 gives the sparsity [2] and the space needed to store the matrix with the data structure in our method (32 bit per element). According to Table 3, the space required is still huge. In order to reduce the memory occupation, the non-linear approximation is used at the rendering time.

Table 4 gives a comparison of the run-time space requirement of the Buddha base face under the 6*32*32 light map and that of the method [2]. In our method, only part of the wavelet coefficients are demanded to compute relighting, while the entire **T** is needed to store in [2]. The reason why we need a double size for all coefficients is that we use 32-bit per data instead of 16-bit per data.

Table 3. Sparsity and Disk Space Occupation of the Radiance Transfer Matrix T

Light	Bunny		Bunny floor		Buddha		Buddha floor	
Res.	Sp.	Size(M)	Sp.	Size(M)	Sp.	Size(M)	Sp.	Size(M)
6×4×4	31.9%	1.75	48.3%	13.5	26.8%	6.91	49.6%	13.5
6×8×8	20.6%	5.20	34.6%	37.8	17.0%	18.6	36.1%	38.5
6×16×16	15.0%	14.9	24.9%	106	12.2%	54.6	26.0%	110
6×32×32	10.8%	42.7	17.8%	302	8.59%	163	18.7%	308
6×64×64	5.72%	82.9	10.3%	691	4.47%	351	10.9%	715

Table 4. Memory Usage of the Radiance Transfer Matrix at Run-time

Terms	20	50	100	200	500	All
Size	5.0M	12.5M	25M	50M	125M	308M
Size[2]	149.4M					

Rendering rate. We have evaluated the performance of our soft shadow rendering technique on the same 3D scenes above. Fig.3 illustrates the rendering rates of the application as compared with Ren's [2] rendering rates. We implement the method both on GPU and CPU. The rendering rates of the GPU version are improved dramatically on the pixel shader with 20 parallel pipelines. For geometry models using vertex sampling, such as Bunny and Buddha, the average performance is about 3.7~8.8 times as fast as Ren's. However, the rendering rate of base faces with texel sampling in these two scenes is about 7.2~19.5 times faster than that of current methods. Much more communication between GPU and CPU in vertex sampling answers for this difference of rendering speeds. All the four figures below also show that the performance of our CPU version exceeds Ren's when only a few terms are selected.

Error analysis. Both non-linear approximations in pre-computation and run-time rendering on GPU would introduce errors to the resulting images. In order to identify the validity of our method, we compare the standardized variances of error L^2 and Sobolev H^1 [2] of these two methods. Fig.4 (a) and (b) illustrate that the values of these two measurements are slightly higher than Ren's method when the numbers of terms are below 100. When we select more wavelet coefficients, the error introduced by the precision of GPU is magnified quickly.

Finally, we compare the images rendered by our approach with Ren's. The 3D scene we use in this experiment is also composed of an object model Buddha and its base face, while the light source is named as Grace Cathedral, which includes many high-intensity light sources with different sizes. The characteristics of all-frequency soft shadows can be exhibited adequately in this situation. The reference image in Fig.5 is rendered with all wavelet terms. In general, the visual result of soft shadows generated by our method is as good as that in [2].

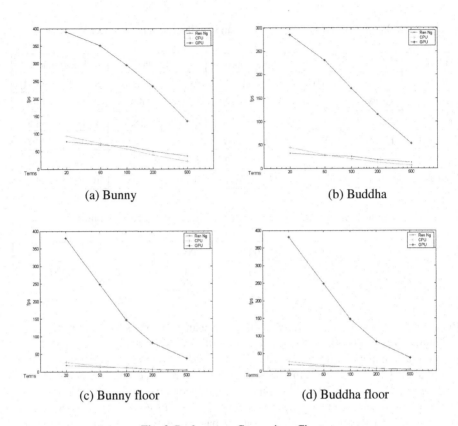

(a) Bunny

(b) Buddha

(c) Bunny floor

(d) Buddha floor

Fig. 3. Performance Comparison Chart

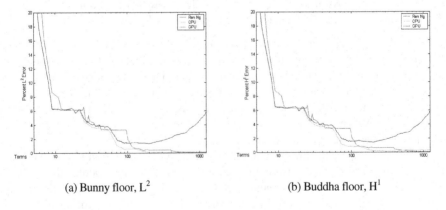

(a) Bunny floor, L^2

(b) Buddha floor, H^1

Fig. 4. Comparison Charts of Errors in Rendering Results

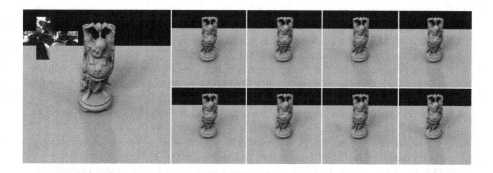

Fig. 5. Rendering Quality Comparison between Our Algorithm and the One in [2] (Reference image:left; [2]algorithm 50, 100,200,500:right up; our algorithm 50,100,200,500 :right below)

6   Conclusions and Future Work

We have proposed a new non-linear approximation on GPU for real-time soft shadow rendering in 3D virtual scenes: relying on the model of relighting scenes with environment maps, it adapts the non-linear approximation on the pre-computed radiance transfer matrix to select the main directions which exert more influence on illumination of every sampling point. It also encodes the resulting radiance transfer matrix into the sparse form, stores it as textures in texture buffers, and organizes the light vector into a cube map to accelerate computation in the run-time process. Therefore, all computations of shadow rendering are performed on GPU, and the parallel processing ability of graphics hardware is fully utilized. This approach balances the workload on CPU and GPU, and yields real-time performance with relatively good image quality. Another benefit is that it can decrease the memory occupation dramatically by selecting wavelet coefficients on the pre-computed radiance transfer matrix, which avoids the large storage cost of the whole **T** in method [2].

Concerning future work, we plan to do some experiments on clustered principal components analysis, and adopt it in our method to increase the compression rate of the radiance transfer matrix and to accelerate the relighting speed. Wavelet coefficients' selection has great influence on error control and image quality, so it would also be valuable to research on the strategies to choose wavelet basis and rearrange wavelet coefficients. Finally, we assume the objects we deal with are purely diffuse ones, and we use the purely diffuse expression as reflection function in this paper. This assumption will limit our method to some applications. How to remove this requirement is till a considerable problem.

References

1. P Sloan, J Kautz, J Snyder. Precomputed radiance transfer for real-time rendering in dynamic, low-frequency lighting environments. In: ACM Transactions on Graphics, 2002, 21(3), pp.527-536

2. R Ng, R Ramamoorthi, P Hanrahan. All-frequency shadows using non-linear wavelet lighting approximation. In: ACM Transactions on Graphics, 2003, 22(3), pp.376-381

3. J Hasenfratz, M Lapierre, N Holzschuch, F Sillion. A survey of real-time soft shadows algorithms. In: Computer Graphics Forum, 2003, 22(4), pp.753-774

4. Randima Fernando, Sebastian Fernandez, Kavita Bala, and Donald P. Greenberg. Adaptive shadow maps.In Computer Graphics (SIGGRAPH 2001), Annual Conference Series. ACM SIGGRAPH,2001. pp.387-390

5. Paul S. Heckbert and Michael Herf. Simulating soft shadows with graphics hardware. Technical Report CMU-CS-97-104, Carnegie Mellon University, January 1997

6. U Assarsson, T Akenine-Möller. A geometry-based soft shadow volume algorithm using graphics hardware. In: ACM Transactions on Graphics, 2003, 22(3), pp.511-520

7. P Debevec. Image-Based Lighting. www.debevec.org/CGAIBL2/ibl-tutorial-cga2002.pdf

8. P Debevec, T Hawkins, C Tchou, H Duiker, W Sarokin, M Sagar. Acquiring the reflectance field of a human face. In: Proceedings of ACM SIGGRAPH 2000. New York: ACM Press / ACM SIGGRAPH, 2000. pp.145-156

9. J Owens. A survey of general-purpose computation on graphics hardware. In: Eurographics 2005, State of the Art Reports. 2005, pp.21-51

10. P Debevec. Rendering synthetic objects into real scenes: bridging traditional and image-based graphics with global illumination and high dynamic range photography, In: Proceedings of ACM SIGGRAPH 2001. New York: ACM Press / ACM SIGGRAPH, 2001. pp.189-198

Predictive Occlusion Culling for Interactive Rendering of Large Complex Virtual Scene

Hua Xiong, Zhen Liu, Aihong Qin, Haoyu Peng,
Xiaohong Jiang, and Jiaoying Shi

State Key Lab of CAD&CG, Zhejiang University,
310027 HangZhou, P.R. China
{xionghua, liuzhen, qinaihong, phy,
jiangxh, jyshi}@cad.zju.edu.cn

Abstract. We present an efficient occlusion culling algorithm for interactive rendering of large complex virtual scene with high depth complexity. Our method exploits both spatial and temporal coherence of visibility. A space hierarchy of scene is constructed and its nodes are rendered in an approximate front-to-back order. Nodes in view frustum are inserted into one of layered node lists, called layered buffers(**LBs**), according to its distance to the view point. Each buffer in the LBs is rendered with hardware occlusion queries. Using a visibility predictor(**VP**) for each node and interleaving occlusion queries with rendering, we reduce the occlusion queries count and graphics pipeline stalls greatly. This occlusion culling algorithm can work in a conservative way for high image quality rendering or in an approximate way for time critical rendering. Experimental results of different types of virtual scene are provided to demonstrate its efficiency and generality.

1 Introduction

Although current GPUs can process above several million triangles per second, interactive rendering of large virtual environment still largely overload their performance. Various acceleration techniques have been proposed including occlusion culling, mesh compression and simplification, parallel rendering, texturing, and imposter, etc. The main goal of these methods is to reduce the triangles flushed into graphics rendering pipeline in each frame while producing images of accurate or approximate visual quality.

Many rendering systems combine several techniques mentioned above. MMR [1] is a rendering framework for massive models which renders near geometry with visibility culling and static LODs while renders far geometry with the textured-depth-mesh. GigaWalk [6] is a parallel rendering architecture which can interactively render tens of millions triangles on multiple graphics pipelines. It integrates LODs, scene graph hierarchy, occlusion culling and parallel rendering. iWalk [9] is a system for out-of-core rendering large models on inexpensive PCs. It builds a hierarchical representation for a scene on disk and uses multiple threads to overlap rendering, visibility computation and disk operation. Quick-VDR [16] uses view-dependent simplification based on clustered hierarchy of

H. Zha et al. (Eds.): VSMM 2006, LNCS 4270, pp. 93–102, 2006.

progressive mesh, occlusion culling and out-of-core rendering. TetraPuzzles [8] employs a tetrahedron hierarchy for out-of-core construction and view-dependent visualization of large surface model. In this paper, we mainly focus on occlusion culling algorithm, i.e., trying to prevent invisible triangles occluded by others from being sent to graphics pipeline on commodity PC.

Contributions: We present an occlusion culling algorithm that is efficient and applicable to general virtual scenes. The method partitions the scene and builds its hierarchy in object space. While rendering, the hierarchy is traversed in a top-to-bottom order with view frustum culling and in an approximate front-to-back order with occlusion culling. We employ a layered buffers to amortize sorting cost. A visibility predictor is used for each node to avoid hardware occlusion queries. The queries are issued for a batch of nodes and are interleaved with rendering process to hide queries latency and to avoid GPU stalls.

Advantages: The method is applicable to general scenes with high depth complexity. It does not need to select occluders from geometry database and requires little preprocessing time. Using image depth buffer to perform occlusion culling addresses the occlusion fusion problem gracefully. For time critical rendering system, it supports approximate occlusion culling to produce most correct image. The algorithm exploits object space coherence by space subdivision with orderly traversal, image space coherence by hardware occlusion queries and temporal coherence by visibility predictor. It optimizes the speed of occlusion culling through reducing occlusion queries count and hiding queries latency.

Limitations: This algorithm explores visibility information of virtual scene from a relatively coarse level. It does not consider the occlusion relationship in each node. Other partition schemes such as vertex hierarchy, clustered hierarchy of progressive meshes and hierarchical surface patches which partition the model following its topology may explore the visibility information in a finer way.

2   Related Work

Visibility computation is a fundamental problem in computer graphics, computer vision and computational geometry. Invisible triangles from the view point can be classified as: projection area less than a pixel, outside of the view frustum, occluded by others. Removing these invisible triangles can be achieved by detail culling or contribution culling, view frustum culling, back face culling and occlusion culling. Detail culling commonly use LODs or imposter to replace those geometry with unnecessary details [19]. View frustum culling and back face culling are easy to implement. But there is no general solution for occlusion culling. Occlusion culling can be computed in object space or image space from a point or a region in a conservative way or an approximate way [15, 7, 4, 10].

Object space occlusion culling. Object space occlusion culling methods use spatial relationship between geometric primitives to compute visibility. They usually require high computation cost and large disk storage space for precomputation. Cells and portals method [2] is applicable to scenes with regular structure such as architecture. For general scenes, it requires selecting large and even convex occluders. Bittner [5] proposed to merge the occlusion volumes of selected occluders and to build an occlusion tree which is used to compute the visible region from a view point.

Image space occlusion culling. Image space occlusion culling methods use depth information to eliminate occluded triangles. If all fragments are further than the corresponding pixels in depth buffer, the triangle is occluded. Performing depth test for each triangle is costly and impractical. This test generally is performed for a bounding box containing a batch of triangles to amortize the cost. A front-to-back traversal order is necessary thus later to be visited boxes will have greater possibility to be occluded. HZB [11] uses a depth pyramid built from the depth buffer to reduce the cost of determining the visibility of a node's bounding box. HOM [17] decomposes the visibility test into a 2D overlap test and a depth test. ATI's HyperZ [14] incorporates a two-level pyramid into hardware to provide early primitive rejection. Delay streams [3] uses a low resolution Z-buffer as an occlusion culling unit. NVIDIA's graphics hardware now supports occlusion queries which returns the count of visible pixels.

Coherent hierarchical culling. Exploiting object space, image space and temporal coherence is important to accelerate occlusion culling. Greene [11] uses an octree to subdivide the scene and traverses it in a front-to-back order. A Z-pyramid is used to exploit image space coherence and a visible node list is maintained to utilize temporal coherence. Klosowski [13] uses Delaunay triangulation and octree for spatial partition and assigns each node a solidity indicating its possibility to be occluded as well as the priority for scheduling order of rendering. Hillesland [12] uses both uniform grid and nested grid decomposition, and traverses all nodes in a slab similar to volume rendering. Bittner [5, 18] adopts K-D tree and their hierarchy updating scheme can eliminate repeated visibility test for partially visible nodes.

3   Hierarchy Construction

There are mainly two spatial approaches to decompose and organize a complex virtual scene into a hierarchical representation. The first uses 3D planes for partitioning, such as regular grid, recursive grid, octree, loose octree, BSP tree, and K-D tree, etc. The second clusters triangles into many localized mesh regions called patches and organizes them into a hierarchy. We adopt the first method mainly for its fast speed. The data structure pertained to each node is defined as follows: a bounding box indicating its position and size, a vertex list and a triangle list, a visibility predictor for skipping occlusion query, and linking node pointers. A triangle is put into all nodes it intersects and a flag is appended to each triangle to guarantee it will be rendered only once in each frame.

Adaptive octree subdivision. An octree hierarchy is constructed in an adaptive and progressive way. The octree root is created with the scene's bounding box. All triangles are inserted into leaf nodes one by one. If the triangles count in a leaf node excesses a predefined threshold, it is split into eight children nodes with equal size and all its triangles are redistributed into the children nodes.

As a result, the scene is partitioned adaptively, i.e. the dense areas of triangles will be subdivided finer. This progressive method can be easily modified to an out-of-core algorithm.

Recursive grid subdivision. The construction of recursive grid subdivision is similar to that of adaptive octree subdivision. The difference is that a node will be subdivided into more children nodes instead of only eight. For populated area of the scene, the depth of adaptive octree will be high. This method can alleviate this problem because triangles will be assigned into more nodes thus the recursive subdivision stops early.

K-D tree subdivision. To obtain better balance of the final hierarchy, we tried subdivision with K-D tree. The position of splitting plane in each node is determined according to the distribution of triangles resulting that both half spaces beside it will include approximately equal triangles count. Instead of selecting the splitting plane in a fixed order such as YZ, XZ, XY, we use the orthogonal plane in the longest dimension of the node's bounding box because the side length of a bounding box usually indicates the distribution of triangles. This kind of subdivision is difficult to perform in a progressive way because the global distribution of triangles should be known for the selection of splitting planes.

Figure 1 gives a comparison of these three space subdivision schemes on a small model. The final hierarchical statistics are listed in Table 1. The maximum count of triangles in a node is limited to 10k and the grid number of recursive grid in each dimension is 3. As shown from the table, the recursive grid hierarchy contains more leaf nodes than the adaptive octree and the K-D tree while its depth is the lowest. The K-D tree hierarchy has the fewest leaf nodes and triangles are distributed with good balance.

Table 1. Statistics of the final hierarchies of space subdivision

Hierarchy Type	Depth	Leaf Count	Max #Tri.	Min #Tri.
Adaptive octree	3	162	9123	2
Recursive grid	2	391	8858	2
K-D tree	6	64	5671	5058

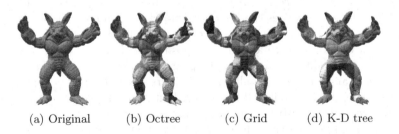

(a) Original   (b) Octree   (c) Grid   (d) K-D tree

Fig. 1. Comparison of three space subdivision schemes

4   Hierarchical Traversal

The scene hierarchy is traversed with view frustum culling and occlusion culling while rendering. For view frustum culling, it is ideal to traverse the hierarchy in a top-to-bottom order so that we can stop testing the visibility of the children nodes if a node is totally inside or outside of the view frustum. For occlusion culling, keeping a front-to-back order is important because later to be visited nodes will have greater possibility to be occluded by previously rendered nodes. The hierarchical traversal is separated into two passes because it is difficult to combine these two different orders together. In the first pass, we traverse the hierarchy in a top-to-bottom order to fully utilize the space object coherence. In the second pass, leaf nodes passing view frustum visibility test are inserted into one layer of a layered buffers depending on its distance to the view point.

In each frame, a predefined number of layers in front are rendered directly without occlusion queries. This will build an initial occlusion representation in the depth buffer. For node in other layers, all triangles in it are rendered only if its bounding box is determined to be visible through hardware occlusion query. Hardware occlusion query is a time consuming operation and may cause graphics pipeline stalls. We attack these problems by using a visibility predictor and adopting an interleaved querying and rendering algorithm.

4.1   Layered Buffers

The layered buffers technique provides an approximate front-to-back order to reduce sorting cost. The distance From the view point to the bounding box of each node is used to compute its layer index. Layers are defined in the following way: the minimum and maximum distances from all nodes are used as the range of the layered buffers, the span between each layer is computed through dividing the range by the layer count which is a user adjustable parameter. Each layer contains a priority list to sort the nodes in it. Our algorithm uses distance as the priority while more complex heuristics may be employed. Figure 2 explains the structure of LBs in 2D plane.

4.2   Visibility Predictor

The direct approach which performs occlusion query for all nodes will decrease the overall performance. We propose to use a visibility predictor to reduce the occlusion queries count. Before issuing an occlusion query for a node, we make a visibility prediction based on its visibility history, i.e., its visibility status in several consecutive frames. If the prediction is being occluded, the occlusion query is issued to hardware and its prediction status is updated when getting the query result. If the node is predicted being visible, the occlusion query is skipped. The prediction scheme is based on the temporal coherence which indicates that once a node becomes visible in a frame then it will remain visible for the successive several frames in a great possibility. Skipping occlusion test will increase the total count of triangles rendered. To overcome this problem, a visible frame counter is kept for each node skipping occlusion query which controls the time to perform the occlusion query on it again. Once a node is determined visible by query, its visible frame counter is set with a variable value considering camera moving and rotating speed. The counter decreases by one after each frame and the occlusion test is performed again when it becomes zero. This scheme is conservative because occlusion tests are always performed for nodes predicted being occluded.

The visibility predictor can work for approximate occlusion culling also, i.e., occlusion tests are skipped either for nodes predicted to be visible or occluded. If a node is determined as being occluded by query in several consecutive frames, it is possible to be occluded in the next frame so we skip its occlusion query. This may discard some actually visible triangles and results partial incorrect pixels. From the experiment results, the ratio of error pixels count is below 10%(tested by item buffer technique). When walking through the scene, it is hard to notice the artifacts because the nodes skipping occlusion test will be checked for visibility status again in the next frame. Figure 3 shows the mechanism of the approximate visibility predictor.

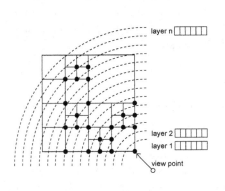

Fig. 2. 2D illustration of LBs

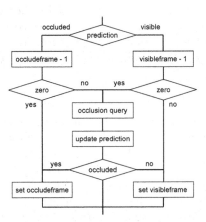

Fig. 3. Mechanism of approximate VP

4.3   Rendering Algorithm

Because of graphics pipeline processing time and data transmission between CPU and GPU, there is a latency to obtain the occlusion test result. To hide this latency, our rendering algorithm interleaves the rendering of visible nodes and the occlusion queries. A batch of occlusion queries are issued to hardware pipeline and a batch of visible nodes are then followed to render. After rendering, the queries results just issued become available. We continue in this way till all nodes are rendered. This scheduling scheme keeps CPU and GPU busy most of time and the pipeline stalls can be reduced greatly. We use OpenGL vertex buffer object technique to accelerate rendering speed. The size of available video memory is limited and generally can not hold the whole scene. We choose to download the visible geometry dataset only. If a node becomes being occluded, we delete its footprint from the video memory.

5   Results

The occlusion culling algorithm is implemented as part of a parallel rendering system for large complex virtual scene. To evaluate the efficiency of this occlusion culling algorithm, other acceleration techniques such as LODs and parallel rendering are disabled. Two different types of scenes are tested: a city matrix consisted of 624 skyscrapers which contains 8M triangles, the UNC Power Plant containing 13M triangles. All tests were conducted on a PC with a 2.4GHz P4 processor, 1GB of RAM and a NVIDIA's GeForce FX 5700 graphics card. Five different rendering approaches are tested for comparison: N, PC, PA, BPC, BPA. N means performing occlusion query first and waiting for rendering till the query result is available. P means using visibility predictor. C and A refer to using conservative and approximate visibility predictor respectively. B means performing the occlusion queries and rendering in batch and interleaving them.

Comparison of different hierarchies: Table 2 gives the statistics of the virtual scenes and their constructed hierarchies. The rendering performance comparison of different space subdivision schemes for the city matrix are given in Figure 4. Both the adaptive octree and the K-D tree subdivision show good performance. But the time of constructing the K-D tree hierarchy is much more than that of the adaptive octree hierarchy.

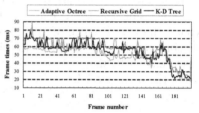

(a) Walking in the city matrix   (b) Frame time comparison

Fig. 4. Performance comparison of different space subdivision schemes on city matrix. Vibration of the recursive grid scheme is obvious like spike in frame 15.

Table 2. Statistics of tested scenes and their hierarchies. Max and Min refer to the maximum and minimum count of triangles in leaf nodes. The triangles threshold in node is 10K and the grid number of recursive grid in each dimension is 3.

Scene	Input file		Adaptive octree			Recursive grid			K-D tree		
	size M	M #Tri	Max	Min	Depth	Max	Min	Depth	Max	Min	Depth
Matrix	364	8	9943	182	4	9996	1	3	8285	7215	10
Plane	479	13	9989	1	9	9880	1	6	7010	5613	11

Visibility predictor efficiency: To test visibility predictor efficiency, we present the occlusion queries count performed with and without visibility predictor. As shown in Figure 5, the queries count is reduced about 25 percentage by using conservative visibility predictor and 50 percentage by using approximate visibility predictor. The results of BPC and BPA are similar to that of PC and PA respectively. The culling efficiency difference between both modes is small. We obtain a culling factor of 70% to 99% in most frames.

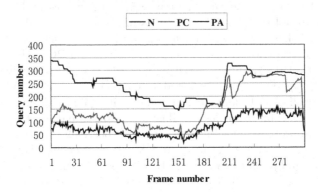

Fig. 5. Query count of Matrix model

Interleaved rendering efficiency: Figure 6 shows the frame time using these five different approaches. Although using visibility predictor may increase the count of triangles rendered per frame and finally will increase the total rendering time, the compensation times obtained from skipping the occlusion queries are more. As a result, the total rendering performance are enhanced. As shown in the chart, the performance of BPC and BPA are better than that of PC and PA demonstrating that the graphics pipeline stalls decrease and the occlusion queries latency is hidden in a great degree. Figure 7 gives some selected rendered frames of the plant model.

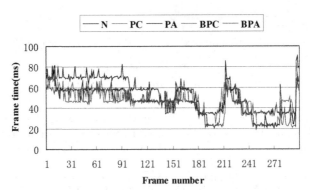

Fig. 6. Frame time of Plant model

Comparison with other approaches: It is hard to directly compare our method with other approaches because of the difference of graphics hardware performance and the tested scenes. The depth complexity of virtual scene is crucial to occlusion culling efficiency. And as far as we know, there is no work in literature on occlusion culling using predictive scheme. Bittner [18] obtained an average speedup of 4.0-4.7 compared to pure view frustum culling and 1.6-2.6 compared to hierarchical stop-and-wait application of occlusion query. Compared with pure view frustum culling and the stop-and-wait occlusion culling, the speedup of our method is 5.0-6.5 and 2.0-4.2 respectively.

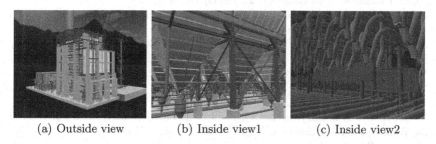

(a) Outside view   (b) Inside view1   (c) Inside view2

Fig. 7. Selected frames of walking through the UNC Power Plant model

6   Conclusions

We have shown using the layered buffers to traverse the scene orderly and to schedule the order of occlusion querying and rendering and applying visibility predictor to reduce count of occlusion queries. Our method exploits object space coherence, image space coherence, and especially temporal coherence. The experiment data presented above proved the efficiency of our occlusion culling algorithm for general complex scene with high depth complexity, mainly taking benefits from layered buffers and visibility predictor. It can be easily implemented and integrated into existing rendering systems.

The major potential in improving the method is to enhance the accuracy and hit ratio of visibility predictor, especially for conservative occlusion culling. Besides exploiting the visibility information in the time dimension, heuristics such as neighboring visibility can be further explored. We also plan to research the parallelism of this occlusion culling algorithm on a PCs cluster.

Acknowledgments

This work is supported by National Grand Fundamental Research 973 Program of China under Grant No.2002CB312105 and the key NSFC project of "Digital Olympic Museum" under Grant No.60533080. The Power Plant model is used with the permission of UNC Walkthru Group.

References

1. D. Aliaga, J. Cohen, A. Wilson, H. S. Zhang, C. Erikson, K. E. Hoff III, T. Hudson, W. Stuerzlinger, R. Bastos, M. Whitton, F. Brooks, and D. Manocha: MMR: An Integrated Massive Model Rendering System using Geometric and Image-based Acceleration. *Proceedings of ACM Symposium on Interactive 3D Graphics.* (1999) 199–206

2. J. Airey: Increasing Update Rates in the Building Walkthrough System with Automatic Model-Space Subdivision and Potentially Visible Set Calculations. *PhD thesis, University of North Carolina, Chapel Hill, USA.* (1991)
3. T. Aila, V. Miettinen, and P. Nordlund: Delay Streams for Graphics Hardware. *ACM Transactions on Graphics.* **22** (2003) 792–800
4. J. Bittner and P. Wonka: Visibility in Computer Graphics. *Environment and Planning B: Planning and Design.* **30** (2003) 729–756
5. J. Bittner, V. Havran, and P. Slavik: Hierarchical Visibility Culling with Occlusion Trees. *Computer Graphics International.* (1998) 207–219
6. W. V. Baxter III, A. Sud, N. Govindaraju, and D. Manocha: GigaWalk: Interactive Walkthrough of Complex Environments. *Proceedings of Eurographics Workshop on Rendering.* (2002) 203–214
7. D. Cohen-Or, Y. L. Chrysanthou, C. T. Silva, and F. Durand: A Survey of Visibility for Walkthrough Applications. *IEEE Transactions on Visualization and Computer Graphics.* **9** (2003) 412–431
8. P. Cignoni, F. Ganovelli, E. Gobbetti, F. Marton, F. Ponchio, and R. Scopigno: Adaptive TetraPuzzles: Efficient Out-of-Core Construction and Visualization of Gigantic Polygonal Models. *ACM Transactions on Graphics.* **23** (2004) 796–803
9. W. Correa, J. Klosowski, and C. T. Silva: iWalk: Interactive Out-of-Core Rendering of Large Models. *Technical Report TR-653-02, Princeton University.* (2002)
10. F. Durand: 3D Visibility: Analytical study and Applications. *PhD thesis, Universite Joseph Fourier, Grenoble, France.* (1999)
11. N. Greene, M. Kass, and G. Miller: Hierarchical Z-buffer Visibility. *Proceedings of ACM SIGGRAPH 1993).* (1993) 231–238.
12. K. Hillesland, B. Salomon, A. Lastra, and D. Manocha: Fast and Simple Occlusion Culling using Hardware-based Depth Queries. *Technical Report TR02-039, Department of Computer Science, University of North Carolina, Chapel Hill.* (2002)
13. J. T. Klosowski and C. T. Silva: Efficient Conservative Visibility Culling using the Prioritized-layered Projection Algorithm. *IEEE Transactions on Visualization and Computer Graphics.* **7** (2001) 365–379
14. S. Morein: ATI Radeon HyperZ Technology. *Proceedings of Workshop on Graphics Hardware, ACM SIGGRAPH.* (2000)
15. C. T. Silva, Y.-J. Chiang, J. El-Sana, P. Lindstrom, and R. Pajarola: Out-of-Core Algorithms for Scientific Visualization and Computer Graphics. *Tutorial 4, IEEE Visualization 2003.* (2003)
16. S. E. Yoon, B. Salomon, R. Gayle, and D. Manocha: Quick-VDR: Interactive View-Dependent Rendering of Gigantic Models. *IEEE Transactions on Visualization and Computer Graphics.* **11** (2005) 369–382
17. H. S. Zhang, D. Manocha, T. Hudson, and K. E. Hoff III: Visibility Culling using Hierarchical Occlusion Maps. *Proceedings of SIGGRAPH 1997.* (1997) 77–88
18. J. Bittner, M. Wimmer, H. Piringer, and W. Purgathofer: Coherent Hierarchical Culling: Hardware Occlusion Queries Made Useful. *Proceedings of Eurographics 2004.* (2004) 615–624
19. M. M. Zhang, Z. G. Pan, and P. A. Heng: A Near Constant Frame-Rate Rendering Algorithm Based on Visibility Computation and Model Simplification. *Journal of Visualization and Computer Animation.* **14** (2003) 1–13

A Study on Perception and Operation Using Free Form Projection Display

Daisuke Kondo[1] and Ryugo Kijima[1,2]

[1] Virtual System Laboratory, [2] Faculty of Engineering,
Gifu University, 1-1, Yanagido, Gifu 501-1193, Japan
daisuke@vsl.gifu-u.ac.jp, kijima@info.gifu-u.ac.jp

Abstract. A Free Form Projection Display using a distortion-eliminating algorithm was constructed. In the system, an object in the curved surface is used and the virtual object is represented by image projection. The virtual object is shown as if it fixed in the curved screen surface and gives the user a sense of motion parallax. Using this construction, the virtual object can be handled directly by the user's hand and examined.

This system seems to be effective in manual operation and shape recognition of virtual object.

In order to evaluate the effectivity, we performed the experiments to compare FFPD and conventional flat display monitor with mouse from the viewpoint of depth perception and manual operation.

Keywords: Free Form Projection Display, object manipulation, motion parallax.

1 Introduction

For constructing a VR/MR system, designing the arrangement of vision output device and manipulation input device is important. Especially, for the system that enables users to handle virtual objects directly by their hand, it is great issue. In general, such systems are constructed with HMD and Phantom, CAVE and game pad, etc. In many cases, an input device and an output device are physically separated, and it causes unnatural interaction.

Object oriented display [1] has been proposed by Inami et al. In their system, image display device and physical object that is manipulated by the user are conjugated. The user can manipulate a real object which is strongly related to the virtual object. It makes natural feeling in interaction with virtual object.

The authors have developed Free Form Projection Display(FFPD). FFPD is an implementation of object oriented display using a projector and a hand-held arbitrary shaped screen on which an image is projected.

1.1 Free Form Projection Display (FFPD)

FFPD is a technology to compensate the projection distortion according to location of the user's viewpoint, location of the projector and the screen's position and shape [2].

H. Zha et al. (Eds.): VSMM 2006, LNCS 4270, pp. 103–109, 2006.

The shape of the screen is measured in advance, and the position and rotation of the screen and the position of the user's viewpoint are measured in real time. FFPD generates an image to project according to the movement of user's viewpoint and the screen. The user can see the projected image on the curved screen surface without distortion. This system gives the user a feel of motion parallax, and displays the virtual object as if it lies inside the actual object as shown in fig.1.

(a) Overview.

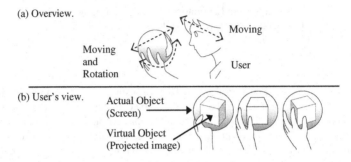

Moving

Moving
and
Rotation

User

(b) User's view.

Actual Object
(Screen)

Virtual Object
(Projected image)

Fig. 1. Representation of virtual object inside the curved screen surface

There ware several studies on representation a virtual object by projection technology. Raskar et al. [3] proposed a distortion cancellation method to project onto the curved surface of a wall without distortion. Our system is able to dynamically handle the whole screen rather than to project the image onto the static curved surface.

FFPD enables the user to handle virtual objects directly by their hand easily. Comparing another device, the error and distortion in the observed image derived from the angular and positional error of the user's head measurement is less than the case of HMD/CAVE system, because the screen is similar to the shape of the virtual object and the virtual object is located near to the surface of screen. [4]

1.2   The Application Using FFPD

Virtual Anatomical Model [4] is an application using FFPD. It is an anatomy education system using a screen in the shape of a human torso model on which images of inner organs are represented by projection, and can be handled directly by the user's hand and examined.

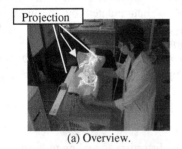

Projection

(a) Overview.

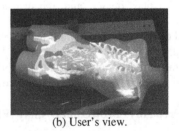

(b) User's view.

Fig. 2. Virtual Anatomical Model

Fig. 2(a) shows the overview of the system, the user can see the image like fig. 2(b). By movement vision and object handling, the user can observe the model of internal organs from various angles. This system was effective to understand the shape, size, positional relationship of organs.

1.3 Perception and Operation Using FFPD

It is expected that the system constructed with FFPD is effective to understand the shape of virtual object by handling and examining.

There seems no research to investigate the effectiveness of the perception and the operation for the case of FFPD. In this paper, we verify this effectiveness by experiments and discussed in terms of the perception and operation.

2 Experiments

FFPD has an effectiveness to enable the user to handle and watch the virtual object easily and naturally. The effectiveness seems to be derived from two merits as follows,

1) Ease of operation:
   The user can operate the virtual object directly by their hands.
2) Ease of perception:
   The system can represent the shape, size and depth by motion parallax. Additionally, user can understand positional relationship of virtual object and screen surface.

In order to verify the effectiveness, we performed experiments from the viewpoint of each of them. And we verified the both effectiveness of FFPD.

In this section, we perform two experiments to verify each merit.

In experiment 1, we investigate the ease of operation using FFPD. In experiment 2, we investigate the ease of perception using FFPD.

2.1 System Construction

In the experiments, the subjects are given the task designed for the experiments and the subjects handle and watch the virtual object to achieve the task using FFPD. The time taken is recorded. In the experiments, an object in curved surface named "screen object" shown in fig. 3 is used. The virtual objects are represented inside the screen object. For comparison, the same task is performed with conventional mouse and monitor. The list of device is shown in table 1.

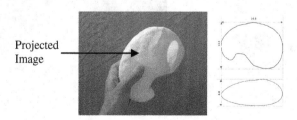

Fig. 3. Screen Object

Table 1. List of input/display device

Device	(A) : FFPD	(B) : Screen Object and flat monitor	(C) : mouse and flat monitor
Input Device	Screen Object		mouse
Display Device	Screen Object	flat monitor	

Device (A):

Device (A) is FFPD. The electro magnetic position sensor is attached on the screen object and the user's head. The screen object is used to move and rotate the virtual object, and the virtual objects are shown on the screen object in the hands directly.

Device (B):

In the case of device (B), screen object is used to rotate the virtual object which is displayed on a flat monitor.

Device (C):

Device (C) is a conventional style of operation with mouse and flat monitor. The user rotates the virtual object by moving mouse.

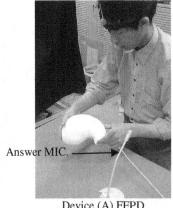

Answer MIC.

Device (A) FFPD

Device (C) Mouse and Flat Monitor

Fig. 4. Experimental System

2.2 Experiment 1: Manual Operation

The purpose of this experiment is to determine the ease of manual operation using FFPD.

In this experiment, three colored ellipses are shown inside the screen object as shown in fig. 5. Ellipses are painted red, orange and green, and sizes of them are different.

Fig. 5. Example of shape and position virtual object

The subjects rotate quickly the virtual object to find the largest ellipse and answer its color by saying the name of the color "red", "green" or "blue". The computer recognizes the voice, and records the time. In this task, quickly handling is required to observe the object from various angles. It is expected that good result is obtained in the case of using screen object.

The number of subjects was ten. The experiment was repeated ten times for each subject, and each times the positions, angles and sizes of ellipses were changed randomly.

Experimental result is shown in table 2.

Table 2. Experimental result 1

Subjects	Average of time			Difference of average time		
	A	B	C	B-A	C-A	C-B
1	3.03	2.48	3.06	-0.55	0.03	0.58
2	4.12	2.85	4.18	-1.27	0.06	1.33
3	1.98	2.19	3.23	0.20	1.25	1.04
4	3.55	3.19	3.58	-0.36	0.03	0.39
5	1.98	2.73	2.24	0.75	0.26	-0.49
6	2.24	2.45	3.05	0.21	0.80	0.59
7	2.39	1.55	2.95	-0.84	0.56	1.40
8	2.11	2.60	3.58	0.49	1.47	0.98
9	3.98	2.61	3.94	-1.37	-0.05	1.33
10	1.39	1.17	2.01	-0.22	0.62	0.84
			ave	-0.295	0.505	0.800
			Std-dev	0.721	0.537	0.570
			t	-1.228	**2.821**	**4.209**

T-test is performed and there were significance of the difference between (C) and (A), and between (C) and (B). Namely, good performance was obtained in the case of device (A) and (B). The result shows that screen object as an input device is effective when the task requires quick operation.

2.3 Experiment 2: Recognition of the Depth and Shape of Virtual Object

The purpose of this experiment is to test the perceptibility of positional relationship between screen object and inner virtual object using each device.

The virtual object used in this experiment is shown in fig 6.

Some colored balls are shown inside the screen object and they are nearby the surface of the screen. The balls are painted on red, orange, and green. Only one ball doesn't contact to the surface. The subjects found the one ball which doesn't contact to the surface and answer its color by their voice. The time taken was recorded.

In this task, motion parallax is required to find positional relationship between screen object and balls.

It is expected that good result is obtained in the case of using FFPD.

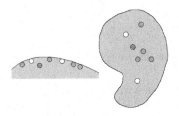

Fig. 6. Example of shape and position virtual object

The number of subjects was ten. The experiment was repeated ten times for each subject, and each times the positions of balls were changed randomly.

Experimental result is shown in table 3.

Table 3. Experimental result 2

Subjects	Average of time				Difference of average time		
	A	B	C		B-A	C-A	C-B
1	6.11	6.45	8.14		0.34	2.03	1.68
2	1.22	2.35	3.09		1.14	1.87	0.74
3	3.26	2.24	4.08		-1.02	0.82	1.84
4	4.76	6.37	5.84		1.61	1.08	-0.53
5	2.93	4.45	5.43		1.52	2.50	0.98
6	2.60	4.14	3.95		1.55	1.35	-0.19
7	4.31	5.54	4.82		1.23	0.51	-0.72
8	1.77	2.03	2.99		0.26	1.22	0.96
9	3.56	4.44	3.61		0.88	0.05	-0.83
10	2.17	2.88	4.25		0.72	2.08	1.36
			ave		0.822	1.352	0.550
			Std-dev		0.806	0.771	1.014
			t		**3.058**	**5.257**	1.568

T-test was conducted. There were significance of the difference between (B) and (A), and between (C) and (A). Namely, good performance was obtained in the case of device (A). The result shows that screen object as a display device is effective when the task requires depth perception.

3 Conclusion

Free Form Projection Display (FFPD) was introduced. FFPD can show the virtual object inside the real object. It is effective in operation and perception.

We expected that FFPD has two merits as follows,

1) ease of operation by hands.
2) ease of perception of shape and depth.

These merits were verified by experiments.

The result of experiments shows that FFPD was more natural and effective to operation and Perception than mouse or flat monitor, as shown in fig 7.

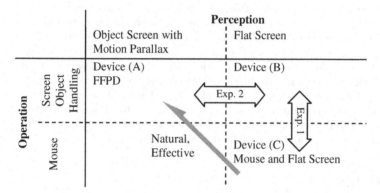

Fig. 7. Compensation matrix

References

1. Visuo-Haptic Display Using Head-Mounted Projector, Masahiko Inami, Naoki Kawakami, Dairoku Sekiguchi, Yasuyuki Yanagida, Taro Maeda and Susumu Tachi, Proceedings of IEEE Virtual Reality 2000, pp.233-240, 2000.3
2. Proposal of a Free Form Projection Display Using the Principle of Duality Rendering, Daisuke Kondo and Ryugo Kijima, Proceedings of 9th International Conference on Virtual Systems and MultiMedia(VSMM2002), pp.346-352, 2002.
3. Ramesh Raskar, Greg Welch, Matt Cutts, Adam Lake, Lev Stesin, and Henry Fuchs, "The Office of the Future: A Unified Approach to Image-Based Modeling and Spatially Immersive Displays", Proceedings of SIGGRAPH '98, pp. 179-188, ACM-SIGGRAPH, 1998.
4. A Virtual Anatomical Torso for Medical Education using Free Form Image Projection, Daisuke Kondo, Toshiyuki Goto, Makoto Kouno, Ryugo Kijima and Yuzo Takahashi, Proceedings of 10th International Conference on Virtual Systems and MultiMedia(VSMM2004), pp.678-685, 2004.

A Service-Oriented Architecture for Progressive Delivery and Adaptive Rendering of 3D Content

ZhiQuan Cheng, ShiYao Jin, Gang Dang, Tao Yang, and Tong Wu

PDL Laboratory, National University of Defense Technology
Changsha, Hunan Province, 410073, China
Spring121cheng@163.com

Abstract. Content adaptation techniques for progressive delivery of 3D models to clients with different rendering capabilities and network connections has been extensively studied in recent years. In this paper, a client-server based novel service-oriented architecture for 3D content delivery and adaptive rendering is presented. The architecture is integrated into the service-oriented architecture (SOA) framework, and it is designed to enhance the client user experience by progressively delivering 3D content stream quickly, reliably, and with high quality based on the adaptive requirements. At the client end the stream is progressively decoded up to the "best" level-of-details as defined by the client computational resources and the user inclination.

1 Introduction

Technologies for processing and transmission of 3D models and multimedia data, also called remote rendering, face an increased demand in professional and private scenarios. This demand has not been filled by software standards and their implementations, leaving a wide potential for technical innovations, such as new pioneering designs and solutions for coding and streaming/broadcasting technologies, as well as technologies and applications for distribution frameworks.

Now, most of the visualization systems are based on the client/server framework for network applications. However, by far there has been no common delivery platform to enable pervasive adoption by users. The design, implementation, and deployment of the architecture are challengeable. To the architecture problems at hand, the service-oriented architecture (SOA) [1] is a promising software engineering approach for adaptive distributed network applications over the conventional alternatives.

In the paper, the remote rendering system is first organized by the SOA with clear logical structures, complete functionality and high performance. Our SOA approach focuses on the interactivity and adaptive processing power utilization issues on the client, by incorporating a real-time control optimization mechanism for high quality interactive visualization using an interactively adapting progressive refinement and simultaneous rendering techniques; while on the server, the view-dependent progressive appearance-preserving 3D models with bounding box in octree structure are built, and a selecting strategy is executed

H. Zha et al. (Eds.): VSMM 2006, LNCS 4270, pp. 110–118, 2006.

based on performance parameters. In section two, we review related work in this field. In section three and four, we present the design of APRR, our component-based SOA framework for the development of remote rendering applications, then the implementation and results are listed. At last, the paper is finished by our conclusion.

2   Related Work

There are already some architecture instances to distribute 3D graphics over networks. In general, architectures for rendering 3D models can be classified into three major categories, mentioned in ARTE[2]: client side method, server side method, and hybrid method, according to where the rendering takes place. Also based on the transmission data format, the architecture can be divided into three types: video, image and geometric object.

1) Video-based: using 3D Video fragments, the method of dynamic free viewpoint 3D video for real-time applications is realized in Motion Picture Experts Group (MPEG)[3] format, visual objects are decoded from elementary streams, organized into a presentation, and extended with Virtual Reality Modeling Language (VRML) scene description to include coding and streaming, timing, and 2D and 3D object integration at the server, then the scene description data received at clients are decoded and represent. Such methods have the advantage that they reduce the geometric complexity of the data being transmitted by replacing it with MPEG. However, determining what a part of a model should be rendered on the server according to the eye position is not a trivial task, and user interaction with the video representation may be limited.

2) Image-based: the rendering is performed by the server, and the resulting stream of pixels is sent over the net. RenderCore[4] provides on-demand, remote access to the server's state. Remote and Distributed Visualization (DiVA)[5] and IBM's Deep Computing Visualization (DCV)[6], which both are grid-based service architecture for high performance scientific visualization can be included in this type. While in SGI's OpenGL Vizserver[7], all rendering is done on the server, which is a SGI supercomputer. The images then are transferred to the client. This offers high-quality graphics, but this approach needs powerful graphics driver, especially if the number of concurrent clients is very high. Furthermore, the transmitted bitmaps represent only 2D information and lack of local interaction.

3) Geometry replication: A copy of the geometric database is stored locally for access by the rendering process. The database can either be available before application start, or downloaded just before usage: one type is what current VRML/X3D browsers do, such as Vizx3D[8], GeoVRML[9], WebCAME[10], and JINX[11]. Furthermore, with the development of network capability, the type of client-server based research becomes a very current topic and many technologies have been exploited, includes flat and progressive coding techniques[12], out-of-core[13] methods as well as space efficient data structures admitting free traversals or visualization algorithms of the compressed[14] representation.

From the preceding discussion, it's obvious that geometry replication rendering at the clients has following better values: lower cost because of no need of high performance visualization server and higher interaction resulting from that the client has the ability to store and render the corresponding data. Though, it needs more network capability, our novel service-oriented architecture for remote rendering takes this type.

3   Adaptive Progressive Remote Rendering Architecture

According to the service-oriented architecture design principle, all development technologies, such as 3D model compression, visibility culling algorithms and etc., should be integrated as services in the remote rendering system. we now turn to the overall logical architecture of ARPP (Adaptive Progressive Remote Rendering) environment, presented by figure 1. It shows service-oriented architecture's three tiers (client, middle service, and EIS tier), which is integrated with adaptation generation and management with performance perceptual model, progressive delivery mechanism. By using universal three-tier architecture, developers can concentrate on their own developing domain with loose-coupled functional modular, achieved by independent service including various attributes, behavior, relationships, and constraints. The middle service layer depends on content retrieval service unit to communicate with enterprise information systems (EIS) tier[15]. In the APRR architecture, the client tier and the middle tier are designed using the "model-view-controller" pattern[16].

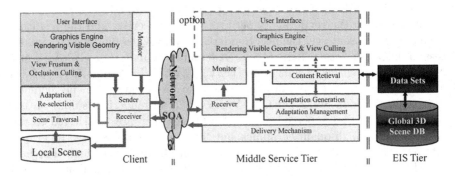

Fig. 1. APRR Logical Architecture: Each color represents an independent design pattern modular. The orange points out view modular, the blue denotes on model modular, and green presents controller modular. Especially, the view modular of middle service tier is optional choice.

When a client makes a request for a 3D model to a server, the server first receives meta-data information about the requested model. This information allows the server framework to retrieve the global 3D scene model database, and to load relevant model into the main memory. The relevant model becomes an adaptive progressive model, after which passes through adaptation generation and management service modular, with estimating its performance characteristics that are synthesized by T, Q, and I parameters similarly to ARTE (T: the estimated time that APRR deliver model from the server to the client, Q the quality which defines how closely a rendering of this representation resembles the rendering of the full-resolution data, and I the level of interaction). The adaptive management mechanism selects the best continuous nidek level available for each model that fits into the budget and progressively delivers it to the client in SOAP. Farther, the progressive model is reverse selected and write to the client's local scene database. Ultimately, the request model is rendered and displayed on the client.

3.1   Client Tier

The client is composed of three independent functional units: model, view, and controller:

- Model module: it includes client's local scene database, scene traversal, and adaptation re-selection functional components. It traverses the scene graph, computes the visible geometry and selects appropriate LOD from the local database or reselect from progressive uncompressed networked LOD.
- View module: the scene, arranged by model, will go through 3D viewing transformation and culling, depth buffer rendering and display in user interface, implemented using OpenSG[17].
- Controller module: the above modules are both monitored by controller, which also contains network's receiver and sender units.

The data, sent by client, are comprised of configuration and state parameters in SOAP format, which are the reification of the T, Q and I parameters. The configuration parameters, sent once at initializing time, consist of viewpoint's position (x, y, z) and orientation $(heading, pitch, roll)$, field of view, and other user preference; while the running state parameters, influencing on the server's adaptation selection management, include display frame rate, aspect ratio of the client's screen, degree of interaction, estimated representing quality, network latency and bandwidth. On the other hand, the data in SOAP format, received by client, are bit-streams of compressed progressive 3D model meshes packets. The structure of packet contains geometric detail, topological detail, external texture file with mapping pattern, and view-dependent refinement information for children nodes.

3.2   Middle Service Tier

The middle service tier takes advantage of the SOA's loose-coupled high-encapsulated reusable functional services based component-based development, and provides a server for automatically generating, managing, and delivering 3D modalities. These functional services have adopted the open standards philosophy and have included a Web services interface. The WSDL defines the interface to communicate directly with the application business logic.

Scene Data Preparation for Content Retrieval. Because of the effective 3D content retrieval requirement based on spatial localization principle, one unified scene hierarchy has to been prepared, which can be generated as a pre-calculation step or on-the-fly. The effective unified scene graph can be achieved by organizing it in octree structure reconstruction, which redefines the objects using a combination of partitioning and clustering algorithms. The partitioning algorithm takes large objects integrated with bounding box, and splits them into multiple objects (top-down strategies). While the clustering step groups objects with low polygon counts based on their spatial localization (down-top strategies). The combination of these steps results in a redistribution of geometry with good localization and emulates some of the benefits of pure bottom-up and up-bottom hierarchy generation. Also octree provides the convenient representation for storing information about object interiors and decreases storage requirements for 3D objects. Integrating with the perceptual requirements, each node in final model octree structure, stored in EIS's database, contains: the bounding box's position relative to the position of the node's parent, per-vertex normal used for lighting calculation, the width of a normal cone used together with the normal for view-dependent culling, referring external texture, and optional per-vertex color. Resulting from the unified octree representation of scene graph with all client's cameras, content retrieval service can take advantage of spatial coherence to reduce the time of searching model nearby client's viewpoint position. Additionally, at client side, the octree representation is used for the viewing frustum, and hidden-surface elimination is accomplished by projecting octree nodes onto the quadtree of viewing surface in a front-to-back order, furthermore, the quadtree representation for the visible surface is loaded into the frame buffer in graphics engine to display.

Adaptation Generation and Management. In the APRR architecture, GLOD tool serves as the LOD generation service, provides a rich set of options for simplification and is used as standalone simplifier as well as the unifying component of the adaptation. Through the adaptation generation, the unified scene hierarchy has transformed to view-dependent progressive meshes with incremental interactive parameters, accounting the max value of Q parameter transmitted through the network from the clients.The configuration and state information provided by the clients with local environment monitor data, such as model priority, determine the time budget (TB) available for management. Starting with the component with the highest importance value, the adaptation management selection algorithm proceeds to identify the most suitable progressive modal level for each client as follows. Among the progressive levels with Time less than TB, the one with the highest quality Q is selected.

Delivery Mechanism. The delivery mesh would be restored at the client side by applying the reverse operations of the adaptation generation process, so the vertices and triangles are inserted into the delivery bit-streams in the order of the reverse adaptation generating sequence. Then it is possible to respectively refine a mesh (i.e. the visual appearance of an element) triangle by triangle at the client based on progressive delivery (illustrated in Fig. 2).The remarkable property of delivery mechanism service is that these structures beyond adaptation generation contain connectivity and the base mesh M0 is dealt as a whole. So the delivery cache entries always provide a consistent representation of the mesh, which is independent to the simplification, refinement, selection and rendering process.

Fig. 2. One typical representation process on client 1 based current delivery mechanism on different state: a) at 3 second with 442 faces, 672 triangles, and 1556 triangles. b) at 5 second with 678 faces, 1031 triangles, and 2387 triangles. b) at 10 second with 1802 faces, 3335 triangles, and 6935 triangles.

3.3   EIS Tier

The EIS tier is designed using ADO.NET, which enables us not only to build high-performance, scalable solutions for 3D model database service provider, but also allows the remote rendering applications to support connectionless database. Through the use of XML, the XmlAdapter and SqlXml Classes, together with the XPathDocument, enables disconnected data manipulation in XML[2]. Data structure stored in datasets can be expressed by XML schema domain (XSD) as follows:

```
<xsd:element name="3dmodel">
 <xsd:complexType>
  <xsd:attribute name="Name" type="xsd:string" />
  <xsd:attribute name="ID" type="xsd:integer" />
  <xsd:attribute name="PreparationState" type="xsd:bool" />
  <xsd:attribute name="OctreeModel" type="xsd:preparingModel" />
  <xsd:attribute name="AdaptationState" type="xsd:bool" />
  <xsd:attribute name="AdaptiveModel" type="xsd:adaptModel" />
  <xsd:attribute name="ExternalFile" type="xsd:string" />
  <xsd:attribute name="JointClient1" type="xsd: connectivity " />
  <xsd:attribute name="JointClient2" type="xsd: connectivity " />
  <xsd:attribute name="JointClient3" type="xsd: connectivity " />
  <xsd:attribute name="JointClient4" type="xsd: connectivity " />
  <xsd:attribute name="Dirty" type="xsd:bool" />
 </xsd:complexType>
</xsd:element>
```

From the XML 3D model data structure, it's easy to learn that octree representation of scene model is marked as "preparingModel", the adaptation generation and management is nominated by "adaptModel" with external reference file, the delivery joint position of each client is mentioned by "connectivity", and data update strategy in main memory is lazy algorithm using "dirty" identifier. The notice is that the "preparingModel" is retrieved just before the time of "adaptModel" created. Once "adaptModel" has been established, the content retrieval service would use it rather than "preparingModel".

4   Implementation and Results

4.1   Implementation and Deployment

The software libraries and remote rendering application system have been implemented on Windows using C++ with OpenGL in Microsoft's Visual Studio .NET Framework with GLUT[18] on five Intel Pentium IV computers running at 2.4GHz with 512 MB DDR and 128MB graphics controller, one computer works as server and others are clients. We have extensively tested our system with a synthetic battlefield environment including a number of military weapon 3D models.

We use portal to present the collection of services, which is a very natural way to provide the location independence, consolidation of functional modules, and the level automation necessary to support remote rendering activities. This achievement is gotten through Visual Studio.Net Framework, therefore the system is configured by assemblies, which are the smallest units of versioning and deployment in the .NET applications. So our APRR system, with one server and four clients, whose screen are captured in figure 4, is deployed by the configuration files with .config suffix.

4.2   Results

Figure 4(a) shows the fidelity quality by time of each client, measured by graphical tool, which points out that our approach has performed an incremental perceptual proximity; while fig. 4(b) illustrates the passing data size received on each client on time, which clearly shows that the client's receiving data packets significantly inverses to client's number. Due to the absence of load balance, the loading time of each client varies from each other.

Client1   Client2   Client3   Client4

Fig. 3. The four clients' remote battlefield environment representation

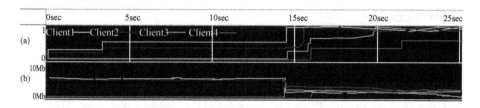

Fig. 4. The four clients' remote battlefield environment representation

4.3 Comparison with **ARTE** and **DiVA** System

Because our APRR is based on service-oriented architecture, it provides more reusable and loose-coupled remote rendering modular than ARTE and DiVA system, through loosely bound service interactions. Additionally, the presented approach provides the following novelties or benefits than them respectively:

- The basic tenet of SOA is that the use of explicit service interfaces and inter-operable, location-transparent communication protocols means that services are loosely coupled with each other.
- APRR' 3D models can be modified and rendered simultaneously, and it always provides a consistent representation of the scene on server and client, even during the simplification and the refinement process.
- The unified scene hierarchy preparation can be generated as a pre-calculation step or on-the-fly, and the process combines the benefits of octree reconstruction with bounding volume hierarchy.

5 Conclusion

We have demonstrated a novel SOA architecture for 3D content adaptive generation and management, network streaming and remote interaction of complex 3D battlefield environment. The design and implementation works with standard SOA three-tier framework, incurs low run-time overhead on the client, and takes advantage of the unified scene Octree hierarchy preprocessing, subtly adaptation synthesizing various factors, compact progressive delivery, and real-time rendering capabilities. This is a solution framework for work in progress with staggered result, while not a prototype system. By far, it is the first SOA based system that can render complex environments at interactive rates with good fidelity.

There are many complex issues with respect to the design and performance of systems for interactive display of remote environments. What should be integrated in APRR, include load balancing, extent of parallelism and scalability beyond current approach, the effectiveness of occlusion culling and issues related to loading and managing large datasets. A second improvement would be to originate and adapt new algorithms for remote rendering. Finally, the performance modular is elementary, and the whole APRR needs improvements.

Acknowledgments. The work is supported by Hunan Province Science Foundation of China (No. 05JJ30124).

References

1. Barry K. D.: Web Services and Service-Oriented Architecture: The Savvy Manager's Guide. ISBN: 1558609067. Morgan Kaufmann Press, New York (2003)
2. Martin M. I.: Adaptive rendering of 3D models over networks using multiple modalities. Technical Report, IBM T. J. Watson Research Center RC 21722, 97821(2000)
3. Daras P., Kompatsiaris I., Raptis T.: An MPEG-4 Tool for Composing 3D Scenes. IEEE MultiMedia **11(2)** (2004) 58–71
4. Rendercore, http://www.rendercore.com/
5. DiVA. http://vis.lbl.gov/Research/DiVA/
6. DCV. http://www.ibm.com/servers/deepcomputing/visualization/
7. Silicon Graphics Inc., OpenGL Vizserver 3.1, http://www.sgi.com/sofeware/vizserver
8. Vizx3d. http://www.vizx3d.com/
9. Reddy M., Iverson L., Leclerc Y.: GeoVRML: Open Web-based 3D Cartography. In Proc. ICC. Beijing ,China (2001) 6–10
10. Helfried T.: WebCAME -A 3D Multiresolution Viewer for the Web. In Proc CESCG. Budmerice castle, Slovakia (2003) 63–72
11. Luciano S., Marcelo K. Z.: JINX: an X3D browser for VR immersive simulation based on clusters of commodity computers. In Proc. Web3D'04, ACM Press, New York, NY (2004) 79–86
12. Sahm J., Soetebier I., Birthelmer H.: Efficient Representation and Streaming of 3Dscenes. Computers Graphics **28(1)** (2004) 15–24
13. Guthe M.l, Klein R.: Streaming HLODs: an out-of-core viewer for network visualization of huge polygon models. Computers Graphics **28(1)** (2004) 43–50
14. Valette S., Gouaillard A., Prost R.: Compression of 3D triangular meshes with progressive precision. Computers Graphics **28(1)** (2004) 35-42
15. Homer A., Sussman D., Fussell M.: First Look at ADO.NET and System Xml v 2.0. ISBN: 0321228391. Addison Wesley, Boston, Massachusetts (2003)
16. Erich G., Richard H., Ralph J., John V.: Design Patterns: Elements of Reusable Object-Oriented Software. ISBN: 0201633612. Addison Wesley, Boston, Massachusetts (1994)
17. OpenSG. http://www.opensg.org/
18. GLUT. http://www.opengl.org/resources/libraries/glut.html

Embedding Image Watermarks into Local Linear Singularity Coefficients in Ridgelet Domain

Xiao Liang, Wei Zhihui, and Wu Huizhong

School of Computer Science and Technology, Nanjing University of Science and Technology, Nanjing 210094, China

Abstract. An adaptive watermarking algorithm operating in the ridgelet domain is proposed. Since the most significant coefficients of the ridgelet transform (RT) can represent the most energetic direction of an image with straight edge, the image is first partitioned into small blocks and RT is applied for each block. Followed by the multiplicative rule, the watermark sequence is casting into local linear singularity coefficients within the highest energy direction of each block. Through analyzing the distribution of the texture in ridgelet coefficients of each block, the feature of luminance masking and texture masking is incorporated to adjust the watermark's embedding strength. Then the embedded watermark can be blindly detected by correlation detector. Experiments show that the proposed algorithm can achieve a better tradeoff between the robustness and transparency.

1   Introduction

Digital watermarking for multimedia including images, video, audio, etc has been drawn extensive intension recently. The image watermarking can be classified into two branches. The first one is called fragile watermarking, while another branch is called robust watermarking. Fragile watermarking can be used in the application of image authentication, proof of integrity, while the robust watermarking is very useful for image copyright protection. It is widely accepted that the frequency-domain watermarking algorithms can easily exploit the perceptual models based on characteristics of the Human Visual System (HVS) to achieve the best tradeoff between imperceptibility and robustness to image processing, and also easy to be implemented in compressed domain. Hence many robust algorithms have been developed in DCT [1]or wavelet domain [2][3][4]. In this paper, we address the issue of how to embed watermark into a recently introduced family of transform-the ridgelet transform (RT)[5]. The RT uses basis elements which exhibit high directional sensitivity and are highly anisotropic. The RT allows obtaining a sparse image representation where the most significant coefficients represent the most energetic direction of an image with straight edges. So it has the advantages for watermarks embedding since the multi-scale edge point according to the noise masking area. However, since edges in nature images are typically curved, in order to obtain an effective image representation through the RT, the image is partitioned into blocks of side-length such that an

H. Zha et al. (Eds.): VSMM 2006, LNCS 4270, pp. 119–127, 2006.

edge appears as a straight line. Within each block, the most significant directions are selected to embed watermark signal. In order to provide a better tradeoff between the robustness and transparency, we propose the noise visible function (NVF) for each block to a local invisible control, while a predefined Peak Signal Noise Rate (PSNR) is used as the invisible constraint to achieve the global invisible control. Experiments show that the proposed algorithm can achieve a better tradeoff between the robustness and transparency.

2   Ridgelet Transform

2.1   Continuous Ridgelet Transform

A substantial foundation for Ridgelet analysis is documented in the Ph.D. thesis of Cand'es[5]. The Ridgelet 2-D function $\psi_{a,b,\theta} : R^2 \to R^2$ is defined by

$$\psi_{a,b,\theta}(x) = a^{-1/2} \cdot \psi((x_1 \cos\theta + x_2 \sin\theta - b)/a) \tag{1}$$

where $a > 0$, each $b \in R$ and each $\theta \in [0, 2\pi)$. so called ridgelets are constant along ridge lines $x_1 \cos\theta + x_2 \sin\theta$,and along the orthogonal direction they are wavelets. Given an integrable bivariate function $f(x)$, we define its ridgelet coefficients by

$$R_f(a, b, \theta) = \int \psi_{a,b,\theta}(x)f(x)dx. \tag{2}$$

A basic tool for calculating ridgelet coefficients is to view ridgelet analysis as a form of wavelet analysis in Radon domain. More precisely, denote the Radon transform as

$$RA_f(\theta, t) = \int_{R^2} f(x)\delta(x_1 \cos\theta + x_2 \sin\theta - t)dx \tag{3}$$

Then the ridgelet transform is precisely the application of a 1-D wavelet transform to the slice of the Radon transform.

$$R_f(a, b, \theta) = \int \psi_{a,b}(t)RA_f(\theta, t)dt. \tag{4}$$

2.2   Digital Ridgelet Transform

In[4], a finite Radon transform (FRAT) is introduced. The FRAT of a real function I defined on a finite grid Z_p^2 being $Z_p = \{0, 1, 2.....p-1\}$ where p is a prime number, is

$$r_k[l] = FRAT_I(k, l) = \frac{1}{\sqrt{p}} \sum_{(i,j)\in L_{k,l}} f[i, j] \tag{5}$$

$L_{k,l}$ Defines the set of points that form a line on the lattice Z_p^2 .Specifically

$$L_{k,l} = \{(i,j) : j = ki + l(\bmod p), i \in Z_p\}, L_{p,l} = \{(l,j) : j \in Z_p\} \qquad (6)$$

being $0 \le k < p$ the line direction (where k=p corresponds to the vertical line) and its intercept. It has been demonstrated that FRAT is invertible, thus providing a representation for a generic image. The invertible finite $IFRAT_I[k,q]$, with $q \in Z_p$, is obtained by taking the 1-D discrete wavelet transform on each FRAT projection sequencefor each direction k .

3 Proposed Watermarking Algorithm

The proposed watermarking algorithm is illustrated as Fig.1. The original image is first partitioned into blocks whose width is such that a curved edge appears to be straight. Then the RT is performed on each block. For each block, the direction having the greater energy is selected. After having collected the coefficients representing the most significant direction of each block, they are marked with the watermark sequence, which are generated by user key and watermark Logo. In order to adaptively adjust the watermark's strength, we propose a local and global invisible control mechanism into the watermarking system. In the local invisible control process, the texture feature of each block is analyzed to model the local luminance masking and texture masking effect, then a local noise visible function (NVF) is defined to control the watermark's strength in each block. While in the global invisible control, the predefined Peak Signal Noise Rate (PSNR) is used as the invisible constraint to compute the global invisible parameter. Finally, the coefficients related to the selected direction are watermarked and the local and global invisible control mechanisms are used to determine the watermark's strength. Finally, the inverse RT is finally performed, thus obtaining the watermarked image.

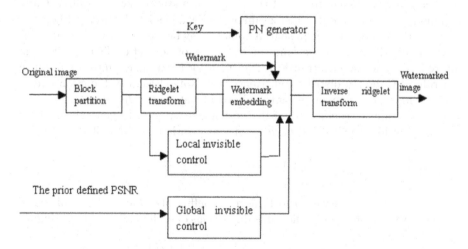

Fig. 1. The block diagram of our proposed watermarking system

3.1   Watermark Generation

In our watermarking system,the meaningful signature such as the logo of the image owner or the information related to the host image such as owner's name, image ID, etc is chosen to generate the embedding signal. The embedding signal $L = [l_1, l_2, ...l_{N_w}]$ with $l_i \in \{0,1\}$ is a bit sequence with length N_w . We modulate the bit sequence by a bit-wise logical XOR operation with a pseudorandom sequence and $s_i \in [0,1]$ to give the watermark sequence $PN = [s_1, s_2, ...s_{N_w}]$ by $w_i = s_i \otimes l_i$.

3.2   Block Partitioning and Local Invisible Control

We Assume that the original image $f(x,y)$ is split into non-overlapped blocks of denoted $B_l, l = 0, 1, 2...B - 1$. That is

$$f(x,y) = \bigcup_l B_l = \bigcup_l f^l(x',y'), 0 \le x', y' \le N$$

for each block, the digital ridgelet transform is applied, thus

$$FRIT_{f^l} = \{FRIT_{f^l}[k,q], (k,q) \in P_{i,j}\} \tag{7}$$

According to the visual masking properties, it is known that the visibility of the superimposed watermark signal is affected by the luminance, the spatial-frequency, and the texture of the background in the following ways[6]. The brighter the background, the lower the visibility of the embedded signal (luminance masking). The stronger the texture in the background, the lower the visibility of the embedded signal (texture masking). Thus it is need to analyze the local luminance masking and texture masking effect.Noise Visibility Function (NVF)[7]is the function that characterizes local image properties, identifying textured and edge regions.There are two kinds of NVF, based on either a non-stationary Gaussian model of the image, or a stationary generalized Gaussian model. According to the histogram of the Lena in spatial domain (Fig.2), we know that the nature image in spatial domain may be viewed as a non-stationary Gaussian distribution. While from the histogram of rideglet coefficients, it is discovered that the ridgelet transform can transform the image into a stationary generalized Gaussian distribution. Hence, the Noise Visibility Function can be modeled in ridgelet domain using the above advantage of ridgelet transform. Assuming the rideglet coefficients of the host image subjects to generalized Gaussian distribution, the NVF at each coefficient position can be written as:

$$NVF(l) = \frac{1}{1 + [\mathrm{var}(FRIT_{f^l})]} \tag{8}$$

Where Var(.) means the variance of ridgelet coefficients. Once we have calculated the NVF, we can obtain the allowable distortions of each block by computing:

$$VS(NVF) = 1 - \frac{\arctan(NVF/c)}{\pi/2} \tag{9}$$

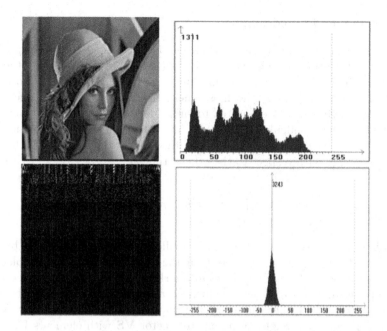

Fig. 2. Upleft: The original Lena, Upright: the histogram of the Lena in spatial domain, Downleft: the ridgelet coefficient image (Scaled into [0,255]), Downright: the histogram of rideglet coefficients

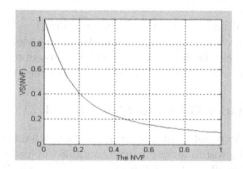

Fig. 3. The curve of the function $VS(NVF)$

Here the parameter c is selected parameter to control the shape of the curve between NVF and allowable distortions of each block as the illustration of Fig.3.From the above Figure 3, the local luminance masking and texture masking effect of each block can be well modeled by the function $VS(NVF)$. If we take the function $VS(NVF)$ as the strength of watermark embedding of each block, then it will be guaranteed that the strength of watermark components embedded into block with weaker texture will be weaker than the block with stronger texture.

3.3   Watermark Embedding

It is well known that the watermark has to be embedded into perceptually significant features of an image,such as the edges in order to improve the robustness and invisibility of the watermarking algorithm. Because the most significant coefficients represent the most energetic direction of an image with straight edges, hence they are selected to embedded with watermarks. For each block, the finite RT is calculated, thus obtaining the ridgelet coefficients for the direction $0 \leq k \leq p$ with $p = N$.Then within the block l, the direction k_h having the highest energy with respect to the others, that is

$$k_h = \max_k \left(\frac{1}{p} \sum_{q=0}^{p-1} \left(FRIT_{f^l}[k,q] \right)^2 \right) \tag{10}$$

In this direction k_h, there are N ridgelet coefficients, let's denote them by the vector $V_l = [I_{l1}, I_{l2}, ... I_{lN}]$ which represent the most energetic edge in block l, thus they are the coefficients to be watermarked. For all the blocks, i.e $0 \leq l \leq B$, all the direction's ridgelet coefficients are collected into the embedded matrix $I = [V_1, V_2, ... V_B]$.Let the remainder ridgelet coefficients denote by $\mathbf{V}_l = [I_{l1}, I_{l2}, ... I_{lN}]$, and the weighting parameter vector $\mathbf{VS}$ with elements $VS(l) = VS(NVF(l))$. Thus according to the multiplicative rule, the watermark signal is superimposed on to each row of the embedded matrix:

$$\mathbf{I^W} = \{\mathbf{I} + \alpha \cdot \mathbf{VS}^T |\mathbf{I}| \mathbf{W}\} \cup \mathbf{I}^c \tag{11}$$

where α is the global invisible control parameter and $|\mathbf{I}| = \{|I_{kl}|\}_{B \times N}$. From above embedding law, it is easily to see that the same watermark signal is embedded into each ridgelet coefficients of the most representative direction of the block under analysis, which improve the robustness of the algorithm.

3.4   The Watermark's Global Invisible Control

Now let us discuss the problem of how to design the global invisible control parameter α.Assume the watermarked image is obtained by inverse RT performing to the watermarked coefficients, and denoted by $f^W = IFRIT(I^W)$. Thus we can assume the watermarked image's visual quality has higher value of PSNR, that is

$$PSNR = 10 \log \frac{f_{\max}^2}{\frac{1}{(B \cdot N)^2} \sum_{i=1}^{M} \sum_{j=1}^{N} \left(f^W(i,j) - f(i,j) \right)^2} \geq T_0$$

where $f_{\max}$ is according to the maximal gray value of original image. From the embedding formula and the Parsval equation of ridgelet transform

$$\sum_{i=1}^{M} \sum_{j=1}^{N} (f^W(i,j) - f(i,j))^2 = \alpha^2 \sum_{j=1}^{N} \sum_{k=1}^{B} (VS(k) |I_{kj}|)^2$$

thus we can obtain the global invisible control parameter , it must be satisfied

$$\alpha \le f_{\max} \cdot B \cdot N \sqrt{\frac{10^{-\frac{T_0}{10}}}{\sum\limits_{j=1}^{N} \sum\limits_{k=1}^{B} (VS(k) |I_{kj}|)^2}} \tag{12}$$

4   Watermark Detection

The watermark detection is the dual procedure of the watermark embedding. For the attacked image with a certain type of attack, the same block portioning and RT transform is performed for each block. The coefficients belonging to directions having the greatest energy within the block are selected and collected into the embedded matrix

$$\mathbf{I}^* = \left[V_1^*, V_2^*, ... V_B^*\right] = \{I_{ij}^*\}_{B \times N}$$

Thus the correlation detector between each row of the embedded matrix $\mathbf{I}^*$ and the watermark $\mathbf{W}$ is calculated and sum over the row, i.e

$$\rho = \frac{1}{N} \sum_{l=1}^{N} \left(\frac{1}{B} \sum_{k=1}^{B} I_{l,k}^* \cdot w_k \right) \tag{13}$$

Similar with the study in the literature[8], we set the detection threshold in the following

$$T_\rho = \frac{1}{N} \sum_{i=1}^{N} \left(\frac{\alpha \cdot VS(i)}{3B} \sum_{j=1}^{B} I_{i,j}^* \right) \tag{14}$$

Then the existence of watermarks is made that when the $\rho > T_\rho$. Otherwise, there is no the embedding watermarks exist. It is clearly that the embedded watermark can be blindly detected by correlation coefficients between the watermarked image and the watermark sequence,without the need of original image.Ofcource,if we want to extract the watermark logo,the original image may be used to achieve the better results.

5   Experimental Results

To demonstrate the validity of our proposed watermarking algorithm, five standard test images including "Lena","Barbara","Baboon","Boat" and "Airplane" with size of 510×510 pixels are used to test our algorithm. They are first partitioned into blocks with17×17 pixels, thus obtaining $B = 900$ blocks. Then the watermark sequence with elements is generated by the method described in section 3.1 using a binary image logo are superimposed in ridgelet domain according to the method described in section 3.3. Experimental results show that the

Fig. 4. Left is the watermarked images "Lena" with PSNR=39.34dB and the middleis the absolute difference between original image and watermarked one. Right is the extracted watermark Logo.

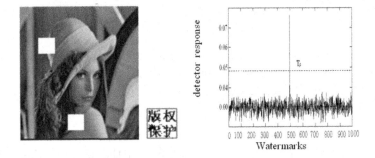

Fig. 5. Left: The cropping attack applied in watermarked Lena. Middle: The extracted watermark logo. Right: The detector response to 999 random watermarks with only the actual embedded watermark.

proposed algorithm can provide good invisibility of the embedding watermarks. If we want the watermarked image has less distortion or has higher PSNR, the propoesed algorithm can adjust the global invisible control parameter.

Fig.4 shows the watermarked images of "Lena", the absolute difference between original and watermarked one and extracted watermark image. It is clearly see that the imperceptibility of the embedded watermarks is well guaranteed. Compared the similar algorithm in ridgelet domain[8], we also use the software of StirMark[9][10] to test our proposed watermarking algorithm's robustness to the different common image processing including 3 3 median filter, Gaussian noise superimposed, Laplace sharping, Image scaling and JPEG compression, etc. Experimental results listed in Table I show that the detector response ρ^{500} is always higher than the detection threshold T_ρ while the second highest detector response ρ^{2nd} always stay below the detection threshold. The detector provides a correlation value far higher than the threshold only for the actual embedded watermark out of the 1000 tested. Experimental results also show that better robustness performance can be obtained for the images with more complex texture, for example "Baboon" image.

Table 1. Comparison of robustness test results in [8]and our algorithm

Agorithms	In [8]			Our		
	T_ρ	ρ^{2nd}	ρ^{500}	T_ρ	ρ^{2nd}	ρ^{500}
median filter	6.24	5.92	25.21	5.04	4.32	25.34
Gaussian noise	6.14	5.64	25.42	5.13	4.41	25.43
Laplace sharping	6.36	5.43	24.42.	5.26	4.21	24.87
Imag scaling(0.75*1.0)	7.69	5.23	26.24	6.34	4.32	26.86
JPEG compression(0.2)	5.57	5.54	25.73	5.29	4.45	26.22

Acknowledgment

This work is supported by Nature Science Foundation of Jiangsu province of China(No.BK2006569),Post-doctor Foundation of Jiangsu province and Youth Foundation of Nanjing university of science and technology(No.NJUST200401)

References

1. Briassouli. A, Tsakalides. P, Stouraitis. A.: Hidden messages in heavy-tails: DCT-domain watermark detection using alpha-stable models. IEEE Transactions on Multimedia. **7** (2005) 700–714
2. B.Mauro, P.Alessandro.: Improved wavelet-based watermarking through pixel-wisemasking. IEEE Transactions on image processing.**10** (2001) 783–791
3. Mobasseri, Bijan G. Berger II, Robert J.: A foundation for watermarking in compressed domain.IEEE Signal Processing Letters. **12**,(2005) 399–402
4. Hernandez Victor, Nakano-Miyatake Mariko,Perez-Meana Hector.: A robust DWT-based image watermarking algorithm. WSEAS Transactions and Communications. **4**,(2005) 1048–1057
5. M. N. Do and M. Vetterli.: The finite ridgelet transform for image representation. IEEE Trans. Image Processing. **12** (2003) 16–28
6. Eyadat Mohammad, Vasikarla Shantaram.: Performance evaluation of an incorporated DCT block-based watermarking algorithm with human visual system model.Pattern Recognition Letters. **26** (2005) 1405–1411
7. Voloshynovskiy. S, Pereira. S, Iquise. V, et al.: Attack modeling: Towards a second generation watermarking benchmark. Signal processing. **8** (2001) 1177–1214
8. Patrizio Campisi, Deepa Kundur, Alessandro Neri.: Robust digital watermarking in ridgelet domain. IEEE signal processing letters. **11** (2004) 826–830
9. R.J.A Fabien, M.G Kuhn.: Attacks on copyright marking systems.In second workshop on information Hiding,Portland, Oregon,April.(1998) 15–17
10. Bogumil.D.: An asymmetric image watermarking scheme resistant against geometrical distortions.Signal Processing. Image Communication. **21** (2006) 59–66

Rotated Haar-Like Features
for Face Detection with In-Plane Rotation

Shaoyi Du, Nanning Zheng, Qubo You, Yang Wu,
Maojun Yuan, and Jingjun Wu

Institute of Artificial Intelligence and Robotics,
Xi'an jiaotong University, Xi'an, Shaanxi Province 710049, P.R. China
{sydu,nnzheng,qbyou,ywu,mjyuan,jjwu}@aiar.xjtu.edu.cn

Abstract. This paper extends the upright face detection framework proposed by Viola et al. 2001 to handle in-plane rotated faces. These haar-like features work inefficiently on rotated faces, so this paper proposes a new set of $\pm 26.565°$ haar-like features which can be calculated quickly to represent the features of rotated faces. Unlike previous face detection techniques in training quantities of samples to build different rotated detectors, with these new features, we address to build different rotated detectors by rotating an upright face detector directly so as to achieve in-plane rotated face detection. This approach is selected because of its computational efficiency, simplicity and training time saving. This proposed method is tested on CMU-MIT rotated test data and yields good results in accuracy and maintains speed advantage.

1 Introduction

In recent decades, face detection techniques have developed very quickly, and the survey of it have been detailed in [1,2]. It could be said without question that the last decade witnessed the most fruitful researches in the field of face detection. First of all, Rowley et al. [3,4] had proposed neural network-based face detection which had greatly improved the accuracy of face detection. Secondly, with great accuracy, Viola and Jones had introduced a fast object detection based on a boosted cascade of haar-like features [5]. Thereafter more importance began to be attached to the research of haar-like features and AdaBoost. Viola had once advanced asymmetric AdaBoost for more robust classification [6]; Lienhart had extended the haar-like features to an efficient set of 45° rotated features and used discrete AdaBoost (DAB), real AdaBoost(RAB) and gentle AdaBoost(GAB) for face detection [7,8].

With the marked improvement of speed and precision in upright face detection, more and more scholars came to focus on the multi-view face detection. FloatBoost presented by Li was used to overcome the monotonicity problem of the sequential AdaBoost learning [9]. Jones had created a fourth type of rectangle filter and applied it to multi-view face detection [10]. Lin addressed MBHboost whose integration with a cascade structure is robust for face detection [11]. Wang had introduced RNDA to handle multi-view face and eye detection [12].

H. Zha et al. (Eds.): VSMM 2006, LNCS 4270, pp. 128–137, 2006.

The above-mentioned techniques had achieved somewhat success, but all of them are based on the framework of retraining samples. That is, those techniques averagely divided a 360-degree in-plane rotated face into 12 different classes, each covering 30 degrees. Within each rotation class, a large number of face samples had to be collected and a corresponding features set had to be designed so that face detectors for each class could be trained to cover the full 360-degree in-plane rotation.

This paper proposed a novel notion that rotated face detectors needn't the retraining of rotated face samples. For the reason of the correspondence of face detectors and their features, rotated face detectors are very likely to be obtained in the way of rotating efficient upright face detector. On the ground of this, with our trained upright face detector and designed set of $\pm 26.565°$ rotated haar-like features, a variety of rotated face detectors can thus be gained to fulfill the task of face detection with 360-degree in-plane rotation. This new proposed approach has been tested in CMU-MIT rotated test set. The test demonstrates our new rotated detectors do not add more computation but can get good results with great accuracy as well. Besides, training time is saved considerably.

This paper is organized as follows. In section 2, the haar-like features have been reviewed, and our rotated haar-like features with corresponding integral images are introduced. In section 3, the framework of in-plane rotated face detection has been presented. Following that is section 4 in which the proposed method is evaluated on CMU-MIT rotated test set and a conclusion is finally drawn in section 5.

2   Features and Its Computation

As we all know, features are important for classification problem. Haar-like features have been widely used in upright face detection for two reasons: 1) Their quantity is much larger than the number of the raw pixels and they can well represent the upright faces. 2) They are simple and can be calculated quickly. Nevertheless, the features only represent the face's horizontal and vertical local features, so they can't be used in rotated faces. For this reason, we have to extend the original haar-like features.

2.1   Previous Work

Haar-like features that can directly represent the local relation between the image regions [5,7,8] perform efficiently in the upright face detector, so they are used for our upright face detection. In this paper, we use the following haar-like features shown in Fig. 1.

The real value of haar-like features can be computed in the way of the pixel sum of the black rectangular region subtracted from that of the white region, and the pixel sum of each rectangular region feature can be obtained by integral images. Fig. 2 illustrates the computation.

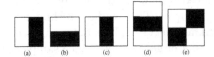

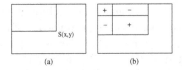

Fig. 1. Haar-like features for upright face detection

Fig. 2. The computation of rectangle feature by the integral image. (a) the upright integral image (b) calculation scheme of the pixel sum of upright rectangle feature.

The integral image at location (x, y) contains the sum of the pixels above and to the left of (x, y):

$$S(x, y) = \sum_{x' \leq x, y' \leq y} I(x', y') \tag{1}$$

where $I(x', y')$ is the pixel value.

$$R(x, y) = R(x, y-1) + I(x, y) \quad S(x, y) = S(x-1, y) + R(x, y) \tag{2}$$

where $R(x, y)$ is cumulative column sum.

The merit of this computation is simple, fast and accurate. Namely, if the integral image is to be computed, we only need to scan the image once.

2.2   Design of Rotated Degrees

The face rotation is generally classified into two categories: in-plane rotation and out-plane rotation. There are mainly two approaches for in-plane rotation. The first is to rotate images for an upright detector to detect faces. The other approach is to design detectors with different degrees directly to detect faces. Compared with the former one conducting relatively bad in its slow speed, the latter has been adopted more often. Based on it, this paper extends the upright face detector to produce different face detectors with in-plane rotation.

Given that images are continuous signals, theoretically, when an efficient upright face detector is rotated to any arbitrary degree, it is supposed to detect faces in the corresponding position. Yet, the fact is not in that case. Since images are discrete digital signals, the arbitrary rotated features for face detectors are usually unable to be computed fast. Consequently, most researchers retrained samples for different detectors. On the contrary, this paper presents a novel technique which can save time without retraining samples any more.

To design rotated features corresponding to face detectors which needn't the retraining of samples, three rules should be followed:

1. Tilted integral images should be computed fast, through which the rotated haar-like features can be calculated.

2. As the upright face detection can detect in-plane rotated faces of $[-20°, 20°]$ and out-plane faces of $[-15°, 15°]$, to ensure that different rotated face detectors, which are obtained by rotating the upright face detector, can detect faces with

360-degree in-plane rotation, the rotated degree between the neighborhood haar-like features (see Fig. 3) ought to be less than $20° \times 2 = 40°$.

3. The above-mentioned rotated degree between the neighborhood haar-like features should be as large as possible, which can make the divided classes of in-plane rotation as few as they could.

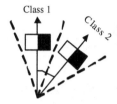

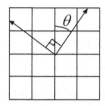

Fig. 3. Rotated degree between neighborhood haar-like features

Fig. 4. Design of rotated degree for fast computation of tilted integral images

On the basis of rule 1, we can find only when the degree θ satisfies $\tan\theta = 1/n, (n = 1, 2, 3, \cdots)$ can the tilted integral images be computed fast in Fig. 4. But according to rule 2, we can get $n \geq 2$. Because of rule 3, n can only equal 2. Hence, the rotated degrees used in this paper are $\arctan 0.5 = 26.565°$ (clockwise) and $-\arctan 0.5 = -26.565°$ (anti-clockwise).

2.3 Rotated Haar-Like Features

In consideration of the design of $\pm 26.565°$ rotated degree, we divide the rotated faces into 12 new classes: $[-13.283°, 13.283°]$, $[\pm 13.283°, \pm 45°]$, $[\pm 45°, \pm 76.717°]$, $[\pm 76.717°, \pm 103.283°]$, $[\pm 103.283°, \pm 135°]$, $[\pm 135°, \pm 166.717°]$, $[166.717°, 193.2\ 83°]$, and the degrees θ of these classes' detectors are $0°$, $\pm 26.565°$, $\pm 63.435°$, $\pm 90°$, $\pm 116.565°$, $\pm 153.435°$, $180°$ respectively, see Fig. 5. The paper redefines the set of haar-like features with the angles $\pm 26.565°$, which are given in Fig. 6.

For the sake of description convenience, two definitions are given here: within-class haar-like features and between-class haar-like features. Within-class haar-like features are a set of features which are used for one detector to detect faces in one class, such as Fig. 6-1(a), 1(d), 2(a), 2(d), 3(a) for upright detector. Between-class haar-like features are the set of same type of features that can be used in different detectors respectively, so they can be transformed each other easily, such as Fig. 6-1(a), 1(b), 1(c).

It is obvious to see that within-class haar-like features Fig. 6-1(a), 1(d), 2(a), 2(d), 3(a) are used for an upright detector $[-13.283°, 13.283°]$. So are features 6-1(b), 1(e), 2(b), 2(e), 3(b) for $26.565°$ detector with the range $[13.283°, 45°]$ and 6-1(c), 1(f), 2(c), 2(f), 3(c) for $-26.565°$ detector with the range $[-45°, -13.283°]$. Rotating these features $\pm 90°$, $180°$ each, the 360-degree frontal face detectors can be obtained with ease.

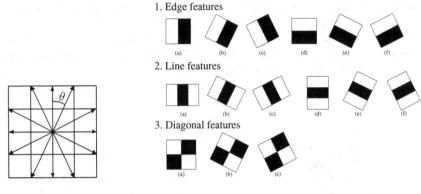

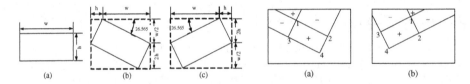

Fig. 5. The distribution of the degrees of 360-degree in-plane rotated detectors

Fig. 6. The set of upright and ±26.565° rotated haar-like features

2.4   Fast Feature Computation

Similar to [7,8], we compute these features by new integral images as well. Firstly, we rotate the basic component, rectangle feature as Fig. 7. The rotated features can't be computed like section 2.1 any longer. To compute the tilted integral images fast, we address the following method.

Fig. 7. The Set of rectangle features. (a) upright rectangle feature (b) 26.565° rotated rectangle features (c) −26.565° rotated rectangle features.

Fig. 8. Computation of rectangle features. (a) the pixel sum of 26.565° rectangle (b) the pixel sum of −26.565° rectangle.

In Fig. 8, the value of every rotated rectangle can be computed by the pixel sum of 4 corners, so our focus is the computation of integral image (see Fig. 9).

In Fig. 9(a), for each pixel point (x, y) , its integral image $S(x, y)$ can be calculated by iteration:

$$R(x,y) = R(x+1, y-2) + I(x,y)$$
$$S(x,y) = S(x-2, y-1) + R(x,y) + R(x-1, y-1) + R(x, y-1) \quad (3)$$
$$+ R(x-1, y-2) + R(x, y-2)$$

where $R(x,y)$, which is denoted as the arrow lines in the figure, is the pixel sum of tilted lines, and $I(x,y)$ is the pixel value.

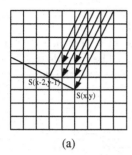
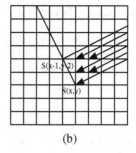

(a)   (b)

Fig. 9. The calculation schedule of rotated integral images. (a) $26.565°$ integral image (b) $-26.565°$ integral image.

Fig. 9(b) lists the similar calculation:

$$R(x,y) = R(x+2,y-1) + I(x,y)$$
$$S(x,y) = S(x-1,y-2) + R(x,y) + R(x,y-1) + R(x+1,y-1) \quad (4)$$
$$+R(x,y-2) + R(x+1,y-2)$$

With these equations, we can easily compute rotated integral images by only scanning images once, so the speed of the computation of the rotated rectangle features is fast.

3   The Framework of Face Detection with In-Plane Rotation

Based on the rotated haar-like features, the following gives the framework of face detection with in-plane rotation.

3.1   Gentle AdaBoost

Compared with other AdaBoost, Gentle AdaBoost (GAB) algorithm is of simplicity and stability [7,8], so GAB is used in this paper for training upright detector. In each update step, GAB uses the Newton method. The algorithm is listed as follows:

1. Initialize the weights: $d_i^0 = 1/N, i = 1, 2, \cdots, N$
2. Repeat for $t = 1, 2, \cdots, T$
   - A regression function $\hat{h}_t(x)$ can be obtained by minimizing a square loss function $E_d\{(y - h_t(x))^2\}$. This regression function can be calculated in the following way:

$$\hat{h}_t(x) = P_t(y = 1|x) - P_t(y = -1|x)$$

   - Update the weights: $d_n^t \propto d_n^{t-1} \exp\{-y_i\hat{h}_t(x_i)\}, i = 1, 2, \cdots, N$
3. Output: $f_T(x) = \sum_{t=1}^{T} \hat{h}_t(x)$

3.2   Cascade Classifiers

In the design of detectors, the cascade classifiers, in which each stage is a strong classifier trained by AdaBoost, are always chosen. The cascade detectors can get rid of much background by only using a few features, so the detection can save much time. Its structure is shown in Fig. 10.

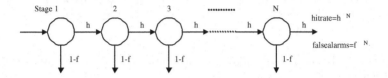

Fig. 10. The design of the detection cascade

Each stage is trained by GAB. Stage one only need a few features that can filter a large number of non-face windows. In the following stages, the number of the features increases very quickly, and the candidate faces are left fewer. After these processes, any efficient technique can be used in the post-process, such as adding the stage numbers or using other detectors.

3.3   The Framework of Face Detection with In-Plane Rotation

In this paper, the in-plane rotated faces are divided into 12 classes like section 2.3. For each class, we can use the new haar-like features to get the corresponding detectors by rotating the upright detector. These new detectors maintain the speed advantage because of the rapid computation of the $\pm 26.565°$ rotated integral images. Our face detection system does not use any method about view estimation, because this paper focuses on the precision of our proposed method and the speed of each detector, but not the speed of the system which is to be researched in our future work. Fig. 11 illustrates the framework of the face detections in our present system.

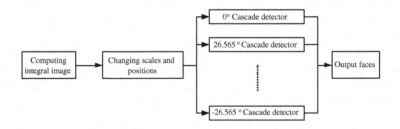

Fig. 11. The framework of face detection with in-plane rotation

4   Experimental Results

The rotated face detection technique is evaluated on CMU-MIT rotated test set [4] which consists of 50 images containing 223 frontal faces with in-plane rotations. We design two experiments to demonstrate our proposed method can get good accuracy. ROC curve detailed in [5] has been given in each experiment.

In the first experiment, the rotation degrees are classified into 12 classes and then 22-layer cascade classifier of the upright face detector is used. To evaluate our method's accuracy, we collect statistics about the number of faces in CMU-MIT for each class and test our method. Most face degrees are in the range $[-13.283°, 13.283°]$, $[13.283°, 45°]$ and $[-13.283°, -45°]$ with 23, 21 and 155 faces respectively, then Fig. 12 gives ROC curves within the three classes.

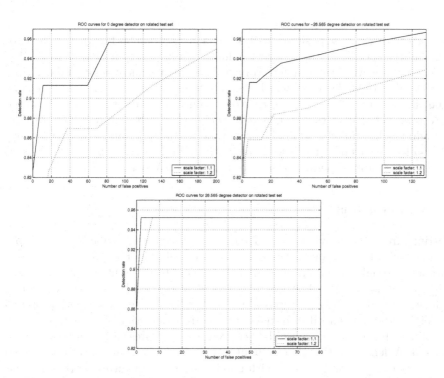

Fig. 12. ROC curve showing the performance of detecting the corresponding classes' faces. (a) ROC curve for $[-13.283°, 13.283°]$ (b) ROC curve for $[13.283°, 45°]$ (c) ROC curve for $[-13.283°, -45°]$.

In the second experiment, to compare with other works on multi-view face detection, we use all detectors to detect the faces in 360°. Fig. 13 gives the ROC curve for a try-all-rotations detector. Rowley et al. had ever reported a detection rate of 89.2% with 221 false positives using a three-stage detector and Jones et al. had a result of 89.7% correct detections with 221 false positives, yet our result

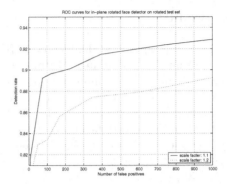

Fig. 13. ROC curve for a try-all-rotations detector on CMU-MIT rotated test set

is 90.1% with 221 false positives with scale factor 1.1 and 86.1% with scale factor 1.2, and the speed of scale factor 1.2 is much faster than that of scale factor 1.1.

The ROC curve of rotated detectors in the first experiment is found much close to that of upright detector, which demonstrates our good accuracy of rotated haar-like features. Moreover, it is in the same case with the time of rotated detectors and that of the upright detector, meaning the rotated detector does not add much computation in detecting process. In the second experiment, with a try-all-rotations detector tested on the CMU-MIT rotated test set, our result works appreciably superior to those of Rowley and Viola.

5 Conclusions

Distinct from the previous face detection techniques, this paper is not constrained with training quantities of samples to build different rotated detectors; instead, through extending upright face detector to different rotated detectors with a new set of haar-like features, face detection with in-plane rotation is achieved. The main contributions of this paper are: 1) The framework proposed by Viola can be extended to in-plane rotated face detection. 2) A new set of rotated haar-like features is described of great use to represent features of rotated faces. 3) A demonstration that without retraining time any more, various rotated face detectors can be obtained with good accuracy. Our future work will focus on view estimation based on using between-class harr-like features to improve the system speed further.

Acknowledgments

This work was supported by the National Natural Science Foundation of China under Grant No. 60021302, and the National High-Tech Research and Development Plan of China under Grant No. 2005AA147060. We thank Jianru Xue for helpful discussions.

References

1. Yang, M.H., Kriegman, D.J., Ahuja, N.: Detecting faces in images: A survey. IEEE Trans. Pattern Analysis and Machine Intelligence, **24** (2002) 34–58.
2. Hjelmas, E., Low, B.K.: Face detection: A survey. Computer Vision and Image Understanding **83** (2001) 236–274.
3. Rowley, H., Baluja, S., Kanade, T.: Neural network-based face detection. In IEEE Trans. Pattern Analysis and Machine Intelligence, **20** (1998) 23–38.
4. Rowley, H., Baluja, S., Kanade, T.: Rotation invariant neural network-based face detection. In Proceedings of the IEEE Conference on Computer Vision and Pattern Recognition, (1998) 38–44.
5. Viola, P., Jones, M.: Rapid object detection using a boosted cascade of simple features. In proceedings of Conference on Computer Vision and Pattern Recognition, (2001) 511–518.
6. Viola, P., Jones, M.: Fast and robust classification using asymmetric adaBoost and a detector cascade. Advances in Neural Information Processing System 14. MIT Press, Cambridge, MA (2001) 1311–1318.
7. Lienhart, R., Maydt, J.: An extended set of haar-like features for rapid object detection. In Proceedings of the IEEE Conference on Image Processing. New York, USA (2002) 155–162.
8. Lienhart, R., Kuranov, A., Pisarevsky, V.: Empirical analysis of detection cascades of boosted classifiers for rapid object detection. In DAGM 25th Pattern Recognition Symposium (2003) 297–304.
9. Li, S.Z., Zhu, L., Zhang, Z., Blake, A., Zhang, H., Shum, H.: Statistical learning of multi-view face detection. ECCV 2002: 7th European Conference on Computer Vision, **4** (2002) 67–81.
10. Jones, M.J., Viola, P.: Fast multi-view face detection. IEEE Conference on Computer Vision and Pattern Recognition (2003).
11. Lin, Y.Y., Liu, T.L.: Robust face detection with multi-class boosting. Proceedings of the 2005 IEEE Computer Society Conference on Computer Vision and Pattern Recognition (2005) 680–687.
12. Wang, P., Ji, Q.: Learning discriminant features for multi-view face and eye detection. IEEE Computer Society Conference, **1** (2005) 373–379.

Contour Grouping: Focusing on Image Patches Around Edges

Shulin Yang[1] and Cunlu Xu[2,*]

[1] Dept. of Computer Science and Engineering, Fudan Univ., PRC, 200433
[2] School of Information Science and Engineering, Lanzhou Univ., PRC, 730000

Abstract. Contour grouping is an important issue in computer vision. However, traditional ways tackling the problem usually fail to provide as satisfying results as human vision can do. One important feature of human vision mechanism is that human vision tends to group together edges that are not only geometrically and topologically related, but also similar in their appearances - the appearances of image patches around them including their brightness, color, texture cues, etc. But in traditional grouping approaches, after edges or lines have been detected, the appearances of image patches around them are seldom considered again, leading to the results that edges belonging to boundaries of different objects are sometimes falsely grouped together. In this paper, we introduce an **appearance feature** to describe the appearance of an image patch around a line segment, and incorporate this appearance feature into a **saliency measure** to evaluate contours on an image. The most salient contour is found by optimizing this saliency measure using a genetic algorithm. Experimental results prove the effectiveness of our approach.

1 Introduction

This paper is concerned with the problem of contour grouping, which aims at finding object contours from images. Solution of this problem provides a necessary pre-step for shape-based object recognition, image segmentation, 3D reconstruction, etc. However, as one of the most challenging problems in computer vision, contour grouping is not well solved, suffering from strong noises, lack of prior knowledge of the resultant contours, etc, and resulting in falsely detected contours.

There have been many schemes tackling the problem of finding contours from gray scale images. In the most commonly used way, first, regions with sharp gray scale discontinuity are highlighted by edges or lines, and then the edges/lines are connected together based on their directional derivatives, gradient directions, distances between them, and certain additional constraints from prior knowledge. For example, in Jacob's [1] and Stahl and Wang's [2] convex grouping methods, convexity is used as a requirement for resultant contours because it is a feature of many natural objects. In the model of Wang and Staib [3], prior shape is incorporated to find boundaries of objects with specific shape features. Another effective way follow a top-down way to detect directly and globally the contour of an object in an image, like the famous snake

---

* Corresponding author.

H. Zha et al. (Eds.): VSMM 2006, LNCS 4270, pp. 138–146, 2006.

model [4], balloon [5], level set [6], etc. These models set initial contours on an image, and then go through iterations of optimization to move the contours to the best places.

However, these schemes suffer from a common problem in distinguishing boundaries of different object while they are physically close to each other, and they always result in falsely connected object contours. In Fig.1, (a) is a real image containing a book and a pen, and (b) is a local area of (a). With traditional approaches, even if edges and lines in image (b) have been precisely and comprehensively extracted as in (c), it is still difficult to distinguish the boundaries of different objects correctly. But if we take a close look at image patches around the edges like the three image patches rounded by circles in (d), it is easy to notice that patch 1 and patch 2 (the two along the boundary of the book) have a similar appearance while patch 3 has not. So it is more reasonable to suppose that the edges in patch 1 and patch 2 are from the same boundary and edge in patch 3 is from another boundary, though the edge in patch 3 is physically more close to the other two. When the appearances of image patches around these edges, including their brightness and texture cues, are taken into consideration, the problem of distinguishing boundaries of different objects can be solved more easily, because it is very possible that edges whose surrounding image patches are similar in their appearances are from the boundary of the same object.

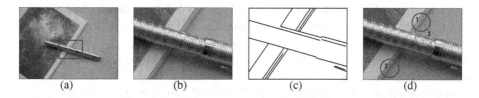

(a)   (b)   (c)   (d)

Fig. 1. It is difficult to distinguish boundaries of different objects for (b) merely by its line detection result (c). In (d), image patches 1 and 2 have a similar appearance while patch 3 has a very different appearance. So, although patch 3 is physically more close to patch 1, it is more reasonable that the edge in patch 1 is grouped together with the edge in 2 than with the edge in 3.

In this paper, we aim at finding contours by connecting line segments from the results of edge detection and line fitting. Our approach is based on the fact that edges and lines tend to have a similar appearance when they are from the boundary of the same object and to have varying appearances when they are from boundaries of different objects. Our approach introduces an **appearance feature** to describe the appearance of image patch around a line segment, and use this feature to apply a morphing to the physical distances between two line segments. Then we propose a **saliency measure** to evaluate a potential contour on an image. A contour with the maximal value for the saliency measure is obtained using a genetic algorithm.

2   Contour Grouping Framework

As in some other contour grouping approaches [1,2], our approach takes as input a set of line segments from the result of edge detection and line fitting. In this proposed approach, a valid contour will be constructed by sequentially connecting a subset of these line segments. We first introduce in our approach an appearance feature to represent the appearance of an image patch around each line segment, and then a distance between two line segments is defined, with a morphing applied to their original physical distance using the difference of their appearance feature. Then, a saliency measure is proposed for contours composed of line segments. The most salient contour can be searched by maximizing the value for the saliency measure.

2.1   Appearance Feature a Line Segment

A set of line segments $\{L_i\}$ ($i = 1, 2, ..., N$, N is the number of line segments) with a minimal length δ_l are first detected from an image using the canny detector [7] and the line fitting algorithm proposed by Nevatia and Babu [8]. These line segments are used to represent gray scale discontinuity on this image. Then image patches with line segments positioned at their centers (as in Fig.2) are inspected for the appearance feature $\mathbf{F}_i$ ($i = 1, 2, ...N$). k attributes are calculated from the corresponding image patch of L_i, $\mathbf{F}_i = (f_i^{(1)}, f_i^{(2)}, ..., f_i^{(k)})$.

The image patch surrounded by dashed line in Fig.2 is used to calculate $\mathbf{F}_i$ for L_i. It is an area of rectangle surrounding L_i with two semicircles at the two ends of the line segment. (The width of the rectangle and the diameter of the semicircles is a parameter δ_w.) The arrow in Fig.2 represents direction of L_i, recorded in a parameter θ_i ($0 \leq \theta_i < 2\pi$). Left side and right side of L_i are determined according to its direction. $S_i^{(1)}$ is the set of pixels at the left side of L_i in the image patch, and $S_i^{(2)}$ is the set of pixels at its right side in the patch. $I(p)$ is the intensity of pixel p in an image, and $|S|$ counts the number of pixels in set S.

In this model, $k = 5$ attributes are considered for $\mathbf{F}_i$: direction of line segment L_i,

$$f_i^{(1)} = \theta_i \qquad (0 \leq \theta_i < 2\pi); \tag{1}$$

average intensity of pixels by the left side of L_i,

$$f_i^{(2)} = \frac{\sum_{p \epsilon S_i^{(1)}} I(p)}{|S_i^{(1)}|}; \tag{2}$$

average intensity of pixels by the right side of L_i,

$$f_i^{(3)} = \frac{\sum_{p \epsilon S_i^{(2)}} I(p)}{|S_i^{(2)}|}; \tag{3}$$

intensity variance of the pixels by the left side of L_i,

$$f_i^{(4)} = \frac{\sum_{p \epsilon S_i^{(1)}} (I(p) - f_i^{(2)})^2}{|S_i^{(1)}|}; \tag{4}$$

intensity variance of the pixels by the right side of L_i,

$$f_i^{(5)} = \frac{\sum_{p \epsilon S_i^{(2)}} (I(p) - f_i^{(3)})^2}{|S_i^{(2)}|}. \tag{5}$$

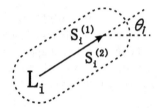

Fig. 2. Image Patch for Extracting Appearance Feature of L_i

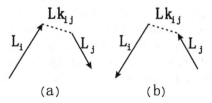

Fig. 3. Two Ways to Decide the Directions of L_i and L_j

These five attributes are used in the model for they can represent the basic features of the appearances of image patches by the two sides of these line segments.

2.2 Distance Between Two Line Segments

Before trying to propose a saliency measure, the distance between two line segments is defined first, which applies a morphing to their original physical distance considering the difference of their appearance feature. With this morphing, line segments that are physically close to each other but have very differing appearance feature would be considered far away, and thus it will be less possible that they are connected in a resultant contour.

The distance between line segments L_i and L_j is based on a link Lk_{ij} between them, and the directions of L_i and L_j are determined by either of the two ways in Fig.3 ((a) and (b)).

After appearance feature of all line segments $\{L_i\}$ are obtained, all the attribute values are normalized to real numbers between 0 and 1 using the maximum values for each attribute over all the line segments $max_{i=1}^{N}\{f_i^{(t)}\}$ $(1 \le t \le 5)$:

$$a_i^{(t)} = \frac{f_i^{(t)}}{max_{i=1}^{N}\{f_i^{(t)}\}} \qquad (1 \le t \le 5) \qquad (6)$$

The distance between line segments L_i and L_j for link Lk_{ij} is,

$$d_{Lk_{ij}} = l_{Lk_{ij}} \prod_{1 \le t \le k} (1 + (a_i^{(t)} - a_j^{(t)})^2)^{\alpha_t} \qquad (7)$$

$l_{Lk_{ij}}$ is the length of link Lk_{ij} - the physical distance of L_i and L_j between their end points that are connected; α_t $(1 \le t \le k)$ are parameters that are used to adjust the emphases on attributes $f_i^{(t)}$ $(1 \leq t \leq k)$. Meanwhile, $\alpha_2 = \alpha_3$ and $\alpha_4 = \alpha_5$, because $f_i^{(2)}$ and $f_i^{(3)}$, $f_i^{(4)}$ and $f_i^{(5)}$ are symmetric attributes of the image patch around L_i.

As can be easily understood, the more different appearance feature of two line segments are, the larger their distance $d_{Lk_{ij}}$ is. And when two line segments have similar appearance feature, their distance $d_{Lk_{ij}}$ would be close to their physical distance.

2.3   Saliency Measure of a Contour

In this part, we focus our attention on defining a saliency measure of each valid contour. The motivation here is simple. On the one hand, a salient contour is expected to cover a sufficient amount gray scale discontinuity of an image, with the objective of including possibly more and longer line segments. On the other hand, a salient contour is expected to be solid - to be thick of line segments - with the objective of improving the ratio of total length of the line segments over total distances between every two sequential line segments in the contour.

A contour c consists of a set of sequentially connected line segment,

$$c = Line_c \bigcup Link_c; \tag{8}$$

where

$$Line_c = \{L_{c_1}, L_{c_2}, ..., L_{c_M}\}; \tag{9}$$

and

$$Link_c = \{Lk_{c_1 c_2}, Lk_{c_2 c_3}, ..., Lk_{c_{M-1} c_M}, Lk_{c_M c_1}\}. \tag{10}$$

The saliency measure of contour c is,

$$E(c) = \lambda ln \sum_{L_i \epsilon Line_c} l_i + \frac{\sum_{L_i \epsilon Line_c} l_i}{\sum_{Lk_{ij} \epsilon Link_c} d_{Lk_{ij}}} \tag{11}$$

where λ is a saliency parameter that balance the prior emphases on the two expectations illustrated above. $\sum_{L_i \epsilon Line_c} l_i$ sums up lengths of all line segments in contour c, and $\sum_{Lk_{ij} \epsilon Link_c} d_{Lk_{ij}}$ sums up distances between every two sequential line segments in contour c. Maximizing the value for the saliency measure $E(c)$ would result in the most salient contour on an image.

3   Saliency Measure Optimization

In this section, a contour with the maximal value for its saliency measure is to be found from an image. Genetic algorithms (GAs) is one of the most widely used artificial intelligent techniques for optimization. A GA is a stochastic searching algorithm based on the mechanisms of natural selection and genetics, and it has been proved to be very efficient and stable in searching for global optimal solutions. Usually, a GA creates a population of solutions in the form of chromosomes and applies genetic operators to evolve the solutions in order to find the best one(s).

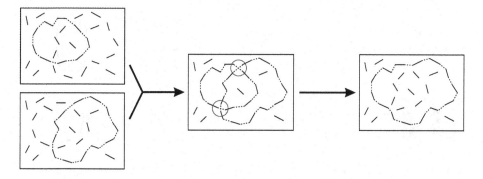

Fig. 4. Crossover of the chromosomes

Fig. 5. Mutation of the chromosomes

In this model, a genetic algorithm is employed to optimize the saliency measure $E(c)$ in (11), searching for the best subset of line segments and the way they are connected into a contour. Details of the genetic algorithm are described as follows:

(1) Chromosome encoding: Each chromosome (a sequence of $'0/1'$) represents a configuration of all the line segments on an image, and an eligible chromosome represents configuration of a contour. Each line segment L_i and each possible connection Lk_{ij} is assigned a gene bit $'0/1'$ in the chromosome, recording whether it is part of the contour the chromosome represents: $'1'$ stands for its existence in the contour and $'0'$ stands for the opposite. A possible connection is a link Lk_{ij} between two line segments L_i and L_j whose distance is within a threshold range $l_{Lk_{ij}} \leq \delta_r$.

(2) Fitness function: The saliency measure $E(c)$ in (11) is used as the fitness function of the GA.

(3) Genetic operations: The crossover operation finds out any possible connection of line segments from the two parent contours respectively, and generates an eligible new contour which is composed of parts from both of the parent contours (Fig.4). The mutation operation makes random modifications to a parent contour, adding, removing or replacing several line segments in it, and results in an eligible new chromosome (Fig.5). Roulette wheel selection is used for selection in this algorithm.

4 Experimental Results and Discussions

In this section, we test our approach on some real images by detecting the most salient contour which has a maximal value for the saliency measure $E(c)$, and the results of

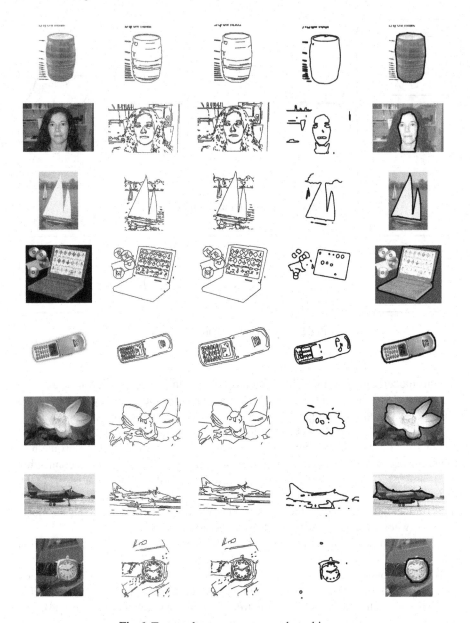

Fig. 6. Test results on some gray scale real images

our approach are compared with the results of the level set method [6] which is used for contour detection and segmentation.

The test images are all gray scale images, and they are normalized to be within the size of 160×160. In our test, parameters α_t ($t = 1, 2, 3, 4, 5$) in formula (6) (the distance definition) are all 1; and the saliency parameter λ in formula (11) (the saliency measure) is 0.8. The minimal length for line segments δ_l and the width threshold δ_w used in finding appearance feature of the line segments are both 20, and the range threshold δ_r for a possible connection of two line segments is 40. Parameters used in the genetic algorithm for optimization goes as $p_c = 0.9$, $p_m = 0.1$, and $N_g = 50$.

Fig.6 shows our test results on 8 real images. Column 1 are the original gray scale image; column 2 are the results of the canny detector. Column 3 are the line fitting results using Kovesi's software ("http://www.csse.uwa.edu.au/ pk/research/matlabfns/"). Column 4 are the results of the level set method, using UCSB's matlab toolbox ("http://barissumengen.com/level_set_methods/index.html").

The most salient contour extracted using the proposed approach are shown in black lines in columns 5. We can see from the test results that our approach avoids connecting edges from boundaries of different objects by making use of the appearance feature of the extracted line segments. Similar appearance feature, short physical distance between sequential line segments and high gray scale discontinuity are all encouraged in the resultant contours.

5   Conclusions and Future Work

This paper presented a contour grouping framework and an optimization technique for finding the most salient contour from an image. The contour grouping framework focuses on three major points. First, it introduces an appearance feature to distinguish line segments at boundaries of different objects by inspecting the appearances of the image patches around them. Second, the distance between two sequential line segments are defined with a morphing to the physical distance between them. And third, a measure is proposed to estimate the saliency of each contour on an image. A genetic algorithm is used as our optimization technique for its stableness in searching for global optimal solutions. Future work can be done on inspecting from the view of vision psychology for a feature vector that can represent more effectively and precisely the appearance of a line segment. Meanwhile, specific constraints can be incorporated into the saliency measure so that this approach can be applied to images of specific categories like remote sensing images or medical images.

References

1. Jacobs, D.: Robust and efficient detection of convex groups. IEEE Trans. Pattern Anal. Machine Intell. **18** (1996) 23–27
2. Stahl, J.S., Wang, S.: Convex grouping combining boundary and region information. (2005)
3. Elder, J.H., Johnston, L.A.: Contour grouping with prior models. IEEE Trans. Pattern Anal. Machine Intell. **25** (2003)
4. Kass, M., Witkin, A., Terzopoulos, D.: Snake: active contour models. INT J Computer Vision (1988) 321–331
5. Cohen, L.D., Cohen, I.: A finite element method applied to new active contour models and 3d reconstruction form cross section. IEEE Trans. Pattern Anal. Machine Intell. **22** (1998) 764–779
6. Osher, S., Sethian, J.: Fronts propagating with curvature dependent speed: algorithms based on hamilton-jacobi formulations. (1988)

7. Canny, J.: A computational approach to edge detection. IEEE Trans. Pattern Anal. Machine Intell. **8** (1986) 679–698

8. Nevatia, R., Babu, K.: Linear feature extraction and description. Comput. Vis., Graph., Image Processing **33** (1980) 257–269

9. Geman, D., Geman, S., Graffigne, C., Dong, P.: Boundary detection by constrained optimization. IEEE Trans. Pattern Anal. Machine Intell. **13** (1990) 609–628

10. Alter, T., Basri, R.: Extracting salient curves from images: an analysis of the saliency network. INT J Computer Vision **27** (1998) 51–69

11. Liu, S., Babbs, C., Delp, E., Delp, P.: Line detection using a spatial characteristic model. IEEE Trans. Image Processing (1999)

12. Zhu, S., Yuille, A.: Region competition: unifying snakes, region growing, and bayes/mdl for multiband image segmentation. IEEE Trans. Pattern Anal. Machine Intell. **18** (1996) 884–900

Synthetic Stereoscopic Panoramic Images

Paul Bourke

WASP, University of Western Australia, 35 Stirling Hwy, Crawley, WA 6009, Australia
pbourke@wasp.uwa.edu.au
http://local.wasp.uwa.edu.au/~pbourke/

Abstract. Presented here is a discussion of the techniques required to create stereoscopic panoramic images. Such images allow interactive exploration of 3D environments with stereoscopic depth cues. If projected in a surround display environment they can engage the two characteristics of the human visual system responsible for immersion, namely stereopsis and peripheral vision.

1 Introduction

Panoramic images are a natural way of capturing a wide visual field of view without the distortion introduced by wide angle or fisheye lens. In their ultimate form they capture the whole 360 degrees about one axis, normally the vertical. Depending on whether they are full spherical panoramas or cylindrical panoramas their vertical field of view will range from ±90 degrees to perhaps as low as ±10 degrees. The earliest panoramic images date back to 1850 and the early days of photography [1]. By 1880 there were a number of commercially available panoramic cameras, the most common variety consisted of a stationary cylindrical strip of film and a rotating camera head. In the early 90's panoramic and stereoscopic panoramic capture was explored in the context of capturing the whole visual field for applications in machine vision [2,3] and scene reconstruction. More recently, interactive digital panoramic images were popularised in 1995 with the advent of QuickTime VR [4] on the early Apple Macintosh computers as a way of interactively viewing a photographically captured environment [5]. These digital panoramic images could be created from dedicated cameras, by stitching together a number of images from standard cameras, or by computer graphics rendering processes. QuickTime VR and now a number of similar software playback solutions allow the user to rotate their viewpoint, zoom in/out, and jump to another panorama that is located at a different position.

In this paper a more recent development will be discussed, namely stereoscopic panoramic images. These consist of two panoramic images, one for each eye, such that when presented correctly to our visual system will give a stereoscopic 3D effect irrespective of which part of the panoramic image is being viewed. The discussion will be targeted at cylindrical panoramic images and how they can be created synthetically. The result will be imagery that, in a suitable immersive environment, can simultaneously satisfy two important characteristics of our visual system, namely stereopsis (humans have two eyes separated horizontally) and peripheral vision (up to 160 degrees horizontally).

H. Zha et al. (Eds.): VSMM 2006, LNCS 4270, pp. 147–155, 2006.
© Springer-Verlag Berlin Heidelberg 2006

2 Stereoscopic Panoramic Rendering

Monoscopic panoramic images are created by rotating a single camera about its optical axis (single viewpoint projection), shown on the left of figure 1. It is easy to show that a stereoscopic panoramic image pair cannot be constructed with simply two offset cameras rotating about their individual optical axes. For example, if the cameras start off pointing parallel to each other for a correct stereo pair then by the time they have rotated by 90 degrees there will be no parallax and effectively two different fields of view. The correct method of capturing stereoscopic panoramic images either photographically or synthetically is shown on the right in Figure 1. Two cameras are separated by the so called interocular distance, the camera view direction is tangential to the circle about which they rotate through 360 degrees. Each camera forms an image from what it "sees" along the view direction through a narrow vertical slit, these are often called circular projections and are a special type of multiple viewpoint projection. The interocular distance relates more to the scale of objects being captured rather than the actual human eye separation, for example, if the virtual model is on the scale of the solar system then the interocular separation, for a satisfying depth effect, may well be on the scale of a few Earth radii.

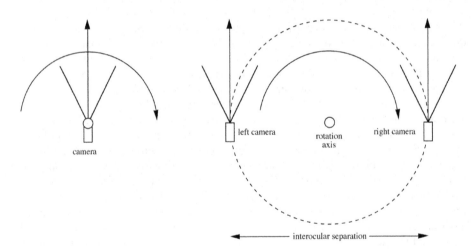

Fig. 1. Idealised camera rig for monoscopic panoramic capture (left) and stereoscopic panoramic capture (right)

Ideally the two cameras would rotate continuously, imaging as they do so. There are some physical cameras [6] designed to capture stereoscopic image pairs that function exactly this way, an example of a stereoscopic pair captured with such a camera is shown in figure 2. Alternatively there are other approaches that form each of the panoramic image pairs by stitching together slices from a large number of images from a camera that rotates in discrete steps.

Correct stereoscopic creation in commercial rendering packages is unusual in itself, and while monoscopic panoramic rendering is fairly common, there are no packages that the author is aware of that create stereoscopic panoramic images in a continuous fashion. While some rendering packages have a sufficiently powerful virtual camera model and scripting language to support continuous capture, that is also relatively unusual. The approach that can be implemented in most packages is a finite slit approximation, the resulting panoramic images get progressively better as the slit width becomes narrower. Typically, while 5 degree slit widths may be suitable for distance imagery, it is usually necessary to use at most a 1 degree slit width and often even narrower angular slit widths. For example, if ½ degree slit widths are chosen, the final panoramic images for each eye will be built up from 720 separate images that are very narrow and as tall as the final panoramic image height. With this approach the cameras are also rotated in discrete steps, the stepping angle is identical to the horizontal aperture of the camera ensuring the image strips forms a continuous composite image, this is illustrated in figure 3 for the left eye camera.

Left eye

Right eye

Fig. 2. Stereoscopic panoramic pair from Hampi in Inidia captured continuously on a roll of film using the RoundShot camera. Left eye (upper) and right eye (lower). Vertical field of view is 60 degrees. Credits: PLACE-Hampi: Sarah Kenderdine, Jeffrey Shaw & John Gollings.

An interesting limitation to the forming of stereoscopic panoramic images compared to traditional monoscopic panoramic images is that in the later one can form the panoramic approximately and even with definite errors without the artefacts necessarily being obvious to the viewer. This is particularly so for photographic panoramic pairs [7,8] that can often include arbitrary stitching and blending of a relatively small number of separate photographs. Because of the additional depth perception in stereoscopic panoramic pairs, approximations and imperfections are usually very noticeable. Additionally, while most panoramic playback applications do not allow camera roll, it was at least possible with monoscopic panoramic images and has been useful for panoramic images where there is no preferred up direction. It is of course not possible to roll (rotation about the view direction vector) inside a stereoscopic panoramic viewer because there is an implied up direction.

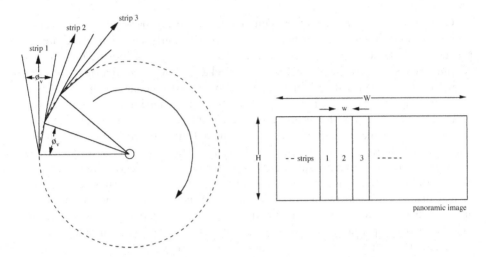

Fig. 3. The horizontal slit aperture ∅ᵥ matches the rotation angle step size for a panoramic image without creating gaps in the imagery

Common to all cylindrical panoramic images is the relationship between the dimensions in pixel units of the panoramic and the vertical angular field of view ϕ_v. This is given by

$$\phi_v = 2 \text{ atan}(H \pi / W)$$

where H and W are the height and width respectively of the panoramic image measured in pixels. When rendering the panoramic in strips the horizontal field of view of the strip ϕ_h in degrees needs to be an integer divisor of 360 degrees in order to achieve a perfect wrap around at the 0 and 360 degree boundary (left and right edge) of the panoramic. The width (w) of the strip in pixels is given by

$$w = W \phi_h / 360$$

where w is also needs to be an integer. This equation can only be solved for quantised values of w, ϕ_h, and W. The relationship between the width of each strip, the height of the panoramic image, and the horizontal and vertical field of view of each strip (assuming square pixels) is given by

$$H \tan(\phi_h / 2) = w \tan(\phi_v / 2)$$

The above relationships define the horizontal and vertical field of view and the aspect ratio, totally defining the frustum of the virtual camera required to render each slit image.

3   Control of Zero Parallax

Of central importance to any stereoscopic image generation and viewing is how to control the distance to zero parallax f_o, that is, at what distance in the rendered scene will objects appear to be at the projection screen depth. Objects closer than f_o will

Left eye

Right eye

Fig. 4. Example of a synthetic stereoscopic panoramic image pair [11] of the Royal Exhibition Building in Melbourne, Australia. Generated using 3DStudioMax and 1 degree slit width. Vertical field of view is 90 degrees.

appear to be in front of the screen (negative parallax), objects more distant than f_o will appear behind the screen (positive parallax). Unlike perspective stereo pairs where horizontally shifting the images with respect to each other to control zero parallax adds occlusion errors, stereoscopic panoramic pairs can be shifted without adding any additional error. For the camera arrangement proposed here the view direction rays are parallel so the final stereoscopic pairs would have zero parallax distance at infinity. The geometry for calculating the relative shift between the image pairs in order to achieve a particular f_o is shown in figure 5. The angle ø between the left and the right camera such that an object is the desired zero parallax distance will be coincident on the left and right eye panoramic image is given by

$$ø = 2 \, asin(r \, / \, f_o)$$

where r is half the camera separation (the radius of the rotation circle). The number of pixels (D) to shift the final panoramic images by horizontally is then

$$D = W \, ø \, / \, (2\pi) = W \, asin(r \, / \, f_o) \, / \, \pi$$

where W is the width of the whole panoramic image measured in pixels. Obviously, when shifting the panoramic image it is performed in a circular fashion, those parts of the image that are shifted past the right hand edge of the panoramic image reappear on the left hand edge and visa-versa.

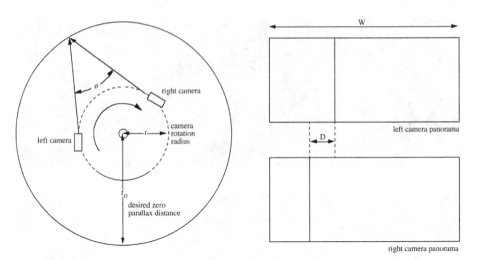

Fig. 5. Geometry for determining the distance to shift the panoramic pairs with respect to each other in order to achieve a particular zero parallax distance

An alternative to parallel cameras is to use what is known in stereoscopic rendering as as "toe-in" cameras. The view direction vector of the two cameras are no longer parallel to each other but rotated inwards and the intersection of their view direction rays determines the distance to zero parallax, see figure 6. While toe-in cameras do not yield correct stereo pairs in traditional perspective stereoscopic image generation (it introduces vertical parallax towards the corners of the image plane), it does not have the same problem when rendering narrow strips for stereoscopic panoramic formation and is a perfectly acceptable solution. As with perspective stereoscopic pairs this approach results in panoramic images with a desired zero parallax distance with no extra post processing required.

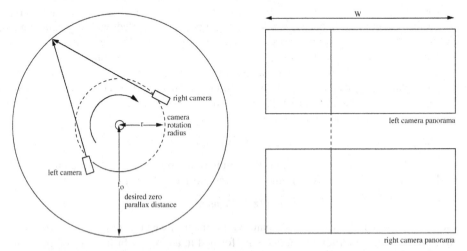

Fig. 6. Toe in camera model for direct zero parallax generation. The panoramic images so created have a preset zero parallax distance.

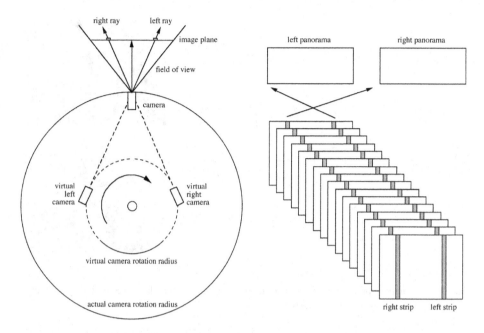

Fig. 7. Single camera capture of stereoscopic panoramic images, more common for real camera capture than computer generated images for efficiency reasons

4 Alternative Approach

There is a technique that is sometimes used for capturing stereoscopic panoramic image pairs with a single real camera [10] and forming the pairs using vertical strips from each side of the resulting images, see figure 7. While there is little reason to employ this method for synthetic panoramic capture, it is mentioned here for completeness. The obvious disadvantage of this approach for synthetic stereoscopic panoramic production is inefficiency, that is, only a very small area of the rendered images is actually employed in the final panoramic images.

5 Viewing

There are a number of options for viewing stereoscopic panoramic images. On a flat screen such as a monitor or a projected image onto a flat screen, the equivalent to a QuickTime VR player has been developed [12]. The standard algorithm uses hardware acceleration such as OpenGL to map the two panoramic images as textures onto two cylinders. Each cylinder is centered on a coincident left and right eye virtual camera position, each camera renders a perspective projection, see figure 8. Each image is presented to the appropriate eye, the details are dependent on the particular stereoscopic projection environment.

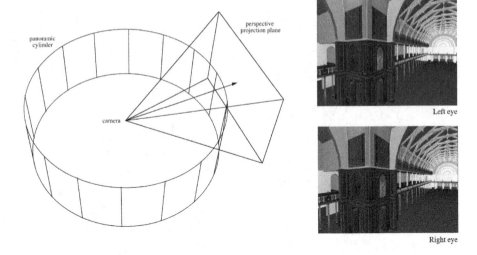

Fig. 8. Perspective projection plane and textured cylinder for flat screen display (upper), examples of resulting stereo pairs (lower)

More immersive environments exist where the entire 360 degrees is presented simultaneously surrounding the viewer or audience [13] as a large cylindrical display. Unlike most stereoscopic surround environments these cylindrical displays do not necessarily need head tracking and are even suited to viewing by multiple simultaneous participants. The image generation and projection details are outside the scope of this discussion but projection into these environments usually involves capturing multiple perspective projections as described above and then applying geometry correction such that the projection of those modified images appear correct on a section of the cylindrical display surface. Each of these sections may additionally need to be edge blended with the neighbouring sections. In such cylindrical environments it is interesting to note that the stereopsis errors that occur towards the periphery of ones vision need not be problematic because they are hidden by the limited field of view of the glasses being worn, but the peripheral vision of the observer is still engaged.

6 Summary

A method of creating synthetic stereoscopic panoramic images that can be implemented in most rendering packages has been presented. If single panoramic pairs can be created then stereoscopic panoramic movies are equally possible giving rise to the prospect of movies where the viewer can interact with, at least with regard to what they choose to look at. These images can be projected so as to engage the two features of the human visual system that assist is giving us a sense of immersion, the feeling of "being there". That is, imagery that contains parallax information as captured from two horizontally separated eye positions (stereopsis) and imagery that fills our peripheral vision. The details that define how the two panoramic images should be created in rendering packages are provided, in particular, how to precisely configure the virtual cameras and control the distance to zero parallax.

References

1. C. Johnson. Panoramas of Duluth, Minnesota. History of Photography, Vol. 16 pp141-146, (Summer 1992).
2. H. Ishiguro, M. Yamamoto, S. Tsuji. OmniDirectional Stereo. IEEE Transactions on Pattern Analysis Machine Intelligence 14(2), pp 257-262, (1992).
3. J. Y. Zheng, S. Tsuji. Panoramic Representation for route recognition by a mobile robot. International Journal Computer Vision, Vol. 9, no. 1, pp. 55-76, (1992).
4. S. Chen. Quicktime VR – an image based approach to virtual environment navigation. In SIGGRAPH '95, Pages 29–38, Los Angeles, California, ACM, (August 1995).
5. H. H. Sham, K. T. Ng, S. C. Chan. Virtual Reality Using the Concentric Mosaic: Construction, Rendering and Compression. Microsoft Research, China, (2000).
6. Roundshot camera, Super 200 VR. Seitz Phototechnik AG, Hauptstr 14, 8512 Lustdorf Switzerland. [http://www.roundshot.ch/]
7. H. C. Huang and Y.P. Hung. Panoramic stereo imaging system with automatic disparity warping and seaming. Graphical Models and Image Processing, 60 (3) pp 196–208, (May 1998).
8. S. Peleg, Y. Pritch, and M. Ben-Ezra. Cameras for stereo panoramic imaging. IEEE Conference on Computer Vision and Pattern Recognition, pp 208--214, (2000).
9. S. Peleg and M. Ben-Ezra. Stereo panorama with a single camera. In IEEE Conference on Computer Vision and Pattern Recognition, pp 395–401, Ft. Collins, Colorado, (June 1999).
10. S. Peleg and M. Ben-Ezra. Stereo panorama with a single camera. In IEEE Conference on Computer Vision and Pattern Recognition, pp 395–401, Ft. Collins, Colorado, (June 1999).
11. Digital Model Of The Royal Exhibition Building (Melbourne, Australia), S. Bekhit, A. Kuek, H. Lie. [http://local.wasp.uwa.edu.au/~pbourke/modelling/reb/]
12. Stereo-capable panoramic viewer. P. D. Bourke.
13. [http://local.wasp.uwa.edu.au/~pbourke/stereographics/stereopanoramic/]
14. AVIE stereoscopic 360 degree panoramic environment, ICinema, UNSW.
15. [http://www.icinema.unsw.edu.au/projects/infra_avie.html]

Building a Sparse Kernel Classifier on Riemannian Manifold

Yanyun Qu[1,2], Zejian Yuan[1], and Nanning Zheng[1]

[1] Institute of Artificial Intelligence and Robotics,
Xi'an Jiaotong University, 710049 Xi'an P.R. China
[2] Computer Science Department,
Xiamen University, 361005 Xiamen P.R. China
{yyqu,zjyuan,nnzheng }@aiar.xjtu.edu.cn

Abstract. It is difficult to deal with large datasets by kernel based methods since the number of basis functions required for an optimal solution equals the number of samples. We present an approach to build a sparse kernel classifier by adding constraints to the number of support vectors and to the classifier function. The classifier is considered on Riemannian manifold. And the sparse greedy learning algorithm is used to solve the formulated problem. Experimental results over several classification benchmarks show that the proposed approach can reduce the training and runtime complexities of kernel classifier applied to large datasets without scarifying high classification accuracy.

1 Introduction

Support vector machines(SVM) have become one of the most successful classification methods, especially the kernel based methods improve the classification and generalization and solve the binary classification problem in feature space. But in large scale problem SVM confront difficulties because the number of basis functions required for an optimal solution equals the number of samples. This requires large storage and computation, which make it impossible to use nonlinear kernels directly. The conventional SVM is slow not only in training for large scale problem, but also in testing. For example, in binary classification problem, a set of training data is given as $\{(x_i, y_i)\}_{i=1}^{l}$, $x_i \in X \subseteq R^d$, $y_i \in \{-1, 1\}$ is the class label. A classification function $\hat{f} : x \rightarrow \{+1, -1\}$ is required to build in order to classify the test data. A kernel based SVM formulate a classifier as $\hat{f}(x) = sgn(f(x))$, where

$$f(x) = \sum_{i=1}^{n} \alpha_i K(\hat{x}_i, x) + b \tag{1}$$

and $\hat{x}_i \in X \subseteq R^d$ is the support vectors, n is the number of the support vectors, $\alpha_i \in R$ is the coefficients corresponding to $\hat{x}_i$, $b \in R$ is the bias and $K : X \times X \rightarrow R$ is a kernel function. In practical problems, the classifier is

H. Zha et al. (Eds.): VSMM 2006, LNCS 4270, pp. 156–163, 2006.

dependent on the number of the support vectors, and the time of calculating equ.(1) is proportional to n. Our aim is to build a classifier with high accuracy and speed. The classification surface is determined by the selected sparse key points $z_1, z_2, \cdots, z_n$, which come from the samples.

There are several methods to build a sparse kernel classifier. In [1], the reduced set method is proposed to determine n ($n < l$) vectors $z_1, z_2, \cdots, z_n$, and their kernel linear combination approximates the kernel classifier built in advance. In [4], the reduced support vector machine algorithm is proposed, and n vectors are selected randomly from the training set. But the obtained classifier may not guarantee good classification performance because the support vectors are chosen randomly. In [3], the relevance vector machine is proposed which assumes a prior of the expansion coefficients which favors sparse solutions. In [5], the sparse large margin classifiers are built by constructing a support vector machine with a modified kernel function, but the computing complexity is higher in training. In [2], the greedy learning algorithm is used to compute the formula :$\|K\alpha - y\|_2 \leq \varepsilon$ and select n columns from the matrix K such that $\|K^n \alpha^n - y\|_2 \leq \varepsilon$, is minimized where K^n is a rectangular matrix formed by choosing a subset of n columns from the original Gram matrix K and α^n denotes the truncated weight vector. In [7], n columns of the matrix K are selected by sparse greedy matrix approximation and the subset is selected randomly in iterations. These work mentioned above did not consider the geometry of original data.

In this paper, we propose an approach to build a kernel classifier which satisfied a given constraint on the degree of sparsity and a regularized constraint. The final classifier map is required to preserve the intrinsic geometry of the data and local structure. So the model is different from the aforementioned methods. In [2] there is no regularized constraint on the classifier. In [7], the classifier subjects to l_2 norm in reproducing kernel Hilbert spaces(RKHS). And in [1,3,4,5], the optimization problems are just like SVM which introduce a cost function that eliminates the contribution of basis function $k(x, x_i)$ corresponding to points which have a large margin.

The rest of this paper is organized as follows. In section 2, we formulate the sparse regularized kernel classifier. In section 3, we use sparse greedy algorithm to solve the problem. Experimental results are given in section 4, and we conclude the paper in the last section.

2 Sparse Kernel Classifier Model

Given an N-samples $\{(x_i, y_i)\}_{i=1}^l$, $x_i \in X \subseteq R^d$ and the target values $y_i \in \{-1, 1\}$, we want to build a classifier in Hilbert space H_K by solving the following problem

$$\min_{f \in H_K} \frac{1}{l} \sum_{i=1}^{l} c(x_i, y_i, f(x_i)) + \frac{\gamma}{2} \int_M \|\nabla f\|_{L^2}^2 \tag{2}$$

The first part is used to fit to the training data, which can be defined as

$$c(x, y, f(x)) = (y - f(x))^2 \tag{3}$$

We also define the classifier on Riemannian manifold, and require that the classifier can preserve the intrinsic geometry of the original data. So we define the second part of equ.(2). Note that minimizing $\frac{1}{2} \int_M \|\nabla f\|_{L^2}^2$ is equal to minimizing $Lf = \frac{1}{2l^2} \sum_{i,j} (f(x_i) - f(x_j))^2 W_{ij}$ on a graph[6], where M is smooth and compact Riemannian manifold, L^2 is the 2-norm defined on the manifold M, and ∇f is the gradient operator of the function on manifold M. It turns out that for any f, we have

$$\frac{1}{2} \sum_{i,j} (f(x_i) - f(x_j))^2 W_{ij} = f^T L f \tag{4}$$

where $L = D - W$ is the Laplacian matrix, D is a diagonal matrix whose entries are column sums of W, $D_{ii} = \sum_j W_{ji}$, W is the weight matrix whose element is defined as

$$W_{ij} = \begin{cases} \exp(-\|x_i - x_j\|^2 / t) & \|x_i - x_j\|^2 < \varepsilon \\ 0 & others \end{cases} \tag{5}$$

or

$$W_{ij} = \begin{cases} 1 & \|x_i - x_j\|^2 < \varepsilon \\ 0 & others \end{cases} \tag{6}$$

The second part of equ.(2) incurs a heavy penalty if neighboring points x_i and x_j are mapped far apart. Therefore, minimizing (4) is to keep the map $f(x_i)$ and $f(x_j)$ are close if x_i and x_j are close. Suppose the classifier can be represented as

$$f(x) = \sum_{i=1}^{n} \alpha_i k(z_i, x) \tag{7}$$

where $z_1, z_2, \cdots, z_n$ are the sparse support vectors, and $k(\cdot, \cdot)$ is Mercer kernel function. Substituting this form in equ.(2), we obtain the following convex differentiable function

$$\min_{\alpha, Z} \frac{1}{l} (K^n \alpha - y)^T (K^n \alpha - y) + \frac{\gamma}{2l^2} \alpha^T (K^n)^T L K^n \alpha \tag{8}$$

where $\alpha = (\alpha_1, \alpha_2, \cdots, \alpha_n)^T$, $Z = \{z_1, z_2, \cdots, z_n\}$, and

$$K^n = \begin{pmatrix} k(z_1, x_1) & k(z_2, x_1) & \cdots & k(z_n, x_1) \\ k(z_1, x_2) & k(z_2, x_2) & \cdots & k(z_n, x_2) \\ \cdots & \cdots & \cdots & \cdots \\ k(z_1, x_l) & k(z_2, x_l) & \cdots & k(z_n, x_l) \end{pmatrix} \tag{9}$$

The derivative of the objective function vanishes at the minimizer if the sparse support vectors are determined first:

$$\alpha = ((K^n)^T K^n + \frac{\gamma}{l} (K^n)^T L K^n)^{-1} (K^n)^T y \tag{10}$$

3 Greedy Learning Algorithm for the Sparse Kernel Classifier

In order to solve the optimization problem (2), we firstly find a good subset K^n beforehand which is not optimal any more. However, if one manages to eliminate irrelevant basis functions, the solution on the subset may be close to optimal. There are many methods to select matrix K^n approximating matrix K, which can be classified into sequential forward greedy algorithms [2,7,8,9], backward greedy algorithms and mathematical programming approaches. Because sequential forward algorithms are computationally cheap and tend to have modest requirements of memory, we take the variant of sparse greedy algorithm proposed in [2].

Let I^{p-1} denote the indices of the columns chosen at the $(p-1)th$ iteration. A new column can be selected at iteration p which leads to the greatest reduction in the residual error. So the new column is obtained by solving the following minimization problems

$$\min_{\mu_j, j \notin I^{p-1}} \left\| r^{p-1} + \mu_j K e_j \right\|_2 \tag{11}$$

The solution of this minimization problem turns out to be

$$\mu_j = -\frac{(r^{p-1}, Ke_j)}{(Ke_j, Ke_j)} \tag{12}$$

and the L^2 norm of the new residual $r^{p-1} + \mu_j K e_j$ can be written as

$$\rho_j^2 = \left\| r^{p-1} \right\|_2^2 - \frac{(r^{p-1}, Ke_j)^2}{(Ke_j, Ke_j)} \tag{13}$$

Let $q_j = \frac{(r^{p-1}, Ke_j)^2}{(Ke_j, Ke_j)}$. We use the algorithm in [2] to solve the problem. Once a new column is chosen, the weight vector μ and the residual error vector are updated. The sparse greedy algorithms used in this paper are described as follows:

Greedy Learning Algorithm
Input: maximum allowable sparsity n
Set $p = 0$, $r^0 = y$, and $I^p = [\,]$
While $p < n$, do
1. $p \leftarrow p + 1$
2. Find $i_p = \underset{j \notin I^{p-1}}{\arg\max} \left| r_j^{p-1} \right|$
3. $I^p = [I^{p-1}, i_p]$
4. $d_j \leftarrow r_j^{p-1} \ \forall j \in I^p$
5. $q \leftarrow Kd$
6. $\beta \leftarrow (r^{p-1}, q)/(q, q)$
7. $r^p \leftarrow r^{p-1} - \beta q$

Compared with the algorithm in [2], this algorithm does not take the exchanging strategy for the purpose of simplicity. Once we select the support vectors $z_1, z_2, \cdots z_n$, we compute equ.(10), and obtain the weight vector α. So the sparse kernel classifier $f(x) = \sum_{i=1}^{n} \alpha_i k(z_i, x)$ is obtained.

4   Experimental Results

We did experiments on the six benchmark datasets: Banana, Breast cancer, German, Image, Waveform, and Diabets [10]. All the experiments were conducted in Matlab6.5. We use Gaussian kernel $k(x_1, x_2) = \exp(-\frac{(x_1-x_2)^2}{\delta})$ to construct the Gram matrix K, and the width of the Gaussian kernel δ was estimated via several fold cross-validation procedures. We set Gaussian kernel width δ and the regularization parameter κ to $[\delta = 0.8, \kappa = 0.5], [\delta = 50, \kappa = 0.5], [\delta = 16, \kappa = 0.5], [\delta = 35, \kappa = 0.1], [\delta = 10, \kappa = 0.01], [\delta = 5, \kappa = 0.01]$, corresponding to Banana, Breast cancer, Waveform, German, Image, and Diabets, where $\kappa = \frac{\gamma}{l}$.

We compare the sparse kernel classifier on Riemannian manifold with conventional SVM, and Minimal residual algorithm[2] in which we did not use exchanging strategy. In the experiments, we construct embedded graph in two ways. One use heat kernel as equ.(5) to assign weight for each edge of the graph where $t = 0.5$, and the other use binary function to assign weight for each edge as equ.(6). For convenience, we denote sparse kernel classifier built in the first way by SK1, and denote the one in the second way by SK2. We average the results over 10 random splits of the mother data for Banana, Breast cancer, German, Waveform, Diabets, Image dataset which are shown in Table 1. It demonstrates that the sparse kernel classifier on Riemannian manifold are better than the greedy learning algorithm in [2] in classification accuracy except Image dataset. The reason that the classification accuracy by SK1 and SK2 is lower than the one by the algorithm in [2] is unknown, and it may result from the set parameters. The ways constructed the embedded graph have similar effect on the experiment results. The support vectors of the proposed algorithm are less than that of the conventional SVM without sacrificing much accuracy. Fig. 1 illustrates the case

Table 1. The classification error and sparsity level of sparse regular kernel classifier for six benchmark datasets

Datasets	Methods							
	SVM		Minmal residual		SRK1		SRK2	
	Error(%)	n	Error(%)	n	Error(%)	n	Error(%)	n
Banana	10.69	145	11.35	41	**10.97**	41	**10.99**	41
B.Cancer	28.05	120	27.53	11	**27.27**	11	**28.31**	11
German	22.97	425	24.13	32	**24.13**	32	**23.93**	32
Image	6.39	420	4.37	175	**5.29**	160	**5.41**	160
Waveform	9.94	171	12.02	27	**10.2**	40	**10.68**	40
Diabetes	24.80	293	25.07	4	**23.13**	10	**23.13**	10

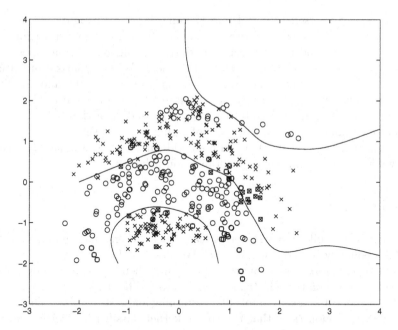

Fig. 1. Sparse kernel classifier on Banana dataset

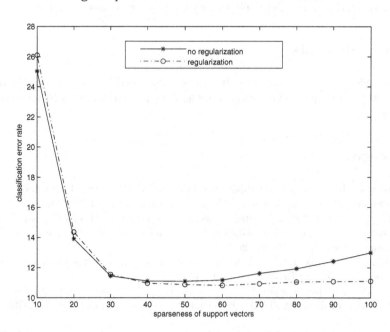

Fig. 2. Comparison between the sparse regularized kernel classifier and the classifier without regularizing on Banana dataset

where we set the sparseness $n = 41$ for Banana dataset. In Figure.1, class 1 is denoted by " × ", class 2 is denoted by " ○ ", the sparse support vectors are denoted by square, and the decision boundaries are signed by solid lines. The proposed approach is also compared with the one without regularization on Banana Dataset. The degree of sparseness ranges from 10 to 100, and the final result is the average of over 10 random splits of the mother data. The result is shown in Fig.2 and demonstrates that the proposed algorithm is more stable and accuracy than the algorithm absence of regularization. We conclude that the sparse kernel classifier on Riemannian manifold can generate a moderate sparse model while keeping competitive generalization behavior.

5   Conclusion

In this paper, we build a sparse kernel classifier on Riemanian manifold which preserves geometry of the original data. We first use forward greedy learning algorithm to choose sparse support vectors, and then we solve the optimization problem based on the selected support vectors. The storage of the proposed algorithm is modest and the complexity in training and testing is low. The experimental results demonstrate that the sparse kernel classifier is efficient and the classification accuracy is competitive with state-of-art SVM. In future work, we consider stop criteria to adaptively determine the sparseness of support vectors.

Acknowledgments

The research work is supported by the Chinese National Nature Science Foundation No.60205004 and the Foundation of Creative Research Group Programming No.60021302 .

References

1. Burges, C. J. C., Simplified support vector decision rules, Proc. 13th International Conference on Machine Learning, Morgan Kaufmann, pp. 71-77,1996.
2. Nair, P. B., Choudhury, A., and Keane, A. J., Some greedy learning algorithms for sparse regression and classification with mercer kernels, Journal of Machine Learning Research, 3, 781-801,2002.
3. Tipping, M. E., Sparse bayesian learning and the relevance vector machine, Journal of Machine Learning Research, 1, 211-244,2001.
4. Lee, Y.J., and Mangasarian, O. L., RSVM: reduced support vector machines, CD Proceedings of the First SIAM International Conference on Data Mining, Chicago, 2001.
5. Mingrui Wu, B. Scholkopf and G. Bakir, Building sparse large margin classifiers, Proceedings of the 22th International Conference on Machine Learning, Bonn, Germany,2005.
6. Belkin,M. and Niyogi,P., Laplacian eigenmaps for dimensionality reduction and data representation.Neural Computation,15(6),1373-1396,2003.

7. Smola, A. J., and Scholkopf,B., Sparse greedy matrix approximation for machine learning, Proceedings of the 17th International Conference on Machine Learning, Morgan Kaufmann, 911-918,2000.

8. Natarajan, B. K., Sparse approximate solutions to linear systems, SIAM Journal of Computing, 25(2), 227-234, 1995.

9. Mallat, S. and Zhang, Z., Matching pursuit in a time-frequency dictionary. IEEE Transactions on Signal Processing, 41, 3397-3415,1993.

10. the repository at http:ida.first.gmd.de/ raetsch/.

Three-Dimension Maximum Between-Cluster Variance Image Segmentation Method Based on Chaotic Optimization

Jiu-Lun Fan[1], Xue-Feng Zhang[1,2], and Feng Zhao[1]

[1] Department of Information and Control, Xi'an Institute of Post and Telecommunications,
Xi'an, Shaanxi, 710061 P.R. China
[2] Department of Electronic Engineering, Xidian University, Xi'an, Shaanxi, 710071, P.R. China
zhangxuefeng3@163.com

Abstract. Chaotic optimization is a new optimization technique. For image segmentation, conventional chaotic sequence is not very effective to three-dimension gray histogram. In order to solve this problem, a three-dimension chaotic sequence generating method is presented. Simulation results show that the generated sequence is pseudorandom and its distribution is approximately inside a sphere whose centre is $(0.5, 0.5, 0.5)$. Based on this work, we use the proposed chaotic sequence to optimize three-dimension maximum between-variance image segmentation method. Experiments results show that our method has better segmentation effect and lower computation time than that of the original three-dimension maximum between-variance image segmentation method for mixed noise disturbed image.

1 Introduction

Image segmentation is the fundamental and first step for image analysis and understanding. Image thresholding selection methods [1] are main and applause segmentation method. Among the thresholding selection methods, Maximum between-class variance method is an attractive one due to its simplicity and effective [1,2]. But in practice, Maximum between-class variance method in one-dimension gray histogram could fail to images with noises. In order to improve the segmentation effect, Liu and Li [3] extended maximum between-cluster variance method to two-dimension gray histogram, their method not only uses the pixels' gray histogram but also uses the pixels' neighborhood's information. Considering the computation time for maximum between-class variance method with two-dimension histogram is large, recursion algorithm was given [3]. Segmentation method based on two-dimension gray histogram can get better segmentation effect for image which is disturbed by single noise. For mixed noise disturbed image, the effect of the method is not good. So Jing et al.[4] extended maximum between-class variance method to three-dimension gray histogram. Considering the computation time for maximum between-class variance method with three-dimension histogram is very large, it is not used broadly. In order to solve this problem, we will present an image segmentation method based on three-dimension gray histogram using chaotic optimization.

H. Zha et al. (Eds.): VSMM 2006, LNCS 4270, pp. 164–173, 2006.

Chaotic systems are nonlinear dynamic behavior, they are pseudorandom and sensitivity to the initialize conditions. Because chaotic systems have good properties, chaotic systems are widely used in communications, optimization, control and image processing et.al[5-8]. For image segmentation, Xiu et.al [9] used Logistic chaotic sequence to optimize one-dimension entropy thresholding method and better segmentation result was obtained. But it is unfeasible to directly extend the one-dimension chaotic optimization method to three-dimension situation, because the generated three-dimension chaotic sequence is proportional distributing in $[0,1] \times [0,1] \times [0,1]$. It should be pointed out that for three-dimension gray histogram, the pixels inside the target class and the background classes' distribution are distributed near the diagonal from $(0,0,0)$ to $(L-1, L-1, L-1)$, so the conventional chaotic sequence is not very effective to image segmentation in the case of three-dimension gray histogram, the problem is how to generate a three-dimension sequence that is pseudorandom and the values of x, y and z in the sequence are approximately equality. In order to solve this problem, the key work is to construct a three-dimension chaotic sequence has the mentioned properties.

Section 2 presents a chaotic sequence generating method based on chaotic system and Bézier curve generating algorithm, Section 3 presents a three-dimension maximum between-cluster variance image segmentation algorithm based on chaotic optimization and also analysis the effect and the efficiency of the method by experimentations. The conclusion is given in Section 4.

2   Chaotic Sequence Generating Method

2.1 Bézier Curve and Its Properties

In 1971, Bézier presented a generating curve method based on Bernstein function and control points [10], this method is widely used in computer aided geometric design (CAGD) because of its good properties. The method is described as follows:

Suppose $P_i = (x_i, y_i, z_i)$, $i = 0,1,\cdots,n$, are control points, where $P_i \in R^3$.

Then the n-rank Bézier curve generated by these $n+1$ points is defined as follows:

$$P(u) = \sum_{i=0}^{n} P_i \cdot B_{i,n}(u) , \quad u \in [0,1] \tag{1}$$

here $B_{i,n}(u) = C_n^i \cdot (1-u)^{n-i} \cdot u^i$ is called Bernstein basic function. When the parameter u changes from 0 to 1, we can get a curve generated by formula (1), which is inside the polygon constituted by control points. The curve is called Bézier curve generated by the control polygon.

In the above processing, the control points are all geometric points in three-dimension space, and the curve is also in the polygon generated by control points. Now let us consider an extended situation. If the control points are nonobjective numeral points, then the points on the curve generated by formula (1) will also be nonobjective numeral points, and we can get a nonobjective numeral curve generated

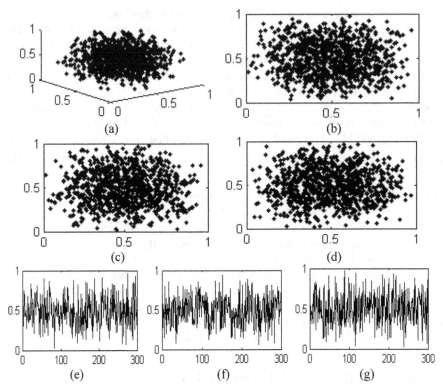

Fig. 1. Sequences generated by formula (3) and (4) (a) three-dimension chaotic sequence (b) xoy plane's randomness analysis (c) yoz plane's randomness analysis (d) zox plane's randomness analysis (e) x coordinator's randomness analysis (f) y coordinator's randomness analysis (g) z coordinator's randomness analysis

by formula (1) which is inside the nonobjective numeral polygon constituted by the nonobjective numeral control points. When the control points are random then we can get a random curve generated by the random control points.

2.2 Extended Chaotic Sequence Generating Method

Based on the statement in section 2.1, we present the extended chaotic sequence generating method based on the above analysis.

Suppose $\{a_1^i, a_2^i, \cdots, a_n^i, \cdots\}$, ($i = 0, 1, \cdots, K$) are known chaotic sequences, and it have the same dimension D and $\{t_1, t_2, \cdots\}$ is a chaotic sequence of one or D dimensions. The extended chaotic sequence $\{a_1, a_2, \cdots\}$ as follows:

$$a_n = \sum_{i=0}^{K} a_n^i \cdot B_{i,n}(t_n) \qquad n = 1, 2, \cdots \qquad (2)$$

when $\{t_1, t_2, \cdots\}$ is one dimension or

$$a_n^j = \sum_{i=0}^{K} a_n^{i,j} \cdot B_{i,n}(t_n^j) \quad n = 1, 2, \cdots \quad j = 1, 2, \cdots, L \qquad (3)$$

when $\{t_1, t_2, \cdots\}$ is D dimensions.

2.3 Three-Dimension Sequence Generating Method

We can show an extended chaotic sequence generated by Arnold chaotic system for $D = 3$. Arnold chaotic system is defined as[11]:

$$\begin{cases} x_{n+1} = (x_n + y_n + z_n) & \mod 1 \\ y_{n+1} = (x_n + 2y_n + 2z_n) & \mod 1 \\ z_{n+1} = (x_n + 2y_n + 3z_n) & \mod 1 \end{cases} \qquad (4)$$

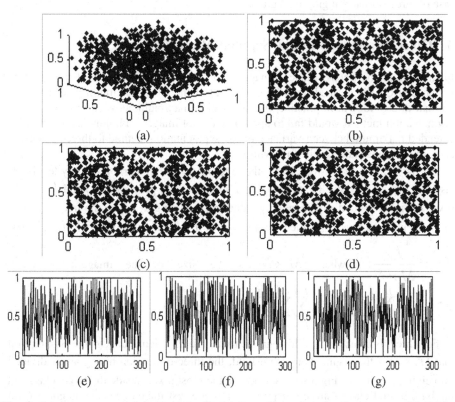

Fig. 2. Sequences generated by formula (4) (a) three-dimension chaotic sequence (b) xoy plane's randomness analysis (c) yoz plane's randomness analysis (d) zox plane's randomness analysis (e) x coordinator's randomness analysis (f) y coordinator's randomness analysis (g) z coordinator's randomness analysis

where mod 1 is defined as: $x \bmod 1 = x - \lfloor x \rfloor$, so the sequence generated by formula (4) is inside the cube $[0,1] \times [0,1] \times [0,1]$.

If we generate the control points and the sequence $\{t_1, t_2, \cdots\}$ using formula (4), then with formula (3), we can get an extended chaotic sequence.

Fig.1 and Fig.2 give the simulation results for Arnold chaotic system and our method, it is shown that the sequence generated by formula (4) are random and proportional distributing in $[0,1] \times [0,1] \times [0,1]$, and the sequences generated by formula (3) are random and its distribution is approximately inside a sphere whose centre is $(0.5, 0.5, 0.5)$. It should be pointed out that for image's three-dimension gray histogram [4], the most pixels inside the target class and the background classes' distribution are distributed near the diagonal from $(0,0,0)$ to $(L-1, L-1, L-1)$, this property means that the most thresholds for image segmentation are distributed near the diagonal from $(0,0,0)$ to $(L-1, L-1, L-1)$. So the sequence generated by formula (3) is superior to the Arnold chaotic sequence for image segmenting in the case of three-dimension gray histogram.

3   Three-Dimension Image Segmentation Method

In maximum between-variance image segmentation method, the between-class variance (BCV) is defined, and the gray level at the BCV maximum determines an optimal threshold. But in practice, one-dimension maximum between-variance image segmentation method would fail to apply in cases of images with noises. Jing et al.[4] extended maximum between-variance image segmentation method to three-dimension case, the detail is stated in the following.

Let the image's gray levels is L, then the pixels' neighbourhood's gray levels are also L. For every point (i, j, k) where i is the pixel's gray value, j and k are the pixel's neighbourhood's average gray value and median gray value, the frequencies of (i, j, k) is written as f_{ijk}, then we can define the joint probability of (i, j, k) as:

$P_{ij} = \dfrac{f_{ijk}}{M \times N}$, where $M \times N$ is the size of the image. We have,

$$M \times N = \sum_{i=0}^{L-1} \sum_{j=0}^{L-1} \sum_{k=0}^{L-1} f_{ijk}, \quad \sum_{i=0}^{L-1} \sum_{j=0}^{L-1} \sum_{k=0}^{L-1} P_{ijk} = 1.$$

For three-dimension gray histogram, there are L^3 elements. On the assumption that (r, s, t) is the segmentation threshold, the three-dimension histogram is divided into eight parts just as Fig.3 shows. Because the most pixels inside the target class and the background classes are consistent, so they are distributed near the diagonal from $(0,0,0)$ to $(L-1, L-1, L-1)$. That means region A and B involve most pixels of target class and background classe, else six regions involve most pixels of edge and the noises.

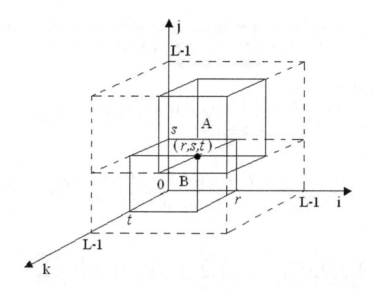

Fig. 3. Three-dimension gray histogram

Now let:

$$P_A(r,s,t) = P(A) = \sum_{i=0}^{r-1}\sum_{j=0}^{s-1}\sum_{k=0}^{t-1} P_{ijk} \ , P_B(s,t) = P(B) = \sum_{i=r}^{L-1}\sum_{j=s}^{L-1}\sum_{k=t}^{L-1} P_{ijk} \qquad (5)$$

The mean values of region A and B are computed as follows:

$$\overline{u}_A = (u_{Ai}, u_{Aj}, u_{Ak})^T = \left(\sum_{i=0}^{r-1} P(i|A), \sum_{j=0}^{s-1} P(j|A), \sum_{k=0}^{t-1} P(k|A) \right)^T$$

$$= \left(\sum_{i=0}^{r-1}\sum_{j=0}^{s-1}\sum_{k=0}^{t-1} \frac{i \cdot P_{ijk}}{P_A(r,s,t)}, \sum_{i=0}^{r-1}\sum_{j=0}^{s-1}\sum_{k=0}^{t-1} \frac{j \cdot P_{ijk}}{P_A(r,s,t)}, \sum_{i=0}^{r-1}\sum_{j=0}^{s-1}\sum_{k=0}^{t-1} \frac{k \cdot P_{ijk}}{P_A(r,s,t)} \right)^T \qquad (6)$$

$$\overline{u}_B = (u_{Bi}, u_{Bj}, u_{Bk})^T = \left(\sum_{i=r}^{L-1} P(i|B), \sum_{j=s}^{L-1} P(j|B), \sum_{k=t}^{L-1} P(k|B) \right)^T$$

$$= \left(\sum_{i=r}^{L-1}\sum_{j=s}^{L-1}\sum_{k=t}^{L-1} \frac{i \cdot P_{ijk}}{P_B(r,s,t)}, \sum_{i=r}^{L-1}\sum_{j=s}^{L-1}\sum_{k=t}^{L-1} \frac{j \cdot P_{ijk}}{P_B(r,s,t)}, \sum_{i=r}^{L-1}\sum_{j=s}^{L-1}\sum_{k=t}^{L-1} \frac{k \cdot P_{ijk}}{P_B(r,s,t)} \right)^T \qquad (7)$$

the whole mean value is computed as:

$$\overline{u} = (u_i, u_j, u_k)^T = \left(\sum_{i=0}^{L-1}\sum_{j=0}^{L-1}\sum_{k=0}^{L-1} i \cdot P_{ijk}, \sum_{i=0}^{L-1}\sum_{j=0}^{L-1}\sum_{k=0}^{L-1} j \cdot P_{ijk}, \sum_{i=0}^{L-1}\sum_{j=0}^{L-1}\sum_{k=0}^{L-1} k \cdot P_{ijk} \right)^T \qquad (8)$$

In many cases, pixels out of region A and B can be ignored. So we can assume that:

$$P_A(r,s,t) + P_B(r,s,t) \approx 1 \ , \quad \overline{u} \approx P_A(r,s,t) \cdot \overline{u}_A + P_B(r,s,t) \cdot \overline{u}_B \quad (9)$$

Now defining the scatter matrix as follow:

$$S_B(r,s,t) =$$
$$P_A(r,s,t) \cdot [(\overline{u}_A - \overline{u}) \cdot (\overline{u}_A - \overline{u})^T] + P_B(r,s,t) \cdot [(\overline{u}_B - \overline{u}) \cdot (\overline{u}_B - \overline{u})^T] \quad (10)$$

The trace of $S_B(r,s,t)$ is defined as:

$$Tr(S_B(r,s,t)) =$$
$$\frac{[(P_A(r,s,t) \cdot u_i - u_{Zi})^2 + (P_A(r,s,t) \cdot u_j - u_{Zj})^2 + (P_A(r,s,t) \cdot u_k - u_{Zk})^2]}{P_A(r,s,t) \cdot P_B(r,s,t)}$$

$$(11)$$

where:

$$u_{Zi} = \sum_{i=0}^{r-1}\sum_{j=0}^{s-1}\sum_{k=0}^{t-1} i \cdot P_{ijk} \ , u_{Zj} = \sum_{i=0}^{r-1}\sum_{j=0}^{s-1}\sum_{k=0}^{t-1} j \cdot P_{ijk} \ , u_{Zk} = \sum_{i=0}^{r-1}\sum_{j=0}^{s-1}\sum_{k=0}^{t-1} k \cdot P_{ijk} \ .$$

The optimal threshold value (r^*, s^*, t^*) is obtained by [4]:

$$(r^*, s^*, t^*) = \underset{\substack{0 \leq r \leq L-1 \\ 0 \leq s \leq L-1 \\ 0 \leq t \leq L-1}}{Arg} \{Tr(S_B(r,s,t))\} \quad (12)$$

Jing's method [4] is validity for mixed noise disturbed image, but the computation time is very large, made the method is not useful in practice. In order to decreasing the computation time, we will use chaotic optimization method to determine the best threshold value. The algorithm is described as follows:

Step1: Input the mixed noise disturbed image, the times of iterative p, the number of the initial points q and the initial conditions of chaotic system. Set the gray levels region: $\{0,1,\cdots,L-1\} \times \{0,1,\cdots,L-1\} \times \{0,1,\cdots,L-1\}$.

Step2: Using formula (3) and (4) to generate the extended chaotic sequences $(R_1,S_1,T_1),(R_2,S_2,T_2),\cdots,(R_q,S_q,T_q)$, discrete it from real number region into integer region, get the sequences $(r_1,s_1,t_1),(r_2,s_2,t_2),\cdots,(r_q,s_q,t_q)$.

Step3: Computing the $Tr(S_B(r_i,s_i,t_i))$ by formula (11), then generate the new chaotic sequences with formula (3) and (4), discrete the sequences from real number region into integer region, at the same time, computing $Tr(S_B(r_i,s_i,t_i))$ of the new chaotic sequence, comparing the new $Tr(S_B(r_i,s_i,t_i))$ with the previous iterative results. Reserve the front q maximum values $Tr(S_B(r_i,s_i,t_i))$ from the obtained $2q$ $Tr(S_B(r_i,s_i,t_i))$ values and its corresponding gray values (r_i,s_i,t_i).

Step4: Continue the computation process for p times and then find the satisfied result in the last q points (r_i,s_i,t_i).

In step 4, the words "satisfied result" relies on the man and the case the image may be used, it may be subjective or objective. For example, we can get a better segmenting result from the last q results based on vision effect. In this paper, in order to compare the efficiency of our method with Jing's method [4], we make the "satisfied result" as the (r_i, s_i, t_i) corresponding to the maximum value of $Tr(S_B(r_i, s_i, t_i))$, this can be consider as a approximate solution for formula (12).

Now we give the simulation results based on Arnold system and the 3×3 neighbourhood. As compare, we also present the results of Jing's method. The image is disturbed with mixed noise of 0.005 Gauss noise and 0.05 salt and pepper noise and the results are tested in the same computer.

Table 1 shows the performances of the two methods, where T means runtime the method expended and the unit of T is second. H means the threshold the method got. Tr means the values of $Tr(S_B(r, s, t))$ corresponding to the threshold we have got.

In the above experiments, we set $q = 25$ and $p = 20$ for our method. It can be seen that the computation time of our method is nearly equal. That is, the efficiency of our method mainly lies on the times of iterative and the number of the initial points. But the efficiency of Jing's method lies on the size of the image thus Jing's method is

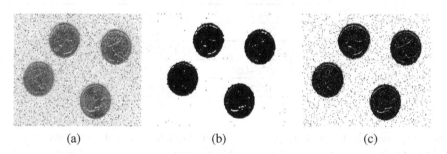

(a)   (b)   (c)

Fig. 4. Results of image segmentation (a) Image with mixed noise (b) Results using our method (c) Results using Jing's method

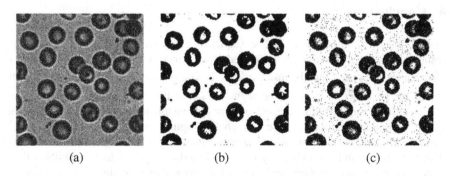

(a)   (b)   (c)

Fig. 5. Results of image segmentation (a) Image with mixed noise (b) Results using our method (c) Results using Jing's method

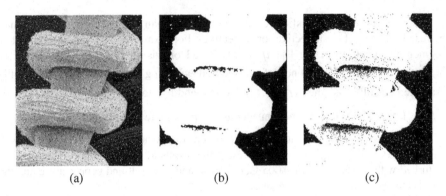

(a)   (b)   (c)

Fig. 6. Results of image segmentation (a) Image with mixed noise (b) Results using our method (c) Results using Jing's method

Table 1. Performances of two methods

		Fig.4	Fig.5	Fig.6
Size of image		397×297	351×325	366×325
Our method	H	(152,181,205)	(136,93,99)	(156,74,77)
	Tr	5.0656e+003	4.4234e+003	9.7685e+003
	T	204	204	205
Jing's method	H	(170,219,225)	(95,129,255)	(95,140,171)
	Tr	7.5097e+003	6.0615e+003	1.3379e+004
	T	1032	2415	2729

not very usefully for real image. In addition, from the simulation results of Fig.4, Fig.5, Fig.6, we can see that the segmentation results using our method is also superior to the Jing's method for mixed noise disturbed image.

4   Conclusions

In this paper, we present a chaotic sequence generating method. The simulation results show that the sequence generated by our method are pseudorandom and its distribution is approximately inside a sphere whose centre is $(0.5, 0.5, 0.5)$, this means the sequence is fit to image segmentation in three-dimension gray histogram. As an application, we also present a three-dimension maximum between-variance image segmentation method based on chaotic optimization. The simulation results show that the effect of segmentation results using our method is good for mixed niose disturbed image and the efficiency of our method is superior to the tradition three-dimension maximum between-variance image segmentation method.

Acknowledgement

The work is supported by National Nature Science Funds project (Grant Number: 60572133), Opening Project of CNIS (Computer Network and Information Security Laboratory) of Ministry of Education, Scientific Research Funds of Education Department of Shaanxi Province (Grant Number: 06JK194).

References

[1] Otsu N. A threshold selection method from gray-level histograms [J]. IEEE Trans on Systems, Man and Cybernetics, 1979 (1): 62-66.

[2] Liu Jian-zhuang, Li Wen-qing. Two-dimension Otsu's Automatic Segmentation method of Gray Image[J]. Automatization Journal. 1993, 19 (1): 101-105.(in Chinese)

[3] Gong J, Li L Y, Chen W N. Fast recursive algorithm for two-dimensional thresholding[J]. Pattern Recognition. 1998, 31(3): 295-300.

[4] Jing Xiao-jun, Li Jian-feng, Liu Yu-lin. Image Segmentation Based on 32D Maximum Between2Cluster Variance [J]. Acta Electronicasinica. 2003, 31(9): 1281-1285.(in Chinese)

[5] Han Hen and Neri Merhav. On the Threshold Effect in the Estimation of Chaotic Sequences[J]. IEEE Trans on Information Theory. 2004, 50(11): 2894-2904.

[6] L. Wang and K. Smith. On chaotic simulated annealing[J]. IEEE Trans on Neural Networks. 1998, 9(4): 716-718.

[7] Claudio R. Mirasso et.al. Chaos Shift-Keying Encryption in Chaotic External-Cavity Semiconductor Lasers Using a Single-Receiver Scheme[J]. IEEE Photonics Technology Letters. 2002, 14(4): 456-458.

[8] Liang Zhao et.al. A Network of Globally Coupled Chaotic Maps for Adaptive Multi-Resolution Image Segmentation[C]. Proceedings of the VII Brazilian Symposium on Neural Networks (SBRN'02).

[9] Xiu Chun-Bo, Liu Xiang-Dong, Zhang Yu-He. Optimal Entropy Thresholding Image Segmentation Based on Chaos Optimization [J].Computer Engineering and Applications, 2004.40(27):76-78. (in Chinese)

[10] Les Piegl, Wayne Tiller. The NURBS Book[M]. Springer, 1995.

[11] Yang Li-Zhen, Chen Ke-Fei. On the orders of transformation matrices (mod n) and two types of generalized Arnold transformation matrices [J]. Science in China Series E. 2004, 34(2): 151-161. (in Chinese)

A Multi-sensor Image Registration Method Based on Harris Corner Matching[*]

Mingyue Ding, Lingling Li, Chengping Zhou, and Chao Cai

Institute for Pattern Recognition and Artificial Intelligence, "Image Processing and Intelligent Control" Key Laboratory of Education Ministry, Huazhong University of Science and Technology, Wuhan, Hubei 430074, China
myding@hust.edu.cn
http://www.imaging.robarts.ca/~mding

Abstract. In this paper, a registration method based on Harris corners is proposed. It is composed of three steps. First, corner extraction and matching. We use the gray level information around the corner to setup the correspondences, then use the affine invariant of Mahalannobis distance to remove the mismatched corner points. From this correspondence of the corner points, the affine matrix between two different images can be determined. Finally, map all points in the sensed image to the reference using the estimated transformation matrix and assign the corresponding gray level by re-sampling the image in the sensed image. Experiments with different types of multi-sensor images demonstrated the feasibility of our method.

1 Introduction

The image captured reflects the property of the scene in the field of view. Different modalities or different imaging systems may obtain different images of the same scene. In other words, different images from different sensors may represent the different properties of the same scene. For instance, CCD camera captures the light illumination and reflection from different surfaces in or around the scene while infrared image represents the temperature distribution on the surface of the objects in the scene. CT image of human body is clearly observable for bones while ultrasound image is suitable for the imaging of soft tissue. Therefore, in order to perform specific tasks, such as object recognition and disease diagnosis, the information contained in one modality image is not enough to make a reliable decision because the limitations of individual sensor. To overcome these problems, a multi-sensor image fusion is needed, which can combine the useful information containing in different images and obtain more correct and accurate interpretations of the scene. Before the fusion of images, a pre-requisite step is to register the images captured from different sensors.

A number of multi-sensor image fusion methods have been proposed in the last 2 decades. It can be categorized into 3 classes.[1,2,3] The first class is grey level-based

---

[*] This work is partly supported by the National Natural Science Foundation of China under the grant of 60135020 FF 030405.

H. Zha et al. (Eds.): VSMM 2006, LNCS 4270, pp. 174–183, 2006.

image registration.[4] The main problem in this class method is that the grey levels are the similar only for the images captured by the same type of sensor. In order to extend it to a registration of different modalities, a mutual information based registration method was developed, [5-6] which now is widely used in medical image registration of multi-modality image. But the problem is that it needs to estimate the probability density, therefore, it is time-consuming.

The second class of registration methods is Fourier transform based registration, such as the phase correlation image alignment method given in Ref. [7] or the other methods in Refs. [8-10]. This method is suitable for linear variation of the grey levels such as the image with a low frequency noise or the grey level change produced by rotation, translation and scale variation.

The third class is feature-based registration. In multi-sensor image registration, the grey levels of the scene are depended on the imaging sensor it used. For multi-sensor images, some of the features, such as the corners or the edges are constant and stable. Therefore, it is not sensitive to the choice of sensor as well as the rotation, translation and the scale changes between images. In Ref. [11], a convex hull of the corner set is defined to solve the affine matrix and recognize the scene. The convex hull provides a new methodology to match the discrete point set but it is only suitable for a simple scene with a limited number of corners. Line segments are other often used features that can be used in registration. Line segment can be extracted by using a Hough transform technique but how to establish the correspondence between the line segments is still challenging.

Among these registration methods, the main problems include:

1)   How to register multi-sensor image
2)   To perform an automatic registration
3)   Fast registration
4)   High accuracy registration under a big alignment shift

In order to solve these problems, a new registration method using Harris corner points was developed. In Section II, first, a diagram of the method is given and the Harris corner detection algorithm is introduced. It is composed of four steps: corner matching, mis-matched corner point removal, grey level mapping and re-sampling. Registration experiments were conducted in Section III while our conclusion is presented in Section IV.

2   Multi-sensor Image Registration Based on Harris Corner Point Matching

The selection of feature is the most important step in registration algorithm. Figure 1 is the diagram of our Harris corner point based registration method. It is composed of the following parts:

1) Corner extraction
2) Corner matching
3) Transformation matrix estimation
4) Point mapping and the image data re-sampling

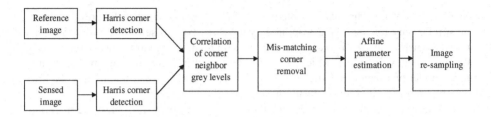

Fig. 1. Diagram of Harris corner based image registration method

2.1 Harris Corner Detection

Our experiment demonstrated that the corner points detected by using Harris corner detection algorithm have a highest detection probability comparing to the algorithms of Kitchen-Rosenfeld,[12] Deriche-Giraudon,[13] SUSAN,[14] and Beaudet.[15] According to Ref. [16], the detection of Harris corners only needs to calculate the first order derivatives of the image and can be calculated from a matrix M:

$$M = G \otimes \begin{bmatrix} I_x^2 & I_x I_y \\ I_x I_y & I_y^2 \end{bmatrix} = \begin{bmatrix} \langle I_x^2 \rangle & \langle I_x I_y \rangle \\ \langle I_x I_y \rangle & \langle I_y^2 \rangle \end{bmatrix} \tag{1}$$

where I_x is the gradient of the image I in x-direction, I_y is the gradient of the image I in y-direction, G is the Gaussian template, $\langle \ \rangle$ represents the convolution of the image I with the Gaussian template. Based on the matrix M, the corner response function is defined as:

$$CRF = \det(M) - k \cdot trace^2(M), \ k = 0.04 \tag{2}$$

where det is the determinant of matrix, trace is the trace of matrix, k is a constant. The local maximum is the corner in image.

Figure 2 is the corner extraction results of a synthetic image. Figure 2(a) is the original image. Figures 2(b)-(f) are the corners detected by five different corner detection algorithms. A comparison of their performance is enlisted in Table 1. From Table 1 it is clear that Harris detector has the lowest error rate and highest detection rate, therefore, we will use the Harris corners as the feature of our registration method.

2.2 Corner Point Matching

Corner point matching plays a key role in registration procedure. First, we establish the correspondence between the corners from the reference and sensed images using the correlation measurement of the grey levels in the neighbors of the corners. The steps are:

Step 1: Calculate the cross correlation coefficients of every corner in the sensed image and reference image with the same template window size. In order to decrease the influence of the image brightness and contrast, a normalized cross-correlation coefficient was used in our method.

Step 2: Find out all corresponding corners that their cross-correlation coefficients are greater than a given threshold. Sort them according to their value and take the top 20 of them as the pre-selected matched pairs.

Secondly, remove mis-matching corners based on the affine invariant of Mahalanobis distance. Mahalanobis distance is a metric defined by an Indian statistician Mahalanobis. For a sample space $X = \{(x_1, y_1)^t, ..., (x_n, y_n)^t\}$ (here t represents the transpose of a vector), the Mahalanobis distance between the point $X_i = (x_i, y_i)^t$ and the mean of the set $\mu = (\mu_x, \mu_y)^t$ is:

$$Md_{(i)} = \sqrt{(\mathbf{x_i} - \mu)\,C^{-1}\,(\mathbf{x_i} - \mu)^t} \quad,$$

(3)

where C is a covariance matrix ; C^{-1} is the inverse matrix of C. The mean μ and the covariance matrix are defined as Eqs. (4) and (5) respectively.

$$\mu = [\mu_x, \mu_y]^t = \left[\sum_{i=1}^{n} x_i, \sum_{i=1}^{n} y_i\right]^t \Big/ n,$$

(4)

$$C = \left[\sum_{i=1}^{n} \begin{bmatrix} x_i - \mu_x \\ y_i - \mu_y \end{bmatrix} [x_i - \mu_x, y_i - \mu_y]\right] \Big/ n .$$

(5)

Suppose the sensed image to be I_1 and the reference image to be I_2 and they are satisfied with an affine transformation. Assume that $X_1 = \{(x_{11}, y_{11})^t, \cdots, (x_{1m}, y_{1m})^t\}$ and $X_2 = \{(x_{21}, y_{21})^t, \cdots, (x_{2m}, y_{2m})^t\}$ are the two corresponding points in I_1 and I_2. From Eq. (3), we can calculate the Mahalanobis distances of X_1 and X_2 are $Md_1 = \{Md_{1(1)}, \quad ..., \quad Md_{1(m)}\}$ and $Md_2 = \{Md_{2(1)}, \quad ..., \quad Md_{2(m)}\}$.

The variance of n statistic variables, $x_1, \cdots, x_n$, can be calculated by:

$$S_n^2 = \frac{(x_1^2 + x_2^2 + \cdots + x_n^2) - n\bar{x}^2}{n}$$

(6)

where $\bar{x} = (x_1 + x_2 + ... + x_n)/n$; when $n=2$, Eq. (6) can be written as:

$$S_2^2 = \frac{(x_1^2 + x_2^2) - 2 \times [(x_1 + x_2)/2]^2}{2} = \frac{(x_1 - x_2)^2}{4}$$

(7)

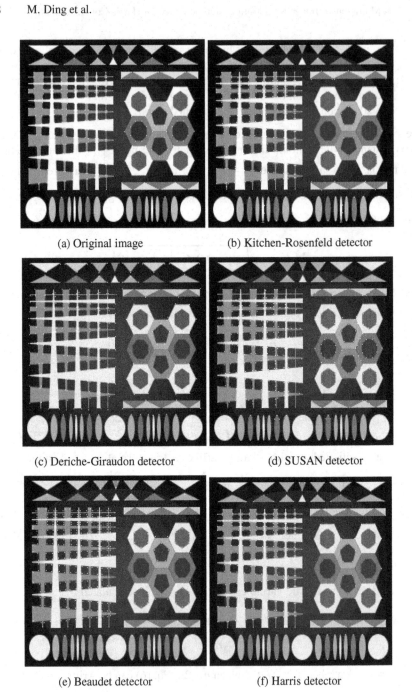

(a) Original image

(b) Kitchen-Rosenfeld detector

(c) Deriche-Giraudon detector

(d) SUSAN detector

(e) Beaudet detector

(f) Harris detector

Fig. 2. Comparison of corner detection using different corner detectors

Table 1. Comparison of five different detectors

Detector	N_D	N_U	N_R	R_E	R_D
Kitchen–Rosenfeld	420	50	32	31.7%	89.4%
Deriche–Giraudon	337	133	0	29.8%	71.7%
SUSAN	370	100	20	27.4%	78.7%
Beaudet	406	64	5	22.1%	86.4%
Harris	**442**	**28**	**0**	**7.2%**	**94.0%**

N_D is the number of detected corners, N_U is the number of undetected corners, N_R is the number of wrong detected corners, R_E is the error rate, R_D is the detection rate.

From Eq. (7), we can define the sum of variances between $\mathbf{X}_1 = \{(x_{11}, y_{11})^t, \cdots, (x_{1m}, y_{1m})^t\}$ and $\mathbf{X}_2 = \{(x_{21}, y_{21})^t, \cdots, (x_{2m}, y_{2m})^t\}$, denoted by *Square,* as :

$$Square = 0.25\sum\nolimits_{i=1}^{m}\left(Md_{1(i)} - Md_{2(i)}\right)^2 \tag{8}$$

According to the affine invariant of Mahalanobis distance introduced in Ref. [17], we have $\mathbf{Md_1}=\mathbf{Md_2}$, *Square*=0. In our experiment, we considered they are correspondent if the value of *Square* is very small.

Now, we have the following mismatching corner removal algorithm:

Step 1: Suppose *th1* to be the threshold of the sum of Mahalanobis distance variances (Our experiment demonstrated that the selection of the value of *th1* is not sensitive to the result. In our experiment, we let *th1*= 0.002). Arbitrarily select 4 pair of corners from the 20 pre-selected matched corresponding points and calculate their square value from Eq. (8). Keep all pairs of the corner points with the *square* less than *th1*.

Step 2: Vote the points appeared in the pair set obtained in Step 1 and sort them in decreasing order. Take the top 4 as the basic pair corners while the rest are stored in an expanded pair set.

Step 3: Suppose *th2* to be a threshold (Our experiment demonstrated that the selection of the value of *th2* is not sensitive to the result. In our experiment, we let *th2*= 0.005). Put any point in the expanded pair set obtained in Step 2 into the basic pair set and calculate the sum of Mahalanobis distance variance again. Find out the point that has a minimum *Square* and the *Square* less or equal *th2*, insert it into the basic pair set. This procedure will be repeated until no more point is found. The basic pair set is the correct corresponding corners that can be used in the estimation of the affine transformation matrix.

2.3 Transformation Parameter Estimation

After determination of the correspondence of at least 3 corner points, the 6 transformation parameters in the affine matrix can be estimated using the Least Square Method (LSM).

Suppose (x_1', y_1'), (x_2', y_2'), ..., (x_n', y_n') to be the fiducial points $n(\geq 3)$, and their corresponding points in the sensed image are (x_1, y_1), (x_2, y_2), ..., (x_n, y_n). If we denote them by $P = \begin{bmatrix} x_1, y_1, 1 \\ x_2, y_2, 1 \\ \bullet, \bullet, \bullet \\ \bullet, \bullet, \bullet \\ x_n, y_n, 1 \end{bmatrix}$, then the solution of affine transformation parameters are:

$$\begin{bmatrix} a_{00} \\ a_{01} \\ t_x \end{bmatrix} = P^+ \begin{bmatrix} x_1', x_2', ..., x_n' \end{bmatrix}^T \quad \begin{bmatrix} a_{10} \\ a_{11} \\ t_y \end{bmatrix} = P^+ \begin{bmatrix} y_1', y_2', ..., y_n' \end{bmatrix}^T \tag{9}$$

where P^+ is the Moore-Penrose inverse matrix of P.[18]

2.4 Image Re-sampling

After the determination of the affine transformation matrix in Section 2.3, we can map the sensed image points to the reference image. Because the coordinates calculated from Eq. (1) may be not exact equal to an integer, we need to resample the image to find the grey level of the mapped point in the reference image. This can be performed using a bi-linear interpolation method.

3 Experimental Evaluation

In order to demonstrate the feasibility of our Harris based image registration method, two experiments were conducted.

3.1 Registration Accuracy

The registration accuracy of our registration method was evaluated by registering a known image pair. The reference image we used is a 200X200 Lena image while the

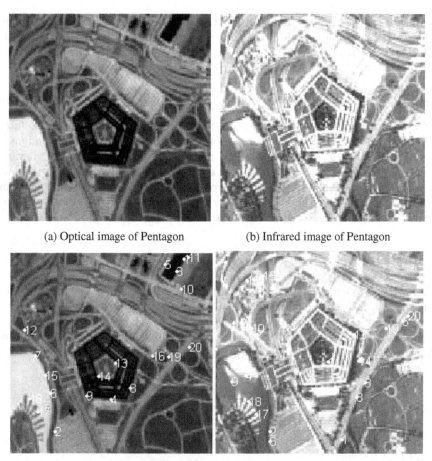

(a) Optical image of Pentagon   (b) Infrared image of Pentagon

(c) 20 pre-selected matched corners from (a)   (d) 20 pre-selected matched corners from (b)

Fig. 3. Registration of optical and infrared images of US Pentagon

sensed image is a 300X300 Lena image. The correct transformation parameters are (0.6667,0,0,0.6667,0,0) while our estimated parameters are (0.6670,0.0001,-0.00058,0.6650,-0.1234,-0.1441). In our experiment, we chose the size of neighbors is 5x5, *th1*= 0.002, *th2*= 0.005.

3.2 Multi-sensor Image Registration

We used different images to evaluate our registration algorithm including Infra-red/optical image, Seasat images and so on. One example of these registrations is shown in Fig. 3. Figure 3 (a) is the optical image of US Pentagon, (b) is the infrared image of (a). Both sizes of (a) and (b) are the same of 225x225. Figure 3(c) and (d) are the 20 pre-selected matched corners. From Fig. 3 (e), it is clear that our algorithm performed a perfect registration. The program is run under Windows XP and takes about 15s for the whole procedure including the extraction of the Harris corners.

4 Conclusions

Image registration, especially multi-sensor image registration is very important for fusion of the images captured from different sensors. In this paper, we developed a new paradigm to register multi-sensor image using the Harris corners. Experiments demonstrated that this method can register the multi-sensor image accurately and automatically. Our future work includes dealing with the fast algorithm and applied it in the fusion of multi-sensor images.

References

1. L.G. Brown. A survey of image registration techniques. *ACM Computing Surveys*, 1992, 24(4): 326 ~ 376
2. Dongfeng Wang, Multi-modality and large image registration technique, PhD thesis, Institute of Electronics, The Academy of Sciences of China, 2002
3. Lixia Shu, Research on image registration method, Master thesis, Institute for Pattern Recognition and Artificial Intelligence, Huazhong University of Science and Technology, 2003
4. A. Rosenfeld, A.C. Kak. Digital picture processing. *London: Academic Press*, 1982
5. P. Violar, W.M. Wells III. Alignment by maximization of mutual information. In: *Proceedings of 5th International Conference on Computer Vision*. Boston, MA, USA.1995: 16 ~ 23
6. P. Violar, W.M. Wells III. Alignment by maximization of mutual information. *International Journal of Computer Vision*, 1997, 24(2): 137 ~ 154
7. C.D. Kuglin, D.C. Hines. The phase correlation image alignment method. In: *Proceedings of IEEE International Conference on Cybernetics and Society*, 1975, 163 ~ 165
8. S. Alliney. Spatial registration of multispectral and multitemporal digital imagery using fast-fourier transform techniques. *IEEE Transactions on Pattern Analysis and Machine Intelligence*, 1993,15(5): 499 ~ 504
9. H.S. Stone, M.T. Orchard, E.C. Chang, et al. A fast direct fourier-based algorithm for sub-pixel registration of images. *IEEE Transactions on Geoscience and Remote Sensing*, 2001, 39(10): 2235 ~ 2243

10. Q.S. Chen, M. Defrise, F. Deconinck. Symmetric phase-only matched filtering of fourier-mellin transforms for image registration and recognition. *IEEE Transactions on Pattern Analysis and Machine Intelligence*, 1994,16(10): 1156 ~ 1168
11. Z. Yang, F.S. Cohen. Image registration and object recognition using affine invariants and convex hulls. *IEEE Transactions on Image Processing*, 1999, 8(7): 934 ~ 946
12. L. Kitchen, A. Rosenfeld. Gray-level corner detection. *Pattern Recognition Letters*, 1982, 1, 95 ~ 102
13. R. Deriche, G. Giraudon. A computational approach for corner and vertex detection. *International Journal of Computer Vision*, 1993, 10(2): 101 ~ 124
14. S.M. Smith, J.M. Brady. SUSAN-A new approach to low level image processing. *International Journal of Computer Vision*, 1997, 23(1): 45 ~ 78
15. P.R. Beaudet. Rotationally invariant image operators. In: *Fourth International Conference on Pattern Recognition*. Tokyo, Japan. 1978: 579 ~ 583
16. C.G. Harris, M. J. Stephens. A combined corner and edge detector. In: *Proceedings Fourth Alvey Vision Conference*. Manchester, U. K. 1988:147 ~ 151
17. Xin Chen, Jianyong Xiang, Yihe Yang, Invariant theory applied to the recognition of air target, Journal of Infrared and Millimeter Waves, 16(1):39-44, 1997
18. Exi Yu, Matrix theory, second version, High education Press, Beijing, 224-244, 1995

Graph Based Energy for Active Object Removal

Yimin Yu, Duanqing Xu, Chun Chen, and Lei Zhao

College of Computer Science, Zhejiang University,
310027 Hangzhou, Zhejiang, P.R. China
yuyym@yahoo.com.cn, xdq@zju.edu.cn,
chenc@cs.zju.edu.cn, zhlzhao@yahoo.com.cn

Abstract. In this paper, we present a system for completing the blank hole in an image list or a video sequence, which can be used in movie-making industry to produce some special montage effect. To achieve this, we apply a 3D coordinate to depict the video clip. As the time information representing different frames is considered, the available information is enriched than the single image. Our method takes the global character into account for avoiding visual inconsistencies. We view the video completion problem as a labeling problem and apply the belief propagation algorithm to minimize the energy defined on the label graph. By measuring the similarity between source and target patches, we could discover the appropriate patch to fill the hole. Furthermore, we introduce some techniques to speedup the belief propagation algorithm for gaining better performance efficiency. Examples demonstrate the effectiveness of our approach and the results are encouraging.

1 Introduction

Active object removal, also called video completion, has many versatile applications in the movie industry for producing special montage effects. The objects could be removed and placed anywhere arbitrarily. The left hole after removal in a frame is completed by background information on the same or other frames. Object removal is a key technique in a variety of research areas. It has been emerged to be a high level understanding task of low level vision content. By means of this technique, most annoying tasks could be automatically achieved very well without human intervention.

There are some mature methods for active object removal. Sand and Telle [7] use two video sequences to match features frame by frame. Bhat et al. [1] extract a moving object from a video sequence by making a mosaic image of the scene. Wexler et al. [9] addresses a problem of completing a moving object which is partly occluded in a video sequence. They use a stationary camera to obtain the video frame. They complete the occluded object areas by filling empty holes with space-time patches which have spatio-temporal consistency. Zhang et al. [10] separate foreground and background objects in multiple motion layers to extract a moving foreground object. The layers are non-overlapping and each of them is completed separately. Although the result is approving but it could not deal with the instance while transformation between frames. There are still some difficulties to be solved, such as visual and time inconsistencies, blurring and artifacts phenomena, etc.

H. Zha et al. (Eds.): VSMM 2006, LNCS 4270, pp. 184–193, 2006.

Our approach is example based texture synthesis. We firstly introduce spatial temporal concept for better operating video sequence. Then we present a well-suited similarity measurement to depict the difference between patches. By speedup belief propagation algorithm, we minimize the energy defined on the 3D graph and advance the procedure by copying the appropriate sample patches from source region to target region. Our technique relates to those used in space-time video completion [9], video object cut and paste [6], image completion with structure propagation [8], motion detection and segmentation [1], video matching [7], and motion layer based object removal in videos [10].

The remaining part of this paper is organized as follows: In section 2, we produce some definitions such as 3-dimension spatial-temporal concept and the difference between two spatial-temporal patches. Section 3 construct a 3D graph and present an energy function defined in this graph. Next we use belief propagation algorithm to minimize the energy and employ speedup technique to accelerate the algorithm execution. Detail experimental results and effect comparison are shown in section 4.

2 Definition

Since video sequences contain dynamic objects correlated with time info, we could combine the space info with time info to an all-in-one framework. We adopt the space-time method [9] to illustrate the content. We extend the planar coordinate in each frame to a cubic coordinate by adding one dimension of time info. Thus, a pixel in the video sequences is denoted as $o(x, y, t)$ instead of $o(x, y)$. Given an input video sequence K, the hole is defined a target region R due to removal of unwanted objects, and a source region S which is subset of K-R.

Definition 1 spatial-temporal coordinate is defined as:
2D planar coordinate: $o(x, y)$ ->3D spatial-temporal coordinate: $o(x, y, t)$

Definition 2 the global visual coherence is defined as:
If each spatial-temporal patch in one video sequence V_1 can be found in other video sequence V_2, then we call the two sequences are global visual coherence.

We hope the missing portion can be filled well, however, how to say the result sequence is better? So we use the definition above to solve the problem. Since we use the video portion of known region S to fill in the unknown region R, we should seek the maximum similarity between region R and S.

Definition 3 the attribute of spatial-temporal pixel is defined as:
In a planar image, we usually take into account the color info of pixels, and it is effective for image completion. However, the video sequence has not only those but also the time information. Since the objects motion along the time is high sensitive to human eyes, we couldn't only take care of the common attribute. In fact, the object motion continuity is more important than the spatial color attribute.

Due to the reason above, an extended attribute is proposed as follows:
Set F for the video sequence containing the gray intensity and the spatial-temporal point is $o(x, y, t)$. Then the spatial and temporal derivatives is (F_x, F_y, F_t). Thus the

horizontal motion can be characterized as: $u = \dfrac{F_t}{F_x}$, this attribute can be used to depict the instantaneous motion along the x direction. The vertical motion can be characterized as: $v = \dfrac{F_t}{F_y}$, and this attribute can be used to depict the instantaneous motion along the y direction. Finally, combining the new two attribute with original color attribute, we can get a 5-dimensional attribute for the ST point: (r, g, b, u, v).

Definition 4 the distance and similarity is defined as:
To estimate the similarity between two ST patches, a straightforward way is to extend the common Sum of Squared Difference (SSD) of color attribute to a new one including time information. Based on the definition 3, we can realize it. Let two ST patches as P_s and P_t, we can get the distance:

$$d(P_s, P_r) = \sum_{(x,y,t)} \left\| P_s(x, y, t) - P_r(x, y, t) \right\|^2 \tag{1}$$

$P_s(x, y, t)$ and $P_t(x, y, t)$ are the attribute vector (r, g, b, u, v) of each pixel on patch P_s and P_t respectively.

Definition 5 the similarity measurement is defined as:
A well-suited similarity measurement between patches is the heart of the algorithm that directly influences the final completion result. The exponential similarity of two patches can be derived from the distance defined in definition 4, and the detail expression can be shown as follows:

$$s(P_s, P_r) = e^{\dfrac{-d(P_s, P_r)}{2\sigma^2}} \tag{2}$$

The σreflects noise, it set to 5/255 graylevels.

3 Object Removal

3.1 3D Graph

Reviewing the image and video completion skills, we can discover that the example-based techniques using texture synthesize have been the most successful in dealing with the completion problem compared to statistical-based or PDE-based methods. In this section, we introduce the texture propagation algorithm. The problem we address is how to synthesize the unknown region by using sample patches in the known region. As noted above, by obtaining the motion parameters from the 5D vector (r, g, b, u, v), we can reduce the portion of the video to search for matching the unknown region.

Based on definition 2, the completion result is satisfied if and only if the two criterions are satisfied:

1) For every ST point o all the ST patches $P_{o1}...P_{ok}$ which contain it agree on the color value at o.
2) All those $P_{o1}...P_{ok}$ appear in the dataset S (known region).

Let o be an unknown point and $o \in R$. Let $C = \{P_{o1}, ..., P_{ok}\}$ be all those ST patches containing o. Let $D = \{P_{r1}, ..., P_{rk}\}$ be the patches in S that are most similarity to $C = \{P_{o1}, ..., P_{ok}\}$ according to equation (2). Then our work is made clearly. We need only search appropriate patches in D to fill the unknown region R, and avoid much unnecessary computing to search the whole video sequence. It gives high efficiency. We set the patch size in the patches set D as 5×5×5, thus there are 125 different patches involve point o. We can transform this patch as larger patch whose center locates at o. So the new patch size is 9×9×9. Thus we reassign the patch set D as $D = \{D(1), D(2), ..., D(n)\}$.

Unlike Wexler's [9] approach, we consider the region propagation in video sequence as a graph labeling problem, where each patch in the video sequence is assigned a unique label. We construct a 3D graph $G = <V, A>$ on the video sequence. V is the node set of ST points in the unknown region, and we set the points $\{o_i\}_{i=1}^m$ as the node of V. The arc set A contains two kinds of arcs: intra-frame arcs A_I connecting adjacent nodes in one frame; inter-frame arcs A_O connecting adjacent nodes across adjacent frames. The intra-frame arcs A_I are constructed by connecting adjacent nodes in one frame, and the inter-frame arcs A_O are constructed by connecting each node to each other node in the adjacent frame $f_{t\pm1}$. The interval of sample patches in D is set to half of the planar patch size to guarantee sufficient overlaps.

For each unknown point o_i, we find a label $l_i \in \{1, 2, ..., n\}$ corresponding to one of the patches in D. Then we just fill the color info of selected patch $D(l_i)$ to the point o_i.

3.2 Energy in Graph

The energy function on the graph G can be defined as follows:

$$E(l) = \sum_{i \in V} E_1(l_i) + \lambda_\alpha \sum_{(i,j) \in A_I} E_2(l_i, l_j) + \lambda_\beta \sum_{(i,j) \in A_O} E_3(l_i, l_j) \tag{3}$$

The E_1 is called likelihood energy and the E_2, E_3 is called prior energy. λ_α and λ_β are relative weights, and their default values are: $\lambda_\alpha = 22$, $\lambda_\beta = 11$. The optimal sample labels $L = \{l_i\}_{i=1}^m$ are obtained by minimizing the energy $E(l)$.
Likelihood energy:

$$E_1(l_i) = \psi_\alpha E_\alpha(l_i) + \psi_\beta E_\beta(l_i) \tag{4}$$

E_1 measures the conformity of the color of o_i to the color of known patch $D(l_i)$. The ψ_α and ψ_β are relative weights. The $E_\alpha(l_i)$ denotes the similarity between the sample patch and the node i in unknown region. Its function term is shown as:

$$E_\alpha(l_i) = \sum_{z \in q^2} s_i \|c(i+z) - c(l_i + z)\|^2 \tag{5}$$

The s_i is the robust parameter that weights the color contrast according to equation (2). $c(i + z)$ and $c(l_i + z)$ are color of point and the q is the area size of patch.

$E_\beta(l_i)$ constrains the synthesized patches on the boundary of unknown region R to match well with the known point in S. $E_\beta(l_i)$ is the sum of the normalized squared differences (SSD) calculated in out of the region R on boundary patches. The portion of $E_\beta(l_i)$ in region R is set to zero.

The prior energy E_2 and E_3 constrains the coherence between adjacent synthesized patches $D(l_i)$ and $D(l_i)$, where l_i and l_j are labels for adjacent nodes. E_2 measure color differences between two adjacent regions in the same frame, and the third term E_3 measures color differences between two adjacent patches in two adjacent frames, and embeds temporal coherence in the optimization process through intra-frame arcs A_I. In a similar fashion, the pair-wise potential $E_{ij}(l, l')$, due to placing patches l, l' over neighbors o_i, o_j, will measure how well these patches agree at the resulting region of overlap and will again be given by the equation similar to equation 5. In fact, E_2 and E_3 are penalty when adjacent nodes are assigned with different labels.

3.3 Energy Minimization

Previously many works such as Criminisi et al. [3] and Drori et al. [4] use greedy way to fill the holes in image or video. Those methods often lead to visual inconsistencies. Belief propagation is an inference algorithm for graphical models containing continuous, non-Gaussian random variables. BP is a specific instance of a general class of methods that exist for approximate inference in Bayes Nets (variational methods) or Markov Random Field.

Belief propagation can be classed as two types of max-product and sum-product. The former maximizes the posterior of each node whereas the latter computes the marginal posterior of each node. With the method [8], the negative log probabilities term can be presented as algorithm 1:

Algorithm 1: video completion with belief propagation

1　Initialize all messages $M_{ij}^0 = 0$ between any two adjacent nodes i and j in graph G.

2　Update all messages M_{ij}^t iteratively from $t = 1$ to T:

$$M_{ij}^t = \min_{l_i}\{E_1(l_i) + E_2(l_i,l_j) + E_3(l_i,l_j) + \sum_{k \neq j,(k,i) \in A} M_{ki}^{t-1}\}$$

3　The optimal label $\hat{l}_i$ for each node i:

$$\hat{l}_i = \arg\min_{l_i}\{E_1(l_i) + \sum_{(k,i) \in A} M_{ki}^T\}$$

We define an n-element vector M_{ij} to denote the message sent from node o_i to node o_j. The vector M_{ij} indicates how likely node o_i thinks that node o_j should be assigned label l_j. The detail process has been shown as the algorithm above. After the optimal labels $\{\hat{l}_i\}_{i=1}^m$ are computed, we simply fill the color of $D(\hat{l}_i)$ to each node o_i.

Belief propagation is based on the criterion: Accuracy Sacrifice = Possible Solution. Thus we can conclude it as the following two steps:

1) Simplified Graph Construction
2) Message Passing until convergence

Its core is iterative message updating procedure. BP works by propagating local messages along the nodes in graph. To be mentionable, BP may not converge, however it seems to work well in practice.

3.4 Speedup Technique

The algorithm above looks very nice, however we can see the label set is very large and it will lead to more time consuming. To overcome this defect, we should employ a speed-up technique to obtain better performance. From [5], we find the Potts model [2] is helpful to the purpose, which assume that labelings should be piecewise constant. Let $h(l_i) = E_1(l_i) + \sum_{k \neq j, (k,i) \in A} M_{ki}^{t-1}$. Then we rewrite the algorithm 1 equation 2 as:

$$M_{ij}^t = \min(h(l_i), \min h(l_i) + c, \min h(l_i) + d) \qquad (6)$$

Where c, d is the cost for different labels and they are positive constant.

The technique can reduce the time of computing a message from $O(k^2)$ to $O(k)$, where k is the number of labels. As a result, we can see that the time of computing message update is linear.

4 Experiments and Comparisons

As is well known, the perceived quality of the completed video frames depends on human perception, rather than mathematical measures, so we show some frames extracted from video sequences to demonstrate the effectiveness of our method. In this section, we mainly produce our algorithm result and the comparison with other ones. Video data used in this paper can be downloaded in:

http://www.wisdom.weizmann.ac.il/~vision/VideoCompletion/.

Figure 1 to 4 demonstrate the results from a two-woman video sequence after one woman has been removed. Figure 1,2,3 shows the completion performance with our method and Figure 3,4 indicate the comparison of the effect obtained by our belief propagation based method with the one obtained by other proposed methods. By our method, the left hole can be completed very well even the hole is very large. Figure 5 indicate the completion effect of a lady on seashore. As the red box shows, our method could produce better effect comparison with Wexler's method. Our method avoids the influence of the blurring and ghost artifacts.

Fig. 1. The original image from video "hopping" containing total 240 frames. Top left to bottom right: frame 5, frame 86, frame 118, frame 163. Video data from [9].

Fig. 2. Overview of the frames in which a person is removed from the original frames of Fig. 1. The blank region is the hole to be completed.

(a)

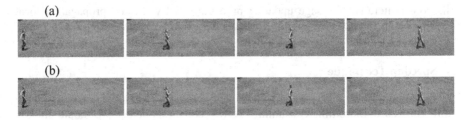

(b)

Fig. 3. Algorithm comparisons. Top row (a) is the result from [9] and bottom row (b) is the result from our approach.

Fig. 4. The zoom-in view of some frames of Fig. 3 around the hole. Left column: results obtained by [9]. Right column: results obtained by our approach.

Fig.4 shows the results of our belief propagation based algorithm on one of the examples used from [9]. As it can be observed by comparing the result from [9] and our completion result, our method does not introduce the edge blur and the ghost artifact. Our result is similar to or slightly better than Wexler's [9].

Fig. 5. The 114th frame of video "crossing_ladies" that contains total 174 frames. Left is result from [9]. Right is result from our method.

We can see differences from the Fig. 5. Small red box shows the lady's foot. The lady's foot in the left image is almost disappeared, while the foot in the right one is better. Big red box shows the lady's skirt. A portion of the skirt in the left image is disappeared, while in the right image, the skirt is preserved better than the left one.

4.1 Comparisons of Time Consuming

According to our spatial temporal derivatives definition and similarity attribution, we can separate moving foreground objects from the background, thus reduce the searching range. However, to the region that each frame has the same pixels such as the still background, there is no need to repeat computing. So in order to decrease unnecessary time consume, we improve our method by avoid searching unrelated fames. We give a definition to decide if a patch belongs to still background:

If in a 5-dimensional attribute representation in definition 3 above, the attribute $u \approx 0$ and $v \approx 0$, then we call the patch belongs to still background and consider the patches of the same position in each frame are the same patch. For example: patch $W_1(x, y, t_1)$ in frame t1, $W_2(x, y, t_2)$ in frame t_2, ..., $W_n(x, y, t_n)$ in frame t_n, if $u \leq h$, $v \leq h$ (h is threshold), we think patch W_1, ..., W_n belong to still background and simply copy the color information of W_1 to other patches with same position in following frames, namely, copy W_1 to patch W_2, ..., W_n directly.

To evaluate the time efficiency of our approach, we experimented with some kinds of video clips and compared their completion time with other approaches.

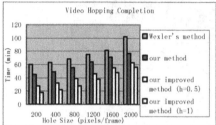
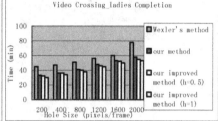

Fig. 6. The time comparison of different completion methods on video hopping

Fig. 7. The time comparison of different completion methods on video crossing_ladies

As can be seen from Fig. 6, the time performance of our improved method is much higher than other one. Because we consider the still background case, if there is few moving object in a video, the time consuming of video completion near image completion. For example, the grass patches in video hopping are seen as still background and we don't repeat computing each frame. However, in Fig. 7, it is not distinct of time consuming between our method and our improved method. The reason of the phenomenon is that the hole on the video crossing_ladies is moving, so there is few patches are seen as still background.

4.2 Comparison Between Video Completion and Image Completion

From Fig. 8, we can see if the patch in hole belongs to still background, such as the grass patch, the result of image completion is good. While the patch in hole belongs to moving object, such as the walking girl, the result of image completion is buggy. Because image completion only search information in one frame, while video completion can obtain available information from other frames.

From Fig.9, a moving car in a video is removed. The experiment result shows that our belief propagation based video completion method can accurately complete the hole induced by moving object removal and the performance of result is encouraging.

Fig. 8. The comparison between video and image completion

Original frame   Car removal frame

Fig. 9. The car is removed from the video

5 Conclusions

We present a novel method for removing the active objects in a video, which is very interesting and useful for movie editing. In view of the video characteristic, especially multi-frame content, the time information introduction is necessary, thus expands the scout scope for breaking through the limitation of example-based techniques. We construct a 3D graph on a video clip which is between two key frames. By iterative steps, we use belief propagation algorithm to minimize the energy defined on the 3D graph. Experiment results show that some previous annoying problems are alleviated or solved.

There are some deficiencies in our method, such as not considering dynamic cameras. It is a challenge work for the background motion and more complex computing. However, it is plenty of applicability in many areas. In the future, we plan to extend the algorithm for dealing with this problem.

Acknowledgement

We would like to thank all that offer assistance to us. This research is supported by the National Grand Fundamental Research 973 Program of China (2002CB312106).

References

1. K. Bhat, M. Saptharishi, and P. Khosla. Motion Detection and Segmentation Using Image Mosaics. IEEE International Conference on Multimedia and Expo, vol. 3, pp. 1577-1580, July, 2000.
2. Y. Boykov, O. Veksler, and R. Zabih. Fast approximate energy minimization via graph cuts. IEEE Transactions on Pattern Analysis and Machine Intelligence, 23(11):1222–1239, 2001.
3. A. Criminisi, P. P´erez, and K. Toyama. Object removal by exemplar-based inpainting. In CVPR, 2003.
4. I. Drori, D. Cohen-Or, and H. Yeshurun. Fragment-based image completion. In ACM TOG. SIGGRAPH, 2003.
5. P.F. Felzenszwalb, D.P. Huttenlocher. Efficient belief propagation for early vision. IEEE Conference on Computer Vision and Pattern Recognition. Volume 1. (2004) 261–268.
6. Y. Li, J. Sun , H.-Y. Shum. Video object cut and paste, ACM Transactions on Graphics (TOG), v.24 n.3, July 2005
7. P. Sand and S. Teller. Video Matching,. ACM Transactions on Graphics, vol. 22, no. 3, pp.592-599, July 2004.
8. J. Sun, L. Yuan, J. Jia, and H.-Y. Shum. Image completion with structure propagation. In SIGGRAPH, 2005.
9. Y. Wexler, E. Shechtman, M. Irani. Space-Time Video Completion. IEEE Conference on Computer Vision and Pattern Recognition (CVPR'04), vol 1, pp. 120-127, July 2004.
10. Y. Zhang, J. Xiao, M. Shah. Motion Layer Based Object Removal in Videos. IEEE Workshop on Application on Computer Vision, Jan 5-6, Breckenridge, Colorado, 2005.

Object-Based Image Recoloring Using Alpha Matte and Color Histogram Specification

Xuezhong Xiao[1], Lizhuang Ma[1], and Marco Kunze[2]

[1] Shanghai Jiao Tong University, China
[2] DAI-Labor, TU Berlin, Germany

Abstract. With the increasing popularity of digital cameras, image editing tools for amateur users are needed. Patrick Pérez and his colleagues generalized that image editing tasks concern either global changes or local changes confined to a selection[1]. Here we focus on local editing of images' color—object-based image recoloring.

In this paper, we introduce a framework for recoloring destination region (desired object) with desired color, which integrates alpha matting and compositing and color transformation algorithms to provide an object-based recoloring tool for common users. There are three steps in the framework: matte extraction, color transformation and alpha compositing. We present a fast color histogram specification as a general method for example-based color transformation. In some cases, our framework to the recoloring problem are quite simple but' works well. We thus feel that the primary contribution of this paper may lie in the organic integration of algorithms totally.

1 Introduction

With the increasing popularity of digital cameras, common users have more and more personal photos. Therefore, image editing tools for amateur users are needed. Patrick Pérez and his colleagues generalized that image editing tasks concern either global changes or local changes confined to a selection[1]. The local changes are given attention because local algorithms can easily extend to global conditions. Here we focus on local image's color editing—object-based image recoloring.

Object-based image recoloring means replacing the destination region's color with a desired one through simple user interaction, and usually the destination region is a meaningful object. It can be considered as a mapping between two three-dimensional color spaces. Conceptually, recoloring includes colorization [2,3], and color-to-gray operation[4,5], if we consider gray-scale image as a special case of color image. Nevertheless, colorization and color-to-gray operation are either one-to-three or three-to-one mappings. The three processing types should be dealt with differently because of their different mathematical essence. Here we focus on the three-to-three mapping of recoloring.

In this paper, we present a framework for recoloring objects in color images, which can be conveniently used by amateur users with effortless interaction and

H. Zha et al. (Eds.): VSMM 2006, LNCS 4270, pp. 194–203, 2006.

produce elaborate results. Traditional image editing tools, e.g Adobe Photoshop CS2, provide a set of tools which can be utilized to recolor images but need more user effort and result in visible seam. To the best of our knowledge, there aren't any publications which have systematically introduced this object-based image recoloring.

Our framework follows the workflow: selecting desired object, then recoloring this object, and last compositing the recolored region with the rest. We contend that there are two key points to this recoloring framework:

- **Effortless user interaction:** The necessary user interaction is needed because it is still far beyond current capabilities of image processing to provide a fully automatic segmentation algorithm. Convenient user interaction can increase the efficiency and keep users' interest.
- **High accuracy:** Apparently, high accuracy is always the goal of many image editing tools. Here the high accuracy means the recoloring result can fit users' desire and is merged seamlessly into the original image.

We incorporate the two key points into our framework that integrates alpha matting and compositing method and color transformation algorithm to provide a tool for object-based image recoloring. The alpha matting and compositing methods can provide an efficient and accurate tool for object selection and the final merging. We propose a fast color transformation method by color histogram specification for recoloring image objects according to users' roughly selection of example image, which needs effortless user interaction.

In some cases, our framework for the recoloring problem is quite simple but works well. We thus feel that the primary contribution of the paper may lie in the seamless integration of the algorithms into one framework, but no so much in technical solutions.

2 Related Work

Image recoloring belongs to the category of image editing. Perez et al.[1] introduced a variety of novel tools for seamless editing of image regions including objects insertion, feature exchange and so on. They also tried to do local color changes, but their results never reach perfect level. As they said in their paper, there is some residual contamination of the destination image outside the object.

Colorization[2,3] and color-to-gray operation[4,5] are closely related with image recoloring because we can consider grayscale image as a special case of color image. Nevertheless, they have different mathematical essences as depicted above. Levin et al.[3] provided several examples of recoloring, but their method does not use real three-to-three mapping. Furthermore, this approach needs professional or experienced persons to deal with the scribbles and their color. Figure 1 shows color pervasion when scribbles' color is changed.

Segmentation is a long established research area in image processing[6] and had been payed attention to by computer graphics community, e.g Graphcut

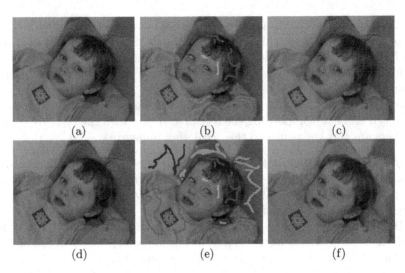

(a)   (b)   (c)

(d)   (e)   (f)

Fig. 1. The color pervasion (the red pane in f) when scribbles' color are changed (b, e): the contrast between the results (c, f) of different scribbles' color when the source image is the same (a, d)

textures[7], Lazy snapping[5] and a large number of other papers which we do not mention here because they are less related to our method. Segmentation algorithms can be utilized to recolor target regions but result in obvious seams[1]. Other methods, such as feathering, also cannot produce satisfying results.

Alpha matting and compositing occupy an important position in our framework. Porter and Duff introduced the alpha component into images' representation and presented the famous compositing equation[9]. Then the alpha component and compositing equation was widely used in blue-screen matting[10], environment matting and compositing [11,12,13], shadow matting and Compositing [14], video matting[15], and natural image matting[16,17,18,19,20,21,22]. From these works, we can see that alpha matting and compositing is a huge research area and has exhibited its powerful vitality. We believe alpha matting and compositing will be used in more wide area. Our framework utilizes alpha matting and compositing through the process from object selection to recoloring the target object. Actually, we use poisson matting[20] in the implementation of our framework. Sun et al. formulated the problem of natural image matting as one of solving Poisson equations with the matte gradient field, and so it was called Poisson matting. It provided global and local operators which can produce elaborated and user-desired results.

Color histogram specification is also an important component in our framework. It is always a intractable problem because of the correlation between the three color components. Grundland and Dodgson introduced a effective color histogram specification method by utilizing histogram warping transformation. But their algorithm needs more computation.

Our method is similar to Irony et al.'s[23], but their algorithm focuses on colorization and their classifier can not be appropriate for general conditions.

3   Our Framework

As mentioned in Section 1, our framework integrates alpha matting and compositing method and color histogram specification algorithm to provide a tool for object-based image recoloring. Figure 2 shows the overview diagram of our approach. There are three steps in image recoloring:

- **Matte extraction:** This step will produce the matte and the desired object's color. First, the user paints a trimap which segments the input image as three parts: the foreground, background and unknown areas, marked by red, blue and green, respectively. The user-desired object which will be recolored is contained in the foreground and unknown areas. Then, a matting algorithm is executed to extract the desired object's alpha matte and color.
- **Color transformation:** Then, the user takes an example image or its portion as a sample for color transformation, and then the object's color is transformed by color histogram specification algorithm according to the user specified sample.
- **Alpha compositing:** Last, the transformed region is seamlessly composited with other regions using the alpha matte obtained in the first step.

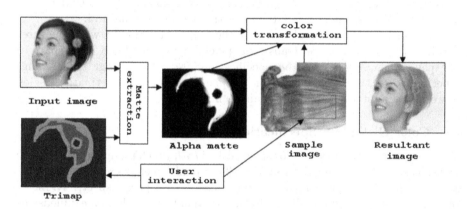

Fig. 2. An overview of our framework for object-based recoloring: There are four components in the process: user interaction, matte extraction, color transformation, and alpha matte compositing. User interaction involves trimap painting and swatch selection which are both simple. First, the accurate matte is extracted according to users' interaction. Then, the transformation of the destination region's color is executed. Last, the transfered region is composited with other regions using the matte gained in the first step.

Apparently, there are four important components in the process: user interaction, matte extraction, color transformation, and alpha matte compositing. User interaction involves trimap painting and sample selection which are both very simple. In actual implementation, we use the poisson matting to extract matte and the desired object's color[20]. Sun et al. formulated the problem of natural image matting as one of solving Poisson equations with the matte gradient field, and provided two operator: the global operator produces a primary matte and the local operator can be used to refine it to an accurate one.

We introduce the color transformation and alpha compositing algorithms in the following section.

4   Color Transformation by Color Histogram Specification

Our color transformation by color histogram specification is inspired by Welsh et al.'s work[2]. They presented a general technique for colorizing gray-scale images by transfering color between a source, color image and a destination, gray-scale image. Their method is a general, fast and user-friendly one. Naturally, transfering color between two color images is considered, which is Reinhard and his colleagues' work before Welsh et al. Reinhard et al.'s method is essentially a color moments-based transformation involving translation and scaling. They utilized the least correlation between the three axes in $l\alpha\beta$ color space to manipulate the transformation on three color components separately. Their method is simple and fast and can produce satisfying result in many cases. But there is one shortcoming: their method can result in truncation errors, since the performed operations might compute color values out of the color domain. Under some extreme conditions, the result of the color transfer looks unnatural.

Our color transformation also utilizes the least correlation between the three axes in $l\alpha\beta$ color space, and transforms pixel values from RGB color space to $l\alpha\beta$ space. Then a color histogram specification (also called histogram matching) is performed on the three components of pixel values of the destination region between the input image and the example image (the sample).

4.1   Color Histogram Specification

Ruderman et al. developed a color space, called $l\alpha\beta$, which minimizes correlation between channels for many natural scenes[25]. Reinhard et al's research approves the feasibility of manipulating on the three axes of $l\alpha\beta$ space respectively. In the following, we just depict one-dimensional condition because the three dimensions can be splitted to three one-dimensional instances.

The pixel values in an image may be viewed as random variables. We use random variables r and s to denote the destination region in the input image and the sample in the example image, respectively. One of the most fundamental descriptors of a random variable is its probability density function. Let $p(r)$ and $f(s)$ denote the probability density functions of random variables r and s, respectively.

Our goal is to find a transformation function $T(r)$ which maps r to s, so the transformed color will look like the sample. We assume that the transformation function $T(r)$ satisfies a condition: $T(.)$ is single-valued and monotonically increasing in r's definition domain. In our method, we specify $[l_r, h_r]$ and $[l_s, h_s]$ as the definition domains of r and s. l_r, h_r, l_s and h_s are the minimum and maximum values in the current data set.

(a) Source image   (b) Target image

(c) Our result   (d) Reinhard's

(e) Source image   (f) Target image

(g) Our result   (h) Reinhard's

Fig. 3. The contrast between our method's results and Reinhard method's results

A basic result from an elementary probability theory is that, if $p(r)$ and $T(r)$ are known and satisfies the above single-valued and monotonically increasing condition, the probability density function $f(s)$ can be obtained using a rather simple formula:

$$f(s) = p(r)|\frac{dr}{ds}|$$

We sort the data set in ascending order, so we get the following equation:

$$\int_{l_s}^{s} f(s)ds = \int_{l_r}^{r} p(r)dr \tag{1}$$

According to Equation 1, our statistics-based color transformation algorithm is depicted as follows:

- Obtain the cumulative distribution density functions $F(s)$ and $P(r)$.
- Interpolate $F^{-1}(\cdot)$ for every F corresponding P but without value in $F(s)$ between F_{min} and F_{max}. The F value corresponding a P can be calculated according the formula: $F = P \cdot \frac{n_r}{n_s}$, while n_r and n_s are the total pixel number in the input destination region and the sample, respectively.
- For every pixel's value in the input destination region, find $F^{-1}(P(r))$.

After the transformation in $l\alpha\beta$ color space, we convert the values back to RGB color space.

Figure 3 contrasts two groups of our results with Reinhard's in the case of a global transfer. The Reinhard's results are produced by a program implemented by us according to their paper[24]. Our method has not any truncation error because the calculation is not beyond the boundary. The difference between the results of the two algorithms is obvious.

5   Alpha Compositing

The compositing operation is implemented in RGB space, which follows the famous compositing equation:

$$C = \alpha \cdot c_{ob} + (1 - \alpha) \cdot c_{re} \tag{2}$$

While c_{ob} and c_{re} denote the transformed pixel color and the original pixel color, respectively; α is the alpha matte; C denotes the compositing color.

6   Results and Discussion

As depicted in the above sections, we use existing or simple algorithms to implement the framework. We use the poisson matting to extract the accurate alpha matte because its local operators can conveniently produce refined results.

Our fast color transformation method essentially is a color histogram specification algorithm. It utilizes the least correlation between the three components

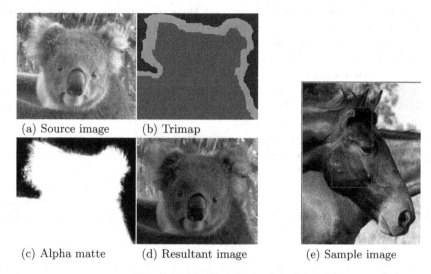

(a) Source image   (b) Trimap

(c) Alpha matte   (d) Resultant image   (e) Sample image

Fig. 4. Recoloring the koala's fur

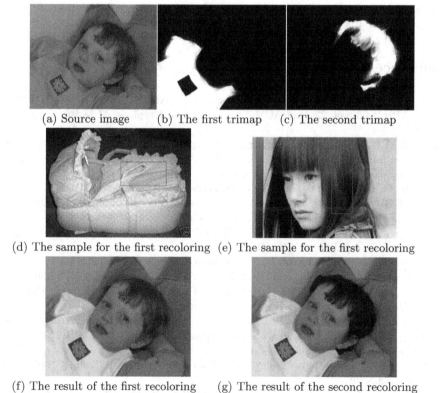

(a) Source image   (b) The first trimap   (c) The second trimap

(d) The sample for the first recoloring (e) The sample for the first recoloring

(f) The result of the first recoloring   (g) The result of the second recoloring

Fig. 5. Recoloring the baby's cloth and hair through two processing

in $l\alpha\beta$ color space and converts the complex three dimensional mapping as three one dimensional transformation. It deals with fractional data and escapes from truncation errors which may occur in Reinhard's approach. Figure 3 shows that our color transformation algorithm can produce believable results which have the effects of enhancement.

In Figure 2, we can see that our framework is simple but works well. User interaction in the framework includes painting the trimap and specifying the sample which are easy and effortless.

Our framework integrates the user interaction, matte extraction, color transformation and alpha compositing as a whole. Figure 4 and 5 shows several convincing results produced by the framework.

We observe that our method converts the sample's feel and look to the selected object but not the textures, e.g., the baby's cloth has not got the sample's dot pattern in Figure 5. Therefore, the framework will be more powerful after adding the function of texture transfer.

Acknowledgements

This work was supported in part by national natural science foundation of China (Grants No. 60403044 and No. 60573147).

References

1. Pérez P., Gangnet M., Blake A.: Poisson image editing. In Proceedings of SIG-GRAPH 2003, vol. 22(3) of ACM Transactions on Graphics, ACM Press, pp. 313-318.
2. Welsh T., Ashikhmin M., Mueller K.: Transferring color to greyscale images. In Proceedings of SIGGRAPH 2002, Hughes J., (Ed.), Annual Conference Series, ACM Press/ACM SIGGRAPH, pp. 277-280.
3. Levin A., Lischinski D., Weiss Y.: Colorization using optimization. In Proceedings of SIGGRAPH 2004, vol. 23(3) of ACM Transactions on Graphics, pp. 689-694.
4. Gooch A. A., Olsen S. C., Tumblin J., Gooch B.: Color2Gray: salience-preserving color removal. In Proceedings of ACM SIGGRAPH 2005, vol. 24(3) of ACM Transactions on Graphics, pp. 634-639.
5. Rasche K., Geist R., Westall J.: Detail preserving reproduction of color images for monochromats and dichromats. j-IEEE-CGA 25, 3 (May/June 2005), 22-30.
6. Gonzalez R. C., Woods R. E.: Digital Image Processing (Second Edition). Publishing House of Electronics Industry and Prentice Hall, 2002.
7. Kwatra V., Schodl A., Essa I. A., Turk G., Bobick A. F.: Graphcut textures: image and video synthesis using graph cuts. In Proceedings of SIGGRAPH 2003, ACM Trans. Graph 22, 3 (2003), 277-286.
8. Li Y., Sun J., Tang C.-K., Shum H.-Y.: Lazy snapping. ACM Trans. Graph 23, 3 (2004), 303-308.
9. Porter T., Duff T.: Compositing digital images. Computer Graphics 18-3 (July 1984), 253-259.
10. Smith A. R., Blinn J. F.: Blue screen matting. In SIGGRAPH (1996), pp. 259-268.

11. Zongker D. E., Werner D. M., Curless B., Salesin D.: Environment matting and compositing. In SIGGRAPH (1999), pp. 205-214.
12. ChuangY.-Y., Zongker D. E., Hindorff J., Curless B., Salesin D. H., Szeliski R.: Environment matting extensions: Towards higher accuracy and real-time capture. In Siggraph 2000, Akeley K., (Ed.).
13. Peers P., Dutre P.: Wavelet environment matting. In Rendering Techniques (2003), pp. 157-166.
14. Chuang Y.-Y., Goldman D. B., Curless B., Salesin D. H., Szeliski R.: Shadow matting and compositing. In Proceedings of ACM SIGGRAPH 2003, vol. 22(3) of ACM Transactions on Graphics, pp. 494-500.
15. Chuang Y.-Y., Agarwala A., Curless B., Salesin D., Szeliski R.: Video matting of complex scenes. ACM Trans. Graph 21, 3 (2002), 243-248.
16. Ruzon M. A., Tomasi C.: Alpha estimation in natural images. In CVPR) (2000), pp. 18-25.
17. Chuang Y.-Y., Curless B., Salesin D., Szeliski R.: A bayesian approach to digital matting. In CVPR (2001), pp. 264-271.
18. Hillman P., Hannah J., Renshaw D.: Alpha channel estimation in high resolution images and image sequences. In CVPR) (2001), pp. 1063-1068.
19. Mitsunaga T., Yokoyama T., Totsuka T.: Autokey: Human assisted key extraction. In Proceedings of SIGGRAPH'95, Cook R., (Ed.), ACM Press, pp. 265-272.
20. Sun J., Jia J., Tang C.-K., Shum H.-Y.: Poisson matting. ACM Trans. Graph 23, 3 (2004), 315-321.
21. A. Levin, D. Lischinski, Y. Weiss. A Closed Form Solution to Natural Image Matting. IEEE Conf. on Computer Vision and Pattern Recognition (CVPR), June 2006, New York
22. Jue Wang and Michael Cohen. An Iterative Optimization Approach for Unified Image Segmentation and Matting. ICCV 2005(oral paper), Beijing, China.
23. Irony R., Cohen-Or D., Lischinski D.: Colorization by example. In Rendering Techniques (2005), pp. 201-210.
24. Reinhard E., Ashikhmin M., Gooch B., Shirley P.: Color transfer between images. IEEE Computer Graphics and Applications 21, 5 (Sept. 2001), 34-41.
25. Ruderman D. L., Cronin T. W., Chin Chiao C.: Statistics of cone responses to natural images:. J. Optical Soc. of America 15, 8 (1998), 2036-2045.

Reconstructing Symmetric Curved Surfaces from a Single Image and Its Application

Jiguo Zeng, Yan Zhang, Shouyi Zhan, and Chen Liu

School of Computer Science and Technology, Beijing Institute of Technology, Beijing, 100081, China

Abstract. Recent advances in single view reconstruction (SVR) have been in modeling 3D curved surfaces and automation. We extend the SVR along the first direction in several ways: (i) We study the reconstruction of curved surfaces under perspective projection rather than orthographic projection. (ii) We illustrate that the horizontally flipped image of the reflective symmetric objects is equivalent to an image photographed from another position under the simplified perspective projection. So the traditional structure from motion techniques can be used to recover the 3D feature points on them. They can be used to create the planar model of the object and be used as position constraints to generate curved surfaces. (iii) New linear constraints, such as perspective projection, are exploited to the linearly constrained quadratic optimization to finding the smoothest surface. We demonstrate these advances in reconstructing real symmetric curved surfaces and objects.

1 Introduction

The rapid development in the fields of virtual reality and electronic game caused relentless increase in demand for 3D models. In this paper, we are interested in the single view reconstruction (SVR): the techniques of creating 3D models from a single image. Recent advances in SVR have been in modeling 3D curved surfaces [1] and automatic photo pop-up [2], which inspired us to study SVR along these directions.

Traditional SVR methods, such as shape from shading, texture and focus, make strong assumptions on shape, reflectance and exposure. So they tend to produce acceptable results for only a restricted class of images. More recent work has shown that moderate user-interaction is highly effective in creating 3D models from a single view. Horry et al. [3] proposed a technique, named tour into the picture, to reconstruct piecewise planar models from paintings or photographs. Subsequent systems [4,5,6] improved the geometric accuracy of SVR.

However, the above systems remained essentially restricted to the scene with strong geometric constraints, such as planarity, orthogonality, parallelism and the geometric property of the surfaces of revolution. These methods [4,5,6] reconstruct more accurate geometry models by exploiting these geometric constraints. For free-form surfaces, Zhang et al. [7] proposed a novel approach to

H. Zha et al. (Eds.): VSMM 2006, LNCS 4270, pp. 204–213, 2006.

generate the smoothest 2.5D Monge patches (or "range image") model satisfying the user-specified constraints. Their main contributions are that they proposed a general constraint mechanism and a convex objective function, which can combine point, curve and normal constraints to yield the smoothest surface. It was an important milestone in SVR of curved surfaces. However, there are several drawbacks: first, the 2.5D Monge patches representation is rather restrictive, representing just one side of the 3D model and always leading to distracting holes near occluding parts. The second weakness is that although the human visual system has the ability to infer 3D shape from a single photograph or painting, but it is hard to input the point depth and the normal accurately. As a result, poor models will be obtained. The third disadvantage is that a considerable user input is required, even for simple models. Prasad et al. [8] extended this scheme by using the standard parametric surface representation and used the silhouettes as the main constraints. The general 3D surfaces representation allows to model truly 3D surfaces rather than 2.5D Monge patches. In addition, silhouettes of the curved surfaces provide more accurate positions and normal constraints under orthographic projection. So the more attractive 3D models can be acquired. More recently, Prasad et al. [1] make a further step to reconstruct the curved smooth surface from its apparent contour in image , including multilocal singularities ("kidney-bean" self-occlusions) and show how to incorporate user-specified data such as surface normals, interpolation and approximation constraints. Compared with the method presented by Zhang et al. [7], curved surface reconstruction method proposed by Prasad et al. [1,8] generates more attractive 3D models with less user interaction. However, there are still some drawbacks: First, it is hard to take the accurate depth estimation in reconstructing general viewpoint images. Second, this method is not able to reconstruct the images with apparent projective distortion. We extend their method by exploiting the reflective symmetric constraints to avoid the above drawbacks and to obtain more accurate curved surfaces.

2   On Symmetry and the Multiple View Geometry

Symmetry is a useful geometric cue to 3D information. Hong et al. [9] provided a principled explanation why symmetry could encode 3D information within a single perspective image. They developed an important principle associated with images of symmetric objects: One image of a symmetric object is equivalent to multiple images. This principle is however not entirely correct since often relationships among such "images" will not be the same as those among conventional images. In fact, it requires careful modifications to existing theories and algorithms in multiple-view geometry if they are to be correctly applied to images of symmetric objects.

However, because we chose a simplified projection model, we can illustrate that the horizontally flipped image of the reflective symmetric objects is equivalent to an image photographed from another corresponding symmetric position. So the existing theories and algorithms in multiple-view geometry can be used to recover the feature points of the objects.

2.1   On Reflective Symmetry and the Multiple View Geometry

A camera is described by the widely used pinhole model.The coordinates of a
3D point $M = [X, Y, Z]^T$ in a world coordinate system and its retinal image
coordinates $m = [u, v]^T$ are related by

$$\lambda[u, v, 1]^T = K[R|t][X, Y, Z, 1]^T, \tag{1}$$

where λ is an arbitrary scale, and (R, t) is the 3D displacement (rotation and
translation) from the world coordinate system to the camera coordinate system.
Assume that the skew parameter is zero, the aspect ratio is one and the principal
point is on the image center, then the intrinsic parameters matrix K can be
illustrated as Eq.(2).

$$K = \begin{bmatrix} f & 0 & I_w/2 \\ 0 & f & I_h/2 \\ 0 & 0 & 1 \end{bmatrix}, \tag{2}$$

where f is the focus, I_w is the image width and I_h is the image height.

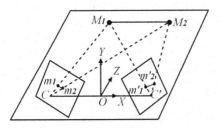

Fig. 1. Photograph the symmetric object from symmetric positions

Consider the case of two cameras as shown in Fig. 1. Let C and C' be the
optical centers of the first and second cameras, respectively. $OXYZ$ is the world
coordinate system. Given a single image of the reflective symmetric objects, the
orientation and position of the first camera is determined. So we place the world
coordinate system $OXYZ$ according to two principles: (1) the plane YOZ is the
reflective symmetric plane of the object; (2) the optical centre of the first camera
is on the axis OX.

The first camera coordinate system can be obtained by rotating the world
coordinate system an angle α along the axis OX and rotating it an angle $-\beta$
along OY, then by translating it $-t_X$ along the initial OX. So the rotation and
translation can be illustrated as follows.

$$R = \begin{bmatrix} \cos\beta & -\sin\alpha\sin\beta & -\cos\alpha\sin\beta \\ 0 & \cos\alpha & -\sin\alpha \\ \sin\beta & \sin\alpha\cos\beta & \cos\alpha\cos\beta \end{bmatrix}, \quad t = -R[-t_X \quad 0 \quad 0]^T \tag{3}$$

The second camera coordinate system is obtained by rotating the world coordinate system an angle α along OX and rotating it an angle β along OY, then
by translating it t_X along the initial OX. The displacement corresponding to
the second camera can be illustrated as the Eq.(4).

$$R' = \begin{bmatrix} \cos\beta & \sin\alpha\sin\beta & \cos\alpha\sin\beta \\ 0 & \cos\alpha & -\sin\alpha \\ -\sin\beta & \sin\alpha\cos\beta & \cos\alpha\cos\beta \end{bmatrix}, \quad t' = -R'[-t_X \quad 0 \quad 0]^T \quad (4)$$

Given a pair of symmetric points, $M_1(-X, Y, Z)$ and $M_2(X, Y, Z)$, their image points in the first image and second image can be denoted as $m_1(u_1, v_1)$, $m_2(u_2, v_2)$, $m_1'(u_1', v_1')$, $m_2'(u_2', v_2')$. So we have:

$$\begin{cases} \lambda_1[u_1, v_1, 1]^T = K[R|t][-X, Y, Z, 1]^T \\ \lambda_2[u_2, v_2, 1]^T = K[R|t][X, Y, Z, 1]^T \\ \lambda_1'[u_1', v_1', 1]^T = K[R'|t'][-X, Y, Z, 1]^T \\ \lambda_2'[u_2', v_2', 1]^T = K[R'|t'][X, Y, Z, 1]^T \end{cases} \quad (5)$$

From Eq. (5), the relations between the m_1' and m_2, m_2' and m_1 respectively can be inferred.

$$\begin{cases} (u_1', v_1') = (I_w - u_2, v_2) \\ (u_2', v_2') = (I_w - u_1, v_1) \end{cases} \quad (6)$$

The Eq. (6) theoretically shows that the image point of the second camera is equivalent to the horizontally flipped image point of the corresponding symmetric space point in the first image. Example of real image is illustrated in Fig. 2. As a result, the traditional structure from motion techniques can be used to recover the feature points on the objects. 3D planar models can be created from these points, as shown in Fig. 3.

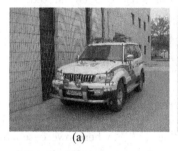 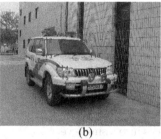

(a)   (b)

Fig. 2. (a) Original image and the feature points. (b) Horizontally flipped image and the corresponding feature points.

2.2   Focus Estimation

As mentioned above, only one parameter in the intrinsic parameters matrix, focus, is unknown. Many self-calibration algorithms can be used to estimate the focus according to the parallel lines in the structure scene [10,11]. Here we can also estimate it directly according to the relationship between the focus and the image size.

$$f = I_h/(2\tan(fov/2)), \quad (7)$$

Fig. 3. Novel views of the recovered planar model

where I_h is the image height, fov is the field of view angle in the vertical direction.

In fact, Bougnoux et al. [12] have illustrated that the reconstructed model doesn't much depend on the camera parameters; this is also the reason of choosing Eq. (7).

3   Smooth Surface Reconstruction Subject to Constraints

3.1   Surface Representation and Generation

Following Prasad et al. [1,8], $r : [0, 1] \mapsto R^3$ is used to represent the standard parametric surface. This representation allows to model truly 3D surfaces rather than 2.5D Monge patches. The continuous surface S is denoted as $r(u, v) = [x(u, v), y(u, v), z(u, v)]^T$. The surface is computed by minimizing a smoothness objective function $E(r)[1,7,8]$.

$$E(r) = \int_0^1 \int_0^1 \| r_{uu} \|^2 + \| r_{uv} \|^2 + \| r_{vv} \|^2 \, dudv \qquad (8)$$

To optimize this we choose a gridded discretization, representing r by three $m \times n$ matrices, X, Y and Z. When solving for the surface, we shall reshape and stack these matrices into a single vector $g = [x^T, y^T, z^T]^T$, where lowercase x represents the reshaping of X into a column vector. Central difference approximations are used for the first and second derivatives on the surface, and are represented by appropriate matrix operators [1]. Thus the first and the second derivative of the point (i, j) is discretely approximated as

$$\begin{cases} X_u(i,j) = X(i+1,j) - X(i-1,j) \\ X_v(i,j) = X(i,j+1) - X(i,j-1) \\ X_{uu}(i,j) = X(i+1,j) - 2X(i,j) + X(i-1,j) \\ X_{uv}(i,j) = X(i+1,j+1) - X(i,j+1) - X(i+1,j) + X(i,j) \\ X_{vv}(i,j) = X(i,j+1) - 2X(i,j) + X(i,j-1) \end{cases} \qquad (9)$$

This is conveniently represented by a constant $mn \times mn$ matrix C_u such that $x_u = C_u x$. A similar matrix C_v computes the central difference with respect to v.

Similarly, the second derivatives are computed using Hessian operator matrices denoted C_{uu}, C_{uv} and C_{vv}. In terms of these, the bending energy (8) can be expressed in discrete form as a quadratic function of g.

$$\begin{cases} \epsilon(x) = x^T (C_{uu}^T C_{uu} + 2 C_{uv}^T C_{uv} + C_{vv}^T C_{vv}) x \\ E(g) = \epsilon(x) + \epsilon(y) + \epsilon(z) = g^T C_{3mn \times 3mn} g \end{cases} \tag{10}$$

The discrete representation of the front part of the police car is shown as Fig. 4(a).

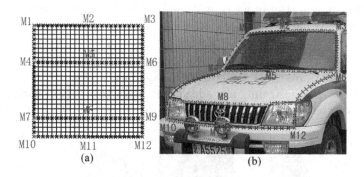

Fig. 4. (a). Discrete representation of the curved surface. (b) Feature curves and the position constraints.

3.2   Constraints

We now introduce linear constraints from the user input of the form $Ag = b$. Without constraints on the surface, the global minimum of $E(r)$ is the singularity $r(u, v) = 0$ [8]. Perspective projection constraints and the plane constraints are new kinds of constraints without mentioned in the previous method [1,7,8].

(1) **Perspective projection constraints.** Generally speaking, we use the first camera coordinate system as the world coordinate system when recovering feature points by structure from motion, so the rotation and translation couldn't be considered. The projection model can be illustrated as the Eq.(11).

$$\lambda \begin{bmatrix} u \\ v \\ 1 \end{bmatrix} = \begin{bmatrix} f & 0 & u_0 & 0 \\ 0 & f & v_0 & 0 \\ 0 & 0 & 1 & 0 \end{bmatrix} \begin{bmatrix} x \\ y \\ z \\ 1 \end{bmatrix} \tag{11}$$

where f is the focus, (u_0, v_0) is the coordinate of the principal point. we can obtain two linear perspective projection constraints as the Eq.(12).

$$\begin{cases} fx + (u_0 - u)z = 0 \\ fy + (v_0 - v)z = 0 \end{cases} \tag{12}$$

As we can see from Fig. 4(b), fourteen feature curves, such as $M1M2$, $M2M3$, $M1M4$ et al., can be acquired from the image of the police car. The discrete image points of these curves are projective constraints as shown in Fig. 4(a).

(2) **Position constraints.** Position constraints are of the form $r(i, j) = [x(i, j), y(i, j), z(i, j)]^T$. There are also partial position constraints act on just one component of r, for example $z(i, j) = z_k$. The z values of the recovered eight feature points,$M1$, $M3$, $M4$, $M6$, $M7$, $M9$, $M10$, $M12$, are partial position constraints as shown in Fig. 4(a).

(3) **Plane Constraints.** The four feature points, $M2, M5, M8, M11$, are on the reflective symmetric plane of the car, as shown in Fig. 4(b). So the plane constraints are added in order to make all points of the curve $u = 1/2$ are on the symmetric plane as Eq.(13).

$$Ax(i, j) + By(i, j) + Cz(i, j) + D = 0 \qquad (13)$$

Where A, B, C, D are the parameters of the symmetric plane.

After all these constraints are added, the attractive curved surface of the police car can be recovered, as shown in Fig. 5.

Fig. 5. Novel views of the recovered curved surface

3.3   Linearly Constrained Quadratic Optimization

All linear constraints can be expressed as $Ag = b$. $E(g)$is a quadratic form and can be expressed as $g^T C g$. Consequently, the linearly constrained quadratic optimization is defined by [7].

$$\begin{cases} g* = \arg\min_{g} \left\{ E(g) = g^T C g \right\} \\ \qquad \text{subject to} \quad Ag = b \end{cases} \qquad (14)$$

The Lagrange multiplier method is used to convert this problem into the following augmented linear system

$$\begin{bmatrix} C & A^T \\ A & 0 \end{bmatrix} \begin{bmatrix} g \\ \lambda \end{bmatrix} = \begin{bmatrix} 0 \\ b \end{bmatrix} \qquad (15)$$

The Hessian matrix C is a diagonally-banded sparse matrix. For a grid of size m by n, C is of size $3mn \times 3mn$. Solution is obtained by using Matlab's sparse backslash operator just as recommended in [1,8].

4   Reconstructing Reflective Symmetric Objects

An image of battleplane obtained from the Internet is used to illustrate the entire process. The image size is 1024×768. Its focus is 1181.83, which is estimated according to the Eq. (7). The feature points are recovered first from the original image and its horizontally flipped image, as shown in Fig. 6. In order to get fine model, more feature points are needed. However, they can't be matched between the two images. So these points can be only recovered according the coplanarity and symmetry constrains from the original image.

Given the camera intrinsic parameters and the image point, the 3D space point can't be uniquely determined by Eq. (11), but it is on the line through the optical center and the image point. If we can find a plane where the space point is on, the 3D position of the point can be uniquely determined. For example, points 2, 3, 12, 13, 14 and 15 are on the same plane as shown in Fig. 6. Given three of them, the plane of them can be determined. So the remainder three points can be determined according the plane. More feature points can be acquired using this principle. As a result, the planar model of the plane can be recovered as shown in Fig. 6(c).

Then we can generate the curved surfaces of the battleplane. The Surface representation is introduced in subsection 3.1, so here only the constraints are introduced. The cockpit is used as an example to illustrate the surfaces' constraints. The feature curve of the cockpit should be first determined as curve A, as shown in Fig. 7(a). Then, n discrete image points are obtained according to the curve A. Assume that all these points are on the plane M1M3M4 or M2M3M4 respectively. Then the n discrete image points of the curve A can be determined, and should be regarded as the position constraints on the curve $u = 3/4$ as shown in Fig. 7(b). Position constraints on the curve $u = 1/4$ can be obtained according to the main reflective symmetric plane. If only the constraints on $u = 1/4$ and $u = 3/4$ are added, then only planar model can be acquired. So inflation point constraints are needed to "inflate" the surface, somewhat like blowing air into it. Five inflation point constraints are added on the curve $u = 1/2$ as shown in Fig. 7(b), which are corresponding to the five points on the main symmetric plane as shown in Fig. 7(a). The five inflation point constraints on the curve $u = 0$ are symmetric points corresponding to the inflation point constraints on the curve $u = 1/2$ according to the plane M1M3M4 or M2M3M4.

In addition to the position constraints mentioned above, Topology constraints [1] should be added. For the plane cockpit of figure 7(a), the points on the $u = 0$ curve are the same points on the $u = 1$ curve. Similarly, their first and second derivatives are also the same.

$$\begin{cases} r(0,v) = r(1,v) & \forall v, \\ r_u(0,v) = r_u(1,v) & \forall v, \\ r_{uu}(0,v) = r_{uu}(1,v) \forall v, etc. \end{cases} \qquad (16)$$

In practice it is simpler to make $X(1,j)$ and $X(m,j)$ neighbors in the derivative computations by modifying the Jacobian operator matrix C_u, as well as the appropriate second derivative operators. Another constraints, $r(u,0) = r(0,0)$

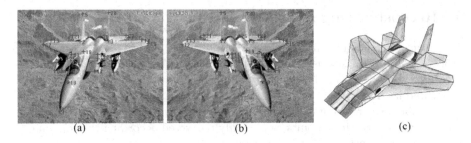

Fig. 6. (a) Original image and the feature points. (b) Horizontally flipped image and the corresponding feature points. (c) Planar model of the battleplane.

and $r(u,1) = r(0,1)$ $\forall u$, should be augmented to ensure that the two ends concentrate on a single point respectively. Now, we can obtain the 3D model of the cockpit, as shown in figure 7(c). Using the same method mentioned above, the missiles and afterbody of the battleplane can be generated according to the curve B and C, as shown in figure 7(a). After all parts of the plane are recovered, the 3D model of the battleplane is created, as shown in figure 8.

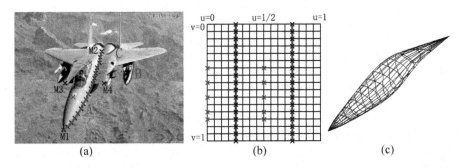

Fig. 7. (a) Feature curves and inflation points. (b) Discrete representation of the cockpit. (c) 3D model of the cockpit.

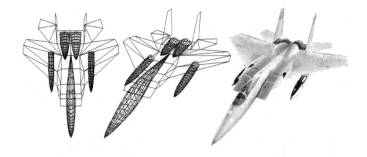

Fig. 8. 3D model of the battleplane

5 Discussion

We extend the previous curved surfaces SVR methods by exploiting the reflective symmetric characteristics. We illustrate that the horizontally flipped image of the reflective symmetric objects is equivalent to an image photographed from another position. So the traditional structure from motion techniques can be used to recover the 3D feature points on them. With the help of these accurate positions, planar parts and curved parts of the objects can be recovered.

However, all the constraints are inputted by user interaction. It is somewhat clumsy and increases the amount of user skill required to determine them. In addition, accurate constraints may not achieve due to noise, so the feature points should be matched carefully by the user. We hope to match the feature points automatically and find ways of determining the constraints easily.

References

1. Prasad, M., Zisserman, A., Fitzgibbon, A.:Single View Reconstruction of Curved Surfaces. Proceedings of CVPR2006. (2006)
2. Hoiem, D., Efros, A. A., Hebert, M.: Automatic Photo Pop-up. ACM Transactions on Graphics. **24** (2005) 577–584
3. Horry, Y., Aniyo, K., Arai, K.: Tour into the Picture: Using a Spidery Mesh Interface to Make Animation from a Single Image. Proceedings of SIGGRAPH97. (1997) 225–232
4. Criminisi, A., Reid, I., Zisserman, A.: Single view metrology. International Journal of Computer Vision. **40** (2000) 123–148
5. Sturm, P., Maybank, S. J.: A method for interactive 3D reconstruction of piecewise planar objects from single images. Proceedings of BMVC. (1999)
6. Colombo, C., Bimbo, A. D., Pernici, F.: Metric 3D reconstruction and texture acquisition of surfaces of revolution from a single uncalibrated view. Pattern Analysis and Machine Intelligence. **27** (2005) 99–114
7. Zhang, L., Dugas-Phocion, G., Samson, J. S., Seitz, S. M.: Single view modeling of free-form scenes. Proceedings of CVPR. (2001) 990–997
8. Prasad, M., Fitzgibbon, A. W., Zisserman, A.: Fast and controllable 3D modelling from silhouette. Proceedings of Eurographics. (2005)
9. Hong, W., Yang, A. Y., Huang, K., Ma, Y.: On Symmetry and Multiple-View Geometry: Structure, Pose, and Calibration from a Single Image. International Journal of Computer Vision. **60** (2004) 241–265
10. Cipolla, R., Drummond, T., Robertson, D.: Camera calibration from vanishing points in images of architectural scenes. Proceedings of BMVC. (1999) 382–391
11. Liu, P., Shi, J., Sun, X.: Reconstruction of Architecture Model by Planar Surfaces. Journal of CAD & CG. **16** (2004) 1045–1050(In chinese)
12. Bougnoux S.: From projective to euclidean space under any practical situationA criticism of self-calibration. Proceedings of ICCV, (1998) 790–796

Constructing 3D Surface from Planar Contours with Grid Adjustment Analysis

Xiaohui Liang, Xiaoxiao Wu, Aimin Liang, and Chuanpeng Wang

Key Laboratory of Virtual Reality Technology of Ministry of Education,
School of Computer Sciences, BeiHang University, 100083, Beijing, P.R.China
lxh@vrlab.buaa.edu.cn

Abstract. This paper researches the method of constructing 3D surface from planar contours. We base our work on distance field function method and mainly concentrate on how to simply and uniformly solve the problems of isosurface generation caused by non-manifold surface. Our work includes three main steps: grid adjustment analysis, volume construction and surface construction. In the first step, we present a new method to process non-manifold contour by adaptively adjusting grid size. In the volume construction and the surface construction steps, we use classic distance field function and Marching Cube method respectively. The experiment shows that our algorithm has more realistic results in constructing 3D surface from planar contour.

1 Introduction

Constructing 3D surface from planar contours is a research aspect of Visualization in Scientific Computing (ViSC). Because the contour data can represent many kinds of objects, such as terrain, etc, many researchers have studied in this field. In general, the work can be divided into two categories:

- Direct Method. This method uses the contours directly and tries to generate a surface by connecting the vertices of adjacent contours [1]. There are three main problems to be solved in this method:
  - Correspondence. How to connect vertices between contours.
  - Tilling. How to create meshes from these edges.
  - Branching. How to cope with slices with different numbers of contours.
- Indirect Method. This method uses the contours indirectly[2][3]. It first generates volume data from the contours using a field function. Then the 3D surface can be generated using classic Marching Cube [4] algorithm. There are two main problems to be solved in this method:
  - Precision. How to reflect the object accurately.
  - Speed. How to generate the volume data quickly.

After the 3D surface is generated, it can be rendered to show the 3D shape of the contours.

In the two methods above, the indirect method has many advantages because it avoids the problems occurring in the direct method by using volume data to

H. Zha et al. (Eds.): VSMM 2006, LNCS 4270, pp. 214–221, 2006.

represent contours and the technologies to generate surface from volume data are mature. Furthermore, in indirect method the surface can also not be generated, the shape of contour can be displayed using direct volume rendering (DVR) algorithms, such as raycasting, footprint etc. Because the development of graphic hardware is very fast and hardware accelerated volume rendering [5][6] has received more and more attention, real time rendering of the volume generated in indirect method is feasible for contour data .

The pipeline of 3D surface construction from contours is shown in Figure 1.

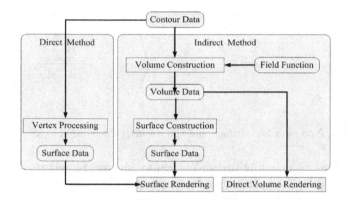

Fig. 1. The Pipeline of constructing surface and rendering from contour data

The two main components of indirect method are the distance field function definition and the density of grid. In fact, the research of distance field function is an important aspect of computer graphics[7]. It can be used in object representation, rendering, metamorphosis etc. Using distance field function to construct volume from contour field also has a long history. Jones [2] defined a distance field function to get a much more satisfactory surface. He also suggested that voronoi diagrams and state function of grid points can be used to minimize the computation needed for calculating the 2D distance field function on a slice. Klein [8] used hardware to accelerate the field function calculation. Kobbelt [9] gave a method of representing special features on surface in a volume sampled distance field by applying a directed distance function. Perry [10] proposed adaptive sampling of distance fields to accelerate rendering, Yamazaki [11][12] used segmented distance field to correct the mistakes caused by non-manifold surface. Nilsson [13] gave a classification of previous work and used a hybrid method to construct surface. In his paper, he used Lagrangian Approach (like direct method in our paper) and Eulerian Approach (like indirect method in our paper) to classify the previous work.

This paper researches the indirect method of 3D surface construction and presents a new algorithm to deal with non-manifold surface conditions listed in [11][12]. Different from previous work, our work mainly concentrates on how to adaptively select the density of grid and gives a grid adjustment analysis step. Section 2 presents the detail of this method and section 3 gives the complete process and main components of 3D surface construction and rendering based on our method. The result is shown in section 4 and section 5 gives the future work.

2   Non-manifold Surface and Grid Adjustment Analysis

Yamazaki defines and presents two non-manifold surface conditions, as illustrated in figure 2.

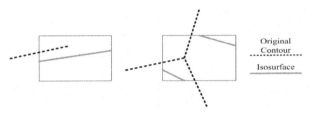

Fig. 2. Non-manifold surface and the isosurface generated in 2D space

Because the non-manifold surface can cause mistakes in isosurface generation of Marching Cube, Yamazaki defined segmented distance field function in [11][12] to solve the problem. He divided the grid in many regions and the distance field is represented by both the distance and the region index. He used Marching Cube method to extract surface from the volume generated using segmented distance field in [11] and using DVR in [12]. The segmented distance field gives a uniform way to solve the non-manifold surface problem. But in general, it is very complicated to use the segmented distance field in 3D surface construction.

The segmented distance field introduces more computation in the volume generation process and more judgment in the surface extraction process. In Fact, non-manifold surface is a very complicated problem. For example, it is difficult to find a proper distance field function to accurately describe the condition in figure 3 because the branch 1 and branch 2 are hard to separate. To solve the problem in figure 3, the only way is to sacrifice the accuracy of the isosurface.

Although it is difficult to find an accurate way to correct all the mistakes caused by non-manifold surface, it is still useful to research a method to deal with non-manifold surface. To make the non-manifold surface problem be solved in a simple and uniform way, we present a new method. The main idea is to

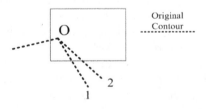

Fig. 3. An example of non-manifold surface

use the non-manifold surface information to resize the grid. We call this a grid adjustment analysis process.

In this paper, we use vertex to imply the joint of the contour and use grid point to imply the voxel of the grid. Furthermore, we use non-manifold vertex to imply the vertex that has less than or more than two neighbors. These definitions are illustrated in figure 4. To make the illustration clear, we use 2D grid to present various conditions.

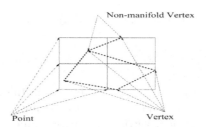

Fig. 4. Different definitions of our algorithm

We analyse the reason that causes the mistakes of isosurface generation. In fact, the boolean segmentation on the grid point generating 16 conditions in the 2D grid or 256 conditions in the 3D cell is sufficient to present the different conditions of volume state. T he mistakes of isosurface generation in non-manifold surface is that the non-manifold vertex does not lying on the grid point, so the boolean condition on the grid point can not reflect the distribution of isosurface. Here we propose a hypothesis, that if all the non-manifold vertices are lying on the grid points and no any two of all the branches connected to the non-manifold vertices are in the same grid cell, as illustrated in figure 5, the problem of non-manifold surface can be solved simply.

This hypothesis can be proved. We suppose all the manifold vertices are lying on the grid point and no any two of all the branches connected to the non-manifold vertices are in the same grid cell, there are only three cases in the grid cell.

Case 1: Contains no segment or vertex of the contour.

Case 2: Contains one part of segment of the contour.

Case 3: Contains one or more vertices belong to V-NV

In all the three cases, because each grid point can only have two conditions: in or out of a contour, the distance field function can separate the grid points

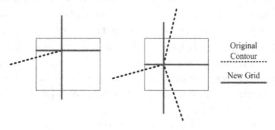

Fig. 5. Non-manifold vertex on the grid point

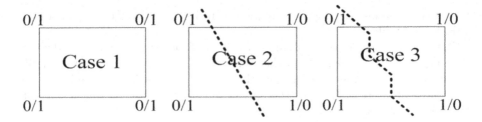

Fig. 6. Three cases of grid cell

by using + or - distance. This will make the isosurface extracted from volume correctly represent the contour.

The hypothesis has two conditions. The first is all the non-manifold vertices are lying on the grid points, and the second is no any two of all the branches connected to the non-manifold vertices are in the same grid cell. Our grid adjustment analysis method is based on the hypothesis and mainly resolves the first condition. To make the method more useful, our method also make some efforts to resolve the second condition.

Because vertex is different from the grid point, the main task is how to reorganize the grid to make the non-manifold vertices lie on the grid points. This is the grid adjustment analysis. Let V denote the set of vertex, P denote the set of grid point and NV denotes the set of non-manifold vertex.

We use $Dist(s,t)$ to denote the Euripides distance between two points in 3D space, $s,t \in V \cup P$. We use $neighbor(s)$ to denote the set of neighbors of s and have:

If $s \in V$ then $neighbor(s) \subset V$

If $s \in P$ then $neighbor(s) \subset P$

The grid adjustment analysis includes four steps.

- Non-manifold vertices looking up step.

  In this step, we look up all the non-manifold vertices on a slice. This work can easily be done by examining the number of neighbor vertices of every vertex on the contour. If the number is not equal to 2, then the vertex is a non–manifold vertex. This step uses following rule:

  if $\|neighbor(v)\| \neq 2$ then add v to NV $(v \in V)$
- Vertex neglect step.

  After the non-manifold vertices are located, it is useful to neglect some unimportant non-manifold vertices to reduce the computation work. We use the distance between two vertices to do this work. Let δ be a small real number. Calculating the distance between the non-manifold vertex and its neighbors, if the distance less than δ , then delete the non-manifold vertex and modify the topology of contour. This step uses following rule:

  if $Dist(s, t) \leq \delta$ then delete s and modify topology $(s \in NV, t \in V)$
- Grid size adjustment step.

  This step adjusts the grid size. After vertex neglect step, some unimportant non-manifold vertices have been deleted. We calculate the distance in x and y dimension between every non-manifold vertex and its neighbors then choose a proper interval size to let most vertices lie on the new grid.

Let η be a small real number.

Let $\Delta X, \Delta Y$ denote the interval size of x and y direction, we use following rule to constrain the $\Delta X, \Delta Y$.

$\Delta X \times \Delta Y \leq \eta$

– Vertex combination step.

After the last step , most vertices have been adjusted to the grid point. But there are still a few vertices which do not lie on grid point. We use the distance between vertex and grid point to combine the vertices to grid point.

Let ε be a small real number.

Calculating the distance between the non-manifold vertex and its nearest grid point, if the distance less than ε , then combine the non-manifold vertex to the grid point, otherwise select a new grid interval and redo this step.

This step uses following rule:

if $Dist(s,t) \leq \varepsilon$ then combine s with t. $(s \in NV, t \in P)$

3   Implementation

Based on the grid adjustment analysis method, we present an algorithm to construct 3D surface from contour. The complete process of our algorithm is in Figure 7.

Our algorithm has three steps to construct 3D surface from contour data. Besides the volume construction step and surface construction step, our algorithm adds one new step, that is gird adjustment analysis.

The grid adjustment analysis step analyses and selects the density of grid before the volume construction step to insure the non-manifold vertex processed properly. In this step, we implement our method in section 2. To make the work easy to do, we select regular grid to produce the volume.

In the volume construction step, we choose the distance field function in [2] to generate volume data, as illustrated in equation 4. Because the calculation for grid points is time-consuming, we use bounding box based method to reduce the grid points distance field calculation.

$$f(x,y) = \begin{cases} -d(x,y) & : & if\ (x,y)\ is\ outside\ all\ contours \\ 0 & : & if\ (x,y)\ is\ on\ a\ contour \\ d(x,y) & : & if\ (x,y)\ is\ inside\ a\ contour \end{cases}$$

Where d(x,y) is the distance from grid point (x, y) to the closest point on the contour.

In the surface construction step, we select marching cube [4] method to extract surface from regular volume data. Based on the work of grid adjustment analysis, the grid cell has a proper size and the 0/1 condition on grid points to generate isosurface is sufficient to extract isosurface from the volume. To save memory

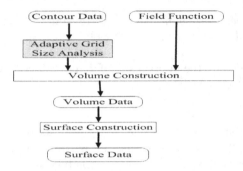

Fig. 7. Process of the Algorithm

and time, we use vertex pool and other techniques. This work will be shown in other paper.

4   Results

Using our improved algorithm, we can generate 3D surface from contour simply and correctly. We give some experiment result of our algorithm. The experiment is completed on a desktop PC, with P4 2.4G HZ CPU and 256M memory. Table 1 illustrates these results.

In above table, Time 1(Second) implies the volume construction time and time 2(Second) implies the isosurface construction time. The contours and results in table 1 are listed in figure 8.

Table 1. Some 3D surfaces generated using our algorithm

Contour	Volume Size	Triangle number	Time 1	Time 2	Result
Contour1	128*128*384	186936	7.5815	5.7450	Result1
Contour2	128*128*128	87812	11.694	2.4946	Result2
Contour3	128*128*640	312888	17.427	12.893	Result3

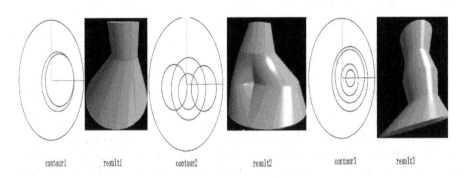

contour1   result1   contour2   result2   contour3   result3

Fig. 8. Contours and Results

5   Conclusion and Future Work

This paper researches the method of constructing 3D surface from contour data. We concentrate on non-manifold surface problems and give a grid adjustment analysis method to adjust the grid size based on the non-manifold vertices information. We also present a complete 3D surface construction algorithm to construct surface from contour data. The experiment shows that our algorithm can construct 3D surface accurately and simply.

The future work includes the subtler distance field function design and uses hardware accelerated method to implement direct volume rendering algorithm on the volume data. Furthermore, we will pay more attention to designing a good structure for out-of-model and rendering large scale data.

References

1. G. Barequet, D. Shapiro, A. Tal. Multilevel Sensitive Reconstruction of Polyhedral Surfaces from Parallel Slices. The Visual Computer, Vol.16: 116-133, 2000.
2. D. Levin. Multidimensional Reconstruction by Set-valued Approximation. IMA Journal of Numerical Analysis, 6:173-84, 1986.
3. M. Jones, M. Chen. A New Approach to the Construction of Surfaces from Contour Data. Computer Graphics Forum, 13(3): 75-84, 1994.
4. W.E.Lorensen, H.E.Cline. Marching Cubes: A High Resolution 3D Surface Construction Algorithm. Computer Graphics, Vol.21, No.4: page 163 169, 1987.
5. K. Engel, M. Kraus, T. Ertl. High-Quality Pre-Integrated Volume Rendering Using Hardware-Accelerated Pixel Shading. Proc. Eurographics/SIGGRAPH Workshop on Graphics Hardware 2001, 9-16, 2001.
6. M. Hadwiger, J.M. Kniss, K.Engel, C. Rezk-Salama,/ High-Quality Volume Graphics on Consumer PC Hardware. SIGGRAPH 2002 Course, Course Notes 42, 2002.
7. S.F. Frisken, R.N. Perry, A.P. Rockwood, and T.R.Jones. Adaptively sampled distance fields: A general representation of shape for computer graphics. SIGGRAPH 2000, 249-254. ACM, July 2000.
8. R. Klein and A. Schilling. Fast Distance Field Interpolation for Reconstruction of Surfaces from Contours. EUROGRAPHICS '99 ,1999
9. L. Kobbelt, M. Botsch, U. Schwanecke, and Hans-Peter Seidel. Feature sensitive surface extraction from volume data. SIGGRAPH 2001, 2001.
10. R. N. Perry,S. F. Frisken. Kizamu: A system for sculpting digital characters. SIGGRAPH 2001, 47-56, 2001.
11. S. Yamazaki, K. Kase and K. Ikeuchi. Non-manifold implicit surfaces based on discontinuous implicitization and polygonization. Geometric Modeling and Processing 2002, 138-146, June 2002
12. S. Yamazaki, K. Kase and K. Ikeuchi. Hardware-accelerated visualization of volume-sampled distance fields. Proc. Shape Modeling International, 264-271, May 2003
13. O. Nilsson, D. Breen, K. Museth. Surface Reconstruction Via Contour Metamorphosis: An EulerianApproach with Lagrangian Particle Tracking. IEEE Visualization 2005,407-414, 2005

Geometric Modeling for Interpolation Surfaces Based on Blended Coordinate System*

Benyue Su[1,2] and Jieqing Tan[3]

[1] School of Computer & Information, Hefei University of Technology,
Hefei 230009, China
[2] Department of Mathematics, Anqing Teachers College, Anqing 246011, China
[3] Institute of Applied Mathematics, Hefei University of Technology,
Hefei 230009, China

Abstract. In this paper we present a new method for the model of interpolation surfaces by the blending of polar coordinates and Cartesian coordinate. A trajectory curve is constructed by circular trigonometric Hermite interpolation spline (CTHIS) and a profile curve is presented by C^2-continuous B-spline like interpolation spline (BSLIS). A piecewise interpolation spline surface is incorporated by the blending of CTHIS and BSLIS. In addition, scaling functions have been introduced to improve the flexibility of the model of the interpolation surfaces. On the basis of these results, some examples are given to show how the method is used to model some interesting surfaces.

1 Introduction

Bézier and B-spline methods are usually used in Cartesian coordinates for constructing piecewise free form curves and surfaces in CAD system. But they have many difficulties in constructing periodic surfaces of revolution. In order to avoid inconveniences, recently, some classes of curves and surfaces modeling in polar, cylindrical and spherical coordinates were proposed. A class of Bézier-type curves and surfaces defined on circular arcs using barycentric coordinates were presented by Alfeld, Cusimano and Morigi et al. ([1], [2], [4], [7]). Sánchez-Reyes and Seidel et al. ([9], [10], [11], [12]) discussed p-Bézier curves and triangular B-spline surfaces in polar coordinates by trigonometric polynomials. Casciola and Morigi ([3]) constructed a product surface in polar-Cartesian mixed coordinates by p-curves and NURBS.

On the other hand, interpolation spline is sometimes requisite for the curves and surfaces modeling. Whereas in constructing interpolation spline we need to calculate the data points conversely using the above-mentioned methods.

* This work was completed with the support by the National Natural Science Foundation of China under Grant No. 10171026 and No. 60473114 and in part by the Research Funds for Young Innovation Group, Education Department of Anhui Province under Grant No. 2005TD03 and the Natural Science Foundation of Anhui Provincial Education Department under Grant No. 2005jq1120zd, No. 2006KJ252B.

H. Zha et al. (Eds.): VSMM 2006, LNCS 4270, pp. 222–231, 2006.

A method (Kochanek and Bartels, [6]) for using cubic interpolating splines was presented, which used three control parameters to change the tension and continuity of the splines with each of these parameters being used for either local or global control. A C^2 continuous spline scheme (Tai and Loe, [14]) was proposed which was called the α-spline and provided weights and tension control. The scheme was based on blending a sequence of singular reparametrized line segments with a piecewise NURBS curve, but the tangent vectors degenerated to zero when the scheme interpolated the control points. In 2001, a B-spline technique was adopted for the blending of Hermite interpolants (Gfrerrer and Röchel, [5]). An alternative method of curve interpolation based on B-spline curves was offered by Piegl et al.([8]). The method used a base curve, which was subjected to constrained shape manipulations to achieve interpolation.

But it is complicated to construct cycloidal surfaces, periodic sweeping surfaces using the above-mentioned methods of interpolation spline.

The main contribution of this paper is the development of a new method based on generalized Hermite interpolation and blended coordinate system. This approach has the following features:

- The introduced method is convenient for constructing cycloidal surfaces, periodic sweeping surfaces and some other interesting surfaces by the blending of Cartesian coordinates and polar coordinates.
- The introduced method is based on the blending of circular Hermite interpolation polynomials and C^2 continuous interpolation spline, which provides a useful tool for geometric modeling of interpolation surfaces.

The rest of this paper is organized as follows. Sect. 2 defines circular trigonometric Hermite interpolation spline. A C^2-continuous B-spline like interpolation spline is introduced in Sect. 3. We present a method for the interpolation surface modeling by the blending of circular trigonometric Hermite interpolation spline and C^2-continuous B-spline like interpolation spline in Sect. 4. Some examples of shape modeling by the introduced method are also given in this section. Finally, we conclude the paper in Sect. 5.

2   Circular Trigonometric Hermite Interpolation Spline

2.1   Barycentric Coordinates on Circular Arcs

The notion of barycentric coordinates on circular arcs was introduced by Alfeld et al. ([1]). Let C be the unit circle in $\mathbb{R}^2$ with center at the origin, and let A be a circular arc with vertices $v_1 \neq v_2$ which are not anti-podal. Then the circular barycentric coordinates of a point v on the circle A with respect to v_1, v_2 are

$$v = b_1 v_1 + b_2 v_2 , \tag{1}$$

where

$$b_1 = \frac{\det(v, v_2)}{\det(v_1, v_2)} , \quad b_2 = \frac{\det(v_1, v)}{\det(v_1, v_2)} . \tag{2}$$

$$\det(r, s) = \begin{vmatrix} r_x & s_x \\ r_y & s_y \end{vmatrix} \text{ for any points } r, s \text{ in } A.$$

We can also express the points on unit circle C in polar coordinates. Suppose

$$v_1 = (\cos\theta_1, \sin\theta_1)^T, \quad v_2 = (\cos\theta_2, \sin\theta_2)^T, \tag{3}$$

with $0 < \theta_2 - \theta_1 < \pi$. Let $v \in C$ be expressed in polar coordinates as $v = (\cos\theta, \sin\theta)^T$. Then the barycentric coordinates of v relative to the circular arc A are

$$b_1(v(\theta)) = \frac{\sin(\theta_2 - \theta)}{\sin(\theta_2 - \theta_1)}, \quad b_2(v(\theta)) = \frac{\sin(\theta - \theta_1)}{\sin(\theta_2 - \theta_1)}. \tag{4}$$

2.2 Circular Trigonometric Hermite Interpolation Spline

Definition 1. *Let A be a unit circular arc, $b_1(\theta)$ and $b_2(\theta)$ denote the corresponding circular barycentric coordinates of the point $v = (\cos\theta, \sin\theta)$. We define the cubic circular trigonometric Hermite interpolation base functions to be*

$$\begin{aligned}
h_0(v) &= b_1(\theta)^3 + \alpha b_1(\theta)^2 b_2(\theta), \\
h_1(v) &= b_2(\theta)^3 + \alpha b_2(\theta)^2 b_1(\theta), \\
g_0(v) &= \beta b_1(\theta)^2 b_2(\theta), \\
g_1(v) &= -\beta b_2(\theta)^2 b_1(\theta),
\end{aligned} \tag{5}$$

where $\alpha = 3\cos(\theta_2 - \theta_1)$ and $\beta = \sin(\theta_2 - \theta_1)$.

We can also rewrite these base functions in polar coordinates by

$$\begin{aligned}
h_0(\theta) &= \tfrac{1}{\sin^3(\theta_2-\theta_1)}(\sin^3(\theta_2 - \theta) + 3\cos(\theta_2 - \theta_1)\sin^2(\theta_2 - \theta)\sin(\theta - \theta_1)), \\
h_1(\theta) &= \tfrac{1}{\sin^3(\theta_2-\theta_1)}(\sin^3(\theta - \theta_1) + 3\cos(\theta_2 - \theta_1)\sin^2(\theta - \theta_1)\sin(\theta_2 - \theta)), \\
g_0(\theta) &= \tfrac{1}{\sin^2(\theta_2-\theta_1)}\sin^2(\theta_2 - \theta)\sin(\theta - \theta_1), \\
g_1(\theta) &= -\tfrac{1}{\sin^2(\theta_2-\theta_1)}\sin^2(\theta - \theta_1)\sin(\theta_2 - \theta).
\end{aligned} \tag{6}$$

Simple calculations verify that these base functions possess the properties similar to the those of normal cubic Hermite interpolation base functions.

Let $[a, b] \subset \mathbb{R}$, and $\Delta : a = \theta_0 < \theta_1 < \cdots < \theta_N = b$ be a partition with $N + 1$ points in the interval $[a, b]$. Suppose $f := (f_i)_{i \in \overline{0,N}}$ are $N + 1$ real numbers.

Definition 2. *Given a knot vector*

$$\Delta : a = \theta_0 < \theta_1 < \cdots < \theta_N = b, \; b - a < \pi.$$

Let

$$\mathbf{CS}^3 = \{s \in C^2[\theta_0, \theta_N] \text{ s.t. } s \in \mathbf{CP}^3 \text{ for } \theta \in [\theta_i, \theta_{i+1}], i = 0, 1, \cdots, N - 1\},$$

where

$$\mathbf{CP}^3 := span\{(b_1(\theta))^3, (b_1(\theta))^2(b_2(\theta)), (b_2(\theta))^2(b_1(\theta)), (b_2(\theta))^3\}.$$

If $s \in \mathbf{CS}^3$ and $s(\theta_i) = f_i$, we call $s(\theta)$ as circular trigonometric Hermite interpolation spline.

From definition 2, we set

$$s_j^3(\theta) = \rho_j h_0(\theta) + \rho_{j+1} h_1(\theta) + m_j g_0(\theta) + m_{j+1} g_1(\theta),\ \theta \in [\theta_j, \theta_{j+1}]\ ,$$
$$j = 0, 1, \cdots, N - 1\ , \tag{7}$$

where ρ_j, $(j = 0, 1, \cdots, N)$, are the function values at the interpolating knots, m_j, $(j = 0, 1, \cdots, N)$, are the corresponding derivative values which are coefficients to be determined and $h_i(\theta)$, $g_i(\theta)$, $(i = 1, 2)$, are the circular trigonometric Hermite interpolation base functions.

In the polar coordinates, we suppose ρ_j are radii and θ_i are polar angles. Then (θ_j, ρ_j), $(j = 0, 1, 2, \cdots, N)$, compose a set of interpolation points in the polar coordinates. From (6) and (7), we know

$$s_j^3(\theta_{j+1}) = s_{j+1}^3(\theta_{j+1}) = \rho_{j+1},\ D_\theta s_j^3(\theta_{j+1}^-) = D_\theta s_{j+1}^3(\theta_{j+1}^+) = m_{j+1}\ ,$$
$$j = 0, 1, \cdots, N - 2\ . \tag{8}$$

So $s_j^3(\theta)$, $(j = 0, 1, \cdots, N-1)$, are C^1 continuous. Let $\delta_i = \theta_{i+1} - \theta_i$, $\Lambda_i = \frac{\rho_{i+1} - \rho_i}{\delta_i}$. We can get the explicit expressions of $s_j^3(\theta)$, $(j = 0, 1, \cdots, N - 1)$, by defining m_j, $(j = 0, 1, \cdots, N)$, as

$$m_0 = \Lambda_0 + \frac{\delta_0(\Lambda_0 - \Lambda_1)}{\delta_0 + \delta_1},\ m_N = \Lambda_{N-1} + \frac{\delta_{N-1}(\Lambda_{N-1} - \Lambda_{N-2})}{\delta_{N-2} + \delta_{N-1}},$$
$$m_j = \frac{\delta_i \Lambda_{i-1} + \delta_{i-1} \Lambda_i}{\delta_i + \delta_{i+1}},\ (j = 1, 2, \cdots, N - 1). \tag{9}$$

But if we suppose that $s_j^3(\theta)$, $(j = 0, 1, \cdots, N-1)$, are C^2 continuous, then we have to compute m_j, $(j = 0, 1, \cdots, N)$, by solving a system of linear equations.

Let

$$D_\theta^2 s_j^3(\theta_{j+1}^-) = D_\theta^2 s_{j+1}^3(\theta_{j+1}^+),\ (j = 0, 1, \cdots, N - 2)\ .$$

We get

$$\lambda_i m_i + 2\mu_i m_{i+1} + \lambda_{i+1} m_{i+2} = \omega_i,\ i = 0, 1, \cdots, N - 2\ , \tag{10}$$

where $\delta_i = \theta_{i+1} - \theta_i$, $\lambda_i = \csc(\delta_i)$, $\mu_i = (\cot(\delta_i) + \cot(\delta_{i+1}))$, $\kappa_i = \cot(\delta_i)\csc(\delta_i)$, $\iota_i = (\cot^2(\delta_i) - \cot^2(\delta_{i+1}))$, $\omega_i = 3(\kappa_{i+1}\rho_{i+2} + \iota_i\rho_{i+1} - \kappa_i\rho_i)$, $(i = 0, 1, \cdots, N-1)$.

If $\delta_i < \pi/3$, $(i = 0, 1, \cdots, N - 1)$, then the tridiagonal matrix is diagonal dominant by (10). So there must exist a circular trigonometric Hermite interpolation spline function which interpolates data $(\rho_i)_{i \in \overline{0,N}}$ at knots $(\theta_i)_{i \in \overline{0,N}}$.

Notes and Comments. For the nonperiodic case, we need to add two additional boundary conditions to obtain a unique solution of (10).

For the periodic spline, we can require that $\rho_N = \rho_0$, $m_N = m_0$. We set $\delta_N = \delta_0$. Computing $\lambda_N, \mu_{N-1}, \kappa_N, \iota_{N-1}, \omega_{N-2}$ by δ_N can yield a periodic circular trigonometric Hermite interpolation spline function by (10).

If we choose equidistant knots, i.e., $\delta_i = \delta$, $(i = 0, 1, \cdots, N - 1)$, we can get the following tridiagonal system of linear equations:

$$m_i + 4\cos(\delta)m_{i+1} + m_{i+2} = 3\cot(\delta)(\rho_{i+2} - \rho_i),\ i = 0, 1, \cdots, N - 2\ . \tag{11}$$

If $\delta < \pi/3, (i = 1, \cdots, N)$, similar results of periodic or nonperiodic cubic circular trigonometric Hermite interpolation spline function can be induced by (11).

3 C^2-Continuous B-Spline Like Interpolation Spline

Definition 3. *[13] Let $b_0, b_1, b_2, \cdots, b_{n+2}, (n \geq 1)$, be given control points. Then a quasi-cubic piecewise B-spline like interpolation spline curve is defined by*

$$p_i(t) = \sum_{j=0}^{3} B_{j,3}(t) b_{i+j}, \ t \in [0,1], \ i = 0, 1, \cdots, n-1 \ , \tag{12}$$

where

$$
\begin{aligned}
B_{0,3}(t) &= \tfrac{1}{4} + \tfrac{t}{2} - \sin \tfrac{\pi}{2} t - \tfrac{1}{4} \cos \pi t + \tfrac{1}{2\pi} \sin \pi t \ , \\
B_{1,3}(t) &= -\tfrac{1}{4} + \tfrac{t}{2} + \cos \tfrac{\pi}{2} t + \tfrac{1}{4} \cos \pi t - \tfrac{1}{2\pi} \sin \pi t \ , \\
B_{2,3}(t) &= \tfrac{1}{4} - \tfrac{t}{2} + \sin \tfrac{\pi}{2} t - \tfrac{1}{4} \cos \pi t - \tfrac{1}{2\pi} \sin \pi t \ , \\
B_{3,3}(t) &= \tfrac{3}{4} - \tfrac{t}{2} - \cos \tfrac{\pi}{2} t + \tfrac{1}{4} \cos \pi t + \tfrac{1}{2\pi} \sin \pi t \ .
\end{aligned}
\tag{13}
$$

From (13), we know that $B_{i,3}(t), (i = 0, 1, 2, 3)$, possess properties similar to those of B-spline except the positive property. Moreover, $p_i(t)$ interpolates the points b_{i+1} and b_{i+2}. That is,

$$p_i(0) = b_{i+1}, \ p_i(1) = b_{i+2} \ , \tag{14}$$

From (12) and (13), we can also get

$$
\begin{aligned}
p_i'(0) &= (\tfrac{\pi}{2} - 1)(b_{i+2} - b_i), \qquad p_i'(1) = (\tfrac{\pi}{2} - 1)(b_{i+3} - b_{i+1}) \ , \\
p_i''(0) &= \tfrac{\pi^2}{4}(b_i - 2b_{i+1} + b_{i+2}), \ p_i''(1) = \tfrac{\pi^2}{4}(b_{i+1} - 2b_{i+2} + b_{i+3}) \ .
\end{aligned}
\tag{15}
$$

So

$$p_i(1) = p_{i+1}(0), \ p_i^{(l)}(1) = p_{i+1}^{(l)}(0), \ l = 1, 2, \ i = 0, 1, \cdots, n-1 \ . \tag{16}$$

Therefore, the continuity of the quasi-cubic piecewise interpolation spline curves is established up to second derivatives. Besides this property, the quasi-cubic piecewise interpolation spline curves have also the following properties:

1. **Symmetry:** From (12) and (13), both $b_0, b_1, b_2, \cdots, b_{n+2}$, and $b_{n+2}, b_{n+1}, \cdots, b_1, b_0, (n \geq 1)$, define the same curve in a different parameterization:

$$p_i(t, b_i, b_{i+1}, b_{i+2}, b_{i+3}) = p_i(1 - t, b_{i+3}, b_{i+2}, b_{i+1}, b_i), \ 0 \leq t \leq 1 \ ,$$

   $i = 0, 1, 2, \cdots, n-1$.

2. **Geometric invariability:** The shapes of quasi-cubic piecewise interpolation spline curves are independent of the choice of coordinates. An affine transformation for the curves can be achieved by carrying out the affine transformation for the control polygon.

4   Surface Modeling by the Blended Coordinate System

In this section, we construct a piecewise interpolation surface by the blending of circular trigonometric Hermite interpolation spline $s_i(\theta)$ in polar coordinates and quasi-cubic piecewise interpolation spline $p_i(t)$ in Cartesian coordinates.

Let us consider the modeling of cycloidal surfaces or periodic sweeping-type surfaces in the 3D space. If the trajectory curves of the sweep-type surfaces can be viewed as the curves defined on the circular arcs which are periodic and pass through some given points, and the profile curves of the sweeping-type surfaces also overpass some other given points in advance in a plane or 3D space. Then we can carry out the representation of the interpolation surfaces by the following assumption.

First, we reconstruct the trajectory curves by the circular trigonometric Hermite interpolation spline $s_i(\theta)$ in polar coordinates.

Second, the profile curves in a plane or 3D space can be represented by the C^2-continuous quasi-cubic piecewise B-spline like interpolation spline $p_i(t)$ in Cartesian coordinates.

At last, the two classes of interpolation spline functions $s_i(\theta)$ and $p_i(t)$ can be incorporated properly to form the interpolation surfaces in demand.

So the profile curves can be represented by

$$p_i(t) = (p_{x,i}(t), p_{y,i}(t), p_{z,i}(t))^T = \sum_{j=0}^{3} B_{j,3}(t)b_{i+j}, \, t \in [0,1] \, ,$$

$$i = 0, 1, \cdots, n - 1 \, , \tag{17}$$

where b_i, $i = 0, 1, \cdots, n + 2$, $(n \geq 1)$, are given points in advance, and $B_{j,3}(t)$, $(j = 0, 1, 2, 3)$, are quasi-cubic piecewise B-spline like interpolation spline base functions.

Similarly, the trajectory curves can be defined as

$$s_j(\theta) = \rho_j h_0(\theta) + \rho_{j+1} h_1(\theta) + m_j g_0(\theta) + m_{j+1} g_1(\theta), \, \theta \in [\theta_j, \theta_{j+1}] \, ,$$

$$j = 0, 1, \cdots, N - 1 \, , \tag{18}$$

where ρ_j, $(j = 0, 1, \cdots, N)$, are the radii, θ is angle of rotation in the polar coordinates, m_j, $(j = 0, 1, \cdots, N)$, are the corresponding derivative values which are coefficients to be determined and $h_i(\theta)$, $g_i(\theta)$, $(i = 1, 2)$, are the circular trigonometric Hermite interpolation base functions.

In order to improve the flexibility of the interpolation surfaces modeling, we introduce scaling functions defined by

$$r_i(t) = (r_{x,i}(t), r_{y,i}(t), r_{z,i}(t))^T = \sum_{j=0}^{3} B_{j,3}(t)c_{i+j}, \, t \in [0,1] \, ,$$

$$i = 0, 1, \cdots, n - 1 \, , \tag{19}$$

where $c_i = (\hat{c}_i, \hat{c}_i, 0)^T, i = 0, 1, \cdots, n + 2$, $(n \geq 1)$, $\hat{c}_i$ are $n + 3$ nonnegative real numbers, which are called scaling factors, and $B_{j,3}(t), (j = 0, 1, 2, 3)$, are quasi-cubic piecewise B-spline like interpolation spline base functions.

Obviously, the scaling functions $r_i(t)$ are C^2-continuous.

On the basis of (17), (18) and (19), we define piecewise interpolation surfaces as follows

$$f_{i,j}(t,\theta) = r_i(t)s_j(\theta) + p_i(t), \ \theta \in [\theta_j, \theta_{j+1}], \ t \in [0,1] \ , \tag{20}$$

where $p_i(t)$ is B-spline like interpolation spline, $s_j(\theta)$ is circular trigonometric Hermite interpolation spline, and $r_i(t)$ is scaling function.

In the spherical coordinate, the piecewise interpolation surfaces can also be defined as

$$f_{i,j}(t,\theta) = \begin{pmatrix} x_{i,j}(t,\theta) \\ y_{i,j}(t,\theta) \\ z_{i,j}(t,\theta) \end{pmatrix} = \begin{pmatrix} r_{x,i}(t)s_j(\theta)\cos(\theta) + p_{x,i}(t) \\ r_{y,i}(t)s_j(\theta)\sin(\theta) + p_{y,i}(t) \\ p_{z,i}(t) \end{pmatrix} . \tag{21}$$

From the (18) and (20), we know that for the fixed $\theta = \theta^*$,

$$f_{i,j}(t,\theta^*) = \sum_{k=0}^{3}(c_{i+k}s_j^* + b_{i+k})B_{k,3}(t) \ , \tag{22}$$

where $s_j^* = s_j(\theta^*)$, and for the fixed $t = t^*$,

$$f_{i,j}(t^*,\theta) = \hat{r}_i^* s_j(\theta) + \hat{p}_i \ , \tag{23}$$

where $\hat{r}_i^* = r_i(t^*)$ and $\hat{p}_i = p_i(t^*)$.

Notes and Comments. Since $c_i = (\hat{c}_i, \hat{c}_i, 0)^T$, we get that $f_{i,j}(t,\theta^*)$ are piecewise C^2-continuous curves as in the case of $p_i(t)$ and the curves $f_{i,j}(t,\theta^*)$ can be obtained by doing the translation transformation on the profile curve $p_i(t)$ that parallel to the xy-plane from the (22).

The curves $f_{i,j}(t^*,\theta)$ can also be attained by the dilation and translation transformation on the trajectory curve $s_i(\theta)$ in the polar coordinate from the (23), where $r_i(t)$ can adjust the shape of interpolation surfaces freely like an elastic band without loss of the smoothness of the interpolation surfaces for its C^2-continuity (See Fig.2 and Fig.3).

Moveover, by computing the first and second partial derivatives of $f_{i,j}(t,\theta)$, we get

$$\frac{\partial^l}{\partial t^l}f_{i,j}(t,\theta) = r_i^{(l)}(t)s_j(\theta) + p_i^{(l)}(t) \ , \quad \frac{\partial^l}{\partial\theta^l}f_{i,j}(t,\theta) = r_i(t)s_j^{(l)}(\theta), \ l = 1,2 \ . \tag{24}$$

So

$$\frac{\partial}{\partial t}f_{i,j}(1,\theta) = (\tfrac{\pi}{2} - 1)((c_{i+3} - c_{i+1})s_j(\theta) + (b_{i+3} - b_{i+1})) \ ,$$
$$\frac{\partial^2}{\partial t^2}f_{i,j}(1,\theta) = \tfrac{\pi^2}{4}((c_{i+1} - 2c_{i+2} + c_{i+3})s_j(\theta) + (b_{i+1} - 2b_{i+2} + b_{i+3})) \ ,$$
$$\frac{\partial}{\partial\theta}f_{i,j}(t,\theta_{j+1}) = r_i(t)s'(\theta_{j+1}) = r_i(t)m_{j+1} \ ,$$
$$\frac{\partial^2}{\partial\theta^2}f_{i,j}(t,\theta_{j+1}) = r_i(t)s''(\theta_{j+1}) \ , \tag{25}$$

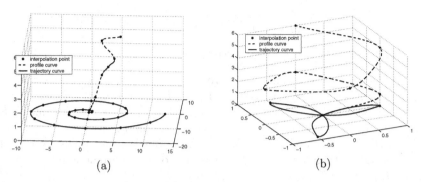

(a)   (b)

Fig. 1. dashed lines: profile curve in Cartesian coordinate, solid lines: trajectory curve in polar coordinate; (a) is the figure in example 1 and (b) is the figure in example 2

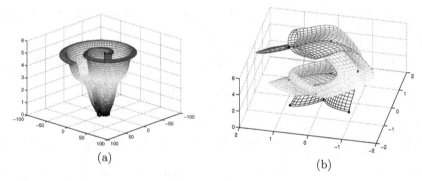

(a)   (b)

Fig. 2. C^1-continuous interpolation surfaces of (a) in example 1 and (b) in example 2 by scaling factor $\hat{c}_i = \{1, 1, 2, 3, 4, 5, 6, 7, 7\}$ and $\hat{c}_i = \{1, 1, 0.8, 0.6, 0.4, 0.6, 0.8, 1, 1\}$ respectively

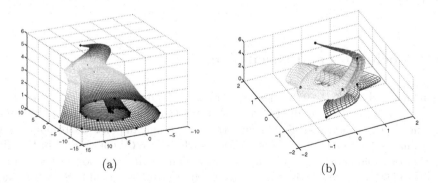

(a)   (b)

Fig. 3. C^2-continuous interpolation surfaces of (a) in example 1 and (b) in example 2 by the scaling factor $\hat{c}_i = \{1, 1, 0.8, 0.6, 0.5, 0.4, 0.2, 0, 0\}$

and

$$\frac{\partial}{\partial t} f_{i,j}(1,\theta) = \frac{\partial}{\partial t} f_{i+1,j}(0,\theta) \ , \ \frac{\partial^2}{\partial t^2} f_{i,j}(1,\theta) = \frac{\partial^2}{\partial t^2} f_{i+1,j}(0,\theta) \ ,$$
$$\frac{\partial}{\partial \theta} f_{i,j}(t,\theta_{j+1}) = \frac{\partial}{\partial \theta} f_{i,j+1}(t,\theta_{j+1}) \ .$$

(26)

Then $f_{i,j}(t,\theta)$ are C^2-continuous with respect to t and C^1-continuous with respect to θ, where m_j, $(j = 0, 1, \ldots, N-1)$, can be defined by (9).

If m_j, $(j = 0, 1, \ldots, N-1)$, satisfy (10), then $s_j(\theta)$ are C^2-continuous. So $f_{i,j}(t,\theta)$ are also C^2-continuous with respect to θ from (25).

That is, if we get piecewise C^1 or C^2 continuous trajectory curves $s_j(\theta)$ in polar coordinate, then we obtain piecewise C^1 or C^2 continuous interpolation surfaces $f_{i,j}(t,\theta)$ in (20).

Example 1. Given interpolation points of profile curve by $b_0 = (0,0,0)$, $b_1 = (0,0,0)$, $b_2 = (1,1,1)$, $b_3 = (2,2,2.5)$, $b_4 = (3,3,3)$, $b_5 = (4,4,3.5)$, $b_6 = (2,2,5)$, $b_7 = (5,5,5)$ and $b_8 = (5,5,5)$.

Suppose the trajectory curve passes through the points (θ_i, ρ_i) in the polar coordinates, where $\rho_i = \theta_i = \pi i/6$.

Then we get piecewise C^1-continuous (Fig.2(a)) and C^2-continuous (Fig.3(a)) interpolation surfaces, where m_i, $(i = 0, 1, \cdots, 24)$, are computed by (9) and (10) respectively. In the Fig.2(a), we choose scaling factor by $\hat{c}_i = \{1, 1, 2, 3, 4, 5, 6, 7, 7\}$, and we set $\hat{c}_i = \{1, 1, 0.8, 0.6, 0.5, 0.4, 0.2, 0, 0\}$ in the Fig.3(a) .

Example 2. Given interpolation points of profile curve by $b_0 = (0,0,0)$, $b_1 = (0,0,0)$, $b_2 = (1,0,1)$, $b_3 = (0,1,2)$, $b_4 = (-1,0,3)$, $b_5 = (0,-1,4)$, $b_6 = (1,0,5)$, $b_7 = (0,1,6)$ and $b_8 = (0,1,6)$.

The trajectory curve passes through the points (θ_i, ρ_i) in the polar coordinates, where $\rho_i = \cos(3\delta_i)$ and $\delta = \pi/6$.

Computing m_i by (9) and (10), $(i = 0, 1, \cdots, 24)$, yields piecewise C^1-continuous (Fig.2(b)) and C^2-continuous (Fig.3(b)) interpolation surfaces respectively. The scaling factors are chosen to be $\hat{c}_i = \{1, 1, 0.8, 0.6, 0.4, 0.6, 0.8, 1, 1\}$ and $\hat{c}_i = \{1, 1, 0.8, 0.6, 0.5, 0.4, 0.2, 0, 0\}$ in Fig.2(b) and Fig.3(b) respectively.

5   Conclusions and Discussions

As mentioned above, we have described a new method for constructing interpolation surfaces by the blending of trigonometric Hermite interpolation polynomials and C^2 continuous B-spline like interpolation spline in polar-Cartesian mixed coordinates. The introduced interpolation surfaces are C^2 continuous in the direction of profile curve and C^1 or C^2 continuous in the direction of trajectory curve so far as m_i satisfy the conditions in (9) or (10). As shown in Sect. 4, some interesting surfaces can be easily constructed by the presented new method in this paper, which, however, used to be complex if implemented by other models, such as normal Hermite polynomials, Bézier and B-splines etc.

References

1. Alfeld, P., Neamtu, M., Schumaker, L. L. : Circular Bernstein-Bézier polynomials. In: Dæhlen, M., Lyche,T. , Schumaker, L. L. (Eds.), Mathematical Methods for curves and surfaces, Vanderbilt University Press, 1995, pp. 11–20

2. Alfeld, P., Neamtu, M., Schumaker, L. L. : Fitting scattered data on sphere-like surfaces using spherical splines. J. Comput. Appl. Math. **73** (1996) 5–43

3. Casciola, G., Morigi, S. : Inverse spherical surfaces. Journal of Computational and Applied Mathematics **176** (2005) 411–424

4. Cusimano, C., Stanley,S. : Circular Bernstein-Bézier spline approximation with knot removal. J. Comput. Appl. Math. **155** (2003) 177–185

5. Gfrerrer, A., Röchel, O. : Blended Hermite interpolants. Computer Aided Geometric Design **18** (2001) 865–873

6. Kochanek, D., Bartels, R. : Interpolating splines with local tension, continuity, and bias control. Computer Graphics (SIGGRAPH'84) **18** (1984) 33–41

7. Morigi, S., Neamtu, M. : Some results for a class of generalized polynomials. Advances in computational mathematics **12** (2000) 133–149

8. Piegl, L., Ma, W., Tiller, W. : An alternative method of curve interpolation. The Visual Computer **21** (2005) 104–117

9. Sánchez-Reyes, J. : Single-valued spline curves in polar coordinates. Computer Aided Design **24** (1992) 307–315

10. Sánchez-Reyes, J. : Harmonic rational Bézier curves, p-Bézier curves and trigonometric polynomials. Computer Aided Geometric Design **15** (1998) 909–923

11. Seidel, H.-P. : An intruduction to polar forms. IEEE Computer Graphics & Applications **13** (1993) 38–46

12. Seidel, H.-P. : Polar forms and triangular B-spline surfaces. In: Du, D.-Z., Hwang, F., (eds.), Euclidean Geometry and Computers (2nd Edition), World Scientific Publishing Co., 1994, pp. 235–286

13. Su, B. Y., Tan, J. Q. : A family of quasi-cubic blended splines and applications. J. Zhejiang Univ. SCIENCE A **7** (2006) 1550–1560

14. Tai, C. L., Loe, K. F. : Alpha-spline: a C^2 continuous spline with weights and tension control. In: Proc. of International Conference on Shape Modeling and Applications, 1999, pp. 138–145

Orthogonal Least Square RBF Based Implicit Surface Reconstruction Methods

Xiaojun Wu[1], Michael Yu Wang[2], and Qi Xia[2]

[1] Harbin Institute of Technology Shenzhen Graduate School, Shenzhen, China
[2] The Chinese University of Hong Kong, Shatin, NT, Hong Kong, China

Abstract. Two contributions on 3D implicit surface reconstruction from scattered points are presented in this paper. Firstly, least square radial basis functions (LS RBF) are deduced from the conventional RBF formulations, which makes it possible to use fewer centers when reconstruction. Then we use orthogonal least square (OLS) method to select significant centers from large and dense point data sets. From the selected centers, an implicit continuous function is constructed efficiently. This scheme can overcome the problem of numerical ill-conditioning of coefficient matrix and over-fitting. Experimental results show that our two methods are efficient and highly satisfactory in perception and quantification.

1 Introduction

Radial Basis Functions (RBF) has been used in several fields because of its accurate and stable interpolation properties [1]. In this paper, we use the LS RBF to solve the problem of surface reconstructions. The problem of surface reconstruction from scattered cloud points has been studied extensively in computer graphics and engineering, in particular, the use of range scanners or laser scanners produce large amount of unorganized point sets in industry, entertainment and archaeology, etc. Traditionally, there are several techniques to accomplish this mission [2–9]. Implicit surface models are popular since they can describe complex shapes with capabilities for surface, volume modeling and complex editing operations are easy to perform on such models.

RBF attracts more attentions recently in multidimensional data interpolation [7,8,9]. It is identified as one of the most accurate and stable methods to solve scattered data interpolation problems. Using this technique, an implicit surface is constructed by calculating the weights of a set of RBFs such that they interpolate the given data points. The surface is represented as the zero level set of this implicit function. In practice, in order to avoid RBF trivial solutions, some interior or exterior constraints along the normal direction, called off-surface points, must be appended to the original samples. But it doubles or triples the number of interpolation centers. Furthermore, RBF interpolation is global support and the coefficient matrix is dense and often ill posed. Therefore, it is difficult to use this technique to reconstruct implicit surfaces from large point sets consisting of more than several thousands of points. Although compactly supported RBF can

H. Zha et al. (Eds.): VSMM 2006, LNCS 4270, pp. 232–241, 2006.

offer a way to deal with large scale point sets since the involved RBF coefficient matrix becomes sparse [9,10,11]. Unfortunately, the radius of support has to be chosen globally, which means the approach is not robust and stable against highly non-uniformly distributed point sets where the density of the samples may vary significantly. Ohtake and Morse's compactly supported RBF [9,11], Carr's greedy algorithm [7], Beatson's GMRES iteration method and Domain Decomposition Method (DDM) [12] and Ohtake and Tobor's Partition of Unity [10,6] offer methodologies to deal with the problem of fast fitting for large point sets. As for fast evaluation of RBF, Beatson's fast multipole method (FMM) is an efficient algorithm [14]. Farfield Technology^{TM} is a commercial toolbox based on the FMM RBF method, which has been successfully employed in archaeology [18]. But the far field expansion of FMM has to be done separately for every radial basis function and its implementation is intricate and complicated.

Since the RBF collocation method uses the scattered points both as data and centers, numerical ill conditioning often occurs due to too small distance between some centers, which will cause linear dependency of coefficients matrix. In order to reduce the computational cost, greedy algorithm or so-called thinning was introduced. In general, the subset of centers is selected randomly or arbitrarily. Such mechanism is clearly unsatisfactory. The method of orthogonal least square (OLS) can be utilized as a forward selection procedure to select set of suitable centers from large data set. This is a regression procedure. The selected set of centers is the regressors, and at each step of regression, the increment to the explained variance of the desired output is maximized [15,16].

In this paper we describe two algorithms to the problem of surface reconstruction from large unorganized point sets based on LS RBF and partition of unity (POU). We adapt the methodology of OLS to select the subset of significant centers for reconstruction. Paper is organized as follows. RBF interpolation is introduced in section 2, and in section 3 the LS RBF scheme is described. Section 4 specifically describes the OLS center selection procedure. The details of algorithm implementation are presented in section 5. Some reconstructed examples are presented in section 6. Part 7 is conclusion section.

2   Radial Basis Functions

The problem of scattered data interpolation can be stated as given a set of fixed points $\{x_i\}_{i=1}^N \in R^n$ on a surface S in R^3 and a set of function values $\{f_i\}_{i=1}^N \in R$, and find an interpolant $\phi : R^3 \to R$ such that

$$\phi(x_i) = f_i, \quad i = 1, 2, \cdots, N. \tag{1}$$

With the use of RBF, the interpolation function is defined as

$$\phi(x) = \sum_{j=1}^N \alpha_j g_j(\|x - x_j\|) + p(x), \tag{2}$$

where $p(\boldsymbol{x})$is a polynomial, α_j are coefficients corresponding to each basis and $\|\cdot\|$ is the Euclidean norm on R^n. The basis function g is a real function on $[0, \infty)$, usually unbounded and global support.

There are many basis functions for use in equation (2). Some popular basis functions include thin-plate spline, Gaussian, multiquadric, inverse multiquadric, biharmonic and triharmonic etc [13]. The polynomial $p(\boldsymbol{x})$ is appended for achieving polynomial precision according to the basis functions. Additional so-called natural constraints are needed. For example, if $p(\boldsymbol{x})$ is a linear polynomial, the coefficients α must satisfy the constraints, $\sum_{j=1}^{N} \alpha_j = \sum_{j=1}^{N} \alpha_j \boldsymbol{x}_j = \sum_{j=1}^{N} \alpha_j \boldsymbol{y}_j = \sum_{j=1}^{N} \alpha_j \boldsymbol{z}_j = 0$.

From equations (1), (2) and the constraints, it gives rise to

$$\phi(\boldsymbol{x}_i) = \sum_{j=1}^{N} \alpha_j g(\|\boldsymbol{x}_i - \boldsymbol{x}_j\|) + p(\boldsymbol{x}_i). \tag{3}$$

The solutions of the system compose of the weighting coefficients and the polynomial coefficients for $\phi(\boldsymbol{x})$. However, it is unpractical to solve the linear system (3) directly for large scale point sets and with complexity of $O(N^3)$ interpolant computing and $O(N)$ evaluation. In this paper, we employ a LS RBF scheme and an OLS square based subcenters selection method to reconstruct surface efficiently.

3   LS RBF Surface Reconstruction

We rewrite the RBF formulation (2) into

$$\phi(\boldsymbol{x}) = \sum_{j=1}^{M} \alpha_j g(\boldsymbol{x} - \boldsymbol{x}_j) = \boldsymbol{g}^T \boldsymbol{\alpha}, \tag{4}$$

where $\boldsymbol{g} = [\boldsymbol{g}_1, \boldsymbol{g}_2, \cdots, \boldsymbol{g}_M]^T$, $\boldsymbol{\alpha} = [\alpha_1, \alpha_2, \cdots, \alpha_M]^T$, M is the number of points used in reconstruction ($M \ll N$), and T is the transpose operator. Function values on the data points $\boldsymbol{h}$ indicating the function value with noisy data. Let $\boldsymbol{G} = [\boldsymbol{g}_1^T, \boldsymbol{g}_2^T, \cdots, \boldsymbol{g}_N^T]_{N \times M}$, we have

$$\phi(\boldsymbol{x}) = \boldsymbol{G}\boldsymbol{\alpha}. \tag{5}$$

The RBF interpolant interpolates the sample points with function values $\boldsymbol{h} = \{f_i\}_{i=1}^{N}$, so the interpolation equations can be derived from the following optimization problem

$$J = \frac{1}{2} \left[(\boldsymbol{G}\boldsymbol{\alpha} - \boldsymbol{h})^T (\boldsymbol{G}\boldsymbol{\alpha} - \boldsymbol{h}). \right]^2 \rightarrow \min \tag{6}$$

To minimize (6), we have

$$\frac{\partial J}{\partial \alpha} = G^T (G\boldsymbol{\alpha} - \boldsymbol{h}). \tag{7}$$

Let equation (7) equal to zero and get

$$G^T G \alpha = G^T h. \tag{8}$$

Then α can be represented as

$$\alpha = (G^T G)^{-1} G^T h. \tag{9}$$

In these equations the low degree of polynomial is not considered. It can be appended in accordance with specific basis functions. When coefficients α are solved, the implicit surface can be reconstructed with much fewer centers ($M \ll N$). The subset of centers, M, can be efficiently selected from the original samples using OLS method.

4   OLS Subsets Selection

The problem of how to select a suitable set of RBF centers from the data set can be considered as an example of how to select a subset of significant points from a given candidate set. OLS method was described in [16] for subset selection of neural networks. But there are a lot of redundant calculations involved in the selection procedure. It holds up the process of fast selection. We adapt this scheme to an efficient center selection algorithm. The regression matrix G from equation (5) can be decomposed into

$$G = WQ, \tag{10}$$

where Q is a $M \times M$ upper triangular matrix with ones on the diagonal, and w is a $N \times M$ matrix with orthogonal columns $\boldsymbol{w}_i$ such that

$$W^T W = D, \tag{11}$$

where matrix D is diagonal with elements d_j, and d_j is defined as

$$d_j = \boldsymbol{w}_j^T \boldsymbol{w}_j = \sum_{i=1}^{N} w_j(i) w_j(i), \quad j = 1, 2, \cdots, M. \tag{12}$$

The space spanned by the set of orthogonal basis vectors is the same space spanned by the set of $\boldsymbol{g}_j$, RBF linear system can be rewritten as

$$h = W\boldsymbol{\eta}. \tag{13}$$

The orthogonal least square solution is given by

$$\boldsymbol{\eta} = H^{-1} W^T h, \text{ or } \eta_j = \boldsymbol{w}_j^T h / (\boldsymbol{w}_j^T \boldsymbol{w}_j), \quad 1 \leqslant j \leqslant M. \tag{14}$$

The coefficients α and vector $\boldsymbol{\eta}$ satisfy the following triangular system

$$Q\alpha = \boldsymbol{\eta}. \tag{15}$$

The well-known Gram-Schmidt method can compute one column of Q at a time and orthogonalize to each $k-1$ previously orthogonalized columns and repeat the operation for $k = 2, \cdots, M$.

An error ration due to $\boldsymbol{w}_j$ is defined as

$$[err]_j = \eta_j^2 \boldsymbol{w}_j^T \boldsymbol{w}_j / (\boldsymbol{h}^T \boldsymbol{h}). \tag{16}$$

This ratio offers a simple and effective means of select subset of significant centers in a forward-regression manner. The significant center selection procedure can be summarized as follows.

- The first selected center
  for $1 \leqslant i \leqslant N$
  $\quad w_1^{(i)} = \boldsymbol{g}_i$
  $\quad [err]_1^{(i)} = ((\boldsymbol{w}_1^{(i)})^T \boldsymbol{h})^2 / (((\boldsymbol{w}_1^i)^T \boldsymbol{w}_1^{(i)})(\boldsymbol{h}^T \boldsymbol{h}))$
  end for
  Find $[err]_1^{(i_1)} = \max [err]_1^{(i)}, 1 \leqslant i \leqslant N$
  And select $\boldsymbol{w}_1 = \boldsymbol{w}_1^{(i_1)} = \boldsymbol{g}_{i_1}$
- At the kth step, where $k \geqslant 2$,
  for $1 \leqslant i \leqslant N, (i \neq i_1, \cdots, i \neq i_{k-1})$
  $\quad$ for $1 \leqslant j < k$
  $\qquad q_{jk}^{(i)} = \boldsymbol{w}_j^T \boldsymbol{g}_i / (\boldsymbol{w}_j^T \boldsymbol{w}_j)$
  $\qquad \boldsymbol{w}_k^{(i)} = \boldsymbol{g}_i - \sum_{j=1}^{k-1} q_{jk}^{(i)} \boldsymbol{w}_j$
  $\quad$ end for
  $\quad [err]_k^{(i)} = ((\boldsymbol{w}_k^{(i)})^T \boldsymbol{h})^2 / (((\boldsymbol{w}_k^{(i)})^T \boldsymbol{w}_k^{(i)})(\boldsymbol{h}^T \boldsymbol{h}))$
  Find $[err]_k^{i_k} = \max [err]_k^{(i)}, 1 \leqslant i \leqslant N, i \neq i_1, \cdots, i \neq i_{k-1}$
  Select $\boldsymbol{w}_k = \boldsymbol{w}_k^{i_k} = \boldsymbol{g}_{i_k} - \sum_{j-1}^{k-1} q_{jk}^{i_k} \boldsymbol{w}_j$
- The process is stopped at the Mth step when the error ration satisfies
  $1 - \sum_{j=1}^{M} [err]_j < \rho$

where $0 < \rho < 1$ is a user defined tolerance which controls the amount of crucial centers.

5   Algorithm Implementation

5.1   OLS Based Subset Selection

When performing the OLS subset selection, an adaptive octree was set up to accelerate the procedure. The octree subdivision will be described in the next subsection. Since the original point sets are the surface samples, the function values h_i are all equal to zero which is not suitable for OLS selection. An extra point, p, is added to each of the non-empty leaf cell of the octree. The function value at this point is set as constant c (in our implementation we set c=1). During selection, if point p is selected as a significant center, it is still retained in the original point set for the next selection.

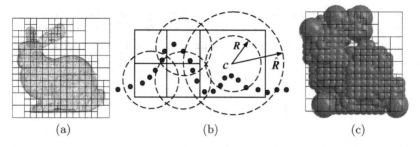

Fig. 1. Adaptive octree subdivision of point data set, (a) Octree of bunny model, (b) Subdomain creation, (c) Subdomains of nonempey octree leaf node of bunny

5.2   Octree Subdivision and Partition of Unity

To divide the scattered point sets into local problems, we use an adaptive octree to organize the point sets as in [10], seeing Fig. 1(a). In order to blend the local patches into a global solution, the technique of partition of unity is employed. The concept of POU is rooted in applied mathematics [19]. The main idea of the partition of unity method is to divide the global domain of interest into smaller overlapping subdomains where the problem can be solved locally on a small scale. The local solutions are combined together by using blending functions to obtain the global solution. The smoothness of the global solution in the overlap regions of two subdomains can be guaranteed by a polynomial blending function. The POU-based RBF surface reconstruction has been applied by Ohtake [10] and Torbor [13]. The global domain Ω is first divided into M overlapping subdomains $\{\Omega_i\}_{i=1}^{M}$ with $\Omega \subseteq \cup_i \Omega_i$. For a partition of unity on the set of subdomains $\{\Omega_i\}_{i=1}^{M}$, we then need to define a collection of non-negative blending functions $\{w_i\}_{i=1}^{M}$ with limited support and with $\sum w_i = 1$ in the entire domain Ω. For each subdomain Ω_i, the data set of the points within the subdomain is used to compute a local reconstruction function ϕ_i that interpolates the data points. The global reconstruction function Φ is then defined as a combination of the local functions

$$\Phi(\boldsymbol{x}) = \sum_{i=1}^{M} \phi(\boldsymbol{x})w_i((x)) \tag{17}$$

The blending functions are obtained from a set of smooth functions W_i by a normalization procedure

$$\omega_i(\boldsymbol{x}) = \frac{W_i(\boldsymbol{x})}{\sum_{j=1}^{n} W_j(\boldsymbol{x})}, \tag{18}$$

where the condition $\sum \omega_i = 1$ is satisfied. In our implementation, we also use a quadratic B-spline $b(t)$ to generate weight functions as in [5]

$$W(\boldsymbol{x}) = b(3|\boldsymbol{x} - \boldsymbol{c}_i|/(2R_i)). \tag{19}$$

In our implementation, the subdomain is defined as sphere centered at c_i and with support radius R_i, shown Fig. 1(b) and (c). R_i is proportional to the diagonal of corresponding octree cell. In the case of the point set with ununiform distribution, the radius should be increased or decreased until the number of points contained in this ball is more than a threshold. In our implementation, we set the threshold $N_{min} = 30$ and $N_{max} = 80$. That is the amount of points in each subdomain must be clamped in range of N_{min} and N_{max}.

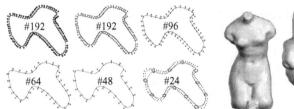

Fig. 2. LS RBF reconstructions in 2D, the result looks good until the point ratio is reduced to 25%

Fig. 3. LS RBF reconstructions in 3D, left is from #10,111, middle from #34,834 and right from #72,545

6   Experimental Results

The above stated algorithms are implemented with VC++ and OpenGL. The hardware configuration is Intel 1.5 GHz with 512 MB RAM and WinXP OS. We tested lots of scattered point dataset with our proposed least square RBF mthod. Fig. 2 shows examples in 2D case; Fig. 2 (a) shows the original curve and samples, the amount is 192. (b) to (f) are reconstructed curves, with the numbers of sub-centers decreasing gradually; say 192, 96, 64, 48, 24 respectively, the maximal errors increase correspondingly. In particular, there are maximal errors in Fig. 2 (f) just using 24 centers marked with ellipsoid. Fig. 3 shows the 3D cases, these examples show highly satisfactory quality. The zero level set is extracted by an extended marching cube (MC) algorithm.

In Fig. 4, dataset (a) is the original samples; we use OLS method to reduce the number of interpolant centers from 34,834 to 11,483 (OLS1) and 7,965 (OLS2) and the thresholds ρ are 0.01 and 0.013, respectively. Figure (d), (e) and (f) are models reconstructed from (a), (b) and (c) respectively. There are no visual differences between these models. Furthermore, we compared the quantitative errors of model (e) and (f) with model (d). Fig. 4 (g) is the error map between (d) and (f). We compute the positive/negative maximum distances (PMD/NMD), average distance (AD) and standard deviation (SD) to evaluate the quality of the reconstructed meshes. Fig. 5 is another example. Table 1 shows three of models processed by our algorithm. Num_pnt means the number of points, Num_tri is the amount of the triangles of reconstructed meshes, and Original means the original

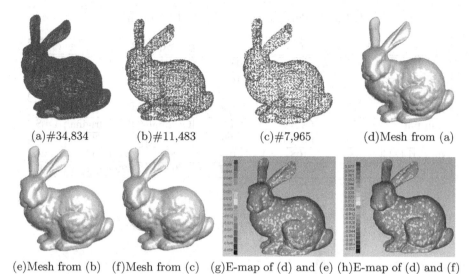

(a)#34,834   (b)#11,483   (c)#7,965   (d)Mesh from (a)

(e)Mesh from (b)   (f)Mesh from (c)   (g)E-map of (d) and (e)   (h)E-map of (d) and (f)

Fig. 4. OLS selected point data sets, reconstructed models and differences between meshes. From (a) to (c), the num. of points is reduced gradually. (d) to (f) are the reconstructed results. Number of triangles is (d) 160k, (e) 108k and (f) 108k respectively. (g) and (h) are error maps. The errors are relatively small. It validates our method using fewer centers to reconstruct accurate models.

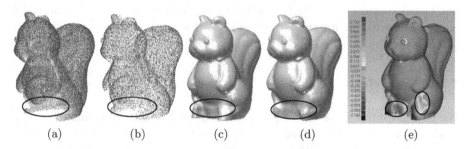

(a)   (b)   (c)   (d)   (e)

Fig. 5. Point set (a) is original with #40,627, (b) is OLS selected point data set from (a),the number of points is 11,321. (c) and (d) are reconstructed models from (a) and (b). (e) is the difference map between (c) and (d), (c) is the reference. (a) and (b) are incomplete in the ellipsoid where the max error appears. It also shows RBF method can fill the hole automatically.

data set. T_time stands for the total time consumption, which includes octree setup, RBF system solving and polygonization. From these figures and Table 1, we can see the mesh models reconstructed from low resolution point sets have high fidelity in comparison with the higher resolution model. But computational timings of these models have great discrepancy. OLS can greatly accelerate the reconstruction and can obtain satisfactory result.

Table 1. Parameters of OSL and Error map

Data sets	Bunny			Squirrel		Igea	
Threshold ρ	—	0.01	0.013	0.002		0.002	
OLS time(s)	—	1.23	0.94	1.45		2.11	
PMD/NMD	—	0.058/-5.8e-3	0.077/-0.077	0.742/-0.742		0.199/-0.199	
AD/SD	—	6.9e-4/4.6e-3	6.7e-4/6.3e-3	3.5e-3/0.062		1.1e-3/0.018	
Num_pnt	Original	OLS1	OLS2	Original	OLS	Original	OLS
	34,834	11,483	7,965	40,627	11,321	72,545	17,945
Num_tri (k)	168	108	108	88	126	111	139
T_time(s)	57.71	17.48	9.17	99.18	16.22	154.23	23.45

Fig. 6. Multi level representations of RBF implicit surfaces

From these examples, we can see OLS is an efficient tool to reduce the computational complexity of RBF based surface reconstruction. Furthermore, by adjusting the threshold, we can obtain a multi-level representation. Fig. 6 displays this statement.

7   Conclusions

We have introduced the least square radial basis functions to estimate the co-efficients on each surface sample and construct a continuous implicit function to represent 3D surface. Its zero level-set is the desired 3D surface. Another scheme proposed in this paper is OLS based center reduction method. These methods can overcome the problem of numerical ill-conditioning and over-fitting of traditional RBF reconstructions and offer a tool to utilize fewer samples to reconstruct models and make geometry processing feasible and practical. The experimental results show that our presented approaches are efficient and ro-bust. In particular, through OLS selection, the computation cost can be reduced substantially. Our implicit surface reconstruction scheme can be served in arche-ology, virtual reality, game development since the precision is not a great concern in these applications.

We can find the coefficients can be solved from equation (15) when getting matrix Q and vector η. But the matrix Q is calculated recursively, which may time consuming. In our future research, we will compute the coefficients from equation (15) directly, which may further speed up the reconstruction procedure.

References

1. Park, J. and Sandberg, J.W.: Universal approximation using radial basis functions network. *Neural Computation, 1991, Vol.3, 246-257.*
2. Hoppe, H, DeRose, T., Duchamp, T., McDonald, J. and Stuetzle, W.: Surface renstruction from unorganized points. *In Proceedings of ACM SIGGRAPH 1992, 71-78.*
3. Amenta, N., Bern, M. and Kamvysselis, M.: A new Voronoi-based surface reconstruction algorithm. *In Proceedings of ACM SIGGRAPH 1998, 415-421.*
4. Carr, J. C., Beatson, R. K., Cherrie, J. B., Mitchell, T. J., Fright, W. R., McCallum, B. C. and Evans, T. R.: Reconstruction and representation of 3D objects with radial basis functions. *In Proceedings of ACM SIGGRAPH 2001, 67-76.*
5. Ohtake, Y., Belyaev, A., Alexa, M., Turk, G. and Seidel, H. P.: Multi-level partition of unity implicits. *ACM Transactions on Graphics, Proceedings of SIGGRAPH 2003, Vol. 22, No. 3, 463-470.*
6. Tobor, P., Reuter, and Schilck, C.: Efficient reconstruction of large scattered geometric datasets using the partition of unity and radial basis functions. *Journal of WSCG 2004, Vol. 12, 467-474.*
7. Carr, J. C., Beatson, R. K., Cherrie, J. B., Mitchell, T. J., Fright, W. R., McCallum, B. C. and Evans, T. R.: Reconstruction and representation of 3D objects with radial basis functions. *In Proceedings of ACM SIGGRAPH 2001, 67-76.*
8. Turk, G. and O'brien, J.: Modelling with implicit surfaces that interpolate. *ACM Transactions on Graphics, 2002, Vol. 21, No. 4, 855-873.*
9. Ohtake, Y., Belyaev, A. G. and Seidel, H. P.: A multi-scale approach to 3D scattered data interpolation with compactly supported basis functions. *In Shape Modeling International SMI, 2003 153-161.*
10. Ohtake, Y., Belyaev, A. and Seidel, H.: 3D Scattered Data Approximation with Adaptive Compactly Supported Radial Basis Functions. *In Shape Modeling and Applications SMI, 2004, 31-39.*
11. Morse, B., Yoo, T.S., Rheingans, P. et al.: Interpolating implicit surfaces from scattered surfaces data using compactly supported radial basis functions. *In Proceedings of Shape Modeling International SMI, 2001, 89-98.*
12. Beatson, R. K., Light, W. A. and Billings, S.: Fast solution of the radial basis function interpolation equations: domain decomposition methods. *SIAM J. Sci. Comput. Vol. 22, No. 5, 2000, 1717-1740.*
13. Tobor, I., Reuter, P. and Schlick, C.: Multiresolution reconstruction of implicit surfaces with attributes from large unorganized point sets. *In Proceedings of Shape Modeling International SMI, 2004, 19-30.*
14. Beatson, B. and Newsam, G.: Fast evaluation of radial basis functions. *Computational Mathematics and Applications, 1992, Vol. 24, No. 12, 7-20.*
15. Chen, S., Billings, S.A., and Luo, W.: Orthogonal least square methods and their application to non-linear system identification. *International Journal of Control, 1989, Vol.50, No.5, 1873-1896.*
16. Chen, S., Cowan, C.F.N., and Grant, P.M.: Orthogonal least square learning algorithm for radial basis function networks. *IEEE Transactions on Neural Network, 1991, Vol. 2, No. 2, 302-309.*
17. Wu J. and Kobbelt, L. P.: A stream algorithm for the decimation of massive meshes. *In Graphics Interface 2003 Proceedings, Halifax, Canada, 2003, 185-192.*
18. Farfield Technology Ltd. http://www.farfieldtechnology.com/.
19. Babuška, I. and Melenk, J.M.: The partition of unity method. *International Journal of Numerical Methods in Engineering, (1997)*

An Interpolatory Subdivision Scheme for Triangular Meshes and Progressive Transmission

Ruotian Ling, Xiaonan Luo, Ren Chen, and Guifeng Zheng

Computer Application Institute, Sun Yat-sen University, Guangzhou, 510275, China
lnslxn@mail.sysu.edu.cn

Abstract. This paper proposes a new interpolatory subdivision scheme for triangular meshes that produces C^1 continuous limit surfaces for both regular and irregular settings. The limit surfaces also have bounded curvature, which leads to improved quality surfaces. The eigen-structure analysis demonstrates the smoothness of the limit surfaces. According to the new scheme, the approach for progressive transmission of meshes is presented. Finally, results of refined models with the new scheme are shown. In most cases, the new scheme generates more pleasure surfaces than the traditional modified butterfly scheme, especially near the irregular settings.

1   Introduction

Subdivision is an effective way to generate surfaces. One can find a great number of literature and ongoing research on the construction of new schemes [5,7]. Simply speaking, a subdivision surface is defined as the limit of a sequence of meshes. Therein each mesh is generated from its predecessor using a group of topological and geometric rules. Topological rules are responsible for producing a finer mesh from a coarse one while geometric rules are designed to compute the position of vertices in the new mesh. These two groups of rules constitute a subdivision scheme.

The present study introduces a new interpolatory subdivision scheme for triangular meshes with arbitrary topology. This scheme is an new modification to Dyn's work [1], which has been widely applied for many years. The new subdivision scheme splits each triangle into 4 by inserting an E-vertex onto each edge. These newly inserted E-vertices are controlled by the rules for regular and irregular settings. Through the smoothness analysis, we numerically prove the limit surfaces are C^1-continuous and have bounded curvature in addition.

In the following sections, we will first review the traditional butterfly scheme in Section 2. New rules for the subdivision scheme are constructed in Section 3 and 4, including rules for regular and extraordinary cases. Convergence and continuity analysis are discussed in Section 5. In Section 6, the rules for applying the new scheme to progressive transmission are presented. The implementation and simulation results are given in Section 7.

H. Zha et al. (Eds.): VSMM 2006, LNCS 4270, pp. 242–252, 2006.

2   Related Work

Interpolatory subdivision surfaces were pioneered by Dyn [1] in which a so called butterfly subdivision scheme was constructed for triangular meshes. Dyn's mask is shown in Fig.1 and the weights of each vertex follow: $w_1 = w_2 = \frac{1}{2}, w_3 = w_4 = \frac{1}{8}, w_5 = w_6 = w_7 = w_8 = -\frac{1}{16}$.

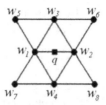

Fig. 1. The mask for Dyn's butterfly scheme

Dyn's scheme generates smooth surfaces for regular setting meshes, however, it exhibits degeneracy when applied to irregular meshes. Zorin [2] presented a modified version by designing new rules for computing newly inserted vertices, which improve the generated surfaces a lot near extraordinary vertices especially. Although Zorin's scheme for the regular setting contains 10 vertices, Zorin suggested that 2 weights in the mask should be zero. In fact, the most popular modified butterfly scheme merely takes 8 vertices into consideration. The irregular rules designed by Zorin is given. Denote n as the valance of a vertex. For $n \geq 5$,

$$w_j = \frac{1}{n}(\frac{1}{4} + \cos\frac{2\pi j}{n} + \frac{1}{2}\cos\frac{4\pi j}{n}), \ (j = 0, \ldots, n-1). \tag{1}$$

For $n = 3$, it takes $w_0 = \frac{5}{12}, w_1 = w_2 = -\frac{1}{12}$, and for $n = 4, w_0 = \frac{3}{8}, w_1 = 0, w_2 = -\frac{1}{8}, w_3 = 0$.

The additional masks by Zorin at the irregular case was constructed with the Fourier transform which has often been used for extending regular masks to irregular cases and this method will be also involved in our derivation.

3   Derivation of Regular Mask

An extension of the 4-point scheme from curve cases to surfaces is presented in this section, which leads to a new butterfly scheme with different weights of vertex in the mask.

Though the smoothness analysis at [6,9,10], it is known that the necessary condition for curvature continuity was discovered. Specially if the six leading eigenvalues of a subdivision matrix have the following structure:

$$1, \lambda, \lambda, \lambda^2, \lambda^2, \lambda^2, \tag{2}$$

then the scheme produces limit surfaces with bounded curvature. Hence, Loop referred the above eigenvalue structure as bounded curvature spectrum [11]. This property is generally employed to improve surfaces quality [12,13]. Now this property is also used in our scheme to construct a new subdivision scheme.

The topological rules of the new scheme proposed in this paper follow the traditional butterfly scheme, which is so called 1-4 splitting. After every step of refinement, the number of triangles in a new mesh is 4 times as that of the previous level of mesh. Fig. 2 shows the mask of E-vertex for regular settings and the inserted vertices are computed as following:

$$q = \sum_{i=1}^{10} w_i p_i^k, \qquad (3)$$

where w_i is the weight of p_i. Notice 2 more vertices are considered in the new scheme than the traditional butterfly scheme. For symmetry reason, it require: (a) $w_1 = w_2$; (b) $w_3 = w_4$; (c) $w_5 = w_6 = w_7 = w_8$; (d) $w_9 = w_{10}$. Since the new

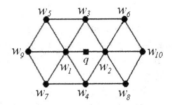

Fig. 2. The regular mask for an E-vertex

scheme is base on 4-point scheme, the weights of vertices should satisfy Eq.(4). Define $w_1 = a, w_3 = b, w_5 = c, w_9 = d$, we have

$$\begin{cases} w_5 + w_1 + w_4 = 9/16 \\ w_3 + w_2 + w_8 = 9/16 \\ w_9 + w_7 = -1/16 \\ w_{10} + w_6 = -1/16 \end{cases}, i.e. \begin{cases} a + b + c = 9/16 \\ c + d = -1/16 \end{cases}, \qquad (4)$$

We establish a subdivision matrix between two invariant stencils around a regular vertex of two subsequent subdivision levels. Here the invariant stencil is selected as the 2-neighborhood of a vertex as shown in Fig.3. Partition the stencil into 6 blocks:

$$B_i^k = (p_{i0}^k, p_{i1}^k, p_{i2}^k, p_{i3}^k)^T \ (i = 1, 2, 3, 4, 5, 6).$$

For convenience of description, $p_{i0}^k (i = 1, 2, 3, 4, 5, 6)$ represent the same vertex here. Denote $B^k = (B_1, B_1, B_2, B_3, B_4, B_6)^T$. Write the vertex vector of the stencil generated after a step of refinement as B^{k+1}. The labeling system is illustrated in Fig.3. We are able to obtain: $B^{k+1} = SB^k$, where S is the subdivision matrix and $S = C(S_1, S_2, S_3, S_4, S_5, S_6)$, here S is a block circulant matrix with 4×4 matrix sequence.

$$S_1 = \begin{pmatrix} 1/6\,0\,0\,0 \\ a/6\ a\ d\ c \\ 0\quad 1\,0\,0 \\ b/6\ a\ d\ b \end{pmatrix}, S_2 = \begin{pmatrix} 1/6\,0\,0\,0 \\ a/6\ a\ d\ c \\ 0\quad 1\,0\,0 \\ b/6\ a\ d\ b \end{pmatrix}, S_3 = \begin{pmatrix} 1/6\,0\,0\,0 \\ a/6\ c\ 0\ 0 \\ 0\quad 0\,0\,0 \\ b/6\ c\ 0\ 0 \end{pmatrix},$$

$$S_4 = \begin{pmatrix} 1/6\,0\,0\,0 \\ a/6\ d\ 0\ 0 \\ 0\quad 0\,0\,0 \\ b/6\ 0\ 0\ 0 \end{pmatrix}, S_5 = \begin{pmatrix} 1/6\,0\,0\,0 \\ a/6\ c\ 0\ 0 \\ 0\quad 0\,0\,0 \\ b/6\ 0\ 0\ 0 \end{pmatrix}, S_6 = \begin{pmatrix} 1/6\,0\,0\,0 \\ a/6\ b\ 0\ c \\ 0\quad 0\,0\,0 \\ b/6\ c\ 0\ d \end{pmatrix}. \tag{5}$$

Combining Eq.(4) and (5) and solving the matrix with some mathematics tool, as the Matlab, we get

$$\begin{cases} a = 17/32 \\ b = 1/16 \\ c = -1/32 \\ d = -1/32 \end{cases}, i.e., \quad \begin{cases} w_1 = w_2 = 17/32 \\ w_3 = w_4 = 1/16 \\ w_5 = w_6 = w_7 = w_8 = -1/32 \\ w_9 = w_{10} = -1/32 \end{cases}. \tag{6}$$

The six leading eigenvalues of subdivision matrix are $1, \frac{1}{2}, \frac{1}{2}, \frac{1}{4}, \frac{1}{4}, \frac{1}{4}$.

It should be noticed that this is not the unique solution that makes the eigenvalues with the bounded curvature spectrum structure, but we have tested that this solution led to the most pleasure surfaces.

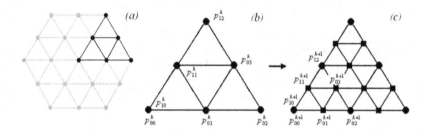

Fig. 3. (a)The 2-neighborhood configuration around a regular vertex. (b)The dark part in (a) with an enlarge view. (c)The mesh in (b) after a step of refinement.

4   Derivation of Irregular Subdivision Mask

We setup the subdivision rules by examining the necessary conditions for a convergent subdivision scheme as found in [6]. In order to keep the subdivision rules as simple as possible we only use the vertices in the 1-neighborhood of extraordinary vertex p_0^k for the computation of the new vertices q. So a new vertex is computed as

$$q = w_0 p_0^k + \sum_{i=1}^{n} w_i p_i^k. \tag{7}$$

For the given configuration we can build the local subdivision matrix M. Firstly, we consider the extraordinary vertex with valence 6 which is a regular

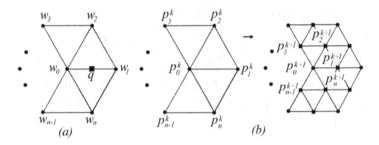

Fig. 4. (a) The irregular mask for an E-vertex. (b) A step of refinement near an extraordinary vertex and its labeling system.

vertex in fact. To extend the regular mask to irregular settings, we only need to extend the 3-point scheme [5] to surface cases. The masks for irregular cases is shown in Fig.4, where w_i is the weight of p_i. When $n = 6$, for symmetry reason, it requires: (a) $w_2 = w_6$; (b) $w_3 = w_5$. Because the irregular cases are base on the 3-point interpolatory scheme, we are able to obtain:

$$\begin{cases} w_2 + w_0 + w_5 = 6/8 \\ w_1 + w_6 = 3/8 \\ w_3 + w_4 = -1/8 \end{cases}, i.e. \begin{cases} w_0 = 1/2 + \alpha + \beta \\ w_2 = 3/8 - \alpha \\ w_3 = -1/8 - \beta \end{cases}, \qquad (8)$$

with $w_1 = \alpha$ and $w_4 = \beta$.

Let us perform one step of refinement near extraordinary vertex, which as shown in Fig.4. Assume p_0^k has valence 6 and denote $A_i^k = (p_0^k, p_i^k)^T (i = 1, 2, 3, 4, 5, 6)$ and $A^k = (A_1, A_1, A_2, A_3, A_4, A_6)^T$. We are able to obtain: $A^{k+1} = M^{(6)}A^k$, where $M^{(6)}$ is the subdivision matrix for irregular settings and $M^{(6)}$ is a block circulant matrix $M^{(6)} = C(M_1^{(6)}, M_2^{(6)}, M_3^{(6)}, M_4^{(6)}, M_5^{(6)}, M_6^{(6)})$ with 2×2 matrix sequence.

$$M_1^{(6)} = \frac{1}{6} \begin{pmatrix} 1 & 0 \\ \frac{1}{2} + \alpha + \beta & 6\alpha \end{pmatrix}, M_2^{(6)} = \frac{1}{6} \begin{pmatrix} 1 & 0 \\ \frac{1}{2} + \alpha + \beta & \frac{9}{4} - 6\alpha \end{pmatrix},$$

$$M_3^{(6)} = \frac{1}{6} \begin{pmatrix} 1 & 0 \\ \frac{1}{2} + \alpha + \beta & -\frac{3}{4} - 6\beta \end{pmatrix}, M_4^{(6)} = \frac{1}{6} \begin{pmatrix} 1 & 0 \\ \frac{1}{2} + \alpha + \beta & 6\beta \end{pmatrix},$$

$$M_5^{(6)} = \frac{1}{6} \begin{pmatrix} 1 & 0 \\ \frac{1}{2} + \alpha + \beta & -\frac{3}{4} - 6\beta \end{pmatrix}, M_6^{(6)} = \frac{1}{6} \begin{pmatrix} 1 & 0 \\ \frac{1}{2} + \alpha + \beta & \frac{9}{4} - 6\alpha \end{pmatrix}. \qquad (9)$$

Performing the Fourier transform on the above matrix sequence, we obtain the following Fourier coefficients

$$\hat{M}_1^{(6)} = \begin{pmatrix} 1 & 0 \\ \frac{1}{2} + \alpha + \beta & \frac{1}{2} - \alpha - \beta \end{pmatrix}, \hat{M}_2^{(6)} = \begin{pmatrix} 0 & 0 \\ 0 & \frac{1}{2} \end{pmatrix},$$

$$\hat{M}_3^{(6)} = \begin{pmatrix} 0 & 0 \\ 0 & 2\alpha + 2\beta - \frac{1}{4} \end{pmatrix}, \hat{M}_4^{(6)} = \begin{pmatrix} 0 & 0 \\ 0 & 3\alpha - 3\beta - 1 \end{pmatrix},$$

$$\hat{M}_5^{(6)} = \begin{pmatrix} 0 & 0 \\ 0 & 2\alpha + 2\beta - \frac{1}{4} \end{pmatrix}, \hat{M}_6^{(6)} = \begin{pmatrix} 0 & 0 \\ 0 & \frac{1}{2} \end{pmatrix}. \qquad (10)$$

We want to determine α and β that make the eigenvalues of the irregular subdivision matrix satisfy the bounded curvature spectrum structure, so the following equations are obtained

$$\begin{cases} 2\alpha + 2\beta - 1/4 = (1/2)^2 \\ 3\alpha - 3\beta - 1 = (1/2)^2 \end{cases}. \tag{11}$$

Solving the equations, we get $\alpha = \frac{1}{3}$ and $\beta = -\frac{1}{12}$.

Since a circulant matrix is uniquely determined by the Fourier coefficients of its element sequence, to gurantee that the subdivision matrix $M^{(n)}$ for a mask containing an extraordinary vertex of valence n is the extension of $M^{(6)}$, we only need to assume $M^{(n)} = C(M_1, M_2, M_3, ..., M_n)$, that the Fourier coefficients $\hat{M}_1, \hat{M}_2, \hat{M}_3, ..., \hat{M}_n$ of the matrix sequence $M_1, M_2, M_3, ..., M_n$ satisfy

(a) If $n = 3 : \hat{M}_1 = \hat{M}_1^{(6)}, \hat{M}_2 = \hat{M}_2^{(6)}, \hat{M}_3 = \hat{M}_6^{(6)}$;

(b) If $n > 3 : \hat{M}_1 = \hat{M}_1^{(6)}, \hat{M}_2 = \hat{M}_2^{(6)}, \hat{M}_n = \hat{M}_6^{(6)}, \hat{M}_i = \hat{M}_3^{(6)} (i = 3, ..., n-1)$.

According to the inverse Fourier transform, we get

$$M_1 = \frac{1}{n} \begin{pmatrix} 1 & 0 \\ \frac{3}{4} & \frac{1}{2} + \frac{n}{4} \end{pmatrix}, M_k = \frac{1}{n} \begin{pmatrix} 1 & 0 \\ \frac{3}{4} & \frac{1}{2} \cos \frac{2\pi k}{n} \end{pmatrix} \quad (k = 2, 3, ..., n). \tag{12}$$

Now we are able to decide the weights in Eq.(7)

$$\begin{cases} w_0 = \frac{3}{4} \\ w_1 = \frac{1}{2n} + \frac{1}{4} \\ w_k = \frac{1}{2n} \cos \frac{2\pi k}{n}, (k = 2, 3, ..., n) \end{cases}. \tag{13}$$

5   Smoothness Analysis

To analyze the smoothness of the limit subdivision surfaces, we consider a simplicial complex similar to the k-neighborhood centered at the extraordinary vertices.

Table 1 shows these eigenvalues of the subdivision matrix M with a vertex of valence n. Notice that the eigenvalues follow Eq.(2) when $n \geq 5$. The eigenvalues analysis shows that the necessary condition of C^1-continuous is satisfied.

To verify the regularity and injectivity of the characteristic maps, we only show the control nets constructed from the eigenvectors of the subdominant eignevalues of the subdivision matrix and results generated by refining the control nets using the proposed subdivision. We have performed this for valence $3 \leq n \leq 50$, while Fig.5 only illustrates the results for valences $n = 3 - 8$. Our results numerically manifest that the corresponding maps are regular and injective.

Following [10], the proposed scheme is numerically proved to be C^1-continuous based on the above eigenvalue analysis of the subdivision matrix and the verification of regularity and injectivity of the characteristic maps. Especially when $n \geq 5$, the limit surfaces also have bounded curvature.

Table 1. Six leading eigenvalues of the subdivision matrix with a vertex of valence n

n	λ_1	λ_2	λ_3	λ_4	λ_5	λ_6
$n = 3$	1	0.5	0.5	0.25	0	0
$n = 4$	1	0.5	0.5	0.25	0.25	0
$n \geq 5$	1	0.5	0.5	0.25	0.25	0.25

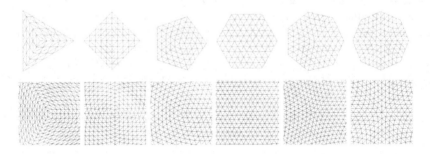

Fig. 5. Visualization of the characteristic maps of valences $n = 3 - 8$. The first row is controlling nets of subdominant eigenvectors and the second row is results after 5 steps of the proposed subdivision.

6   Progressive Meshes

Subdivision schemes are quite useful tools for generating curves and surfaces. The reverse subdivision schemes are also an effective method to simplify meshes and it is easy to apply reverse scheme to progressive transmission [3,4]. In this section, new rules of our subdivision scheme are constructed for progressive transmission.

According to the approach presented in [3], three steps are consisted in the procedure of simplification: splitting, predicting and updating. Now a modification of the three steps is performed to apply our new scheme to progressive transmission.

Splitting step is to distinguish reserved vertices and eliminated vertices in meshes. For convenience of expression, we name the group of reserved vertices as even group and the group of eliminated vertices as odd group. The splitting step can be denoted by the following equation:

$$M^{k-1} = EVEN^k = M^k - ODD^{k-1}, \qquad (14)$$

where M^k is the mesh and $EVEN^k$, ODD^k are the even group, odd group in mesh M^k respectively.

Fig.6 illustrates an example of splitting, where the vertices of dark triangles are in odd group, the rest vertices are in even group. The meshes, which are to be split, must satisfy the following constraint:

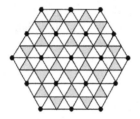

Fig. 6. An example of splitting

$$Distance(P^i_{EVEN}, P^j_{EVEN}) = 2^m, \ m = (0, 1, 2, \ldots), \tag{15}$$

where P^i_{EVEN}, P^j_{EVEN} are 2 arbitrary vertices in even group.

Predicting step is to compute the errors before eliminating the vertices in odd group. These errors are used to adjust the vertices in even group for reducing the geometric error between the original mesh and the simplified mesh. When applying our subdivision scheme in refining models, the vertices of odd groups are generated from the vertices in even groups. When applying our reverse scheme, we can also compute a new position of every vertex in odd group by the vertices in even groups. These new positions, in most cases, are not the same as their original positions. Then we take the difference between the new position and the original position of an eliminated vertex as its error. This process can be expressed by Eq.(16):

$$error^k = ODD^k - Predict(EVEN^k). \tag{16}$$

After computing all the error of vertices in odd group, the updating step can be performed. The updating step is to adjust the positions of reserved vertices. Observing the eliminated vertices around a reserved vertex, the rule for updating can be computed as following:

$$Update(e) = \frac{\eta}{n}(\frac{17}{32}\sum e^1 + \frac{1}{16}\sum e^2 - \frac{1}{32}\sum e^3), \tag{17}$$

where n is the valence of the centric even vertex and η is a coefficient to control the updating step. $e^i (i = 1, 2, 3)$ are the error of odd vertices with distance 1, 2, 3. This paper uses $\eta = 2$ in the step and it turns to generating more pleasure simplified meshes.

Given the operation of splitting, predicting, updating, the progressive transmission can be performed. By iterating the reverse subdivision process, a more coarse mesh and a sequence of errors are obtained. These errors are the details of the original mesh, i.e. the progressive mesh representation of the original mesh is as follows:

$$(M_n) \rightarrow (M_{n-1}, e_{n-1}) \rightarrow \cdots \rightarrow (M_0, e_0, e_1, \cdots, e_{n-1}). \tag{18}$$

When a transmission session is started, the coarsest base mesh is sent first. The client displays the base mesh when the transmission is finished. Then, if a more detailed surface is required, a command string is sent from client to server by requesting the next level of details. The client reconstructs a denser mesh with those details.

7 Examples

To test the proposed new subdivision scheme, we present some examples in this section. The proposed subdivision scheme has been implemented on a personal computer with a Pentium 1.6 GHz CPU and 512MB RAM running Windows XP operation system.

Fig.7 and Fig.8 show the difference between our scheme and the modified butterfly scheme [2]. Obviously our scheme generates more pleasure surfaces. More refined models with the new scheme is demonstrated in Fig.9, Fig.10 and Fig.11.

Fig. 7. A plane with a cusp. (a) The original model. (b) The result with the modified butterfly scheme. (c) The result with our new scheme. Both (b) and (c) are the corresponding results after 5 steps of refinement.

Fig. 8. A polygonal pyramid with an extraordinary vertex with valence 20. (a) The original model. (b) The result with the modified butterfly scheme. (c) The result with our new scheme. (d) The result near irregular setting with the modified butterfly scheme. (e) The result near irregular setting with our new scheme. (b)-(e) are the corresponding results after 6 steps of refinement.

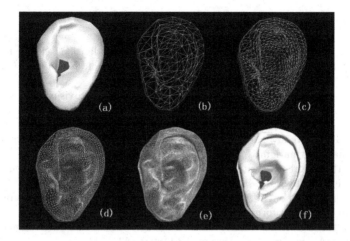

Fig. 9. An example of refinement of a mannequin ear model: (a) The original model. (b) The original mesh. (c) The mesh after 1 step of refinement. (d) The meshes after 2 steps of refinement. (e) The mesh after 3 steps of refinement. (f) The model of the mesh in (e).

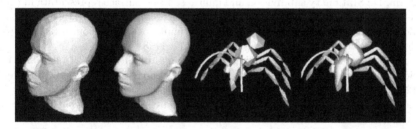

Fig. 10. A mannequin head model, an ant model and their refinement results. Both of the two refined models are after 4 steps of refinement.

Fig. 11. Illustration of a progressive mesh. From the left to right: the initial model and its mesh, the mesh after one step of simplification, the mesh after two steps of simplification and the model of its mesh after two steps of simplification.

Acknowledgement

The work described in this article is supported by the National Science Fund for Distinguished Young Scholars (No.60525213) and the Key Project (No.60533030) of the National Natural Science Foundation of China .

References

1. Dyn, N., Levin, D., Gregory, J. A.: A butterfly subdivision scheme for surface interpolatory with tension control. ACM Transactions on Graphics. **9** (1990) 160–169
2. Zorin, D., Schröder, P., Sweldens, W.: Interpolating subdivision for meshes with arbitrary topology. In: Computer Graphics Proceedings, Annual Conference Series, ACM SIGGRAPH. (1996) 189–192
3. Zheng, G.: Progressive meshes transmission over wireless network. Journal of Computational Information Systems. **1** (2005) 67–71
4. Hoppe, H.: Progressive meshes. In: Proceedings of the 23rd Annual Conference on Computer Graphics and Interactive Techniques. (1996) 99–108
5. Li, G., Ma, W., Bao, H.: A new interpolatory subdivision for quadrilateral meshes. Computer Graphics forum. **24** (2005) 3–16
6. Reif, U.: An unified approach to subdivision algorithms near extraordinary vertices. Computer Aided Geometric Design. **12** (1995) 153–174
7. Labsik, U., Greiner, G.: Interpolatory $\sqrt{3}$ subdivision. Computer Graphics Forum. **19** (2000) 131–138
8. Dyn, N., Gregory, J. A., Levin, D.: A 4-point interpolatory subdivision scheme for curves design. Computer Aided Design. **4** (1987) 257–268
9. Zorin, D.: Stationary subdivision and multiresolution surface representation. Ph.D. Thesis, California Institute of Technology, Pasadena, California. (1998)
10. Zorin, D.:A Method for Analysis of C^1-continuity of subdivision Surfaces. SIAM Journal of Numerical Analysis. **37** (2000) 1677–1708
11. Loop, C.: Smooth ternary subdivision of triangle meshes. In A. Cohen and L.L. Schumaker (eds), Curve and Surface Fitting: St Malo, Nashboro Press, Brentwood. (2002)
12. Loop, C.: Bounded curvature triangle mesh subdivision with the convex hull property. The Visual Computer. **18** (2002) 316–325
13. Stam, J., Loop, C.: Quad/triangle subdivision. Computer Graphics Forum. **22** (2003) 1–7

Geometric Hermite Curves Based on Different Objective Functions

Jing Chi[1], Caiming Zhang[1,2], and Xiaoming Wu[3]

[1] Department of Computer Science and Technology, Shandong Economic University,
Ji'nan 250014, P.R.China
[2] School of Computer Science and Technology, Shandong University, Ji'nan 250061,
P.R.China
[3] Shandong Computer Science Center, ji'nan 250014, P.R.China

Abstract. Based on the objective function defined by the approximation of the curvature variation formula of the curve, a new method for
constructing composite optimized geometric Hermite (COH) curves is
presented in this paper. The new method can deal with some cases in
which neither of the existing methods those are based on minimum curvature variation or minimum strain energy can get pleasing shape. The
comparison of the new method with the existing methods are given,
which shows that none of the new method and the existing ones can deal
with all the cases well. The experiments show that combination of the
new method with the existing methods can achieve a good result in all
cases.

1   Introduction

In computer aided geometric design and computer aided design, Hermite interpolation is a widely used method for constructing a smooth curve with given
endpoint conditions (positions and tangent vectors). The given endpoint conditions can determine a Hermite curve. Although the Hermite curve has the
minimum strain energy among all C^1 cubic polynomial curves satisfying the
same endpoint conditions [12], its shape may be unpleasant. It may have loops,
cusps or folds, namely, not geometrically smooth. Hence, additional degrees of
freedom are needed to meet the geometric smoothness requirements. Obviously,
adjusting the magnitudes of the given tangent vectors can achieve the goal, and
such Hermite curve is known as geometric Hermite curve that is extended from
the standard Hermite technique and is the focus of the recent research.

Research on geometric Hermite curves can be classified into two categories.
The first one focuses on building a low degree geometric Hermite curve with
high order geometric continuity and approximation accuracy [1,2,3,4,8,9]. The
second one focuses on producing a G^1 geometric Hermite curve without loops,
cusps or folds [6,7,10,11,13]. Yong and Cheng [10] present a new class of curves
named optimized geometric Hermite (OGH) curves, such a curve is defined by
optimizing the magnitudes of the endpoint tangent vectors in the Hermite interpolation process in order to minimize the strain energy (MSE, choosing the

H. Zha et al. (Eds.): VSMM 2006, LNCS 4270, pp. 253–262, 2006.

integrated squared second derivative of curve as objective function to approximate the strain energy) of the curve, and they give the geometric smoothness conditions and techniques for constructing 2-segment and 3-segment composite optimized geometric Hermite (COH) curves. Hence, an explicit way can be used to quantize the smoothness of a curve in the geometric Hermite interpolation process both mathematically and geometrically. However, the COH curves constructed by Yong's methods have unpleasant shapes in some cases. Hence, in paper [5], we use minimum curvature variation (MCV) as the smoothness criterion of curve and choose the integrated squared third derivative of curve as the approximate form of the curvature variation, i.e., objective function. Similarly, the extended definitions of OGH and COH curves, the tangent angle constraints (tangent direction preserving conditions and geometric smoothness conditions) based on the objective function are given, and new methods for constructing 2-segment and 3-segment COH curves are also presented. Comparisons of the methods in paper [5] with Yong's methods in paper [10] show that, in some cases, the COH curves constructed by the former are more pleasant than the latter, and in some cases, the latter are more pleasant than the former. Unfortunately, there still exist some cases in which neither of them has pleasant shape.

For above disadvantage, a new method for constructing COH curves based on MCV is presented in this paper. By transforming and uniforming to the existed good methods, the new method can deal with the cases in which neither of the methods in paper [5] or [10] can get pleasing result. In section 2, the related knowledge of OGH and COH curves based on MCV is described. In section 3, the basic idea and detailed steps of the new method are given. In section 4, examples of comparison of COH curves based on different objective functions are given. Additionally, the conclusion that which of these methods should be adopted in certain tangent angle region is drawn.

2 Related Knowledge

The extended definition of an OGH curve based on MCV is given first.

Definition 1. *Given two endpoints P_0 and P_1, and two endpoint tangent vectors V_0 and V_1, a cubic polynomial curve $P(t), t \in [t_0, t_1]$, is called an optimized geometric Hermite (OGH) curve with respect to the endpoint conditions $\{P_0, P_1, V_0, V_1\}$ if it has the smallest curvature variation among all cubic Hermite curves $\overline{P}(t), t \in [t_0, t_1]$, satisfying the following conditions:*

$$\overline{P}(t_0) = P_0, \quad \overline{P}(t_1) = P_1, \quad \overline{P}'(t_0) = \alpha_0 V_0, \quad \overline{P}'(t_1) = \alpha_1 V_1, \tag{1}$$

where α_0 and α_1 are arbitrary real numbers.

The cubic Hermite curve $\overline{P}(t), t \in [t_0, t_1]$ satisfying the constraints in (1) can be expressed as

$$\begin{aligned}
\overline{P}(t) &= (2s+1)(s-1)^2 P_0 + (-2s+3)s^2 P_1 \\
&\quad + (1-s)^2 s(t_1 - t_0)\alpha_0 V_0 + (s-1)s^2(t_1 - t_0)\alpha_1 V_1
\end{aligned} \tag{2}$$

where $s = (t - t_0)/(t_1 - t_0)$.

The objective function, i.e., the approximate curvature variation of the curve $\overline{P}(t)$ on $[t_0, t_1]$ is defined as

$$E = \int_{t_0}^{t_1} [\overline{P}'''(t)]^2 dt,$$

where $\overline{P}'''(t)$ is the third derivative of $\overline{P}(t)$.

The following theorem gives the existence of such an OGH curve.

Theorem 1. *Given two endpoints P_0 and P_1, two endpoint tangent vectors V_0 and V_1, and a parameter space $[t_0, t_1]$, the value of α_0 and α_1 related to an OGH curve $P(t), t \in [t_0, t_1]$ with respect to the endpoint conditions $\{P_0, P_1, V_0, V_1\}$ is obtained as follows:*

if V_0 and V_1 are unparallel, then

$$\begin{cases} \alpha_0 = \dfrac{2[(P_1 - P_0) \cdot V_0]V_1^2 - 2[(P_1 - P_0) \cdot V_1](V_0 \cdot V_1)}{[V_0^2(V_1^2) - (V_0 \cdot V_1)^2](t_1 - t_0)}, \\ \alpha_1 = \dfrac{2[(P_1 - P_0) \cdot V_1]V_0^2 - 2[(P_1 - P_0) \cdot V_0](V_0 \cdot V_1)}{[V_0^2(V_1^2) - (V_0 \cdot V_1)^2](t_1 - t_0)}. \end{cases} \tag{3}$$

if V_0 and V_1 are parallel, then α_0 and α_1 satisfy the equation

$$\alpha_0 V_0^2 + \alpha_1 V_0 \cdot V_1 = \frac{2(P_1 - P_0) \cdot V_0}{t_1 - t_0}. \tag{4}$$

α_0 and α_1 defined in Eqs. (3) and (4) are called the optimized coefficients of the tangent vectors of $P(t)$ at t_0 and t_1, respectively.

Tangent angle constraints contain tangent direction preserving conditions and geometric smoothness conditions. The former ensures that the endpoint tangent vector directions of the OGH curve are same to the given ones, i.e., α_0 and α_1 in theorem 2 are both positive, and the latter ensures that the OGH curve is geometrically smooth, i.e., loop-, cusp- and fold-free. The theorems are as follows:

Theorem 2. *$P(t), t \in [t_0, t_1]$, is an OGH curve with respect to the endpoint conditions $\{P_0, P_1, V_0, V_1\}$, then $P(t)$ preserves the directions of V_0 and V_1 if and only if the following tangent direction preserving conditions*

$$\begin{aligned} &\sin(\theta - \varphi) \neq 0 \quad and \quad \cos\theta > \cos(\theta - 2\varphi) \quad and \quad \cos\varphi > \cos(\varphi - 2\theta) \\ or \quad &\theta = \mu \quad\quad and \quad \cos\theta > 0 \\ or \quad &\theta - \varphi = \pm\pi \end{aligned} \tag{5}$$

are satisfied, where θ is the counterclockwise angle from vector $\overrightarrow{P_0P_1}$ to V_0, φ is the counterclockwise angle from vector $\overrightarrow{P_0P_1}$ to V_1, $\theta, \varphi \in [0, 2\pi)$, and θ, φ are named tangent angles.

Theorem 3. $P(t), t \in [t_0, t_1]$, *is an OGH curve with respect to the endpoint conditions* $\{P_0, P_1, V_0, V_1\}$, *then* $P(t)$ *is geometric smoothness if it satisfies the conditions:*

$$\sin(\theta - \varphi) \neq 0 \quad and \quad \tan\theta \tan\varphi < 0$$

$$or \quad \sin(\theta - \varphi) = 0 \quad and \quad 0 < \alpha_0 \cos\theta < 2\cos^2\theta \tag{6}$$

where α_0 *and* θ, φ *are defined in theorem 2 and 3, respectively. Conditions (6) is called the geometric smoothness conditions.*

The proofs of theorems 3 and 4 can be refer to paper [5], and are not concerned here.

From theorems 3 and 4, we conclude that conditions (5) and (6) can both be satisfied when $(\theta, \varphi) \in (0, \pi/2) \times (3\pi/2, 2\pi) \cup (3\pi/2, 2\pi) \times (0, \pi/2)$. Obviously, if the given tangent angles are in the region, the corresponding OGH curve is the most ideal for having minimum curvature variation, preserving tangent vector directions and loop-, cusp- and fold-free. However, the curve is not pleasing if either (5) or (6) cannot be satisfied, hence, we should consider COH curves, which can achieve the whole smoothness requirements by ensuring automatic satisfaction of conditions (5) and (6) for each OGH segment. The definition of a COH curve is as follows:

Definition 2. *A piecewise cubic polynomial curve is called a composite optimized geometric Hermite (COH) curve if the curve is* G^1 *and each segment of the curve is an OGH curve.*

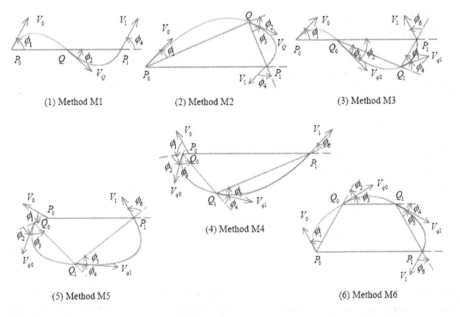

(1) Method M1   (2) Method M2   (3) Method M3

(4) Method M4

(5) Method M5   (6) Method M6

Fig. 1. Methods for constructing 2-segment and 3-segment COH curves

We have presented six methods for constructing 2-segment or 3-segment COH curves in paper [5]. As shown in Fig.1, (1)-(2) are methods for constructing 2-segment COH curves. The joint and the tangent vector at the joint of the two OGH segments are denoted Q and V_Q, respectively. The counterclockwise angles at the endpoints of these OGH segments with respect to their base lines are denoted ϕ_1, ϕ_2, ϕ_3 and ϕ_4, respectively. (3)-(6) are methods for constructing 3-segment COH curves. The joints and the tangent vectors at the joints of the three OGH segments are donated Q_0, Q_1, V_{q0} and V_{q1}, respectively. The counterclockwise angles at the endpoints of these OGH segments with respect to their base lines are donated $\phi_1, \phi_2, \phi_3, \phi_4, \phi_5$ and ϕ_6, respectively.

Method M1. If $(\theta, \varphi) \in [0, \pi/2) \times (0, \pi/2)$, then Q and V_Q are determined by setting

$$\phi_1 = \begin{cases} \theta, & \theta \in (0, \pi/2) \\ \varphi/4, & \theta = 0 \end{cases}, \qquad Q \text{ on the perpendicular bisector of } \overline{P_0 P_1},$$

and $\phi_2 = \begin{cases} (\theta + \varphi)/3, & \theta \in (0, \pi/2) \\ (\theta + \varphi)/6, & \theta = 0 \end{cases}$.

Method M2. If $(\theta, \varphi) \in (0, \pi/2] \times (\pi, 3\pi/2]$, then Q and V_Q are determined by setting

$$\phi_1 = \theta/2, \quad \phi_4 = (2\pi - \varphi)/2, \quad \text{and} \quad \phi_2 = \phi_3.$$

Method M3. If $(\theta, \varphi) \in [0, \pi/2) \times [\pi/2, \pi]$, then Q_0, Q_1, V_{q0}, V_{q1} are determined by setting

$$\phi_1 = \begin{cases} \theta, & \theta \in (0, \pi/2) \\ \pi/18, & \theta = 0 \end{cases}, \quad \|\overline{P_0 Q_0}\| = \|\overline{P_0 P_1}\|/3, \quad \phi_2 = \phi_1, \quad \phi_3 = \phi_2/2,$$

$$\phi_6 = \begin{cases} \varphi/2, & \varphi \in [\pi/2, \pi) \\ 4\pi/9, & \varphi = \pi \end{cases}, \quad \text{and} \quad \phi_4 = \phi_5.$$

Method M4. If $(\theta, \varphi) \in [\pi/2, \pi] \times (0, \pi/2]$, then $Q_0, Q_1, V_{q0}, V_q 1$ are determined by setting

$$\phi_1 = \begin{cases} \pi/3, & \theta = \pi/2 \\ 7\pi/8 - 3\theta/4, & \theta \in (\pi/2, \pi] \end{cases}, \|\overline{P_0 Q_0}\| = \|\overline{P_0 P_1}\|/8, \quad \phi_2 = \phi_1, \quad \overrightarrow{Q_0 Q_1}$$

bisecting the counterclockwise angle from V_{q0} to $\overrightarrow{Q_0 P_0}$, $\phi_6 = \varphi/2$, and $\phi_4 = \phi_5$.

Method M5. If $(\theta, \varphi) \in (\pi/2, \pi] \times (\pi/2, \pi)$, then Q_0, Q_1, V_{q0}, V_{q1} are determined by setting

$$\phi_1 = 5\pi/6 - 2\theta/3, \|\overline{P_0 Q_0}\| = \|\overline{P_0 P_1}\|/6, \ \phi_2 = \phi_1, \ \overrightarrow{Q_0 Q_1} \text{ bisecting the coun-}$$

terclockwise angle from V_{q0} to $\overrightarrow{Q_0 P_0}$, $\phi_6 = \begin{cases} 5\pi/8 - \varphi/4, & \varphi \in [17\pi/30, \pi] \\ \varphi - \pi/12, & \varphi \in (\pi/2, 17\pi/30) \end{cases}$,

and $\phi_4 = \phi_5$.

Method M6. If $(\theta, \varphi) \in (\pi/2, \pi] \times [\pi, 3\pi/2)$, then Q_0, Q_1, V_{q0}, V_{q1} are determined by setting

$$\phi_1 = \begin{cases} \theta/2, & \theta \in (\pi/2, \pi) \\ 7\pi/16, & \theta = \pi \end{cases}, \quad \|\overline{P_0 Q_0}\| = \|\overline{P_0 P_1}\|/2, \quad \overrightarrow{Q_0 Q_1} // \overrightarrow{P_0 P_1},$$

$$\phi_6 = \begin{cases} \pi - \varphi/2, & \varphi \in (\pi, 3\pi/2) \\ 7\pi/16, & \varphi = \pi \end{cases}, \quad \phi_2 = \phi_3, \quad \text{and} \quad \phi_4 = \phi_5.$$

Obviously, the tangent angles of each OGH segment of the COH curves generated by above methods are all in the region $(0, \pi/2) \times (3\pi/2, 2\pi) \cup (3\pi/2, 2\pi) \times (0, \pi/2)$, so these methods can guarantee automatic satisfaction of conditions (5) and (6) for each segment and consequently, the satisfaction of the whole smoothness requirements of the COH curve. However, there still exist some tangent angle regions in which the COH curves generated by these methods are unpleasant. As shown in Fig.2 (a), in the region $(\pi/2, \pi] \times (\pi/2, \pi)$, the curves constructed by above methods (the red curve) and Yong's methods (the green curve) are both undesired. We hope the curve has the shape in (b) rather than (a), so a new method based on MCV is presented to generate the desired curves.

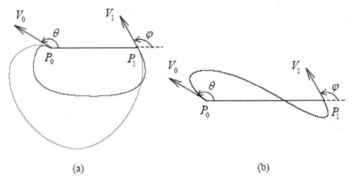

(a)   (b)

Fig. 2. Comparison of the curve shapes (a) undesired shape (b) desired shape

3   New Method for Constructing COH Curves

When $(\theta, \varphi) \in (\pi/2, \pi] \times (\pi/2, \pi)$, we adopt the following new method to construct the COH curves. It consists of three steps: firstly, transform the given tangent angles to the region $[0, \pi/2) \times (0, \pi]$; secondly, use the known method M_1, or M_3 and its extension M_3^{RT} in the relevant region to construct the COH curve; finally, apply converse transformation to the constructed curve to get the final curve which satisfies the given tangent angles. As shown in Fig.3, without loss of generality, we assume given endpoint positions are $P_0 = (0, 0)$, $P_1 = (1, 0)$, tangent angles are θ and φ, and tangent vectors $V_0(= \overrightarrow{P_0 A})$ and $V_1(= \overrightarrow{P_1 B})$ are both unit vectors, i.e., $A = (x_0, y_0) = (\cos\theta, \sin\theta)$, $B = (x_1, y_1) = (1 + \cos\varphi, \sin\varphi)$. After transformation, endpoint positions are $P_0' = P_0$, $P_1' = P_1$, tangent angles are θ' and φ', tangent vectors $V_0'(= \overrightarrow{P_0' A'})$ and $V_1'(= \overrightarrow{P_1' B'})$ are still unit vectors, i.e., $A' = (x_0', y_0') = (\cos\theta', \sin\theta')$, $B' = (x_1', y_1') = (1 + \cos\varphi', \sin\varphi')$. The detailed process of the new method is as follows.

Step 1. If $\theta > \varphi$, then $\theta' = \pi/2$, $\varphi' = \varphi - (\theta - \theta')$,
    else if $\theta < \varphi$, then $\varphi' = \pi/2$, $\theta' = \theta - (\varphi - \varphi')$,
        else $\theta' = \varphi' = \theta/2$.

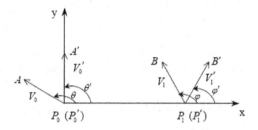

Fig. 3. Transformation in step1

Obviously, $\theta' \in (0, \pi/2]$, $\varphi' \in (0, \pi/2]$. The corresponding transformation formula is

$$\begin{cases} x' = a_0 x + a_1 y + a_2 \\ y' = b_0 x + b_1 y + b_2 \end{cases} \tag{7}$$

where (x, y) is point in the original coordinate system, and (x', y') is point in the transformed coordinate system. a_0, a_1, a_2, b_0, b_1 and b_2 are unknown coefficients. Obviously, the six coefficients can be determined uniquely by six conditions. We use three point pairs $B \to B'$, $P_0 \to P_0'$ and $P_1 \to P_1'$ to resolve the linear equation (7). Substitute the values into Eq.(7), we get

$$\begin{cases} a_0 = 1 \\ a_1 = (x_1' - x_1)/y_1 \\ a_2 = 0 \\ b_0 = 0 \\ b_1 = y_1'/y_1 \\ b_2 = 0 \end{cases}$$

The transformation matrix equivalent to (7) is

$$\begin{bmatrix} x' \\ y' \end{bmatrix} = \begin{bmatrix} a_0 & a_1 \\ b_0 & b_1 \end{bmatrix} \begin{bmatrix} x \\ y \end{bmatrix} + \begin{bmatrix} a_2 \\ b_2 \end{bmatrix}. \tag{8}$$

Step 2. Use corresponding method M_1, or M_3 and its extension M_3^{RT} in the transformed region to construct the COH curve.

Step 3. Transform conversely the tangent angles of the curve constructed in step 2 to the original region to get a new curve. The new curve is the final curve satisfying the given endpoint conditions. The converse transformation matrix is easily obtained from Eq.(8), that is

$$\begin{bmatrix} x \\ y \end{bmatrix} = \frac{1}{a_0 b_1 - a_1 b_0} \begin{bmatrix} b_1 & -a_1 \\ -b_0 & a_0 \end{bmatrix} \begin{bmatrix} x' - a_2 \\ y' - b_2 \end{bmatrix}.$$

The new method can be generalized to commoner cases, in which given endpoint positions can be arbitrary values. In those cases, it only needs to adjust the transformation coefficients in (8) correspondingly. We name the new method M_N. As shown in Fig.2, the given tangent angles are $\theta = 5\pi/6$, and $\varphi = 2\pi/3$. The red COH curve in (a) is constructed by method in paper [5], and the green is constructed by Yong's method in paper [10]; the blue COH curve in (b) is constructed by new method M_N. It can be seen that the curve generated by M_N is more pleasant than those by the methods in paper [5] and [10].

4   Comparison of the COH Curves Based on Different Objective Functions

The new method presented above can be combined with methods $M_1 - M_6$ to form a group of methods for constructing COH curves based on the objective function of MCV. Yong's methods are based on the objective function of MSE. We now compare the COH curves generated by different methods based on different objective functions, and draw the conclusion of which of these methods is better in different tangent angle regions.

As shown in Fig.4, (1)-(10) are examples of the COH curves based on MCV being better than those based on MSE (where, curves based on MCV in (1)-(8) is constructed by $M_1 - M_6$, and in (9)-(10) by new method M_N); (11)-(16) are

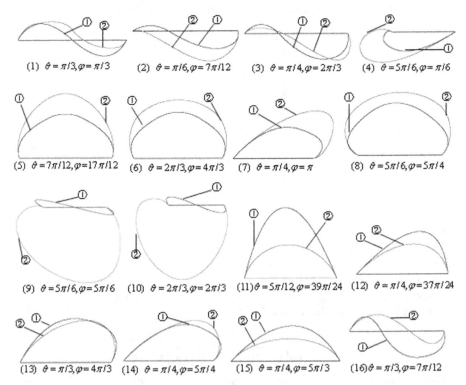

(1) $\theta = \pi/3, \varphi = \pi/3$ (2) $\theta = \pi/6, \varphi = 7\pi/12$ (3) $\theta = \pi/4, \varphi = 2\pi/3$ (4) $\theta = 5\pi/6, \varphi = \pi/6$

(5) $\theta = 7\pi/12, \varphi = 17\pi/12$ (6) $\theta = 2\pi/3, \varphi = 4\pi/3$ (7) $\theta = \pi/4, \varphi = \pi$ (8) $\theta = 5\pi/6, \varphi = 5\pi/4$

(9) $\theta = 5\pi/6, \varphi = 5\pi/6$ (10) $\theta = 2\pi/3, \varphi = 2\pi/3$ (11) $\theta = 5\pi/12, \varphi = 39\pi/24$ (12) $\theta = \pi/4, \varphi = 37\pi/24$

(13) $\theta = \pi/3, \varphi = 4\pi/3$ (14) $\theta = \pi/4, \varphi = 5\pi/4$ (15) $\theta = \pi/4, \varphi = 5\pi/3$ (16) $\theta = \pi/3, \varphi = 7\pi/12$

Fig. 4. Comparison of the COH curves based on different objective functions

examples of the COH curves based on MSE being better than those based on MCV. Note: Symbols ① and ② in figure denote the COH curve based on MCV and MSE, respectively.

From the examples, we can draw the conclusion as follows:

$$\text{when } \begin{aligned} (\theta, \varphi) \in {}&[0, \pi/3] \times [0, \pi] \cup [2\pi/3, \pi] \times (\pi/2, 3\pi/2) \cup (\pi/2, 2\pi/3] \times [\pi, 4\pi/3] \\ &\cup [2\pi/3, \pi] \times [\pi/6, \pi/2] \cup [\pi/3, 2\pi/3] \times [4\pi/3, 3\pi/2], \end{aligned}$$

shapes of the COH curves based on MCV are more pleasant, and the corresponding methods $M_1 - M_6$ and M_N should be applied.

$$\text{When } \begin{aligned} (\theta, \varphi) \in {}&[0, \pi/3] \times (\pi, 2\pi] \cup [\pi/3, \pi/2] \times [\pi, 4\pi/3] \\ &\cup [\pi/3, 2\pi/3] \times [\pi/3, 2\pi/3] \cup [\pi/3, 2\pi/3] \times [3\pi/2, 5\pi/3], \end{aligned}$$

shapes of the COH curves based on MSE are more pleasant, and the corresponding methods of Yong's should be applied.

We mark the above two regions R_1 and R_2, respectively. After symmetry-based extension [5], they can cover tangent angles of all possible cases, i.e., the entire $\theta\varphi$ -space, $[0, 2\pi) \times [0, 2\pi)$, and the results of comparisons in the extension regions are the same as their respective original regions. From the above conclusion, we can see that different methods based on different objective functions should be adopted when the tangent angles are in different regions in order that good results can be achieved.

5 Conclusion

A new method for constructing COH curves based on MCV is presented in this paper, examples of comparison of methods based on different objective functions are given, and the conclusion that which method generates better curves when the tangent angles are in different regions is drawn. Our discussion shows that combination of the new method M_N with the known methods $M_1 - M_6$ and Yong's methods can achieve a much better result in the entire $\theta\varphi$ -space, $[0, 2\pi) \times [0, 2\pi)$.

References

1. Chen, Y., Beier, K.-P., Papageorgiou, D.: Direct highlight line modification on NURBS surfaces. Computer Aided Geometric Design **14 (6)** (1997) 583–601
2. de Boor, C., Höllig, K., Sabin, M.: High accuracy geometric Hermite interpolation. Computer Aided Geometric Design **4** (1987) 269-278
3. Höllig, K., Koch, J.: Geometric Hermite interpolation. Computer Aided Geometric Design **12 (6)** (1995) 567-580
4. Höllig, K., Koch, J.: Geometric Hermite interpolation with maximal order and smoothness. Computer Aided Geometric Design **13 (8)** (1996) 681-695
5. Jing Chi, Caiming Zhang, Lin Xu: constructing geometric Hermite curve with minimum curvature variation. Ninth International Conference on CAD/CG **1** (2005) 58-63

6. Meek, D.S., Walton, D.J.: Geometric Hermite interpolation with Tschirnhausen cubics. J. Comput. Appl. Math **81 (2)** (1997a) 299-309
7. Meek, D.S., Walton, D.J.: Hermite interpolation with Tschirnhausen cubic spirals. Computer Aided Geometric Design **14 (7)** (1997b) 619-635
8. Reif, U.: On the local existence of the quadratic geometric Hermite interpolant. Computer Aided Geometric Design **16 (3)** (1999) 217-221
9. Schaback, R.: Optimal geometric Hermite interpolation of curves. In: Dahlen, M., Lyche, T., Schumaker, L.L. (Eds.), Mathematical Methods for Curves and Surface **II** (1998) 1-12
10. Yong, J., Cheng, F.: Geometric Hermite curves with minimum strain energy. Computer Aided Geometric Design **21** (2004) 281-301
11. Zhang, C., Cheng, F.: Removing local irregularities of NURBS surfaces by modifying highlight lines. Computer-Aided Design **30 (12)** (1998) 923-930
12. Zhang, C., Zhang, P., Cheng, F.: Fairing spline curves and surfaces by minimizing energy. Computer-Aided Design **33 (13)** (2001) 913-923
13. Zhang, C., Yang X. and Wang J: Approaches for Constrained Parametric Curve Interpolation. Journal of Computer Science and Technology **18(5)** (2003) 592-597

Aligning 3D Polygonal Models with Improved PCA

Liu Wei and He Yuanjun

Department of Computer Science and Engineering, Shanghai Jiaotong University,
Shanghai, 200240, P.R.China

Abstract. PCA is a useful tool for pose normalization in 3D model retrieval, in this paper, we analyze its basic principle, point out its shortcoming and give our solution. Experiments show that our methods can enhance the robustness of PCA and align 3D models well.

Keywords: PCA, alignment, pose normalization, uniform sampling.

1 Introduction

The wide use of 3D models has led to the development of 3D shape retrieval systems which can retrieve similar 3D objects according to the given query object. One of the main works in this context is the mapping of 3D object into compact canonical representations referred to as descriptor or feature vector, which serve as search keys during the retrieval process. At present, they can be divided into two types: Rotation-Invariant descriptors and Rotation-Variant descriptors. The first type includes: shape spectrum, topology matching, shape distributions, etc; and the second type includes: depth buffer matching, silhouette comparison, multi-resolution moments, etc. Vranic compared 19 kinds of 3D model descriptors in his Ph.D Dissertation and drawn a conclusion that the Rotation-Variant descriptors outperform the Rotation-Invariant ones[1]. While for Rotation-Variant descriptors, an additional step must be done to normalize the pose of the 3D models which usually adopts the method of PCA(Principal Component Analysis). But traditional PCA does not provide a robust normalization for many cases. In this paper, we analyze the reason why sometime it will fail and propose a novel way to enhance the robustness of PCA, which remarkably meliorate the performance of the retrieval in the later experiments.

2 Our Analysis

2.1 Basic Principle of PCA

General speaking, 3D models are given in arbitrary units, position, and orientation. Since many kinds of features need to be extracted in a canonical coordinate frame, the poses of 3D models should be normalized in advanced. The most important tool for pose normalization is PCA, which is also called as Karhunen-Loeve transform, or Hotelling transform in the fields of signal processing, statistics, compression, and

H. Zha et al. (Eds.): VSMM 2006, LNCS 4270, pp. 263–268, 2006.

neural computing[2]. The PCA is based on the statistical representation of a random variable as following:

Let $P = \{P_1, P_2, \cdots, P_n\}$ $(P_i = (x_i, y_i, z_i) \in R^3)$ be the set of vertices on the surface of this model. The goal of PCA is to find an affine map: $\tau : R^3 \rightarrow R^3$ in such a way that a 3D model of any translation, rotation and scaling can be put normatively with this transformation. The translation invariance is accomplished by finding the barycenter of the model firstly:

$$x_c = \frac{1}{n}\sum_{i=1}^{n} x_i \,,\, y_c = \frac{1}{n}\sum_{i=1}^{n} y_i \,,\, z_c = \frac{1}{n}\sum_{i=1}^{n} z_i$$

So the point $P_c(x_c, y_c, z_c)$ is the center of this model, we move P_c to coordinate origin. That is to say, for each point $P_i = (x_i, y_i, z_i) \in P$, a corresponding transformation $P_i' = (x_i - x_c, y_i - y_c, z_i - z_c)$ is performed. Based on the transformation we define points set $P' = \{P_1', P_2', \cdots, P_n'\}$. Then we calculate the covariance matrix C .

$$C = \sum_{i=1}^{n} P_i'^T P_i' = \begin{bmatrix} \sum\limits_{i=1}^{n} x^2 & \sum\limits_{i=1}^{n} xy & \sum\limits_{i=1}^{n} xz \\ \sum\limits_{i=0}^{n} xy & \sum\limits_{i=1}^{n} y^2 & \sum\limits_{i=1}^{n} yz \\ \sum\limits_{i=1}^{n} xz & \sum\limits_{i=1}^{n} yz & \sum\limits_{i=1}^{n} z^2 \end{bmatrix}$$

Obviously the matrix C is a real symmetric one, therefore its eigenvalues are non-negative real numbers. Then we sort the eigenvalues in a non-increasing order and find the corresponding eigenvectors. The eigenvectors are scaled to Euclidean unit length and we form the rotation matrix R which has the scaled eigenvectors as rows. We rotate all points in P' and a new point set is formed: $P'' = \{P_i'' \mid P_i'' = P_i' R, P_i' \in P', i = 1, \cdots, n\}$.

When this step has been done, the model is rotated so that the X-axis maps to the eigenvector with the biggest eigenvalue, the Y-axis maps to the eigenvector with the second biggest eigenvalue and the Z-axis maps to the eigenvector with the smallest eigenvalue.

The scaling invariance is accomplished by zooming the model to an appropriate size. Firstly let r_{ave} be the average distance from the set of vertices to coordinate origin. Then r_{ave} can be calculated as following: $r_{ave} = \frac{1}{n}\sum_{i=1}^{n}\sqrt{x_i''^2 + y_i''^2 + z_i''^2}$,

$(x_q'', y_q'', z_q'') = P_q'' \in P'', q = 1, \cdots, n$. Next for each point in P'' ,we must do the third transform and obtain the final points set:

$$P''' = \{(\frac{x_i''}{r_{ave}}, \frac{y_i''}{r_{ave}}, \frac{z_i''}{r_{ave}}) \mid (x_i'', y_i'', z_i'') = P_i'' \in P'', i = 1, \cdots, n)$$

The new model composed of points set P''' and has the same topology structure as the original model is just the result of process of pose normalization.

2.2 Shortcomings of Traditional PCA

The most important step is to rotate the model, while it is also the easiest one to fail. The failure can be divided into three types. Firstly, the eigenvectors are only defined up to a multiple of ± 1, thus, there is ambiguity in choosing which direction of the eigenvector to choose, and alignment performance is hampered if the wrong direction is chosen(Fig.1, Left two models). Secondly, if the two eigenvalues are of slight difference, then the corresponding eigenvectors are easy to make misplaced(Fig.1, Middle two models). Thirdly, there is no guarantee that when two models are each aligned to their own principal axes then they are also optimally pair-wise aligned(Fig.1, Right two models). Fig.1 shows three groups of contrasts in which the two models belonging to three pairs respectively are similar in shape while they have different results after PCA has acted on them.

Fig. 1. Failures of alignment after PCA

For these shortcomings, several improved methods have been proposed in which two kinds: "Weighted PCA"[3] and "Continuous PCA"[4] obtain better performance. But for the first former, the matrix R is only approximated as not all the points of the set P' are treated in the same way. Thus, the principal directions cannot be computed exactly and, for instance, the orientation of a symmetrical object can deviate from the desired one. And for the later, complicated calculation costs plentiful of time which deteriorates the efficiency of this arithmetic.

2.3 Our Improvement

We notice that one important factor that affects the preciseness of PCA rests with the non- uniform distribution of the points on the surface of 3D model, for example, a large quadrangle on the surface of a model can be decomposed into two triangles and four points while some fine detail needs hundreds of triangles and points. So in this paper we propose a novel method with its basic idea being that we sample points uniformly on the surface of the model to replace its original vertices set P. An effective arithmetic for uniformly sampling introduced by Osada[5] is as following:

First, we iterate through all polygons, splitting them into triangles as necessary. Then, for each triangle, we compute its area and store it in an array along with the cumulative area of triangles visited so far. Next, we select a triangle with probability proportional to its area by generating a random number between 0 and the total cumulative area and performing a binary search on the array of cumulative areas. For each selected triangle with vertices (A, B, C), we construct a point on its surface by generating two random numbers, r_1 and r_2, between 0 and 1, and evaluating the following equation: $P = (1 - \sqrt{r_1})A + \sqrt{r_1}(1 - r_2)B + \sqrt{r_1}r_2C$. In this formula, $\sqrt{r_1}$ sets the percentage from vertex A to the opposing edge, while r_2 represents the percentage along that edge (see Fig.2a). Taking the square-root of r_1 gives a uniform random point with respect to surface area. This arithmetic is very robust and easy to calculate. Let M be the sampling amount and N be the number of the triangles on the surface of 3D model, then its has a complexity of $M \log_2 N$. Fig.2b shows the original model, Fig.2c is its sampling points and Fig.2d is the model after pose normalization.

Fig. 2. Uniform sampling

But only uniform sampling doesn't guarantee completely correct result for all cases. For those models which have accessories on their main bodies, their resulting pose may not accord with apperception of human beings. For example, the handle of the cup make X axis deviate its principal axis as Fig.3a shows, while the ideal situation we expect is showed in Fig.3b.

Fig. 3. Effect of handle

An effective way is to detect the symmetrical face of the 3D model with respect to a plane cutting the model through the center. An approach for measuring the symmetry distance between parts of the model lying on the opposite sides of the cutting plane and getting the most perfect plane is presented in [6, 7]. Let (a, b, c) be the normal of the cutting plane and since the plane pass through the center of the model which superposes the origin, the constant item of plane equation is 0. There may or may not a small angle between the cutting plane and XOY plane, and if may there must be a middle plane between them. Then we project X-axis and Y-axis onto this plane to replace their foregoing layouts and form new Z-axis with right hand rule(see Fig.4). At last we rotate the 3D model to the new reference frame. Our motivation is to adopt symmetrical face detection to emendate the deviation of PCA and it is effectual for those 3D models with accessories like cups in practice.

But the two measures above can only reduce the third shortcoming described in Section 2.2 and but probably be helpless for the first and the second cases. As the orientation is limited, we can enumerate all the situations. Fig.5 shows 6 orientations from the center of the cube to the center of its faces, called as main orientations superposed by the X-axis of the 3D model. For each main orientation, we rotate the model around it per 90 degrees and get 4 postures, and if we take reflection into account, we can get total $6 \times 4 \times 2 = 48$ postures.

Since each orientation's symmetrical situation is also within the 48 cases, when aligning two 3D CAD models, we can assume that one remains fixed while the other adjusts its pose to the 48 cases, if D_1, D_2, $\cdots$, D_{48} be the matching distances, then the actual difference between them can be denoted as $D = \min(D_1, D_2, \cdots, D_{48})$.

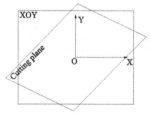

Fig. 4. Emendation by symmetrical face

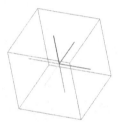

Fig. 5. 6 main orientations

3   Experiments and Result

The essence of 3D model retrieval is to find correspondences between the query model and the candidate ones, and PCA is a common tool to align 3D models to make them in an appropriate layouts. In contrast to single solution of traditional PCA, we propose three measures to improve its performance according to the reasons why the shortcomings should come into being. Experiments show that the rate of success and robustness of PCA have been enhanced. Fig.6 shows three types of 3D models after pose normalization using our method.

Since many kinds of 3D model retrieval arithmetic depend on pose normalization, our enhancement of PCA optimizes the alignment of 3D models, which will do great benefit for 3D model comparison and retrieval.

Acknowledgements

This research has been funded by The National Natural Science Foundation of China (60573146).

fish-like   **dog-like**   **plane-like**

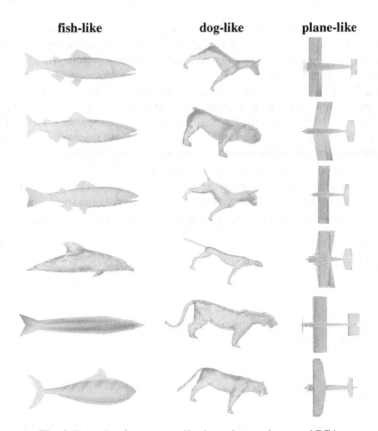

Fig. 6. Example of pose normalization using our improved PCA

References

1. Vranic D. 3D model retrieval. Technical University of Vienna, Ph. D. Dissertation, 2004
2. Vranic D, Saupe D, Richter J. Tools for 3D object retrieval: Karhunen-Loeve transform and spherical harmonics [A]. In: Proceedings of the IEEE 2001 Workshop Multimedia Signal Processing , Cannes, France, 2001.1, 293-298
3. Tangelder J, Veltkamp R. Polyhedral model retrieval using weighted point sets [J]. International Journal of Image and Graphics, 2003, 3 (1): 209-229
4. Ankerst M, Kastenmüller G, Kriegel H. 3D shape histograms for similarity search and classification in spatial databases [A]. In: Proceedings of the 6th International Symposium on Large Spatial Databases (SSD'99), Hong Kong, 1999.1, 207-226
5. Osada R, Funkhouser T, Chazelle B and Dobkin D. Shape distributions. ACM Trans. on Graphics, 2002, 21(4): 807-832
6. Kazhdan M, Chazelle B, Dobkin D, etc. A reflective symmetry descriptor. In: Proceedings of European Conference on Computer Vision 2002, Copenhagen, May 2002, 642-656
7. Kazhdan M, Chazelle B, Dobkin D, etc. A reflective symmetry descriptor for 3D models. Algorithmica, 2004, 38(1): 201-225

A Crowd Evacuation System in Emergency Situation Based on Dynamics Model

Qianya Lin, Qingge Ji, and Shimin Gong

Department of Computer Science, Sun Yat-Sen University, Guangzhou, 510275,
P.R.C.
issjqg@mail.sysu.edu.cn

Abstract. This paper presents a system for crowd evacuation in emergency situation based on dynamics model to offer a base platform for further researches. Starting with the implementation of base functions, our focus is on the stability and expandable of the platform to offer new functions easily according to our needs latter. To improve the independence of the module, the function into layers and dividing the data are separated into blocks. To reach efficient system implementation, the 3D building is translated into a 2D graphics by turning the map into a group of nodes. Furthermore, the element called node plug is used to enhance the expansibility of the system. Experiments are carried out to analyze the crowd's evacuation efficiency in a given building. The impact caused by mass behavior, the structure of the building and the number of people inside are also construed qualitatively in the experiments.

1 Introduction

As a branch of virtual reality, crowd animation is becoming more and more important and challenging. It is widely applied in city planning, building design and entertainment industry and so on, and involves a great many fields, such as physics, psychology, sociology, physiology, computer graphics, and computer network, etc.. The key point of researches focuses on how to simulate a lot of complicated and changeful human behaviors, activities and situations by a computer.

The goal of this paper is to build up a platform for the research of the mutual influences between crowded individuals in emergency. Moreover, the influence on the crowd by the emergency extent and the environment is another emphasis of our research. To reduce the complexity, we use Helbing's dynamic model[1] to analyze the behaviors of individuals and crowd.

The paper is organized as follows. Section 2 covers related work in the field of crowd animation. Section 3 shows the rough characters of this system to give a clear impression to readers. Section 4 describes the details about the system. In section 5, experiments and results are presented to support the system. Conclusions and future work are presented in section 6.

H. Zha et al. (Eds.): VSMM 2006, LNCS 4270, pp. 269–280, 2006.

2   Related Work

2.1   General Studies of Crowd Animation

Crowd animation mainly includes crowd visualization, modeling of crowd behavior and crowd simulation, modeling of crowd behavior is the emphasis of this paper.

The research of crowd animation in prophase adopts rule-based schemes. Reynolds[2] is one of the pioneer researchers that proposed crowd animation. His distributed behavior model simulated the behaviors such as flocks of birds, schools of fishes and controlled their behavior with three principal rules. Tu and Terzopoulos[3] studied simulating the behavior of artificial lives and present the model of artificial fishes with interaction, synthetic visions and exhibited realistic behaviors. Reynolds[4] strided a step forward by implementing some steering behaviors such as seek, pursuit and obstacle avoidance on his original model, that can provide fairly complex behaviors by combining the simple one together.

Layered model appears to reduce the complexity, in which agent is endowed with different degrees of autonomy, social relationship and emotional state. Perlin and Goldberg[5]'s Improv system uses a blackboard for the actors to communicate with each other. They introduced a layered behavior model to break down the complex behaviors into simpler scripts and actions. Franco et al.[6] proposed a 2D-grid with a four-layered structure platform to simulate crowds in the city that each layer is used to reflect a different aspect of an agent's behavior so as to implement complex behaviors. Soteris et al.[7] used the top-down approach where the movement of the pedestrians is computed at a higher level, and the lower level deals with the detailed and realistic simulation to reduce the computing burden. Musse and Thalmann[8] presented the ViCrowd model to simulate crowds with different levels of autonomy. Based on this work, Musse, Thalmann and Kallmann[9] put forward a system which collected actors together if they share a common goal and controls them as one group.

Bouvier et al.[10] used particle system to simulate human behaviors. Each agent is regarded as a particle, endued with a state and a feedback function to dominate its behavior and all agents' behaviors constituted the whole system's performance. Still[11] studied the crowd in a physical aspect and abstracted the model by watching real crowds in his PhD thesis. Helbing and his research group adopted particle system to study the crowd behavior in emergency situation based on social psychology and dynamics. Adriana et al.[12] went further that they added up individual's characteristic and relational behavior to vivify the evacuation. We should notice that distinct from other research methods, particle theory looks on things in a general view that one of the individuals may not act correctly when the crowd performs vividly.

Nowadays, many new ideas are turning up in the study. Vallamil et al.[13] brought out the new idea that defines the agent and group in parameterization. As an old technique, cellular automaton reignited because of its simplicity and expeditiousness. Blue and Adler[14] used cellular automata model to solve the crowd evacuation problem in emergency situation. Yang et al.[15] imported relational behaviors into the cellular automata model. There are countless ways to generate human-like behaviors, such as hydromechanical model and psychologic model etc. As people pay more and more attention to crowd animation, more and more original and effective ideas will be introduced to the study.

2.2 Behavior Simulation in Emergency Situation

The obstacles of behavior simulation can be summarized into two types: how to compose natural and gliding behavior and how to generate appropriate path planning. Crowd simulation in emergency situation usually concentrates on the latter, e.g., Hebling's particle model mentioned above. Musse goes further based on Helbing's research. Besides, Musse also brings out a random distributing behavior model to study the relations between autonomy and mass behaviors. Adler's cellular automata model offers a new way for crowd simulating research. L.Z. Yang et al. imported relational behaviors into cellular automata model and reached the conclusion that mass behavior is not always harmful.

3   General View

A crowd animation system in emergency situation based on Helbing's dynamic model is presented in this paper to offer a basic platform for the study of crowd evacuation behaviors and effects. In this sytem, the main focus is the basic functions for easily improving new functions according to our subsequent needs.

Generally speaking, the Helbing's dynamic model can be summed up as the following formula:

$$a = m_i \frac{d\vec{v_i}}{dt} = m_i \frac{v_i^0 \vec{e}_i^0 - \vec{v_i}(t)}{\tau_i} = \sum_{j(\neq i)} \vec{f_{ij}} + \sum_w \vec{f_{iw}} \tag{1}$$

The $\vec{f_{ij}}$ and $\vec{f_{iw}}$ in the formula are interpreted by the next two formulas:

$$\vec{f_{ij}} = [A_i^{\frac{r_{ij}-d_{ij}}{B_i}} + kg(r_{ij} - d_{ij})] \cdot \vec{n_{ij}} + kg(r_{ij} - d_{ij}) \triangle v_{ji}^t \vec{t_{ij}} \tag{2}$$

$$\vec{f_{iw}} = [A_i^{\frac{r_i-d_{iw}}{B_i}} + kg(r_i - d_{iw})] \cdot \vec{n_{iw}} + kg(r_i - d_{iw})(\vec{v_i} \cdot \vec{t_{iw}})\vec{t_{iw}} \tag{3}$$

Fig.1 shows the general structure of the proposed system which is divided into two execution layers and two store modules. The higher layer is the operation layer, which is responsible for computing the whole crowd and agents' states, escape direction and evacuation effect, while the lower layer is the description layer, assigned to render the local 3D scenes. Separating computing and scene rendering can enhance the efficiency, reduce coupling extent among modules and make sure that each module concentrates on its own mission.

The data store modules supply various data to two layers. Different layers communicate by gaining data from the two store modules instead of calling each

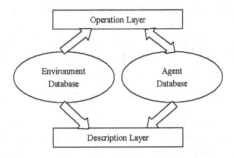

Fig. 1. General structure of the system

other. One of the characteristic of the system is separating the function into layers and dividing the data into blocks.

In detailed design, based on Soteris et al.[7]'s ideas of dividing the areas, the 3D building is transferred into a 2D graphic by making the room, the porch and the stairs as a node. In addition, inspired by Sung et al.[16]'s pluggable architecture, the node plug is clipped to enhance the expansibility. In path planning and dynamical analysis, simple arithmetic based on Helbing's dynamic model is put forward for pre-computing.

4   Crowd Animation System in Emergency Situation

As mentioned before, this system is divided into operation and description layer, moreover, the environment and agent database are added to separate data and computing. Fig. 2 shows the whole system structure.

4.1   Environment Database

Environment database includes the map and the node plug.

Map. The map records the building's size, the amount of floors, how the room is divided, the location of walls and doors and so on. In other words, map is the digital presentation of the building.

Partitioning of Map. Each partitioning of the map is defined to be a node. If node A connects to node B with an exit, then there is directed edge from A to B.

First, the building's map information is read in from predefined external files. The compositions of the building, such as rooms, porches and stairs, are marked as nodes. A door that connects two areas is an exit, which suggests that there is a bidirectional edge between these two nodes. Stairs is a special node that bridges the nodes of different floors. Finally, a 3D building can be turned into a 2D oriented graph by partitioned into a number of nodes and edges(Fig. 3(a)). The nodes format is shown in Fig. 3(b).

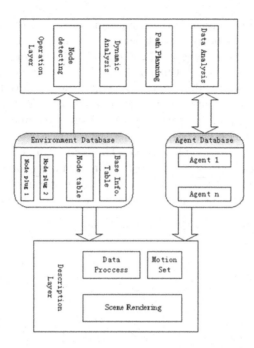

Fig. 2. Detail structure of the system

Types of Nodes. There are various types of nodes of which the figurative properties are quite different. Room and porch can be regarded as the same type since they are in one plane. Stairs whose collision arithmetic is also quite different, which is another kind of node, so is the tumble motion.

The concept of "Node plug" is advanced to encapsulate different properties into different node plugs. When a new node plug is added up, without modifying the whole structure, the expansibility and applicability of the system later can be enhanced.

Fig. 3(c) shows the structure of a node plug as following.

- Name: The identifier which distinguishes it from others.
- Description Information: Optional parameters that describe this plug.
- Attractive Coefficient: The attractive extent shows the higher the coefficient is, the more attractive this node is, and also the larger probability that people flow to it. Attractive coefficient gains a autonomous right to the user by adding user-defined node plug.
- Dynamical Analysis Arithmetic: It means the arithmetic analyzing the force that an agent suffers. Further explanation will be presented in the coming section.
- Motion Set: It is a set of motions belonging to some kind of node. When description layer is rendering the scene, it chooses appropriate motions from the motion set according to the individuals' states. The motions vary from one kind of nodes to anther.

Connecting Table. It records the connecting degree of the nodes using connecting coefficient. Connecting coefficient is a real number between 0 and 1 ($\theta \in [1,0]$) that stands for whether two nodes are linking or not. It's the probability that people from node A flow to node B. If two nodes are block, $\theta = 0$. When θ is higher, the probability so does agents from A move to B. Element in row m, line n is the probability that node m moves to node n. Given node A has four edges, linking to node B, C, D, E respectively, then in connecting table, it is depicted as follows(Fig. 3(d)).

The connecting table is unidirectional. The connecting coefficient in row m, line n may not be equal to the one in row n, line m in that people incline to run out of a room towards to porch, but not run back to the room.

The way to calculate the connecting coefficient will be shown in the next few sections.

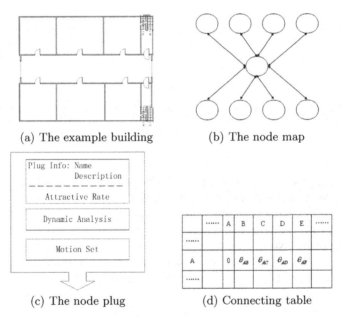

(a) The example building   (b) The node map

(c) The node plug   (d) Connecting table

Fig. 3. Map and Node

4.2   Agent Database

Agent database stores each agent's data. The information includes:

- Agent ID: The unique identity of each agent.
- Coordinates: The location of agent in the map, which has three dimensionalities (X, Y, Z).
- Speed: The current speed, including its coefficient and direction, which also has three dimensionalities (X, Y, Z).
- Node ID: The node ID that agent is in. Detailed information can be found out through node id.

- Quality
- Diameter: Agent's width of shoulder is looked on as the diameter.
- Alive State: It has two states (alive and dead).
- Default State: State that includes stand, move, tumble, injury and so on.
- Escape Time: A period of time that starts from the beginning of escape. If the agent escapes successfully, its escape time stop.

4.3   Operation Layer

Operation layer is responsible for computing and has four modules. Three of them are important and detailed in the following.

Node Type Detecting Module. We'll show the steps of Node Type Detecting Module. First, Node Type Detecting Module reads information from agent database, then find out the node through node id. Second, after detecting the node type, it informs dynamic analysis model to adopt corresponding acting and description layer to call corresponding motion set.

Path Planning Module. Agent's intention direction relies on some sub-factors. First, the more number of doors, the lower probability of passing through one of them. Second, people prefer to leave from exit most near them. Third, the user-define property, attractive coefficient, reflecting the popularity of the node, grant rights to user to adjust the path mildly.
    The connecting coefficient from room A to room B through door i is

$$\theta' = \frac{1}{n} \times \frac{\frac{1}{d_i}}{\sum_{j=1}^{n} d_j} \times \frac{Atr_b}{Atr_a} \tag{4}$$

n is the total number of room A's exit. d_i is the distance from agent to door i. $\sum_{j=1}^{n} d_j$ stands for the total distance. Atr_a and Atr_b are attractive coefficients. When $Atr_b > Atr_a$, room B is more attractive. As $\sum_{j=1}^{n} d_j$ is the same for each exit in a room, we can simplify the formulation as follows:

$$\theta = d_i \cdot \frac{Atr_b}{Atr_a} \tag{5}$$

In emergency situation, an interesting crowd behavior is called mass behavior. Agent is influenced by self-consciousness and crowd-consciousness. An urgent coefficient U is defined to be the emergency degree. $U \in [0, 1]$. $U = 0$ means that the individual is not influenced by others at all, while $U = 1$ shows that it's totally controlled by the crowd.
    Agent has its own direction $\vec{e_i}$, but it is also influenced by agents nearby in the form of average direction. The final direction of the target agent is:

$$\vec{e_i^t} = \frac{(1 - U_i)\vec{e_i} + U_i \cdot \vec{e_i^\partial}}{\|(1 - U_i)\vec{e_i} + U_i \cdot \vec{e_i^\partial}\|} \tag{6}$$

Dynamic Analysis Module. Helbing's dynamic model can be concluded in a formula:

$$\alpha = m_i \frac{d\vec{v_i}}{dt} = m_i \frac{v_i^0(t)\vec{e}_i^0(t) - \vec{v_i}(t)}{\tau_i} + \sum_{j(\neq i)} \vec{f_{ij}} + \sum_w \vec{f_{iw}} \qquad (7)$$

Since Helbing's model is only fit for a plane, his model can be addressed as the dynamic analysis algorithm of nodes like rooms or porch.

4.4   Description Layer

Description layer is composed of three modules. Data Process Module is engaged in data reading and processing. It reads the situation and map information from environment database, fetches agent's states from agent database and does some preparation for rendering. Motion Set module consists of some motion models pre-tailored by 3D modeling tools while Scene Rendering Module fetches corresponding motion which is prepared by the motion set in order to render the 3D scene in real time.

5   Experiment Result

We have designed an evacuation scenario for application based on the above system framework. For simplicity and practice, Helbing's model is adopted as the algorithm of our node plug, which suggests that our test only focuses on a building with one floor, regardless of stairs.

5.1   Initialization of the Parameters

Fig. 4 shows the building which is a dormitory with one floor. According to the work of Helbing, τ_i is $0.5s$. Usually, the crowd's expecting evacuation speed reaches $v_i^0 = 5m/s$, but in fact, an agent is unable to escape in such a high speed because of the limit of environment that based on Helbing's observation, the speed comes to $0.6m/s$ in free state, $1m/s$ in common state, and in urgent state, it can only reach to $1.5m/s$.

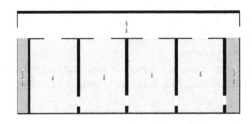

Fig. 4. The given building

Similarly, the constant parameters is :

$$A_i = 2 \times 10^3 N$$
$$B_i = 0.08m$$
$$k = 1.2 \times 10^5 kg/s^2$$
$$\kappa = 2.4 \times 10^5 kg/ms$$

We suppose the average quality of an agent is $60kg$. In order to be close to the reality, the radius r_i is defined as ($r_i \in [0.25m, 0.35m]$).

5.2 Experimental Results

Analysis of Evacuation Time. Fig. 5 shows the curve while escaping in different door width. We observe that $1.60m$ is the turning point of door width. When door is narrower than $1.6m$, the time of escaping increases obviously, and when it's wider than $1.60m$, the influence to time by door width is not obvious.

Fig. 6 shows the impact given by different number of people with urgent coefficient 0.4, and doors width $1.6m$. Obviously, the more people, the longer time for evacuation. In the point of 30 or 80 people, evacuation time increases quickly along with the increasing of people. 80 is a notable point since when there're more than 80 people, jam and block will occur to stop the leaving.

Jam and Block. When there are too many agents and too narrow exits, fanlike jam will appear in the bottleneck of the exit as showed in Fig. 7.

Similarly, the flow of people will be blocked in the bottleneck when there are too many agents and too narrow exits, therefore sometimes few agents can pass through and other times, nobody can leave, as showed in Fig. 8. When it occurs, the flow is blocked, the leaving curve is discrete.

Mass Behavior. The mass behavior under the urgent coefficient is also observed. The more urgent the situation is, the weaker the agent's self-consciousness, the stronger influenced by others and the clearer the mass behavior, assumed that agent is easily inflected by people that five meters around

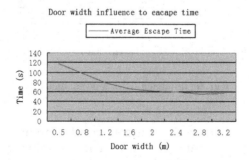

Fig. 5. Door width influence to escape time

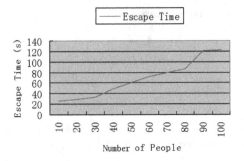

Fig. 6. The influence by agent's number

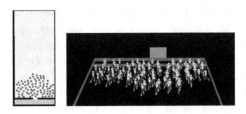

Fig. 7. The fanlike jam

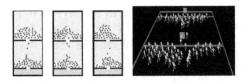

Fig. 8. The block of flow

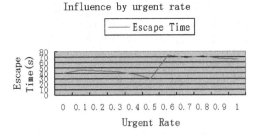

Fig. 9. Influence by urgent coefficient

it in the same room. Finally Fig. 9 is got according to different urgent cases. From Fig. 9, it is found that mass behavior is not always harmful and some extent of mass behavior will contribute to evacuation. There is a turning point in $U = 0.5$, indicating that when the crowd in a panic with a degree of 0.5, the efficiency of evacuation climb up to the peak. When the panic gets into more deeply and the mass behavior runs into more intensively, the escape efficiency falls more steeply. This conclusion matches L.Z. Yang and Helbing's observation. But in Helbing's results, the turning point occurs in 0.4, which is different from our analysis, due to the different of two experiment environments.

6   Conclusions and Future Work

This paper presents a simple and expandable crowd evacuation system in order to offer a platform for the study. For improving the independence of the modules, the function is separated into layers and the data is divided into blocks. For efficient implementation, the 3D building are translated into a 2D graphic by turning the map into a group of nodes. In addition, a new element called node plug is applied to enhance the expandability of the system.

In the future work, more motions can be added into the motion set to enrich the performance of agent and make it act vividly. In regard to the great amount of calculation, new techniques can be introduced to improve the concurrency. We believe that as the development of virtual reality, crowd animation system based on dynamics model will become one of the most important assistant tools for analysis of building structure or crowd evacuation.

Acknowledgements

We would like to express our thanks to Prof. Xiaola Lin at Sun Yat-Sen University for his kind suggestions on english writing and Dr. Xianyong Fang at Anhui Univeristy for many helpful discussions with him on this paper. This research is supported by National Science Foundation of P.R.China(grant No. 60473109) and Guangdong Province Natural Science Foundation of P.R.China (grant No. 04300602).

References

1. D. Helbing, I. Frank, T. VicseSimulating dynamical features of cscape panic. Nature. **28**(2000) 487-490
2. CWReynolds: Flocksherdsand schoolsA distributed behavioral model. Proceedings of the 14th annual conference on Computer graphics and interactive techniques. (1987) 25-34
3. X. Tu, D. Terzopoulos: Artificial fishes: Physics, locomotion, perception, behavior. Proceedings of the 21st annual conference on Computer graphics and interactive techniques. (1994) 43-50
4. C.W. Reynolds: Steering behaviors for autonomous characters. Proceedings of Game Developers Conference 1999. (1999) 763-782
5. K. Perlin, A. Goldberg: Improv: A system for scriping interactive actors in virtual worlds. In Compuer GraphicsProc. of SIGGRAPH '96(1996) 206-216

6. T. Franco, L. Celine, C. Ruth, C. Yiorgos: Agent behaviour simulator (ABS):A platform for urban behavior development. The First International Game Technology Conference and Idea Expo (GTEC'01). (2001)
7. S. Soteris, M.F. Marios, C. Yiorgos: Scalable pedestrian simulation for virtual cities. Proceedings of the ACM symposium on Virtual reality software and technology 2004. (2004) 65-72
8. S.R. Musse, D. Thalmann: A model of human crowd behavior: Group inter-relationship and collision detection analysis. Proceedings of Workshop Eurographics Computer Animation and Simulations 1997. (1997) 39-52
9. D. Thalmann, S.R. Musse, M. Kallmann: From individual human agents to crowds. Informatik/Informatique-Revue des organizations suissesd'informatique. 1(2000) 6-11
10. E.Bouvier, E. Cohen, L. Najman: From crowd simulation to airbag deployment: Particle systems, a new paradigm of simulation. Journal of Electronic Imaging. bf 6(1) (1997) 94-107
11. G. K. Still: Crowd dynamics. PhD Thesis. Mathematics Detartment. Warwick University (2000)
12. B. Adriana, S. R. Musse, P. L. Luiz, de Oliveira, E.J. Bardo: Modeling individual behaviors in crowd simulation. Proceedings of Computer Animation and Social Agents 2003.2003 143-148
13. M.B. Vallamil, S.R. Musse, L.P. L. de Oliveira: A Model for generating and animating groups of virtual agents. Proceedings of 4th International Working Conference on. Intelligent Virtual Agents. (2003) 164-169
14. V. Blue, J. Adler: Celluar automata model of emergent collective bi-directional pedestrian dynamics. Artificial Life VII, The Seventh International Conference on the Simulation and Synthesis of Living Systems (2000) 437-445
15. .Z. Yang, D.L. Zhao, J. Li, T.Y. Fang: Simulation of the kin behavior in building occupant evacuation based on cellular automaton. Building and Environment. 40(3) (2005) 411-415
16. M. Sung, M. Gleicher, S. Chenney: Scalable behaviors for crowd simulation. Computer Graphics Forum. 23(3) (2004) 519-528.

Come Closer: Encouraging Collaborative Behaviour in a Multimedia Environment

Cliff Randell[1] and Anthony Rowe[2]

[1] Department of Computer Science, University of Bristol, UK
`cliff@cs.bris.ac.uk`
[2] Interactive Media, Arts Institute Bournemouth, U.K. and Squidsoup
`arowe@aib.ac.uk, ant@squidsoup.org`

Abstract. Come Closer describes a combined research and art installation using wearable technology and collaborative interaction to explore and challenge the sense of personal space and proximity to others. Participants become acutely aware of each other; aware of their presence in both physical and virtual space. They are encouraged to probe and investigate the boundaries that define personal space, to test them and to cross them. Interaction is defined entirely by position in a room, and the distances between them and others. The movements of the participants are logged and analysed for expected and unexpected behaviours.

1 Introduction

In this paper we present an interactive art installation designed to encourage participants, or players, to overcome traditional notions of personal space in a public area. Edward Hall first identified the concept of proxemics, or personal spaces in his book, The Hidden Dimension [1]. He describes the subjective dimensions that surround someone and the physical distances one tries to keep away from other people according to subtle cultural rules. This project provides an exploration of ways in which an interactive art installation can break down these inbuilt restraints, or inhibitions.

The name Come Closer draws on the locative element of the project, combined with notions of shared experience and collaborative space. The closer people get to each other, the more acutely aware of each others presence they become. This may be playful, comforting or disquieting. With more people in a room, complex relationships and harmonies can begin to form and disappear, allowing scope for cooperation and confrontation, intimacy and rejection. It also allows people to begin to play the space in collaborative and creative ways.

In an immersive experience dominated by sound and digital projection, conscious awareness of the physical presence of others diminishes as participants focus instead on the virtual. However, if the virtual space works as a mirror on reality, with each person represented in the virtual space, awareness of others begins to return. If representations in the virtual space are affected by the proximity of other people, and if things begin to happen when participants approach each other, this should have an effect on the behaviour of those using the space,

H. Zha et al. (Eds.): VSMM 2006, LNCS 4270, pp. 281–289, 2006.

and their behaviour can to an extent be controlled - or at least encouraged in certain directions. We know how space is supposed to unfold before us when we move through it - sonically as well as visually. When these relationships are altered, connected in new and different ways, we become acutely aware of them and try to rationalise the changes. The effects can be unnerving yet ultimately rewarding as we master the new relationships and make them work for us in creative ways.

The notion of shared experience is central to the project, and this needs to work at the crossover between virtual and real. A wall projection is used as a virtual mirror; movement in real space is seen in the reflection - an abstracted mirror image of the real space.

We first describe the installation and its development, then present subjective comments from the participants with our observations, followed by an objective analysis of the logged movements and interaction, and lastly present our conclusions and thoughts for future work.

2   The Installation

There have been several phases in the development of the installation and these provide the background to the concepts and thinking that led to Come Closer (2005).

2.1   Background and Earlier Work

Squidsoup, the creative developers of Come Closer, have a history of creating works that explore the possibilities of creative interaction. Come Closer builds on their experience in this field; projects such as Alt-space [2], Ghosts [3] and Freq [4] deal with the relationship and interfaces between people and virtual spaces in a range of guises.

Come Closer is most closely related to their ongoing Altzero project [5], particularly in the use of physical and virtual space to dissect and explore sound and spatial musical composition. In early 2001, altzero2 was premiered at the ICA, London, U.K. The piece looked at the possibilities of navigating through a piece of music composed in virtual space. It used a 3.5m x 3.5m semi-enclosed active square to control movement through a virtual space projected on a single wall; position tracking was achieved using a single camera. Standing forward made the square, which was transposed into an infinite virtual space, move forwards. Standing on the left made the square bank left, and so on. As participants move through the virtual space, they see and hear what is in proximity to them, so movement equates to exploring the spatialised musical composition.

The piece was effective as an immersive experience, and also as a means of experiencing and navigating through a piece of music, but was less successful in dealing with collaboration in virtual space, as people were generally unaware of how the piece worked when multiple participants were involved. Direct user feedback was blurred with several people in the space simultaneously attempting to control the direction of virtual flight. If a second person walked into the space (the first person may be unaware of this), the direction of movement changed as it was now controlled by the average of two people's positions rather than the direct relationship with a single user.

Another reason was also suspected for this confusion: we observed that if two people are in an enclosed area they will naturally, and subconsciously, gravitate to opposite corners of the space. This notion of encroaching on others personal space was the primary inspiration for developing Come Closer.

2.2   Initial Research and Trials

The Come Closer project started with further dissection of this problem. It was felt that we might overcome the confusion if the position detection system was sufficiently accurate and responsive, and opted to use an ultrasonic position detection system designed by the University of Bristol [6] with hardware developed by HPLabs, Europe [7]. This used a head-mounted transducer connected to a belt-worn networked PDA.

Initial experiments were carried out with a design identical to Altzero2 in terms of user interaction: multiple participants collaboratively controlling movement through an infinite virtual space through their position in a shared physical space. The environment was semi-abstract and immersive, consisting of randomly placed virtual floating dandelion seeds, using anaglyphic stereoscopy to enhance depth perception (see Figure 1a). This approach showed that the problems were not to do with accuracy or responsiveness. Participants need direct and immediate audiovisual responses to their own interactions taking an average of all positions results in a lack of clarity and personal connection with the piece.

It was only by altering the relationship between the physical and virtual spaces that the combination of results we were searching for could be achieved: shared audiovisual experience, direct one-to-one feedback, collaborative interactivity and an uninhibited awareness of others in both the physical and virtual spaces. The viewpoint of the projection was thus altered to become an abstracted mirror image of the physical space - a static virtual camera in a moving space, rather than the converse. Each person would see an iteration of themselves (and others) on the screen, and the audiovisual experience could then be controlled directly from the distances between participants.

Two virtual spaces were created for public presentation and reaction. The first was a simple space containing up to four elongated cascading towers (or columns - see Figure 1b). Each tower represented one participant, its position in the projected space reflecting the participants position in the real space. Sound consisted of a series of sine waves whose frequency related to the distance between each pair of people. The second space was an adaptation of the dandelion seeds but, whereas before the seeds were static and participants moved through the space, in this incarnation the seeds and people moved, but the virtual view

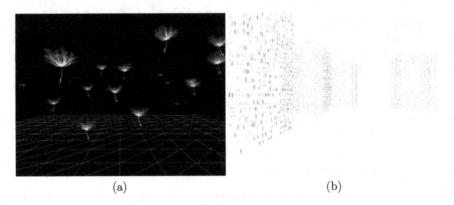

(a)   (b)

Fig. 1. Early versions a) Dandelions and b) Columns

was static. By moving, participants generated virtual wind and gusts of air
that pushed the seeds around. Sound, as before, was emitted by the seeds as
they were pushed out of the visible area. An undulating surface was added to
the floor of the virtual space that bulged wherever the participants were to
indicate their position. Both spaces were audiovisual trials to explore the levels
of complexity that can be entertained in such a setup. Responses from the trials
were very positive people generally understood the connection between what
they did and what they saw; opinions on which version (simple interaction with
the columns against more abstracted link between cause and effect with the
dandelions) were varied. Several hundred visitors took part in the trials, of which
some 137 contributed comments including the following:

*"Really enjoyed the columns version as it was clear what effect my position and
movement was having; the link with 'your' column was strangely endearing and
made me feel part of the art; found the 'columns' easier to unravel quickly; really
enjoyed the experience and finding out how it reacts to your movement/group
movement; feeling of control over intangible things; I liked experimenting with
new movements (swinging yourself around with someone else); you felt part of
a performance; artistically and psychologically interesting - e.g exploring sensations of personal space, racial difference; bit freaky - tried to avoid people as much
as possible; interesting to watch the way people explore in this new environment
and how they create(?) or remain more stationary this from a psychologist's perspective with obvious interest in the potential information to be gathered in this
forum; fascinating and positively weird - I liked wandering while watching - circling each other etc; liked the dandelion seed but not so sure about the other one."*

In order to complete the process, however, a new audiovisual experience was
needed that would properly use the collaborative techniques developed. Additionally, a bespoke ultrasonic system needed to be developed. In its current state
it was over-complex, cumbersome for the user (relying on handheld devices) and
erratic. A new ultrasonic tracking system was devised based on another University of Bristol design [8] enhanced with RF synchronisation giving approximately
5cm accuracy at 3Hz with transponders fitted into baseball caps. Designed for

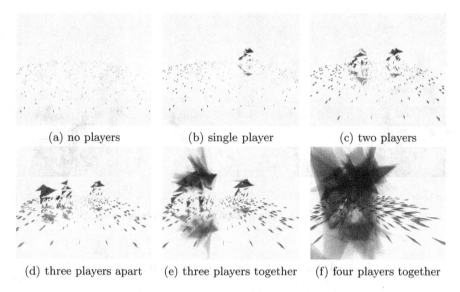

(a) no players   (b) single player   (c) two players

(d) three players apart   (e) three players together   (f) four players together

Fig. 2. Come Closer (2005) - screengrabs

four simultaneous players, this system was easy to use and did not rely on the wireless networking of the previous design.

2.3   The Final Version - Come Closer (2005)

Visually, the final version is an abstract representation of the position and movement of people in virtual space; as the virtual space is a reflection of the real space and the position of participants in it, the projection acts as a mirror (see Figure 2). Similarly, the sounds are designed to highlight the spatial relationship between participants. Each person has a threshold - a personal space that, once encroached upon, triggers clusters of MIDI piano notes. The more people enter into each others personal space, the more complex the note clusters.

In trials it was readily apparent that, once participants had understood this process, they began to play with and explore these boundaries, getting much closer to each other than in previous experiments and even forgetting (albeit temporarily) their own standards of personal space (see Figure 3). Analysis of user feedback seems to confirm our hopes that people generally understood more of the systems in place, and appreciated the ability of the piece to let people assign their own meaning to the experience (like playing windchimes, underwater sonata etc).

The final version of Come Closer was premiered at Lovebytes 06 in Sheffield, U.K. Around 150 people participated and provided feedback; all positional data was also recorded for subsequent analysis. The feedback and analysis are presented and discussed in the following section.

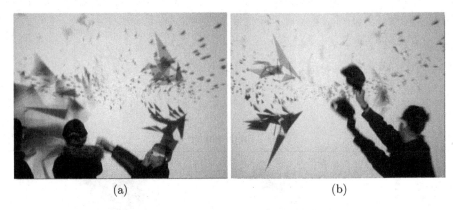

(a)   (b)

Fig. 3. Come Closer (2005) - player interaction

3   Feedback and Behavioural Observations

3.1   Audience Feedback

Again, participants were invited to leave comments on their subjective experience of the installation. These were generally positive and provided support for our aspirations. 34 responses were obtained and an edited selection is given here:

"Mysterious; Strange; Nice, I like the tracking technology. Needs more sound. Good! Great fun - would love to do with more people; Great. More sound and bigger room would be good, but good stuff! Encourages people to go against instinct to move away - beautiful images; Interesting to see the consideration of multi-user interaction; Wondering what kind of movements create the sound. Different; Confusing, made my eyes go weird; Fun; Like Satie but with better headgear; Very interesting - a great interactive experiment; Very very interesting. Playful, immersive . Beautiful; Impressive; Very good, intriguing; Good shapes; Trippy - scary applications??; Very good, funny; V. delicate + moving piece; Brilliant, interesting; Fantastic; Inspiring; Got a lot from visuals - not as much from sound (I understood this was because I was alone); Felt very playful; Like a dancefloor; Fantastic; Moving space; Really cool. So much you could do with this idea!; Wow! A visible approach to the effects of inter/intra personal dynamics, BRAVO!; It truly was an audio representation of the relationship between myself and one of my peers."

From the comments it is clear that many of the participants clearly understood the nature and purpose of the installation, and thoroughly enjoyed participating. Interestingly, some players commented on the dynamic aspects of the piece with comparisons to a dancefloor, and to the playful elements of the installation. This was also reflected in the recorded data as described in the data analysis.

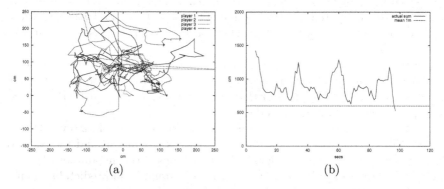

Fig. 4. Typical results plots (a) path and (b) proximity

3.2 Data Analysis

Data was recorded during two 6 hour sessions. From these, fifteen 4 person interactions lasting over one minute were identified with an average session lasting 2min 52secs. Participants were briefed of the nature of interaction to be expected - that the display would change according to their position in the room, and that the musical effects would increase as they 'came closer' together. Thus they were anticipating the nature of the intended effects, but nevertheless a learning, or calibration, stage was expected.

We observed that in over 65% of the tests people would initially move together within 20 seconds of starting the experience. Others were more hesitant and could take 40 seconds or more to gain an initial impression. This could be regarded as the calibration stage. The nature of learning how to interact with the display and sounds incorporated direct reinforcement through spatial correspondence; self-administered awareness of the immediate interaction; as well as observation of the effects of the other participants moving around the floor-space. Other than the initial instruction there was no element of being taught how to use the installation.

The data collected from the installation was analysed graphically in three ways. Firstly, all periods when the full four players were present for over one minute were identified and the relevant log data extracted. This was then used to create, firstly, a real time 'movie' overview of the players movements; secondly, a 2D plan view showing the cumulative tracks of the players was plotted (e.g. see Figure 4a); and, lastly, a plot of the total 'closeness' - or proximity - of the players was made against time for each of these periods (e.g. see Figure 4b). A total of fifteen of these periods taken over the two days were plotted.

From the movies, typical behaviours included:

Hovering - standing in one spot and slowly moving around. This would be typical behaviour in an art gallery as a visitor stands relatively still and looks at an exhibit. This pattern was noted in over 80% of the tests.

Grouping - moving together, and then apart, in a regular cycle. This was the behaviour we anticipated from the design of the installation and was observed in over 65% of the tests. However the cyclical pattern was a surprise and is further analysed below.

Coupling - moving around in pairs, often two pairs. Again this would be normal behaviour at a conventional art installation where couples were visiting together. Observed in 40% of the tests. This was reinforced by the couples moving, as well as standing, together.

Circling - walking round the perimeter of the installation, often several times. In over 45% of the tests we observed participants moving around the edges of the floor-space, presumably exploring the limitations of the installation. This behaviour appears instinctive and, with hindsight, would seem predictable though it did not correspond with any significant display or audio effects.

From the proximity plots we observed a distinct pattern in which the players converged, and then diverged, and then converged again repeatedly. Eight of the periods were suitable for objective analysis of this phenomenon and we found a mean period of 34 seconds with a standard deviation of 11.5 seconds. This behaviour was completely unexpected and seemed to resemble some form of instinctive group dance inspired by the piece.

Applying Hall's analysis [1] for Americans to the measured distances between the players, we observe that players are moving closer together than the expected 1.2-3.5m associated with *social* interactions among acquaintances. The under 1.2m *personal* distance represents interactions typically found among good friends. According to research by Michael Watson, these distances are also likely to be appropriate for English players [9]. Therefore this indicates that Come Closer was successful in bringing players closer together than would normally be expected in a social environment.

4   Conclusions and Future Work

Come Closer (2005) has shown that it is possible to overcome traditional inhibitions of gallery visitors with multimedia interaction, resulting in an engaging experience where visitors begin to lose, albeit temporarily, their reservations and feelings of personal space. As well as predicted behaviour, unexpected movement patterns have been identified which indicate that it may be possible to initiate group, and individual, behaviours with suitably designed interactive multimedia displays.

Further experiments in a more controlled environment could enable a more detailed analysis, perhaps using principal components analysis, or even Felicific calculus [10]. It may be worthwhile to preselect the participants to explore different age, gender and cultural representations; and also to examine the influence of prior acquaintance. Controlled experiments with such groups could also focus on the relative influence of the visuals and audio components of the installation. However by using a controlled environment we risk losing the instinctive responses of the players. The design of further installations is thus anticipated building on the experiences gained from the development of Come Closer, with the prospect of learning more about how people interact with multimedia art.

Acknowledgements

Come Closer is a squidsoup project, developed with funds from the Clark Digital Bursary and Arts Council England (Grants for the Arts). The initial development was supported by Watershed Media Centre, Mobile Bristol, JA Clark Charitable Trust, Arts Council England and The University of the West of England. Further development was funded by the Arts Council, England, and the Watershed Media Centre. Additional research funding and support was provided from the U.K. Engineering and Physical Sciences Research Council, Grant No. 15986, as part of the Equator IRC.

References

1. Edward T. Hall. *The Hidden Dimension*. Bantam Doubleday Dell Publishing Group, 1745 Broadway, New York, USA, 1963.
2. Peter Waters and Anthony Rowe. Alt-space: Audiovisual interactive software for developing narrative environments. In *In CADE 2004 Proceedings of Computers in Art and Design Education Conference*, June 2004.
3. Ghosts website. www.squidsoup.com/ghosts.
4. Freq website. www.squidsoup.org/freq2.
5. Altzero website. www.squidsoup.org/altzero.
6. C. Randell and H. Muller. Low cost indoor positioning system. In *UbiComp 2001: International Conference on Ubiquitous Computing*, pages 42–48, September 2001.
7. R Hull, J Reid, and E. Geelhoed. Delivering compelling experiences through wearable computing. *IEEE Pervasive Computing*, 1(4):56–61, 2003.
8. Paul Duff, Michael McCarthy, Angus Clark, Henk Muller, Cliff Randell, Shahram Izadi, Andy Boucher, Andy Law, Sarah Pennington, and Richard Swinford. A new method for auto-calibrated object tracking. In *Proceedings of the Seventh International Conference on Ubiquitous Computing*, pages 123–140. Springer-Verlag, September 2005.
9. O. Michael Watson. *Proxemic Behavior: A Cross-Cultural Study*. The Hague: Mouton, 1970.
10. Jeremy Bentham. *An Introduction to the Principles of Morals and Legislation*. Oxford University Press, Great Clarendon Street, Oxford, UK, 1789.

The Component Based Factory Automation Control in the Internet Environment

Hwa-Young Jeong

Faculty of General Education, Kyunghee University
1, Hoegi-dong, Dongdaemun-gu, Seoul 130-701, Korea
hyjeong@khu.ac.kr

Abstract. In the factory automation, the communication information between the Control part and the GUI part usually contains the product, control and the operational information. The operations in the GUI part transfer the information between the user and the operational system part. Detailed analysis of the communication information and the process is an important factor to the system. And current software development process is changed over component and internet environments. In this paper, I was design and implement the control system for factory automation in component and internet environments. The component logic makes up the remote status view of the GUI communication modules which has associating the message interrupt method and the timer. This research aimed the IC test handler and this system can display on the web for review and analysis. The proposed method improves the analyzability by catching the operational data under various operation statuses. And it is able to come under a system manager's observation.

1 Introduction

The automation technique, as an illustration of the concept of performance gap, is expected to provide company with the enhancement of efficiency in labor utilization, machine operation, working environment and production management[1]. The effective engineering technique is required to obtain the optimization of all component factors related to the automation process. The engineering technique is defined as the integrated concept of producing technique of the various mechanical components and their operating mechanism, designing of the optimal production process and the technique of using those machines and the information oriented technique of the productivity improvements by maximizing the efficiency of the mechanical components and the process components. When the system of special purpose is developed, it could be practically composed from the standard set of the system components and the users could select and combine the system components from the set, too[2,3]. Accordingly, each part, such as software and hardware component for system, and the mutual data exchange among the system components are the most important matters in the production of the automation machinery and its efficiency. Data cannot be processed without the data interchange among the automation systems. Even after the

H. Zha et al. (Eds.): VSMM 2006, LNCS 4270, pp. 290–299, 2006.

data exchange initiates the automation system, the error which occurs during the data exchange can terminated the operation at any time, which means a great economic loss in the process of the automation. Automation system design technique should be based and stabilized on the integration of proper software, hardware, communication protocol and the user interface in order to perform the static data analysis as well as the dynamic data analysis. Moreover, it is necessary to understand the status of the manufacturing system and reflect it in production planning. To realize the manufacturing system, a remote access system to check the manufacturing system status is required[11].

In this paper, I was design and implement the control system for factory automation. I was design using UML and implement using Visual .Net for this system. For internet environment, I was implementing using ASX. In the control system, the major function is made component under COM(Component Object Model). The component logic makes up the remote status view of the GUI communication modules which has associating the message interrupt method and the timer. This research aimed the IC test handler and this system can display on the web for review and analysis. The proposed method improves the analyzability by catching the operational data under various operation statuses. And it is able to come under a system manager's observation.

2   Factory Automation Control on the Web

2.1   CBD(Component Based Development)

WSystem development using the CBD approach becomes selection, reconfiguration, adaptation, assembling and deployment of encapsulated, replaceable and reusable, building blocks with hidden interior called components, rather than building the whole system from scratch[12]. That is, These improvements result from reuse: building software from existing well tested building blocks is more effective than developing similar functionalities from scratch[13]. To ensure that a composed application is consistent with respect to the expectations and assumptions of each of its constituent components, interfaces can be used. The most basic type of interface only lists the services that a component provides or requires[14]. The interface of a component should be all we know about the component. It should therefore provide all the information on what the component does, i.e. its operations, (though not how it does it) and how we can use the component, i.e. its context dependencies[15]. And COM is a software architecture that allows applications to be built from binary software components. COM is the underlying architecture that forms the foundation for higher-level software services, like those provided by OLE. OLE services span various aspects of commonly needed system functionality, including compound documents, custom controls, inter-application scripting, data transfer, and other software interactions.

2.2   Communication for the Factory Automation

The industrial communication network aims to connect directly to the devices which control and supervise the manufacturing process. The tasks which are executed in the PLC(Programmable Logic Controller) in the industry computer may have some time constraints in the starting or terminating points. It can cause some disability over the operation of the system and the function of the various devices[4, 5]. This kind of disabilities can be caused from the loss of the data from the difference between the data processing time and the communication time in the interface of the control system. The error state which occurs during the operation can be divided into two categories, one that can achieve the original purpose without terminating the operation and the other that requires the complete termination of the operation[6, 7]. Both are critical to the operation of the automation facilities. The communication technique which are used in the industrial communication devices are Parallel Digital I/O Interface, IEEE-488 GPIB(General Purpose Interface Bus) Interface and Serial Communication Interface(RS232C). The serial interface is economic because it uses the internal slot, requires no additional board and can be easily implemented using the software to consider the necessary factors like the board rate (borate)[9]. The GUI systems based on the PC are widely used in the Industrial Automation because of the low cost, reliability and the feasibility of the maintenance[9].

2.3   Communication for the Factory Automation

The World Wide Web provides a best way to materialize the remote access for control and check the machine from a distance. Web server provides the authorization service as the system allows one user at a time to experiment with the machine. Cabello[10] have proposed the remote access to FA controller. In

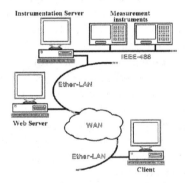

Fig. 1. Remote measurement system scheme

these studies, the different parts that integrate the whole remote access measurement system are: the measurement instrument, controller equipment that will be called instrumentation server, a web server and the client computer from which the user accedes to the system as shown Fig. 1. Kazuhiro[11] shows Fig. 2 that the structure of the FA controller access software through which that software communicates with FA controllers in a LAN (Local Area Network) or serial line. That consists of three processing functions: user interface processing, access command processing, and a communication data processing. In order to use such software via the Internet, a communication protocol conversion function to change TCP/IP and the datalink layer protocol in the Internet to the real communication protocols (transport, network, and datalink layer) for FA controllers must be supported.

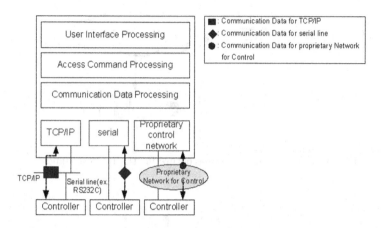

Fig. 2. Communication connected Architecture of controller access software

3   The Design and Implementation of the Factory Automation Control

3.1   The Structure of the Factory Automation Control

This research aimed the IC test handler. Fig. 3 shows the structure of this system. IC test handler consists of two parts: GUI system, Actuator control system. GUI system operates the User interface processing and remote status view processing on the WEB using PC. The User interface processing performs dialog processing between the software and the user. The remote status view processing performs communication processing on the WEB. It sent operation data to server, remote access systems. In remote access systems, they provided an HTTP server in the target control systems. In the HTTP server, the remote access software can access controllers only by using CGI (Common Gateway Interface) programs. The actuator control system operates to control actuator part such as motor, cylinder, sensor using VME board. That is, actuator control processing contains an I/O control program for the production line, and that program runs recursively. Fig. 4 shows the process structure this system. I make user interface processing to components, ReceiveDataRegistry.dll and NotifyDataProcess.dll.

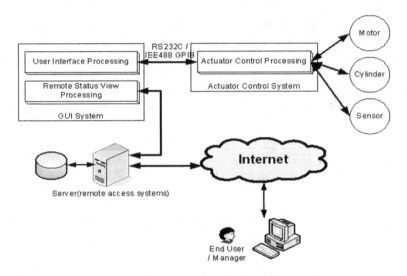

Fig. 3. The Communication structure for the IC Test Handler

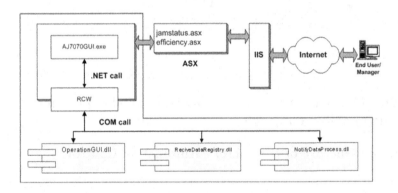

Fig. 4. The Diagram of Communication structure

OperationGUI.dll component perform total control view process. This system use asx and IIS(Internet Information Service) for internet service.

3.2 The Communication Between User Interface Processing and Actuator Control Processing

The communication of user interface processing performs the received data at the point of the data retrieval time. The GUI system proposed in this paper could be used under Windows XP environment and coded with Visual .NET. In OperationGUI.dll component, when it was created window form, the initial setup for the communication port has been required as the followings.

```
Public class FormAJ7070 : System.Windows.Forms.Form {
 private void InitializeComponent( ) {
  device number = OpenComm(communication port,
                   receive buffer size, send buffer size);
  if(communication port opens successively) {
  Select the communication port;
  setup value;
     }
}
```

After communication port has been selected, the GUI system uses Message Interrupt Method to set up the data initiation part;

```
SetCommEventMask( );
EnableCommNotification(communication ID, buffersize);
```

In ReceiveDataRegistry.dll component, it contains the data receive part which actually receives the message in the following. It inputs the received data through the communication port into the circle wait array. In order to retrieve the received data in the data processing part it increases the data receiving pointer by the length of the received data and terminates the task of the data receiving part to be ready for the next data arrival.

```
Public void Commnotify( ) {
    if(data receiving message appeared?) {
        Inputs the received data into the circle wait array ;
        Increases the data receiving pointer by the length
          of the received data ;
        }
}
```

After the processing of the data receiving part described above has been terminated, in NotifyDataProcess.dll component, it calls the Commnotify( ) on the GUI whenever the receiving data has been arrived from the communication network. Data processing part initiates the timer as described in the following to use the GUI process for the first time.

```
Public void ButtonClickStart( ) {
   Timer timerstart;
   Private void OperationStart(object sender,
                         system.EventArgs e) {
      if(StartFlag) {
         timerstart.stop();
      } else {
         timerstart.start();
      } ChangeButton(StartFlag);
   }
}
```

The timer message calling part retrieves the received data, processes them and terminates the operation of the data processing part.

```
Private void timerstart_Tick(object sender, system.EventArgs e) {
    if(value of data receiving pointer = value of data
                processing pointer) {
        function call for the received data processing;
        Increases the pointer value of circle wait
            array by the processed data length;
    }
}
```

4   Application

Fig. 5 shows the IC test handler machine. And I implement component based control system by proposal method. Fig. 6 shows the main screen in the GUI system for control of the IC test handler.

Fig. 5. The IC test handler machine for test semiconductor chip

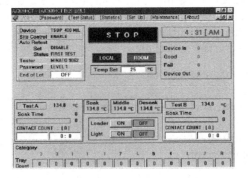

Fig. 6. Main screen of component based control system for IC test handler machine. This system was embedded machine itself. Operator is able to control that machine using this program and receive an operation status message using internet from the other operator at the long distance.

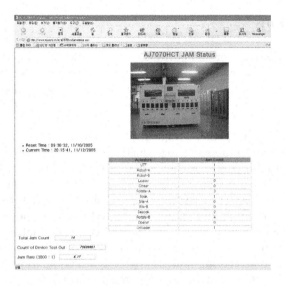

Fig. 7. The jam status information on the WEB

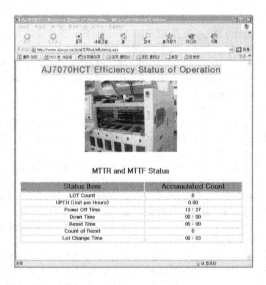

Fig. 8. The jam and operate information on the WEB

Fig. 7 shows is the jam status information and Fig. 8 shows the operation status information(UPEH, down time, etc) on the Web during the IC test handlers running.

5   Conclusions

The communication is very important part for the operation of the FA. It is also necessary to provide a way to detect failures, analyze the reasons for the failures, and recover from a failure quickly. Instead of dispatching maintenance staff, a remote access method to the FA system through a network is required.

This research is developed and implemented component based GUI system for FA machine control. Component logic made GUI system, communication systems between actuator control system and GUI system. Also, it is able to display operation status of FA machine from a distance by internet. The RS232C and IEE 488(GPIB bus) used the communication between actuator control system and GUI system. The operation data send to server(remote access system) and display user or operation manager the data of each information on the WEB. Consequently, we have applied the technique to the IC Test Handler of the Semiconductor Manufacturing Machine System which Samsung Semiconductor Company and UTC Company in Taiwan are currently using.

References

1. R. H. Hayes and S. C. Wheelwright, Restoring Our Competitive Edge: Competing through Manufacturing, New York : John Wiley and Sons, (1984)
2. P. M. Noker, CNC's Fast Moves, Manufacturing Engineering, (1995)
3. J. V. Owen, Open Up Control Architecture, Manufacturing Engineering, (1995)
4. http://www.industry.net
5. http://islsun20.snu.ac.kr/technology/rain.html
6. J. J. Gertler and K. C. Anderson, An Evidential Reasoning Extension to Quantitative Modelbased Failure Diagnosis, IEEE Transaction on System, Man and Cybernatics, vol 22, (1992)
7. R, J, Patton and J. Chen, Review of Parity Space of Approaches to Fault Diagnosis for Aerospace Systems, Journal of Guidance, Control, and Dynamics, vol 17, (1994)
8. Michael F. Hordeski, Control System Interfaces / Design and Implementation using Personal Computers, Prentice Hall, (1992)
9. Kevin Borthwick, Pardip Thind, and Philip Fransen, PC-Based Operator Interface, IEEE Industry Application, 4(4), July/August (1998)
10. R. Cabello, M. Dieguez, I. Gonzalez, F. J. Gomez, Javier Martniez and M. Cervera, Remote Control of Electronic Equipment. An Application to the Practical Formation of University Students, First Technical Workshop of the Computer Engineering Department, March 31, (2000)
11. Kazuhiro Kusunki, Isao Imai, Tomonori Negi, Nori Matsuda, and Kazuo Ushijima, Proposal and Evaluation of a Method of Remote Access to FA Controllers via the Internet, Electronics and Communications in Japan, Part 1, Vol. 85, No. 6, (2002)
12. Stojanovic Z., A. Dahanayake, Components and Viewpoints as integrated Separations of Concerns in system Designing, International Conference on Aspect-Oriented Software Development, April (2002)
13. Miguel Goulao, ."CBSE: a Quantitative Approach.", Proceeding of ECOOP 2003, (2003)

14. Chris Luer, Andre van der Hoek, Composition Environments for Deployable Software Components, Technical Report 02-18, Department of Information and Computer Science, University of California, Irvine, August, (2002)
15. Kung-Kiu Lau, The Role of Logic Programming in Next-Generation Component-Based Software Development, Proceedings of Workshop on Logic Programming and Software En-ginering, July, (2000)

Database, Communication and Creation – A Research on Cultural Heritage-Based Educational Models

Ling Chen

School of Journalism and Communication
Tsinghua University, 100084 Beijing, China
Lingc@tsinghua.edu.cn

Abstract. This paper will discuss new cultural heritage-based communication and education models that are inspired by the ideas and arts of ancient Asia. Some examples of the models used will be given to show how knowledge from around the world can be shared. The goal of this research is to provide new data-based Communication Models that can be used to achieve education with a global background. Our research has just begun, and we are currently working at the theoretical level. The models we discuss here will be examined in greater detail during the next stage of our work.

1 The Museum Database

In recent years, museums all over the world have made extraordinary progress in the use of technology to digitize their collections; in addition, a number of large museums have constructed sophisticated databases. So far, the databases in most museums are used chiefly for information retrieval, management, museum organization, education, etc. The ways adopted are basically unilateral and fixed. The question to be addressed in museum-based communication, education and entertainment is the following: how can a museum's archive be brought into play at the global level and used for communication and creative educational proposes?

The museum information system supported by computer and network technology is presented in a variety of forms, such as simple images, 2D, 3D, and movies. At present, most museum information systems are independent and dispersed, and like the physical museums themselves, the museum's digital resources have their own space. Indeed, it could be said that invisible walls now divide most digital museums. The WWW-based platform has made it possible to integrate museum resources beyond the limits of their physical environment. The interconnection of digital museums in different countries and areas can transform a small museum into a large one and a unilateral museum into a multilateral one. Given this capability, a multilateral museum could freely combine and exchange any cultural heritage information located in a variety of museum archives. A multilateral or interconnected museum could also exchange data and help to construct a distributed museum in the future, thereby overcoming physical obstacles and virtual separation and making it possible to share humanity's historic heritage and its arts.

H. Zha et al. (Eds.): VSMM 2006, LNCS 4270, pp. 300–307, 2006.
© Springer-Verlag Berlin Heidelberg 2006

We are happy to see that some researchers have now reached the initial stages in the creation of goal-sharing museum archives and have developed intelligent search engines: e.g., SCRAN and Informedia projects. SCRAN (the Scottish Cultural Resource Access Network) was begun in 2002 as one of a number of Millennium Projects. It was organised by the Scottish Museums Council and the National Museum of Scotland for the purpose of integrating all of Scotland's museum resources and building a nation-based museum archive that could be transformed into a database for educational purposes. At the present time, a part of that database (from 400 Scottish museums) is available for school and university users.

The Informedia Project at Carnegie Mellon University's School of Computer Science was begun in 1994 as one of six Digital Library Initiative (DLI) projects funded by NSF, DARPA, and NASA. The goal of Informedia is to develop an intelligent search system that will automatically summarize, visualize, and present distributed text, images, audio and video in the form of a single abstract. Informedia will also have access to the international digital library collaboration of Europe and Asia with its multi-cultural platform.

Since old copyright policies, access systems, and security technologies do not address digital databases such as movies, copyrights are now becoming a major problem in the sharing of databases and resources. As a result, while some museums have made the choice to open their digital doors completely to the public, others have decided to keep them closed. Nonetheless, there are some positive examples in Europe, like the Uffizi Gallery in Italy, which has divided its database according to pixels to accommodate a variety of needs. To make the world's heritage-sharing possible, a multimedia database and information system and cross-domain resource discovery must first be developed.

In the course of our research on database-based communication models, we have found that a common ground exists between today's network-based databases and the prevailing ideas of ancient Asia, namely the idea that all things in the world are integrated and connected to one another. This research has led us to ancient oriental art patterns that reflect this idea, patterns like Indra's Net in India and the multiple viewpoints of early Japanese space constructions known as Rakutyuurakugai, as well as the famous Mandalas of Tibet. Indeed, we have come to regard these reflections of ancient knowledge patterns as an underlying framework for the construction of a cultural heritage information space characterized by dispersal, interactive communication, and sharing. The "network" of Western technology is now reaching out to these ancient ideologies and arts.

2   The Historical Knowledge Mining

The beginnings of the ensuing dialogue among physicists, biologists, physiologists, and artists can be traced back to the 1960s. It was at that time that Dr. Suzuki[1] first translated his Zen Buddhism into English, and the appearance of Zen philosophy strongly influenced the Western world. Physicists began to apply modern physics and systems theories to Buddhism and Taoism. Artists like John Cage created a music of

---

[1] D.T. Suzuki (1870-1966) was the first Japanese who introduced Zen Buddhism to the West.

silence based on the teachings of Zen, and the very popular work by Fritjof Capra, The Tao of Physics, appeared. Capra's book explored existing parallels between modern physics and Eastern mysticism.

This dialogue between Western technology and Eastern philosophy, which emerged from developing technologies in the 20th century, focused on the structure of the world as a holographic model. One of the first pioneers of the dialogue was Stanford neurosurgeon Karl Pribram, the author of "The Languages of the Brain." Benefiting from developing technologies, Pribram was able to confirm the traditional theory that the "higher centers" of the brain controlled the lower ones. His studies in brain memory and function led him to the conclusion that the brain operates, in many ways, like a hologram. He accumulated convincing evidence to support the belief that the brain's "deep structure" was essentially holographic.

At about the same time, English physicist David Bohm, who had worked with Einstein, suggested that the organization of the universe itself might be holograph. According to Bohm, beneath the explicate realm of separate things and events lay an implicate realm of undivided wholeness, which was simultaneously available to each explicate part. In other words, the physical universe itself functioned like a gigantic hologram; each part of which contained the whole.

We can find this same idea of holographic world in Tibetan Mandalas, In Sanskrit, the word "Mandala" means a circle or a polygon. It is often conceived as a place with four gates, each of which faces in one of the four directions. As a symbolic representation of the universe, it is most commonly associated with Indian tantra, the Vajrayana school of Buddhism in Tibet. Mandala is a perfect example of the way in which a single aspect of life can be used to represent all of life itself. In that sense, a Mandala can be said to be an undivided universe.

Fig. 1. The image of the Tibetan sand Mandala

A most extraordinary ancient description of a network of interconnections is found in certain Indian Buddhist sutras. As Fritjof Capra explains in his Tao of Physics,".. particles are dynamically composed of one another in a self-consistent way, and in that sense can be said to 'contain' one another. In Mahayana Buddhism, a very similar notion is applied to the whole universe. This cosmic network of interpenetrating things is illustrated in the Buddhist Sutra by the metaphor of Indra's net." As Fritjof Capra describes it in his Tao of Physics:

"In the new paradigm, the relationship between the part and the whole is more symmetrical. We believe that while the properties of the parts certainly contribute to our understanding of the whole, at the same time the properties of the parts can only be fully understood through the dynamics of the whole."

Fig. 2. Computer graphics illustrate the image of Indra's Net

Fig. 3. The Painting of Japanese Rakutyuurakugai Picture

A style of screen painting known as Rakutyuurakugai picture that we often associate with the"cubism"of the 1890's in the West appeared in the Late Momoyama and early Edo Periods in Japan. Typically, The pictures showed ordinary people in the streets and shops of Edo, but the way the scenes were portrayed was indeed uncommon, in view of the fact that they were painted long before the invention of airplanes and aerial photography or even the erection high buildings. Nonetheless, it is beyond dispute that the pictures demonstrate an excellent command of the city's geography and the artist's own interpretation thereof. Unlike the use of perspective in the West, the artists of the Edo Period integrated information about the city in plan form by means of full-orientation construction.

The ancient Asian ideas and arts mentioned above all demonstrate the same concept from different points of view, namely that the world is an undivided entity and that all knowledge of that entity is interconnected and associated with its various parts. Just as a Mandala represents a symbolic universe and the unified structure of the world, Indra's net offers an insight into the construction of the world of knowledge and its relationships. The screen painting of Rakutyuurakugai, on the other hand, contained philosophical and artistic ideas on how to view and organize a city's information. These ancient ideologies and approaches to art will serve as the theoretical framework for our present-day research on the development of cultural heritage-based communication and education models.

3 A New Database-Based Communication Paradigm

I would now like to discuss the new database-based communication models we are working on. Let us first take a look the character-search engines, such as google, yahoo and/or museum information systems. If, for example; we enter the key words "Francisco Goya", we will get innumerable results that contain the words "Francisco Goya", but there will be little if any relationship between the items listed, whether it be date, life story, or works of art. To find relevant relationships takes a lot more search time and perhaps two or three returns to the original results. What's more, in the course of searching, one of the items found may even take us to a website that has nothing to do with "Francisco Goya", deviating entirely from the original search.

But with the new data-based models as follows, users can use a PC, a PDA, or a mobile phone, etc. to connect to the Inter-Museum System and the Inter-Museum Models, including the Time and Space Combination Model, the Bootstrap Model, the Free Association Model, the Tree Model, and the Multi-Viewpoint Model. These could all offer new approaches to education, research, entertainment, arts creation, tourism and the making of presentations.

Through keyword retrieving/searching, users can, by choosing any one of the above patterns, get the data they require from the museum database and freely combine it in virtual space in accordance with such different categories as "history," "biography," "aesthetics," and "works." In this way, they can construct a new virtual knowledge space that centers around vision.

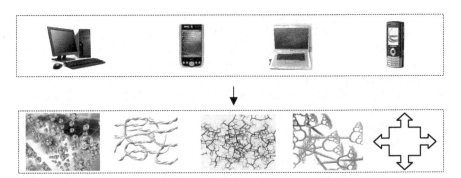

The data-based communication models; 1-A Time and Space Combination Model; 2- bootstrap; 3-A Free   Association Model; 4-A Tree Model; 5-A Multi-View Point Model

For: Education; Research; Entertainment; Arts Creation

Meanwhile, an interactive heritage communication can transfer museum data (used mainly to save and retrieve) into an active space for spreading knowledge and creating art. In virtual space, students, according to their own needs, can choose the corresponding knowledge construction pattern to construct their own space from a variety of museum data information systems. They can then reconstruct the database resources in time and space by means of transfiguring, copying and interpreting the original heritage resources by means of their own creative activity. I would now like to show you some examples;

Fig. 4 and 5. The image of Kabuki, before and after

The Center for Media Esthetics in Koyto Zoukei University is a place in which people are now working on database creation activities. By accessing Koyto's network-based database, which includes ancient paintings, architecture, and handicrafts, students can freely copy and download the images and, if they wish, combine new images with old images to make original works of art. By means of the process of copying and digitizing, they can derive the different values of ancient Kyoto. Without digital technology, this would not be possible. For example, one can enlarge an ancient silk fabric, combine new information with the old pattern and create a new work of art. Figure 4 and 5 show how to digitize an original Kabuki drawing and make it into a new image by means of the digital image system, correcting the colors and clearing up the lines in the picture. In the connected museum system, the world is an open space in which traditional cultural elements can be transformed into a myriad of hybrid formats.

I would also like to give a few examples of some of the projects we completed over the past few years and discuss the role a data-based heritage source can play in the virtual presentation of China's cultural heritage.

Fig. 6, 7 and 8. The way in which users take part in the "Five Animal Exercises"

Fig 6,7 and 8 are two of the interfaces for the "Five Animal Exercises" that we designed for the "Virtual Olympic Museum Project" 2. They show how we learned about ancient sports and culture by transferring the images from a physical space to a virtual space. In doing this, we realised the importance of emphasising the concept of harmony between man and nature in ancient China. Our work was based on a huge database with many documents, paintings, and images that related to this prototype. In essence, it showed by means of images how ancient sports and ancient cultures related to the concept of harmony, something that the users could not otherwise have seen. This was the real power that underlay and supported the dynamic artistic experience.

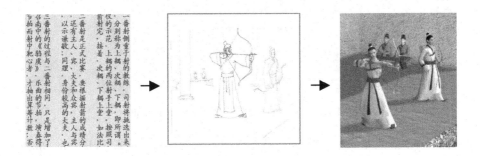

Fig. 9, 10 and 11. The process of transformation from the document to the virtual image

Fig 9, 10 and 11 are another example drawn from the "Virtual Olympic Museum Project", "The representation of an Ancient Archery Competition", for which we re-created the competition by means of 3D technology. During the course of our creation, we realised that it would not be possible to understand this sport without some basic knowledge of ancient Chinese Liyi culture. It would also not have been possible to fully understand the key point of the project – the difference between ancient Chinese and ancient Greek sports, the techniques they exemplified, and the cultures that generated them. We were, therefore, very grateful to Prof. Penglin, an expert from the history department of Tsinghua University, who shared his knowledge of this subject with us and provided us with original materials that made it possible for us to recreate the ancient competition and the culture.

"An Excursion to West Lake - Beyond Time and Space" 3is the name of an older project that I directed in 2000. This provides a good example of how we integrated 800 years of West Lake's history, art, poetry, and architecture throughout different dynasties over time and space axles. It also shows, in the design of the interface, the different relationships that prevailed between the landscape, the culture, and the people of those times.

---

2 VOM is a co-operative project among Beijing University of Aeronautics and Astronautics; Tsinghua University; Beijing University of Physical Education and Capinfo. We took the part of concept & interface design and the 3D graphics creation.

3 A project sponsored by MMCA (Multimedia Contents Association of Japan) and Ministry of Economy trade and Industry (METI).

Fig. 12 and 13. The interfaces of West Lake, the time and space design

4 Conclusion

In China, the digitization of museums began in the late 1990's and, at present, most Chinese museums are in the process of setting up the equipment they need and constructing database systems. With this in mind, it is important to point out that an inter-museum system represents the realization of the union of Western technology and the ancient wisdom of the East. As such, we are convinced that it will play an important role in the creative education of the students. Indeed, it is our sincere hope that a culturally rich and interactive museum-based system will help our students to open their minds to the many possibilities of the new global culture.

As Vannevar Bush, the inventor of the network, said in 1954 in his paper "As we may think," "The human mind does not work that way. It operates by association. With one item in its grasp, it snaps instantly to the next that is suggested by the association of thoughts, in accordance with some intricate web of trails carried by the cells of the brain. It has other characteristics, of course; trails that are not frequently followed are prone to fade; items are not fully permanent; memory is transitory. Yet the speed of action, the intricacy of trails, the detail of mental pictures, is awe-inspiring beyond all else in nature." From this point of view, the Inter-Museum Information System is nothing less than the dream of the internet technology.

References

1. The Tao of Physics; an exploration of the parallels between modern physics and Eastern mysticism / Fritjof Capra, Toronto New York Bantam Books, 1984
2. Wholeness and the implicate order/ David Bohm/ London Boston Routledge & Kegan Paul, 1981
3. The Holographic paradigm and other paradoxes: exploring the leading edge of science / Ken Wilber Boulder Shambhala, 1982.
4. InterCommunication No. 25,1998
5. InterCommunication No. 18,1996
6. SCRAN Project, EVA-GIFU'98, Japan
7. http://www.cchn.cn
8. http://www.informedia.cs.cmu.edu/
9. http://scran.ac.uk
10. Thoughts on Education for Global Citizenship, Lecture by Daisaku Ikeda at Columbia University, 1996 http://www.sgi.org/english/sgi_president/works/speeches/thoughts.htm

An Adaptive Reliable QoS for Resource Errors Running on Ubiquitous Computing Environments

Eung Nam Ko

Department of Information & Communication, Baekseok University,
115, Anseo-Dong, Cheonan, ChungNam, 330-704, Korea
ssken@bu.ac.kr

Abstract. The ARQ_RE model is proposed for supporting QoS resource errors detection-recovery in the situation-aware middleware. An example of situation-aware applications is a multimedia education system. QoS guarantees must be met in the application, system and network to get the acceptance of the users of multimedia communication system. There are several constraints which must be satisfied to provide guarantees during multimedia transmission. They are time, space, device, frequency, and reliability constraints. We propose a method for increasing reliability through an Adaptive Reliable QoS for Resource Errors (ARQ_RE) model for ubiquitous computing environments. The model aims at guaranteeing it through application QoS.

1 Introduction

Ubiquitous computing environment is a computing environment which provides useful services to users by embedding computers in the physical environment and being aware of the physical circumstances. Therefore, the situational information is very important for deciding service behaviors in the ubiquitous computing environment. The situational information of entities is called context. An entity is a person, place, or object that is considered relevant to the interaction between a user and an application, including the user and applications themselves [1, 2]. Context awareness(or context sensitivity) is an application software system's ability to sense and analyze context from various sources; it lets application software take different actions adaptively in different contexts[3]. In a ubiquitous computing environment, computing anytime, anywhere, any devices, the concept of situation-aware middleware has played very important roles in matching user needs with available computing resources in transparent manner in dynamic environments [4, 5]. An example of situation-aware applications is a multimedia education system. Education system for distributed multimedia holds the promise of greatly improving all forms of remote education and training [6]. However, since this new education system must be developed in a way that combines various field of technologies, including group communication and distributed multimedia processing which are the basis of packet based videoconferencing systems, integrated service functions such as middle ware are required to support it[7,8,9]. QoS guarantees must be met in the application,

H. Zha et al. (Eds.): VSMM 2006, LNCS 4270, pp. 308–317, 2006.

system and network to get the acceptance of the users of multimedia communication system. There are several constraints which must be satisfied to provide guarantees during multimedia transmission. They are time, space, device, frequency, and reliability constraints [10].

We propose a method for increasing reliability through an Adaptive Reliable QoS for Resource Errors (ARQ_RE) model for ubiquitous computing environments. The model aims at guaranteeing it through application QoS. Section 2 describes related works as QoS-layered model for the multimedia communication system. Section 3 denotes the ARQ_RE architecture and algorithm. Section 4 describes simulation results of our proposed ARQ_RE model. Section 5 presents conclusion.

2 Related Works

Traditional QoS (ISO standards) was provided by the network layer of the communication system. An enhancement of QoS was achieved through inducing QoS transport services. For multimedia communication system, the QoS notion must be extended because many other services contribute to the end-to-end service quality. As shown in Figure 1, the organization of QoS-layered model for the multimedia communication system include 4 layers. The four layers consist of a user QoS layer, an application QoS layer, a system QoS layer and a network QoS layer[10].

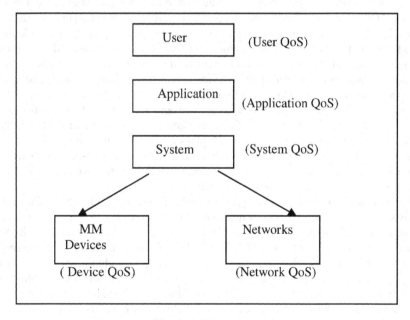

Fig. 1. QoS Layering

3 The ARQ_RE Model for Situation-Aware Middleware

The QoS layered model based on RCSM is described in section 3.1, and integrated white model on RCSM is proposed in section 3.2. ARQ_RE(Adaptive Reliable QoS for Resource Error) is presented in section 3.3.

3.1 QoS Layered Model Based on RCSM

A conceptual architecture of situation-aware middleware based on Reconfigurable Context-Sensitive Middleware (RCSM) is proposed in [3]. All of RCSM's components are layered inside a device. The Object Request Broker of RCSM (R-ORB) assumes the availability of reliable transport protocols; one R-ORB per device is sufficient. The number of ADaptive object Containers (ADC)s depends on the number of context-sensitive objects in the device. ADCs periodically collect the necessary "raw context data" through the R-ORB, which in turn collects the data from sensors and the operating system. Initially, each ADC registers with the R-ORB to express its needs for contexts and to publish the corresponding context-sensitive interface. RCSM is called reconfigurable because it allows addition or deletion of individual ADCs during runtime (to manage new or existing context-sensitive application objects) without affecting other runtime operations inside RCSM.

Other services have many agents. They consist of AMA(Application Management Agent), MCA(Media Control Agent), FTA(Fault Tolerance Agent), SA-UIA(Situation-Aware User Interface Agent), SA-SMA(Situation-Aware Session Management Agent), and SA-ACCA(Situation-Aware Access and Concurrency Control Agent), as shown in Figure 2. AMA consists of various subclass modules. It includes creation/deletion of shared video window and creation/deletion of shared window. MCA supports convenient applications using situation-aware ubiquitous computing. Supplied services are the creation and deletion of the service object for media use, and media share between the remote users. This agent limits the services by hardware constraint. FTA is an agent that plays a role in detecting an error and recovering it in situation-aware ubiquitous environment. SA-UIA is a user interface agent to adapt user interfaces based on situations. SA-SMA is an agent which plays a role in connection of SA-UIA and FTA as situation-aware management for the whole information. SA-ACCA controls the person who can talk, and the one who can change the information for access. However, it did not include QoS support in the architecture.

We assumed throughout this paper the model shown in Figure 2. This model consists 4 QoS layer: User QoS(including Situation-Aware Application Objects), Application QoS(including Optional Components and Other services in RCSM), System QoS(including ADCs, R-ORB and OS), Network QoS(including Transport Layer Protocols for Ad Hoc Networks) and Device QoS(including Sensors). In this paper, we concentrate in the application QoS layer. There are several constraints which must be satisfied to provide guarantees during multimedia transmission. They are time, space, device, frequency, and reliability constraints. Time constraints include delays. Space constraints are such as system buffers. Device constraints are such as frame grabbers allocation. Frequency constraints include network bandwidth and system bandwidth for data transmission. In this paper, we focus on how to represent application QoS during fault tolerance method.

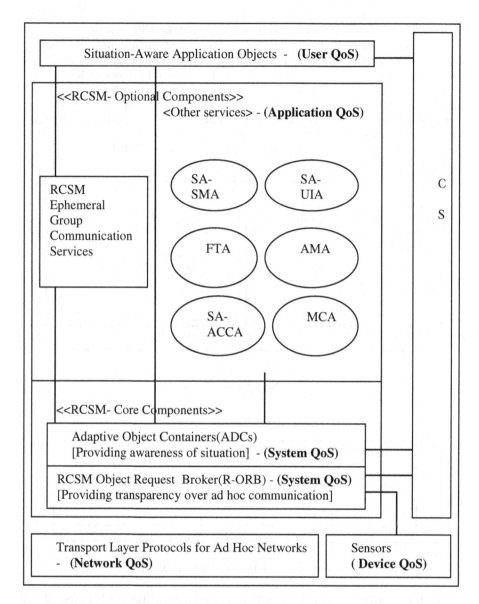

Fig. 2. RCSM and Other Services for Situation-Aware Ubiquitous Computing

3.2 Integrated Whiteboard Model on RCSM

As shown in Figure 3, you can see the relationship between Whiteboard Instance and Whiteboard SM(Session Manager). This system is used to be one of services that are implemented on Remote Education System. This Remote Education System includes several features such as Audio, Video, Whiteboard and WebNote running on Internet environment which is able to share HTML. We have implemented Whiteboard function to do so either. While session is ongoing, almost all participants are able to exchange HTML documents. For this reason, we need the URL synchronization. To win over such dilemma for centralized or replicated architecture, a combined approach, CARV(the centralized abstraction and replicated view) architecture is used to realize the application sharing agent. This system is used to be one of services that are implemented on Remote Education System. This Remote Education System includes several features such as Audio, Video, Whiteboard, WebNote running on Internet environment which is able to share HTML(Hyper Text Mark-up Language). We have implemented Whiteboard and WebNote function to do so either. While session is ongoing, almost all participants are able to exchange HTML documents. .

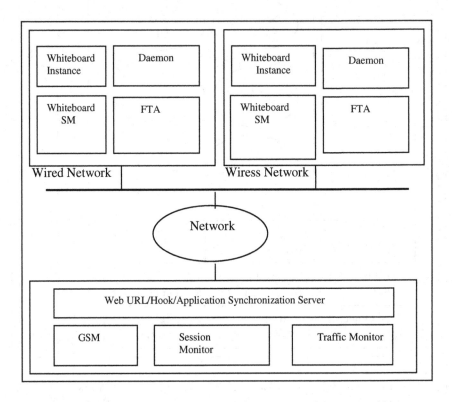

Fig. 3. Relationship between Whiteboard Instance & Whiteboard SM

This paper proposes an URL synchronization function used in Whiteboard and WebNote with remote collaborative education system based on situation-aware middleware for CBM(Computer Based Multimedia). It retrieves the common characteristics of these tools and designs an integrated model including all these methods for supporting concurrent collaborative workspace. As shown in Figure 4 and Figure 5, this paper describes an integrated model which supports object drawing, application sharing, and web synchronization methods of sharing information through a common view between concurrently collaborating users. This proposed model consists of multiple view layout manager and each layout control, a unified user interface, and defines the attributes of a shared object.

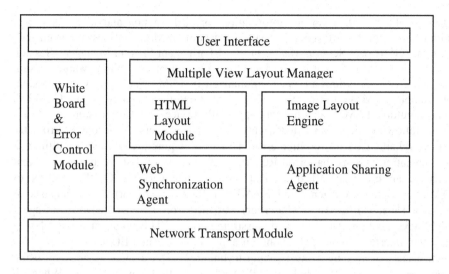

Fig. 4. An Integrated Model with Web Synchronization

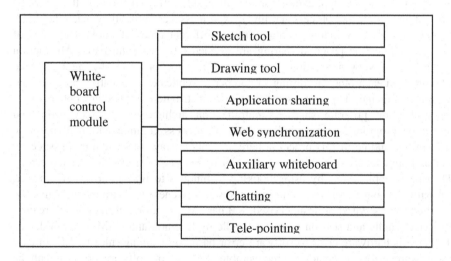

Fig. 5. User Interface

3.3 Adaptive Reliable QoS for Resource Errors

ARQ_RE consist of FTA(Fault Tolerance Agent), UIA(User Interface Agent) and SMA(Session Management Agent). UIA is an agent which plays a role as an interface to interact between the user and FTA. UIA is a module in ARQ_RE. UIA has functions which receive user's requirement and provides the results for the user. SMA is an agent which plays a role in connection of UIA and FTA as management for the whole information. SMA monitors the access to the session and controls the session.

It has an object with a various information for each session and it also supports multitasking with this information. SMA consists of GSM(Global Session Manager), Daemon, LSM(Local Session Manager), PSM(Participant Session Manager), Session Monitor ,and Traffic Monitor. GSM has the function of controlling whole session when a number of sessions are open simultaneously. LSM manages only own session. For example, LSM is a lecture class in distributed multimedia environment. GSM can manage multiple LSM. Daemon is an object with services to create session.

The following algorithm detects, classifies, and recovers the resource errors for adaptive reliable QoS for resource error. To ensure required reliability of multimedia communication systems based on RCSM, FTA consists of 3 steps that are an error detection, an error classification, and an error recovery. ARQ_RE consists of EDA(Error Detection Agent) and ERA(Error Recovery Agent). EDA consists of ED(Error Detector), EC(Error Classifier) and EL(Error Learner). EDA is an agent which plays a role in detecting, and classifying errors. ED is an agent which plays a role as an interface to interact among an application, EC and EL. ED has functions which detect an error by using hooking techniques. EDA detects an error by using hooking methods in MS-Windows API(Application Program Interface). When an error occurs, A hook is a point in the Microsoft Windows message-handling mechanism where an application can install a subroutine to monitor the message traffic in the system and process certain types of messages before they reach the target window procedure. Windows contains many different types of hook. The roles of error and application program sharing are divided into two main parts; Abstraction and sharing of view generation. Error and application program sharing must take different from each other according to number of replicated application program and an event command. This proposed structure is distributed architecture but for error and application program sharing, centralization architecture is used. Error and application program sharing windows perform process communication of message form. In the middle of this process, there are couple ways of snatching message by error and application sharing agent. ED informs EC of the results of detected errors. ED inspects applications by using hooking techniques to find an error. EC and EL deal with learning in reactive multi-agent systems. Generally, learning rules may be classified as supervised or unsupervised. KB has a registration information of creation of service handle and session manager handle by Daemon and GSM. EC can decide whether it is hardware error or software error based on learning rules by EL. In case of hardware error, it cannot be recoverable. In case of software error, it can be recoverable. This approach is based on the idea of comparing the expected error type which is generated by an EL with the actual error occurred from sites.

The scheme of error recovery method is different each other. It can be classified as many cases. In unrecoverable case, the system has to be restarted by manual when error occurred in hardware This approach has no consideration of domino effect between processes as follows in recoverable case.

(1) Error Detector request to GSM session information
(2) GSM give response Error Detector session information
(3) Error Detector request to Daemon for recovery
(4) Daemon announce to Remote-Daemon for recovery

(5) Remote-Daemon announce to Participant Session Manager for recovery
(6) Remote-Daemon receives an acknowledgement for recovery packet.
(7) Daemon receives an acknowledgement for recovery packet
(8) Daemon create Local Session Manager
(9) Local Session Manager create Whiteboard or Media server
(10) Whiteboard or Media server create Whiteboard or Media server Instance
(11) Whiteboard or Media server Instance make an acknowledge to Local Session Ma
     nager
(12) LSM create application
(13) Daemon inform GSM of an information for recovery

The strong point of this system is to detect and recovered automatically in case that
the session's process come to an end from a software error.

4 Simulation Results

Our approach has distinct features such as the SoC principle support and dynamism of
situation-aware support. For existing QoS management techniques: In OS-level
management, QoS management schemes are limited to CPU, memory, disk, network,

Table 1. Analysis of Conventional Multimedia Distance Education System

Function	Sha- Stra	MER- MAID	MM- conf	CE- CED
OS	UNIX	UNIX	UNIX	UNIX
Development Location	Purdue Univ. USA	NEC, JAPAN	CamBridge USA	SRI, International
Development Year	1994	1990	1990	1993
Structure	Server /client	Server /client	Centralized or Replicated	Repli- cated
protocol	TCP/IP	TCP/IP	TCP/IP	TCP/IP multicast
Whiteboard Function running on RCSM	No	No	No	No
Error Control Function running on RCSM	No	No	No	No

and so on [11, 12]. In application-level management, a limitation of the schemes is in monitoring states of necessary resources from applications steadily or periodically. To extend the limitation, QoS is managed in the middleware level to satisfy integrated QoS of several applications over the network [13, 14, 15]. However, these approaches are also limited and not flexible in dynamically changing situations, comparing with our situation-aware QoS management using the ARQ_RE model.

As shown in Table 1, conventional systems for multimedia distance education are Shastra, MERMAID, MMconf, and CECED. You can see the characteristic function of each system function for multimedia distance education.

There are two different structures. Those are CACV and RARV. In this paper, we discuss a hybrid software architecture which is adopting the advantage of CACV and RARV. CACV is centralized architecture where only one application program exists among entire sharing agents and centralized server takes care of input processing and abstraction is the same. RARV is replicated architecture at which application data input(event) that is generated when sharing takes place is transferred and executed. This means that only event information is separately performed. We proposed an adaptive reliable QoS for resource errors based on a hybrid software architecture which is adopting the advantage of CACV and RARV for situation-aware middleware.

5   Conclusion

A QoS resource error detection-recovery model called "ARQ_RE" was proposed for situation-aware middleware as RCSM. ARQ_RE model was used to detect and recover the QoS resource errors among actions. An example of situation-aware applications is a multimedia education system. Education system for distributed multimedia holds the promise of greatly improving all forms of remote education and training. However, since this new education system must be developed in a way that combines various field of technologies, including group communication and distributed multimedia processing which are the basis of packet based videoconferencing systems, integrated service functions such as middle ware are required to support it. QoS guarantees must be met in the application, system and network to get the acceptance of the users of multimedia communication system. There are several constraints which must be satisfied to provide guarantees during multimedia transmission. They are time, space, device, frequency, and reliability constraints. We proposed a method for increasing reliability through an Adaptive Reliable QoS for Resource Errors (ARQ_RE) model for ubiquitous computing environments. The model aims at guaranteeing it through application QoS. Our future works are QoS-aware middleware for ubiquitous and heterogeneous environments.

References

[1] Anind K. Dey and Gregory D. Abowd: Towards a Better Understanding of Context and Context-Awareness, Workshop on the What, Who, Where, When, and How of Context-Awareness, CHI 2000, The Hague, The Netherlands, Aprl, 3, (2000).
[2] Eunhoe Kim and Jaeyoung Choi: An Ontology-Based Context Model in a Smart Home LNCS 3983, pp. 11-20, May, (2006).

[3] S. Yau, F. Karim, Y. Wang, B. Wang, and S. Gupta: Reconfigurable Context-Sensitive Middleware for Pervasive Computing, *IEEE Pervasive Computing*, 1(3), pp. 33-40, July-September, (2002).

[4] S. S. Yau and F. Karim: Adaptive Middleware for Ubiquitous Computing Environments, *Proc. IFIP 17th WCC*, Vol. 219, pp. 131-140, August, (2002).

[5] S. S. Yau and F. Karim: Contention-Sensitive Middleware for Real-time Software in Ubiquitous Computing Environments, *Proc. 4th IEEE Int'l Symp. on Object-Oriented Real-time Distributed Computing ISORC 2001*, pp. 163-170, May, (2001).

[6] Palmer W.Agnew, Anne S. Kellerman, Distributed Multimedia, ACM Press, (1996).

[7] Jae Young Ahn, Gyu mahn Lee, Gil Chul Park, Dae Joon Hwang: An implementation of Multimedia Distance Education System Based on Advanced Multi-point Communication Service Infrastructure: DOORAE, In proceedings of the IASTED International Conference Parallel and Distributed Computing and Systems October 16-19, Chicago, Illinois, USA (1996).

[8] ITU-T Recommendation T.122: Multipoint Communication Service for Audiographics and Audiovisual Conferencing Service Definition, ITU-T SG8 Interim Meeting 18th Oct, (1994), mertlesham, issued 14th Mar, (1995).

[9] Eung-Nam Ko, Dae-Joon Hwang, Jae-Hyun Kim: Implementation of an Error Detection-Recovery System based on Multimedia Collaboration Works: EDRSMCW, MIC'99 IASTED International Conference, Innsbruck Austria, Feb., (1999).

[10] Ralf Steinmetz and Klara Nahrstedt: Multimedia: computing, communications & Applications, Prentice Hall P T R.

[11] D. Xu, et al.: QoS and Contention-Aware Muiti-Resource Reservation", 9th IEEE International Symposium on High Performance Distributed Computing (HPDC'00), (2000).

[12] P. Bellavista, A. Corradi, and R. Montanari: An Active Middleware to Control QoS Level of Multimedia Services, Proceedings of the Eight IEEE Workshop on Future Trends of Distributed Computing System. (2001).

[13] D. Xu, D. Wichadakul, and K. Nahrstedt: Resource-Aware Configuration of Ubiquitous Multimedia Services, Proceedings of IEEE International Conference on Multimedia and EXPO 2000(ICME 2000), (2000).

[14] K. Nahrstedt, D. Xu, and D. Wichadakul: QoS-Aware Middleware for Ubiquitous and Heterogeneous Environments", In IEEE Communications Magazine. (2001).

[15] J. Huang and Y. Wang, and F. Cao: On Developing Distributed Middleware Services for QoS- and Criticality-Based Resource Negotiation and Adaptation, Journal of Real-Time System, (1998).

Learner's Tailoring E-Learning System on the Item Revision Difficulty Using PetriNet

Hwa-Young Jeong

Faculty of General Education, Kyunghee University
1, Hoegi-dong, Dongdaemun-gu, Seoul 130-701, Korea
hyjeong@khu.ac.kr

Abstract. E-learning models are attempts to develop frameworks to address the concerns of the learner and the challenges presented by the technology so that online learning can take place effectively. So it usually used the item difficulty of item analysis method. But item guessing factor in learning results has to be considered to apply the relative item difficulty more precisely. So, for e-Learning system support to learner considering learning grade, it need item revision difficulty which considered item guessing factor. In this paper, I designed and embodied the learner's tailoring e-learning system on the item revision difficulty. For an efficient design, I use PetriNet and UML modeling. In building this system, I am able to support a variety of learning step choice to learners so that the learner can work in a flexible learning environment.

1 Introduction

E-learning can take the form of courses as well as modules and smaller learning objects. E-learning may incorporate synchronous or asynchronous access and may be distributed geographically with varied limits of time[1]. One of the most important(if least appealing) tasks confronting faculty members is the evaluation of student performance. This task requires considerable skill, in part because it presents so many concerning the method, format, timing, and duration of the evaluative procedures. Once designed, the evaluative procedure must be administered and then scored, interpreted, and graded. Afterwards, feedback must be presented to student. Accomplishing these tasks demands a broad range of cognitive, technical, and interpersonal resources on the part of faculty[2]. Web based courseware specification is the process of identifying the aims and objectives of the material, placing this in the context of the student population and their assumed previous knowledge and describing the detailed syllabus[3]. An e-learning course should not be designed in a vacuum; rather, it should match students' needs and desires as closely as possible, and adapt during course progression[4]. Also, individualization learning that presents learning contents and method separately according to learning ability of individuals is deficient. And the most of e-learning system was developed the program according to process oriented method by CGI. But this method is difficult to reuse, maintain and repair after development.

H. Zha et al. (Eds.): VSMM 2006, LNCS 4270, pp. 318–327, 2006.
© Springer-Verlag Berlin Heidelberg 2006

This paper discusses the need to operate e-learning system considering efficient learning item difficulty. For this purpose, I designed and embodied learner's tailoring e-learning system by the item revision difficulty. Item revision difficulty is item difficulty which considered item guess parameter. In this system, learners can select learning item difficulty which tailored to him. I used UML for design and PetriNet[5, 13, 11] for analysis. And I made main business logic with EJB component for efficiently implementation and development. So, throughout this system, I showed that advanced learning score by training this system, rapidly.

2   Relate Work

2.1   E-Learning Contents and Course

Generally, an e-learning system comprises three key components, they are infrastructure, services and content. Infrastructure is the software that allows learning to be created, managed, delivered and measured. Services involve the planning, customization, integration and management of the e-learning application. Content can be categorized according to subject, preferred format, students progress and language requirements[6]. To make a new e-learning course really good, a team of authors, didactic workers and programmers and media designers has to participate in its creation. Traditionally, the course development goes like this: Content authors and didactic workers (sometimes one person) prepare the course content by means Known to them e.g. MS Word or PowerPoint. Due to their professional orientation, skills and practice, in most cases, these authors are not qualified to use and operate sophisticated development tools. But now, In the source documents of the course, the content authors and didactic workers give instruction on the required interactive features of the course (callbacks, gradual uncovering, reactions to the students actions or simulations) and multimedia (pictures, animations, videos or sounds)[7]. Web-based courseware in e-learning increasingly focuses on active self-learning and therefore includes constructive concepts, namely interactive illustrations and virtual laboratories[8].

2.2   The Item Revision Difficulty

Item analysis "investigates the performance of items considered individually either in relation to some external criterion or in relation to the remaining items on the test"[14]. As difficult as it can be to write a good test, it can be equally difficult to interpret its results[9]. The equation for the three-parameter model is item difficulty parameter, item discrimination parameter and item guessing parameter[11]. Item difficulty is a measure of the percentage of students answering a question correctly[9] and Cangelosi[14] divides items into difficult item, proper item and easy item. The calculation formula is as the following.

$$P = \frac{R}{N} \tag{1}$$

(N : Number of total learners, R : Number of learners who answers correctly)

Item guessing parameter represents the value of learners who gave an answer correctly by guess among all learners who answer correctly in truth. That is as the following.

$$G_R = G * \frac{1}{Q}, G_W = G * \frac{Q-1}{Q} = W, G = \frac{WQ}{Q-1} then G_R = \frac{W}{Q-1} \quad (2)$$

(G_R : the number of learners who answer correctly by guess, G : the number of learners who guess the answer, Q : the number of answers, W : the number of learners who guess an answer but can not give a correct answer)

Item guessing parameter, the ratio of learners who don't know the answer but give the correct answer by guess, is presumed by the following formula.

$$P_{GR} = \frac{G_R}{N} = \frac{(\frac{W}{Q-1})}{N} \quad (3)$$

(P_{GR} : Item guessing parameter, N : Number of total learners)

The item revision difficulty represents the relative difficulty that excludes Item guessing parameter, the ratio of learners who give the correct answer by guess, and is calculated as the following.

$$P_C = P - P_{GR} \quad (4)$$

(P_C : Item revision difficulty, P : Item difficulty)

2.3   PetriNet

PetriNets[12] are a well-founded process modeling technique. Since then Petri nets have been used to model and analyze all kinds of processes with applications ranging from protocols, hardware, and embedded systems to flexible manufacturing systems, user interaction, and business processes. Petri nets are marked by the availability of many analysis techniques. These techniques can be used to prove properties (safety properties, invariance properties, deadlock, etc.) and to calculate performance measures(response times, waiting times, occupation rates, etc.)[13]. Basic PetriNet structure consists of finite set of place and transition, finite set of arcs and sets of tokens that define initial marking. Arcs have input and output function and these functions represent the flow to token from Place to Transition and from Transition to Place. PetriNet represents as like (P, T, A_i, A_o, m_0). Each character represents followings. P: Place set, T: Transition set, A_i : Input Incidence Matrix, m_0 : Initial marking. Consequently, Input/output relations of Place and Transition represent as the following.

$$\bullet p = \{t|a(t,p) \neq 0, t \in T\}, p\bullet = \{t|a(p,t) \neq 0, t \in T\} \quad (5)$$

$$\bullet t = \{p|a(p,t) \neq 0, p \in P\}, t\bullet = \{p|a(t,p) \neq 0, p \in P\} \quad (6)$$

Also, the enable rule of Transition to input Place is as the following.

$$\forall p \in \bullet t, a(p, t) \leq m(p) \tag{7}$$

After Transition t was enabled, the firing rule to this is as the following.

$$\forall p \in \bullet t, m'(p) = m(p) - a(p, t) \tag{8}$$

$$\forall p \in t\bullet, m'(p) = m(p) - a(t, p) \tag{9}$$

3 Learner's Tailoring E-Learning System on the Item Revision Analysis

3.1 Decision of Learning Step on the Item Revision Analysis

In this paper, I applied the item revision difficulty containing item guess parameter. I divide items 5 steps, very difficult, difficult, normal, easy and very easy. It is calculated and stored to next test for learning. And then, as learning proceeds, the item revision difficulty set at the first time is calculated and reapplied by learning result of learner. Table 1 shows the application standard of the item revision difficulty containing Item guessing parameter. The item revision difficulty was calculated as like $P_C = P - P_{GR}$ by the relative item difficulty and Item guess parameter of item analysis method.

Table 1. Evaluation standard by the item revision difficulty

Learning class	Item revision difficulty	Type of problem
High	$0 \sim 0.2$	Very difficult
Normal-High	$0.21 \sim 0.40$	Difficult
Normal	$0.41 \sim 0.60$	Normal
Easy-Normal	$0.61 \sim 0.80$	Easy
Easy	$0.80 \sim 1$	Very easy

3.2 Design of Learner's Tailoring E-Learning System

Business logic is the basic function of programming module. In case of component software, business logic is in charge of basic process include input parameter, process and output parameter. Software(or software component) was constructed function by several business logics which related target system. Brief process diagram of tailoring e-learning system is shown Figure 1. It has three steps, step 1 for prepare and select learning item, step 2 for learning and step 3 for analysis and save item revision difficulty.

These system was designed with UML and constituted with dispersed server having main server and EJB component server and EJB parts was embodied with stateless session bean. Cloudscape of Informix company built in J2EE was used as database. Fig 2 shows use-case diagram of this system.

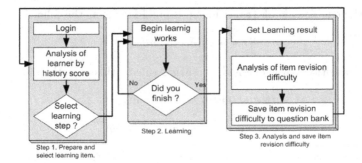

Fig. 1. Structure diagram of e-learning system considering item revision difficulty

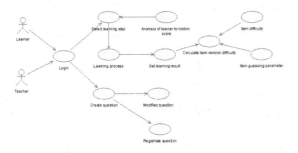

Fig. 2. Use-case diagram

Fig 3 shows class diagram for whole system composition. Question class, a part that provides question to student, has question number, question contents and question from example No. 1 to example No. 5. QuestionResult class, a part that analyzes learning results, has question number which student solved and a number of an examination paper and verifies answers. DifficultyHome is home interface class and DifficultyRemoteEJB is remote interface class of EJB component. That is, Question that is application class request and process item difficulty via EJB's interface. DifficultyRemoteEJB class calculates the relative correction of item difficulty and sets questions classified by learning level. QuestionResult can get process result of Question class. Fig 4 shows internal class of EJB component that handles the relative correction of item revision difficulty.

DifficultyHome is class to register component from the outside. DifficultyEJB class has the relative correction of item difficulty and actual business logic to set questions and has ItemDifficulty class to calculate the relative item difficulty, Pcr class to calculate Item guess parameter and Pc class to calculate the relative correction of item difficulty. Questions corresponding to learning level chosen by student are extracted randomly according to the relative item difficulty collection from question information database in CheckQuestion, internal method. Extracted questions have information of each items set in Result class

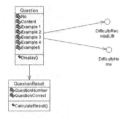

Fig. 3. Class diagram of question class

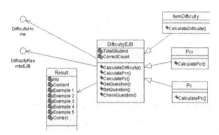

Fig. 4. Class diagram of internal EJB component for calculation of item revision difficulty

and provide students questions. Component diagram that describe relation of application and component is as like Fig 5. DifficultyEJB component provide DifficultyHome and DifficultyRemoteEJB interface. Therefore, Question application request and process item difficulty via EJB's interface

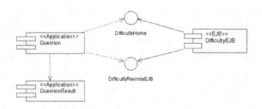

Fig. 5. Component diagram of E-learning system

3.3   System Analysis Using PetriNet

PetriNet of total system describe message flow protocol of each state. Fig 6 shows message flow protocol of the item revision difficulty in EJB component.

Place pl_1 represents the state that question extraction component was created by the item revision difficulty. A part of calculation of the item revision difficulty in question extraction component is as followings. pl_2 represents value

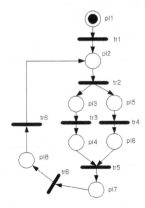

Fig. 6. Analysis of the item revision difficulty

of learning result of learner to calculate the item revision difficulty. The relative item difficulty and Item guess parameter need to calculate the item revision difficulty. In a part of calculation of the relative item difficulty, pl_3 represents data value to calculate the relative difficulty and pl_4 represents value of the relative item difficulty. n a part of calculation of Item guessing parameter, pl_5 represents data value to calculate Item guess parameter and pl_6 represents value of Item guessing parameter. By the relative item difficulty and Item guess parameter calculated, pl_7 shows the item revision difficulty. From the item revision difficulty, pl_8 represents value of learning level which was reset. Transition tr_1 represents request of learning result value of learner, tr_2 is the relative item difficulty and guess ratio divergence, tr_3 is calculation handling of the relative item difficulty and tr_4 is calculation handling of Item guessing parameter. tr_5 represents calculation of the item revision difficulty by summing up the relative item difficulty and guess ratio. tr_6 represents handling of resetting learning level of item by the item revision difficulty and tr_7 represents storing of learning level value of relevant item. Initial marking(m_0) is (1,0,0,0,0,0,0,0). Therefore, token for Place pl_1 is $m(pl_1)=1$. Since arc number from pl_1 to tr_1 is $a(p_1,t_1)=1$, enable rule about Transition tr_1 is formed, $m(p_1)$ becomes 0 and $m(p_2)$ becomes 1 by firing rule. tr_2 is ignited by $a(pl_2,tr_2)=1$ in Place p_2 and then token of pl_2 disappears and token is created as many as $a(tr_2,pl_3)=1$ and $a(tr_2,pl_5)=1$ respectively. Therefore, we can calculate the relative item difficulty and Item guess parameter on the basis of value of learning result.

3.4   Application of E-Learning System

In this research, I make E-learning system of English. After login, learner can select learning level according to item revision difficulty as shown Fig 7(a) and Fig 7(b) displays the question by learning step.

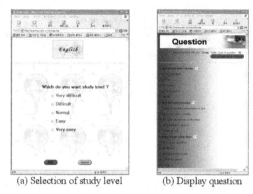

| (a) Selection of study level | (b) Display question |

Fig. 7. Selection of learning level and display question

After finish learning process, learner can see learning result shows as Fig 8.

Fig. 8. Learning contents and result screen

4   Results and Analysis

It tested initial 10 times application results of this research system to learners. Since questions are presented according to learning level selected by learner among total questions, the number of learners (N) and the number of learners who give a right answer (R) is different by each item. Therefore, the whole values become different. When it applied 30 times, that is, according to variation of the number of learners and the number of learners who give a right answer, the relative item difficulty (P), Item guess parameter (P_{GR}) and the item revision

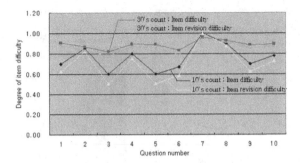

Fig. 9. Question and correct answer state by testing

difficulty (P_C) are calculated and learning level (Step) is readjusted on the basis of Table 1.

From these results, this research shows that learning level for each question is reset by reflecting learning result according to increase the number of times of learning of various learners on the item revision difficulty continuously. Therefore, more relevant items can be presented in learning level selected by learner. Fig 8 shows each question and correct answer state by 10's and 30's testing.

5   Conclusions

In this research, I designed and embodied question extracting component considering the item revision difficulty and applied English question learning system. I let learners select the relative difficulty by themselves according to 5 learning levels (highest, higher, middle, lower and lowest) by the item revision difficulty and can expect more appropriate learning effect. Most of web-based learning system considered only the relative item difficulty in setting-question system but, in this research, I calculated and applied the item revision difficulty considering guessing factor of learners who gave a correct answer. Getting out of existing development process in system development, I embodied core business logic as component and could increase development efficiency, reusability, maintainability and repairability. For these purposes, I used UML in system design and used PetriNet to analyze handling algorithm of system. I made modification, maintenance and repair of embodied logic easy by embodying the item revision difficulty parts which is main business logic as component using EJB. Also, in developing learning system similar to this, the item revision difficulty calculating parts can be applied with component of this research without newly embodying. As a further research subject, it is necessary to prepare the theoretical basis to verify objectivity about the relative difficulty which is set at the first question registration by examiner. Also, with running parallel with detailed classification works such as learning chapter and so forth, learner should be able to choose not only learning level but also learning chapter and subjective questions should be applied in company with objective multiple-choice questions followed by 5 options.

References

1. Consuelo L. Waight, Pedro A. Willging, Tim L. Wentling, Recurrent Themes in E-Learning: A Meta-Analysis of Major E-Learning Reports, Academy of Human Resource Development Annual Conference 2002, (2002)
2. Raymond M. Zurawski, Making the Most of Exams: Procedures for Item Analysis, The National Teaching & Learning Forum, Vol 7 No 6. (1998)
3. David Benyon, Debbie Stone, Mark Woodroffe, "Experience with developing multimedia courseware for the World Wide Web: the need for better tools and clear pedagogy", International Journal of Human?Computer Studies 47, 197?218, (1997)
4. Sabine Graf, Beate List, An Evaluation of Open Source E-Learning Platforms Stressing Adaptation Issues, International Conference on Advanced Learning Technologies 2005, (2005)
5. Tommi Junttila, "On the symmetry reduction method for petri nets and similar formalisms", Helsinki University of Technology Laboratory for Theoretical Computer Science Research Reports 80, Espoo, (2003)
6. Jesshope C. R. and Zhang, Z. A content management system for the TILE managed learning environment, Proc of the Third International Conference 2002, (2002)
7. E-learning Content's Creation Issue, http://www.e-learn.cz, (2006)
8. Frank Hanisch, Authoring and Linking of Highly Interactive Content within Web-based Courseware, Challenges and Solutions for Virtual Education (NL 2002), Technical University of Berlin, (2002)
9. Stephen F. Hulse, et al, Test Statistics, instructional techniques, Vol. 61, No. 2, (2006)
10. Susan Matlock-Hetzel, Basic Concepts in Item and Test Analysis, Texas A & M University, January, (1997)
11. Frank B. Baker, The basics of item response theory, ERIC Clearinghouse on Assessment and Evaluation, (2001)
12. A. Fronk, J. Pleumann, Relation algebraic Analysis of Petri Nets: Concepts and Implementation. PetriNet News Letters, (2005)
13. W.M.P. van der Aalst, The Application of Petri Nets to Workflow Management, The Journal of Circuits, Systems and Computers, (1998)
14. Cangelosi,J.S., Designing tests for evaluating student achievement, New York: Longman, (1990)

A Time-Controlling Terrain Rendering Algorithm

Lijie Li, Fengxia Li, and Tianyu Huang

School of Computer Science and Technology, Beijing Institute of Technology, Beijing, 100081, China

Abstract. The paper proposes a time-controlling algorithm for large-scale terrain rendering, which can't be efficiently dealt with by LOD technique. In this algorithm, the terrain is divided and organized by quad-tree structure. Each terrain patch is assigned a certain time according to the total rendering time given in advance. The multi-resolution levels rendered are determined by visual apperception. To solve the T-junction and popping, an approach of stitching the level boundaries and geomorphing are respectively performed on GPU. The algorithm guarantees that each frame is rendered in preset time independent of the terrain or the eye position. The slow or jerky phenomena during roaming, which are usually caused by unstable rendering frame rate, can be successfully avoided. This terrain rendering algorithm is demonstrated in a massive terrain flyover application. The experiment proves that this algorithm is feasible and efficient.

1 Introduction

Terrain rendering [1][2][3] is a challenge research and indispensable job of virtual outdoor environments visualization, as applied in virtual battlefield environments [4], computer games, in particular, flight and driving simulators. Generally, terrain in such instance contains millions of sampling information of both color and elevation. The Brute Force algorithm is far from the requirement of real-time rendering. LOD [5][6] and recent LOD extensions [2][3][7][8] are kinds of view-dependent solutions for real-time rendering. However, constant-fidelity LOD rendering suffers from uncontrolled delay with increased rendering demand, and results in the display of high detail models influent and unstable. In this paper, we focus on the real-time rendering of large-scale terrain to solve the two issues above.

The general extended LOD algorithm accelerated the terrain rendering and handled the balance workload between CPU and GPU, however, constant-fidelity LOD rendering suffers from uncontrolled delay with increased rendering demand, and results in the display of high detail models influent and unstable. [9] presented an algorithm that used hierarchical LOD to render large and detailed city models with TIN (Triangular Irregular Networks) for interaction. However, the T-junction and popping phenomenal are unsolved when the transition from one level of LOD to another. Terrain made of RSG (Regular Square Grid) has many

H. Zha et al. (Eds.): VSMM 2006, LNCS 4270, pp. 328–337, 2006.

outstanding criteria than that of TIN for terrain processing. In this paper, we proposed a time-controlling algorithm to render the large-scale RSG terrain with stable frame-rate and smoother interaction. Our method maintains a specified frame rate by allocating rendering time in advance, solves the T-junctions by zero-area-triangle algorithm, and incorporates geomorphing into GPU computing to achieve efficient rendering and seamless transition.

The paper proceeds with a presentation of related work in section 2. Section 3 introduces the terrain data management. Section 4 describes the time-controlling strategy in details, including methods of time allocation, priority computation, conditions of ending subdivision and terrain LOD adjustment. Section 5 and section 6 respectively give the solutions for T-junction and popping. In section 7, the time-controlling applications are provided and the rendering results are analyzed. We make a discussion and present future work in Section 8.

2   Related Work

For large-scale terrain rendering, LOD control is necessary to adjust the terrain tessellation and realize a multi-resolution display, which ensures real-time and realistic. In addition, adaptive display is important for the purpose of interactive and stable roaming. In this section, the research on terrain rendering is expatiated in two aspects: terrain rendering based on LOD and adaptive display technique.

2.1   Terrain Rendering

There has been extensive research on terrain LOD. The typically schemes adopt refinement based on both the view and the local terrain geometry. There are two categories: Progressive Mesh [6] (PM) algorithm based on TIN and Real-Time Optimally Adapting Meshing (ROAM) algorithm based on RSG [5]. The view-dependent LOD algorithms control the LOD levels based on viewpoint and reach extra refinement. However, the computing cost for triangulation is time-consuming and they are not able to fully utilize the graphics hardware accelerations since the geometry changes frequently. To reduce the per-triangle workload, the aggregated LOD [2][3][7][8] was proposed by composing pre-assembled terrain patches during run-time. To alleviate the CPU/GPU bottleneck, [8] extended the ROAM algorithm by statically freezing and saving the sub-trees of the bin-tree in a pre-processing phase, similar to [9], which dynamically processed clusters. Batched Dynamic Adaptive Meshes (BDAM) [2] suggested replacing triangles in the re-meshing process by a batch. Stripping the TIN prior to rendering made BDAM highly efficient. The chunked LOD algorithm accelerated the terrain rendering and balanced the workload between CPU and GPU. However, with increased rendering demands, constant-fidelity LOD rendering causes uncontrolled delay and influent display.

2.2   Adaptive Display Algorithm

The classical algorithms perform the view-dependent and coarse error optimization to choose a LOD, and the frame rate is changeable and unstable from different view position and direction, which results in the delayed rendering and uncontrolled roaming. Recently, the adaptive display algorithms [10][11][12][13] were studied to solve the problem of frame rate. [13] presented a selection method for real-time rendering on hierarchies of discrete and continuous representations and integrated point rendered objects with polygonal geometry. [14] described an adaptive display algorithm for interactive frame rates during visualization of the complex virtual environments, but the algorithm relied upon a hierarchical model representation at multiple levels of detail. [15] used a temporally adaptive framed sampling scheme that adaptively controlled frame rate to minimize simultaneously the error created by reduced rendering fidelity and by reduced rendering update. [9] applied the cost and benefit approach of the adaptive display algorithm to deal with a city scene represented by TINs, which are hard to process geomorphing. Our work is similar to [9], but we are looking forward to designing a time-controlling display algorithm for RSG terrain, especially, on which the T-junction can be fixed by filling zero-area-triangle and popping by morphing.

3   Terrain Data Management

In our approach, a large-scale terrain is partitioned into the same size LOD tiled patches, which are organized by quad-tree. Supposing that the terrain elevation is $(2^N + 1) \times (2^N + 1)$, and the size of each patch is $(2^n + 1) \times (2^n + 1)$, the whole terrain can be divided into $(N - n)^2$ most refined patches. The $i + 1$-level LOD patch is computed by sparsely sampling from four neighboring i-level LOD patches. The terrain vertex data are stored as (x, y, z, y_l). Here, (x, z) denotes the horizon coordinate, and y is the height of (x, z). y_l, which is used for geomorphing on GPU, is the height of its father patch at the position (x, z).

The quad-tree structure of terrain improves the rendering efficiency and simplifies the algorithm of time allocation. In our algorithm, the triangle-strip idea is adopted to accelerate rendering, and the indexed vertex arrays are used to speed the data transferring. For the reason that each patch costs the same rendering time with the same size, the allocation of the time can be simplified.

4   Time-Controlling Strategy

4.1   Time Allocation

For the rendering purpose, processing each terrain patch should be limited in a certain time, which satisfies the real-time interaction. We define a time slice in advance, and then restrict the terrain data to the fixed time slices. By this way, it can be ensured that the total rendering time is equal to the pre-defined time slices. A time slice is defined as

$$timeSlice_i = shareTime_i \times \frac{priority_i}{\sum_{t \in sib(i)} priority_t}, \tag{1}$$

where $timeSlice_i$ is the time allocated for node i, $shareTime_i$ is the time allocated for its father node and initialized by a constant $C_{targetTime}$, $sib(i)$ is the visible sibling of node i, and $priority_i$ represents the priority of rendering.

First a preset time slice is allocated to the root node. Then the time slice is recursively subdivided and assigned to its children's node. This procedure of subdivision will stop until the ending conditions are satisfied. Thus, the latest LOD level is the terrain patch for rendering. Finally, the algorithm outputs all terrain patches requiring render and the LOD level of rendering.

4.2   Priority Computation

For the sibling nodes, it is necessary to compute the priorities to determine the time allocation, since they are belonging to the same LOD level of the rendering quad-tree.

By back-culling and frustum culling for the terrain bounding box, we can obtain the visibility of each terrain patch. The priority of node manifests the importance in the view. It is computed as following:

$$\begin{cases} priority_i = \frac{staticPriority_i \times foreShorten_i}{distance_i^2} & \text{block } i \text{ is visible} \\ priority_i = \sum_{t \in child(i)} priority_t & \text{part of block } i \text{ is visible} \\ priority_i = 0 & \text{bock } i \text{ is invisible} \end{cases} \quad . \quad (2)$$

$distance_i$ is defined as the distance from patch i to the viewpoint. $foreShorten_i$ is the variable angle between terrain patches and the sight. $staticPriority_i$, denoted by equation 3, represents the properties of the terrains, such as area, surface roughness and so on. For the sake of the independence of viewpoint, $staticPriority_i$ can be computed in the pre-processing phase to accelerate the computing while roaming.

$$\begin{cases} staticPriority_i = \sum_{t \in tri(i)} area_t & child(i) \text{ not exist} \\ staticPriority_i = \sum_{t \in child(i)} staticPriority_i & child(i) \text{ exist} \end{cases} \quad , \quad (3)$$

where $tri(i)$ represents the triangles contained in patch i, child(i) all children of patch i, and $area_t$ the area of triangle t. $foreShorten_i$ is used to measure the terrain towards the viewer, denoted by

$$foreShorten_i = 1 + (\boldsymbol{view} \cdot \boldsymbol{avgNormal} \times C_{fore}). \quad (4)$$

Here, $\boldsymbol{view}$ is the direction of the viewpoint, C_{fore} is a weight constant. $\boldsymbol{avgNormal}$, the average normal vector, is pre-computed by

$$\boldsymbol{avgNormal} = \frac{\sum_{t \in tri(i)} \boldsymbol{normal_t}}{\left\| \sum_{t \in tri(i)} \boldsymbol{normal_t} \right\|}, \quad (5)$$

where, $\boldsymbol{normal_t}$ represents the normal of triangle t.

4.3   Conditions of Ending Subdivision

In the recursion of the time allocation, three conditions are given to end the subdivision, shown as follows:

Condition 1: if the time allocated is insufficient to render its visible children nodes, the subdivision ends. The condition is described by inequation 6.

$$sliceTime_i \leq V_{timeNeed} \times numChild_i, \tag{6}$$

where $V_{timeNeed}$ is the total time for rendering a terrain, and $numChild_i$ is the number of its visible children nodes. $V_{timeNeed}$ is a variable that is adjusted in a feedback loop by comparing actual time with the estimated render time, so that our algorithm is adapted to any rendering speed dynamically.

Condition 2: If the node is a leaf node, which is the most refined LOD terrain, the subdivision ends.

Condition 3: If the precision of rendering satisfies the inequation 10, which means that the size of triangles is close to the pixels, the subdivision ends.

As illustrated in figure 1, eye is the viewpoint, h is the distance from the viewpoint to the projection plane, and $distance$ is the distance from viewpoint to the terrain patch. From this figure, we can deduce a proportional equation as

$$\frac{verticalArea_i}{distance_i^2} = \frac{minArea}{h^2}, \tag{7}$$

where $verticalArea_i$ is the area of a vertical terrain in sight, $minArea$ is the minimum patch area in projection area, denoted by

$$minArea = (pixLength \times m \times 2^n)^2, \tag{8}$$

where $(2^n + 1)$ is the size of terrain patch, and m is the minimal pixel-number of displaying a side of a triangle. $pixLength$, computed by equation 9, is the length of one pixel.

$$pixLength = \frac{h \times \tan(\theta/2)}{height/2}, \tag{9}$$

where $height$ is the number of pixels in the vertical side of view, and θ is the vertical perspective.

Since the terrain is not keeping vertical with sight while rendering, the proportional equation can be adjusted by $foreShorten$. Thus, the distance for maximum division is computed by

$$\frac{staticPriority_i \times foreShorten_i}{distance_i^2} \leq \frac{minArea}{h^2} \times C_{pix}, \tag{10}$$

where C_{pix} is a constant.

4.4   Terrain LOD Adjustment

Though the rendering time is allocated for each terrain patch as time slices, there is some time remained by the three ending conditions, so a further adjustment

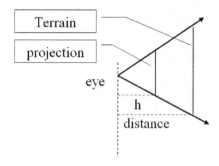

Fig. 1. The projection of terrain patches

for the time allocation is required. We use a table to register the patch for rendering in time allocation, and the procedure is repeated till no time remained as following steps: (1) Look for the patch with the highest priority. (2)If this patch can be subdivided but stopped by condition 1, the subdivision can keep going on. (3) Delete it from the table, and then add its visible sub-patches. By this way, the predefined time $C_{targetTime}$ is totally assigned to the terrain patches, and the LOD of the terrain is determined.

5   Solution for T-Junction

The connection between different LOD terrain patches may result in T-junction because of the triangle-strip rendering way, illustrated as Figure 2. To solve this problem, we need locate the transition border first, and lookup those borders need to be mended. If the neighboring terrain patches share the same LOD, there is no gap between them. If they are in different LOD levels, a repair is need for the border of the refined one. We are looking for those terrain patches that have higher LOD than their neighbors.

To perform the border location, each terrain patch is marked with different state, i.e. division, culling, rendering, when computing for time allocation. By analyzing these states of patches, it is easier to locate the borders for repairing. For one patch, if its neighbor with rendering mark in the same direction, they are in the same LOD; if its neighbor marked with division, the neighbor one has higher LOD; if its neighbor is marked with culling, it no need to be repaired; if its neighbor has undefined state, there are two instances: 1) the LOD of neighbor is lower than it, which means the neighbor's forefather has been rendered, it need to be repaired 2) the neighbor's forefather has been culled, it no need to be repaired. All of the neighbors' forefathers are checked recursively till that the state is culling or rendering.

We adopt the algorithm of zero-area triangles to fill the gaps caused by T-junction. Give an example as figure 2, T-junction appears at the junctions of $block_a$, $block_b$ and $block_c$ by rendering with triangle strips. The gaps can be

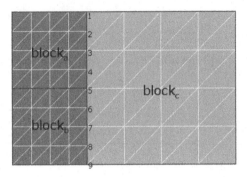

Fig. 2. The connection of terrain patches

filled by rendering triangles $(1, 2, 3)$, $(3, 4, 5)$, $(5, 6, 7)$ and $(7, 8, 9)$. For the same size of patches, the patches are rendered by the indexed vertex arrays. We define a unified index table for recording all vertexes need to be mended, so as to improve the efficiency of seeming.

We fill the gaps by morphing the border vertexes on the GPU. Given a case in Figure 2, coordinates of vertex 2, 4, 6 and 8 are transformed to the superposition of the $block_c$, i.e. $y = y_l$.

6   Geomorphing

We apply geomorphing to solve the popping phenomena caused by LOD chang-ing. The distortion variable f is measured by the terrain patch priority from the rendering table, and sent to GPU as the interpolation coefficient to compute $y = y \times f + y_l \times (1 - f)$. The borders are not changed so as not to destroy the connection of the terrain patches.

In vertex program of GPU, three variables are provided, including the transi-tion variables $trans$, interpolation coefficient f and the terrain border variables, which distinguish the border vertexes and center vertexes board. On GPU, y_l is assigned to y when the vertex on the border; else, the height y is adjusted by interpolation $y = y \times f + y_l \times (1 - f)$.

7   Experiments and Results

We have implemented the time-controlling algorithm with C++ and OpenGL, and performed on an Intel PIV 2.8GHz computer with 1G RAM, 128M display memory. Our experiments were tested on the terrain data—Puget sound area, which contains 20492 grids, and each terrain patch are 172. Figure 3 shows terrain rendered with the target time of 33 milliseconds for a fly-through.

Shown in figure 4, we made statistic for the fps and patches while roam-ing in the terrain with such a routine: from frame 0-200, walk-through with

Fig. 3. The terrain rendered to the target time of 33 ms by fly-through

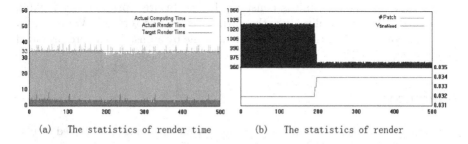

(a)   The statistics of render time   (b)   The statistics of render

Fig. 4. The statistics of roaming with the target render time of 33 milliseconds

20-meter height; drive-through from frame 200-300 with 300 meters; fly-through from frame 300-500. Figure 4(a) is the time statistics according to frame rate, and figure 4(b) shows the patch statistics.

In figure 4(a), computing time is represented by dark blue color, and light blue color shows the rendering time. It shows, independent of the drive-through ways, the computing time takes less than 10 percent from the rendering time, the rendering speed is keeping 33millseconds, and with the frame rate of 30 fps. Figure 4(b) shows that, $V_{timeNeed}$ for each patch covers 0.032-0.034ms, and 960-975 patches, each containing 512 triangles, are rendered at each frame even when changing to fly-through.

Experiments show that our algorithm rendered the terrains at steady frame rate. Even with 500 thousand triangles, it still guaranteed the render frame rate of 30fps. However, ROAM algorithm only process 20 thousand triangles with the same frame rate and configuration. For our algorithm can render more triangles, which are satisfied the vision requirement, the terrain get higher rendering quality shown as figure 3. In a word, the proposed algorithm achieved better render quality, higher render speed and stable frame rate.

8   Conclusion and Discussion

We demonstrated a time-controlling algorithm to achieve more efficient and steady rendering on 3D terrain data. Comparing with other methods, the main contributions are following: (1) Simple data structure. All terrain patches are divided into the same size and easily managed. (2) High-speed rendering. Pre-processing helps reduced the rendering time. In addition, index-vertex-array and triangle-strip rendering speeds the rendering. (3) Constant rendering frame rate. The rendering time is confined to the pre-defined time, and independent of view-point position. (4) High-quality rendering.The huge amount of rendered triangles makes the result more realistic.

Our presented work supplies an effective and real-time algorithm of rendering terrains. Render time of each frame is equal to the pre-provided time, which ensures that the render time is constant. In the future work, we are looking forward to render the utilities on the surface as well as terrains. We argue to realize the constant time render of the whole scene by adjusting the pre-provided time dynamically.

References

1. Losasso, F., Hoppe, H.: Geometry clipmaps: terrain rendering using nested regular grids. In Proc.ACM SIGGraph 2004. (2004) 769–776
2. Cignoni, P., et al.: BDAM - Batched dynamic adaptive meshes for high performance terrain visualization . Computer Graphics Forum **22** (2003) 505–514
3. Wagner, D.: Terrain geomorphing in the vertex shader. In ShaderX2: Shader Programming Tips and Tricks with DirectX 9. Wordware Publishing (2004)
4. Xingquan, C., et al.: Research of Dynamic Terrain in Complex Battlefield Environments. Lecture Notes in Computer Science **3942** (2006) 903–912
5. Mark, D., Murray, W., et al.: Roaming Terrain: Real-Time Optimally Adapting Meshing. IEEE Visualization 1997. (1997) 81–88
6. Hoppe, H.: Smooth view-dependent level-of-detail control and its application to terrain rendering. IEEE Visualization 1998. (1998) 35–42
7. Davis.: ROAM Using Triangle Clusters (RUSTIC). Master's thesis, U.C CS Dept. (2000)
8. Levenberg, J.: Fast view-dependent level-of-detail rendering using cached geometry. IEEE Visualization 2002. (2002) 259–266
9. Lakhia, A.: Efficient Interactive Rendering of Detailed Models with Hierarchical Levels of Detail. In Proceedings of the 2nd International Symposium on 3D Data Processing, Visualization, and Transmission. (2004) 275–282
10. Parkhurst, D., Niebur, E.: A feasibility test for perceptually adaptive level of detail rendering on desktop systems. In Proceedings of the ACM Applied Perception in Graphics and Visualization Symposium. (2004) 105–109
11. Gobbetti, E.,Bouvier, E.: Time-critical Multiresolution Scene Rendering. Proceedings of the conference on Visualization 1999. (1999)
12. Alper, S., Ugur, G., Bulent, Y. O.: Walkthrough in Complex Environments at Interactive Rates using Level-of-Detail. Turkish Journal of Electrical Engineering and Computer **10** (2002) 57–72.

13. ach, C., Mantler, S., Karner, K.: Time-critical Rendering of Discrete and Continuous Levels of Detail. Proceedings of the ACM symposium on Virtual reality software and Technolog. (2002)
14. Funkhouser, T. A., S'equin, C. H.: Adaptive display algorithm for interactive frame rates during visualization of complex virtual environments. Computer Graphics **27** (1993) 247-254
15. Woolley, C.,Luebke, D., Watson, B., Dayal A.: Interruptible Rendering. Proceedings of the 2003 symposium on Interactive 3D graphics. (2003)

Developing and Analyzing Geographical Content Display System by Using RFID

Hiroshi Suzuki[1], Tadahiko Sato[2], Koji Yamada[1], and Akira Ishida[1]

[1] Institute of Advanced Media Arts and Science,
3-95 Rvoke-cho, Ogaki, Gifu 503-001 Japan
{Hiroshi, Koji, Akira}, s-kihiro@iamas.ac.jp
[2] Trigger Device Co., Ltd 2-12 Ohno, Yoroucho, Yoro-gun, Gifu 503-1383 Japan

Abstract. As a new management tool in place of the barcode, RFID (radio frequency identification) applied in various industrial fields. The distinguishing feature of RFID is it's ability for contactless information transmission, making it possible to retrieve information about previous activities from people without their knowing.

In this research, Geographical Content Display System Development and it's tested and experimental use was conducted as one example of the use of RFID technology in the field of education. By using RFID technology in a hands-on workshop, we investigated how the data obtained could be analyzed and we show future possibilities.

1 Introduction

In the workshop, understanding the participants' interest in the theme, learning processes, and learning outcome is an extremely important element in addition to creating an efficient workshop curriculum and educational materials. However, while it is possible to measure the effectiveness of learning outcome through paper tests, it is difficult to calculate interest in theme and learning process. In general, methods can be taken where surveys are done through questionnaires and interviews and the workshop is recorded on video and scrutinized in detail, but this take an enormous time to accomplish.

However, by using the elements of RFID technology (contactless data transmission) to try to naturally obtain the participants' actions in the workshop scenario, it becomes possible to track the participants actions and behavior with little difficulty.

By analyzing and evaluating this history of actions, it becomes possible to produce quantitative measurements regarding the participants interest in the workshop and learning processes, which was no easy feat in the past. Further, by measuring and analyzing the results, it becomes possible to evaluate the level of difficulty for the workshop scenario, and aids in modifying the curriculum.

In summary, this research:

- Is research and development on systems and workshop scenarios that can naturally track the movements of children.

H. Zha et al. (Eds.): VSMM 2006, LNCS 4270, pp. 338–348, 2006.

- Examines the effectiveness of the system by examining the methods of analysis possible after obtaining movement history and learning outcomes of children both with the system and without the system.
- By analyzing the movement history during the workshop, one can explore possibilities for quantitative evaluations of the workshop itself.

2 System Outline

As a system that could use RFID in workshops, this research developed a geographic content display system. Figure 1 shows an image of this system in use.

Because the features of RFID can be utilized even further when using it with positional information such as maps, globes can be considered material that would amply utilize these features.

The developed geographic contents display system was constructed out of the following three materials and a server.

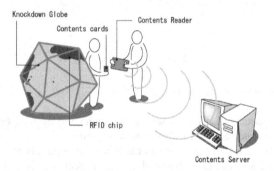

Fig. 1. Image of system in use

Knockdown Globe

The knockdown globe is constructed from 20 map panels in the shape of 90cm equilateral triangles and a frame. RFID chips are pasted on the backside of the map panels so that 30 points on the globe can be identified. The RFID chips can be pasted anywhere on the panels, so it is possible to change the positions according to the contents.

IDs are allocated to the RFID chips to be used to retrieve video or sound contents stored in a database.

Contents Cards

Content cards hold information such as characters and illustrations that are used in the contents. Like the panels, the cards are embedded with RFID chips. The number of cards used can raised proportionally to the number of RFID chips used, but in this case we made 30 cards corresponding to the map panels.

Contents Reader

The contents reader is a handheld terminal that the participants use during the workshop. The contents reader play two roles: 1) to read the RFID chips on the contents card and map panels; 2) to play still shots and music, video, etc.

Contents Server

The contents server processes the information received from the contents reader, and transmits videos, photographs, and other contents from the contents database to the contents reader. 3. System Configuration

We will now explain the functions of this system's educational materials and server. Figure 2 is a configuration figure of the geographic contents display system.

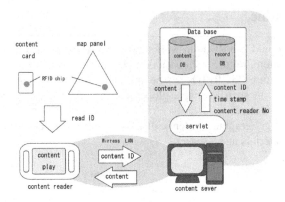

Fig. 2. System configuration figure

This has the following four functions:

1. The contents reader and contents server are connected by wireless LAN enabling them to transmit and receive information in real time.
2. When the RFID chips in the contents cards and map panels are read through the contents reader, and the IDs allocated to the contents cards and map panels, the contents reader number, and the timestamp is transmitted to the contents server.
3. The contents server responds with the necessary action according to the information transmitted. For example, it retrieves the video relevant to the contents from the database, records the contents card and panel order, and according to order and the card and panel the participant made read, it is possible to change the contents that are retrieved.
4. The RFID chip read history is constantly transmitted to the contents server and accumulated in the history database.

3 Workshop Outline

Intended Audience for the Workshop

Because this system uses globes as materials, the intended audience for the workshop is upper elementary school and students who are beginning to learn geography in class up to middle school students.

Workshop Theme

The theme of the workshop is dealing with world geographic information while using folk performance arts as content to spur the children's interest.

There are a multitude of peoples that exist in the world, and nearly all of them have traditional folk performance arts such as music and dance. Embedded within the costumes, masks and makeup in the folk performance arts are each of the peoples' gods and demons, death, wishes which are multifarious and unique to each region. Furthermore, the costumes the performers wear, and the music they perform is strongly represents each of their cultures and customs.

The objective of this research is to deepen children's understanding of the world and its cultures by enabling them to observe and compare various folk performing arts and imagine the peoples' geographic position and culture. To do this, we created a workshop scenario using geographical information, culture and climate of folk performing arts as key factors.

4 Workshop Scenario

The scenario is basically a plot from a movie or play, or the equivalent to a script. For the workshop itself, it is necessary for the instructors conduct the workshop following every step, and to have a scenario to allow observation of what route the participants take to progress and learn. In this research, the following scenario was used for folk performing arts workshop using a terrestrial contents display system.

This workshop has a two-part structure, divided into a first and second half. The children followed each step of the scenario shown in Figure 3.

(1) The children are individually or as a group given one contents reader and several contents cards (here after folk performance arts cards). The performance arts cards contain photographs of performance arts.

(2) By comparing the folk performance arts cards with map panels, the children predict what region on the globe the peoples on the folk performance arts cards.

(3) When the folk performance arts cards are read with the contents readers, an explanation of the folk performance arts is displayed on the contents readers. Further, when the contents readers approach the map panels, music from the folk performance arts of that region can be heard.

(4) The children guess what region each of the folk performance arts are from according to the costumes and appearances of the folk performance arts on the contents cards, as well as the explanations from reading the folk performance arts cards or the cultural or climate atmosphere of the folk performance arts music.

(5) Once the children guess what region the folk performance arts on the contents reader are from, they read the RFID chips from the folk performance arts card with the contents reader to check their answers.

(6) Next, they press the contents reader against the map panels they guessed to read the RFID on the panels. If the folk performance arts card and the panel RFID chips match, then they are correct, if not, then they are incorrect.

(7) If they are correct the contents reader with play a video of the relevant folk performance arts.

(8) If they are incorrect, an image will display showing them their answer is incorrect.

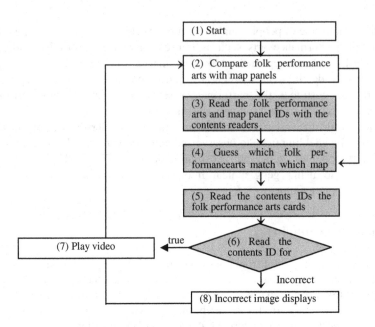

Fig. 3. Children's scenario for using the system

In the first half of the workshop, this continuation of procedures is done with the map panels disassembled. By disassembling the map panels, the children must guess the region of the people by connecting the folk performance arts cards with the music. In the second half, the map panels are assembled to form a globe, and the children must now guess with consideration to geographic information.

5 Verification Experiment

Experiment outline

In this research, a workshop not using this system (experiment 1) and a workshop using this system (experiment 2) were each conducted once to serve as a verification experiment.

Using this system, the action history for steps (3) through (6) in the scenario was obtained. The objective was to verify whether differences in evaluating the workshop would appear based according to whether this history data was obtained or not.

For experiment 1, which did not use this system, the map panels were set up so that when speakers where inserted into them, the folk performance arts music would play in place of the function (3) of Figure 3.

Further, to replace the assessment function of (6), letters were marked on the map panels and an answer form to fill in contents numbers and letters was prepared.

In the interactive workshop, a video camera recorded the workshop being implemented in order to obtain feedback for the workshop.

Experiment 1 (Not using the RFID system)

On January 14, 2006, we conducted the Folk Performing Arts Workshop at the Ogaki Information Studio for five students in the range of 5th grade elementary to 2nd grade junior high school students. Please refer to Figures 4 & 5 for photos of the experiment.

Folk performing arts from ten countries were prepared as contents, and the workshop time period was 90 minutes.

Since the workshop changes slightly when not using the system, the workshop flow is listed below.

1. Folk performance arts cards were distributed by number of people.
2. Globe panels are laid out on the floor. The children listen to the folk performance arts music by inserting a compact speaker in a minijack coming out of the map panel.
3. The map panels have letters written on them, and the students predict which folk performance arts cards match with which music they hear when they insert the speakers in the map panels.
4. The children then write on the answer sheet the folk performance arts card number together with the letter of the map panel for their predictions. (First half of their answer)
5. After the children write all of their matches, they assemble the globe while looking at the world map written on the surface of the panels for reference.
6. After assembling the globe, they predict again which folk performance arts cards match which music. The content is the same as the first half.
7. The children predict which folk performance arts cards match which map panels and write their answers on the answer sheets. (Second half of answer)
8. When all participants finish writing, they exchange answers.

Fig. 4. Listening to the folk arts music after inserting the speaker

Fig. 5. Listening to the music from each region after assembling the map panels

Experiment 1 Results and Analysis

Answer results from the answer sheets are shown in Table 1. The country with the most correct answers in the first and second halves was Japan, in the second half, Canada, Turkey, and Zimbabwe were also high.

Overall percentage of correct answers were higher in the second half after the globe was assembled than in the first. Further, in the first half there was some variation in answers, but in the second half three children had identical answers, which resulted in the same percentage correct. It can be surmised through these results that the children discussed the answers together.

With regard to the video recorded, it was possible to grasp the overall flow and atmosphere of the workshop by observing the content, but since no one child's actions were entirely recorded, it was impossible to determine the correct number of times each childe listened to the music of each region or which regions' music were compared.

Table 1. Experiment 1 answers

		Answer	a		b		c		d		e	
			1	2	1	2	1	2	1	2	1	2
A	UK	1		5	5	5		5			1	1
B	Mongolia	2		2	10	2	1	2	2	6		2
C	Mexico	3		3		3	2	3	8	3	9	
K	Canada	4		4		4		4	4	4		10
F	Nogliki, (Russia)	5		6		6		6	5	5	7	5
L	Australia	6	4	2	5	2	4	2		2		6
G	Turkey	7	7	7		7		7		7	5	4
H	Japan	8	8	8	8	8	8	8		8	8	8
I	Sri Lanka	9	9	1	8	1		1	1	6		7
E	Zimbabwe	10		10	7	10	7	10	9	10	3	9
	Total		3	6	1	6	1	6	1	5	2	5

To summarize the results for Experiment 1, through the paper test results and observation through video, it was possible by to grasp that percentage of correct answers increased in the second half after assembling the knockdown globe compared to the first half. Also, it was possible to determine to a certain extent that several children submitted identical answers, and the difficulty of the content such as which countries were easy to answer. However, it is unknown how often the folk arts music was listened to or for what duration.

Experiment 2 (Using the RFID System)

On February 25, 2006, the Folk Arts Workshop was implemented at the IAMAS 2006 Graduate Exhibition hosted at Softopia Japan. The subjects were five children in the range of 5th grade elementary school to 2nd grade elementary school students, who had not previously participated and the workshop duration was again 90 minutes.

This time, the five children were separated into two groups, each with one contents reader and were challenged to contents from 30 countries in 90 minutes. The actual system used and workshop are shown in Figures 6 and 7.

Experiment 2 Results and Analysis

The results of Experiment 2 are shown in Table 2. The column *tries* in Table two refers to the children pressing the card reader to the predicted region of the contents card read in the contents reader.

Fig. 6. Reading a map panel with the contents reader

Fig. 7. Assembling the map panels

Table 2. Participant's number of tries and correct answers

	Total Tries	Correct Answers	Correct Percentile
Group A	26	15	58%
Group B	66	22	33%
Total	92	37	40%

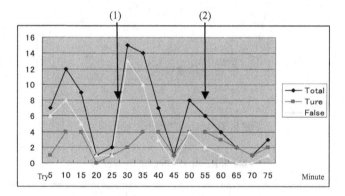

Fig. 8. Number of tries every five minutes

The children made a total of 92 tries in the workshop with an average correct percentile of 40%.

Figure 8 are the collected totals of tries, correct answers and incorrect answers every five minutes.

Overall incorrect answers exceed correct answers in the beginning. However, gradually in proportion to the number of tries correct answers increase, and about 55 minutes into the workshop correct answers exceed incorrect answers. This indicates that the children were making intuitive answers at first, but then began thinking more about their responses as the workshop progressed. Looking at the graph, the following interpretations can be made.

Point (1) on Figure 8 shows the time period when the knockdown globe was assembled according to the video recorded. Compared to other time periods, the number of tries severely drops. After assembly, around 25 minutes into the workshop, the number of tries sharply rises, and one can see that this is the most active time period for the children. Point (2) on Figure 8 is the time period when the instructors conducting the workshop give advice to the children. This time period marks the point when correct answers tend to exceed incorrect answers indicating that the advice given influenced the children's tries.

Figure 9 is a graph of the time until the children submitted answers. As the figure suggests, when the children answer after a few seconds the number of incorrect answers exceeds correct answers and as the time increases before answering the number of correct answers exceeds incorrect answers. According to the graph, it can be thought that after reading the folk arts cards with the card reader, when the children submit answers in a short time they are answering intuitively. Reversely, when they submit answers after a longer time, the percentile of correct answers increases suggesting that they are answering more carefully.

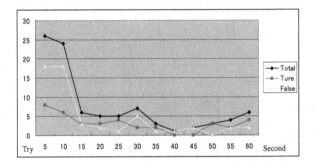

Fig. 9. Time spent before answering

Table 3. Results collected by region

	1	2	3	4	5 or more	Average	Total Countries
Asia	5	2	2	1	2	2.6	12
Africa	3	2	0	0	0	1.4	5
Oceania	1	1	2	0	0	1.7	4
Europe	1	2	0	0	0	2.3	3
N. America	2	0	0	0	0	1.0	2
S. America	0	1	1	0	2	6.0	4
Total	12	8	5	1	4		30
%	40.0%	26.7%	16.7%	3.3%	13.3%		

Table 3 is the collected total number of tries for each region by the children in the workshop. As the table suggests, the children answered almost all contents correctly within three tries occupying an overall percentile of 83%. However, the results to answers for South America were severely lower than answers to any other region. Presumably, the South America region was difficult for the children to imagine.

From the results of Experiment 2, the children were simply guessing which folk arts card matched which region, but incorrect answers increased and through trial and error they began to grasp the features of each folk art, leading them to the correct answers. With regard to the level of difficulty, it was simple to answer questions about the three regions of Africa, Europe, and North America, but relatively difficult to answer questions about the two regions of Asia and South America. It became clear that this trend must be addressed when considering the contents for each folk art (photo and music selection) for the next workshop.

6 Considerations

In Experiment 1, it was not possible to obtain a record of how many tries the children made for each of the contents or on which try they answered. In Experiment 2, by using this system in the workshop, it was possible to the correctly obtain the action history of the participants (children) of how often they tried each of the contents and on which try they arrived at the correct answer.

Further, by running the gained action history of the children with the workshop scenario, it was possible to analyze the children's most active period and the transitions in correct and incorrect answers in the workshop.

By analyzing the action history as above, it was possible to show that it is possible to grasp the workshop participants' (the children) assertiveness, trends in action, and level of difficulty for the problems.

7 Conclusion and Further Development Research Conclusion

In this research, research and development for a geographic contents display system as one use of RFID technology in the field of education and its verification and experiment of use was conducted. According to the results of Experiment 1 and Experiment 2, it was determined that the children's activity, as well as quality of the children's actions (number of tries in the experiment and the time taken for each answer) and the difficulty of the contents was easily grasped.

In the future we would like to conduct more workshops and we expect the following results by using action histories from more people.

Create more accurate educational materials
Since we are able to obtain which contents were difficult for the participants and their action histories along the workshop scenario, the procedure for contents explanation and selection criteria for photographs, music and videos becomes clearer, making it possible to create more comprehendible education materials for the participants.

Useful information for workshop instructors

It is difficult to understand the progress of the participants toward the problems. If there were information about which problems the intended participants often answer wrong, then it would be possible to offer assistance or hints. In the workshop format, there is a need for guidance responsive to each participant. If it were possible to see the participants' action history, it would be possible to provide more appropriate guidance.

Future development

We propose connecting the contents reader to the Web as a future development. Doing so would allow logging action history for more participants (in other regions) and make it simple to collect more data.

We also expect development of workshops with competitive and collaborative elements such as having opponents in remote areas and the first to answer correctly wins, or sharing workload to tackle the same problem.

Application to various contents

This system is based on use of a globe, so the range of application for other kinds of contents (geographic information, the world's architecture, language, etc.) is wide, and updates and changes of the contents can be done by simply updating the contents server database. We would like to expand application to new contents based on this experiment.

Acknowledgements

We would like thank Planning Division Sakai City, Osaka and Clear Light Image Products for contents materials in this research and development of this system.

References

[1] Koji Yatani, Masanori Sugimoto, Fusako Kusunoki, "Musex: A System for Supporting Children's Collaborative Learning in a Museum with PDAs," wmte, p. 109, 2nd IEEE International Workshop on Wireless and Mobile Technologies in Education (WMTE'04), 2004.

[2] Hiroaki Ogata and Yoneo Yano: Knowledge Awareness Map for Computer-Supported Ubiquitous Language-Learning, IEEE WMTE2004, Taiwan, March 23-25, 2003.

[3] Workshop—New learning and places of creation—Tamio Nakano, Iwanami Shoten, 2001.1 in Japanese

[4] Research in Workshop Practice, Yoichi Takahashi, Musashino Art University Press, 2002.4 in Japanese

[5] RFID Now and in the Future, NTT COMWARE, Ohmsha, 2005 in Japanese

Determination of Ancient Manufacturing Techniques of Ceramics by 3D Shape Estimation

Hubert Mara and Robert Sablatnig

Vienna University of Technology,
Institute for Computer Aided Automation
Pattern Recognition and Image Processing Group
Favoritenstrasse 9/183-2, A-1040 Vienna, Austria
{mara,sab}@prip.tuwien.ac.at

Abstract. We propose a rotational symmetry evaluation method that is used to determine the manufacturing technique of rotationally symmetric pottery like vessels. With the help of scanned 3D data of the surface of the vessel the symmetry is determined which is used to derive the manufacturing technique for this particular vessel. For example it can be determined whether or not a turning wheel was used to manufacture the vessel. Results for trditionally manufactured new vessels and ancient vessels are given and the applicability of the method in archaeology is shown.

1 Introduction

Documentation of ceramics is a main task in archaeology, because ceramics are the most common findings, which haven been used and produced in large numbers by humans for several thousands of years. Archaeologists use them on a daily basis to reveal information about the age, trading relations, advancements in technology, art, politics, religion and many other details of ancient cultures by analysis of ceramics [7]. The basis of this documentation is a manually drawn horizontal intersection of the ceramics, which is called profile line [7]. As the ceramics are found in tens of thousands at virtually every excavation, these drawings require a lot of time, skill and man-power of experts. Therefore we are assisting archaeologists in interdisciplinary projects [5,2] by using an automated system for acquisition and documentation of ceramics using a 3D-Scanner based on the principle of structured light [3,8]. Previous work [11] was focused on fragments of ceramics (sherds) of living places. These sherds virtually never reassemble a complete object, because in general only one or two dumped sherds of an object are found. Therefore no real ground truth exists about the object a sherd belongs to. As archaeologists are also excavating burial places, where unbroken ceramics or complete sets of sherds are found, we are presenting a method to determine the manufacturing process of ceramics, which reveals information about the technological advancement of an ancient culture. Furthermore this method can be applied on, but is not limited to, unbroken or reconstructed vessels.

The following section gives an overview about previous work regarding 3D-acquisition and processing of ceramics for traditional archaeological documentation. As we are using 3D-acquisition, we get 3D-models, which can be used to answer

H. Zha et al. (Eds.): VSMM 2006, LNCS 4270, pp. 349–357, 2006.
© Springer-Verlag Berlin Heidelberg 2006

further questions from archaeologists like the manufacturing quality and the manufacturing technique of ceramics. The principle of our method to answer these questions is shown in Section 3. The experiments and results are shown in Section 4 and 5. Finally a conclusion and an outlook are given in Section 6.

2   Data Acquisition and Processing

Developing a documentation system for archaeology is a challenging task, because it should be accurate, portable, inexpensive, easy-to-use and robust against all kind of odds of foreign climate, which can range from desert via jungle to arctic. This means several technologies like computer tomography and other laboratory equipment is often not suitable for the daily work of archaeologists - especially not for ceramics.

As photography has already proven its reliability for archaeology, we choose to use a camera and a light-source for 3D-acquisition. Our first prototype [16] in our laboratory was using structured light [3]. Its predecessor was a digital still camera with a special flashlight called *Eyetronics ShapeSnatcher* [2]. This camera was developed and used in the 3D-MURALE project [2].

Nowadays we use 3D-Scanners from the *Konica-Minolta Vivid* [9,10] product range, because of their resolution (≈ 0.1 mm), which meets the requirements given by archaeologists for their documentation. Figure 1 shows the setup of our 3D-Scanner from recent experiments at the excavations in the Valley of Palpa [15], Peru.

Furthermore Figure 1(a) shows the triangulation principle [9] using a laser (bottom) and a camera (top) having a well-known distance and orientation. Additionally the turntable - also shown in this Figure - is used to get a complete 3D-model of the ceramic. The number of 3D-scans depends on the complexity of the ceramic and it typically ranges from two scans for sherds up to eight scans for vessels. The 3D-scans are registered using [17] reassembling the 3D-model.

After the registration, noise from dust and other objects like holding devices (e.g. clamps or plasticine) are removed from the 3D-model. Then the orientation is estimated based on the assumption that ceramics are rotationally symmetric objects [9], because they were generally manufactured on rotational plates. The principle of our orientation method is fitting of circle templates [4]. In comparison to the computerized, but manual method of [12] our orientation method can be used fully- automatic and semi-automatic [6]. Furthermore our system is capable to store the 3D-model and further archaeological information (e.g. description, photographs, etc.) in a database. For solving the puzzling problems and other - typically industrially manufactured - rotational objects, methods like [14,19,13] can be applied.

Having an orientated 3D-model a vertical cross-section, at the highest point is estimated. This cross-section is the so-called profile line, which concludes the traditional archaeological documentation. As such a rather simple two- dimensional profile line does not reflect any information about the manufacturing quality leading to the manufacturing technique, we decided to enhance our system by giving the archaeologists a tool to gather further information about the acquired 3D-model. These enhancements are shown in the following sections.

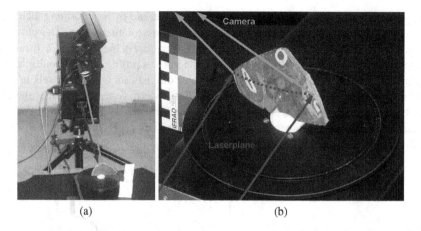

(a)   (b)

Fig. 1. *Konica-Minolta Vi-9i* 3D-Scanner (a) projecting a laser-plane (bottom arrow) on to a sherd, while the camera (top) acquires the projection of the laser. Having a well-known distance and orientation of the laser-plane and the field of view of the camera the distance (range) can be estimated. (b) Detail of this setup showing a sherd mounted with plasticine on the turntable, which is used for controlled acquisition of all sides of an object.

3   Analysis of the Manufacturing Process

Technological advancement, is determined by archaeologists between ceramics, that have been produced either or on slow or fast turning rotational plates. Another example would be an ongoing discussion between archaeologists about the existence of rotational plates for manufacturing ceramics in South America. The general opinion is that in this region the wheel was not invented and therefore ceramics were produced without a rotational plate (wheel) [18] on the other hand-side there is evidence that rotational plates were used [1].

As we use structured light as 3D-acquisition method, we can not make an assumption about the internal structure of a ceramic like [18], but we can estimate the surface with high resolution (0.1 mm). Therefore we can analyze the symmetry and estimate features like deviation of real surfaces in respect to a perfectly symmetrical surface. Such features can help archaeologists to decide about the technological advancements of ancient cultures.

To begin with our investigation in answering questions about the manufacturing process of ceramics, we choose to use two modern pots, which were manufactured in traditional way. Therefore this data can be interpreted as mixture between synthetic and real data, because we used real objects, but in contrast to real archaeological fragments, we know how it was produced.

Furthermore we decided to use the method for finding the orientation of a sherd [11]. We start with the profile line, which can be estimated in a similar way like for sherds. The difference is, that for complete vessels the bottom plane can be used for orientation, because it is the counterpart for the rotational plate, which defines the (orthogonal) axis of rotation.

We estimate multiple profile lines, which can be overlaid by transforming them into the same coordinate system, where the y-axis equals the rotational axis. Therefore the distance between profile lines can be estimated. Figure 2(a,b,e,f) shows a front and side-view of our pots. Figure 2(c,d,g,h) shows the longest profile line and multiple profile lines combined with the side-view, like archaeologists show such vessels in their documentation. In case of the multiple profile lines, we have estimated, that the distance between the profile lines differs and therefore these pots and their profile lines are unique. The maximum distance between two profile lines of the first pot was $9.8\ mm$ and $21.2\ mm$ for the second pot.

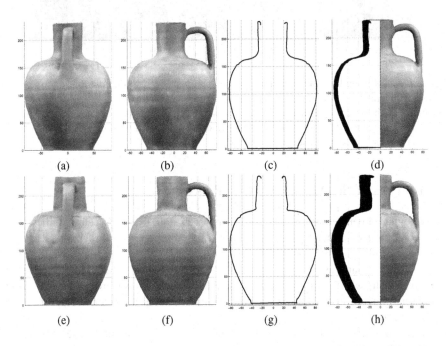

Fig. 2. (a,e) Front-view, (b,f) side-view, of modern ceramics, manufactured in traditional way, which are supposed to be identical. (c,g) Longest profile line and (d,h) multiple profile lines.

4   Experiments

The multiple profile lines shown Figure 2(d,h), the distance, measured parallel to the x-axis, between profile lines is not equal. If the profile lines were parallel, this would mean, that the pots have an elliptic (horizontal) cross-section. As it appears, the asymmetry is more complex. Therefore, we choose to analysis the pots slice-by-slice along the rotational axis supposed as orthogonal to the bottom plane.

Figure 3a,c shows the horizontal intersection, we applied with a distance of $10\ mm$ along the rotational axis. The distance of $10\ mm$ corresponds to the manufacturing process, which has left its traces as rills as seen in Figure 2(a.e). These rills are spaced $10\ mm$, which corresponds to the width of finger or tool used to "grow" the pot along the axis of the rotational plate. The intersections at height 160 mm and 170 mm have been discarded, because they intersect the "shoulder" of the pot with a very low angle ($\ll 5°$), resulting in an intersection having a non-representative, random curvature.

Dividing ceramics into sections by characteristic points (like the "shoulder") is done by archaeologists for classification. Therefore we choose to analyze the segmented object into a lower and an upper part. This means, we have two fragments, where an axis estimation can be applied, like for sherds (fragments). The estimation of the axis is shown in Figure 3b,d. The numeric results for the axis are, that they have a minimum distance of 4 mm towards each other and to the axis defined by the bottom plane. Furthermore the angles between the axes differ for $5°$ to $7°$.

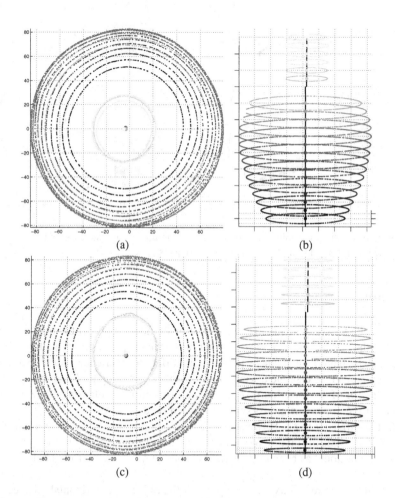

Fig. 3. (a,c) Top-view and (b,d) side-view of the horizontal cross-sections - the level of gray corresponds to the height. The axis of rotation for the lower and upper part is shown as black line, defined by the centers of the concentric circles (shown as dots).

Using the rotational axis of the lower and upper fragment, we repeated the estimation of the profile lines, which are shown in Figure 4 for the upper part and for the lower part of the objects. The maximum distance between the profile line is 7 mm for the upper and 2 mm for the lower part. Therefore the first conclusion is, that the upper and lower part do have different axis of rotation, which means, that these parts have been produced separately and combined without the use of the rotational plate.

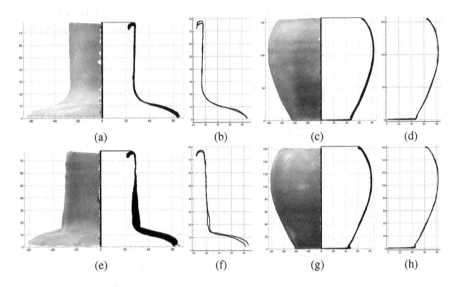

(a)   (b)   (c)   (d)

(e)   (f)   (g)   (h)

Fig. 4. Axis of rotation and multiple profile lines of the upper part (a,e), lower part (c,g) and (b,d,f,h) the longest profile lines of the parts of the objects

5   Results

We can conclude, based on the different deviation to the multiple profile lines shown in Figure 4 of the upper parts, that the upper part has been made in a lesser quality than the lower part, which has been made by potters with different experience and/or on a slower rotational plate. Vice versa the deviation of the upper part of up to 7 mm compared to less than 2 mm of the lower part, shows that a faster turning rotational plate has been used and for the upper part more experience is required.

From the differing angle between the axis of rotation based on the bottom plane compared to the axis of rotation of the upper and lower fragment, we can conclude that the either the bottom has been post-worked or the pot has been contorted before it was fired in the oven.

Even with the corrected axis for the parts of the object, the horizontal intersections are not perfectly circular. The horizontal intersections are elliptic. Therefore we estimated the direction of the major and minor axis of the ellipses. We could estimated that the minor axis has the same direction as the orientation of the handle. This means that the symmetry of the pots were broken, when the handle was attached, while the pots were still wet. Figure 5 show the pots, intersected by a plane, defined by the center of gravity of the pot and the direction of the major axis of the ellipses. The angle between the minor axis and the handle of the pot was 7° and 14° for the second pot.

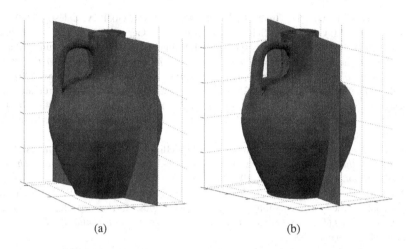

(a)   (b)

Fig. 5. Planes of symmetry of the (a) first and (b) second object

We additionally conclude that ellipses fitted [4] to the horizontal cross-sections can be used as further feature. Therefore the distance between the foci of the ellipse is estimated. Ceramics with a distance converging towards zero (circular cross-sections) are made of higher quality.

The proposed method has also been tested on 17 real vessels [10], from the NASCA-period [1], which have been found in the Valley of Palpa, Peru [15]. Therefore we could seperate these vessels into three classes determined by the symmetry. The vessesls (60%) of two of these three classes have not been produced on rotational plates. Beside this answer about the use of rotational plates in South America, this classification is used by archaeologists of the *German Institute for Archaeology* (DAI, Bonn) for refinement of their classification schemes.

6   Conclusion and Outlook

The proposed method regarding the analysis of the manufacturing process is part of an enhanced archaeological documentation system, which will replace the traditional documentation system of manual drawings by a fully computerized system, which can be used beyond the estimation of profile lines of sherds. Furthermore this system can document sherds with increased accuracy compared to manual drawings and it makes it possible to investigate other archaeological questions. Such questions concern the quality of production of ceramics, which are reflected by its symmetry or information about the manufacturing process can be revealed. Future work will be the automated estimation of classification rules based on complete vessels to classify sherds, which is currently done by an expert system.

References

1. Patrick H. Carmichael. NASCA Pottery Construction. In *Nawpa Pacha*, volume 24. Berkeley, California, 1986.
2. J. Cosmas, T. Itagaki, D. Green, E. Grabczewski, L. Van Gool, A. Zalesny, D. Vanrintel, F. Leberl, M. Grabner, K. Schindler, K. Karner, M. Gervautz, S. Hynst, M. Waelkens, M. Pollefeys, R. DeGeest, R. Sablatnig, and M. Kampel. 3D MURALE: A Multimedia System for Archaeology. In *Proceedings of the International Conference on Virtual Reality, Archaeology and Cultural Heritage*, pages 297–305, Athens, Greece, November 2001.
3. Fred W. DePiero and Mohan M. Trivedi. 3-D Computer Vision Using Structured light: Design, Calibration, and Implementation Issues. *Advances in Computers*, 43:243–278, 1996.
4. W. Gander, G.H. Golub, and R. Strebel. Least-squares fitting of circles and ellipses. *BIT*, 34:558–578, 1994.
5. Martin Kampel and Robert Sablatnig. On 3d Modelling of Archaeological Sherds. In *Proceedings of the International Workshop on Synthetic-Natural Hybrid Coding and Three Dimensional Imaging*, pages 95–98, 1999.
6. M. Lettner, H. Mara, A. Müller, R. Sablatnig, M. Singer, and M. Krenn. PAT: Profile Analysis Tool for the Documentation of Archaeological Finds. In *Proc. of Electronic Imaging & the Visual Art (EVA'06 Vienna) - Digital Cultural Heritage - Essential for Tourism*, page accepted / to appear, 2006.
7. U. Leute. *Archaeometry: An Introduction to Physical Methods in Archaeology and the History of Art*. John Wiley & Sons, December 1987.
8. C. Liska. Das Adaptive Lichtschnittverfahren zur Oberflächenkonstruktion mittels Laserlicht. Master's thesis, Vienna University of Technology, Vienna University of Technology, Institute of Computer Aided Automation, Pattern Recognition and Image Processing Group, April 1999.
9. Hubert Mara. Documentation of rotationally symmetrical archaeological finds by 3d shape estimation. Technical Report PRIP-TR-103, Vienna University of Technology, Inst. of Computer Aided Automation, Pattern Recognition and Image Processing Group, 2003.
10. Hubert Mara and Niels Hecht. 3D-Acquisition and Analysis of freehand manufactured NASCA Ceramics. In *Proc. of CAA06: Computer Aplications an Quantitative Methods in Archaeology*, page to appear, April 2006.
11. Hubert Mara and Martin Kampel. Automated Extraction of Profiles from 3D Models of Archaeological Fragments. In Orhan Altan, editor, *Proc. of CIPA2003: XIX CIPA Int. Symposium: New Perspectives to Save Cultural Heritage*, pages 87–93. CIPA 2003 organising committe, 2003.
12. F. J. Melero, A. Leon, F. Contreras, and J.C. Torres. A new system for interactive vessel reconstruction and drawing. In *Proceedings of CAA'03: Computer Applications in Archaeology*, pages 8–12, April 2003.
13. X. Orriols. *Generative Models for Video Analysis and 3D Range Data Applications. Ph.D. thesis*. Universitat Autonoma de Barcelona, Spain, 2004.
14. H. Pottmann and T. Randrup. Rotational and helical surface approximation for reverse engineering. *Computing*, 60:307–322, 1998.
15. Markus Reindel and J. I. Cuadrado. Los Molinos und La Muna. Zwei Siedlungszentren der Nasca-Kultur in Palpa, Südperu. In Philipp von Zabern, editor, *In Beiträge zur Allgemeinen und Vergleichenden Archäologie*, volume 21, 2001.
16. R. Sablatnig, C. Menard, and P. Dintsis. A Preliminary Study on Methods for a Pictorial Acquisition of Archaeological Finds. Technical Report PRIP-TR-010, Vienna University of Technology, Institute of Computer Aided Automation, Pattern Recognition and Image Processing Group, 1991.

17. S. Tosovic. Adaptive 3D Modeling of Objects by combining Shape from Silhouette and Shape from Structured Light. Master's thesis, Vienna University of Technology, Vienna University of Technology, Institute of Computer Aided Automation, Pattern Recognition and Image Processing Group, February 2002.

18. Alfried Wieczorek and Michael Tellenbach. Exkurs zur Frage der Drehscheibenkeramik. In *An die Mächte der Natur - Mythen der altperuanischen Nasca-Indianer. Katalog zur Ausstellung im Reiss-Engelhorn-Museum. Mainz: Philipp von Zabern.*, pages 54–63. 2002.

19. R. Willis. *Stochastic 3D Geometric Models for Classification, Deformation, and Estimation. Ph.D. thesis.* Brown University, Rhode Island, USA, 2004.

CG Restoration of a Historical Noh Stage and Its Use for Edutainment

Kohei Furukawa[1], Choi Woong[1], Kozaburo Hachimura[2], and Kaori Araki[3]

[1] Center for Promotion of the COE, Ritsumeikan University, Japan
[2] College of Information Science and Engineering, Ritsumeikan University, Japan
[3] Kawamo Art Research Institute, Japan

Abstract. Japan's oldest Noh stage has been restored using CG. The painting of pine trees on a wall, which is severely damaged by the weather, has been restored and painted based on several historical and aesthetical investigations. The painting was texture-mapped onto the CG model giving the atmosphere of the stage when it was originally built. By using the CG Noh stage and motion capture data of a Noh play performed by a professional player, several kinds of edutaiment contents have been produced. Not only an ordinary character animation of a Noh play on the restored stage, but also walk-through animation of a scene which might be observed by the player during a play was created, which might be useful for introductory enlightenment.

Keywords: Cultural heritage, Motion capture, Character animation, Intangible cultural properties.

1 Introduction

Today, a considerable number of studies have been conducted on digital archiving of cultural properties. Attempts have been made of recording and preserving both tangible and intangible materials with digital technologies. Visualization with computer graphics (CG) and virtual reality (VR) are promising for these kinds of digital archives, or digital heritage. One of the authors, Furukawa, has been studying the production of visual contents by using CG, especially for the restoration of historical ruins and buildings [1,2].

Also, by using the motion capture technique we can measure and digitize human body motions during traditional dance and archive the data for preservation. Research on numerical analysis of dance movement including Japanese traditional dance has been conducted based on archived motion data [3,4,5].

We can also reproduce the archived dance motion by using CG character animation. However, for performing arts, not only a dancer's body motion itself but also a theater, stage, clothing, make-up and lighting are very important. Therefore, movement reproduction by CG character animation is not sufficient, and it is important to reproduce dance motion in a suitable environment for these dances. A group of our colleagues in our university is coping with CG restoration of an old theater building where Kabuki plays have long been performed [6]. They

H. Zha et al. (Eds.): VSMM 2006, LNCS 4270, pp. 358–367, 2006.

intended to use the 3D CG model for producing digital contents concerning not only traditional Kabuki plays but even some of today's entertainment.

In [7], a research on a real-time interactive digital narrative and real-time visualization of animated Namaz pray in the virtually restored mosque was presented. This kind of trials of integrating tangible cultural heritage and intangible human body motions will be essential for the cultural heritage especially for performing arts like dance.

From this viewpoint, we intended to artificially restore Japan's oldest Noh stage still surviving in the precinct of Nishi-Honganji Temple located in Kyoto by using 3D CG as an environment for the reproduction of archived Noh plays. The Noh stage was built in the 16th century and is one of the national treasures in Japan. Because the stage has been in an open air environment, paintings pained on the wall were severely degraded by the whether. One of our authors, Araki, who is a specialist in restoration of historical fine art objects tried to restore the painting based on historical and aesthetical knowledge.

Since the Noh play is very classical and it is not necessarily easy to understand for people of today, especially young people, some of the persons concerned in the Noh play are willing to educate people who have less interest in the art by using various methods including IT. In these circumstances we have been trying to develop digital contents that can be used for education and promotion of the Noh play by using archived motion data and a restored environment including the stage. We created a new expression of the Noh play, namely, an animation of the scene as viewed from the Noh player, by using information of the Noh player's head motion obtained via motion capture.

2   CG Restoration of Noh Stage

2.1   Modeling

We used the software LightWave for the modeling of the Noh stage. We modeled a scene that can be seen from a Noh player on the stage, namely the whole Noh stage, the corridor, and the exterior of surrounding buildings. As for the modeling of the Noh stage, we were able to use measured drawings recorded during the dismantling repair done in 1928. The drawings were provided by the Department of Cultural Asset Protection, Kyoto Prefecture. Fig. 1 shows one of the drawings.

When modeling the stage, we were very careful to accurately model every board on the stage floor, ridgepoles, beams, and boards on the roof, one by one. This might cause an increase of the number of polygons in the scene. We had to be conscious of both accurate modeling and reduction of the number of polygons.

2.2   Texture Mapping

Texture mapping is useful for keeping the quality of the resulting CG images while suppressing the number of polygons and computing load when rendering

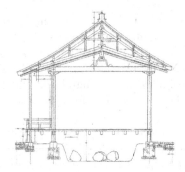

Fig. 1. Example of measured drawings

the scene. We prepared texture image data by using the photograph that had been actually taken on site. Detailed patterns and textures of the surface of woods were rendered by using bump maps made from photographs. We also took care of avoiding disunited impression in the representation of colors and textures by using a smooth shading method .

2.3   Restoration of the Pine Tree Painting

The target Noh stage was, actually, presented by the Shogun, Ieyasu Tokugawa, to the Nishi-Honganji Temple, and the stage was confirmed as the oldest existing one in Japan, because a document, on which letters indicating the year of 1581 were written, was found when the repair by dismantling was undertaken in 1928.

One of the most characteristic and common parts of Noh stages in general is a picture of pine trees painted on the wall of a stage. The pine tree paintings have been used for giving some distinctive features to the stage. However, the painting of this stage has been severely worn by weather as shown in Fig. 2. Only the marks of the leaf bush of the pine tree barely remain. Kawamo Art Research Institute once surveyed these marks of the painting in 1997, and one of the authors, Araki, from the Institute made an investigation for the digital restoration again this time. Since the painting has been severely damaged, restoration had to be made on conjectural bases and with the academic investigation.

We think that the level of this building is unusually high because this building was presented by the Shogun, and good quality timbers were used. Therefore, the pine tree painting must be the work done by one of the leading painters of the age.

At that period, Eitoku Kano was the top artist of the Kano school, and painters of the school painted pictures in many noble places. Eitoku died in 1590. However, the year 1581 was thought to be the period when Eitoku was still actively painting. Therefore, we presume that this pine tree painting is a work of Eitoku Kano who was a retained painter hired by the famous general Nobunaga Oda.

Fig. 2. Current status of the pine tree painting

We can visually find marks of moss drawn on the trunk of the pine tree, marks of pigments on the leafed bush areas of the pine tree, and the marks of lines of twigs depicted with Indian ink. A thick trunk should exist in the center of the board, however, we could not find any marks of pigments used for painting the trunk there. Expression of pine leaves drawn one by one, and powerful expression of the twigs were able to be confirmed by using an oblique lighting (Fig. 3).

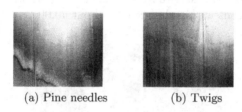

(a) Pine needles   (b) Twigs

Fig. 3. Marks of the painting seen with oblique lighting

In this restoration work, we investigated other famous pictures painted by Eitoku to understand the mood of his paintings. Consequently, the result, shown in Fig. 4, has come up with the style considerably different from the pine tree paintings found in other Noh stages. However, because marks that remain do not have signs of re-painiting, these marks must be the ones of the original painting. Thus, we think that this painting restored on resumption bases gives a good estimate of the original painting in that period.

Fig. 4. Restored pine tree painting

2.4 Procedure for Modeling and Rendering

The outline of our modeling and rendering procedures is as follows.

1) First, we modeled the ground, and then created some simple objects like pillars and boards of the floor based on sizes obtained from the drawings. It was assumed that the ground surrounding the Noh stage is basically flat. Next, the pillars were assembled by consulting the drawing.

2) Parts with complex curved surfaces were modeled by first scanning the drawings and then manually tracing the outline of the parts displayed on a screen. The depth information is given to the traced parts, and the 3D shapes of the parts are determined.

3) After the larger parts were roughly assembled, detailed decorations were modeled as described in step 2).

4) The surface textures were decided by investigating the actual photographs, and were used for texture mapping. Also, the restored pine tree painting was digitally photographed, and the image was texture mapped on the wall of the stage.

5) Next, the lighting condition was set. This time, an atmosphere with a soft impression was produced by using a relatively strong ambient light and a planer light source. Fig. 5 shows the wire frame model of the whole scene. In this case, the number of polygons within the scene is about 40,000.

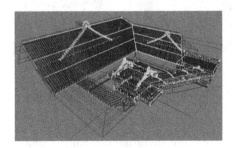

Fig. 5. Wire frame model

2.5 Results of Rendering

Examples of the resulting rendered images are shown in Fig. 6 and Fig. 7.

3 Edutainment Contents

The origin of the Noh play dates back to the middle of the 14th century. This classical play has been successfully inherited up to now by Japan's unique succession system kept by head families. However, Noh is not necessarily well accepted by today's younger generation because the plays are mainly based on the classics, and difficult to comprehend. Some of the actors in Noh plays are willing to educate people via various methods including information technologies. In this

Fig. 6. CG restored Noh stage

(a) The pine tree painting   (b) The Noh stage in the daylight

Fig. 7. Noh stage rendered in other conditions

background we have been trying to make some edutainment content that can be used by interested people to learn the Noh play.

In this section some of the trials will be introduced, all of which employ motion-captured body motion data of Noh plays as well as the CG restored stage.

3.1   Character Animation on the Stage

As the simplest implementations, we produced character animation on this digital Noh stage. Character animation becomes possible by assigning the motion data to the character model of Fig. 8(a), which has been modeled with Maya. We employed the motion capture data of a Noh play called "Ama" played by a leading professional Noh player, Mr. Kiyoshi Katayama. Finally, the character animated by the motion-captured data is placed on the above-mentioned Noh stage as shown in Fig. 8(b). At this time, to express the Noh play more attractively, we reproduced the camera work and the effect of the lighting. Fig. 9 shows snap shots of the animation.

(a) Character model   (b) Animation on the stage

Fig. 8. Character animation

Fig. 9. Snapshots of the animation

3.2 Walk-Through Animation Seen from Noh Player's Viewpoint

As a new style of edutainment content using the CG restored Noh stage, the animation scene viewed from Noh player's view point was produced. For this purpose, information of the actor's viewpoint and gaze direction is necessary. It is not possible to accurately estimate the gaze direction that includes the movement of the actor's eyes. Therefore, we derived the coordinates at the center of eyes and the direction of gaze from the positions of four markers attached to the dancer's head as shown in Fig. 10.

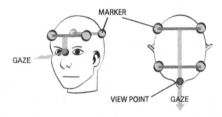

Fig. 10. Estimation of a viewpoint and gaze direction

We can make an animation sequence just like making an ordinary walk-through animation by using estimated eye position and gaze direction obtained from the motion captured data of the player as explained above for a camera path and focus direction respectively. This time, we used the same motion capture data of "Ama" played by Mr. Katayama as described earlier. Several snapshots of the animation scene are shown in Fig. 11. The resolution of the picture is 640 × 480 pixels.

Fig. 11. Snapshots of animation seen from a viewpoint of the Noh player

3.3 Character Animation Overlaid on Walk-Through Animation

Edutainment content was developed, which displays both animation seen from the player's viewpoint and ordinary character animation in one screen. Users can observe animations from two viewpoints, namely subjective and objective viewpoints, at the same time.

First of all, we apply movement data of the Noh player to a 3D stick figure character model, and the stick figure character animation of the Noh play seen from a fixed viewpoint as shown in Fig. 12 is produced. Next, the stick figure character animation is overlaid onto the actor's viewpoint animation using the video editing software, with synchronization being kept accordingly. At this time, to be able to see both animations, the degree of transparency of the overlaid foreground screen was set to 40% as shown in Fig. 13.

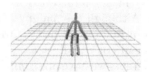

Fig. 12. Stick figure character animation

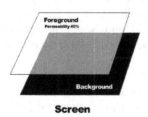

Fig. 13. Translucent foreground layer overlaid

A snapshot of the resulting animation is shown in Fig. 14. The animation video clip was produced at a resolution of 1280 × 500. This is for suppressing flicker in thin lines that appear at a lower resolution. The audio data of instruments and chanting were also added to the animation video clip.

Fig. 14. Viewpoint animation with stick figure animation overlaid

4   Conclusions

In this research, we first restored a Japanese national treasure Noh stage by using 3D CG. We were able to model it accurately owing to the use of detailed measured drawings. Moreover, the atmosphere of the Noh stage was successfully restored with the pine tree painting on the wall.

At the same time, we made several types of edutainment content by using character animation generated with motion-capturing a professional Noh player's motion. We think that we have achieved content with reasonable significance at this moment. Among them the most characteristic is the animation scene viewed from the player's viewpoint. Although the making of an animation seen from a Noh player's viewpoint was our first experience, we were able to produce a vivid video scene which audiences can not usually see.

As for the edutainment contents we have not completed an adequate objective assessment so far. However, we obtained evaluation comments from the Noh player, Mr. Katayama, whose motion data was used for making these contents:

1) These contents are interesting as a form of new entertainment and may give rise to the interest of peoples.

2) The estimated gaze direction is something not correct. We have to improve this by estimating the movement the Noh Player's eyes.

Acknowledgments. This research has been partly supported by the "21st Century COE Program", the "Open Research Center Program" and the "Grant-in-Aid for Scientific Research" of the Ministry of Education, Science, Sports and Culture, No.(B) 16300035. We would like to thank Mr. Kiyoshi Katayama for providing superb Noh plays and valuable comments and Prof. Ross Walker of Ritsumeikan University for checking our English manuscript.

References

1. Kohei Furukawa, Takahiro Yonemura, Sadahiko Nagae: Presenting Educational Contents by Using a Non-contact Viewer (in Japanese), Journal for Geometry and Graphics, Volume 6, No.2, pp.213-219, 2002.
2. Kohei FurukawaCTakahiro YonemuraCKenichi HiroseCSadahiko Nagae: A prorposal on Interactive Educational Contents by Using Visual Symbols (in Japanese), The Japan Society for Graphic ScienceCJournal of Graphic Science of Japan, No.107, pp.19-24, 2005.
3. Kozaburo Hachimura: Digital Archiving of Dancing (Invited Talk), Extended Abstract of the First South-Eastern European Digitization Initiative Conference, pp.42-45, 2005.
4. Mitsu Yoshimura, Hideki Murasato, Tamiko Kai, Akira Kuromiya, Kiyoko Yokoyama, and Kozaburo Hachimura, Analysis of Japanese Dance Movements Using Motion Capture System, Systems and Computers in Japan, Vol.37, No.1, pp.71-82, 2006.
5. Kozaburo Hachimura, Katsumi Takashina, and Mitsu Yoshimura: Analysis and Evaluation of Dancing Movement Based on LMA, Proc. IEEE International Workshop on Robot and Human Interactive Communication, pp.294-299, 2005.
6. Naoko Oomoto, Kyoko Hasegawa, Hirotsugu Motojima, Susumu Nakata, and Satoshi Tanaka: 3D Model of Kyoto Minami-za Theater and its Application (in Japanese), IPSJ symposium series vol.2005, No.21, pp.109-112, 2005.
7. G. Papagiannakis, A. Foni, and N. Magnenat-Thalmann: Real-Time Recreated Ceremonies in VR Restituted Cultural Heritage Sites, Proc. 19th CIPA International Symposium, pp.235-240, 2003.

Surveying and Mapping Caves by Using 3D Digital Technologies

Wei Ma and Hongbin Zha

National Laboratory on Machine Perception, Peking University, 100871, China

Abstract. In this paper, we propose an original three-dimensional (3D) computer-aided approach for surveying and mapping caves to get line drawings. By introducing 3D digital technologies into the line drawing, our approach has advantages in improving the drawing accuracy while cutting a lot of time costs. The 3D digital technologies are used to reconstruct accurate 3D models of real scenes. Then, the lines on the model surfaces are extracted by analyzing the model geometry. To demonstrate the advantages, we compare our approach with the traditional method usually used by archaeologists. Results show that our approach is much more convenient and accurate than the previous method.

1   Introduction

Line drawings (plan, elevation and profile) are a necessary part of archaeological reports for caves. To get line drawings, archaeological workers usually use a traditional manual method. For example, to draw a profile of a cave, the workers do the following steps:

1. decide two standard baselines perpendicular with each other by poles and ropes. One is parallel to the horizon along a profile plane, while the other is vertical to the horizon;
2. mark important features manually on the walls of the cave;
3. measure each feature by using rulers or spreading grids based on the coordinate system determined by the two baselines. To facilitate surveying, additional lines parallel to the baselines are added, each with a soft ruler attached, as shown in Fig. 1(a);
4. draw the features in a millimeter paper and connect them to produce a smooth drawing.

The traditional procedure above is labor intensive and time consuming. Furthermore, most of the sculptures in grotto sites are weathered, eroded and oxygenated to be seriously mottled [1]. It is difficult to recognize their original carved appearances as shown in both pictures of Fig. 1. In this case, manual surveying is subjective and inaccurate.

Since the traditional methods are subjective and time consuming, it is necessary to find a new method to simplify and automate the procedure. Therefore, the School of Archaeology and Museology, the National Laboratory on Machine

H. Zha et al. (Eds.): VSMM 2006, LNCS 4270, pp. 368–376, 2006.

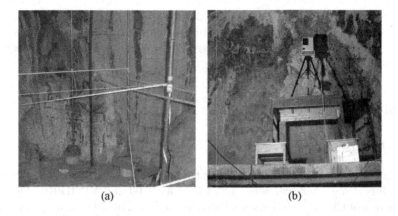

(a)   (b)

Fig. 1. (a) A traditional working site; (b) a scanning working site

Perception at Peking University and the Longmen Grottoes Research Academy make an experiment on line drawings aided by three dimensional (3D) digital technologies in the Leigutai area of Longmen Grottoes. Parallel projection maps without any colors and perspective distortions are provided by our laboratory. Archaeological workers in Longmen Grottoes are responsible for the line drawing from the maps. The paper describes the whole process in detail.

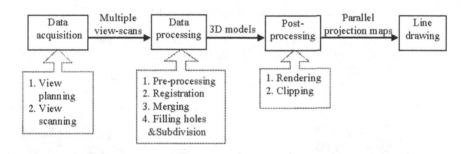

Fig. 2. Pipeline of our procedure

Our working pipeline is shown in Fig. 2. In the first step, we scan an object from multiple planned viewpoints by using laser scanners. Then we pre-process each view-scan, register all the scans into a single coordinate system, merge them to be a whole model and fill holes on the surface of the model. During post-processing, we render the model in proper lighting conditions and clip it into different parts for its plan, elevation and profile parallel projection maps under the instruction of archaeological workers in Longmen Grottoes. At last, the workers spread each map under a millimeter paper, and draw lines on the basis of the maps.

In Section 2, we describe how to model a real object, which includes two steps: data acquisition and data processing. In Section 3 we show how to create line drawings from 3D models. Experiment results are given in Section 4. Section 5 presents conclusions.

2   Model Reconstruction

2.1   Data Acquisition

To create an accurate 3D model, we scan the surface of a real object from multiple viewpoints using laser scanners, such as Cyrax 2500 and VIVID910. The main parameters of the two scanners are listed in Table 1. For efficiency, we use Cyrax 2500 (Fig. 3(a)) with lower precision to scan large caves, and VIVID910 (Fig. 3(b)) with higher precision for fine details. We change viewpoints by moving scanners. Before scanning the object, we first decide the positions of all needed viewpoints around the object. This procedure is called view planning. The goal of the view planning for the object is to cover its whole surface with as few as possible view-scans, while keeping neighbour scans partially overlapped as illustrated in Fig. 3(c). For surfaces inaccessible from the ground, special shelves for the scanners are built. Fig. 1(c) shows a planned position for scanning a high and concave part in the south cave of the Leigutai area.

Table 1. Parameters of Cyrax 2500 and VIVID910

Scanners	Scan range	Field of view	Precision
Cyrax 2500	$< 150m$	$40^0 \times 40^0$	2mm
VIVID910	$< 2.5m$	$80^0 \times 60^0$	0.008mm

 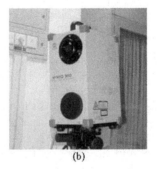 

        (a)   (b)   (c)

Fig. 3. (a) Cyrax 2500; (b) VIVID910; (c) a two-viewpoint illustration

2.2   Data Processing

We acquire the data of an object view by view as described in section 2.1. Some obtained view-scans may contain noisy parts because of self-occlusions, etc. During pre-processing, we delete the obvious noisy parts. On the other hand, processing large data with high precision is difficult even with graphic workstations. We decimate the original scanning data also in the pre-processing step.

(a)   (b)

Fig. 4. The Bodhisattva on the main wall of the middle cave (a) after registration; (b) after merging

Scanning a large cave using Cyrax2500 or a fine statue using VIVID910 often produces tens of view-scans. These scans are independent and each has its own coordinate system. We use the IMAlign module in Polyworks, a software produced by InnovMetric Software Inc., to register all the scans and put them into a common coordinate system [2]. The main steps are:

1. import two view-scans, and choose their corresponding feature points respectively;
2. regarding the first scan's coordinate system as the world one, compute the second one's transformation matrix relative to it based on the matched points and transfer the second scan into the world coordinate system;
3. obtain an optimal alignment using the ICP (Iterative Closest Points) algorithm by minimizing the 3D distances between surface overlaps.

Taking the two scans as a whole, we then import a third one and follow the three steps. The same operations are carried out to the other scans, until all of them are in the same coordinate system, as shown in Fig. 4(a) with different colors denoting different view-scans. After the registration, we use the IMMerge module in Polyworks to merge the different view-scans into a monolayer triangle mesh model as shown in Fig. 4(b).

Due to occlusions, some surfaces are impossible to scan, resulting in holes on the surfaces of 3D models. Holes on simple and smooth surfaces can be repaired automatically with allowable errors. We fill these holes with triangles and subdivide the triangles into finer ones with uniform surface resolutions by using the IMEdit module of Polyworks. Yet, holes lying on complex surfaces are difficult to be filled automatically and accurately with existing hole filling algorithms [3, 4]. Repairing them manually is inaccurate and time consuming. Instead of filling these holes here, we keep them until the line drawing step, where archaeological workers add feature points manually on the missing parts of the line drawings by measuring their corresponding points on the real objects.

3   Line Drawing

After getting an object's 3D model, we render it under proper lighting conditions and clip it to get the model's plan, elevation and profile parallel projection maps. Then, archaeological workers spread each map under a millimeter paper, and finish line drawing by referring to the maps. Fig. 5 shows a plan parallel map of the north cave at 1.3 meters high and its line drawing.

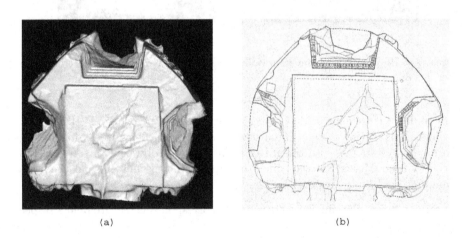

(a)   (b)

Fig. 5. A plan of the north cave at 1.3 meters high. (a) Parallel projection map; (b) line drawing.

In the research of 3D digital geometry processing, feature lines on model surfaces can be extracted automatically based on the surface variations [5, 6]. Decarlo [5] detects lines by setting a threshold for the inter-angles between the normal direction of each point on the model surface and a current view direction. Points with angles larger than the threshold are defined as feature points. Yoshizawa [6] introduces crest lines on the model surface as features. The crest lines detection is based on estimating curvature tensors and curvature derivatives via local polynomial fitting. Fig. 6(a) shows a line drawing extracted by us using Decarlo's method. However,usually the lines extracted automatically do not satisfy the requirements of archaeological reports. An archaeological line drawing (as shown in Fig. 6(b)) needs to be partially emphasized. Realizing these requirements rely on archaeologists' subjective judgements and artistic knowledge.

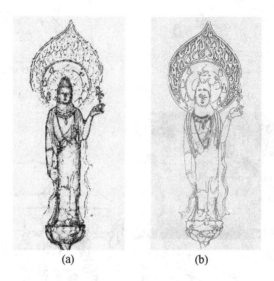

(a)   (b)

Fig. 6. The Bodhisattva on the main wall of the middle cave. (a) Lines extraced automatically; (b) lines drawn manually.

Although an automatically extracted line drawing does not satisfy archaeological requirements, it includes all needed features and seems closer to an archaeological one than its corresponding projection map. In the future, instead of the line drawing by projection maps, we hope to provide archaeologists an ideal platform which can extract accurate and necessary feature lines from a 3D model automatically and also includes an interactive interface for users to edit the lines. With this platform, people can get archaeological line drawings conveniently.

4   Results

Fig. 7(a) and (c) are the parallel projection maps of the Buddha statue on the main wall of the north cave and the outside elevation of the Leigutai area

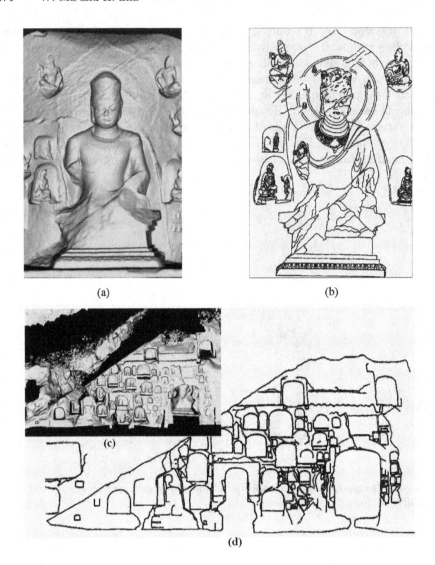

Fig. 7. The Buddha in the north cave. (a) Parallel projection map; (b) line drawing. The outside elevation, (c) Parallel projection map; (d) line drawing.

respectively. Fig. 7(b) and (d) are their corresponding line drawings. Table 2 presents the time costs for the traditional method and our method on surveying and mapping three different objects: the Bodhisattva on the main wall of the middle cave (Fig. 4, Fig. 6), the Buddha statue on the main wall of the north cave (Fig. 7(a) and (b)), and the outside elevation (Fig. 7(c) and (d)) in the Leigutai area. Comparing with the traditional method, our method saves 52 hours for the Bodhisattva in the middle cave, 324 hours for the Buddha in the north cave, and 448 hours for the outside elevation. The larger and the more seriously eroded

Table 2. Comparison between the computer aided method and the traditional method in time costs

Objects	Size(m^2): width×height	View number	computer aided(h): modeling+line drawing	Traditional method(h)	Saved time(h)
Bodhisattva in the middle cave	0.8 × 2.9	29(VIVID)	4+40	96	52
Buddha in the north cave	2 × 3.4	21(Cyrax)	4+32	360	324
Outside elevation	20 × 8.5	41(Cyrax) +42(VIVID)	8+24	480	448

the object, the more the time saved. We present one line drawing for each of the three objects above. Generally, all kinds of drawings (plan, elevation and profile) for an object can be produced quickly once its 3D model has been reconstructed as described in Section 3. Such a batch production ability for one object is a new feature as compared with the traditional method.

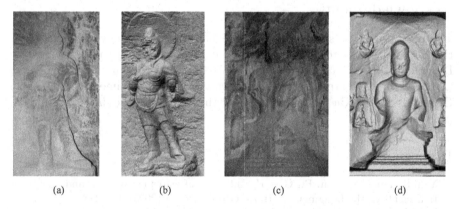

| (a) | (b) | (c) | (d) |

Fig. 8. A Warrior in Liutian cave. (a) Photo; (b) parallel projection map. The Budda on the main wall of the north cave. (c) Photo; (d) parallel projection map.

In accuracy, we make no quantitative comparison between the traditional method and our method for now. However, the traditional method suffers errors due to manual measuring, perspective distortions and the disturbances of mottled colors. In contrast, the measuring errors of our laser scanners are ralatively small and parallel projection could be easily realized in computers. In addition, our method is based on the geometric shapes of 3D models rather than any color information. Fig.8 (a) and (c) are photos of a Warrior statue in Liutian cave and the Buddha statue on the main wall of the north cave respectively. Fig.8 (b) and

(d) are their corresponding projection maps used for the line drawing. Archaeologists seeing the maps were strongly impressed because they never felt before that these statues were carved so elaborately. These examples show that the computer aided line drawing without any color disturbances are certainly more accurate than the traditional manual method. In some other applications, such as building a digital museum [7], we generally take photos as textures for reality. However, there is no necessity to do the work for the line drawing purpose.

5   Conclusions

In this paper, we integrate 3D digital technologies into surveying and mapping caves and describe the whole process. By comparing with the traditional manual method, we show that the new approach is much more efficient and accurate.

However, there still exist two issues unresolved. One is the lack of an accurate and automatic hole-filling algorithm as described in Section 2.2. The second problem is the limitation of computer hardware for processing high precision scanning data so that we have to decimate the original data for practice. If the two problems were resolved, the quality of line drawings would be improved largely.

Acknowledgment

The pilot project is supported by the School of Archaeology and Museology, the National Laboratory on Machine Perception at Peking University and the Longmen Grottoes Research Academy. We would like to thank Prof. Chongfeng Li, one of the main organizers, for his direction on the experiment, and Danhong Huang, Tao Luo, Xin Li, Tao Wei etc for their efforts in the data scanning and processing.

References

1. Yan, S., Fang, Y., Sun, B., Gao, H.: Influence of water permeation and analysis of treatment for the Longmen Grottoes. Geoscience **19** (2005) 475–478
2. InnovMetric Software Inc.: Polyworks user's guide (2001)
3. Davis, J., Marschner, S., Garr, M., Levoy, M.: Filling holes in complex surfaces using volumetric diffusion. The First International Symposium on 3D Data Processing Visualization and Transmission. (2002) 19–21
4. Jun, Y.: A piecewise hole filling algorithm in reverse engineering. Computer-Aided Design **37** (2005) 263-270
5. DeCarlo, D., Finkelstein, A., Rusinkiewicz, S., Santella, A.: Suggestive contours for conveying shapes. ACM Transactions on Graphics. **22** (2003) 848–855
6. Yoshizawa, S., Belyaev, A., Seidel, H.: Fast and robust detection of crest lines on meshes. ACM Symposium on Solid and Physical Modeling. (2005) 227-232
7. Li, X., Feng, J., Zha, H.: 3D modelling of geological fossils and ores by combining high-resolution textures with 3D scanning data. The ninth Intenational conference on Virtual Systems and Multimedia. (2003) 686-693

On the Use of 3D Scanner for Chinese Opera Documentation

Hao Zhou and S.P. Mudur

Department of Computer Science and Software Engineering, Concordia University, Montreal, Quebec, H3G 1M8, Canada

Abstract. Chinese opera, a heritage performance art with many different styles and of great popularity in the mid 20th century is undergoing a major decline in recent times. There are ongoing efforts initiated by the Chinese government to document this heritage of humanity based on photographs and audio records of renowned master artists. All these efforts are based on the use of technologies for still and video imaging, with their own serious difficulties, as enunciated by the project leaders. With rapid and tremendous advances in 3D graphics, use of 3D virtual humans is an exciting new medium of documentation. In this paper we discuss our efforts towards this approach. Our documentation proposal makes use of 3D body scanning technology for capture of facial expressions for combining it with the well established motion capture technology for capturing body movements from young artists, along with audio from master artists. Our initial efforts have been devoted to facial expression capture and synthesis using 3D scan data. The paper brings out major issues, problems and some of our proposed solutions in using this approach for documentation.

1   Chinese Opera

Chinese opera with its distinct styles has undergone a serious decline over the last few decades. Several of Chinese opera styles are on the verge of extinction. On eighteenth of May 2001, Kunqu, the 500-year-old Chinese Opera, was proclaimed by United Nations Education, Science and Culture Organization (UNESCO) as being among the first nineteen Masterpieces of Oral and Intangible Heritage of Humanity [1]. In the most flourishing times for this art form, Chinese opera became fashionable even among ordinary people. Performances were watched in tearooms, restaurants, and even around makeshift stages. Chinese opera together with Greek tragic-comedy and Indian Sanskrit Opera are the three oldest dramatic art forms in the world [2]. Some documentation efforts are in place for preserving this precious heritage of humanity. Our work described in this paper addresses the problem of choosing appropriate technology for such documentation; In particular, we describe some results of our investigations on the use of 3D graphics and 3D scanners for this purpose.

H. Zha et al. (Eds.): VSMM 2006, LNCS 4270, pp. 377–386, 2006.

2   Documentation Technologies

The most flourishing time for Beijing Opera was from 1940s to 1960s. Many renowned master artists emerged during this period. While, there are lots of photographs and audios of their performances, there are very few videos because of paucity of video recording devices in those times. In order to make up this lost heritage, China has launched a videotape project, which has 2 stages lasting nearly 20 years (See Fig. 1) [3]. The videotaping is made by integrating the singing of 47 prominent Beijing opera artists, mostly recorded from the 1940s to the 1960s, with performances by their younger-generation followers. The project saw the completion of 582 videotapes in the first stage and 104 videotapes in the second stage [4]. As clearly enunciated by Li Ruihuan, previous chairman of the

Fig. 1. An Example Illustrating Video Documentation of Peking Opera

National Committee of the Chinese People's Political Consultative Conference, who proposed and masterminded the project, videotaping is extremely difficult. First, the young performers have very little enthusiasm because it is very difficult to get into the depth of original master artists performance. Second, it is hard to make the new performance to fit the audio. Third, since the performance is in a recording studio, it lacks the atmosphere of opera theatre, so essential to motivate the artist [5].

With tremendous advances in 3D graphics technology, another promising medium of documentation is virtual opera performances using 3D geometric modeling and 3D computer animation techniques. Compared to the video record-ing approach, virtual opera performance has the following advantages. 1) We can create the character (virtual) of the artist herself/himself by the techniques of geometric modeling and reconstruction from pictures and look-alikes. 2) We can capture motion from young performers and then map it to the virtual character to create natural looking physically realistic body motion. 3) We can use 3D fa-cial animation techniques for facial expressions. 4) It may be easier to synthesize the 3D animation to fit the audio, than to get a young performer to do the same. Accordingly we have been working over the last three years at building such an experimental system for this purpose. Initial efforts in this direction have been presented in [6]. In this paper we report on considerable more progress made using a 3D half body scanner.

3   Brief Review of Related Work

The most widely known example of the use of 3D scanning system and point based solution for documenting heritage data is the Digital Michelangelo project from Stanford University [7]. Virtual humans have been demonstrated exten-sively in the work on Virtual Marylyn Monroe [8]. In the field of facial anima-tion, since the pioneering work of Frederic I. Parke in early 1970s, many research efforts have attempted to generate realistic facial expressions [9]. In [10], Parke and Waters categorize and describe facial animation in detail. Most work on facial animation makes use of morphing between two or more facial poses which are represented in the form of triangle meshes or in some cases NURBS sur-faces. In all these cases, there is a one-to-one correspondence that needs to be specified/established for every geometric element in each of the poses. Noh and Neumann [11] provided a method for facial expression cloning based on 3D mor-phing. They transfer vertex motion vectors from a source face model to a target model having different geometric proportions and mesh structure (vertex num-ber and connectivity). Pyun et al [12] proposed an approach of scattered data interpolation. They succeeded in composting two key-models of different aspects automatically, but the shape blending imposes too much burden. In general, there has not been much work on morphing directly with point based represen-tations of poses.

4   The Need for Combining Facial Expression and Body Animation

Beijing Opera has "chang" (singing),"nian" (dialogue),"zuo" (acting)and "da" (martial arts) as its basic performing forms. "chang" is mainly performed in the tunes of "xipi" (used for expressing strong emotions) and "erhuang" (used for expressing deep and sorrowful feelings)."Nian" is mainly done in the tones of "yunbai" and "jingbai". "Zuo" means the body movements (dancing and acting) of the actor or actress. "Da" is the martial art with acrobatic actions

[13]. From the above it is clear that both facial (lips, mouth, eyes movements, etc.) and body motion (joint movements, postural changes) are important in the Chinese opera documentation. Further, being an oral tradition, voice is also equally important. Motion capture devices are very popular in the 3D animation domain. A variety of motion capture technologies have evolved and are in regular use in industries such as cinema, gaming, industrial simulation, new media artworks, etc. It is our belief that this technology has matured sufficiently to be of practical use and can be used to gather body motion data from young performers which can then be mapped onto virtual human performers. In motion capture, typically, a human performer wears a set of markers at each joint and then performs the motion to be captured. The sensors track the position or angles of the markers, optimally, at least twice the rate of the desired motion. The motion capture computer program records the positions, angles, velocities, accelerations and impulses, thus providing an accurate physically valid digital representation of the motion. Often, the limb dimensions of the human performer and the virtual character are not the same. In this case, the captured motion data has to be processed and suitably transformed to suit the actual dimensions of the virtual human [14].

However, motion capture devices are not very suitable for facial animation since facial animation is very gentle global shape changes that are very hard to detect by sensors. And, we can not stick sensors on the full face of Chinese opera performer. Instead, we propose the use of techniques involving 3D scanning of facial expression poses to incorporate facial animation in the performances of the virtual performers. This can then be combined with body movements simulated using motion capture and then synchronised with pre-recorded voices of the master artists. Figure 2. shows the individual pipelines of data processing tasks in facial animation and body. We are aware that the task of combining facial animation from scan data with body movements produced from motion capture is a daunting one and will need considerable investigation. Particularly, taking into account the need for audio synchronization. At present, we are put in our efforst into creating facial animations using 3D scans of facial poses.

5   Facial Animation Experiments

5.1   Overview of Process of Facial Animation

Our system is based on the use of 3D scanners for facial pose capture in the form of point based models and the facial animation method is that of simulating the Chinese opera facial expressions by direct morphing of the point based face models.

5.2   Scanning Facial Expression Poses

The process of scanning is as follows: 1. Set up the Scanner and console system (PC) 2. Have human performer pose, adjust the digitizer and lights; 3. Scan with multiple camera heads (takes only a faction of a second); 4. Repeat steps

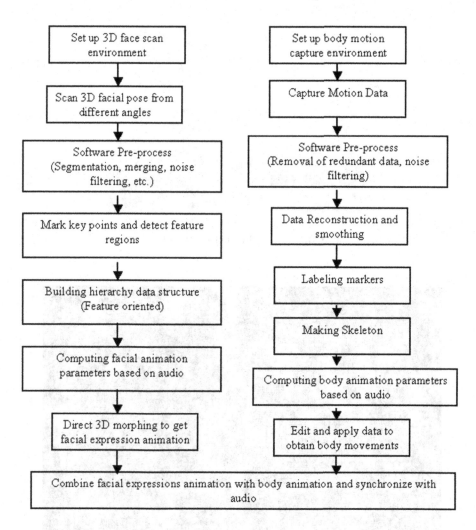

Fig. 2. Processing pipelines for combined facial expression and body animation for virtual 3D performers

2 and 3 for other poses. 5. Software processes include: selecting valid scan volume, stitching surface segments, noise removal and smoothing, model editing. 6. Output 3D scan data as point cloud geometry.

5.3   Scanning Hardware and Software

In our project, we use Mega Capture DF series digitizers made by Inspeck Inc.. The 3D Mega Capturor DF is designed to offer two different fields of view using two mega-pixel cameras built into the system. The [Small Field] camera is perfect for small volumes like faces or heads for example, as it will give you very

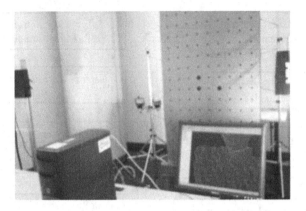

Fig. 3. Two head camera installation

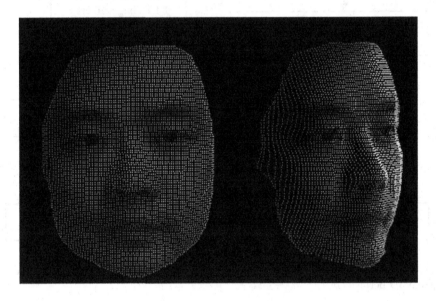

Fig. 4. Scanned face model

high resolution. On the other hand, the [Large Field] camera will capture larger objects/subjects but with lesser details. Besides, Inspeck supports Multi-head system, which use more than one digitizer. Each digitizer takes acquisitions from different view, and those views are intergraded in software. In our experiments, we use a bi-digitizer system (see Fig.3 above)). We use Inspeck EM software to optimize our scanned model. It supports many functions, such as merging, measurement, smoothing and editing.(Fig.4 shows plots of an example scanned face model).

5.4 Difficulties in Using 3D Scan Data for Face Models

As we mentioned above, we have to carry out certain preprocessing operations on the scanner output data before we can use it.

First of all, we have to select valid scanning volume and cut off some redundant 3D data such as the visible background and other extraneous objects that were visible to the camera along with the human performer. Noise removal is a must, because some noise is caused because of the light reflection or shadow; some noises are caused because of scanning view. For example, the hair part of the model always has much noise. Second, a model will miss some parts in scanning due to the view of scanning. For example, it is hard to get the data on a plane parallel to the scanning axle. In this case, we have to scan from a different view, and merge the patches. In the merging process, we could select some reference points on each scanning patch, and merge them with the scanning software.

5.5 Direct Morphing

In any two 3D scans of facial poses, even of poses belonging to a single expression, there is no one-to-one correspondence in the sampled points obtained for each of the poses. The same facial region may be represented by different number of points in the two scans. Traditionally, 3D scan data is used by first transforming/fitting the data into a surface model (triangulated mesh, NURBS etc.). This is a highly cumbersome largely manual process made even more complex by the requirement that we have one-to-one correspondence among all the facial poses. In our work, we have preferred to use the scan data directly as point based models without explicitly fitting any continuous surface geometry. Hence the problem of direct morphing of point based models needs to be addressed in a satisfactory manner. Below, we briefly describe the solution we have adopted for this purpose. Using a simple interaction tool that we have developed for this, we first identify the small number of corresponding key points on the different facial poses. Using these key points we group all of other sample points into feature regions. Correspondence of facial regions is automatic based on correspondence of key points. Finally, we construct a hierarchy feature region oriented hierarchical data structure similar to a spatially organized hierarchy. Now, given two data structures representing two facial poses, we will find that each feature has a corresponding feature region at the same level in the tree. Since we use the same subdividing method, each sub-region or even each scanned point has its corresponding sub-region or point. However, since the number of points in corresponding regions varies, the point correspondence could be one-to-many or many-to-one. Fig. 5 shows scans of two poses from an open mouth expression. It can be clearly seen that points corresponding to tongue and teeth are present in the scan shown on the right in the figure and are completely absent from scan shown on the left. Once this correspondence is established, we track the movement of the points during morphing and thus create facial animations.

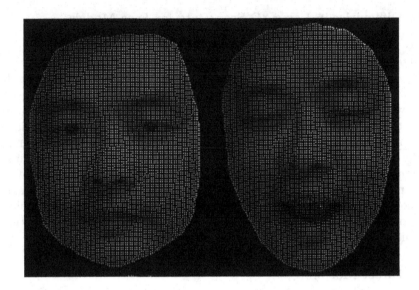

Fig. 5. 3D scans of two poses from a single expression(tongue present only in the scan on the right)

6   Conclusions

We have prototype implementations of the above. Fig. 6 shows morphed in-betweens for a facial expression. Since most of the tasks are carried out in the pre-processing stage, the final morphing is computationally straightforward and can be performed fast enough to give us real time frame rates. We have experimented with a number of Chinese opera facial expressions, and also synchronized with captured audio. At present, one of most laborious tasks is that of marking feature points. For the immediate future, we will be working on providing automation support in combining facial expression animation with body motion. At present, the overall tasks involved in creating virtual humans to perform in a believable manner are truly daunting. However, with the kind of rapid progress and evolution that one sees in the field of 3D graphics and animation, many of these tasks may be considerably simplified through appropriate automation support tools and techniques. The overall effort for authentically documenting this masterpiece of oral heritage may seem too much, but may well be worth it for all future generations.

Acknowledgements

We gratefully acknowledge NSERC for an equipment grant that enabled the second author to set up the 3D scanning facility, and also Discovery grants for graduate research support.

Fig. 6. Samples of in-between morphed point models for some facial expressions involving eyes, lips etc

References

1. *http : //www.unesco.org/bpi/intangible_heritage/china.htm*, Retrieved on June 27, '06
2. *http : //www.travelchinaguide.com/intro/arts/chinese − opera.htm*, Retrieved on June 27, '06
3. *http : //www.chinaqw.com.cn/node2/node116/node1486/node1494/node1569/ userobject6ai209094.html*, Retrieved on July 14, '06
4. *http : //english.people.com.cn/200209/05/eng20020905_102705.shtml*, Retrieved on July 14, 2006
5. *http : //www.chinaqw.com.cn/node2/node116/node1486/node1494/node1569/* userobject6 ai89565.html. Retrieved on July 14, '06

6. H. Zhou and S. P. Mudur, "Application of 3D Facial Animation Techniques for Chinese Opera Documentation", "Hybrid Reality: Art, Technology and the Human Factor", ISBN:1-895130-12-3, pp.165-175

7. M. Levoy, K. Pulli, B. Curless, S. Rusinkiewicz, D. Koller, L. Pereira, M. Ginzton, S. Anderson, J. Davis, J. Ginsberg, J. Shade, and D. Fulk. The digital michelangelo project: 3d scanning of large statues. Proceedings of SIGGRAPH 2000, pages 131C144, July 2000. http://graphics.stanford.edu/papers/dmich-sig00/dmich-sig00-nogamma-comp-low.pdf

8. Kalra, P., Magnenat Thalmann, N., Moccozet, L., Sannier, G., Aubel, A., Thalmann, D. Real-time Animation of Realistic Virtual Humans. IEEE Computer Graphics and Applications,Vol.18, No.5, pp.42-55, 1998

9. Parke, F. 1990. State of the Art in Facial Animation. Siggraph Course Notes 26.

10. Parke F. I. M, Waters K., Computer facial Animation, 1996, ISBN 1-56881-014-8, A. K. Peters Ltd.

11. Jun-Yong Noh, Ulrich Neumann, Expression Cloning (2001), SIGGRAPH 2001, Computer Graphics Proceedings

12. H Pyun, Y Kim, W Chae, HW Kang, SY Shin, An Example-Based Approach for Facial Expression Cloning, Proceedings of the 2003 ACM SIGGRAPH/Eurographics Symposium on Computer Animation, 2003.

13. *http : //english.peopledaily.com.cn/features/music/peking.html* Retrieved on July 12, 06.

14. B Bodenheimer, C Rose, S Rosenthal, J Pella - Computer Animation and Simulation, 1997

3D Data Retrieval of Archaeological Pottery

Martin Kampel and Robert Sablatnig

Vienna University of Technology
Image Processing and Pattern Recognition Group
Favoritenstrasse 9/183
1040 Vienna, Austria
{kampel,sab}@prip.tuwien.ac.at

Abstract. Motivated by the requirements of the present archaeology, we are developing an automated system for archaeological classification and reconstruction of ceramics. This paper shows different acquisition techniques in order to get 3D data of pottery and to compute the profile sections of fragments. With the enhancements shown in this paper, archaeologists get a tool to do archaeological documentation of pottery in a computer assisted way.

1 Introduction

Data acquisition is the first and the most important task in a chain of 3D reconstruction tasks, because the data quality influences the quality of the final results [1]. El. Hakim specifies in [4] the quality of the data by a number of requirements:

high geometric accuracy, capturing all details, photo-realism, full automation, low cost, portability, flexibility in applications, and efficiency in model size. It would be ideal to have one single acquisition system that satisfies all requirements, but this is still the future. F. Blais gives in [3] an overview on state of the art of range scanners by describing the last 20 years on range sensor development. The order of importance of the requirements depends on the application, for example cost is a major concern in the field of archaeology.

For the acquisition of archaeological pottery we identified the following four applications:

- Profile acquisition [5]: The goal is to provide data in real time for the manual classification done by archaeologists [10].
- Fragment acquisition [6]: Computation of a range image of two views of a fragment. The data acquired is used for the documentation and archival of the fragment, thus it is the data to be assembled into one object.
- Recording of complete objects [8]: Data is used as virtual representation of the real object.
- Color acquisition [7]: On the one hand the data is used as texture of the fragments recorded; on the other hand it serves as an attribute for the automatic classification of the finds.

This paper focuses on a selection of acquisition devices designed or adapted to facilitate the recording of profile sections and fragments. Our main contribution is the

H. Zha et al. (Eds.): VSMM 2006, LNCS 4270, pp. 387–395, 2006.
© Springer-Verlag Berlin Heidelberg 2006

investigation of state-of-art scanning techniques for the acquisition of archaeological pottery. In a preceding, national funded project "3D acquisition of archaeological finds" different strategies for recording of pottery with respect to the mentioned requirements were studied. Besides a comparative study of the devices we present practical experiences from field trips.

In Section 2 we describe four devices that meet requirements of the archaeologists in different ways. Section 3 shows results and compares the different approaches. A summary is given at the end.

2 Acquisition Devices

In the following we describe the setup of four different acquisition devices and its technical principles.

Two Laser Method

In order to generate a profile section in real time we developed a two laser technique resulting in a two dimensional image of the profile. The acquisition system consists of the following devices:

- two monochrome CCD-cameras with a focal length of 16mm and a resolution of 768x576 pixels.
- two red lasers with a wavelength of 670nm and a power of 10mW. The lasers are equipped with a prism in order to span a plane out of the laser beam.

The two lasers are mounted in one plane on both sides of the fragments, so that one camera takes the picture of the laser-plane projected on the outer side (see Fig. 1a) and the other camera the inner side of the sherd as seen in Fig. 1b. These images are combined manually, so that a profile line containing the inner and outer profile is generated. The resulting image is filtered by an adaptive threshold that separates the background from the laser. Afterwards the laser line is thinned, so that a profile line - similar to the lines drawn by hand from archaeologists - is extracted.

(a)

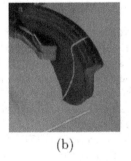
(b)

Fig. 1. 2D-acquisition with two lasers and two cameras: (a) Camera 1 acquires laserline 1, (b) Camera 2 acquires laserline 2

The method has some drawbacks for using it in an automated system:

- The sherd has to be oriented manually, because no axis of orientation can be estimated from the recorded data.
- The diameter of the whole object has to be determined manually.
- The position of the fragment, laser and camera in the acquisition system has to be selected, so that there are a minimum of occlusion effects of the laser plane and that the longest profile line is recorded.

LCD-Projector

In order to overcome the limits from the two laser method, a system for the automated acquisition of the profile line based on active triangulation [2] was developed. The acquisition system consists of the following devices:

- one monochrome CCD-camera with a focal length of 16mm and a resolution of 768x576 pixels.
- a Liquid Crystal Display (LCD640) projector.

Fig. 2a illustrates the acquisition system. The LCD projector is mounted at the top in order to illuminate the whole acquisition area. The angles between the optical axis of the LCD projector and the camera are chosen to minimize camera and light occlusions (approximately 20°). The volume of the fragments to be processed ranges from 3x3x3cm3 to 30x30x50cm3.

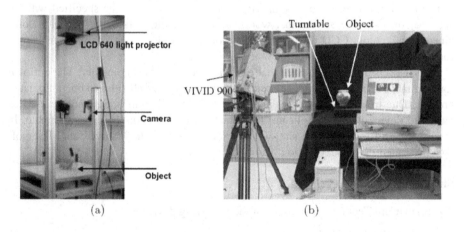

Fig. 2. 3D-acquisition with: (a) LCD Projector, (b) Minolta VIVID 900

The projector projects stripe patterns onto the surface of the objects. In order to distinguish between stripes they are binary coded [9]. The camera grabs gray level images of the distorted light patterns at different times. The image obtained is a 2D array of depth values and is called a range image [9].

Fragments of vessels are thin objects, therefore 3D data of the edges of fragments are not accurate, and this data cannot be acquired without placing and fixing the fragment manually which is time consuming and therefore not practicable. Ideally, the fragment is placed in the measurement area, a range image is computed, the fragment is turned and again a range image is computed. This step consists of sensing the front and backsides of the object (in our case a rotationally symmetric fragment) using the calibrated 3D acquisition system. The resulting range images are used to estimate the axes of rotation, in order to reconstruct the fragment.

There is no manual orientation of the fragment necessary, because it is computed automatically (see [6]). Since this acquisition system is not portable and therefore not usable outside the laboratory, we used the ``Minolta Vivid 900'' Technology, presented in the next section for recording fragments outside.

Minolta Vivid 900

The Vivid 900 3D Scanner developed by MINOLTA in our setup consists of the following devices:

- one CCD-camera with a focal length of 14mm and a resolution of 640x480 pixels, equipped with a rotary filter for color separation.
- one red laser with a wavelength of 670nm and a maximal power of 30mW. The laser is equipped with a galvanometer mirror in order to open loop control the laser beam scanning motion.

Fig. 2b illustrates the acquisition setup consisting of the Vivid 900 Scanner connected to a PC and the object to be recorded. Optionally the object is placed on a turntable with a diameter of 40cm, whose desired position can be specified with an accuracy of 0.1°. The 3D Scanner works on the principle of laser triangulation combined with a colour CCD image. It is based on a laser-stripe but a galvanometer mirror is used to scan the line over the object.

Vivid 900 is a portable device that does not require a host computer. The optional rotating table is used to index the scanned part and capture all sides in one automated process. Due to its weight (11kg) and size (213x413x271mm3) it cannot be used as handheld device which complicates the acquisition process on the excavation site. In order to record fragments on site, we therefore also used the ``ShapeCam'' Technology, presented in the next section.

ShapeCam Technology

The ShapeCam Technology consists of the following devices:

- a Sony TVR-900E digital camera
- a Leica slide projector

Fig. 3 illustrates the ShapeCam: a digital camera and a specially designed flash device are mounted on a lightweight frame. The flash device projects a predefined grid or pattern onto an object or a scene which is viewed by a camera from a (slightly) different point of view. The camera also grabs the texture information which can be mapped on the resulting 3D geometry of the object.

Camera   **Slide projector**

Fig. 3. Eyetronic's ShapeCam

The ShapeCam technology is a commercially available technique improved in the EU project MURALE [11] that allows the generation of 3D models based on the use of a single image taken by an ordinary camera.

As this system is a handheld device, the shapes can be recorded in situ. We carried out on site tests to capture 3D pot sherds and other finds from excavation sites. The ShapeCam hardware has been adapted to facilitate such work.

3   Results and Accuracy

In order to demonstrate the output of the presented acquisition systems, examples for each method are given below. Acquisition speed and accuracy of each system are compared to each other at the end of this section. The range accuracy describes the measurement uncertainty along the depth axis, i.e. Z axis. It is estimated by comparing measurements of known objects with measurements of the recorded object: the average deviation along the Z axis gives the range accuracy.

Two lasers

In order to show the applicability of the approach two examples are given (Fig. 4 and Fig. 5) Each figure contains the data acquired (a), the thinned profile and final presentation of the profile section (c). In order to visually compare the computer aided results with the manual results, a manual drawing of the same fragment is given (d).

The results achieved visually correspond to the manual drawing of the fragment, showing the feasibility of the approach. Since the images are combined and orientated manually, the precision of the final profile section depends on the resolution of the camera and on the experience of the user, consequently the results are not objective. The profile is acquired in real time, because acquisition takes only the time necessary to grab an image. Experiments have shown that the actual speed for the acquisition of a profile section by an experienced archaeologist lies between 10 and 30 seconds, because time is spent for the manual orientation of the fragment.

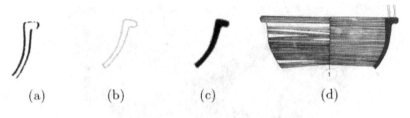

Fig. 4. Profile acquisition of fragment 70-1

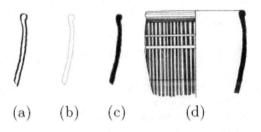

Fig. 5. Profile acquisition of fragment 78-2

LCD projector

Applying the non portable acquisition system, two views of 40 fragments have been recorded. The data was mainly used for testing the classification tasks, because these fragments have been available in the laboratory, which has simplified the evaluation of the automatic classification. See Fig. 6 for two resulting range images of one fragment. The front view contains 37176 points and the back view contains 31298 points.

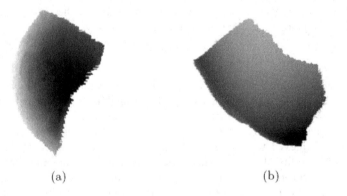

Fig. 6. Range Image of two views of a fragment, (a) front view (b)

Range accuracy is specified between 0.68mm to 1mm. Most of the acquisition time (5sec; +/- 0.5sec) is needed for the projection of the light patterns. Total acquisition time is around 5.5 sec (+/- 5 sec) on a Pentium 233MMX with 256 MB RAM using non-optimized code.

Minolta VIVID 900

Using the VIVID 900 we have recorded 2 to 15 views of 500 archaeological frag-ments. The number of data points ranges from 3.000 to 150.000 points. Fig. 7 shows a decorated fragment with 17781 points and 33981 triangles. The acquisition time de-pends on the number of range points (size of the object), for 150.000 points it is ap-proximately 1.5 sec. The achieved range accuracy lies between 0.2mm and 0.7mm.

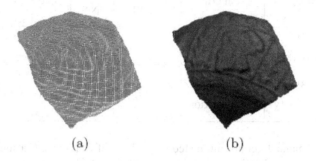

(a)   (b)

Fig. 7. (a) Wireframe representation and (b) textured representation of a fragment

ShapeCam Technology

Using the ShapeCam Technology we have recorded 2 to 7 views of 70 fragments. These fragments served as test material for assembling a complete vessel, because some of them came from one and the same object. Knowing that fragments belong together simplify the evaluation of the assembly. The range accuracy lies between 0.7mm to 1mm which matches the specification of the manufacturer. The acquisition time depends on the number of range points (size of the object), for 30.000 points it is approximately 2sec.

Comparison of the systems

In order to compare the acquisition systems presented in Table 1 summarizes the results. For each technique the type of the computed results, the underlying measuring method, the precision in terms of range accuracy, portability and acquisition speed is given. The result of the two laser method is a 2D plot of the profile line, consequently no range accuracy is given. The most accurate and fastest system is the VIVID 900, but it is also the most expensive one which makes it difficult to use at archaeological excavations. The advantage of the ShapeCam is its portability, efficiency in model size and flexibility in applications. The use of LCD projector which is not a portable system allows full automation from the acquisition until the reconstruction.

Field trips

In 2004 we joined the TELDOR Excavation [12] together with the Department of Physics from the Weizmann Institute of Science. The goal was to do a systematic

Table 1. Comparison of the acquisition devices used

Device	Output	Measuring Scanner	Precision [mm]	Port- able	Speed	Cost
Two **Laser**	2D Profile Line	Laser Scanner	-	No	Real time	Prototype
LCD	Range Image	Pattern projection	0.6 - 1	No	50.000 pts in 5.5 sec	10.000 EUR
Shape **-Cam**	3D Geometry	Pattern projection	0.7 – 1	Yes	30.000 pts in 2 sec	20.000 EUR
Vivid- **900**	3D Geometry	Laser Triangulation	0.2 – 0.7	Yes	150.000 pts in 1.5sec	50.000 EUR

comparison of manual versus automated acquisition of Ceramics. For the comparison of accuracy between hand drawings, profilograph and 3D scanner, we scanned 35 different sherds which were selected by archaeologists. Archaeologists selected these sherds among daily finds with the criteria that their size is small and their curvature is low, so that the axis of rotation is also difficult to find by manual orientation. The expected failure rate for all methods was high because the sherds contained flat and/or small pieces and pieces with handles.

For the performance evaluation we set up the 3D scanner, such that we could scan sherds from small 4x3cm to large size 27x20cm. In order to increase the number of sherds per scan we placed small and medium sized sherds into a frame. We could than scan up to 6 sherds per scan, which resulted in a rate of 40 sherds per hour. For a detailed description of the results see [13].

The Commission for Archaeology of Non-European Cultures (KAAK) of the German Archaeological Institute (DAI), in Bonn is conducting an investigation project about the pre-hispanic occupation of the Palpa Valley, Peru. During the field-trip in 2005 we brought our 3D-Scanner to Palpa. Aim of this cooperation was to test the possibilities for documentation of freehand manufactured ceramics by using a 3D-Scanner.

For our experiments we acquired 38 sherds and 102 complete vessels found in the area. The sherds were used to test the estimation of the axis of rotation using a circular template matching [14] on NASCA sherds, because this kind of ceramic is not supposed to be manufactured on rotational plates, but they appear to be rotational symmetric. The results described in [14] show that Nasca ceramic has not been manufactured on rotational plates.

5 Summary

In this paper a selection of acquisition devices which meet the requirements of pottery acquisition has been described. The setup of each acquisition system and its technical principles were shown. Results of the methods described show the accuracy and applicability of the selected approaches.

References

1. J.A. Beraldin, C. Atzeni C., G. Guidi, M. Pieraccini, and S. Lazzari S. Establishing a Digital 3d Imaging Laboratory for Heritage Applications: First Trials. In Proceedings of the Italy-Canada 2001 Workshop on 3D Digital Imaging and Modeling Applications, Padova, 2001. on CD-ROM.
2. P.J. Besl. Active, optical range imaging sensors. Machine Vision and Applications, 1(2):127–152, 1988.
3. F. Blais. A Review of 20 Years of Range Sensor Development. In SPIE Proceedings, Electronic Imaging, volume 5013, pages 62–76, 2003.
4. S. F. El-Hakim, J. A. Beraldin, and M. Picard. Detailed 3D Reconstruction of Monuments using multiple Techniques. In W. Boehler, editor, Proceedings of ISPRSCIPA Workshop on Scanning for Cultural Heritage Recording, pages 13–18, Corfu, 2002.
5. M. Kampel. 3D Mosaicing of Fractured Surfaces. PhD thesis, Vienna University of Technology, 2003.
6. M. Kampel, H. Mara, and R. Sablatnig. Investigation on traditional and modern ceramic documentation. In Vernazza G. and Sicuranza G., editors, Proc. Of ICIP05: Intl. Conf. on Image Processing, volume 2, pages 570–573, Genova, Italy, September 2005.
7. M. Kampel and R. Sablatnig. Color Classification of Archaeological Fragments. In A. Sanfeliu, J.J. Villanueva, M. Vanrell, R. Alquezar, A.K. Jain, and J. Kittler, editors, Proc. of 15th International Conference on Pattern Recognition, Barcelona, volume 4, pages 771–774. IEEE Computer Society, 2000.
8. M. Kampel, R. Sablatnig, and S. Tosovic. Volume based reconstruction of archaeological artifacts. In W. Boehler, editor, Proc. of Intl. Workshop on Scanning for Cultural Heritage Recording, pages 76–83, 2002.
9. R. Klette, A. Koschan, and K. Schl¨uns. Computer Vision - Räumliche Information aus digitalen Bildern. Vieweg, 1996.
10. C. Orton, P. Tyers, and A. Vince. Pottery in archaeology. Cambridge University Press, Cambridge, 1993.N. Nescio, Instructions for the Preparation of a Camera-Ready Manuscript. IOS Press, Amsterdam, 1991.
11. A. Gilboa, A. Karasik, I. Sharon, and U. Smilansky. Towards computerized typology and classification of ceramics. Journal of Archaeological Science, 31:681–694, 2004.
12. M. Kampel, H. Mara, R, Sablatnig, "Investigation on Traditional and Modern Ceramic Documentation", in G. Vernazza, and G. Sicuranza (Eds.), ICIP05: Intl. Conf. on Image Processing, Genova, Italy, pp. 570-573, Sept 2005.
13. H. Mara, R. Sablatnig, 3D-Vision Applied in Archaeology, Forum Archaeologiae 34/III/2005 (http://farch.net).

Participation as a Model
the Canadian Heritage Information Network

Kati Geber

Canadian Heritage Information Network
www.chin.gc.ca

Abstract. The presentation at VSMM'06 will consider concepts related to the participatory culture that is developing throughout the Internet. It will also look at some of the ways in which CHIN has been taking up participatory applications to further the goals of its 1200 member institutions and respond to public expectations. With online projects such as the Virtual Museum of Canada (VMC), Community Memories, Agora and the Knowledge Exchange come new challenges that question established business models, learning patterns, the public sphere and collective memory.

Keywords: digital cultural content, participation, collaboration, education, museum, virtual exhibit, audiences and change.

1 Introduction

As with all sectors of society, memory institutions are increasingly turning to new technologies to engage their audiences in conversations about heritage. While the transition to digital holds out the promise of innovative relationships with audiences and a range of new cultural and social interaction models, we should nevertheless be aware that the creation of a cultural digital environment imposes significant challenges on memory institutions.

These challenges become obvious when we focus on two of the main aspects of a digital environment: the increased participation of institutions and citizens in the communication process, and the trustworthiness of the communicated messages.

The impact of these two aspects is before anything else a socio-cultural one. We are witnessing the emergence of a participatory culture, which is both decentralized and collaborative.

2 Presentation at the 12th International Conference on Virtual Systems and Multimedia, Xi'an, China

The presentation will include (i) <u>an overview</u> of some of CHIN's participatory, interactive, multimedia, Internet products and services:

The *Virtual Museum of Canada* engages audiences of all ages in Canada's diverse heritage through a dynamic Internet service freely available to the public in French and English.

H. Zha et al. (Eds.): VSMM 2006, LNCS 4270, pp. 396–398, 2006.

Fig. 1. VMC Participatory Map

Fig. 2. VMC Exhibits (www.virtualmuseum.ca)

Community Memories is an aggregation of multimedia objects and local history online exhibits drawing from the collections of museums and reminiscences of individuals from those communities.

Fig. 3. Community Memories

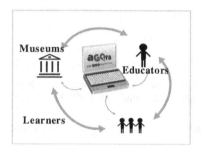

Fig. 4. Agora

Agora connects teachers, students and museum educators through an interactive online environment that offers a compilation of customizable learning resources.

Knowledge Exchange is an online space in which museum professionals and volunteers can learn, collaborate and share, thereby promoting community engagement through the use of relevant technologies.

(ii) <u>Research and experimentation</u> exploring the explicit public value and social impact of participation, diversity, decentralization with aggregation and audience engagement.

A discussion on the (iii) <u>role of cultural heritage institutions</u> within the emerging participatory culture, and their central role in supporting learning.

(iv) <u>The Digital Cultural Content Forum</u> (dCCF) - an international partnership dedicated to the promotion of digital library and museum content for education and learning. The DCCF is supported by the Institute of Museum and Library Studies (US), CHIN (Canada) and the Museums and Libraries and Archives Council (UK).

3 The Canadian Heritage Information Network (CHIN)

Réseau canadien d'information sur le patrimoine
Canadian Heritage Information Network

Fig. 5. CHIN

The Canadian Heritage Information Network (CHIN) is an agency of the Department of Canadian Heritage. It supports an active network of over 1,200 not-for-profit member heritage institutions across Canada, serving as a national centre of excellence that provides a visible face to Canada's heritage through the world of networked information. CHIN's vision is to connect Canadians and worldwide audiences to Canada's heritage by promoting the development, presentation and preservation of Canada's digital heritage content for current and future generations of Canadians.

To reach these goals, CHIN is focusing on:

Enhancing the skills of member museums by leveraging emerging technologies to develop convenient, participatory, personalized, and interactive online services;

Furthering the use of heritage content in education by enabling virtual learning environments, supported by a compelling repository of Canadian museums content;

Increasing public interest and participation by analyzing audiences to better target needs, and implementing effective communication strategies;

A collaborative research program designed to advance our collective understanding of issues associated with new technologies and digital content, particularly in the areas of social impact, intellectual property and online audiences.

References

1. What Is Web 2.0 - Design Patterns and Business Models for the Next Generation of Software, by Tim O'Reilly, http://www.oreillynet.com/pub/a/oreilly/tim/news/2005/09/30/what-is-web-20.html, accessed: August, 1, 2006
2. The Economics of Open Content, http://www.intelligenttelevision.com/opencontent.htm, accessed August 1, 2006
3. About CHIN, http://www.chin.gc.ca/English/About_Chin/overview.html, accessed: August 1, 2006
4. Beyond Productivity: Culture and Heritage Resources in the Digital Age, http://www.chin.gc.ca/English/Digital_Content/Dccf_Workshop/index.html, accessed: August 1, 2006
5. Content Scope Evaluation: Determining Audience Interest in Virtual Exhibits, http://www.chin.gc.ca/English/Digital_Content/Content_Scope/evaluation.html, accessed August 1, 2006
6. Web 2.00 - blogs, Flckrs and folksonomies - can a museum really hand it all over? Susan Hazan, Collecting, Connecting and Conserving? Salzburg, 21-22 June 200

3D Digital Archive of the Burghers of Calais

Daisuke Miyazaki[1], Mawo Kamakura[1], Tomoaki Higo[1], Yasuhide Okamoto[1],
Rei Kawakami[1], Takaaki Shiratori[1], Akifumi Ikari[1], Shintaro Ono[1], Yoshihiro Sato[1],
Mina Oya[2], Masayuki Tanaka[2], Katsushi Ikeuchi[1], and Masanori Aoyagi[2]

[1] The University of Tokyo, 4-6-1 Komaba, Meguro-ku, Tokyo 153-8505, Japan
{miyazaki, mawo, higo, okamoto, rei, siratori, ika, onoshin,
yoshi, ki}@cvl.iis.u-tokyo.ac.jp
http://www.cvl.iis.u-tokyo.ac.jp/
[2] National Museum of Western Art, 7-7 Ueno-koen, Taito-ku, Tokyo 110-0007, Japan
{oya, tanaka}@nmwa.go.jp, msnryg@attglobal.net
http://www.nmwa.go.jp/

Abstract. Auguste Rodin is the most celebrated sculptor of the 19th century. His works, such as The Gates of Hell, The Thinker, and The Burghers of Calais, are famous worldwide. To our knowledge, no art historians have analyzed three-dimensional data of Rodin's work. This paper describes our project to fill this need by digitally archiving the bronze statue, The Burghers of Calais. First, we scanned the geometrical shape of the sculpture by using a laser range sensor. After that, we analyzed the resulting three-dimensional data using expert knowledge in the field of art history and technology developed in the fields of computer vision and graphics.

Fig. 1. Rodin's three bronze statues in National Museum of Western Art, Tokyo, Japan: (a) The Gates of Hell, (b) The Thinker, (c) The Burghers of Calais

1 Introduction

Historical buildings and cultural assets are subject to the risks of being damaged, destroyed, or ruined by weathering, natural disasters, or man-made disasters. Therefore, it is important to digitally archive these properties [1]. Among archiving methods, three-dimensional (3D) digital archiving [2] is notable for its use of cutting-edge technology. Specifically, 3D digital archiving has significance in the area of information science in two fields: archaeology and information technology.

From the viewpoint of archaeology, permanently preserving the current state of existing cultural assets as digital data is an important subject. Analyzing 3D digital data

H. Zha et al. (Eds.): VSMM 2006, LNCS 4270, pp. 399–407, 2006.
© Springer-Verlag Berlin Heidelberg 2006

by computers provides new aspects for research in archaeology and art history. Moreover, there is a societal advantage: any number of people can examine computer-generated images of these cultural assets, seeing different colors and more viewpoints than are possible to observe in the real world.

From the viewpoint of information science, digitally archiving cultural assets provides a strong motivation to promote the development of information technology, since the preservation of cultural assets is important both nationally and worldwide. The technology of measurement is also promoted by this subject since obtaining archive data requires special sensors that capture the complex shapes and colors of cultural assets. Also, developing software to process or show the immense amount of data typical of large-sized cultural assets provides a frontier that must be crossed by new and creative methods.

To what fields should we apply these new methods? Until now, many sites, architectures, and statues have been three-dimensionally archived. Previous works have been largely directed to rock- and stone-like objects, but we believe that these methods might be successfully applied to bronze statues. To test this theory, we have attempted to capture 3D data for certain sculptures created by the most famous sculptor of the 19th century, François-Auguste-René Rodin [3].

Rodin's best-known works include The Gates of Hell, The Thinker, and The Burghers of Calais (Fig. 1). Among these, The Burghers of Calais (subsequently referred to as The Burghers) is a sculpture commissioned by the city of Calais, France. The work is based on the historical fact that six citizens of Calais volunteered to sacrifice their lives to England's Edward III in 1347 to save the lives of their fellow citizens. The city wanted the statue placed on a lofty pedestal, showing high-blown fortitude and courage. Instead, Rodin placed the group near ground level, where they were more accessible to viewers, and showed the men exhibiting the sullen, worn, and even fearful expressions of bare human emotion. Rodin first made plaster casts of the figures, and from these plaster casts bronze statues were made. Among Japanese public organizations, the National Museum of Western Art owns The Burghers as a group of bronze sculptures, and eleven more works exist in other place in the world. It is usual to create multiple bronze statues from same cast; however, The Burghers is unusual in that the same cast was used in two different parts in The Burghers, even though those parts are of different people.

We obtained a 3D digital model of the approximately 2-m tall The Burghers in the National Museum of Western Art using a 3D digital archiving technique. We generated an image from an upper view which is difficult to achieve for a real statue, generated an image of a plaster figure which Rodin first made, and compared the similarity of two parts from the statue which are believed to be made from same cast. This paper is therefore organized as follows: In Section 2, we present our procedure to create a 3D model. In Section 3, some analyses and discussions of this work from the standpoint of art history are presented. In Section 4, we discuss the Museum displays of our images generated from the 3D model, and the reactions of museum visitors. In Section 5, we conclude that art historians are correct: certain casts were indeed reused within the group.

2 3D Digital Archive

3D digital archiving is achieved by a laser range sensor, which measures the surface shape of the object in high precision (Fig. 2) [4]. The process to obtain the shape of the object can be divided into three steps: scanning, alignment, and merging. We will explain these three steps in this section.

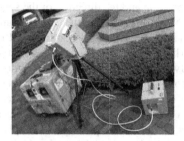

Fig. 2. Laser range sensor

2.1 Measurement (Scanning)

The field of view of the laser range sensor is limited; thus, the sensor only obtains a partial shape of the object during each scan. To generate a 3D model of the object, we need to measure the partial 3D data many times from different positions and directions (Fig. 3) and correlate the data.

Fig. 3. Obtained data

Fig. 4. Scanning from different position: (a) From ground, (b) from car, (c) from scaffold, (d) from roof

The Burghers is kept outdoors; it is outside the National Museum of Western Art. We scanned the statue from ground level, from a parked car, from a scaffold, and from the roof of the museum building (Fig. 4).

2.2 Registration (Alignment)

Each of the partial 3D models obtained by a laser range sensor has different coordinate systems depending on the position and the direction of the sensor. Therefore, we have to align these partial models in order to represent the data in a unified coordinate system.

Iterative Closest Point (ICP) algorithm [5] is often used for estimating the relative position between two overlapped models. This method first search for a pair of corresponding points between two models, and then estimate the relative position between two models such that the total squared distance for all pairs of corresponding points is minimized. The solution is obtained when this iterative process converges.

If we sequentially align each pair of partial models, the models do not align well due to accumulation errors. To avoid this problem, we apply a method which simultaneously estimates the relative position for all partial models (Fig. 5) [6].

Fig. 5. Aligned data

2.3 Integration (Merging)

Aligned data have overlapping regions; thus, we have to merge all partial models into one integrated model.

One of the merging algorithms is the Volumetric method [7,8]. It first projects all partial models into a voxel space, and then extracts the surface model from the voxel space where the signed distance field becomes zero. The extracted volumetric data are then converted into mesh data by using the Marching Cubes method [9]. In our work, we used Sagawa's method, which is based on the Volumetric method, for merging the data (Fig. 6) [10].

Fig. 6. Merged data

3 Analyses from the Aspect of Art History

3D digital model obtained from laser range sensor has many advantages such as the fact that we can inspect the object from arbitrary viewpoints, we can change the surface material virtually, and we can produce images with different illuminations. In this section, we analyze and represent the 3D digital data from the aspect of art history.

3.1 Arbitrary Viewpoint

Since we have the whole shape as a digital data set, we can choose arbitrary viewpoints. It is said that Rodin struggled to find the best position in which to settle the statue; that he considered carefully how it looked when seen by viewers. By changing the viewpoint of the 3D digital model, we can look at the statue not only horizontally, but also from the bottom or the top (Fig. 7).

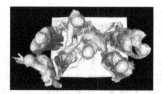

Fig. 7. Rendered image of an upper view

3.2 Rearrangement

Editing the shape of the 3D digital model is undoubtedly easier than changing the shape of a real object. Rodin tried to express the movement of the human body in static statues by this group of sculptures and its arrangement of six heroes. Figure 8 demonstrates the image of the six people rearranged into a line, by cutting each statue away from the others. The figure clearly shows their individual facial expressions and the inclinations of their bodies, which can be difficult to recognize when seeing them as a group.

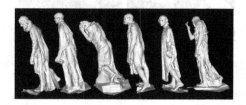

Fig. 8. Rendered image of lining up the group's six individuals

3.3 Candle Light

It is easy to change the illumination and generate synthetic shadowing when a 3D digital model is available. Like all of Rodin's work, the bronze statue of The Burghers is widely exhibited and compared with its plaster model. However, Rodin preferred to look at his white plaster model when it was lit by candlelight. Figure 9 is an image of the white plaster model lit by candlelight, which is reproduced from 3D digital model.

Fig. 9. Rendered image of white plaster figures lit by candlelight

3.4 Different Environment

It is easy to create an image in different synthetic environments using a 3D digital model. The Burghers are located in different parts of the world, and people can find them in many situations. We can reproduce these situations with computer graphics. Figure 10 shows some images of the bronze sculptures reproduced from the 3D digital model under different illumination distributions. The reflection property of the bronze material to render these images is set manually. Illumination distribution data are obtained from a web site [11]. We can see how The Burghers look if they are situated in a different place.

Fig. 10. Rendered images of bronze sculptures under different environments: (a) Funston Beach at Sunset, (b) Galileo's Tomb, Santa Croce, Florence, (c) Kitchen at 2213 Vine St, (d) Grace Cathedral, San Francisco

3.5 Same Motif

It is said that Rodin created many kinds of casts of human parts such as heads and hands, and created many works by combining these parts. Art historians say that two hands of different persons in The Burghers are produced by the same cast. To verify this historical fact, first we cut out two hands which are said to be made from the same cast, and then we aligned these two shapes by using our alignment algorithm. We obtained convincing evidence that these two hands were created from same cast (Fig. 11).

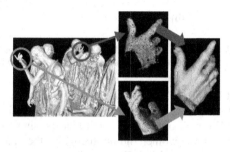

Fig. 11. The result of aligning the two hands created from same cast

4 Demonstrations Using Mobile Computer

From April 29th, 2006 to May 7th, 2006, we demonstrated our computer graphic animations to people who visited the National Museum of Western Art. An audio guide is often used in museums to help people understand the exhibits more deeply; we went one step further and provided a video guide. This video guide, which included our computer animations, was produced by the Japan Broadcasting Corporation [12]. It ran on a mobile computer developed by the YRP Ubiquitous Networking Laboratory (head manager: Prof. Ken Sakamura of The University of Tokyo) [13].

4.1 Opinions from Visitors

After each demonstration, we asked each visitor to complete a questionnaire. Fig. 12 is the answer to their overall satisfaction with our computer graphic animations. 44% of the visitors expressed a favorable answer while only 13% expressed an unsatisfied feeling.

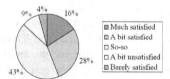

Fig. 12. The answer to the question, "Were you satisfied with the computer graphic animation?"

We demonstrated the animations of the candlelight scene (Fig. 9), the upper view scene (Fig. 7), and the lining-up scene (Fig. 8). We asked visitors whether or not they felt that the animations were realistic, and also whether they were interesting. The answer is shown in Fig. 13. Some people did not recognize the candlelight scene as being computer graphics, possibly due to the illumination effects of candlelight. We believe that if we do not add any illumination effects to our computer graphics, we cannot achieve realism.

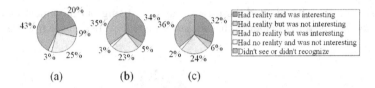

Fig. 13. The answer to the question, "Were you satisfied with the computer graphic animations of (a) the candlelight scene, (b) the upper view scene, and (c) the lining up scene?"

Fig. 14 shows that there is a gender difference between men and women in these responses. The question is that of Fig. 12, "Were you satisfied with the computer graphic animations?" Women, interestingly, felt that the simulations were more realistic than did men. Also, some women did not recognize the video as computer graphics due to its high degree of realism. We speculate that women tend to accept new ideas, and quickly accept the look and feel of our computer graphics as being reality. We further speculate that, on the other hand, because men are well-acquainted with computer graphics through movies or video games -- more so than women -- they only perceive realism when computer graphics are of very high quality.

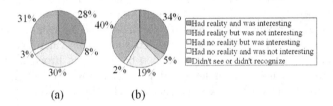

Fig. 14. The answer to the question, "Were you satisfied with the computer graphic animations?", from (a) men and (b) women

5 Conclusions

We have created a 3D digital model of a bronze statue, The Burghers of Calais, sculpted by the most famous sculptor of the 19th century, Auguste Rodin, who is also famous for his works, The Gates of Hell and The Thinker. First, we scanned the sculpture by laser range sensor from different positions and directions; then, we aligned all our valid datasets of vertices and merged these datasets into a 3D digital model. After that, we created computer graphic animations and demonstrated these animations using a mobile computer to the visitors of the Museum. Our animations produced many favourable visitor impressions.

We also presented a result of the comparison between the hands of two different figures in The Burghers. From this result, we concluded that these two hands were indeed made from the same cast, thus proving assertions previously made by art historians.

All these analyses could not have been carried out unless a 3D digital model had been developed. This work therefore yielded especially valuable information because of collaboration between computer scientists and art historians.

Acknowledgements

Our development of a 3D digital archiving technique was supported in part by the Ministry of Education, Culture, Sports, Science and Technology under the Leading Project: Development of High Fidelity Digitization Software for Large-Scale and Intangible Cultural Assets. 3D measurement of The Burghers of Calais was performed as a part of the Wel.com Museum Project [14]. The Wel.com Museum Project was conducted by the National Museum of Western Art and its director Masanori Aoyagi, as well as Prof. Ken Sakamura of The University of Tokyo, Prof. Katsushi Ikeuchi of The University of Tokyo, Nissha Printing Co., Ltd., YRP Ubiquitous Networking Laboratory, and NHK Educational Corporation. The authors thank Kyoko Kuramori and Kenji Yokoo of Japan Broadcasting Corporation, and Hisato Arai of the National Museum of Western Art for their great help. The authors thank Joan Knapp and Robert Knapp for proofreading and editing this manuscript.

References

1. UNESCO Archives Portal, http://www.unesco.org/webworld/portal_archives/
2. K. Ikeuchi and Y. Sato, Modeling from Reality, Kluwer Academic, Boston, 2001.
3. Musée Rodin, The Complete Guide to Rodin, Tankosha, Kyoto, Japan, 2005. (in Japanese)
4. Cyrax 2500, http://www.leica-geosystems.com/
5. P. Besl and N. McKay, "A Method for Registration of 3-D Shapes," IEEE Trans. On Pattern Analysis and Machine Intelligence, 14(2), 239-256, 1992.
6. T. Oishi, A. Nakazawa, R. Kurazume, and K. Ikeuchi, "Fast Simultaneous Alignment of Multiple Range Images using Index Images," Proc. Int'l Conf. on 3-D Digital Imaging and Modeling, 476-483, 2005.
7. B. Curless and M. Levoy, "A Volumetric Method for Building Complex Models from Range Images," Proc. SIGGRAPH, 303-312, 1996.
8. M. Wheeler, Y. Sato, and K. Ikeuchi, "Consensus surfaces for modelling 3D objects from multiple range images," Proc. Int'l Conf. on Computer Vision, 917-924, 1998.
9. W. Lorensen and H. Cline, "Marching cubes: a high resolution 3d surface construction algorithm," Proc. SIGGRAPH, 163-170, 1987.
10. R. Sagawa, K. Nishino, and K. Ikeuchi, "Adaptively Merging Large-Scale Range Data with Reflectance Properties," IEEE Trans. on Pattern Analysis and Machine Intelligence, 27(3), 392-405, 2005.
11. Light Probe Image Gallery, http://www.debevec.org/Probes/
12. Japan Broadcasting Corporation, http://www.nhk.or.jp/
13. YRP Ubiquitous Networking Laboratory, http://www.ubin.jp/
14. Wel.com Museum Project, http://www.nmwa.go.jp/jp/files/wel.pdf (in Japanese)

The EPOCH Multimodal Interface
for Interacting with Digital Heritage Artefacts

Panagiotis Petridis[1], Daniel Pletinckx[2], Katerina Mania[1], and Martin White[1]

[1] Department of Information Technology, University of Sussex, United Kingdom
{p.petridis, k.mania, m.white}@sussex.ac.uk
[2] Visual Dimension bvba, Lijnwaadmarkt 47, B-9700 Ename, Belgium
daniel.pletinckx@visualdimension.be

Abstract. In recent years, 3D and virtual reality have emerged as areas of extreme interest as methods for visualizing digital museum artefacts in context, and particularly over the Internet. The technology associated with these new visualization techniques has until now been very expensive. The advent of cheap computing and graphics cards coupled with increasing Internet 'broadband' access has made possible the implementation of effective virtual museums both online and within the museum. Virtual museums are valuable for the end-user for efficient and remote learning about their local heritage in a diverse multimodal manner. Multimodal access to museum artefacts can help the user to better understand and appreciate the objects and stories that the museum brings forward, but also creates a closer psychological bond between the user and his past. If we now couple cheap computing technologies, 3D and virtual reality with appropriate 3D interaction techniques based on formal usability evaluations, museums are able to implement high fidelity exhibitions that are intuitive for the museum visitor. This paper reports on the latest technological additions to the EPOCH Multimodal Interface, which is used as an interaction interface that can be implemented as part of a virtual museum interactive system.

1 Introduction

Museums small or large play a unique role in preserving our heritage and exhibiting that heritage in the traditional way, i.e. through exhibitions within the museum. Depending on the type of museum, e.g. the Natural Science Museum in the UK, and the like, interactive exhibitions loosely engineered into so called 'kiosk' based systems are quite popular.

However, innovative multimodal visualisation technology is now starting to make an appearance, that of virtual and augmented reality [16, 18, 22, 30]. Integrating 3D content, for example, into a museum's website has been shown to enhance the experience of learning acquired by a visitor's interaction with an online exhibition, either within the museum or on the Internet. Further, virtual reality interfaces offer curators new technological tools for preservation and access. The curator could utilize these tools to extend their already existing digital preservation techniques by adding digital 3D models of artefacts to their digital archives, and then repurpose these digital surrogates for presentation in visualisation systems (perhaps built into kiosks) that also allow access online by the citizen.

H. Zha et al. (Eds.): VSMM 2006, LNCS 4270, pp. 408–417, 2006.

Museum artefacts can now be digitised accurately, using laser, photogrammetry and cheap software, and thus create photorealistic 3D models for display online. Innovative interaction systems can be designed that expand on the traditional museum approach of displaying an artefact in a glass case with the curators' viewpoint on a simple card. In short, we can liberate the physical artefact in the form of a digital surrogate and interact with it through physical touch and tactile handling [22]. Of particular interest for a museum is the ability to create interaction systems composed of replicas of a museum's physical artefact linked to a 3D model (digital surrogate) of that artefact organised to deliver a contextual heritage view on the artefact.

One can imagine such a system in a museum whereby the actual artefact as before is displayed in its glass case, perhaps by a wall, and a large display is situated next to the glass case. Further, a robust physical replica of the artefact is linked to the display, which presents a virtual environment containing a 3D model of the artefact. The museum visitor can then explore the artefact simply by picking up the replica and observing that, as they turn the replica, the 3D model turns in unison. Thus, the visitor will obtain tactile information that is traditionally impossible, and by selecting attached sensors on the replica they can also explore a 3D world that digitally narrates the story of the artefact on the display. This paper reports on the latest technological developments of such a system and investigates key issues in virtual heritage environments that serve to drive such implementation systems.

2 Background

There are several key issues which should be considered when designing museum interactive systems:

1. Museum interactive systems should be as cost effective as possible given the limited funds available to the average museum.
2. 3D content should be created as cheaply as possible in addition to digitisation of supporting data.
3. Consideration should be given to the costs of maintaining the museum interactive systems because this implies new skills that need to be acquired by the museums, etc. The museum may in effect be converting itself from a learning institute to a so called hybrid institution [5, 24] where the institution exhibits not only analogue (i.e. the physical artefact), but also the digital surrogate or resources. In this context, it is important that authoring tools contain all tools necessary for proper digital curation.
4. Appropriate interaction techniques should be devised to augment the digital resource so as to effectively engage the user. In order to identify suitable interaction techniques for the end-user but also the curator, formal usability evaluation studies are necessary. Relevant skills are, therefore, needed.
5. Museum hardware and software should be repurposed in order to create innovative museum interactive systems cost effectively. This is achieved by accommodating generic hardware such as PC systems with appropriate museum based management and visualisation software such as that demonstrated by the ARCO system [11, 12, 18, 30] and EPOCH multimodal interface [16, 19, 21, 22].

6. Any museum interactive system should present the information as a story that reinforces the heritage behind the artefact that is on display targeted at different users and age groups. Using the new opportunities that digital storytelling [33] offers requires to extend the skill set of museum curators and their staff.
7. Perceived 'presence' [27] is shown to be enhanced when modalities such as sound and 3D content are added in a museum interactive system in order for the visitor to feel part of the virtual exhibition.

The museum community has now recognized the benefits of virtual museums towards efficient learning about their local heritage. Off-the-shelf technologies allow cheaper digitisation of collections, however cost does vary with complexity; digitising software for capturing internet quality 3D can cost as little as a few hundred dollars.

One of the limitations in the development of virtual museums by traditional establishments is the need for 3D content, which has been up to now expensive because 3D modelling is a time consuming and complex process. However, cheap software for 3D modelling allows even the smallest museum to create virtual artefacts using simple photography skills [24]. EPOCH partners are developing highly qualitative but efficient and cheap workflows for 3D digitalisation of museum objects in the 3DKIOSK activity [34]. These models can easily be exported as VRML/X3D models and incorporated into a virtual environment designed to offer interactive virtual content that provides a valuable experience for remote users [15] in addition to seeing an artefact in a museum glass case with a simple description on a card. Implemented virtual museums including a thorough collection of 3D content has transformed the so called learning institutions (e.g. museums, libraries, online catalogues, etc.) into "hybrid institutions" that accommodate both analogue and digital resources [18, 25, 30].

Interaction techniques and devices employing novel virtual reality interfaces are currently developing at a rapid pace [2]. Interaction technologies such as the space mouse, game pad controller, motion and orientation trackers, etc. are now available that can be integrated into multi-modal virtual and augmented reality interactive interfaces. Innovative 3D interaction techniques can now be developed and coupled to the virtual museums cost effectively. Such a virtual museum could be created in the form of a museum kiosk. An example museum interactive kiosk could consist of a simple but powerful PC desktop system rather than a bespoke and expensive kiosk that only has one use. A major advantage of this approach is that standard PCs with cheap interfaces can be re-purposed for new virtual exhibitions simply by replacing repository content, and display method [11, 12, 17, 18, 30].

3D content and virtual interfaces in virtual exhibitions do not just present virtual objects and descriptions; such content should be set in a story that reinforces the visitors learning and understanding of the cultural context in place. Therefore, one of the goals of museum interactive systems is to communicate and enhance the feeling of 'presence' related to a past era. Presence in virtual reality world (or virtual environment) can be explained as the participant's sense of 'being there'; the degree to which the users feel that they are somewhere other than they physically are, while experiencing a computer generated simulation [31]. It has been shown that both visual and tactical senses enhance perceived 'presence' while exposed to a virtual environment [29]. Thus, it is worthwhile investigating whether any multimodal interface enhances perceived presence in comparison to traditional interfaces. Formal usability evaluation studies have been recently conducted to investigate this issue [22]. Studies on the impact aspects of multimodal interfaces need to be carried out, to investigate if improved presence and access to the object changes the visitor engagement and appraisal of that piece of heritage and creates personal involvement in the sense of "this is my heritage".

The incorporation of new technologies in museums signifies challenging research opportunities having as main goal to provide novel ways to present regional or national heritage, as well as offering new consultation methods for archaeological or cultural sites and museums [4]. Our previous work has focused on systems for building virtual museums while our current work and the focus of this paper is on developing interaction systems and appropriate input devices.

3 Interaction Devices

In this paper, we are focusing on multimodal interaction with a digital surrogate of a museum artefact. We are particularly concerned in how effective 3D manipulation using the artefact as an input device is in comparison with lower fidelity interaction devices such as a simple mouse or keyboard [1, 3, 6, 8, 9, 16]. User interfaces for computer applications are becoming more diverse, e.g. 2D interaction devices such as mice, keyboards, windows, menus and icons are still prevalent but non traditional devices and interfaces can now be created rapidly and cost effectively. These include spatial input devices using motion and orientation trackers, 3D pointing devices, whole hand devices and three dimensional multi-sensor output technologies such as stereoscopic projection displays, head mounted displays, spatial audio systems, and haptic devices [3].

The method of interacting with typical 2D devices is common place; however interacting with 3D devices needs more consideration of the tasks involved. Interaction tasks according to Wuthrich [32] can be broken down into three elementary actions: selection/grabbing, positioning with N degrees of freedom and deforming [1]. Research carried out by Subramanian [28] has shown that an increase in the number of available DOF (degrees of freedom) in an interaction device can improve performance. By exploiting the interface requirements of specific tasks, the complexity of the 3D interface could be ultimately reduced, however, diverse application needs can also be identified [7]. For example, adding modalities such as sound, text or tactile feedback could enhance relevant visualization metaphors.

Our multimodal interface allows tactile feedback, sound, text and any manner of multimedia feedback to occur. Multimodal input systems process two or more combined user input modes in a coordinated manner with the multimedia system [20]. Our method matches the shape and appearance of the virtual object with the shape and appearance of the physical object so that the user can both 'see' and 'feel' the virtual object. By physically touching a virtual object (mixing the real objects and virtual reality) the quality of the virtual experience can be improved [8, 9].

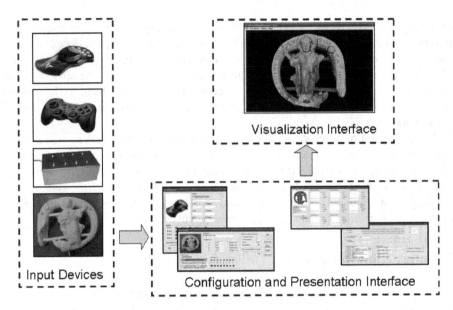

Fig. 1. Overall System Architecture of the EPOCH Multimodal Interface

4   The EPOCH Multimodal Interface

We have developed several example applications in which our multimodal interface is demonstrated. In one application the multimodal interface has been integrated with a standard web browser including information content delivered as a part of an Internet based virtual museum [21]. A standalone version which is a separate application has been developed and it was analysed in detail at VSMM2005 [22]. This version had only the ability to integrate one input device, the museum object ("Kromstaf") replica. This paper presents new technological developments which are implemented in a standalone application. The overall system architecture is shown on Fig. 1.

The EPOCH Multimodal interface now incorporates many new features including:

1. The ability to use different input devices, Fig. 1 illustrates:
   o The original Kromstaf input device reported in [19, 22]
   o A simple 'box' interface that has all the functionality of the Kromstaf but without the 'tactile' feel—includes orientation tracking and touch sensors.
   o A space mouse, which is a common input device for controlling 3D models in CAD software.
   o A Game pad, which provides a good interface for children used to playing games using this type of input.
   o The ability to add other input devices by simply creating a new input driver.
2. A new configuration and presentation interface incorporating:
   o A setup interface for the touch sensors.
   o A variety of input device interfaces, e.g. space mouse shown in Fig. 1.

○ A simple content management system that allows the museum to assign content for display to each of the touch sensors.

○ A calibration interface for the orientation tracker.

The main purpose of the EPOCH Multimodal interface is to expand the presentation of a methodology that provides an alternative exhibition of an artefact through the use of a safe hybrid 2D/3D multimodal interface based on the integration of an orientation tracking device and touch sensor electronics with a physical artefact replica to provide tactile feedback [16, 19, 21, 22]. However, because we now include support for several orientation trackers from Intersense [10] (Intertrax, IS-300, IS-600, IS-900 and IS-1200), a SpaceMouse and support for any type of joystick/game pad the multimodal interface is very flexible. It can be adapted to the build of other bespoke input devices as demonstrated by the simple 'box' interface or if a museum did not want to go the expense of developing such an interface other cheaper input devices such as the space mouse or game pad can be used. Furthermore, in addition to the support of the above input devices, speech was integrated to the system and a simple content management tool has been added.

5 Alternative Input Devices

In the latest version of the EPOCH multimodal interface we foresaw the need to provide cheaper alternatives to the development of a bespoke input device such as the Kromstaf. As reported in [22] the development of an artefact replica involves laser scanning of the artefact in order to build both the 3D model and the rapid prototyping of the replica. The cost of developing the replica can be saved by using perhaps a less effective input device. Further, a cheaper alternative to developing a replica, which gives the same functionality, is to use the same orientation tracker and electronics in a simple box—or shape of choice. Even cheaper still is to use off-the-shelf 3D input devices. The box interface uses exactly the software setup interface as the Kromstaf. The two new setup interfaces are the for the space mouse and game pad.

The Magellan SpaceMouse plus XT [26] is a USB device providing a six degree-of-freedom (6DOF) mouse and a nine button menu interface, see Fig. 2. All nine buttons are programmable. The user can program the buttons to perform several graphics operations and the user can now programme into the buttons so called 'information actions', i.e. calls to supporting information on web pages or other presentation media, e.g. movies, etc., or other events in the virtual world.

The cheapest input device, which can be had for less that 40 dollars is a typical 'game pad', which can easily be integrated using the standard Microsoft 'Joystick' drivers. This provides an easy to use input device in comparison with the other input devices. Each button of the game pad is fully programmable.

In our case three buttons are used to enable basic transformations, one button resets the scene and eight buttons are used to provide information about the cultural object such as historical information and a multimedia presentation of the artefact. The number of the buttons may vary according to the type of the joystick or game pad used.

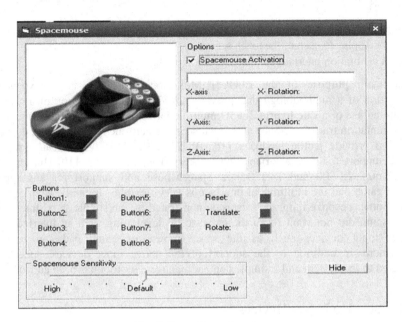

Fig. 2. SpaceMouse Interface

An interesting development is the new game pad input device that comes with the Sony PlayStation 3. This game pad is both wireless (nothing new there, we have tested wireless game pads currently available) and is reported to include a motion tracker. Such a game pad would provide a very effective and cost effective equivalent to the box interface. We mentioned above that support for several trackers have been added to the system in order to provide the user with more flexibility.

Finally, in order to add multimodal input to the presentation methodologies speech has been integrated into the system. The software architecture is build around Microsoft Speech SDK SAPI 5.1 [14]. A typical use scenario here is that the museum enters some text associated with a particular touch sensor (button) on the input device. A check box is then selected on the input interface to select whether the user wants to see the text display in the virtual environment or the text converted to audio and played when the button is oppressed, or both.

6   Evaluation of the EPOCH Tangible User Interface

A formal usability evaluation has been performed in order to assess the usability of the EPOCH Tangible User interface by comparing a physical mock-up of the artefact (Kromstaf) with a Spacemouse and a blackbox for manipulating 3D Content. Fifty-four participants were recruited from the University of Sussex undergraduate and postgraduate population and were asked to interact with the system. The participants were divided into three groups corresponding to the three types of the interface (i.e. Kromstaf, blackbox and Spacemouse). Each group was balanced in terms of age, gender and their background. The experiment was divided into two stages. During the first stage we tested the written memory recall of the cultural artefact by manipulating either the artefact replica, the SpaceMouse or the plain black box for a brief exposure to the system. During the second stage we assessed the users' perceived level of presence and user satisfaction across all conditions. By analysis the data we collected from the two stages we discovered that the participants using the Kromstaf interface performed better in terms of memory recall performance compared to the other devices. Furthermore although there was a clear difference between the replica as well as the blackbox and the SpaceMouse provoking better user satisfaction, an overall statistically significant difference was not observed between the replica and the blackbox. For a more detailed analysis of the results of this evaluation study please refer to [23].

7 Conclusions

A user-friendly and interactive visualisation interface specifically designed for interacting with virtual museum and associated virtual artefacts has been described. Our system combines several types of interactions utilizing sophisticated devices such as the spacemouse, game pad, orientation trackers and touch sensors. This transforms the EPOCH Multimodal Interface from an interface designed for a specific task (manipulating only the Kromstaf replica) to a generic multimodal interface that the user can manipulate different items by using several input devices.

Further improvements to the system will be the addition of input devices such as virtual reality gloves, the integration to the system with the ARCOLite architecture reported in [11, 12, 17, 21] and extending the system so that it can be used with mobile devices.

Acknowledgements

The Provincial Archaeological Museum Ename, headed by Marie-Claire Van der Donckt, provided the scan data and photography of the ivory object, and the information for the stories that are embedded in the object. Animations with virtual monks were made by the Computer Graphics Lab at EPFL. The realisation of the interactive replica was done at the Ename Center.

This work has been partly supported by the European Union FP5 and FP6 projects ARCO (IST28336) and EPOCH (IST-2002-507382) allowing the integration of ARCO results with EPOCH multimodal interface showcase results.

References

1. Aliakseyeu, D., Martens J. B., Subramanian, S. , Rauterberg, M. . Interaction Techniques for Navigation through and Manipulation of 2D and 3D Data. in In proceedings of Eight Eurographics conference on Virtual Environments 2002.
2. Billinghurst, M., Kato, H., Poupyrev, I. The MagicBook: A Traditional AR Interface. in Computer and Graphics. 2001.
3. Bowman, D., Kruijff, E., LaViola, J., Poupyrev, I., An Introduction to 3D User Interface Design. Presence: Teleoperators and Virtual Environments, 2001. 10(1): p. 96-108.

4. Brogni, A., Avizzano, C.A., Evangelista, C., Bergamasco, M. . Technological Approach for Cultural Heritage: Augmented Reality. in Proc. of 8th International Workshop on Robot and Human Interaction. 1999.

5. Digicult Progress Report. Digicult Progress Report. [Internet] 2006 [cited 01/06/2006]; Available from: http://www.digicult.info/pages/index.php.

6. Frohlich B., P.J., Wind J., Wesche G., Gobel M., Cubic-Mouse-Based Interaction in Virtual Environments. IEEE Computer Graphics and Applications, 2000. 20(4): p. 12-15.

7. Hinckley, K., Pausch, R.,Goble, J. C., Kassell, N. F. . A survey of design issues in spatial input. in In Proceedings of the Symposium on User Interface Software and Technology. 1994: ACM Press.

8. Hoffman, H., Groen, J., Rousseau, S., Hollander, A., Winn, W., Wells, M., Furness, T. Tactile Augmentation: Enhancing presence in virtual reality with tactile feedback from real objects in In American Psychological Society. 1996. San Francisco, CA.

9. Hoffman, H. Virtual Reality: A New Tool for Interdisciplinary Psychology Research. in CyberPsycology & Behaviour. 1998.

10. Intersence. [Internet] 2006 [cited 04/07/06]; Available from: http://www.isense.com/.

11. Liarokapis, F., White, M., Lister, P.F. Augmented Reality Interface Toolkit. in IEEE Proc. International Symposium on Augmented and Virtual Reality, IV04-AVR. 2004. London.

12. Liarokapis, F., Mourkoussis, N. , White, M., Darcy, J. , Sifniotis, M. , Petridis, P. , Basu, A. , Lister, P.F. Web3D and Augmented Reality to support Engineering Education. in World Transactions on Engineering and Technology Education, UICEE. 2004.

13. Mase, K., Kadobayashi, R., Nakatsu, R. Meta-museum: A Supportive Augmented Reality Environment for Knowledge Sharing. in Proceedings of International Conference on Virtual Systems and Multimedia. 1996.

14. Microsoft. [Internet] 2006 [cited 01/07/2006]; Available from: http://www.microsoft.com/downloads/details.aspx?FamilyId=5E86EC97-40A7-453F-B0EE-6583171B4530&displaylang=en.

15. Milosavljevic, M., Dale, R., Green, S.J., Paris, C., Williams, S. Virtual Museums on the Information Superhighway: Prospects and Potholes. in Proceedings of CIDOC '98, the Annual Conference of the International Committee for Documentation of the International Council of Museums. 1998. Melbourne, Australia.

16. Mourkoussis, N., Mania, K.,Petridis, P.,White, M., Rivera, F., Pletinckx, D. . An analysis of the effect of technological fidelity on perceptual fidelity. in To appear in proceedings of the IEA 2006 (International Ergonomics Association), 16th World Congress on Ergonomics. 2006. The Hague, Netherlands.

17. Mourkoussis, N., Liarokapis, F., Basu, A., White, M., Lister, P.F. Using XML Technologies to Present Digital Content with Augmented Reality. in Eurographics Ireland Chapter Workshop Proceedings. 2004. Cork

18. Mourkoussis, N., Liarokapis, F., Darcy, J., Pettersson, M., Petridis, P., Lister, P., White, M.. Virtual and Augmented Reality Applied to Educational and Cultural Heritage Domains. in In proceedings of Business Applications of Virtual Reality, Workshop. 2002. Poland, Poznan.

19. Oosterlynck, D., Pletinckx, D., White, M., Petridis, P., Thalmann, D., Clavien, M. ,. EPOCH Showcase 2.4.2: Multimodal Interface for Safe Presentation Of Valuable Objects. in VAST 2004. 2004. Brussels, Belgium.

20. Oviatt, S. Multimodal Interfaces. in Handbook of Human-Computer Interaction. 2002. Lawrence Erlbaum: New Jersey.

21. Petridis, P., White, M., Mourkousis, N., Liarokapis, F., Sifiniotis, M. Basu, A., Gatzidis, C. Exploring and Interacting with Virtual Museums. in CAA 2005: The World in your eyes. 2005. Tomar,Portugal.

22. Petridis, P., Pletinckx, D., White, M. , A Multimodal Interface for Presenting and Handling Virtual Artifacts. in Proceedings of the Eleventh International Conference On Virtual Systems and Multimedia. 2005. Belgium, Ghent.

23. Petridis, P., Mania, K., Pletinckx, D., White, M., Usability Evaluation of the EPOCH Multimodal User Interface: Designing 3D Tangible Interactions. To appear in ACM Symposium on Virtual Reality Software and Technology. 2006. Cyprus.

24. PhotoModeler.   [Internet]   2006   [cited   05/02/2006];   Available   from: http://www.photomodeler.com.

25. Roussou M. Immersive Interactive Virtual Reality in the Museum. in In Proc.of TiLE (Trends in Leisure Entertainment). 2001.

26. Spacemouse.   [Internet]   2006   [cited   04/07/06;   Available   from: http://www.3dconnexion.com/.

27. Starner, T., Mann, S., Rhodes, B., Levine, J., Healey, J., Kirsch, D., Picard, R. W., Pentland, A. , Augmented Reality through Wearable Computing. Presence: Teleoperators and Virtual Environments, 1997. 6(4): p. 386-398.

28. Subramanian, S., Aliakseyeu, D., Martens, J. B. Empirical Evaluation of Performance in Hybrid 3D and 2D Interfaces. in In Human Computer Interaction - Interact'03. 2003. Zürich, Switzerland: OS Press, (c) IFIP.

29. Van Dam, A., Forsberg, A. S., Laidlaw, D. H., LaViola, J. J., Simpson, R. M., Immersive VR for Scientific Visualization: A Progress Report. IEEE Computer Graphics and Applications, 2000. 20(6): p. 26-52.

30. White, M., Mourkoussis, N., Darcy, J., Petridis, P., Liarokapis, F., Lister, P., Walczak, K., Wojciechowski, R., Cellary, W., Chmielewski, J., Stawniak, M., Wiza,W., Patel, M., Stevenson, J., Manley, J., Giorgini, F., Sayd, P., Gaspard, F. . ARCO-An Architecture for Digitization, Management and Presentation of Virtual Exhibitions. in In IEEE Proceedings of 22nd International Conference on Computer Graphics. 2004. Greece, Crete.

31. Witmer, B.G., Singer, M. J., Measuring Presence in Virtual Environments: A Presence Questionnaire,. Presence: Teleoperators and Virtual Environments, 1998. 7(3): p. 225-240.

32. Wuthrich, C.A. An analysis and a Model of 3D Interaction Methods and Devices for Virtual Reality. in Proc. of the Eurographics Workshop. 1999.

33. Daniel Pletinckx, Neil A. Silberman and Dirk Callebaut, Heritage Presentation through Interactive Storytelling : A New Multimedia Database Approach, Journal of Visualization and Computer Animation, Wiley, June 2003

34. EPOCH Network of Excellence [Internet] 2006 [cited 04/07/06, available from http://www.epoch-net.org/, 3DKIOSK info is available in the Research Section.

Virtual Manuscripts for an Enhanced Museum and Web Experience 'Living Manuscripts'

Jessica R. Cauchard[1,2], Peter F. Ainsworth[1], Daniela M. Romano[2], and Bob Banks[3]

[1] Dpt of French, University of Sheffield, Arts Tower, Sheffield S10 2TN UK
{jessica.cauchard, p.f.ainsworth}@sheffield.ac.uk
[2] Dpt of Computer Science, Sheffield U, 211 Portobello Street, Sheffield, S1 4DP, UK
d.romano@sheffield.ac.uk
[3] Tribal Education and Technology, St Mary's Court, 55 St Mary's Road, Sheffield S2 4AN
bob.banks@tribalgroup.co.uk

Abstract. Due to preservation and conservation issues, manuscripts are normally kept in research libraries far from public gaze. On rare occasions, visitors can see these priceless objects, typically separated from them by a sealed case, with only a fixed double page spread visible from a manuscript that may contain hundreds of folios. This restricts the amount of knowledge offered by these books. This paper proposes the creation of virtual manuscripts as exhibits in their own right in a museum context, and as part of a web-based virtual learning environment offering visitors the unique opportunity of engaging with the manuscripts, providing further possibilities for accessing the heritage and cultural information contained in them. A database supplying information about and from the manuscripts, held in a virtual environment, creates the illusion of their "real" presence and materiality. 'Living Manuscripts' aims to stimulate and encourage engagement with vulnerable materials via an innovative virtual experience.

1 Introduction

Ancient manuscripts are great treasures and an important part of our heritage; full of narratives, they give us access to the wealth, culture and imaginative capital of the past. Researchers in several branches of the Arts and Humanities study them as texts, images or both; more recently scholarship of this kind has begun to engage with e-Science (collaborative and interdisciplinary approaches using new technologies), whilst the agenda of conservators and curators is to protect and preserve their holdings in order to give to everyone today, but also tomorrow, the possibility of continuing if restricted access to these treasures. Due to conservation issues, on the rare occasions when these manuscripts are exposed to public view, they are typically displayed under glass in sealed cabinets, and opened to show just one fixed double-page spread. It is sometimes possible to find an explanatory label on the side or front of the showcase, indicating the name of the author as well as the approximate year of creation of the manuscript and details (if known) of its provenance. Unless a specialist, the visitor will not have access to the multi-layered knowledge that these

H. Zha et al. (Eds.): VSMM 2006, LNCS 4270, pp. 418–427, 2006.

manuscripts teem with. Catalogues go some way towards resolving this issue, but tend to be limited in scope and potential appeal.

This project proposes to make use of virtual reality (VR) technology to bring these manuscripts from long distant centuries to life. Electronic exhibits installed inside a museum will allow visitors to engage interactively with these valuable artefacts in a more complete manner. Amongst requirements for the project, a key objective is the creation of an innovative, powerful, and large scale viewer to show the manuscripts from any angle. The book itself will be recreated in three dimensions, its "pages" being derived from high-resolution photographic files (TIF files) of the real folios, specially prepared as part of a Leverhulme Research Fellowship [1] (Ainsworth, University of Sheffield) by a team comprising scholar, digital photography consultant and curator. Visitors thus have the opportunity of viewing the entire (digitised) manuscript while enjoying an immersive experience and navigate inside the environment. For example, users can turn the pages in an intuitive way and zoom in and out, as well as read a translation into modern English of the text of the current page. Visitors can also navigate from the environment to underlying material stored in ad hoc created databases accessed from a grid-enabled portlet. This enhances their potential appreciation of the content, stories, and historical background to the manuscripts. A novel navigation system of virtual hot spots placed on the relevant part of the pages has been specially created. Furthermore the virtual manuscripts will offer a personalised experience of the book by providing different information, whether the visitor is an average visitor, a child, a researcher, a non-native speaker or has a disability. A key objective of the project is to amaze and delight museum's visitors and web users, to give them the impression that they are dealing with something radically different from anything they have experienced before – as a prelude to a more pleasurable and personally engaging learning process.

2 Virtual Environments for Entertainment

Technology is often used in museum exhibitions, where touch-screens or simple computers offer a multimedia exhibition experience. Can virtual reality technology offer a more involving experience with the artefacts than currently used multimedia? Joseph Bates describes virtual reality as a "new medium, new entertainment, a new and very powerful type of art." [2] (p.1). Virtual Reality is the next step beyond books, television and cinema; as a visualisation technology that can be applied for medicine, science, architecture, and elsewhere such as heritage, education, literature, museums, galleries and art. The manuscripts featuring in this exhibition are resources for historians, with the stories they tell; for pupils and teachers, for their knowledge of the past; and even for artists and art historians, on account of their remarkable and beautiful illuminations. Bates (1992) still considered that there was a lack of presentation resources for virtual worlds, explaining that: "in film, the feeling of the underlying world is greatly influenced by the lighting, camera angles, focus, editing" [2] (p.5). Today, computing technologies allow the integration of all these components within virtual environments. VR is therefore certainly a suitable tool for displaying such manuscript material. Bates (1992) also notes that one is accustomed to having normal control over their bodies and perceptions, finding the lack of control confusing and perhaps unpleasant. Consequently care must be taken to ensure that the interaction with the virtual exhibit occurs as naturally, agreeably and spontaneously as possible. Moreover, the environment needs to be rich enough to give the user the possibility of interacting with as many elements as possible. "This must be done in such a way as to leave the user with an undiminished feeling of free-will"; [2] (p.6) calling for the application of Human-Computer Interaction (HCI) principles.

3 Virtual Museums as Enhancement of Real Museums' Experiences

A museum is defined by the International Council of Museums (ICOM) as: "A non-profit making, permanent institution in the service of society and of its development, and open to the public, which acquires, conserves, researches, communicates and exhibits, for purposes of study, education and enjoyment, material evidence of people and their environment. (...)" [3]. Some studies have been made taking into consideration this issue. Yonk-Moo Kwon (2003) [4] states that the essential functions of all kinds of museums, including virtual museums, are 'exhibition, communication, research, acquirement, and conservation' [4] (p.1). The solution proposed certainly fulfils the main "exhibition" function. To decide whether or not the project embodies a fully communicative aspect, an adequate definition is needed for communication in such a context. Communication is commonly defined as 'the activity of conveying information' [5]. The project's virtual manuscript allows people to read and have ready access to the information contained in the folios and the linked database communicating with the visitors. From the standpoint of research value, the fact of being able to read a manuscript from a remote site provides worldwide researchers with the possibility of studying the manuscript book, and maybe even annotating it or responding via a collaborative environment. Moreover, at least one dimension of the conservation issue is addressed by the project as described above, since the virtual manuscript can neither age nor deteriorate. For the "acquirement" function, the virtual artefacts program as conceived also allows for display of any suitably digitized manuscript. In sum, the project as defined has a very good fit with the conceptual framework for a virtual museum exhibit. The exhibit uses the possibilities offered by new technologies to display a so-called virtual heritage. Although it will not compete with the real museum, it complements them. Each, moreover, retains its own appeal.In his project, Y.-M. Kwon [4] considers that a 'virtual museum consists of roughly two parts, a museum server and interface orbit. A museum server conveys the museum services based on databases. Interface orbit is a conceptual term to represent user's applicability according to devices' [4] (p.2). The project described in the present paper somehow resembles Kwon's solution as it will have all the resources open to the visitors stored in databases containing the digitised manuscript(s), translations, links to specific URLs or documentary films and video clips. In addition a range of interfaces will expand throughout the project. Y.-M. Kwon's project is equipped with both Mixed and Virtual Reality technology; available on the museum's site. An immersive experience is proposed where visitors can navigate virtually inside Namsan – a Korean mountain granted World Heritage status by UNESCO – through an immersive theatre or a CAVE [6]. The solution proposed will provide a solution viewable in environments with different level of immersion form a CAVE to a hand-held device.

Fig. 1. SEE's screenshot of a board [7]

4   Learning and Entertaining in 3D Worlds

By bringing a virtual exhibit inside the museum, the project aims to introduce people safely and engagingly to extremely valuable manuscripts, and furthermore to offer them the possibility of learning while enjoying this immersive experience. Studies have already been conducted into the potential for associating entertainment and education in virtual environments. A particularly interesting exemplar is "The Shrine Educational Experience (SEE): Edutainment In 3D Virtual Worlds" [7] (Figure 1). In this project, Di Blas, Paolini and Hazan [7] state that, by re-using the experience of the Virtual Leonardo Project [8], they use the '3D graphic environment (…) as a "container" to display "objects" of the museum'. Similarly the solution proposed can be seen as having every single digitised folio as an object in its own right and the book as a its container. Di Blas et al [7], who focussed an important part of their work on the possibilities offered by real-time, were using the software CUSee-Me to broadcast the exhibition all day from the gallery; transforming local visitors in "spontaneous players on the live stage" (p.1). It is also hoped that our solution will be broadcasted in real-time to other mirror exhibition sites. Di Blas et al. (2003) also did a lot of collaborative work in the environment, allowing people to visit simultaneously and together the environment. For the SEE they used what they described as an "indispensable" virtual "museum guide" taking the view that users might easily feel lost in the virtual environment. The manuscripts project presents the virtual manuscript book without an accompanying guide. The interest of the visitor for the artefact is sustained by the entertaining and engaging nature of the exhibit; ensuring that the visitors see the entire potential of the virtual manuscript. One of the objectives is to let people learn as well as interact with each other and also play in the environment. Di Blas et al. (2003) tested the concept, of making students engage with the cultural content while enjoying themselves at the same time, with high school and junior high school pupils. At the beginning, the students received an introduction to the environment from the virtual guide; next, they received some cultural information; after that, they played two cultural and educational games, and finally received feedback on their experience. The result was that the game encouraged the students to move inside the environment and to move progressively throughout all the artefacts. On the other hand,

Di Blas, Paolini and Hazan [7] conclude that '3D worlds are clearly not appropriate architectures for disseminating large amount of information, as neither lectures nor expansive documents work well with new means of communication' [7] (p.7). Personalised delivery of knowledge might be the solution to this problem delivering the right information to the right audience, since clearly the complexity and quantity of information underlying a manuscript might not be deliverable all at once or to all audience. 3D worlds also support discovery and experiential learning and navigation, and therefore are well suited for personalised delivery of knowledge.

5 Existing Viewers

Some manuscripts viewers are already available on the Web or on CDs. A very famous one is the "Turning the pages" collection and software produced by the British Library [9]. The software is available on a CD containing one complete, digitized manuscript per product. It allows one to view each page of the manuscript and to turn the page in view, or to go to the next or preceding page. The book is typically displayed on two open pages. The British Library recreated a book as a "host" environment for the product. However, the book is realised in two-dimensions and even if the execution is impressive, the limitations of using 2-dimensional representation are readily apparent. A sensation of depth (depending on the number of pages left on either side of those displayed) is not afforded; nor is it possible to determine how many pages are left, or when the last page has been reached, save for a line which says that the end of the manuscript has been reached. The British library team also equipped their viewer with a zooming tool. When this is activated, the image is decomposed into four parts. At the top left the page displays a section in zoom format, while at the bottom right a miniature image of the book is shown, with a rectangle representing the position of the part in zoom in the whole page. They also provide some explanatory material about the content of the page in view at the top right, plus some descriptive information about the part shown in zoom format at the bottom left. The British Library TTP collection offers an interesting interpretation of the viewing tool. Unfortunately, the possibilities offered are quite limited. The user cannot go directly to a page, has to navigate through each and every page; and must use the mouse to turn each page. Moreover, if the user has a pad rather than a mouse, the operation can be strenuous. Another drawback is that the zoom is fixed; the user is therefore unable to zoom in more or less at his convenience on a particular detail. The zooming feature also has a predetermined magnification that cannot be changed by the user. Another remarkable viewer available online belongs to the "Library of The Jewish Theological Seminary" project [10]. They have some manuscripts available online, accessible to any visitor from their website. The interaction is exceptionally pleasant to use. At the beginning, the visitor chooses a book from a shelf (*Figure 2*). The book is opened in a new window. It is then possible either to turn the pages one by one using the mouse or clicking on a button; furthermore, the visitor can also choose to go directly to a page, selecting it by its number. For each page turned, an animation is displayed giving the impression of a real page turning.

Fig. 2. Screenshot of Louis Marshall's bookcase **Fig. 3.** Floating Zoom 4X [11]
Fig. 2 and 3. Courtesy of The Library of The Jewish Theological Seminary [10]

In this viewer, the number of the pages currently in view is visible at the bottom of pages, compared to the total number of pages contained within the manuscript. This allows the visitor to know how many pages still remain to be seen and also when the end of the book has been reached. This software is also equipped with a zoom feature. Its display mode is that of a floating magnifying glass (*Figure 3*); the user is free to move in the page, moreover to magnify at 4x or 2x. For the 'living manuscripts' project, the aim is to deliver a product allowing greater flexibility from the user's point of view. The user will be in a position to check any particular detail, or to go straight to a particular folio. Users will have the impression of dealing with the real manuscript, and not only with the electronic folios. The technology employed for the two previously described viewers makes use of Macromedia Flash Player. In our case, the development environment uses an Oriented-Object language and a three–dimensional API. The final result will therefore necessary be different in concept and realisation at least from the use of 3-dimensions.

6   Existing On-Site Exhibits

The project will imply the virtual device to be brought into a public museum. Some museums already possess some state-of-the-art technology devices. Amongst the existing one, some are particularly interesting as on the archaeological site at Ename (Belgium). The town of Ename has an open-air museum of archaeological remains [12]. These have regrettably been badly preserved and are not intelligible to non-professionals visitors. In order to give visitors an overview of what the site used to be like; a virtual device, called TimeFrame (TimeScope for the prototype) was developed, allowing people to see the buildings that used to be there, shown together with virtual representations of their original inhabitants (*Figure 4*). Technically, 'TimeScope 1 consists of a video camera, a computer system, two monitors, and a touch screen. A specially designed on-site kiosk houses the system and protects visitors from the elements. The video camera is directed toward a particular section of the archaeological remains and it transmits real-time video images of those remains to the monitor screens in the kiosk' [11] (*Figure 5*).

Visitors can interact with TimeScope using a touch screen, and navigate successively through the different stages of the reconstruction of the building and its

Fig. 4. Animated Sequence of TimeScope1©[13] **Fig. 5.** Kiosk and projection ©[12]

structures. Users also have access to some multimedia material, some photos, maps and virtual animations; all describing the evolution of the site and its buildings'. Another advantage of TimeFrame is acts as a multi-user exhibit, allowing the visitors to go inside a wooden cabin and experience the display as a group. A survey asking visitors for their impressions has shown that everybody has been really pleased to discover these remains in a comprehensible way. They also have been enthusiast using these new interactive technologies. In the similar way, 'living manuscript' will provide visitors with virtual access to treasures on parchments. It is interesting to notice that the Ename project deploys a multi-user exhibit, whilst only one person at a time can actually interact with the touch screen. 'Living manuscripts' proposes to adopt a similar approach, all the more since the interaction is made using one big displaying device inputting haptics.

7   The Proposed Solution

First, the virtual manuscripts will be created in three-dimensional form, to host the digitised pages. Second, the pages are inserted inside their "container" (*Figure 6*). This operation is done automatically by the program in order to permit scrutiny of any manuscript accessible and selectable for viewing. A text file describing the content of each of the digitised manuscripts to be displayed is created and used by the program to generate the equivalent 3D version. Then a mechanism to move inside the environment and to see the book from further away from their vantage-point or from closer at hand is implemented. Animations are then realised. The first of the latter is a facility for opening or closing the book. The second addresses the action of turning the pages. This stage is more complicated than it seems: due to memory limitations, it will not be possible for all of the pages to be displayed simultaneously. Furthermore, one has to be sure that the proper, consequent page is in view, in the right sequence. The sensation of visual depth and volume is given by the thickness of the book depending on how many pages have already been turned. The next features to be implemented are the navigation tools. Some hotspots are created for location at the top of the virtual manuscript on the relevant part of the book's folios or a tool will be created in order to leave curators and specialists the freedom to place hotspots at positions they consider important. A floating bookmark is produced allowing the hotspots to appear and disappear. This function is essential so as to avoid detracting from the manuscripts' intrinsic visual and aesthetic presentational value.

Fig. 6. Screenshot of the opened book © Bibliothèque d'Étude et de Conservation, Besançon, France; MS 865 f. 1r [14] **Fig. 7.** Screenshot of 'Living Manuscripts' © Stonyhurst College Library, UK; MS 1, f 1r [15]

The hotspots give users the possibility of navigating inside the environment and to go to underlying material such as translations, videos or related pictures supplied from given databases. The implementation can be hosted in an immersive environment such as the RAVE using visualisation technology and navigation tools available in our laboratory or a portable 3D projectors version for the museum exhibition. The user's position is known using the sensors embedded in the 3D Glasses. The movements of the user will be tracked in order to enable movement inside the scene. The main idea is to let the visitor interact with the book in a manner that is as natural as can be contrived. Similarly the virtual artefact will be viewable within a web page and the navigation will take place with standard mouse and keyboard. Different scenarios will be implemented depending on the user. Subtitles in the native language of the visitor might be used (though the number of potential languages is an inhibiting factor), and proposals are afoot for interactive, digital-DVD-video games and competitions for children, together with more specialised underlying material for researchers or students, enhancement of volume and soundscapes for hearing-impaired persons, plus navigational aids for visually-impaired visitors.

One of the aims of 'living manuscripts' is to create a virtual environment to host the digitised image files for each page of the manuscripts. The manuscript has been recreated in 3-Dimensional format and hosts the pages inside it, as in a real codex. The pages are created as bendable polygons to create the illusion of naturally "falling" onto the board when the user turns them. Once the book and the pages are created, the digitized corresponding images are applied as textures. For memory reasons, all of the created pages of the book cannot be displayed at the same time. In practice, all the pages do not in fact "exist"; only a few do at any given time. As the pages are turned, a different texture is applied to the current page in view. In order to choose which texture is in view, a .txt file containing the name of all the book's pages is perused. Now that the environment is almost created in full, the book requires animation to be applied. This is to provide the basis for interaction between user and book. The book is constructed hierarchically in order to perform the animation calling a minimum of functions and so to reduce the time needed by the system to realize the operation. One important function is the one turning the pages. As a matter of fact, the user has to be able to turn the pages of the book (*Figure 7*) in a natural way, and to turn the exact number of pages in the book.

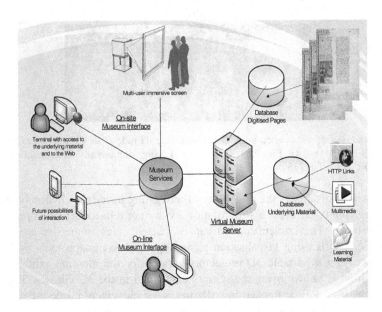

Table 1. Architecture of Living Manuscripts

The architecture for 'living manuscripts' is represented as Diagram 1. The museum will be at the centre of the project. The amount of interaction available will rely on the services offered by each museum. The information displayed will be stored in databases accessible via a virtual museum server. For each manuscript displayed, a corresponding database containing the digitized images of the pages will be accessible from the server. The underlying material will vary depending on how much information is available for a particular manuscript or exhibition. Concerning the user interface, part of the virtual museum will be available on-site during the exhibition either using an immersive screen, a terminal or possibly a hand-held device; whereas the other part will be available online using a personal computer.

8 Evaluation and Testing

To test the sustainability of the 'living manuscripts' project, we will first organize an evaluation on the prototype displayed both using PCs for the online version and a RAVE for the on-site version. In a second time, we have a 6-month national exhibition planned for the second semester 2007; where we will collect data on how the museum visitors and the web visitors use the different tools, how they interact with the virtual manuscripts, what they learn from this experience and what is their global satisfaction. These results will be used as feedback on the virtual museum and allow improving the tools. The 2007 exhibition has the ambition to be broadcasted in different museums at the same time.

9 Conclusion

A solution has been proposed for the preservation and appreciation of ancient arte-facts belonging to our heritage, such as medieval manuscripts. As the paper has sought to demonstrate, 'Living manuscripts' aims to bring vellum manuscripts to life using virtual reality technology. The 'living manuscripts' are 3D interactive photo-realistic representation of the original manuscripts; they also provide additional man-ner to explore the content and the layers of knowledge that are related to the real arte-facts. The virtual manuscripts can be deliverable to a wide audience as exhibits in a museum or on the web. The solution proposed will be tested within a planned simul-taneous exhibition in several museums and on the web, to measure the impact of vir-tual learning environments such as the living manuscripts.

References

1. http://www.leverhulme.org.uk/
2. Bates J., Virtual Reality, Art and Entertainment, *Presence: Teleoperators and Virtual Environments, 1(1), 133-138. (1992)*
3. International Council Of Museums – http://icom.museum/definition.html
4. Kwon Y-M. et al., Toward the Synchronized Experiences between Real and Virtual Museum, *APAN 2003 Conference in Fukuoka*
5. Online dictionary: http://www.wordreference.com/definition/communication
6. Cruz-Neira C. et al., The CAVE: Audio Visual Experience Automatic Virtual Environ-ment, *Communications of the ACM, Vol. 35, No. 6, June 1992, pp. 65-72.*
7. Di Blas N., Hazan S., Paolini P., The SEE Experience: Edutainment in 3D Virtual Worlds, in Proceedings *Museums and the Web 2003*
8. Virtual Leonardo Project: http://www.museoscienza.org/english/leonardovirtuale/
9. CDs, The British Library Board 2002 ©, Turning the pages ®.
10. Special Treasures form the Library of The Jewish Theological Seminary, http://www.jtslibrarytreasures.org
11. MS 8255, fol. 5b (Siddur Italian rite, Italy 1471)
12. Ename open-air museum http://www.ename974.org/
13. Images © Ename 974 http://www.ename974.org/
14. Photographs of Besançon MS 865 by *Scriptura* (Colin Dunn), reproduced by kind permission of the Bibliothèque d'Étude et de Conservation, Ville de Besançon, France
15. Photographs of Stonyhurst MS 1 by *Scriptura* (Colin Dunn), reproduced by kind permission of Stonyhurst College, United Kingdom

Note-Taking Support for Nurses Using Digital Pen Character Recognition System

Yujiro Hayashi[1], Satoshi Tamura[2], Satoru Hayamizu[2], and Yutaka Nishimoto[3]

[1] Graduate School of Engineering, Gifu University
[2] Faculty of Engineering, Gifu University
[3] Gifu University School of Medicine

Abstract. This study presents a novel system which supports nurses in note-taking by providing a digital pen and character-recognition system laying stress on user interface. The system applies characteristics of a digital pen for improving the efficiency of tasks related to nursing records. The system aims at improving the efficiency of nursing activities and reducing the time spent for tasks for nursing records. In our system, first, notes are written on a check sheet using a digital pen along with a voice that is recorded on a voice recorder; the pen and voice data are transferred to a PC. The pen data are then recognized automatically as characters, which can be viewed and manipulated with the application. We conducted an evaluation experiment to improve efficiency and operation of the system, and its interface. The evaluation and test operations used 10 test subjects. Based on the test operation and the evaluation experiment of the system, it is turned out that improvement for urgent situations, enhancement of portability, and further use of character recognition are required.

1 Background and Purpose of the Study

During their daily work, some nurses take notes related to information such as patients' condition and doctors' instructions on the backs of their hands or forearms when no writing pads are immediately available. Then, they sit in front of a PC for considerable time everyday transcribing the notes written on their hands, forearms and papers into electronic medical records. Taking notes on their hands and forearms, however, requires transcription and reduces the level of hygiene. Those salient disadvantages cause heightened concern among these nurses.

For such situations, this study is intended to support nurses in note-taking by providing a digital pen (c.f. Figure.1) and character-recognition system[1]. The Digital Pen is a writing device which records information such as handwriting strokes automatically. The information can be

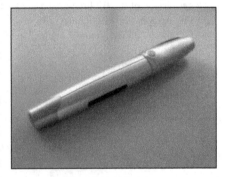

Fig. 1. Digital pen

H. Zha et al. (Eds.): VSMM 2006, LNCS 4270, pp. 428 – 436, 2006.

transferred to PC. The system applies characteristics of a digital pen [2] for improving the efficiency of tasks related to nursing records.

2   Past Studies

A conventional study using a digital pen is the *"Snail System: Classroom Interaction Support System with Digitized Pens and PDAs* [3]". This is a learning system comprising sub-systems for teachers and students. It makes practical use of a feature of digital pens: *extraction of written information.* This system imports information written by students with a digital pen into a PDA equipped with a wireless LAN, through which the information is sent to the teacher system. The teacher system then displays a list and details of students' handwriting and allows annotations to be added. Consequently, it contributes to the improvement of classroom interaction. The report also notes that a digital pen fundamentally follows the conventional form of learning primarily through writing in the act of writing on a piece of paper, which helps reduce the resistance that the students might feel by the use of a new device.

Another system using a digital pen is the PaperIQ[4], which allows users to use pen and paper to organize their personal information. The system provides handwritten character recognition, fax transmission and a web-based digital archive of their notes available for download as common formatted documents.

In addition, we conducted studies on home-nursing support with digital pens involved in medical care [5]. This study is intended for improving the efficiency of home nursing care by allowing the families of home patients to easily check the condition of the patient using a digital pen and transfer the digital data. The digital pen used in this case was useful in the sense that they were easy to handle and allowed hand-written data transfer.

Another study [6] examined the achievements of the reduction of time spent for tasks related to nursing records and the sharing of nursing records that are anticipated from computerization of nursing records such as electronic medical records. According to that study, the reduction of time spent for tasks related to nursing records and sharing of nursing records seemed to have been achieved overall to a considerable extent. That study, however, suggests that challenges remain in the method of sharing nursing records and the information system for real-time recording and its use.

This paper describes a nurse support system of note-taking in hospitals as an extension of a previous study [5]. We use digital pens' feature of extracting written information, along with the reduced resistance to a new interface, which was common in previous studies. A digital pen has the characteristic of "Portability", as we can carry a digital pen to everywhere. For nursing application, portability is very important for practical use as nurses need intense movement and busy daily works. In addition, log information can be used to show the time of written strokes. The portability and use of time information are the novel characteristics of this study.

With the system used in our study, we also attempts to improve the efficiency of nursing activities by building a system that reduces the time spent for tasks for nursing records, thereby supporting nurses in note-taking.

In this paper the authors propose note-taking support system for nurses using digital pen character recognition system. This paper is organized as follow:

In section 3, about the characteristic and components of the note-taking support system.

In section 4, about improving the user interface through test operations.

In section 5, about an evaluation experiment to verify the usefulness of user interface, operational procedure and components in the system which had been built according to results from test operations

In section 6, about summary included the result and consideration of in this study.

3 Note-Taking Support System

3.1 Benefits of Digital Pens

The benefit of digital pens is that the written notes can be stored as data in the pen, which can subsequently be transferred to a PC. This consequently eliminates the necessity of transcribing the notes on another medium. Digital pens also record the time when the notes are taken in a log, allowing the users to know the point in time of each event. In addition, the act of writing on a piece of paper is fundamentally the conventional style of note-taking, which helps reduce resistance that typically accompanies the use of a new device.

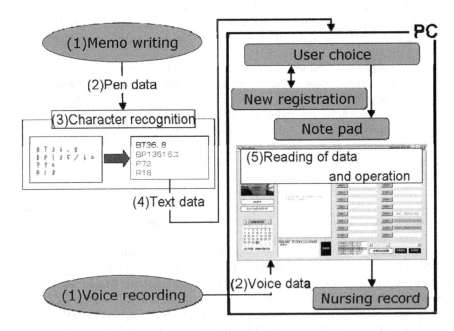

Fig. 2. Flow of the system

3.2 Benefits of Character Recognition

By converting the scripts, into text data through character recognition, the document can easily be used on a PC, which is expected to facilitate the sharing of nursing records. The system can also contribute to data entry for electronic medical records.

3.3 Overview of the System

Opinions of nurses who are currently on the job regarding the proposed system were collected. The note-taking support system was developed so that actual opinions that were gained at the healthcare sites would be reflected.

The overview of the system is shown in Figure 2.

(1) Take notes on the check sheet (exclusive paper specifications in Figure 3) using a digital pen. Use a voice recorder to record voice information if necessary.

(2) Transfer the note data and recorded voice to a PC.

(3) The note data are recognized as characters by character recognition software, "Form OCR v 3.0 of Media Drive Corp."

(4) The result of the character recognition in (3) is produced as text.

(5) The text data are converted from the notes by the application; they are displayed and the recorded voice data can be replayed.

* Steps (3)–(5) are performed automatically.

First, notes are written on a check sheet using a digital pen along with a voice that is recorded on a voice recorder; the pen and voice data are transferred to a PC. The pen data are then recognized automatically as characters, which can be viewed and manipulated with the application.

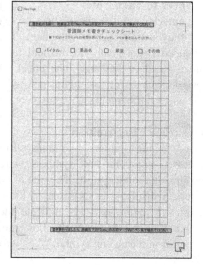

Fig. 3. Check sheet

3.4 A Sample Scenario Using the Proposed System

Nurses are supposed to carry paper sheets on which special dot patterns are printed. They write memos on the sheets with a digital pen during their work with patients and doctors. They bring the sheets and the digital pen back to their office. They put the digital pen to the dock module which is plugged with the PC by USB connection. The information of written strokes is transferred to PC automatically. The images of written strokes are recovered from the transferred information. Using the images, character recognition is done and the text information is extracted from the images.

Then, the recognized character information is used as the input data for the nursing record.

These operations allow the users to input the nursing records efficiently. Instead of key-board input seeing the written memos, the system helps the users even those who are not used to PC. Therefore, the note-taking support system using a digital pen and character recognition assists the users by shortening the input time during their works.

3.5 Specifications and Functions of the System

This system consists primarily of a digital pen and the character recognition system. The benefits of using each component are explained below.

■ Where to Take Notes

The nurses carry the check sheet on which they take notes along with the worksheet that they usually carry with them. The worksheet refers to the list of instructions produced from electronic medical records, which indicates the daily tasks that the nurses need to perform. The check sheet mentioned above is a sheet of custom designed paper for the digital pen, which has a grid printed on it for writing notes. The paper has been made exclusively for use in the study.

■ Character Recognition

Based on the opinions of nurses currently on the job, Japanese katakana, English alphabet, numbers, and symbols were selected as the types of characters to be recognized by the system. The rate of character recognition with this setting was 93%. Figure 4 displays an example of the character recognition results. In Figure 4 the characters in the left box indicate the hand-written characters, and the right box recognized ones respectively. For example, in red frame in Figure 4, the character recognition means the symbol "/" is wrongly recognized as the number "1".

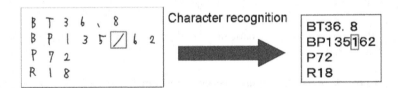

Fig. 4. Result of character recognition

■ Display of Time and Person

The log information of the note data will be saved when the note data are transferred from the digital pen to the PC. The time when the notes are taken is displayed in the log information. The person, who has written the notes, is identifiable according to the unique ID of the pen, which is also included in the log information.

■ Audio-recording Function

Among the opinions of the nurses about the system, there was a request to add an audio-recording function that would allow them to replay the voice to help them take long notes or when they failed to capture or forget some of the doctors' instructions or other messages. For that reason, this system is equipped with a voice recorder to allow voice information replay. We used a portable voice recorder (53g) for a recording device.

■Categories of Notes

The check sheet has been made in such a way that it allows categorization of the notes. Before taking notes, one check box on the sheet that represents the category of the notes to be taken is marked, which will appear in the PC application to allow quick categorizing of the notes.

3.6 Application

The written characters will be recognized automatically and thereafter the application will start when the digital pen is connected to a PC. The text data resulting from character recognition of pen data are sent out to the application.

The operational procedure of the application is as follows:

(1)Login the user
(2)Register a new user *
(3)Notepad (read, view and edit the data)
(4)Enter nursing records
* Only when using the application for the first time.

The user can check the content of the notes and source images, import and replay recorded audio data and display the note log. Furthermore, a nursing record function has been added to reproduce the workflow from confirming and referring to the notes to entering nursing records. Note that this set of nursing records has been developed for the test operation and evaluation test in this study. It differs from the actual records.

4 Test Operation

Because the system is intended for use in medical scenarios, the user interface is particularly important in view of its efficiency and ease of use. Therefore, we aimed at constructing the system by improving the user interface through test operations.

The steps were as follows: test subjects took notes, recorded voice information and used the application (steps (1)–(4) in section 3.4) according to the instruction sheet (Test Operation Procedure) prepared in advance. Thereby, they evaluated the system.

The system was improved based on their evaluation of the test operation, subsequently completed.

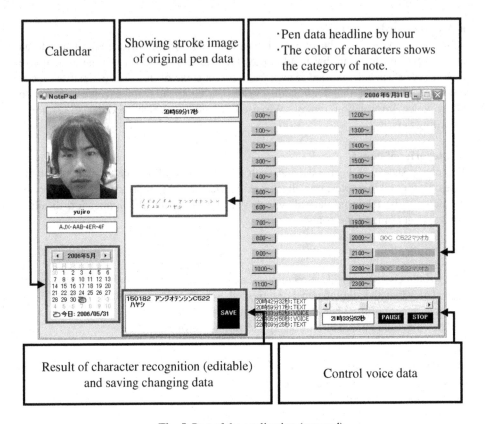

Fig. 5. Part of the application (notepad)

5   Evaluation Experiment

An evaluation experiment was conducted using 10 test subjects to verify the usefulness of user interface, operational procedure and components in the system which had been built according to results from test operations.

In this experiment, the test subjects operated the system following the same procedure as in the test operation. They evaluated it in more detail than in the test operation while adding a numerical method. Evaluation was made based on the following criteria, which used a scale of seven levels of -3 to +3 ([A, B] indicated on the right-hand side of each criterion represent A = -3 and B = +3).

I. Evaluation of the application in total
a. Screen composition   [difficult to see / easy to see]
b. Replay function for recordings   [difficult to use / easy to use]
c. Note search   [difficult to search / easy to search]
d. Note editing   [difficult to edit / easy to edit]
II. Voice recorder
a. Flow from recording to PC connection   [difficult to use / easy to use]
b. Size and weight   [difficult to use / easy to use]

III. Digital pen
a. Ease of writing   [difficult to write / easy to write]
b. Size and weight   [difficult to use / easy to use]
IV. Evaluation of the overall flow of the system based on the actual record entry while referring to the notes
a. Whether the system is useful in actual note-taking (whether appropriate during rushed activities)   [unusable / usable]
b. Whether the system reduces the actual time consumption
                                      [It does not. / It does.]
V. Free answer: remarks, impressions, etc. other than the above

Figure 6 shows the results of the above questionnaire expressed in numerical values. The labels of the horizontal axis represent the evaluation numbers, the blue points represent the average scores and the length of the lines extending above and below the blue points represents the standard deviation.

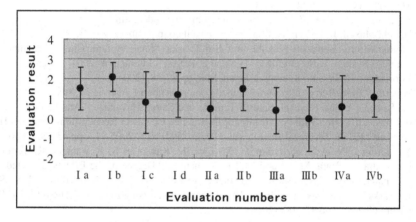

Fig. 6. Results of the evaluation experiment

In general, we got positive evaluation results in this experiment. But the results make us become aware of the dispersion of evaluation of a digital pen by the test subjects. Improvement is necessary in the application and flow of the input devices from to PC connection and so on. Those issues should be solved to facilitate the practical use of note-taking support system for nurses.

6 Summary

In this study, a system was developed that supports nurses in taking notes using a digital pen and character recognition software. Based on the test operation and evaluation experiment of the system, the issues that must be addressed for practical use of the system to support nurses' note-taking have been identified:

• Improve support for urgent situations (voice recognition, usability of the notepad)
• Improve portability (digital pen, check sheet)
• Consider other methods to use the character recognition function.

We will also need to have nurses' experiment and evaluate the improved system in their actual daily work.

Acknowledgements

The author would like to thank Mr. Hironori Seiyama of Media Drive Corporation, for his support.

This research was carried out as a part of the knowledge cluster initiative (commissioned by the Ministry of Education, Culture, Sports, Science and Technology).

References

1. MediaDriveCorp."FormOCRv.3.0"
   http://biz.mediadrive.jp/products/package/formocr03/index.html
2. Hitachi Maxell, Ltd. "Pen it", http://www.maxell.co.jp/penit/
3. Motoki Miura, Buntarou Shizuki, and Jiro Tanaka. "Snail system: Classroom Interaction Support System with Digitized Pens and PDAs." Interaction 2004 Paper Collection, Information Processing Society of Japan, Mar, pp.87-88, (2004)
4. PaperIQ. "BlackBerry" http://www.paperiq.com/blackberry_overview.mspx
5. Go Sawada, Yujiro Hayashi, Satoshi Tamura, and Satoru Hayamizu. "Automatic Correction of Misidentification with Application of Digital Pen Character Recognition System in Home Nursing." IEICE Technical Report, vol. 105, no. 594, NLC 2005-113, pp.43-48, (2006)
6. Y. Kurihara, N. Asai, R. Ishimoto, M. Oka, K. Kawazoe, S. Kawamata, R. Terada, S. Nakamura, M. Hara, M. Futami, and R. Yamanaka. "Degree of the Effects Expected from Computerization of Nursing Records that Have Been Achieved – Reduction of Time Spent for Tasks Related to Nursing Records and Sharing of Nursing Records – The Fifth JAMI-NS paper collection, pp.97-100, (2004)

Human-Robot Interaction in a Ubiquitous House

Simon Thompson, Satoshi Kagami, and Yoshifumi Nishida

Digital Human Research Center, AIST, Aomi Tokyo-to 135-0064, Japan
`simon.thompson@aist.go.jp`

Abstract. This paper reports on the development of a mobile robot system for operation within a house equipped with a ubiquitous sensor network. Human robot interaction is achieved through the combination of on-robot laser range sensing and ultrasonic sensors mounted in the ceiling of the ubiquitous environment. Places, objects or inhabitants within the environment are tagged with ultrasonic transmitters from which approximate location can be estimated. Fusing these position estimates with on-robot sensor information, the robot can navigate to the transmitter location, approach the target and await further interaction.

1 Introduction

Robot service providers for the family house require basic functions such as autonomous navigation and methods for initiating or responding to human robot interaction. Such functions can be difficult to realize in an autonomous robot because of technical difficulties in sensing uncertain environments. In particular in a home based environment, human robot interaction can often be initiated by people outside the robot's sensor range, for example in a different room. To alleviate this problem, as well as for providing other services in it's own right, a ubiquitous sensor network embedded within the house can provide information to facilitate human robot interaction.

The proposed system works in this manner: an autonomous mobile robot with on-board sensors, operating within a ultrasonic sensing network equipped house, is connected via wireless ethernet to a server providing the locations of various ultrasonic tags throughout the environment. Given a command, the robot can plan autonomously plan a path within a known map to the targeted transmitters location and using on-robot sensor information, approach the object nearest the target location in preparation for human robot interaction.

The paper is organised as follows: Section 2 describes the hardware specifications of the robot platforms and the ubiquitous sensor network. Section 3 then briefly describes the autonomous navigation capabilities of the mobile robot system such as on-board sensing, localisation, and path-planning. Ultrasonic tag position estimation by the ubiquitous sensor network is also described. Next, Section 4 presents a method for approaching ultrasonic tag designated targets and fusing such targets with on-robot sensor data. Section 5 then describes an experiment which shows the system performing such an approach to a ultrasonic tagged person. Finally Section 6 presents some conclusions.

H. Zha et al. (Eds.): VSMM 2006, LNCS 4270, pp. 437–445, 2006.

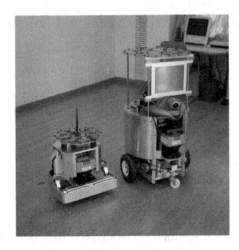

Fig. 1. Mobile Robot Platforms: each with non-holonomic steering and 2D laser range finder sensors

2   Robot Platforms and Ubiquitous Environment

The two mobile robot platforms are small two wheel (with casters) differential driven robots which move non-holonomically. They range from 30-55cm in height and have a diameter of 35 and 50cm. They are equipped with dual Xeon 3.0GhzCPU's which run RT-Linux. On board sensors include wheel odometry, 2D laser range finders, 32 channel microphone arrays, stereo camera systems and a video conference system.

The ubiquitous house is shown in Figure 2. It has sensor clusters mounted in the kitchen, two bedrooms, the entrance and the living rooms, with a total of 16 sensor clusters. The sensor clusters are conical in shape and consist of 15 ultrasonic receivers set in a cone, surrounded by 8 microphones arranged in a ring. A sample sensor cluster and ultrasonic transmitter tag is shown in Figure 3 along with a floodplain of the ubiquitous house.

3   Autonomous Navigation and Ubiquitous Sensing

The system described operates in a distributed environment, with component modules running on various computers within the ubiquitous house and on-board the mobile robot. The system architecture is shown in Figure 4. In brief, robot sensing and actuation control is situated on robot, while higher level robot control software such as localisation and path planning are executed off-board on a separate machine. Also on board the robot is a module for processing data from the local microphone array (speech recognition). The on-robot software acts as a server to the higher level client. In the same fashion, the higher level client reads ultrasonic tag position location from the ubiquitous network server.

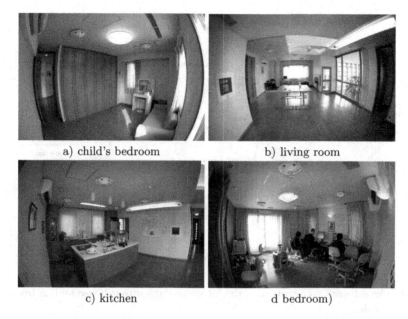

a) child's bedroom   b) living room

c) kitchen   d bedroom)

Fig. 2. Views of the house with ubiquitous sensor network

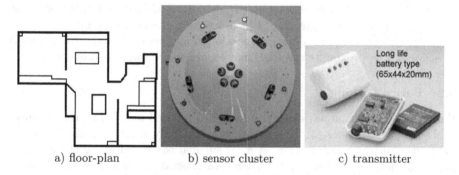

a) floor-plan   b) sensor cluster   c) transmitter

Fig. 3. Ubiquitous House: a) floor plan of ubiquitous house; b) sample ubiquitous sensor: ultrasonic transmitters mounted on conical frame and surrounded by a microphone ring; and c) ultrasonic transmitter

3.1 Localisation

Localisation is the process of determining where a robot is within a known map. The framework behind the localisation system developed in this work is that of particle filter localisation [1]. This is now a widely used method for mobile robot localisation which uses sampling of the robots position to approximate its location probability density function. A motion model is used to predict a sample's future position according to control or odometry information, and predicted positions are evaluated according to how their expected sensory view

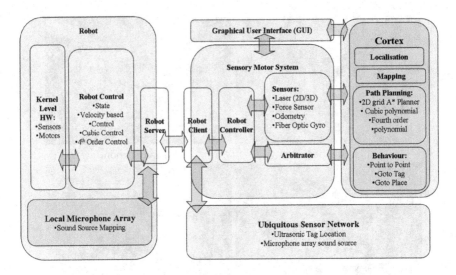

Fig. 4. The software architecture of the integrated ubiquitous house and mobile robot control system

matches the current sensor view. Resampling of the predicted positions based on this evaluation ensures the sampled positions remain distributed about the correct localisation estimate. For 2D sensory data, the matching process can be done efficiently enough to allow a large enough number of particles (or samples) to accurately approximate the PDF and ensure continuous localisation.

3.2   Path Planning

Path planning is achieved using the method proposed in [2]. The method uses a 2D A* path planner [3] to generate the optimally shortest path through a 2D grid map to a goal location. A local subgoal is created along the 2D path (at about $5m$) and is used as the target for generating cubic and fourth order curvature polynomials. These local trajectories are continuous in curvature and allow the robot to make smooth motions through the environment.

3.3   Ubiquitous Sensing

The ubiquitous sensor network can calculate the position of ultrasonic tags which move the house [4]. Ultrasonic transmitters, which can be mounted on objects within or inhabitants of the ubiquitous house emit ultrasonic pulses which are then detected by the various sensor clusters throughout the house. Through multi-lateration, a form of redundant trilateration, the time of flight of the transmitted pulse to ultrasonic sensors can be used to produce an estimate of the transmitters position [4]. While the accuracy of the estimated position is quite accurate close to sensor cluster mount locations, estimation error increases with distance from the sensors as well as with proximity to walls.

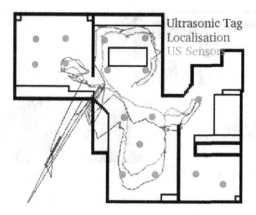

Fig. 5. Map of ubiquitous house and sample ubiquitous sensor: ultrasonic transmitters mounted on conical frame and surrounded by a microphone ring

An experiment to measure ultrasonic tag position estimation was conducted by mounted such a tag on a mobile robot and moving the robot throughout the environment. The results were compared with the localisation based position estimate of the mobile robot and a plot of both estimated paths is shown in Figure 5. As can be seen the ultrasonic position estimate can vary greatly with the localisation estimate, especially in places such as doorways.

4   Approach a Tagged Object

A crucial part of robot based services is that of initiating human robot interaction. As mentioned in the introduction, one method of facilitating this interaction is through the use of a ubiquitous sensing environment. An example of this facilitation, and the focus of this paper is the use of ultrasonic tags to allow for easy position estimation of objects or inhabitants of the ubiquitous environment. Upon receiving an estimate of the target location the robot can then plan a path to nominated objects without directly sensing them. When such objects come within sensor range, the robot must then match objects in it's local sensor view with the noisy ultrasonic tag estimate, and approach the corresponding object. To do this the robot must have a method to segment and approach local objects, a method to approach distance unseen target positions and a method to fuse the local sensor information with the rough tag estimate.

4.1   Map Segmentation

Current sensor data can be divide into object/background categories based on the known map. From the current estimated position of the robot, an expected laser-view can be generated which represents all expected laser-map intersections. Using a threshold distance, this expected view can be used to segment previously unknown objects from the current sensor data.

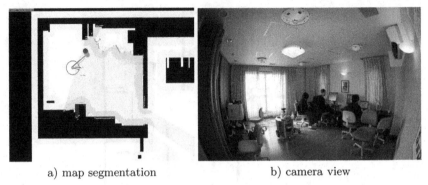

a) map segmentation   b) camera view

Fig. 6. An example of map segmentation of local laser view and the associated camera image

Fig. 7. An example of planning to a target designated by estimated ultrasonic tag location

4.2   Approaching Segmented Objects

Detected object sensor data points can then be further processed to identify specific objects to approach. In this work, because the aim is to approach objects identified by nearness to an ultrasonic tag's estimated location, as an intermediate step, the object to approach was identified by the closest object. By identifying the closest point and calculating a position 50cm in front of the object (in the direction of the robot's approach) a target position can be nominated for path planning and subsequent robot approach. An example of segmenting the closest object and planning an approach to the object is shown in Figure 6. Current laser data is shown in green, with segmented objects (laser data not matched to map) shown in blue. The closest object is designated by a yellow circle.

4.3 Approaching Ultrasonic Location

Once a command is given to go to an ultrasonic tag the robot navigation system will attempt to navigate to that goal position. The robot-control software reads the position (x, y) of the ultrasonic tag from the ubiquitous sensor network server and assigns this position as the target in the path planning task. An example of such a planning task is shown in Figure 7, with the plan shown in light blue and the estimated tag position in maroon.

4.4 Fusing Sensed Objects and Ultrasonic Tag Location

Because the sensor tag location can be inaccurate and located within the 2 dimensional bounds of a physical object, it is desirable to associate locally sensed objects with the ultrasonic tag location, and approach the object most likely to be carrying the ultrasonic tag. To do this there must be some fusion between the location identified by the ubiquitous sensor and the local sensor data captured on-board the robot.

This work uses the RANSAC (RANdom SAmpling Consensus)[5] to propose and evaluate likely object centroids in a Gaussian distribution around the tag location. Evaluate of potential centers involve a voting system based on nearness of segmented object sensor data to a hypothesised object radius. The object radius on which data points should lie, is set to 20cm to roughly approximate the size of a human "object". The object center which is evaluated as the most likely given the current laser view is then designated as the object to approach. As in the preceding section the robot control software then plans to approach within 50cm of this object.

5 Experiment

An experiment was conducted to confirm the ability of the system to facilitate the beginning of interaction between an out-of-view object and the mobile robot. The mobile robot is given the task of navigating to a ultrasonic tag located in a another room of the house. Given the position of the tag by the ubiquitous sensor network the robot plans a path, and navigates to the room containing the ultrasonic tag. Upon entering the room, the robot associates objects segmented from local sensor data with the estimated tag position and approaches the object. Screen-shots of the experiment captured from the GUI interface of the system are shown in Figure 8.

6 Conclusion

This paper has described the integration of a ubiquitous sensor network with a mobile robot navigation system to facilitate human-robot interaction. An autonomous mobile robot system was developed with an interface to communicate with a ubiquitous sensor server which provides estimates of the location of ultrasonic tag transmitters within the environment. This information can be used

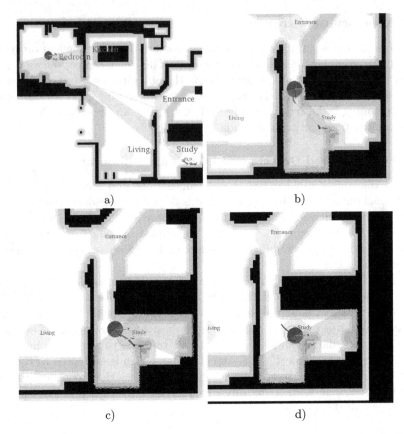

Fig. 8. An example of approaching a tagged object within the ubiquitous house. Figure a) shows the planned path to estimated tag location, while b), c) and d) show the robot approaching a local goal identified by fusing the transmitter location with locally detected objects.

to plan paths to, and approach objects and inhabitants of the environment, even if they are out of view of the robot. The details of the mobile robot system and the ubiquitous sensor network were described and a method to fuse local sensor data with a rough transmitter position estimate for approaching target objects was proposed. An experiment illustrating such an interaction was presented.

References

1. S. Thrun, W. Burgard and D. Fox. *Robust Monte Carlo Localisation for Mobile Robots*, Artificial Intelligence 128, pp99-141, 2001
2. S. Thompson and S. Kagami. *Smooth Trajectory Planning with Obstacle Avoidance for Car-Like Mobile Robots*, Proceedings of the 23rd Conference of the Robotics Society of Japan, 2005.

3. J. Kuffner. *Efficient Optimal Search of Euclidean-Cost grids and Lattices*, Proceedings of the IEEE/RSJ International Conference on Intelligent Robots and Systems, 2004.

4. Y. Nishida, H. Aizawa, T. Hori, N. Hoffman, T. Kanade and M. Kakikura. *3D Ultrasonic Tagging System for Observing Human Activity*, Proceedings of the IEEE/RSJ International Conference on Intelligent Robots and Systems, 2003.

5. M. Fishler and R. Bolles. *Random Sample Consensus: A Paradigm for Model Fitting with Application to Image Analysis and Automated Cartography*, Communication of the ACM, Vol 24, June 1982, pp. 381-395.

Development and Evaluation of a Hybrid Shared Tele-Haptic System

Shinji Yamabiraki, Tsuneo Kagawa, Nishino Hiroaki, and Kouichi Utsumiya

Department of Computer Science and Intelligent Systems,
Oita University, 700 Dannoharu, Oita, 870-1124, Japan
{yamabira, kagawa, hn, utsumiya}@csis.oita-u.ac.jp

Abstract. A constitution method of a distributed virtual environment using haptic devices is shown. In recent years, the force-feedback devices have been developed and they have gotten a lot of attentions to realize a new interaction modality between human begins and computer systems. The haptic channels, however, are more sensitive to the network QoS (quality of service) such as delays and packet losses than the visual and acoustic channels. Therefore, we propose a new constitution method for realizing an effective virtual environment even in the low-quality network. The proposed method adopts a hybrid approach using the client-server and peer-to-peer models. In this paper, we describe our proposed method, an implemented system, and the results of a preliminary experiment to evaluate the scalability of the proposed architecture.

1 Introduction

In recent years, distributed virtual environments (DVEs) have dramatically evolved depending on the progress of network technologies and computer system performance. In traditional DVEs, interaction modalities have been restricted to be the visual (3D computer graphics, movie) and acoustic (sound, voice) channels. Recent advances in force-feedback technologies or haptic devices, however, enable to incorporate the sense of touch into the traditional DVEs. The DVEs empowered by the haptic devices can realize a highly realistic communication environment to allow collaborative work such as lifting and deforming 3D objects in a virtual space and shake hands with remotely separated users.

The haptic device information, however, needs to be updated at extremely high frequency to present users natural forces through the device, because the human touch sensation is very sensitive. The update rate of the haptic attributes should generally be 1KHz compared with the 30Hz in the case of visual channel. Therefore, communicating and sharing haptic information over the network must overcome the degradation of network QoS and haptic rendering quality caused by the delays and packet losses. Moreover, a traditional client-server model's disadvantage is that the whole system response degrades according to the increase of client systems because of the server's overload.

We are studying a constitution method of DVEs that can provide the natural and stable force sharing between remotely separated users. In recent years, the network

H. Zha et al. (Eds.): VSMM 2006, LNCS 4270, pp. 446–455, 2006.

speed between Japan and Korea has been upgraded so rapidly. A marine fiber cable called KJCN (Korea-Japan Cable Network) becomes available in mid 2001 between Japan and Korea. Today, the network supports multimedia-based communications such as e-Learning and medical collaborations using high-quality video conference technologies [1]. We, a VR research group at Oita University, are conducting a collaborative research project with KIST (Korea Institute of Science and Technology) in Seoul and Kyushu University in Japan, designing and implementing a technical framework to realize a haptic-empowered DVE [2].

In this paper, we describe a feature and implementation method of the proposed architecture for realizing high-speed haptic processing and a scalable system, and show the results of a preliminary experiment to validate the system scalability.

2 Related Work

There are many related projects who applied the haptic technologies to make more realistic and effective systems than the traditional ones using only visual and acoustic channels [3]. We found that the working time of collaborative tasks using both haptic and visual channels is about three times shorter than the one using only visual channel.

There is a fundamental study about the communication technology to effectively support the haptic channel and construct an active DVE system. But their target environment for the study is a homogeneous campus network and no consideration on a heterogeneous network environment such as the common Internet. Hasegawa et al. proposed a server-centric architecture [4]. In their architecture, the server is responsible for all principal transactions such as handling the haptic devices, keeping the virtual space attributes up to data, and synchronizing an image with a force-feedback in a small amount of time (normally 1 millisecond for the haptic update). They don't validate how well the proposed architecture can scale. Hikichi et al. devised another approach by breaking a DVE transaction into the server and client parts [5]. In their approach, the server manages the DVE attributes up to date while the client is responsible for the haptic device handling. They reported that the acceptable limit for network delay is about 20 milliseconds if the client handles the haptic operations. The limit, however, goes up to 80 milliseconds if the server takes care of the haptic devices. Their experimental system consists of two client systems and has no considerations on larger systems configured by more than two clients.

Consequently, most previous approaches are only dealing with the DVE system consisting of two (a pair of) clients, and their experiments cannot validate the scalability of general DVEs with more than two clients. Therefore the behaviours of the DVEs using the large number of haptic devices are still unclear. We design a DVE architecture enabling to flexibly increase the number of clients, and perform an experiment to evaluate the system scalability when supporting more than two clients.

3 System Implementation

Our method is slightly similar with the client-server approach proposed by Hikichi et al [5]. We further improve the architecture by synthesizing the client-server's data consistency and the peer-to-peer's scalability in a hybrid fashion. While the client-server model preserves the consistency of DVE attributes, the scalability is poor because the server tends to be a bottleneck. On the other hand, the peer-to-peer model can't assure the consistency, but it can scale well. By the proposed method, we realize both the consistency of the virtual space attributes and the responsive haptic interactions.

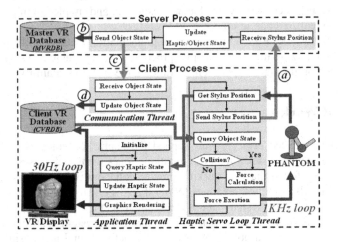

Fig. 1. Process flow between server and client

3.1 Communication Between Server and Clients

Figure 1 shows a process flow between the server and a client in our proposed method. In the method, DVE attributes such as 3D objects, participants' information and haptic cursors (the position of the PHANTOM stylus tip) are managed in an integrated fashion by the VR database. The VR database consists of the client VR database (CVRDB) and the master VR database (MVRDB). The CVRDB is the locally copied VR database retained in each client, and the MVRDB is a unique VR database resided in the server.

The client system has two threads, the application thread for graphics rendering (30Hz) and the haptic servo loop thread for haptic processing (1KHz). The application thread has a role to update the VR state information such as the virtual objects' position, orientation and haptic cursor position in the virtual space and renders an updated graphics image for every 1/30 second. The haptic servo loop thread processes all tasks required to maintain the stable touch sensation via the haptic devices. It performs the tasks such as the stylus tip (haptic cursor) position acquisition, the collision detection between the haptic cursor and the virtual objects, and the reaction force calculation and exertion if the collision occurs. The servo loop needs to maintain the 1KHz update loop to generate the stable haptic sensation. Therefore, keeping the extreme high update rate (1KHz) in the haptic channel is a crucial requirement for implementing the successful VR system empowered by the touch sensation.

The processing flow between the server and each client is as follows:

(Figure 1 –a) each client senses the haptic states such as position, orientation and a button state of the PHANTOM stylus and sends them to the server. The CVRDB is not updated at this time.

(Figure 1 –b) the server updates the MVRDB attributes based on the haptic cursor information sent from all participating clients.

(Figure 1 –c) the server delivers the updated MVRDB attributes to all participating clients using the multicast protocol.

(Figure 1 –d) each client updates the local CVRDB attributes by reflecting the latest MVRDB attributes received form the server and render the updated virtual space.

In this way, the system preserves the consistency of the virtual space for all participating clients. Because the synchronization between each client's CVRDB and the server's MVRDB is done through the server, our method is considered to be very similar with the client-server approach.

3.2 Responsive Haptic Interaction

As already mentioned in the previous section, there is a big difference between the update rates for the haptic and visual channels (1KHz in the haptic and 30Hz in the visual). In the traditional client-server system, information about the virtual space attributes and the haptic states is delivered to all participating clients via the server. Therefore, the end-user QoS for both visual and haptic channels can easily degrade if the server becomes a bottleneck. The users particularly feel uncomfortable sensations with even a small amount of delays between the stylus tip sensing and the reactive force exertion, because the haptic device behaves as a bi-directional input-output device. Additionally, the end-user QoS for the haptic channel goes down if the network performance degradations such as increasing delays, packet losses and jitters occur.

Therefore, we propose a hybrid architecture as shown in figure 2. The peer-to-peer model directly sends and receives all haptic information between the participating clients without going through the server. This method realizes the force sharing between all clients by guaranteeing the 1KHz update rate. Meanwhile the virtual space attributes synchronization between all participating clients is managed via the server as described in **3.1**, each client renders the updated graphics image with 30Hz update rate. Accordingly, we improve the system scalability and stability by simultaneously implementing the asynchronous/high-speed haptic channel and the synchronous/low-speed visual channel. There are separated communication paths for the haptic and visual channels.

Moreover, we presume that the visual channel is dominant and works superior to the haptic channel in human sensations. Srinivasan et al. reported that the visual channel supersedes to the haptic channel especially for recognizing the stiffness and surface materials of the 3D virtual objects [6]. In other words, if the haptic channel is maintained with the 1KHz update rate, the users can operate 3D objects without any uncomfortable feelings due to the visual channel superiority even if there are some mismatches between the visual and haptic states cased by the network performance degradation or the overloaded server. The proposed method uses the superiority of visual channel to share a natural and stable force feedback between the remote users. Therefore, it can accommodate even a long-distance heterogeneous network such as the one between KIST and Oita University that cannot preserve the 1KHz update rate for the haptic channel.

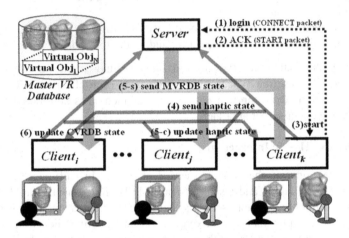

Fig. 2. Proposed DVE system architecture

4   Evaluation Experiments

We conducted some experiments to verify the effectiveness of the proposal method. First, we explore an acceptable limit of the network QoS parameters allowing the collaborative tasks without losing the operational stability. Next, we measure the network QoS parameters between KIST and Oita University as a preliminary experiment to construct the real DVE system. Finally, we evaluate the scalability of the proposed architecture.

4.1   Task for Experiment

We developed a VR application to inspect two haptic sharing options supported in the proposed method, the object sharing and device sharing options. The object sharing is an option to allow the users to collaboratively lift up and move the virtual objects in the virtual space. The device sharing is a mode to let the users shaking hands remotely through the network. Figure 3 shows a snapshot of the application. The small spheres labelled as "haptic cursors" in the figure show the cursor positions of the participating clients. This figure shows that the virtual space consists of four clients. In the object sharing mode, the users can hold the same virtual object and collaboratively lift up the

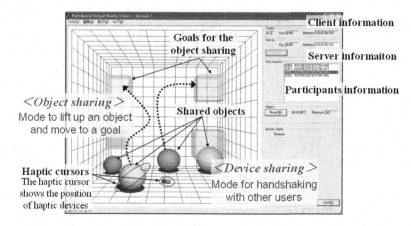

Fig. 3. An application for experiments

grabbed sphere toward one of the goals which are the four transparent boxes placed in the shared space.

In the object sharing mode, the users indirectly feel and share the other clients' forces through the grabbed object, because they can collaboratively hold and lift up the same virtual object. Therefore, the object sharing is considered to be a coarse-grained force sharing task. On the other hand, the device sharing is a fine-grained force sharing option, because the users virtually share only one haptic device with others by accurately synchronizing all clients' haptic devices. Because the tighter force sharing consumes more system resources, the network QoS and server responses become worse than the object sharing mode.

4.2 An Acceptable Limit of Network QoS

As mentioned in section 1, stable haptic communication highly depends on the network QoS parameters such as delays, packet losses, and jitters. Therefore, we firstly implement the application on the campus network in Oita University to assess the correlation figures between the user-level QoS and the network QoS parameters. We add the queuing function inside the server to intentionally simulate the delays, packet losses, the jitters on the real network. Six subjects are employed to perform three experimental sessions (two clients a session). We asked them to do both of the object sharing and the device sharing tasks as described in **4.1** with various network QoS parameters [7].

The three graphs in figure 4 show the results of the experiment. Figure 4(a) shows the correlation between the user-level QoS (degree of satisfaction for operability) and the simulated delays. Figure 4(b) and 4(c) present the packet losses and jitters in the same way, respectively. According to the subjects' introspective reports, we identified the 3.5 is an acceptable rate to perform collaboration without losing the operability. The acceptable limits quantify the threshold limits for the delays, packet losses, and jitters as shown in figure 4.

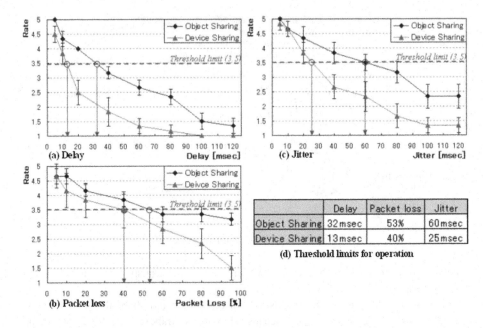

Fig. 4. Threshold limit of network QoS

4.3 QoS Measurement Between KIST and Oita University

As mentioned in the previous section, one of our goals is to construct the DVE system between KIST and Oita University. Therefore, we measured the network QoS parameters on the real network between KIST and Oita University.

The proposed method guarantees the consistency of virtual space information of all clients by collectively managing and synchronizing them through the MVRDB on the server. Therefore, the consistent haptic behaviour performance highly depends on the round-trip time between a client and the server. Consequently, we measured the delays and packet losses occurred in the round-trip haptic transactions between two sites.

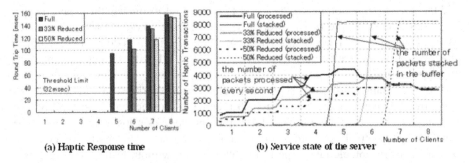

(a) Haptic Response time   (b) Service state of the server

Fig. 5. System scalability. The server is HP XW6200 (Xeon 3.6GHz, 2GB MMU).

The result shows that the dominance effect of visual channel can effectively compensate for the time-critical haptic communications. If the visual images can be updated within 30Hz, the users have an illusion that they are feeling the appropriate haptic responses conforming the visual information in spite of insufficient network speed to keep the 1KHz haptic update rate. The result shows that the visual update rate can be maintained in 30Hz because the average round-trip delay time between KIST and Oita University is 16.9 milliseconds.

4.4 Evaluation of System Scalability

Figure 5(a) shows the correlation between the system response time and the number of participating clients. The response time is a round-trip time between the server and a client. The leftmost blue bar labelled as "full" presents the response times measured when all haptic states (1,000 packets a client) detected from the haptic devices are delivered. The haptic state is the PHANTOM stylus tip three-dimensional position. The mid green bars labelled as "33% reduced" and rightmost white bars labelled as "50% reduced" are cases that 33% and 50% haptic states out of the whole data are thinned out to reduce the traffic, respectively. The horizontal thin red line in the figure shows the threshold limit of the delay (32 milliseconds) for the object sharing task as shown in figure 4(d).

The result of the experiment shows the maximum number of clients to support for a stable force sharing is four. Additionally, we found that the response time drastically degrades at a certain number of clients independently of the data reductions. The result indicates that the maximum number of clients to support in the DVE system needs to properly be set, because the response time drastically degrades when the clients exceed the maximum number.

4.5 Discussion

Figure 5(b) presents the number of haptic states processed by the server every second. The graph also shows the number of packets stacked in the system buffer and waiting to be processed by the server. The server is the HP XW6200 (Xeon 3.6GHz, 2GB MMU) in the experiment. There are six lines in this figure: the three thick lines shows the number of haptic states processed by the server in a second, the three thin lines shows the number of stacked packets in the buffer according to the server loads. As mentioned in **4.4**, the response time drastically degrades at a certain number of clients. When the number of exchanged haptic states exceeds the number of treatable packets per unit time by the server, the buffer quickly overflows and the haptic response drastically degrades. In the case of no data reduction (full data) illustrated as the solid black line in figure 5(b), the number of haptic states processed in a second increases about 1000 packets when a client is added in the system. For example, assume that the number of participating clients is two, about 2000 packets are sent to the server, and about 4000 requests are sent when the number of clients becomes four. Figure 5(b) indicates that the server can process all packets when the clients are less than five. When the number of clients reaches five (about 5000 packets are sent to the server in a second), 500 packets are stacked in the buffer in a second because the server can process at most 4500 packets. In this way, the users may feel uncomfortable senses on the haptic channel caused by the sudden degradation of the haptic response. This phenomenon happens when the number of participating clients exceeds the maximum connectable clients.

As shown in figure 5, we can improve the maximum connectable clients by reducing the communication data because the number of packets to process decreases. Immoderate reduction of haptic data communication, however, induces uncomfortable and unstable haptic interactions. Therefore, a data reduction method to eliminate the undesirable discomfort for the haptic interactions is needed to improve the scalability.

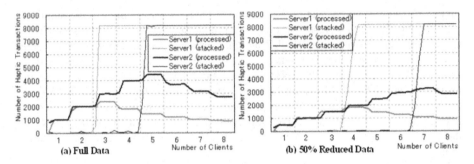

Fig. 6. Comparison by two servers

The server1 is TOSHIBA Dynabook (Pentium4–M 1.8GHz, 768MB MMU).
The server2 is HP XW6200 (Xeon 3.6GHz, 2GB MMU).

Figure 6 shows the compared data using two different servers with different performance. The server1 is TOSHIBA Dynabook (Pentium4-M 1.8GHz, 768MB MMU), and the server2 is HP XW6200 (Xeon 3.6GHz, 2GB MMU) in the figure. Figure 6(a) shows the case for the full data to communicate, and figure 6(b) shows the case for the 50% data reduction. As similar with figure 5(b), the thick lines shows the number of haptic states processed by the server every second, and the thin lines shows the number of stacked packets in the buffer. The maximum connectable number of clients for the server1 is two, and the number for the server2 is four. In the case of using the 50% data reduction, the numbers are three for the server1 and six for the server2. From this result, we found that the maximum connectable number of clients strongly depends on the server's available hardware resources because the server2's maximum number is twice as high as the server1's and the server2's CPU speed is about twice as fast.

5   Conclusion

In this paper, we described the constitution method of DVEs using haptic communication channels and some experiments to discover correlations between the user-level QoS, the network QoS, and the system scalability. Because the human's sense-of-touch modality only accepts micro-delays for stable interaction, we designed a new DVE architecture to implement a practical system on the long-haul international network such as the one between Korea and Japan. We adopted the peer-to-peer model to immediately share the haptic state between the participating clients, and the client-server model to manage the shared data in an integrated fashion. In recent years, many research projects of the DVEs incorporate the haptic interface into the shared virtual environment The number of clients to support in their experiments, however, is limited to a pair (two) and the behaviour of the DVE system consisting of more than two clients is unclear. Therefore, we conducted some experiments to validate the scalability of the proposed DVE architecture by allowing more than two clients be configured in the experiment. According to the results of the experiments, we found that the maximum connectable number of clients is four with no data reduction, the number grows to five if 33% of the whole data is reduced, and the number becomes six when 50% data can be reduced. Moreover, we found that the maximum connectable number of clients should properly be set to realize the stable DVE system empowered by the haptic interface.

References

1. K. Araki, K. Okamura, and M. Hirabaru: Korea-Kyushu Gigabit Network: A Frontier Network Research Project beyond the Strait, Proc. International Workshop on Informations & Electrical Engineering (IWIE2002), pp.289-292, 2002.
2. H. Nishino, S. Yamabiraki, Y.-M. Kwon, Y. Okada, and K. Utsumiya: A Distributed Virtual Reality Framework for Korea-Japan High-Speed Network Testbed, Proc. of the IEEE 20th Int'l Conf. on Advanced Information Networking and Applications (AINA2006), Vol.1, pp. 443-438, 2006.
3. X. Shen, J. Zhou, A. E. Saddik, and N. D. Georganas: Architecture and Evaluation of Tele-Haptic Environments, Proc. IEEE DS-RT2004, pp.53-60, 2004.
4. T. Hasegawa, Y. Ishibashi, and S. Tasaka: A Causality and Inter-Destination Synchronization Control Scheme for Haptic Media in Distributed Virtual Environments, Tech. Report of IEICE, CQ2002-133, pp.19-24, 2002 (in Japanese).
5. K. Hikichi, H. Morino, I. Matsumoto, K. Sezaki, and Y. Yasuda: Proposal and Evaluation of Systems for Haptics Collaboration, Trans. Of the IEICE, Vol.J86-B, No.2, pp. 268-278, 2003 (in Japanese).
6. M. A. Srinivasan, G. L. Beauregard, and D. L. Brock: The impact of Visual Information in the Haptic Perception of Stiffness in Virtual Environments, Proc. ASME Dynamic System and Control Division, DSC, Vol.58, pp.555-559, 1996.
7. S. Yamabiraki: A Framework for Realistic Haptic Communication Using Gigabit Network, APII Workshop Poster Presentation, http://anf.ne.kr/news/APII_Workshop_2005.htm, 2005.

Experimental Investigation on Integral Cognition by Multiple Senses

Kazuo Tani[1], Takuya Kawamura[1], and Satoshi Murase[2]

[1] Gifu University, Yanagido, Gifu 501-1193, Japan
tani@info.gifu-u.ac.jp
[2] Fujitsu Chubu Systems Limited, 2-9-29 Nishiki, Nagoya 460-0003, Japan

Abstract. Humans cognize images of events by perceiving through senses the stimuli generated by events. VR started the idea to let an artifact event generate the stimulation equal to that generated by the original event. For further generalization, we investigated the possibility of letting a human cognize an equivalent image from non-equal stimulation. In the experiment, variable integral stimuli of force, visual, and auditory senses are presented to a subject and integral cognition is compared in the measure of integral intensity. This will hopefully lead to a broader region of cognition possible using limited equipment for presenting stimulation.

Keywords: Multiple senses, Integral cognition, Integral intensity.

1 Introduction

The recent advancement of Virtual Reality (VR) technology is striking and VR is beginning to be used in many aspects in human lives. A human generally perceives an event using his/her five senses in an integrated process. Traditional VR has worked on presentation in each sense, such as visual or auditory sense, separately and developed sophisticated presentation systems. However, research on "multiple-sense integral presentation systems", in which multiple senses are used interrelatedly, has just started.

For effective integral presentation of multiple senses, knowledge about human perception is indispensable. Former researches have reported that multiple senses have interrelated influence on human perception. We expect that, using such interrelation between senses, perception of higher degree of reality is possible by means of multiple-sense integral presentation. Even if we use only modest presentation devices of individual senses, we could present higher reality by using these devices in an integrated way.

This paper experimentally seeks for the possibility that a certain integral stimulation is perceived as equivalent to another integral stimulation. We hope the experimental results lead us to broader knowledge.

2 Events, Senses, Stimuli, Perception, and Cognition

Here we try to define senses, perception, and cognition [1]. A "sense" is regarded as a communication channel consisting of a physical form of stimulation and a type of

H. Zha et al. (Eds.): VSMM 2006, LNCS 4270, pp. 456–465, 2006.

responding receptors, and its behavior. "Perception" is to capture, by processing the signals from receptors, the group of stimuli as a distinct cluster. "Cognition" is to classify the result of perception by creating an image of an event. Stimuli are regarded to be generated by events in the real world. Cognition is a device to capture the events as correctly as possible.

Events generally generate stimuli of plural senses. A human perceives stimuli through plural senses and cognizes as images of events. We will call the processes of the group of signals of multiple senses for perception and cognition "integral perception" and "integral cognition". Generation of stimuli of multiple senses for this purpose is called "integral stimulation".

We assume that sets of events, stimuli, perception, and cognition constitute respective spaces, namely "event space", "stimulation space", "perception space", and "cognition space". An event is represented as a single point in the event space. The event generates a group of stimuli which is represented as a single point in the stimulation space. The group of stimuli is projected, through multiple channels of senses and perception functions, onto a single point in the perception space. The single point in the perception space is projected by the cognition function, usually onto a single point in the cognition space.

It is difficult to differentiate perception from cognition. In our study, however, we consider they are different and so are the perception space and the cognition space. For example, the famous picture of two faces or a vase is projected onto one point in the perception space but is switched to and fro between two points in the cognition space.

Traditional VR makes an effort to present, by means of artifact events, the same stimuli as produced by original events, thereby inducing one to cognize the images of original events. It is an effort to devise a projection from different points in the event space to one point in the *stimulation space* [2]. Our concept, on the other hand, is the assumption of projections from different points in stimulation space onto one point in the *cognition space*, and our work is to investigate experimentally the possibility of such projections. Fig. 1 shows our concept.

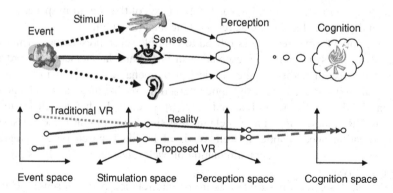

Fig. 1. Concept of integral cognition

It is sometimes the case that, for humans, perception of stimuli of one sense is related to that of other sense. Pain is sometimes perceived from cold. One feels warmth from a hand over a dead stove. One recognizes the motion of the train one is on when one sees the next train outside, but actually the next train starts moving. This case is an illusion across senses. There is a phenomenon called "synaesthesia" [3] for some people, in which a stimulus of one sense involuntarily evokes perception of other sense, such as "When I look at a word, I see a color." and "I see a shape from a taste." Synaesthesia is not common to people.

From these facts, it is considered that humans do not perceive separately in senses but perceive integratedly.

3 Purpose of Our Research

The practical purpose of our research is to investigate the possibility of different integral stimuli evoking the same integral cognition, or in other words evoking the same images of events. Recent VR systems often have stimulation of several senses. Then the idea is a matter of course to generate integral stimuli of so many senses in an organized way. Our concept assumes many-to-one correspondence between integral stimulation and integral cognition. If this correspondence is found, we need only to use a smaller region in the stimulation space to cover a particular region in the cognition space than in a conventional method. In this way, a multi-sense presentation device, though limited in its ranges, can cover a broader region in the cognition space. This method will hopefully permit us to present broader area of event images with cost-limited devices such as game machines.

What method is appropriate to investigate the integral cognition in our study? It is not yet the time when we have any standards to rely on to make investigations and experiments. We will define and conduct experiments arbitrarily, obtain and analyze results, and repeat this process before we may find something that works as a standard.

Based on this expectation, we have conceived two kinds of experiments. In the experiments, we adopted "integral intensity" as an axis of the cognition space, to scale the strength the subject feels when he receives the integral stimuli.

There are some former researches related to multiple sense presentation. Tanaka et al. [4] propose the synchronized presentation in visual and haptic senses in order to create a high sense of reality for the physical phenomena such as collisions. Fang et al. [5] provide museum visitors with haptic interactions so that they can touch and feel texture and hardness of objects. Bae and Jang [6] developed a haptic suit for tactile feedback in VR games. Zang et al. [7] claims that simulation of cutting soft tissues in surgical operation needs haptic as well as visual feedback based on an integrated model. These works try to present stimulation of each sense as accurately as possible according to physical models.

Some recent researches have interests in the interrelation between senses. Hara et al. [8] investigated the illusion occurring in visual-haptic interrelation. Garancs [9] developed artistic "metaphor" in his immersive artwork, explored the extremes of audiovisual perception, and conducted experiments to explore "artificial synaesthesia" or how the senses are interrelated. Our work is rather on this line and tries to investigate the interrelation quantitatively.

4   Investigation Experiment

4.1   Experimental Setup

Fig. 2 shows the setup used in the experiment. A system is build which can present integral stimulation in the force, visual, and auditory senses. The force sense here includes the sense of motion. A haptic interface PHANToM is used for force presentation, a 17-inch color liquid crystal display (LCD) for visual presentation, and headphones for auditory presentation.

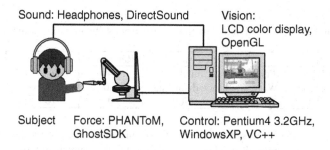

Fig. 2. Experimental setup

4.2   Presentations in the Experiment

Two types of experiments were conducted. Experiment A: rubbing a wavy surface and Experiment B: explosion.

Experiment A. Experiment A looks like playing an instrument "guiro". It is a simulation of rubbing a wavy board surface with a stick. Two flat surfaces are shown on LCD. The subject holds the PHANToM stylus and, as pushing it down, moves it to the right and left (in the x-axis). The stick on LCD moves according to the stylus movement. As for the force stimulus, the upward reaction force is presented on the stylus, which is proportional to the deformation occurring when the stick is pushed against the assumed elastic board with a wavy surface, and therefore varies when the stick moves along the x-axis. For the visual stimulus, the wave of the surface is shown with gradation while the stick is on that surface. For the auditory stimulus, a rubbing sound is presented on the headphones. As shown in Fig. 3, two surfaces are shown in the left and right for reference and comparative presentations, respectively.

Background scene is shown for realistic atmosphere.

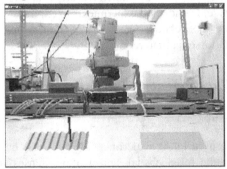

Reference surface: Comparative surface:
Wave is shown when stick   Wave is not shown when
is moving on the surface.   stick is away.

Fig. 3. Display in Experiment A: wavy surface rubbing

Table 1. Specification of stimuli in Experiment A: wavy surface rubbing

Stimulus	Specified term	Reference	Range	Step
Force [N]	Force for wave amplitude	0.40	0.16 – 0.64	0.048
Vision [pixel]	Wave amplitude displayed	2.0	0.0 – 4.0	0.4
Sound [dB]	Volume of DirectSound	0	−10 – 10	2

The stimuli of the three senses are specified and the reference values, ranges, and step values are determined as shown in Table 1. The ranges are divided into ten intervals and thus eleven levels (level 0 to level 10) are determined, the middle ones (level 5) being the reference values. It is a big problem what physical values should be specified to the levels of stimulation. The reference values are determined as "comfortably accepted stimuli" and the lower limits of the ranges as "barely perceived stimuli". The stimuli presented integratedly are represented using the level numbers such as $(F, V, S) = (3, 7, 8)$, the reference being $(5, 5, 5)$. In the experiment, the stimulation space is represented by this coordinate system.

Experiment B. Experiment B simulates an explosion. After a fixed introductive stage (early vibration), stimuli of variable magnitudes are presented. Vibration is presented for force stimulus, a red circle for visual (Fig. 4), and an explosion sound for auditory.

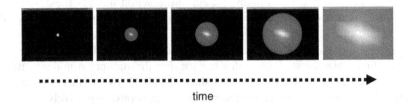

time

Fig. 4. Display in Experiment B: explosion

Table 2. Specification of stimuli in Experiment B: explosion

Stimulus	Specified term	Reference	Range	Step
Force [N]	Vibration force amplitude	3.0	1.4 – 4.6	0.4
Vision [pixel]	Radius of red circle	32	32 – 128	12
Sound [dB]	Volume of DirectSound	0	−16 – 16	4

The stimuli of the three senses are specified as shown in Table 2. The ranges are divided into eight intervals and nine levels (level 0 to level 8) are determined, the middle ones (level 4) being the reference values.

4.3 Experiment Methods and Results

The reference integral stimulus and the comparative integral stimulus with various levels of stimulation are presented to the subject. The subject is asked which integral stimulus he feels stronger and forced to select one. So far we have conducted experiments for a male subject of 22 years. The presentation, comparison, and selection were done quickly.

Experiment A. In Experiment A, there are 1331 patterns of comparative stimuli. Each pattern is presented, in contrast with the reference stimuli, ten times randomly among others. The probability of comparative stimuli being felt stronger, which we call "cognition probability", is calculated for each pattern.

In the stimulation space the comparative stimuli are represented by 1331 points. For each point the cognition probability is obtained. Fig. 5 shows the probabilities in the V-S section planes at F levels of 0, 5, and 10. The thick points show 60 % or more, middle points 50 %, and thin points 40 % or less. Fig. 5 also shows those in the F-V and F-S sections.

These section figures suggest that the levels of force stimuli have large influence on the integral intensity, while the levels of visual stimuli have considerable influence and the levels of auditory stimuli have small influence.

The comparative integral stimuli with 50 % of cognition probability are regarded as reference-equivalent integral stimuli. These equivalent stimuli are plotted in the stimulation space. The regression plane for the equivalent stimuli is obtained with V and S as the independent variables and F as the dependent variable. The root-mean-square value of the residues and the correlation factor between the experimental values and the regression values of F are obtained. The same procedure is carried out for the stimuli with cognition probability of 40–60 %.

50 % : $F = -0.451V - 0.113S + 8.025$ Residue 0.676 Correlation factor 0.894
40–60 % : $F = -0.457V - 0.089S + 8.078$ Residue 0.899 Correlation factor 0.849

Fig. 6 shows the plots. The coordinate systems are rotated so that the regression planes appear as straight lines. The coefficients of V (0.451) and S (0.113) as compared to 1 for F reconfirm the influences of the levels of stimuli on the integral intensity stated above.

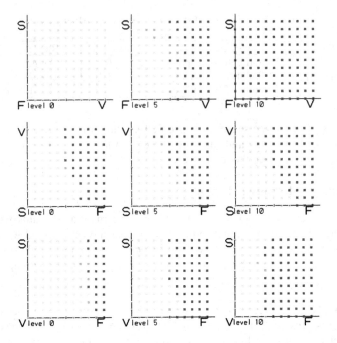

Fig. 5. Sections at F, S, and V levels

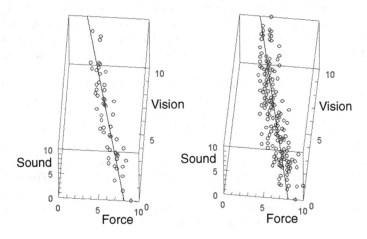

Fig. 6. Reference-equivalent integral stimuli in Experiment

Experiment B. In Experiment B, there are 729 patterns of comparative stimuli. Each pattern is presented alternately with the reference stimuli, ten times randomly. The cognition probability is calculated for each pattern.

50 % : $F = -1.211V - 0.403S + 13.226$ Residue 0.991 Correlation factor 0.931
40–60 % : $F = -1.219V - 0.492S + 13.596$ Residue 0.966 Correlation factor 0.929

Similar procedures are executed for the data obtained in Experiment B. Fig. 7 shows the plots. The coefficients of V (1.211) and S (0.403) as compared to 1 for F suggest that the levels of visual stimuli have the larger influence on the integral intensity, the levels of force a little smaller influence, and the levels of auditory small influence.

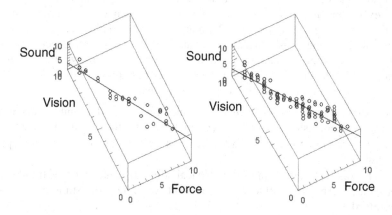

Fig. 7. Reference-equivalent integral stimuli in Experiment B

If we take V with the largest influence as the dependent variable, the regression planes will be as follows.

50 % :   V = −0.342S −0.715F +10.450 Residue 0.762 Correlation factor 0.942
40–60 % : V = −0.398S −0.708F +10.568 Residue 0.736 Correlation factor 0.943

4.4 Discussion on the Experimental Results

The plots of reference-equivalent comparative integral stimuli are distributed very closely on a flat plane, suggesting that the influences of stimulus levels of each sense are considerably linear. In Experiment A, force stimuli have the largest influence on the integral cognition, visual stimuli about half as large, and auditory about 1/10 as large. In Experiment B, visual stimuli have the largest influence, force stimuli about 3/4, and auditory about 1/3. Why are the influences of stimuli different between experiments?

In Experiment A, the subject is active in making the motion to push down the stylus and move it while he receives any stimuli. So the subject is sensitive to the force presentation for it is the response to the motion he makes. In Experiment B, on the other hand, the subject is entirely passive in receiving the stimuli in all senses. This explains the reason why the influences of stimuli are different between experiments.

5 Discussion

In the experiment, integral stimuli of force, visual, and auditory senses which simulate certain events are presented and positioned in the stimulation space. The cognition space is provided with an axis called "integral intensity" which scales the strength of integral stimuli the subject feels.

It is a matter of course that some of the different integral stimuli are project onto one point if we use only one axis of integral intensity to evaluate the integral stimuli. So, the significance of the experiment depends on whether we can find any relationship among stimuli projected onto one point of integral intensity.

The experimental results show that the stimuli which give reference-equivalent integral intensity are distributed on a flat plane in the stimulation space. This suggests that the integral intensity is a linear combination of intensities in respective senses. If we adopt the one-dimensional cognition space of integral intensity, all the stimuli on the flat plane can be the substitutes for the reference stimuli.

The following questions may be imposed on the experiments.

- Do the experimental results have significance on VR as they only deals with the simplest one-dimensional scale of integral intensity for the cognition space?
- Could the present experiments have effects in two-dimensional cognition space or even higher?
- Is the arbitrary determination of the physical stimulus values for the stimulus levels appropriate? Are the influences dependent on how the stimulus levels are determined?
- Is the arbitrary determination of events: wavy surface rubbing and explosion, appropriate?
- Could there be more complicated or dynamic relationship between stimuli?

These questions look reasonable. It seems that we have but to make appropriate hypotheses and prove them experimentally.

6   Conclusions

A human perceive an event by receiving stimuli generated by the event through his/her five senses and integrating them. Concerning with this, we have proposed the concept of integral stimulation, integral perception, and integral cognition. As a way of understanding VR, we have proposed the idea of event space, stimulation space, perception space, and cognition space. VR is understood as an effort to find different points in the event space projected onto one point in the cognition space.

We have a hypothesis that different points in the stimulation space can be projected onto one point in the cognition space. We have conducted experiments of two kinds of assumed events: wavy surface rubbing and explosion, in which a stimulation space is considered with force, visual, and auditory senses. We have provided the cognition space with an axis of integral intensity which scales the strength the subject feels when he receives the integral stimuli. It is a matter of course that some of the integral stimuli are projected onto one point if we use only one axis of integral intensity. The experiment, however, have shown that the stimuli which give reference-equivalent integral intensity are distributed on a flat plane in the stimulation space, and that if we adopt the one-dimensional cognition space of integral intensity, the integral intensity is a linear combination of intensities in respective senses, and all the stimuli on the flat plane can be the substitutes for the reference stimuli.

References

1. Schmidt, R.F. (ed.): Fundamentals of Sensory Physiology, Springer-Verlag (1986)
2. Tachi, S., H. Arai, H.: Design and evaluation of a visual display with a sensation of presence in tele-existence system, J. Robotics Society of Japan, Vol.7, No.4 (1989) 314–326 (in Japanese)
3. Harrison, J.: Synaesthesia, The Strangest Thing, Oxford University Press (2001)
4. Tanaka, K., Masaru, K., Abe, N., Taki, H.: Synchronization of visual, haptic and auditory sense using a haptic display and a virtual sound device, Proc. VSMM2002 (2002) 673–680
5. Fang, S., Zhou, H., Palakal, M., Tennant, S.: Haptic interaction for virtual museum, Proc. VSMM2003 (2003) 96–103
6. Bae, H., Jang, B.: Haptic suit for tactile feedback on VR game, Proc. VSMM2003 (2003) 539–545
7. Zhang, H., Payendeh, S. Dill, J.: The look and feel of virtual progressive cutting, Proc. VSMM2003 (2003) 764–771
8. Hara, M., Yabuta, T., Higuchi, T.: Reproduction of perceptual illusion in virtual reality using haptic interface, CD proc. 20th Conference of Robotics Society of Japan, (2004) 2D12 (in Japanese)
9. Garancs, J.: Audiovisual "surgery on space": series of VR environments for tempo-spatial exploration and artificial synaesthesia, Proc. VSMM2004 (2004) 536–543

Object Detection for a Mobile Robot
Using Mixed Reality

Hua Chen[1], Oliver Wulf[2], and Bernardo Wagner[2]

[1] Learning Lab Lower Saxony (L3S) Research Center, Hanover, Germany
chen@l3s.de
[2] Institute for Systems Engineering, University of Hanover, Germany
{wulf,wagner}@rts.uni-hannover.de

Abstract. This paper describes a novel Human-Robot Interface (HRI)
that uses a Mixed Reality (MR) space to enhance and visualize object
detection for mobile robot navigation. The MR space combines the 3D
virtual model of a mobile robot and its navigating environment with
the real data such as physical building measurement, the real-time acquired robot's position and laser scanned points. The huge amount of
laser scanned points are rapidly segmented as belonging either to the
background (i.e. fixed building) or newly appeared objects by comparing them with the 3D virtual model. This segmentation result can not
only accelerate the object detection process but also facilitate the further process of object recognition with significant reduction of redundant
sensor data. Such a MR space can also help human operators realizing
effective surveillance through real-time visualization of the object detection results. It can be applied in a variety of mobile robot applications
in a known environment. Experimental results verify the validity and
feasibility of the proposed approach.

1 Introduction

Last two decades have seen the popularization of Virtual Reality (VR) that
attempts to use virtual environments to convey a sense of reality. A virtual environment is the representation of the computational geometric modeling of a
real environment in a 3D visual simulation created with computer graphics techniques [1]. Since real objects that are difficult to access can be represented by
virtual objects in a virtual environment, VR finds applications in many fields
such as military training, medicine and education etc. Especially, VR has huge
potential in robotics [2] and it has facilitated the development of new kind of
Human-Robot Interface (HRI). Through VR, human operators are able to interact with the real robots that work in a remote, hazardous, micro or macro
environment in an intuitive, natural way.

According to the correlation between the real world and the virtual environment, the VR-based HRI tools fall into two main categories. One is using
virtual environments as a front-end interface for controlling a robot such as the
applications in telerobotic manipulation [3,4]. Physical robots and their working space are represented in the virtual environments that provide visual cues,

H. Zha et al. (Eds.): VSMM 2006, LNCS 4270, pp. 466–475, 2006.
© Springer-Verlag Berlin Heidelberg 2006

constraints or predicted trajectory for more accurate and safe execution of the operator's commands. The other kind of HRI constructs virtual environments to simulate the behavior and working space of a robot. In this case, the physical robot and its surroundings are not even required. Currently, robotic system is still expensive and fragile, which may preclude most students from having "hand-on" experience and also prevents researchers from trying any robotic algorithm freely because of some safety issues. Therefore, virtual environments used for simulations can make robotics not only more accessible to students as a learning tool [5] but also more flexible to researchers as a testbed [6]. Furthermore, it is necessary to use virtual environments to simulate some specific environments such as disaster areas for the investigation on robots that undertake the Urban Search-And-Rescue (USAR) tasks [7].

Recently, the importance of developing a HRI that meets the users' needs and requirements has received more attention [8]. In semi-autonomous mobile robots applications, some real information such as paths to survivor [10] or navigation map [11] is visualized in a virtual environment using Mixed Reality (MR) technique. Introduced by [17], MR technique aims at making use of both the flexible computer modeling and rich knowledge information in the real world within a MR space. It has received much interest due to its potential of helping humans in some practical activities such as industrial design [9]. This kind of MR-based HRI assists human operators in situation awareness, monitoring and control for surveillance during the collaboration with mobile robots. This paper addresses a novel MR-based HRI for mobile robot applications.

Given a prior known environment, indoors as well as outdoors, a MR space is constructed to enhance and visualize the object detection during mobile robot navigation. Here the object is defined as the newly appeared object in the environment. The MR space integrates the 3D virtual model of a robot and its known navigating environment with the real data such as the physical building measurement, the real-time acquired robot's position and laser range data. By comparing with the 3D virtual model, the huge amount of laser range data is rapidly segmented as belonging either to the known background (i.e. fixed building) or newly appeared objects. This segmentation result can not only speed up the object detection process but also facilitate the following object recognition process with significant reduction of redundancy in sensor data. The MR space provided in the proposed HRI can improve the robot intelligence on object detection through the comparison with the virtual model and it can also help human operators realizing effective surveillance through real-time visualization of the detection results. Such a HRI tool can be applied in a variety of mobile robot applications such as exploring indoor environments (e.g. office/house buildings) to detect victims, survivors and fallen obstacles for rescue task or navigating outdoor environments (e.g. a parking square) to detect occupied spaces and further find spaces for parking.

This paper is organized as follows. Section 2 introduces the sensor system that is used to acquire range data in our experiments. Section 3 describes the method of object detection in detail. Experimental results are given in section 4. Finally, the conclusions and some future work are summarized in section 5.

2   Range Data Acquisition

Range data that indicate the distances from obstacles to a robot are inherently suited for the object detection task. Based on different sensor systems, various methods have been provided to acquire range data. Sonar sensors use the transmission and reflection of sound wave to find obstacles [12], but they suffer from poor directionality, specular reflections and wrong distance measurement caused by crosstalk. A camera-stereo pair can be used to derive 3D information from a calculated disparity map [13], but the captured image is sensitive to light conditions (e.g. shadows).

Currently, laser scanners that provide better resolution are getting used widely within the robotics community. Among various laser scanners, the laser scanner based on the measurement of Time-Of-Flight (TOF) is most suitable for fast scanning during mobile robot navigation and it is used in this work. The distance between the scanner and the object surface is measured by the time between the transmission and the reception of the laser beam. Many commercial 2D TOF laser scanners are available for the distance measurement on one plane.

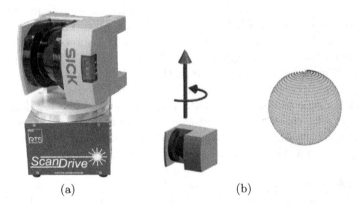

(a)   (b)

Fig. 1. The solution to 3D scanning (a)A 3D scanning system consisting of a 2D scanner and a servo drive (b)The yawing scan pattern

For 3D object detection, a laser scanner that can measure distance in 3D space is desired. However, there are no commercial 3D scanners available for this purpose at present. In our system, a commercial 2D scanner and a mechanical actuator are combined to achieve 3D scanning (see Fig. 1a). The actuator is a self-build servo drive that turns the 2D scanner around the upright axis (i.e. yawing scan pattern) to reach the third dimension (see Fig. 1b).

The usability and reliability of a 3D scanning system are evaluated by some main criteria such as the ability of fast and continuous scanning while driving, accurate synchronization of the laser measurement and the scanning device etc. After our previous optimization work [15] such as mechanical improvements of the scanning device and compensation of systematic measurement errors, this 3D scanning system can be used to acquire an undistorted 3D point cloud in a range about 30m with centimeter accuracy. In our experiments, during the navigation of a robot equipped with this scanning system, the undistorted 3D point cloud is acquired at intervals of 2.4s with 2° and 1° resolution at horizontal and vertical directions, respectively.

3   Object Detection in a MR Space

With prior knowledge of a mobile robot navigating environment, objects here are defined as newly appeared objects in the known environment. In this section, the construction of a 3D MR space corresponding to a robot navigating environment is firstly described. Further, the object detection within the MR space is presented.

3.1   MR Space Construction

Here the MR space is constructed by combing the virtual model of a mobile robot and its navigating environment with the real data such as the physical building measurement, the real-time acquired robot's position and laser scanned points.

Firstly, a static 3D virtual scene model corresponding to the physical mobile robot navigation is built using some popular 3D design tool (e.g. 3D MAX). The size of the 3D model is appropriately scaled to ensure the desired quality and speed of 3D rendering. Then the designed 3D model is exported to a Virtual Reality Modeling Language (VRML) file that is a ratified International Organization for Standardization (ISO) standard (ISO 14772) file format for description of the geometry and behavior of 3D computer graphics. In a VRML file, a virtual scene is described by a scene graph in which virtual objects are represented as VRML nodes and organized in hierarchical structure. Since a web browser with a VRML plug-in is able to show a VRML-based virtual scene by interpreting the corresponding VRML file, VRML is largely used to distribute 3D applications via the World Wide Web and it is widely supported by current prevalent 3D design software. Here the static VRML-based virtual scene is composed of a virtual robot and a virtual building model that correspond to the physical robot and its navigating environment respectively.

During the mobile robot navigation, the robot pose (i.e. position and orientation) is obtained using our novel robust localization method that integrates a 3D laser scanning into a Monte Carlo Localization (MCL) system [16]. Range data are acquired from the scanning systems described above. These dynamic real data are required to be integrated with the virtual scene to form the dynamic MR space. This integration is accomplished by using Java Applet to communicate between the robot system and the MR space via VRML External Authoring

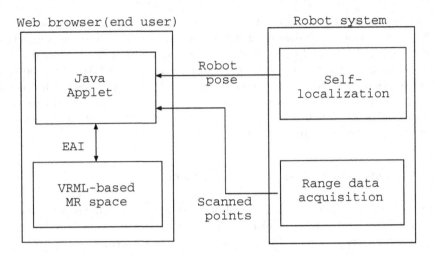

Fig. 2. The dynamic MR space interface architecture

Interface (EAI) that defines a set of functions to allow an external program to access VRML nodes (see Fig. 2).

A Java applet running in the end user's web browser needs to be firstly signed as a trusted applet for the permission of a safe connection with the robot system. Then the signed Java Applet receives the dynamic data produced by the navigating mobile robot in real-time via network using the TCP/IP protocol. These dynamic 3D data are transformed to be represented in an appointed world coordinate frame for data consistency. Finally, VRML EAI allows this external Java Applet to update the VRML-based MR space such as set the virtual robot to have the same pose with the real robot, render the MR space according to the current viewpoint of the real robot and create 3D graphic objects that represent laser scanned points. Note that creating and rendering the huge amount of 3D graphic objects is an extremely time-consuming process under current non-specialized hardware condition. One way to accelerate the rendering process is to preload the 3D graphic objects off-line and transform them to the corresponding positions in real-time during on-line process.

3.2 Object Detection

The object here is defined as the newly appeared object at some different position from a known robot's navigating environment. As described above, the robot's navigating environment can be represented by a virtual building model. Thus any scanned point that differs in position from the virtual building model is segmented as belonging to an object. To implement this segmentation process, a table can be built to pre-store the 3D measurement of a virtual building model. Each line in the table indicates a geometrical surface in the model. Take a unit cube as an example. The 3D data stored in a table represent six faces of the cube at each line respectively (see Fig. 3).

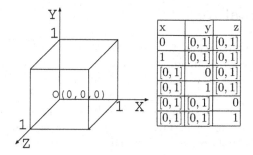

x	y	z
0	[0, 1]	[0, 1]
1	[0, 1]	[0, 1]
[0, 1]	0	[0, 1]
[0, 1]	1	[0, 1]
[0, 1]	[0, 1]	0
[0, 1]	[0, 1]	1

Fig. 3. (left) A unit cube model; (right) A table representing six faces of a unit cube

With the proposed table that represents all the geometrical surfaces of a model, the following steps can be used to determine whether a given point belong to an object or the model:

1. Compute the distances from the given point to the surfaces represented by each line in the table respectively
2. Find the minimum of the distances resulted from step (1)
3. The given point belongs to an object if the minimum value is above an appointed threshold

In ideal case, the given point belongs to an object if the minimal distance does not equal 0, which means it is not on any surface of the model. In practice, the noise, the measurement error and the accuracy of sensor data all need to be taken into account. So in step (3), the given point is determined to be on an object if it is enough far (more than a threshold value) away from the nearest surface of the model.

Based on the principle above, the object detection for a mobile robot can be performed by comparing the laser scanned points with the table that stores the 3D data of the virtual building model corresponding to the robot's navigating space. Such a table is built along with the design of the virtual environment. In practice, the real navigating environment may consist of a large number of complex geometrical surfaces, which will drastically increase the size of the table for 3D data storing. Comparing each scanned point with each surface represented by each line in the huge-sized table will slow down the detection process. Our solution is using a valid segment of the table for comparison. The valid segment indicates a certain part of the virtual building model corresponding to the nearest region that the sensor data can reach. It can be implemented based on the structured model and the recorded positions of scanned points related to the robot. For example, in our experiment, a forward scanned point only needs to be compared with the current forward-looking surfaces of the robot within its reachable range of 30m. Finally, the detection result is represented by the laser scanned points that belong to newly appeared objects within the MR space.

4   Experimental Results

For experimental verification, the corridor of our institute has been selected as a typical indoor environment for robot navigation. A 3D virtual building model corresponding to the institute environment has been constructed. Two mobile robots that are equipped with a commercial 2D TOF laser scanner and the proposed 3D scanning system respectively were used to navigate along the corridor at the speed about 0.7m/s. The range data are continuously acquired during the robot navigation. Two virtual robots corresponding to these two mobile robots have also been built. At the user end, a HRI runs on a notebook PC (with a 1.69 GHz CPU and a 512 MB RAM) that is connected with the robot system via 11Mbit/sec Wireless Local-Area Network (WLAN). The HRI shows a MR space in a web browser (e.g. Internet Explorer) with a VRML plug-in (e.g. Cortona [14]). Fig. 4 and Fig. 5 give the experimental results of a robot with the 2D scanner and the 3D scanning system respectively.

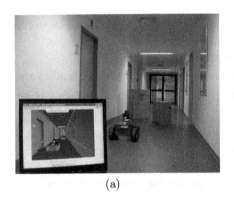 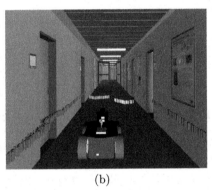

| (a) | (b) |

Fig. 4. Robot navigation with a 2D laser scanner (a) A HRI corresponding to the physical navigation environment (b) The HRI shows a MR space where detected objects are highlighted in yellow

Fig. 4(a) presents the physical corridor environment where a robot with a 2D scanner is navigating and the corresponding MR space displayed on the notebook PC as a HRI for the user. Fig. 4(b) demonstrates a virtual robot navigating in the MR space, which corresponds to the physical robot navigation. The position and orientation of the virtual robot are the same with those of the real robot. The 2D scanned points are visualized with 3D graphic objects (i.e. small cylinders) at corresponding positions in the MR space. Here about 720 scanned points are acquired for a 360° scan on one horizontal plane with 0.5° resolution. Scanned points belonging to objects, i.e. two newly appeared boxes in the corridor, are highlighted with yellow color to show the detection result.

Fig. 5(a) gives the physical navigating environment of a robot with a 3D scanning system. Fig. 5(b) visualizes the 3D scanned point cloud with 3D graphic objects (i.e. small spheres) in the MR space. The highlighted scanned points in

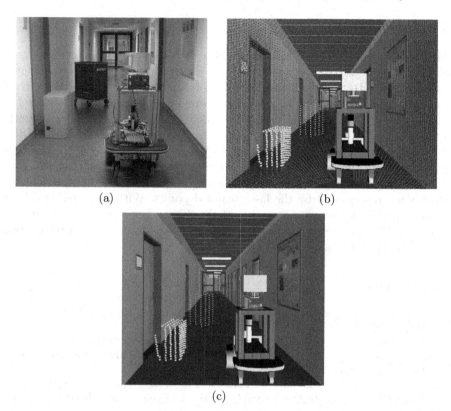

(a)   (b)

(c)

Fig. 5. Robot navigation with a 3D laser scanning system (a) Physical navigation environment (b) The 3D scanned point cloud is visualized in the MR space where the detected objects are highlighted in yellow (c) Only the scanned points belonging to the detected objects are visualized in the MR space

the MR space indicate the detected newly appeared objects. Fig. 5(c) visualizes the scanned points that only belong to the detected objects in the MR space.

Note that the amount of the 3D scanned points acquired by aforementioned 3D scanning system with 2° and 1° resolution at horizontal and vertical direction respectively is actually huge (about 32400). It is still difficult to render the MR space with so huge amount of 3D graphic objects in real-time with current non-specialized hardware. However, the MR space rendering can be substantially accelerated without visualizing the large amount of redundant scanned points as shown in Fig. 5(c). In our experiments, the system is able to visualize the detection result within the MR space in real-time. That is, during the mobile robot navigation, the virtual corridor, the virtual robot and 3D graphic symbols of laser scanned points belonging to newly appeared objects are dynamically updated in the MR space at each interval of laser scanning.

5   Conclusions

This paper presents a novel HRI that utilizes a MR space to enhance and visualize the object detection for mobile robot navigation in a known environment.
This kind of HRI has dual functions. One is that the 3D data of the virtual
environment corresponding to a real known navigating space of a mobile robot
can be used by the robot to improve its intelligence on fast detection of newly
appeared objects, and the other is that the real-time visualization of the object
detection result is beneficial to human operators for effective surveillance purpose. The huge amount of laser range data has been considerably reduced to the
data that only belong to the newly appeared objects. Currently, the detected
objects are represented by the laser scanned points. With these reduced laser
scanned points, a fast reconstruction of the 3D surface corresponding to each
object could be further investigated to facilitate real-time 3D object recognition
during mobile robot navigation.

References

1. Y. Ohta and H. Tamura (eds.), Mixed Reality: Merging Real and Virtual Worlds,
   Springer Verlag, 1999.
2. E. Natonek, L. Flckiger, Th. Zimmerman and C. Baur, Virtual Reality: an intuitive approach to robotics, in Proc. of SPIE Telemanipulator and Telepresence
   Technologies, Vol. 2351, pp. 260-270, 1994.
3. L. B. Rosenberg, Virtual fixtures: Perceptual tools for telerobotic manipulation, in
   Proc. IEEE Virtual Reality Annual International Symposium (VRAIS), pp. 76-82,
   1993.
4. A. Monferrer and D. Bonyuet, Cooperative robot teleoperation through virtual
   reality interfaces, in Proc. of the Sixth International Conference on Information
   Visualisation, pp. 243 - 248, 2002.
5. T. L. Dunn and A. Wardhani, A 3D Robot Simulation for Education, in ACM
   Proc. of the 1st International Conference on Computer Graphics and Interactive
   Techniques in Australasia and South East Asia, pp. 277-278, 2003.
6. D. Gracanin, M. Matijasevic, N.C. Tsourveloudis, K.P. Valavanis, Virtual reality testbed for mobile robots, in Proc. of the IEEE International Symposium on
   Industrial Electronics (ISIE), Vol. 1, pp. 293 - 297, 1999.
7. J.J Wang, M. Lewis and J. Gennari, A game engine based simulation of the NIST
   urban search and rescue arenas, in Proc. of the Winter Simulation Conference,
   pp.1039-1045, 2003.
8. J. A. Adams, Critical Considerations for Human-Robot Interface Development, in
   Proc. of the American Association for Artificial Intelligence (AAAI) Fall Symposium on Human-Robot Interaction, pp.1-8, 2002.
9. Hua Chen, Real-time video object extraction for Mixed Reality applications, Dissertation, Technical University of Clausthal, ISBN 3-89720-844-x, Germany, 2005
10. M. Daily, Y. Cho, K. Martin and D. Payton, World embedded interfaces for human-
    robot interaction, in Proc. of the 36th Annual Hawaii International Conference on
    System Sciences, pp. 125-130, 2003.
11. S. Tejada, A.Cristina, P. Goodwyne and et al., Virtual Synergy: A Human-Robot
    Interface for Urban Search and Rescue, In Proc. of the American Association for
    Artificial Intelligence (AAAI) Mobile Robot Competition, pp. 13-19, 2003.

12. R. Kuc, A spatial sampling criterion for sonar obstacle detection, in IEEE Transactions on Pattern Analysis and Machine Intelligence, Vol. 12, Issue 7, pp. 686-690, 1990.

13. K. Berns, V. Kepplin and R. Dillmann, Terrain and obstacle detection for walking machines using a stereo-camera-head, in IEEE Proc. of the 24th Annual Conference of the Industrial Electronics Society (IECON), Vol. 2, pp.1170-1175, 1998.

14. http://www.parallelgraphics.com/products/cortona/

15. O. Wulf and B. Wagner, Fast 3D-Scanning Methods for Laser Measurement Systems, in International Conference on Control Systems and Computer Science (CSCS), 2003.

16. O. Wulf, M. K. Allah and B. Wagner, Using 3D Data for Monte Carlo Localization in Complex Indoor Environments, 2nd European Conference on Mobile Robots (ECMR), 2005.

17. P. Milgram and F. Kishino, A Taxonomy of Mixed Reality Visual Displays, in IEICE Transactions on Information Systems, Vol. E77-D, No.12, pp.1321-1329, 1994.

A Humanoid Robot to Prevent Children Accidents

Altion Simo[1], Yoshifumi Nishida[1], and Koichi Nagashima[2]

[1] AIST Advanced Industrial Science and Technology, DHRC, 2-41-6, Aomi, Koto-ku,
Tokyo 135-0064, Japan
altion.simo@aist.go.jp
[2] R-Lab, 1-44-15, Asagayaminami, Suginami Ward, Tokyo 166-0004, Japan

"Mistress, the baby won't eat. If he doesn't get some human love, the Internet pediatrics book says he will die." "Love the damn baby, yourself. "Robot Model number GenRob337L3, serial number 37942781—R781 for short—was one of 11 million household robots [7].

Abstract. We describe in this paper the implementation and experimentation of a humanoid robot system, aimed at the prevention of children accidents in everyday indoor activities. The main focus of this research work is placed on the "on demand" interaction between the robot and the child in the relevant context that the robot is used (preventing child accidents). Different controlling strategies and attractive interfaces were considered in designing this system, to result in an effective use of the robot when attempting to prevent child accidents. This is achieved through an active attraction of child attention as well as passive interaction. Some experimental results are given and conclusions are drawn, and some future implications are considered in refining not only the independent robot control, but also the effectiveness of this system.

Keywords: Children Accidents, Robotics, Ubiquitous Living Environments.

1 Introduction

Recent development in robotics has brought forward quite a few applications that address childcare in the context of a personal robot [3, 10]. At the same time unintentional injury is the leading cause of death for children after the first year of their life.

The development of different service robots is getting more and more public awareness and robots are already being used in the everyday life in Japan. From here we have derived our goal of integrating certain services and added values into these commercially available robots.

Instead of having a watchful eye through immobile cameras that wirelessly can transmit passive images; an active approach is proposed through a robotic solution in our research. Being at the right place and time, the robots can save lives, and avoid different accidents that can escalate in the course of time.

We have tackled this issue earlier in our research [11] and through our results have proposed different solutions in modelling children behaviour especially those related

H. Zha et al. (Eds.): VSMM 2006, LNCS 4270, pp. 476–485, 2006.
© Springer-Verlag Berlin Heidelberg 2006

to accidents. The accumulated children's behaviour related data are used to model a comprehensive behaviour model which is then used to pioneer evidence-based services, which can be offered in different ways to the wide public. In general, after predicting high risk injuries for children we can then apply this knowledge in educational applications or hardware actuators (this paper is one of these proposals).

Benesse Corporation has already launched a massive service based on the above research, serving at the same time as a web-based sensing channel for us in assuring the necessary feedback for our problem [12]. This gives us a tremendous wealth of data in order to increase the evidence when inferring children behaviour related to accidents. Recently in Japan, there are quite a few robots that are intended to serve indoors.

Irobi robot (Figure 1.) is a commercial robot which can offer different services including remote interactive communication and guarding for children, amongst other things. However one noticeable drawback of this robot is that it will not approach children if a dangerous situation is detected. Instead, it passively monitors them as they move around the indoors environments of the house [10].

Fig. 1. Irobi and its applications

Another service robot prototype that is intended for childcare is Papero [3]. Meant to be part of children's groups at daycare centers/homes, kindergartens and elementary schools it is claimed that the robot is capable of recognizing and verbally communicating with people, sending images by mobile phone to persons far away, as well as playing games and singing along with others. Again this robot falls short of recognition and active responding in situations where children might be involved in indoor activities that have a high level of risk, with respect to imminent accidents. The approach taken by Kozima et al [6] investigates human social development and interpersonal communications of children with robots, but lacks different aspects which are crucial and important in our research. First, there is not that much action when interacting with a robot as the amount of information that should be exchanged between the participants (i.e. child and the robot) is not balanced. More importantly, this robot does not fit our requirements because he is static and can not move around the room, when trying and interact with the child, in a macro level. Since children are more aware of a vivid interaction that follows their actual mood, a variety of interaction should be actively and spatially offered.

However it was very interesting to observe the phases which they suggest when introducing children to robots (though our robot was an actively moving entity and this has a different psychological effect on the child). The three proposed phases

(Neophobia, Exploration, and Interaction phase) were of use in an introduction pre-session, that we applied as well, ahead of the experiments that we were conducting.

We want to extend a little bit more the Active versus Passive intervention concept for preventing accidents. It is a fact that the actual development status of robots can not handle complicated tasks, such as physically dealing with children, and don't have an autonomous intelligence for the wide variety of situations occurring in everyday life. But one important point in our experiment is the active approach (rather than passive) the robot takes in attracting the child attention, sometimes even interfering in the physical way towards an object related to a potentially risky probable accident. Attracting the child attention is more passive in a second stage, and results effective with respect to our experiments. The study presented in [2] explored people's perception for robots, as a very important aspect of interaction, and attitudes towards the idea of a future robot companion for home. Though this research reports that household tasks were preferred to child/animal care tasks, the research found that humanlike communication was desirable for a robot companion among children, whereas humanlike behavior and appearance were less essential. Similar general steps with our research were taken when trying to robotize the entire home, mainly based on the function distributed collaborative infrastructure [9]. The goal is to obtain a clear understanding of human behavior in the robotized home and similarly realize new services based on such an understanding.

Human robot interaction and cooperation has been used for different purposes as in [8]. The idea of combining a robot gesture and a feedback through a LCD touch panel comes closer with our implementation, though the experimental setting and information flow differs essentially. Inferring the next human action, based on the past actions can support the reach of certain goals in everyday life.

When comparing with others, using IC Tags (ubiquitous environment sensing), similar to ultrasonic sensing techniques that we employ is becoming a common practice now, though the LCD support in the above mentioned experiment is used in another instance. Also interesting is the scenario sequence robot control which gives a good handle on combining the robot behavior with that of the humans.

Solutions for the needs in our case, were studied from literature, invented and adopted by our team or were provided to us during similar experiments we conducted on probabilistic children behavior modeling [11].

Actually we see the elderly and children as the two extreme group-ages of the society, with whom the robots (at the state of the development they are now) can deal better with.

Robots are psychologically, logically and physically able to fully challenge children of different ages (up to 8-9 years). When it comes to attracting their attention and also inferring their behavior robots are able to respond within a ceratin accuracy. Especially in societies with a high scale of technological development, robots are accepted more and more psychologically from children as part of their environment. The interaction of preschool children has been analyzed with different robotics pets and was given a strong emphasizing on the behavioral interaction [4]. The perception of the robots when compared to toy pets has social and moral impact. We used their results in consolidating the child-robot relationship that is crucial for our final purpose. The reciprocity attempts and the avoidance of impoverished relation growing in time, after few interactions, were among several points considered.

In summary when seeing the boom of the indoor service robots, equipped with different services related functions, we thought that it was the right time to experiment in this direction with children.

2 The Proposed System

The developed system consists of a humanoid robot in Figure 2., which is called H3 (developed near Tokyo University). Though it was modified on its lower part with a Pioneer 2 wheel base, it looks like a humanoid, mainly because of its upper body, which is custom built (Figure 2).

Its height is around 1meter (and this makes it suitable for interaction with children) and its center of gravity is very low, making it difficult to be tumbled accidentally by children during their interaction, in addition to being stable and moving smoothly.

Ultrasonic Emitters   Touch LCD Panel (A/V)

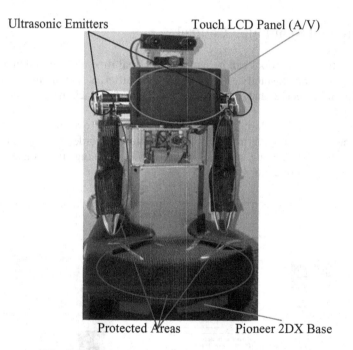

Protected Areas   Pioneer 2DX Base

Fig. 2. The hybrid humanoid H3, a custom built robot

Furthermore a touch LCD screen (incorporated speakers) which serves for the interaction of children with the robot is mounted on its front. In order to preserve its human like outlook, this interactive part is placed such, that doesn't prevent the robot from moving its arms and form different figures and gestures that can appeal the child. The LCD screen can be adjusted according to the child height. The Robot communicates wirelessly through a series of TCP/IP sockets in executing commands and giving feedback about his status. Also the graphics and the sound control which are running onboard can be controlled remotely.

Related to safety issues during the experiment different measures were taken. First of all we want to clarify why H3 was chosen among different humanoids we considered for our experiment. While being a humanoid in the upper body part which brings this robot closer to human-like relation with children, it would be dangerous to use a pure humanoid due to its instability in walking. The robot is far more solid the way it was modified taking into account and the vivid child interaction.

A light camouflage was used for the arms and its lower sharp edges to assure a smooth impact in case the child would crash into the robot. Front and rear bumpers for H3 were considered, this not only because the robot becomes safer, but also because it facilitates its movement in the sensor room among the objects that lay on the floor whose location can be reconfigured anytime from the child playing.

The experiments were taking place in a ubiquitous ultrasonic wireless sensors environment [13] which gives wealthy and accurate information for the whereabouts of the robot, child and different objects.

3   Event and Simulation Control

As we mentioned the robot can be controlled in real time and the system can update all its components instantly. Figure 3, shows different communication channels employed in a secure and effective control and feedback between the different system's parts.

For security reasons during the experiments we were overriding the autonomous robot control with a slave-master control interface in order to simulate the exact needed behaviour, having the possibility of intervening immediately, in case something gets out of control.

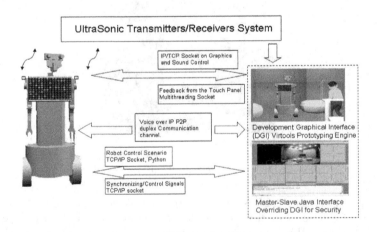

Fig. 3. Signal Flow Chart

A combined fish eye camera in the sensorized environment, and a robot onboard camera, makes it possible to override remotely robot's autonomous control and control the robot with a very high accuracy. Through a Voice over IP audio channel in addition to the implemented robot's commands sound matrix we had a good grasp for the executed audio on the robot side. We developed this feature as during the experiments we noticed that the child was ignoring sometimes robot's articulated words, and therefore thought that the parents' voice (via robot speakers) would be more familiar and appeal to the child better.

The autonomous control of the robot was initially chosen to take place through a generated scenario protocol for several reasons. In planning interactive storytelling [1] different techniques were considered. Similarly, the robot control can be like in [5]. We considered the generation of a scenario affected by the environmental events as a proper and adequate technique.

The real time update of this scenario according to a certain goal (child accidents prevention) and the events happening in the environment seem to fit our implementation purpose. Again related to security reasons, the system can issue a special command p3.stop() which immediately stops the robot in case the child apperas very near. A safety space always remains between the moving robot and the child in any case.

4   Experimental Results

The experimental settings were such that when the child enters the sensorized room he has a vast range of toys choices to play with, so his attention is not necessarily on the robot. Initially the robot is not active (no sound/graphics/movement) though it can read all the related sensors location data. As shown in Figure 4, from above and left to right, in the course of time the robot approaches after sensing a proximity of the child for an extended amount time near tagged objects which represent an increased risk.

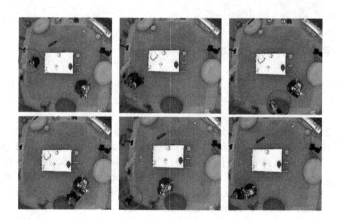

Fig. 4. Experimental settings and the experiment flow in the course of time (the red circle shows the child when he was not interacting with the robot and did things on his own)

These objects might be an operating electrical stove, a glass vase full of flowers, a hot water container, etc. In these cases after the robot gets the child's attention (this by calling his/her name, while approaching), it tries to keep him engaged through an interesting interaction (games) on the touch panel. Afterwards, while backing up slowly, the robot tries to take the child into safe areas, and stop then the interaction. In the course of ~40 minutes, as shown in Figure 4 slides, the robot was able to successfully perform this interactions on demand several times.

During the experiment we employed often the audio attraction of parents' voice as an effective way to get and keep the child attention or issue desires/order that favoured the smooth run of the experiment. The child has to go through the suggested psychological steps of neophobia further into exploration and interaction. There exists a breakpoint when children realize that the robot can move and can fully talk/interact with them (i.e. they begin to further consider it as a social entity). Figure 5 shows a case of socializing issues. For the girl, aged 3 years, a very protective behavior, in the presence of her mother was initially observed.

Her neophobia transition period was much longer and more dramatic. Actually she was not able to stay alone with the robot and the interaction "on demand" from the robots side, was always taking place in the presence of her mother. However, she was developing with time a more appealing attitude towards the robot interaction. And finally she totally accepted the robot.

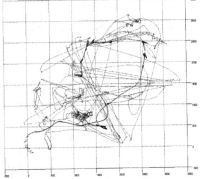

Fig. 5. Socializing Issues: Neophobia, Exploration, Interaction, Socialize, Parental Support, Physical Interaction, full Communication/Relation

In order to evaluate the adequacy of the proposed system, we measured different parameters, during experiments with several children, among which (1) the support that the LCD gives in attracting children's attention in an active interaction (this by measuring the interaction of that child on the screen), and (2) the support that the robot gives with its active movement, (this measured through the plotted trajectories of the robot and the child during the experiment).

All the interactions that the child was performing on the LCD screen can be detected and recorded quantitatively and qualitatively (if continuously touching the screen or not, how many times the screen was touched, etc) by the system. For the first factor we accounted a very high interaction frequency (more than 90% of time), this due to the attractive interface and its high multimedia capabilities.

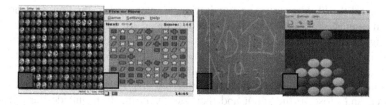

Fig. 6. Game interfaces to attract child attention in order the interaction can take place on demand. The colors next to each game interface correspond to the graphs in Figure 7.

Both these factors are discussed further with the help of Figure 7 and the captured video footage. In order to keep the attention of the child always toward the robot, the system can remotely switch, according to the situation, different interfaces.

We employed several open source games part of the GNOME Linux system (Figure 6), which were modified to fit children of the according ages. In addition we developed/modified 2D drawing software which allows children to draw different objects on the screen. Different functions in the above mentioned software can be remotely performed and they are played full screen.

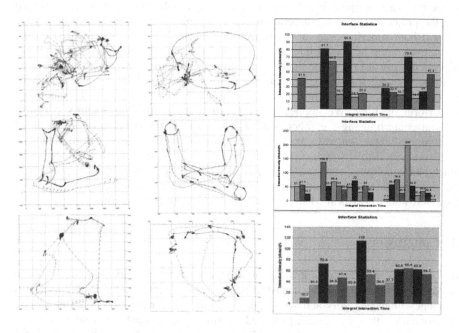

Fig. 7. Plotted trajectories of child and robot during the experiment, and normalized interaction parameters graphs (colors corresponding to game interfaces in Figure 6). Each row corresponds to ~3, ~4, ~5 y. o. child gathered data. From left to right plotted trajectories are separated in two frames in the course of time for better viewing.

In general the children were responding quite interested to the "on demand" robot attention request. A special interface was developed for very young children. It was including an animated three big buttons keyboard, interfaced via USB with the computer, from which they could affect the animation flow in the touch panel. Their interest was present even after repeating the experiment for several times. Different behavioural patterns for the robot were inferred hypothetically (keeping the child interested and close to the robot and then slowly luring him outside the potentially high risk areas, similar to mother's behaviour) but this doesn't compromise the experimental goal. In Figure 7, we have shown the plotted trajectories and normalized values for few interaction parameters (calculated based on the video footage of the experiment). LCD interaction time was normalized against the total time that the child was in front of the robot.

To see child's interest on different games interfaces we normalized the interaction time (clicks on the screen) for different games against the total time that game was displayed. Certain age groups liked drawing more than other games. To insure robustness of this method several times the child was encouraged to play with other toys in the environment. The correlation between attracting child's attention through LCD and robot's ability to move around the room seem to affect these parameters.

As it can be inferred from Figure 7, where trajectories of the child and robot are plotted, most of the time robot was successful in attracting child attention in function of their age and keeping him engaged for the requested time. Also we have plotted and the projected changing direction of the child (blue arrows) and the robot (black arrows) both superimposed on the trajectory curves. The child was focused on the robot, even when he wasn't interacting with it. This might be interpreted as a relative dependency toward the robot, therefore we always limited the interaction time.

Robot moving speed was another issue. Moving too fast is dangerous and makes the control difficult, while moving too slow might be unacceptable as the robot fails to perform on time. We applied a conservative speed (this for security reasons), without compromising the robot goal in achieving his target on time. In search of appropriate interaction ways, children used different means, varying from their bare fingers, to small toys which occasionally were in their hands, in spite of a suggested touch pen which was easily accessible on the robot body. However after several tries the children were able to understand the interaction rules and proceedings. Therefore they were able to perform when in front of unknown games/situations.

5   Conclusions

By comparing and evaluating different ways of interaction, this combined with an active robot intervention; we measure this robot's acceptance by children and his efficiency in successfully and safely guarding indoors (for the considered interface). We concluded that the current proposed interface was optimal for children 4-5 y.o. this due to several mentioned factors. Therefore in order we balance the interface for different ages, we are thinking to work in more suitable interfaces for 2~3 y.o. children (in spite of drawing, or passive animated stories).

Future work will focus in a more intensive data gathering process (by using a bigger children's population) in order we confirm better our findings. A 24 hours long experiment is underway in order we see the alternated attention span for children when interacting with robots. This will be realized through a pair of identical H3 robots (already available) which can fast-charge themselves alternatively on demand and play their care giving role complementarily. Also experiments with extreme age groups of ~2 y.o. and up to ~8 y.o. children are scheduled to be conducted, in a living environment comprising different living spaces (kitchen, bath, bedroom, etc) in order the experimental conditions get more realistic. We plan to experiment further with more than one child as there are quite a few issues; in spite of the robot's recognition for the dominant child, the influence of whom must be balanced interactively from the robot's side.

References

1. Charles F., Lozano M., Mead S.J., Bisquerra A.F., Cavazza M., Planning Formalism and Authoring in Interactive Story Telling, Proceedings of the 1st International Conference on Technologies for Interactive Digital Storytelling and Entertainment TIDSE 2003, (March 2005, Darmstadt, Germany), 254-261.
2. Dautenhahn K. Woods S., Kaouri C., Michael L. W, Kheng L. K, Werry I. What is a Robot Companion- Friend, Assistant or Butler? Proceedings of IEEE International Conference on Intelligent Robots and Systems IROS 2005, (August 2005, Edmonton, Canada), 788-795.
3. Fujita Y. Personal Robot PaPeRo and its application as Childcare Robot. Proceedings of ROBOCASA Workshop 2005 at Waseda University (Tokyo, Japan, September 2005), 36-42
4. Kahn P., Friedman B., Perez-Granados D., Freier N., Robotic pets in the Lives of Preschool Children Proceedings of Conference on Human Factors in Computing Systems CHI 2004, (April 2004, Vienna, Austria), 1449-1452.
5. Kanda T., Ishiguro H., Imai M., Ono T., Mase K. A Constructive approach for developing interactive humanoids robots, Proceedings of IEEE/RSJ International Conference on Intelligent Robots and Systems IROS 2002 (October 2002, Lausanne Switzerland), 1265-1270.
6. Kozima H., Nakagawa C. Yano H., Using Robots for the Study of Human Social Development, Developmental Robotics, Proceedings of 2005 AAAI Spring Symposium, DevRob 2005 (March 2005, Stanford, USA), 111-114.
7. McCarthy J., Robot and the Baby, Available at http://www-formal.stanford.edu/jmc/robotandbaby/robotandbaby.html
8. Nakauchi Y., Fukuda T., Noguchi K., Matsubara T., Intelligent Kitchen: Cooking Support by LCD and Mobile Robot with IC-Labeled Objects, Proceedings of IEEE/RSJ International Conference on Intelligent Robots and Systems IROS 2005 (August 2005, Edmonton, Canada), 76-84.
9. National Institute of Information and Communication Technology Keihanna Human Info-Communication Research Center Distributed and Cooperative Media Group the UKARI Project Available at http://www2.nict.go.jp/al35/eng/research/ukari_project.html
10. Yujin Robots Company,Korea. Irobi Robot Available at http://www.irobi.co.kr/english/irobi_English.files/frame.htm
11. Simo A., Kitamura K., Nishida Y., Behavior based Children Accidents' Simulation and Visualization: Planning the Emergent Situations. Proceedings of 4th International Conference on Computer Intelligence CI 2005, (Calgary, Canada, July 2005), 61-69.
12. Benesse Corporation, Children Accidents Prevention and Simulation Web Service, Available at (Japanese only): https://www.shimajiro.co.jp/ikuji/kiken/login.php
13. Nishida Y. Aizawa H. Hori T. Hoffman N.H. Kanade T. Kakikura. T. 3D Ultrasonic Tagging System for Observing Human Activity. Proceedings of IEEE International Conference on Intelligent Robots and Systems IROS 2003, (October 2003, Las Vegas, USA), 785-791.

Facial Sketch Rendering and Animation for Fun Communications

Yuanqi Su[1], Yuehu Liu[1], Yunfeng Zhu[1], and Zhen Ren[2]

[1] Institute of Artificial Intelligence and Robotics,
Xi'an Jiaotong University, Xi'an, P.R.China, 710049
yqsu@aiar.xjtu.edu.cn, liuyh@mail.xjtu.edu.cn
[2] France Telecom R & D Beijing Co., Ltd., Beijing, China, 100080
zhen.ren@francetelecom.com

Abstract. The ability to analyze a human's facial expressions and reproduce them is important for fun communication. In this paper, a novel model is presented for generating the facial sketch of pen-and-ink style and reproducing facial expressions in facial sketch animation. Facial sketch rendering is implemented by combing the painting path and line template, in which personalized painting path ensures the generated facial sketch to fit the specific face, and line templates bring different styles to it. The animation of facial sketch, which is based on pseudo-muscle model, reproduces some specific expressions in 2D facial sketch. These works are significative for multimedia application in low bandwidth communication environment.

1 Introduction

Versatile services have been developed for communication and experience-sharing for geographically separate people: various value-added services are ceaselessly adopt for satisfying personality demand of cell phone subscribers, and more popular real-time chat applications such as MSN let people exchange messages in Internet. But they are devoid of appreciable emotion reproduction in facial sketch animation.

Communicating empathy and aesthesia is a strikingly attractive research region, which has three primary elements: content capture, recognition and reproduction[1]. Chandrasiricite[2] developed a system that animates 3D facial agent based on real-time facial expression analysis techniques and research on synthesizing facial expressions, which was used to reproduce facial expression.

To reappear 2D facial expression, Hong Chen proposed a face-cartoon generation method[3], which used a group of facial sketches drawn by a specific artist to generate the non-photorealistic rendering of the face. Given a photo of face, the feature points of the face are extracted firstly, non-parametric sampling is introduced for generating the estimated facial drawing, and the most probable drawing path is then segmented to generate the facial sketch. Bruce Gooch[4] resorted to combing the separately thresholded luminance and brightness images for generating human facial illustration. By exaggerating the difference between

H. Zha et al. (Eds.): VSMM 2006, LNCS 4270, pp. 486–494, 2006.

the particular face and the average face, a so-called caricature could be generated. Aaron Hertzmann[5] modeled the stroke based non-photorealistic rendering (SBR) problem as an optimization process, different optimization strategies were then used to generate the non-photorealistic rendering images of different styles.

In this paper, a novel model is presented for generating the facial sketch of pen-and-ink style and facial expression animation. Proposed facial sketch rendering includes two primary concepts: One, called the painting path, decides the layout of the strokes; and the other, called the line template, decides the looking of the strokes. By combining the two parts together, a person-specific facial sketch can be generated, which reflects the input face and implies the specific artistic style. Then the pseudo-muscle model is introduced for animating the generated facial sketch. The animated results include the facial sketch with specific expressions and a sequence of facial sketches for rendering the facial motion of some expressions.

2   Personalized Painting Path Generation Using Model Adaptation

To generate a styled facial sketch from the person-specific face, the facial contour is necessarily extracted for constructing the painting path, which decides the layout of the strokes. AdaBoost algorithm can be firstly used for detecting the region of the face, then predefined facial feature points are extracted with an active shape model (ASM). By connecting the extracted feature points, a facial painting path can be generated, which is coarsely representing the contour of the original face. However, for generating more advanced painting path, extra strategies should be introduced.

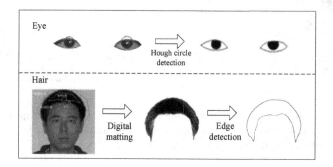

Fig. 1. The painting path generation for eyeball and hairstyle

In proposed method, facial components are modeled separately since their different characteristic. The painting path of eyes and eyebrows is directly decided by connecting their feature points; the contour of eyeball is detected by Hough transform, which is modeled as circle. The profile of hair serves as the initial shape, used for segmenting its texture region with matting, whose edge is then used to decide the painting path as shown in figure (1).

The contours of nose and mouth are used as reference shapes for generating personalized painting path using model adaptation, which is necessary for rendering some artistic style for facial sketch.

Model adaptation[6] is based on the fact that generic facial component prototype can be transformed into the one of specific face by comparison of their feature points. In order to implement model adaptation, a painting path database must be pre-built as generic prototype of each facial component, and the corresponding feature points are collected as shown in figure 2(a). Given a specific face, proper prototype is selected from the database for representing each component of the specific face. By comparing the feature points of the specific face with those of the prototype, the selected generic prototype is adapted to fit the specific facial component, the process is shown in figure 2(b)(c). Prototype model adaptation can further be divided into two phases: global adaptation and local adaptation.

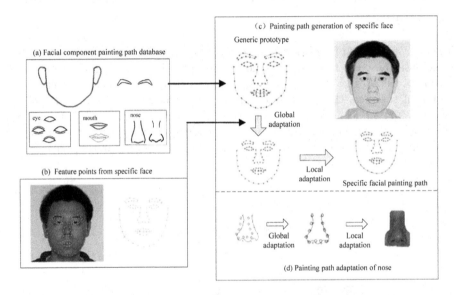

Fig. 2. The flowchart of painting path generation based on model adaptation, generic prototype which is selected from database is transformed to fit specific facial component by global adaptation and local adaptation

2.1   Global Adaptation for Facial Components

Global adaptation is responsible for tuning the facial component prototype's position, direction and ratio along the XY direction, which leads to coarse fit for the specific face. Suppose that feature points of the specific facial component are $\mathcal{T} = \{\mathbf{t}_i | i = 1, \cdots, N\}$, where $\mathbf{t}_i = (x'_i, y'_i)^T$; those of the selected prototype are $\mathcal{S} = \{\mathbf{s}_i | i = 1, \cdots, N\}$, and $\mathbf{s}_i = (x_i, y_i)^T$. The least square fitting of two 2D point sets[7] is used to adapt facial component prototype. By calculating an optimized affine transform from $\mathcal{S}$ to $\mathcal{T}$, the generic prototype can be transformed to coarsely fit the specific face.

Suppose that $\mathbf{R}$ and $\mathbf{c}$ are transformation matrix and displacement vector of affine transform separately, an optimized pair of $\mathbf{R}$ and $\mathbf{c}$ is necessary for making two point sets fit each other, which is described as formula (1).

$$\min_{\mathbf{R},\mathbf{c}} \left\{ f(\mathbf{R}, \mathbf{c}) = \sum_{i=1}^{N} \|\mathbf{Rs}_i + \mathbf{c} - \mathbf{t}_i\|^2 = \sum_{i=1}^{N} (\mathbf{Rs}_i + \mathbf{c} - \mathbf{t}_i)^T (\mathbf{Rs}_i + \mathbf{c} - \mathbf{t}_i) \right\} \tag{1}$$

The optimized $\widehat{\mathbf{R}}$ and $\widehat{\mathbf{c}}$ is finally calculated with formula (2).

$$\begin{cases} \left(\sum_{i=1}^{N} (\mathbf{s}_i - \bar{\mathbf{s}})(\mathbf{s}_i - \bar{\mathbf{s}})^T \right) \widehat{\mathbf{R}} = \left(\sum_{i=1}^{N} (\mathbf{t}_i - \bar{\mathbf{t}})(\mathbf{s}_i - \bar{\mathbf{s}})^T \right) \\ \widehat{\mathbf{c}} = \bar{\mathbf{t}} - \widehat{\mathbf{R}} \bar{\mathbf{s}} \end{cases} \tag{2}$$

Where, $\bar{\mathbf{s}} = \frac{1}{N} \sum_{i=1}^{N} \mathbf{s}_i$, $\bar{\mathbf{t}} = \frac{1}{N} \sum_{i=1}^{N} \mathbf{t}_i$.

With $\widehat{\mathbf{R}}$ and $\widehat{\mathbf{c}}$, each point in generic prototype is transformed, resulting in a new shape of facial component, which is coarsely fitting the specific face. Then, the local adaptation is introduced to get a fine fitting.

2.2 Local Adaptation Based on RBF

The geometric deformation makes the generic prototype to fit the specific face in the local manner, which is called local adaptation. Various deformation algorithms can be used for the purpose, the warping method based on radial basis function (RBF) is selected for its simplicity.

Assume that feature points of new shape are $\{(x_i, y_i) | i = 1, \cdots, N\}$, and let $\mathbf{X}_i = (x_i, y_i)^T$, the deformation based on the RBF can be expressed as formula (3).

$$\mathbf{B}(\mathbf{X}) = \sum_{i=1}^{N} \alpha_i g(\|\mathbf{X} - \mathbf{X}_i\|) + \mathbf{A}(\mathbf{X}) \tag{3}$$

$g(\cdot)$ is called pure radial basis function, the form of $g(\cdot)$ determines the characteristic of the deformation; $\mathbf{X}_i$ is the feature point and α_i denotes the corresponding coefficient; $\mathbf{A}(\mathbf{X})$ is the affine component of the deformation function, which can be replaced as $\mathbf{X}$ since the global adaptation.

$$\begin{cases} B_x(X) = \sum_{i=1}^{N} \alpha_{ix} g(\|X - X_i\|) + x \\ B_y(X) = \sum_{i=1}^{N} \alpha_{iy} g(\|X - X_i\|) + y \end{cases} \tag{4}$$

The 2D deformation can be decomposed into two 1D deformations just as formula (4). $\{(x_i', y_i') | i = 1, \cdots, N\}$, where $\mathbf{X}_i' = (x_i', y_i')^T$, are the destined coordinates of the feature points, the full form of can be drawn by equations (5).

$$\begin{bmatrix} g\left(\|X_1 - X_1\|\right) & \cdots & g\left(\|X_1 - X_N\|\right) \\ \vdots & \ddots & \vdots \\ g\left(\|X_N - X_1\|\right) & \cdots & g\left(\|X_N - X_N\|\right) \end{bmatrix} \begin{bmatrix} \alpha_{1x} & \alpha_{1y} \\ \vdots & \vdots \\ \alpha_{Nx} & \alpha_{Ny} \end{bmatrix} = \begin{bmatrix} x_1' - x_1 & y_1' - y_1 \\ \vdots & \vdots \\ x_N' - x_N & y_N' - y_N \end{bmatrix} \tag{5}$$

3   Facial Sketch Rendering

Hsu[8,9] proposed a model called "skeletal strokes" for combining the painting path and arbitrarily selected pictures. By controlling the global deformation of specified pictures along the predefined path and selecting different joint types, diverse styles of skeletal strokes can be generated, presenting fascinating results. Same as skeletal strokes, the generated line templates are deformed along the synthesized painting path, forming pen-and-ink stylistic facial sketch rendering.

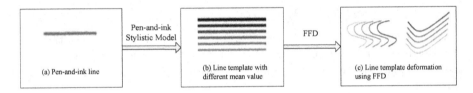

Fig. 3. The process of line template generation and deformation

3.1   Line Template Generation Based on Statistical Model

As for line template generation, a group of pen-and-ink lines are collected from the real world. By dint of these lines, line templates with different styles can be directly synthesized using statistical model.

The statistical model can generate different style line template based on a statistical variable with normal distribution, whose probability density function is denoted as formula (6).

$$f(\mathbf{X}) = \frac{1}{(2\pi)^{\frac{n}{2}} |\Sigma|^{\frac{1}{2}}} e^{-\frac{(\mathbf{X}-\mu)^T \Sigma^{-1} (\mathbf{X}-\mu)}{2}} \tag{6}$$

Where, n is the dimensionality of the multivariate distribution, representing the width of generated line template; μ is the mean value of the multivariate distribution, implying the mean gray level of the generated line; Σ is the variance-covariance matrix, deciding the changing styles of the spatial gray level of line template. By tuning μ, Σ and n, line templates with different styles can be generated.

Figure (3) gives an example of pen-and-ink line with $n = 6$, each slice along the direction of line width is seen as a sample, denoted as $\{\mathbf{p}_i | i = 1, \cdots, N\}$, where $\mathbf{p}_i = (p_{i1}, \ldots, p_{in})$. By calculating the mean and variance of these samples, its properties μ and Σ can be drawn by equation (7).

$$\widehat{\mu} = \frac{1}{N} \sum_{i=1}^{N} \mathbf{p}_i, \widehat{\Sigma} = \frac{1}{N} \sum_{i=1}^{N} (\mathbf{p}_i - \widehat{\mu})(\mathbf{p}_i - \widehat{\mu})^T \tag{7}$$

With the calculated properties $\widehat{\mu}$ and $\widehat{\Sigma}$, line template can be directly generated, and synthesized result is shown in figure (3). Then by changing the mean and variance, line templates with different styles can be generated as shown in figure 3(b).

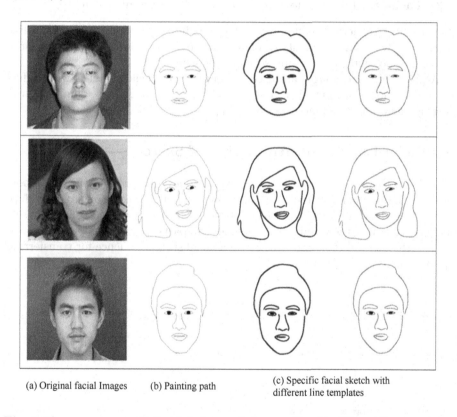

(a) Original facial Images   (b) Painting path   (c) Specific facial sketch with different line templates

Fig. 4. Three person-specific facial sketch rendering results with different line templates

By observation, it can be found that the generated line template looks almost identical to the pen-and-ink line from the real world in the original scale. However, when all zoomed in, the difference arises while the change of the gray level of pen-and-ink line looks more continuous than that of generated line template. This is brought by the independent sampling, thus the continuity of the neighboring region can't be guaranteed.

3.2   Line Template Deformation Using FFD

To render facial sketch in pen-and-ink style, free form deformation (FFD)[10,11] is selected for combining line template and painting path. In FFD, the shape of an object, described by free form splines, is subsequently changed with each control point's transition.

To bend the line template along the painting path based on FFD, three steps must be taken: defining the control points on the line template, searching for the coordinates of the control points along the painting path, and interpolating the coordinates of the points other than control points. The results of line template deformation are shown in figure 3(c).

3.3   Facial Sketch Rendering Based on Component Model

Facial sketch rendering is the process for combining the painting path and line template. By changing the styles of painting path and line template, versatile facial sketches with pen-and-ink style can be generated.

A group of facial images are used to generate the facial sketches with different styles shown in figure (4). Through observation, it can be found that the correspondence of most faces can be recognized.

4   Facial Expression Animation of Sketch

The ability to analyze a human's facial expressions and reproduce them is important for fun communication. The animation of sketch is explored to reproduce some specific expressions in 2D facial sketch, which is based on pseudo-muscle model. Animating the facial sketch includes two parts: generating specific expression on the facial sketch, and generating a facial sketch sequence for transferring specific emotion information.

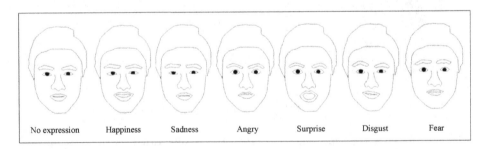

No expression   Happiness   Sadness   Angry   Surprise   Disgust   Fear

Fig. 5. Sketch rendering results of six typical facial expression

To implement the pseudo-muscle model[12] on the 2D facial sketch, a group of pseudo-muscles are predefined for controlling the motion of painting path. The pseudo-muscle is a 2D vector which influences its neighboring region through motion propagation. And the extent of the influence at a point is decided by its inclination and distance to its pseudo-muscle. To generate a specific expression on the facial sketch, empirical values are assigned to each pseudo-muscle as the facial motion vector; then by tuning the facial motion of nearby regions around pseudo-muscles, the painting path of the facial sketch can be transformed to reproduce some facial expression as shown in figure (5). Six typical expressions are implemented on the generated facial sketch; and by tuning the parameters of each pseudo-muscle, extra expressions can be achieved.

When the process of the transformation is set to be continuous, a sequence of painting path of the facial sketch can be generated, transferring personal emotion information. As shown in figure (6), a sequence of facial sketch is generated for rendering the facial motion of surprise.

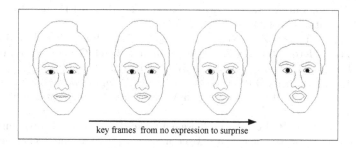

key frames from no expression to surprise

Fig. 6. A sequence of facial sketches for animating surprise

5   Conclusion and Further Works

A new model is proposed for generating the facial sketch with pen-and-ink style. In this model, model adaptation is introduced for generating the painting path of some facial components with artistic styles, and statistic model is used for generating so called "line template" with pen-and-ink style. By combing two parts together, facial sketch is generated. However, current work concentrates only on the sketch information of a specific face.

Based on the generated facial sketch, pseudo-muscle model is introduced for animation, which results in facial sketches with specific expressions, and a sequence of facial sketches for reproducing some emotions. It can be drawn that the results can successfully reproduce some expressions.

Further works will focus on rendering the facial sketch in advanced artistic style using texture information and exploring low time-consuming deforming algorithm.

Acknowledgment. This work was supported by the NSF of China (No.60021302, No.90412010). The authors would like to thank Dr. Eude and Dr. Haila Wang of France Telecom R&D, for contributing to the ideas in this paper.

References

1. Y. KataGiri: Toward a Media Environment for Communicating Empathy and Aesthesia, The Journal of the Institute of Electronics, Information and Communication Engineers, Vol. 89, No.1 (2006) 2-6.
2. N.P.Chandrasiri, T.Naemura: Internet Communication Using Real-Time Facial Expression Analysis and Synthesis, IEEE MultiMedia, Vol.11, Issue 3 (2004) 20-29.
3. Hong Chen, Ying-Qing Xu, Heung-Yeung Shum, Song-Chun Zhu, Nan-Ning Zheng: Example-based facial sketch generation with non-parametric sampling, ICCV2001, Vol.2 (2001) 433-438.
4. Bruce Gooch, Erik Reinhard, Amy Gooch: Human facial illustrations: Creation and psychophysical evaluation, ACM Transactions on Graphics (TOG), Vol.23, no.1 (2004) 27-44.
5. Aaron Hertzmann: A Survey of Stroke-Based Rendering, IEEE Computer Graphics and Applications, Vol.23, Issue 4 (2003) 70-81.
6. Yuehu Liu, Yunfeng Zhu, Yuanqi Su, Zejian Yuan: Image based Active Model Adaptation Method for Face Reconstruction and Sketch Generation, Edutainment 2006, LNCS 3942, Springer Verlag Berlin Heidelberg(2006) 928-933.
7. KS Arun, TS Huang, SD Blostein: Least-squares fitting of two 3-D point sets, IEEE Transactions on Pattern Analysis and Machine Intelligence, Vol.9, Issue 5 (1987) 698-700.
8. S. C. Hsu, I. H. H. Lee, N. E. Wiseman: Skeletal Strokes, Proceedings of the 6th annual ACM symposium on User interface software and technology, ACM Press(1993) 197-206.
9. S. C. Hsu, Irene H. H. Lee: Drawing and animation using skeletal strokes, Proceedings of the 21st annual conference on Computer Graphics and Interactive Technique, (1994) 109-118.
10. J Gomes, L Darsa, B Costa, L Velho: Warping and Morphing of Graphical Objects, Morgan Kaufmann(1997) 243-265.
11. Thomas W. Sederberg, Scott R. Parry: Free-form deformation of solid geometric models, ACM SIGGRAPH Computer Graphics, Vol.20, Issue 4 (1986) 151-160.
12. K.Waters: A Muscle Model for Animating Three-dimensional Facial Expression, ACM SIGGRAPH'87, Vol. 21, Issue 4 (1987) 17-24.

Implementation of a Notation-Based Motion Choreography System

Shun Zhang[1], Qilei Li[1], Tao Yu[1], XiaoJie Shen[1],
Weidong Geng[1], and Pingyao Wang[2]

[1] State Key Lab of CAD&CG, Zhejiang University, Hangzhou, PR China
[2] Professional College of Ningbo, Ningbo, PR China

Abstract. Motion choreography is a design process of creating, structuring and forming body movements. We proposed and implemented a notation-based motion choreography system, LabanChoreographer version 0.1. Given the user specified movement notations, it will firstly perform Laban-based motion retrieval to find the most similar motions from a motion capture database notated with Labanotation, and snap together these retrieved motion clips into a continuous rough motion sequence that match the input Laban sequence as much as possible. Secondly, Laban-based motion editing algorithm is employed to semi-automatically revise and refine this candidate motion sequence such that the resulting motion data can best approximate the desired motion in the user's mind. The choreographer is able to move flexibly back and forth between Labanotations and its rapid-prototyped motion data. It well supports the iterative and interactive development of movement ideas at a conceptual level.

1 Introduction

The movement notation language is a popular tool to specify and choreography motions for human characters. The animator often creates, communicates and archives animated motions via notation language such as Labanotation. The role of Labanotation for motion data is the same as the role of the music score for music performance. It is easy for us to roughly grasp the body motion by browsing the movement notation scores in Laban sequence [1]. The musician can compose music by the music staff. Therefore, computer animators began to dream when they can directly author and choreograph motions by the movement notation language. The challenging part of this problem is that: authoring and choreographing human motion is a complex synthesis task for animators. They have to choreograph many degrees of freedom so that human figures will move in a coordinated and a human-like fashion. Moreover, these movement notations mainly are qualitative temporal and spatial abstraction of human motions. It only provides a rough control specification, and this inaccurate feature makes it difficult to automatically convert the qualitative depiction into precise quantitative motion data desired by the user. Even for human animators, they also need lots of training to get the ability of reconstructing motions through reading movement notation language such as Labanotation.

H. Zha et al. (Eds.): VSMM 2006, LNCS 4270, pp. 495 – 503, 2006.

Some pioneers started the research on notation-based motion authoring and choreography tools in 1970s. They developed computer-based editing tools to assist the creation of Labanotation and explored approaches to generating motion clips from notation language [2] [3] [4]. In order to support the conception and development of human movements via Labanotation, computer-based creative design tools had also been investigated [5] [6]. Recently, Neagle did a survey on movement notational systems and computer tools for editing and animating dance notations [7]. In the LabanDancer project [8], they developed an interpretation system to animation Labanotation, Calvert et al also suggested the future integration of the movement notation with motion captured data for animations in games [9]. However, most existing choreography tools employ model-based approaches to generating character motion by kinematic, dynamic, or biomechanical models. It can sometimes be difficult to construct and control, or may fail to generate natural-looking motions if the models do not sufficiently constrain the motion. But in computer graphics community, intensive use of motion capture data has become a common strategy for producing plausible movements. Therefore, we intend to combine them together, and implemented a novel data-driven approach to assisting motion choreography via a movement notation language – Labanotation. Based on a motion capture database, it aims at providing the iterative and interactive development of movement ideas expressed in Labanotation, and enabling the animator to create and synthesize appealing motions by notations in an immediate and responsive way.

The remainder of this paper is organized as follows. We first give a brief description of Labanotation and related tools in Section 2. We explain the choreography pipeline of LabanChoreographer in Section 3. Then we describe how to retrieve and compose similar motions from a motion capture database in Section 4. Section 5 presents how to edit and refine motion sequence by Labanotation. We show the experimental results and conclude with a discussion of our approach in Section 6.

2   Overview of Labanotation and Relevant Tools

Labanotation, devised by Rudolf Laban in the early 20th century, has been used in recording body motions of ballet and dance [10]. It is easy for us to roughly understand the body movements by simply browsing the notation scores in Laban sequence. Each Labanotation symbol gives four pieces of information. Calvert et al have given a very concise and comprehensive description of Labanotation as follows [9]: the symbol's shape depicts the direction of motion. Its shading shows the level of a movement; diagonal strokes for high, a dot for middle, and blackened for low. Moreover, the symbol's length indicates duration of the movement. The staff is read from the bottom up; moving ahead in time. The tick marks on the center line divide the time into counts and the horizontal lines correspond with the bar lines in the music. Movements written on the same horizontal line occur simultaneously; movements written one above another occur sequentially. Finally, the symbol's placement on the column within the staff suggests that which part of the body is being described. Symbols to the left side of the center line refer to the left-hand side of the body, and those to the right side refer to the right hand side. Symbols for movement are shown in Figure 1a.

a) Laban symbols for movements.   b) Laban signs for body parts.

Fig. 1. Symbols and signs in Labanotation

The signs to identify body parts are in front of each column, as shown in Figure 1b. motion choreography enables animators to conceptualize and develop the movement idea via a notation language, which can greatly facilitate the evolution and communication of motions.

The role of computer in human movement choreography includes assistance in notating, illustrating human movements, re-creation of historic works from notation, and devising motions for script-based animations etc. [11]. The earlier work on computer-based motion choreography can be traced back to the end of 1970. Brown and Smoliar developed a graphical tool to assist the editing and creation of Labanotation sequence for human choreographer [2]. Badler & Smoliar discussed how to generate the digital representation of human movements by notation languages [12]. The automatic approaches to converting motion capture data into coded and compact description using Labanotations have also been investigated and implemented [1] [13]. Calvert et al developed computer based notation systems to edit and interpret Labanotation by a model based approach [3] [4]. In light of the iterative and interactive nature of the choreographic process, they also investigated how to support the choreographer in compositional process, and developed a visual idea generator with intuitive interface of Stage-, Body-, and Stance- Editors [5] [6]. Kojima et al developed an interactive graphical editor for writing and editing Labanotation scores, and the user can input and edit human body movement of dance with alternate view of 3D human body animation [14]. Calvert et al analyzed the performance of LabanWriter and LabanDancer, and presented how to translate dance notions into animation via inverse kinematics model [9]. Most of these existing efforts focus on computer based tools to assist movement notating, and intuitive interfaces to devise and create a notation-based choreography with the visual feedback of 3D body animation.

3 The Choreography Pipeline in LabanChoreographer

Motion choreography is to arrange and coordinate the overall motion performance and the local movement details in a time sequence. During the process of conceptualization and development of movement ideas, a choreographer will always need to move between the design of overall human motion and the design of more detailed levels of particular movements, gestures or stances. The computer based choreography system is designed to assist, not to replace this process.

In LabanChoreographer, the motion choreography process is modelled as a loop of content-based retrieval and optimization that tries to choose the fitted motion clips from a

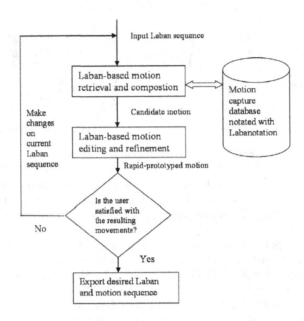

Fig. 2. The pipeline of motion choreography by LabanChoreographer

motion library, and effectively snap them together so that the resulting motion is continuous and closely matches to movement notations in Laban sequence. The motion library is composed of motion capture data associated with corresponding Labanotations. A Laban generation tool is developed to automatically convert motion capture data into Labanotation sequence according to algorithms in [1] [13]. When a motion clip is stored into the database, its corresponding Labanotation sequence is created in advance, and then the computer correlates them in motion library. As shown in Figure 2, a single-step loop of such a data-driven choreography process is described as follows: given the user specified Labanotation sequence, it will firstly perform Laban-based retrieval and composition to find the most similar motions from motion capture database, and then snap together these retrieved motion clips into a continuous rough motion sequence that matches the input Laban sequence as much as possible. Secondly, Laban-based motion editing and refinement are launched to semi-automatically revise and refine these candidate motion sequences such that the resulting motion data can best approximate the input Laban sequence. If the current motion is not desirable yet, the user can interactively make changes on Labanotation, and the system will enter into the next loop of Laban-based motion retrieval, composition, editing and refinement. This choreography process can be iterated until the user gets the desired motion or choreographed work.

4   Laban-Based Motion Retrieval and Composition

During motion choreography process, the user expresses the desired motion by Labanotation. In order to visually evaluate these motions, we need to convert the user specified Laban sequence into concrete motion data first. Our strategy is to find the desirable motion sequence from an existing set of motion capture data. Such a Laban to motion conversion problem is therefore transformed into searching in a motion library for motion clips that best fits the input Laban sequence. The system should locate and extract the similar motion segments that are the same action or action sequence expressed by the user specified Labanotation, and then snap them together to create the best-fit candidate motion sequence matched to the input Laban sequence.

In our motion library, the movements have been associated with the corresponding Labanotations. Therefore, the input Laban sequence can be directly compared with Laban depiction in the motion Library. The system will first identify the most similar Laban sequence from the motion library, and then pick out their corresponding movement data in terms of the relationship between motions and Laban sequences. Labanotation sequence is in essence a temporal data sequence where each beat describes the posture of character in a specific time interval. Many retrieval techniques for temporal data are proposed in database community. We employ the DTW (dynamic time warping) algorithm to measure the similarity of two Laban sequences [15]. Its algorithmic idea is that we firstly check the similarity between the corresponding beats, and then construct a warping curve in the distance grid along a time axis. If the average warping cost of the curve is within the specified threshold, they will be considered as similar.

Fig. 3. An instance to evaluate Laban distance metric and best-fit motion retrieval

The effectiveness of Laban distance metric function and retrieval algorithm are evaluated by a series of experiments. We convert a source motion capture data into a Laban sequence, and use this Laban sequence to search for best-fit motions in a motion library. The resulting motions are then visually compared with the source motion captured data. We tested out tens of motion clips for martial arts techniques performed by the upper part and lower part body respectively. Figure 3 shows one of these tests. The frames from the source motion capture data is in the center, and the surrounding regions display four motions retrieved from the library using the aforementioned Laban distance and search algorithm.

5 Laban-Based Motion Editing and Refinement

In motion choreography, a basic requirement for motion evaluation is that rapid-prototyped motion data should match to the user desired motion expressed in Laban sequence. As mentioned in section 4, Laban-based motion retrieval can only guarantee that the candidate motion is closely similar to the desired motion in Labanotation form. It needs the post-processing steps to match them as much as possible. For this purpose, Laban-based motion editing and refinement is developed to alter the candidate motion sequence such that the rapid-prototyped sequence can best approximate the desired 3D human motions in the mind of choreographer. The motion sequence represented in Labanotation may have many variants. Therefore we employ a coarse-to-fine method to semi-automatically build the rapid-prototyped motion. It firstly makes their Laban sequence be the same by the constraint-based algorithm. The system automatically convert the difference of movement notations between two Laban sequences into temporal and spatial constraints, and then a constraint-based solver is used to make changes on the candidate motion via optimization.

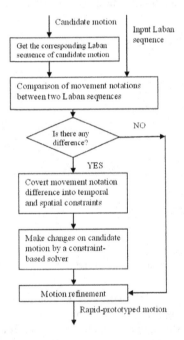

Fig. 4. The pipeline of Laban-based motion editing and refinement

After their Laban sequences are matched to each other, the user can interactively refine the motion using low-level frame and position constraints etc. Its algorithmic details are given in [16]. The pipeline of Laban-based motion editing and refinement are shown in Figure 4.

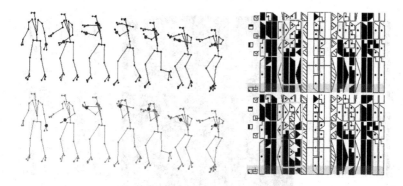

Fig. 5. An example of Laban-based motion editing. The difference between two Laban sequences is on left-wrist joint. The frames from source and target motion are drawn in black and red respectively.

Figure 5 gives an experimental result of a Laban-based motion editing. The left-wrist joint is moved to a higher position in its Laban sequence, and the resulting motion data is changed accordingly. After the motion sequence has been made to match to the query Laban sequence, it does not mean that the current motion also exactly match the desired motion in the user's mind, as movement notation is not an accurate representation of motion. Therefore, motion refinement is introduced to allow the user to interactively alter the current motion. The user can enforce low level constraints, and the system will accordingly make the adjustments on the target motion data via motion refinement while keeping its Labanotations unchanged.

6 Results and Discussion

Notation-based motion choreography can rapid-prototype realistic motions via Labanotation at the early stage of the motion design. It helps the motion composer not only to evaluate the choreography work, but more importantly, to follow and develop the intent of movement idea in an animation sequence. In script-based animation for virtual characters etc., it can potentially bridge the gap between semantic script words and the animation data, as movement notation language is a neutral qualitative representation with less numerical data, it may be better and easier to translate the animation script into a neutral notation language, other than directly into a concrete key-frame sequence. It is also suited as a tool for the education and training of rhythmic movements such as dance and martial arts.

The LabanChoreographer is implemented using Visual C++. We employ an extended version of Labanotation that has 17 joints to represent the posture of human body. The motion library contains more than 90,000 frames of captured martial arts motions (around 300 different martial arts forms). Its user interface to choreograph two persons' movement is shown in Figure 6. The rapid-prototyped motion data is displayed in central region. The users can iteratively make changes on the Laban sequences on the fly, and the system will accordingly generate the latest desirable motion data for visual evaluation.

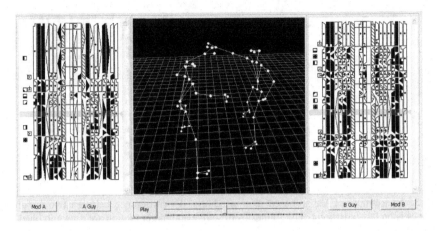

Fig. 6. The interface of motion choreography for two persons

Compared with annotation-based choreography, the advantages of notation-based choreography are obvious. Annotations are subject to individual interpretation, and for complex motions, it is difficult to generate annotations that most users can identify the same images of motions without misunderstanding the content. More importantly, annotations lack the capability of accurately clipping the proper segments of the motion data [17]. But movement notations show more hints about the content of motions. The beats in Laban sequence can decompose its motion sequence into motion segments accordingly. In most cases, we can easily communicate motions by Labanotations without misunderstandings.

The major limitation of LabanChoreographer is that it will fail to work if the system can not find any matched motion segments for the input Laban sequence. The current solution to deal with this case is that we let the user browse the motion library, and interactively choose and form a candidate motion sequence for Laban-based motion editing and refinement. In the future, we plan to integrate it with script-driven animation for virtual character. With the capability of natural language understanding, it is possible to translate the animation scripts into movement notations in specific game scenarios, aiming at automating the generation of variant movements of virtual characters in real-time.

Acknowledgements

This work was supported by NSF of China (60373032), by the research funds of Science and Technology Department of Zhejiang Province, and by Bureau of Science and Technology of Ningbo City.

References

1. Hachimura, K., Nakamura., M.: Method of generating coded description of human body motion from motion-captured dada. In IEEE International Workshop on Robot and Human Interactive communication(2001), 122–127

2. Brown, M. D., Smoliar., S. W.: A graphics editor for labanotation. In Proc. SIGGRAPH'76, (1976), 60–65
3. Calvert, T.W., Chapman, J., Patla, A.: The integration of subjective and objective data in animation of human movement. In Proc. SIGGRAPH '80(1980), 198–203
4. Calvert, T.W., Chapman, J., Patla, A.: Aspects of the kinematic simulation of human movement. IEEE Computer Graphics and Applications(1982), 2(9):41–50
5. Schiphorst, T., Calvert, C., Lee, C., Welman, C., Gaudet, S. : Tools for interaction with the creative process of composition. In Proceedings of the SIGCHI Conference on Human Factors in Computing Systems(1990), 167–174
6. Calvert, T. W., Bruderlin, A., Mah, S., Schiphorst, T., Welman, C.: The evolution of an interface for choreographers. In Proceedings of SIGCHI Conference on Human Factors in Computing Systems (1993), 115–122
7. Neagle, R.J.: A survey on application for editing and animating dance notations. In http://www.comp.leeds.ac.uk/royce/htmlpaper/nea-0303-001-sur.html, 2004
8. Wike, L.: Calvert, T., Ryman, R., Fox., I.: From dance notation to human animation: The labandancer project. Computer Animation and Virtual Worlds(2005), 16:201–211
9. Calvert, T., Wilke, L., Ryman, R., Fox, I.: Applications of computers to dance. IEEE Computer Graphics and Applications(2005), March/April , 6–12
10. Hutchinson, A.: Labanotation. Theatre Arts Books(1977)
11. Lansdown, J.: Computer-generated choreography revisited. In Proceedings of 4D Dynamics Conference(1995), 89–99
12. Badler, N. I., Smoliar, S. W.: Digital representations of human movement. ACM Computing Surveys(1979), 11:19–38
13. Hachimura, T. K., Nakamura, M.: Generating labanotation from motion-captured human body motion data. In Proceedings of International Workshop on Recreating the Past – Visualization and Animation of Cultural Heritage(2001), 118–123
14. Kojima, K., Hachimura, K., Nakamura, M..: Labaneditor: Graphical editor for dance notation. In Proceeding of the 2002 IEEE Int. Workshop on Robot and Human Interactive Communications(2002), 59–64
15. Yu, T., Shen, X., Li, Q., Geng, W.: Motion retrieval based on movement notation language. Computer Animation and Virtual Worlds(2005), 16:273–282
16. Shen, X., Li, Q., Yu, T., Geng, W., Lau, N.: Mocap data editing via movement notations. In Proceedings of CAD and Graphics 2005(2005), 463-470
17. Arikan, O. , Forsyth, D.A., O'Brien, J. F.: Motion synthesis from annotations. In Proc. SIGGRAPH '03(2003), 402–408

Nomadic Perspectives:
Spatial Representation in Oriental Scroll Painting and Holographic Panoramagrams

Jacques Desbiens

École des Arts Visuels et Médiatiques (E.A.V.M.), Doctorat en Études et Pratiques des Arts
Université du Québec à Montréal (U.Q.A.M.), Montréal, Québec, Canada
www.i-jacques.com

Abstract. Experiments in composition and effects of holographic panoramagrams (computer generated holography), demonstrate an analogy between this three-dimensional imaging process and Oriental horizontal scroll painting. These two ways of representing space share a similar conception of spatial representation in which multiple points of view are spread horizontally, parallel to the scene. The similarities are not only geometrical and conceptual, they also reveal a direction in the development of new spatial representation technologies in which the observer isn't only a passive receiver of visual information from a fixed position, but an active observer. This paper is based on analysis of the holograms structure as well as on artistic experiments in composition and art history researches.

For centuries, artists and scientists have tried to represent space in a way that the image conveys the illusion of dimensions and distances. Perspectivists have relied on several geometrical methods to project space appearances on a flat surface. These methods are essentially egocentric: in panoramic perspective for example, the artist is placed in the center of the world, representing the environment surrounding him by rotating his unique point of view from a fix location. As for binocular perspective, or stereoscopy, it is barely entering the world of spatial imaging by adding a second point of view that gives a sensation of distance between objects. Viewing apparatus and limited number of points of view may have prevented stereoscopy and autostereoscopy to expand its field of applications. In holography, sensibility to vibrations, technical complexity and limitations of subject matter has prevented it from becoming an accessible 3D imaging technique. Thus, spatial imaging is still in need for a practical freeviewing[1] 3D representation method. While most imaging systems inherit their geometrical and optical characteristics from the occidental perspective tradition, some of them, like computer generated holographic

---

[1] Freeviewing: in 3D imaging, freeviewing is the ability to view three-dimensional images and perceive artificial 3D without using a viewing device like prism glasses, polarized filters, goggles, etc.

H. Zha et al. (Eds.): VSMM 2006, LNCS 4270, pp. 504–513, 2006.

panoramagrams[2], draw up a link with oriental representation of space as seen in horizontal scroll painting. Its hybrid conception of spatial representation offer new possibilities in spatial imaging as well as in the presentation of visual information, and gives to the observer the liberty to choose its point of view and interact naturally with the 3D space.

1 Multiple Points of View Perspective

In the computer generated holographic process I use, a three-dimensional scene is created in a 3D graphic software in which the space is defined by the standard *(x, y, z)* coordinates, *"x"* being the horizontal axis, *"y"* is the vertical axis and *"z"* is depth. A virtual camera moves laterally, on the *"x"* axis, in front of this 3D scene recording a large number of conical perspective images corresponding to a series of juxtaposed points of view. These images provide us with the necessary viewing angles to recreate horizontal parallax perception. This set of images is used to expose a holographic film using a holographic imager developed recently in Montreal (Canada) by XYZ Imaging inc.. This machine is an automated printer in which a pulsed RGB laser and an optical system produce small overlapped holographic pixels on large format high resolution emulsions. When the resulted hologram is displayed and lighted by a point source white light, it reconstructs the full colour three-dimensional appearances of the represented space. When observers move laterally in front of the hologram, they perceive successively and stereoscopically the juxtaposed points of view, consequently, the spatiality of the scene and its volumetric content. Since the hologram is made of a large number of images that will be viewed over time with the observer's movements, short animations can be added to the scene. Therefore, holographic panoramagram are not only three-dimensional, but also dynamic in interaction with the viewer's positions and movements.

Fig. 1 and 2. Virtual camera setup of a computer generated holographic panoramagram

It is interesting to note that, from antiquity up to the development of a coherent perspective system during the renaissance, attempts in perspective representation were constructed from many points of view but, lacking a unified geometrical

---

[2] Holographic panoramagram are often called "holographic stereogram". The term "panoramagram" should be employed since they allow continuous parallax viewing. OKOSHI, Takanori, Three-Dimensional Imaging Techniques, Academic Press, NewYork, 1976, p. 247.

composition approach, these experiments resulted in incoherent spatial representation. In the history of perspective systems, while the viewer's eye is considered unique and immobile in Alberti's and Piero Della Francesca's[3] approaches, the recognition of the dynamic and multiplicity of points of view as a requirement for coherent perspective representation of space was present in northern European renaissance[4]. However, experiments in this field became mostly optical curiosity and didn't survive the utilitarian applications that directed perspective development since the XVIth century.

We tend to see the invention of the stereoscope in the XIXth century[5] as the beginning of multiple points of view imaging. In fact, the first stereoscopic drawing is attributed to Giovanni Battista Della Porta around 1600. Unfortunately, to be viewed correctly, stereoscopic images need a special optical display apparatus. Without it freeviewing is difficult and uncomfortable, if not impossible, and most of the time the result is double images, obvious distortions or headaches. As for autostereoscopy or lenticular imaging, while they offer stereoscopy without viewing devices, the limited number of points of view prevents this approach to be able to provide continuous parallax and volume realism. As you may have noticed, these 3D images tend to flatten volumes as if objects were cut-out images with distances between them. Autostereoscopy is, by definition, a multiple points of view perspective system but it is, by far, unable to provide the quality of 3D visual information available in holographic panoramagrams.

Since the invention of holography by Denis Gabor[6] in 1948, several important developments have transformed this diffraction based imaging process. One of which is the multiplex hologram developed by Lloyd Cross[7] in 1972. Computer generated holographic panoramagrams are a variation on the composite approach of the multiplex hologram principle. Instead of using film or video images, the source images are computer generated and the compositing of a full 3D hologram is made by exposing a large number of small holographic pixels. This method allows much more possibilities in contents and visual effects.

What the holographic panoramagram technology offers, is a coherent multiple points of view perspective system. In this 3D imaging process, geometrical parameters of the 3D scene are determined by the optical characteristics of the imaging system and the size of the hologram. The format of the hologram (height and width), in relation to the pixel size (0.8mm or 1.6mm), will determine the camera field-of-view, its distance from the hologram plane and the image resolution to render. It will also determine the number and point of view positions for the juxtaposed images to render. These parameters are used to circumscribe the three-dimensional scene constructed in the 3D graphic program. What we obtain with this approach, is a multiple perspective images that are combined in an optical viewing device, the hologram itself, to reconstruct the appearances of continuous parallax, as if we were observing a real wide field of view three-dimensional space.

---

[3] BRION-GUERRY, L., *Jean Pélerin Viator – sa place dans l'histoire de la perspective*, Société d'Édition les Belles Lettres, Paris, 1962, p.46.

[4] Idem, pp.79-81.

[5] Mirror stereoscope: Charles Wheatstone, 1838. Prism Stereoscope: David Brewster, 1849.

[6] Denis Gabor (1900-1979), Nobel prize 1971.

[7] Lloyd Cross. In 1972, he used cinematographic images to expose a holographic emulsion resulting in animated images. These multiplex holograms are also called "holographic stereograms".

The landscape hologram (fig. 8) for example, is 380mm X 1200mm, the holographic pixels size is 0.8mm, the virtual camera in the 3D software was at a distance 2494mm from the hologram plane and it moves laterally on a distance of 1600mm, each side of the center of the x axis. This virtual camera registered a set of juxtaposed images at a resolution of 5501 X 475 pixels. With these parameters, the resulting hologram presents a spatial structure that resembles a double truncated pyramid jointed by its small base delimited by the hologram plane. 3D objects appear behind and in front of the hologram plane, in full volume, and a large panoramic view of the scene is offered to the observer, thanks to the 1280 juxtaposed points of view.

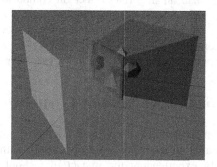

Fig. 3. Spatial structure of a computer generated holographic panoramagram

2 Spatio-temporal Observation of Holographic Panoramagrams

My first experiment in spatio-temporal composition of holographic panoramagrams included content closely related with time. It was a simulation of the 1999 total eclipse over Europe (fig. 4). It presented one hour of the astronomical phenomenon, showing the moving shadow on earth synchronised with a clock showing the time, the appearance of a few cities when the eclipse was total over them, the position of the sun and a view through a telescope of the eclipse with its flash. When the observer moves from left to right, the event is viewed chronologically. In this experimental hologram, the hour is only a reference since the observer can view the whole event in a few seconds. If he moves from right to left, the eclipse is reversed. Content is presented on the basis of synchronisation of information instead of a linear presentation over time.

Fig. 4. « Simulation of the 1999 total eclipse over Europe »; Jacques Desbiens, 2004

Experiments like this have shown that some spatial features of the holographic panoramagram have a strong influence on composition choices and on perceptual effects. Spatial contradictions can occur: *"time-smear"* are distortions or blurring caused by animation speed and patterns can create *"moiré"* effects. One feature makes this imaging approach very particular: time distortions can be caused by viewing conditions. For example: *"Simultaneity"* occurs when two observers see different points of view and therefore two different moments at the same time. *"Reversibility"* in which an animated scene created to be viewed from left to right will be seen in reverse if an observer moves from right to left, as described in the eclipse hologram experiment. *"Speed incoherence"* is also an important effect on compositional characteristics: it doesn't matter if a represented movement is slow or fast, continuous or jerky, speed appearance will depend on the movement of the viewer. Observers can move fast or slow, go back and forth or they can stop whenever they want. Consequently, holographic panoramagrams are non-cinematographic, space is given, time is given up.

3   Points of View Shifting as Nomadic Perspective

These spatio-temporal characteristics make the holographic panoramagram a distinct media, with its own spatial structure, its own relationship with time, its own way to convey information. By experiencing the impact of technological features on the composition of holographic images, it became clear to me that this 3D media posses conceptual similarities with ancient spatial representation approaches that tries to include multiple points of view perspective and observer's movement.

In the composition of a 3D scene for a holographic panoramagram, the virtual camera is setup to render a set of individual images corresponding to each point of view needed to reconstruct horizontal parallax. Each of these images are conical perspective views of the scene, but the virtual camera gradually shift its position on the x axis transforming this traditional occidental perspective into a multiple points of view system of spatial representation. Even though we use the term "panoramagram", this camera movement isn't a "panoramic rotation", but a "travelling". The observer, as the camera, moves in space.

This viewing movement, this continuous point of view shifting as a mean of spatial representation is central to the holographic panoramagram process, and it is rarely found in occidental art and imaging history. On the other hand, in oriental history of spatial representation, the multiple points of view approach is widespread. In Chinese landscape scroll painting, the space is represented as a series of points of view from which the artists depicted objects, lakes and streams, trees, houses, hills, mountains and clouds, while travelling in the landscape. Scroll paintings may not produce the optical illusion of distance and three-dimensionality, but as in the holographic panoramagram, space is visualized dynamically through many points of view.

Fig. 5. Kuo Hsi, "Clearing Autumn Skies Over Mountains and Valleys", 11th century

These long scrolls link the representation of space to the representation of time which are transferred to the viewing experience itself. As in the holographic panoramagram, control over viewing time of a long landscape scroll painting isn't available. Forms, brush strokes, hue, intensity, spatial organisation is constructed, composed. Time, speed and direction are left to the observer's choices.

This analogy between holographic and scroll painting dynamics became apparent through experimentation. While I was composing a 3D scene for a hologram, I made experimental drawings in concertina format Chinese sketchbooks. These very long drawings (fig. 6) represented imaginary landscapes viewed from a series of juxtaposed points of view. I also made, the same way, several long format computer generated landscapes (fig. 7). The influence of format on composition, the impact of point of view shifting and movement as a way to conceive space, transformed my conception of 3D composition for computer generated hologram.

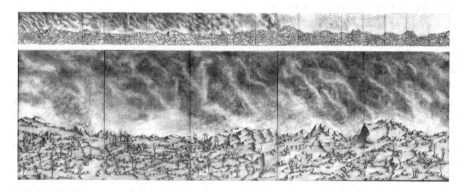

Fig. 6. "Landscape", Jacques Desbiens, 2005, graphite on paper, concertina sketchbook & detail, 337cm X 25cm

Fig. 7. "Computer generated landscape", Jacques Desbiens, 2004

The holographic panoramagram "The broken window" (fig. 8) is the latest in this series of experiments in representing space through the observer's movement. This hologram represents a scroll unrolling when the observer move from right to left. The 3D image depicted is a window through which we can see a deep landscape. The glass in the left pane is broken by a tree branch that appears in front of the hologram plane.

From all those experiments, it became clear to me that multiple point of view imaging is a distinct approach to perspective in which movement through space is the principal mean of depicting our own relationship with the spatial structure. It is travelling, it is nomadic perspective.

Fig. 8. "The Broken Window", Jacques Desbiens, 2006. Central point of view of the source images for a holographic panoramagram, 120cm X 38cm.

4 Three Holographic Zones

When working on composition of 3D scenes for holography, one becomes very aware of the importance of the geometrical structure of space, the positions of objects in relation with the hologram plane, but also of the role of void between objects. Distances, overlapping, occlusion, juxtaposition, objects movements, become more than esthetical components, they are tools in shaping space, in creating the illusion of volumes and presence. A shadow will convince the observer that the object is in front of another and occlusion of some objects by others will reinforce the appearance of depth. "In front" and "behind" are concepts spread in the whole set of points of views.

Holographic space can be divided in three zones (see fig. 3): the foreground in which objects appear in front of the hologram plane, this is a real image as defined in optics terminology; then there is the hologram plane itself which is a flat surface position on the emulsion; and finally there is the background in which the objects appear behind the hologram plane, this is the virtual image. When composing a hologram, these three holographic zones are very similar to the "three distances" (san yuan) as described by Kuo Hsi in his XIst century painting treatise "Lofty Messages of Forests and Springs" (Lin ch'üan kao chih)[8].

Kuo Hsi's three distances concepts, "high distance" (gaoyuan), "deep distance" (shenyuan) and "level distance" (pingyuan), are obviously different from the holographic foreground, hologram plane and background zones, and it is surely different from occidental perspective constructions. Nevertheless, by introducing a distance relationship between content and appearances, these concepts find their application in the composition of a hologram scene by analogy to the positioning of objects in the holographic space and the effects of depth of field. Indeed, the sharpness of an object in the virtual holographic space will decline with distance, as in most oriental landscape painting, the background is blurry. On the other hand, the visual quality of objects appearing in front of the hologram plane, as a real image, can

---

[8] Kuo Hsi (XIst century), *Lofty Messages of Forests and Springs* (Lin ch'üan kao chih), published as *An Essay on Landscape Painting*; translated by Shio SAKANISHI, John Murray, London, 1935.

be affected by convergence when they are too far from the hologram plane. So distances of objects, in relation to the holographic zones, are related to sharpness and visibility. But moreover, the three distances concepts help us understand the process of, not only positioning objects in relation to each other, but also of composing space itself in relation to multiple and dynamic points of view. The role of fog, void, contrast and superposition in shaping volume and distance between object in oriental painting is similar to positioning objects in the empty illusionary space of holograms. Luminance and chromaticity, emptiness and occlusion, play important parts in the visibility of spatial relationships.

When the composition represent a non-geometric subject, like a landscape, these composition elements are critical to an efficient perception of three-dimensional space. And again, multiple points of view and the observer's movement are the main components in providing this spatial illusion. A real or an imaginary landscape invites the viewer to wander, to change points of views, to move. However, our tradition of flat imagery, observed from a unique point of view, made us accustomed to representation and observation in inertia, through a fix window. Often, when I show one of my holograms to people who never seen computer generated holographic panoramagrams before; they position themselves toward the center of the hologram and stay there. I have to tell them to move, to change points of view. We can understand that it is rare to find spatial representations asking for observation in movement thus, the proliferation of such spatial imaging technologies may change our physical relationship with the image. The creation of such images will have to consider our movement, in natural or artificial environments, as part of the representation.

5 Narration Through Multiple Points of View Perspective

There is some example of geometrical perspective associated with multiple points of view in long scroll format. However, these are not conical perspective but rather parallel perspective constructions[9] which allowed the artist to maintain apparent coherence while shifting points of view and moving through the scene. Apparently, this technique facilitated the introduction of narrative content. While we can find a few example of narrative content depicted in very long horizontal composition in occidental art, they are either a chronological depiction of events without any spatial representation of three-dimensionality, like the Bayeux tapestry[10], or a fix representation of space and time as in most cylindrical panoramas[11].

---

[9] WELLS, Wilfrid H., *Perspective in early Chinese painting*, Edward Goldston ltd., London, 1935.

[10] The Bayeux tapestry is a 70m by 50cm embroidered cloth depicting the 1066 battle of Hastings. The images are describing chronologically the events leading to the conquest of England by the Normans.

[11] Many painted panoramas were created in Europe during the XVIIIth and XIXth centuries. These images were painted inside a large cylindrical room usually depicting war scenes, cityscapes and historical events.

Fig. 9. Zhang Zeduan, "Upper River during Qing Ming Festival", XIIth century. Detail of parallel perspective in a long scroll painting.

Chinese scroll painting however, presents a wide representation of space and time with a multiple points of view spread in real space, as well as many examples of narrations of either chronological or parallel subjects. This way of presenting content in space and time, link with the movement of the artists and, by extension, of the observer, make oriental scroll painting and holographic panoramagrams related in their approaches of presenting narrative content. In both cases, the observer can view the content by shifting its point of view and by synchronising the different elements for each sequence. Linearity may be suitable, but again, it is left to the observer's choices.

In computer generated holographic panoramagrams, visual information is spread out through its multiple points of view spatial structure. Synchronisation of content in space becomes the dominant way of conveying information. Instead of having the content given in a flowing linear and chronological manner as in cinema, the observer has to participate in finding the links between the different elements of content. His movements and choices of angles of viewing allow him to reconstruct the message. This characteristic makes holographic panoramagram a very different method of presenting visual information and narration. This is different from fix 2D images, kinetic media like cinema or video, interactive media like the internet, or even traditional optical holography. It is also very different from 3D imaging systems like virtual reality because the observer's movements are real and interactivity is limited to direct freeviewing.

It is quite extraordinary that one of the oldest forms of spatial representation, oriental scroll painting, is analog to one of the most recent technological advancement in spatial imaging. These structural and conceptual analogies emphasise the fact that, by merging oriental and occidental conception of spatial representation, we are moving into nomadic perspectives. With new interactive imaging technologies, beyond stereoscopy, the observer's movements may be the requirements for an efficient illusionist spatial representation. These new technologies of three-dimensional imaging may change, not only the way we represent space with geometry and optics, but also our very conception of spatial representation and our role in its dynamics. Chinese scroll paintings and holographic panoramagrams may be very different in visual effects, in structure and in techniques; nevertheless, they share a similar conception of spatial representation. The fixity of traditional perspective is evacuated. The artist and the observer are not in the center of the world anymore, they are passing through the environment. These similarities show us new ways of representing the space we share and the artistic and scientific heritage on which we build our future.

Jacques Desbiens
Artist & Researcher
École des Arts Visuel et
Médiatiques
Université du Québec à Montréal
July 2006
Montreal, Qc, Canada
www.i-jacques.com

Urban-Planning Game

L. Benčič and M. Mele

Institute and Academy for Multimedia, Ljubljana, Slovenia

Abstract. The project Urban-planning game represents a way of democratic
involvement of the public in the shaping of the future of historic towns by way
of an interactive game. It is based on cooperative behavior between the
inhabitants, the experts and the government. The object of the game is acquiring
ideas and guidelines for a lasting development on the basis of people's needs
and problems. As a possible way of communication I propose a publicly
accessible cooperative nonzero-sum game on the playground of Geographic
information system technology. The player has a free use of symbolic
infrastructural elements. He can arrange them in the urban space according to
his experience, needs and wishes and in agreement with his co-players. The end
of the game is supposed to represent work and life in a modern town, organized
according to the player's plans.

1 The Circumstances for the Formation of the Project

The idea for the Urban-planning game appeared in Split in Croatia in 2004. The town
of Split is an obvious example of the gap between 2000 years of history of the
urbanistically unsurpassable Diocletian's palace and between the present which shows
a disorganized picture and its everyday problems.

2 Comparable Projects and Theoretic Findings

I got very few useful practical cases that could serve me as a model or comparison
and that I could test (CLUG [02], SimCity [07], DuBes [08]…).

Three parts of the theoretical basis of the game were formed: democracy, future of
towns and game theory.

These chapters confirm my original idea and its benefits for protection of cultural
heritage and help understand the backgrounds of urban systems [03], [04].

Crowding, swarming and socializing are a basic right and frequent phenomena in
the modern society. Crowds create goods and exploit them. But they also have to
strike and keep the balance. This balance could be called - the Social game. One
segment of the social game works in the sphere of urban systems. This segment could
be called – the Urban-planning game.

H. Zha et al. (Eds.): VSMM 2006, LNCS 4270, pp. 514–519, 2006.
© Springer-Verlag Berlin Heidelberg 2006

This is a game that would in practice be worth as much as there would be knowledge, experience and advice of the players in it. So it has to be a mass game.

The more there would be active communication, that is, understanding, negotiating, learning between the players, the greater and more precious would the stock of knowledge be.

Knowledge of social behaviour, on which the proposals for the realization of the lasting development are based, is always insufficient and all information is welcome [05], [06].

This kind of game and the information from its contents can be used by experts to predict the future and lasting development of towns as one of the methods for gaining and supplementing their bases of knowledge [01]. (It does not replace the existing methods of sociological research.)

3   Concept of My Urban-Planning Game (Fig. 1.)

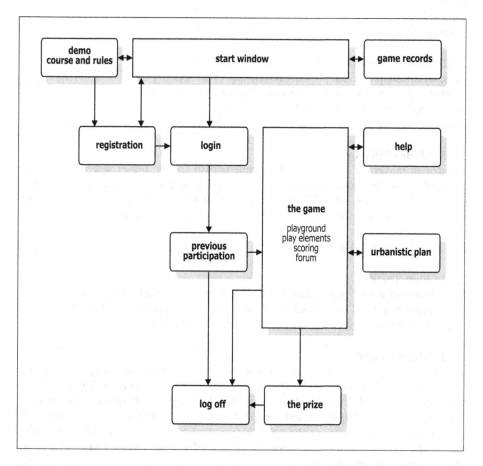

Fig. 1. To illustrate the concept I will use a sketch which otherwise shows the navigation in the user interface of the game

3.1 Rules of the Game

3.1.1 Object of the Game
The object of the game is defined according to the basic guidelines of the urbanistic plan:

Promotion of city government and its orientation towards an open dialogue with citizens
Tools for data collection and communication with citizens (following their thoughts and doubts, their distress and enthusiasm…)
Social cooperation which encourages involvement of citizens and their interaction on the level of the game (find out the opinions of others, negotiate with other citizens, allow for, understand and accept the freedom of thinking which is different from theirs…)
Collecting ideas - guidelines for predicting future development and cultural heritage protection
Education
Awareness

3.1.2 Elements of the Game
basic components: actual projects anticipated in urbanistic plan
place-area: game surface is a GIS map of town or part of town
roles: players are all citizens in their actual roles
events: arranging elements on the playground, forum, marking, prize coupons

3.1.3 Mode of Playing
Number of players is not limited. The game is over for the player when he arranges the symbols on the game surface, scores the sufficient amount of points and gets the coupon. The starting points for players are given in the description of the symbols which represent the projects, in UP (urbanistic plan) and in Help window.

3.2 Game Levels – Model

3.2.1 First Third
Registration of a new or login of a registered player. The registration comprises user name, password, local appurtenance, status of the player, profession of the player.
    Demo window shows the course and the rules of the game.

3.2.2 Second Third
The player proposes his selection on the map by indicating, selecting and placing icons-symbols of projects (buildings) into places on a GIS map according to his real world experience. He can also demolish some of the existing buildings. The projects are divided into obligatory and optional ones. It is necessary to arrange all compulsory ones and some of the optional ones without exceeding the proposed joint value. The player has at his disposal the rules of the game in text form and a short presentation of the urbanistic plan.

Players, registered with the same role and local appurtenance can see each other's decisions and can discuss, negotiate and evaluate the projects in the forum window. After discussion the player independently decides on final arrangement and selection of projects, saves it and submits it for marking.

According to location's suitability for realization and cost and logistics justification the player is awarded points. More points represent a more suitable solution from the viewpoint of above stated criteria.

3.2.3 Third Third

On Mosaic – a lottery game the player's prize appears (if justified). The prize is a randomly chosen mosaic square representing one of the game sponsors and as such the sponsor's prize. The coupon is printed; the player collects it and logs off.

Best scores of previous games are available to players regardless of their participation. They represent temporary arrangement of projects and are the indicators of the will and needs of citizens. They are presented by a GIS map and statistic data.

4 Scenario of My Urban-Planning Game

4.1 Course of Game

The player arranges symbols of urbanistic elements on the game surface according to real life needs and tries to score as many points as possible. While playing the game he can consult other players on the forum and compare his solutions with theirs. By scoring points he can win the prize.

4.2 Players (Activities, Actions)

Every citizen of the town where the game is placed or every visitor who wishes to express his opinion and propose solutions for environmental problems and preservation of the cultural heritage can be the player. The player enters the game after registration and login. His task is to select symbols representing elements of urbanistic development, drag and place them on the chosen part of the playground (GIS map) representing the part of town according to his data. He repeats the procedure until all obligatory and some optional elements are arranged. The player has a greater chance for better score if he discusses the game with other players. He can do so in the forum window. The player has access to other player's solutions by indicating and selecting the game surface of his decisions. After a cooperative discussion the player gains more knowledge and experience and indirectly more possibilities for a reasonable, useful and cheaper selection. The player returns to his main game window and decides about his symbol arrangement. He saves the arrangement and submits it to marking according to three criteria. If he wants a better score which can be awarded, he can repeat the arranging, saving and marking. The player can temporarily exit the game, take time to think or check something in real world. He can continue the game by resuming registration anywhere and anytime. More players create a cooperative atmosphere; maximum number of players can only be limited technically. All players, regardless of their role in the game have equal possibilities for point scoring and prizes.

4.3 Elements of Game (Use, Aims, Communication, Interdependence)

Elements of the game are the playground (GIS map), existing and planned buildings and locations which are the subject under discussion of the urbanistic plan for the area on GIS map.

Playground: An indispensable layer in GIS application is a map of the area, a register of environmental units or database of all buildings in the area. Descriptions in the base offer data about contents, purpose, use and quality of environmental units, proprietors, managers, price and conditions of environmental unit acquisition and all other data necessary for making selections and decisions, for example for public transport planning, finding the most suitable locations for shops, hospitals, schools etc. When we roll the mouse over a marker on a map a flag with the address and data appears. So we can check at the beginning of the game all environmental elements which are available as game elements, and after arranging all elements which have been placed on the map and complement missing locations or substitute former buildings.

4.3.1 Existing Buildings

Static: changes not possible (for example cultural heritage)
Dynamic: it is possible to change the purpose, renovate, demolish, change into static (indicate, select, delete, edit data, go back to previous or starting positions). Changes affect the value of the building.
    Value in points changes.

4.3.2 Locations

Static: changes not possible (for example archaeological site)
Dynamic: it is possible to build, change into static location (indicate, select, delete, edit data, go back to previous or starting positions). Changes affect the value of the building.
    Value in points changes.

4.3.3 Planned Buildings

Dynamic: it is possible to determine a suitable location for realization (to indicate, select, delete, edit data, go back to previous or starting positions).
    Existing buildings and locations are located on a GIS map. They have all existing GIS data and the information about the actual score (number of points).
    Planned buildings are shown as symbols outside the GIS map and have data necessary for making decisions and justifying the choice of future location and the information about the actual score (number of points). The player selects, drags and places the symbols of environment elements on the game surface.
    Dynamic elements can be marked, selected, dragged and deleted, the data can be edited and it is possible to go back to previous or starting positions. While arranging selected elements on the map the existing database is supplemented with new, just selected elements and their characteristics and new relations in the environment are made.

4.4 Artificial Intelligence and Marking (Desired Behaviour)

The tools of artificial intelligence deal with the evaluation of the value and quality of proposals. During the game, after every move of the player calculating realization costs, acquiring and collecting logistic information and predicting possible development of town is in course. The player gets the new value of points scored. Location suitability, cost justification and logistics of new proposals are evaluated. Above average score enables the player to participate in prize-winning competition. Evaluation takes place according to rules and criteria established in urbanistic, economic and logistic field. Methods, already tested in such analyses are used. The total sum of all three analyses represents the player's final score.

4.5 Multi-player Possibilities of the Game

The relations between players are cooperative. On the forum the players discuss possible solutions of their problems. Players, registered with the same role and local appurtenance can see each other's decisions in the forum window and can discuss, negotiate and evaluate the projects. After discussion the player independently decides on final arrangement and selection of projects, saves it and submits it for marking. Proposals and decisions of the other players do not affect marking and awarding prizes.

5 Conditions for Realization

The next phase anticipates the realization.

I designed a Urban-planning game. I prepared the concept. I planned the scenario (playing technique, navigation, list of elements and functional claims of the user interface).

I devised the realization plan.

The game is realizable under following conditions:

- finding an investor who will secure finances,
- expert and legal support of the government agencies,
- engaging a selection of an adequately qualified team of co-workers,
- using modern technology support.

6 Conclusion

The urban-planning game represents an example of a concept of democratic involvement of the public in the shaping of the future of a town by way of an interactive game. It is based on cooperation and anticipates thinking and creative players.

References

1. Cecchini, A., Indovina, F. (1992). Strategie per un futuro possibile, Franco Angeli, Milano.
2. Feldt, A. G. (1972). CLUG Community Land Use Game, New York.
3. Gantar, P. (1985). Urbanizem, družbeni konflikti, planiranje, Založba Krt, Ljubljana.
4. Hočevar, M. (2000). Novi urbani trendi, FDV, Ljubljana.
5. Pogačnik, A. (1988). Kvantitavne metode v prost. in urb. planiranju, FAGG, Ljubljana.
6. Toš, N. (1988). Metode družboslovnega raziskovanja, DZS, Ljubljana.
7. simcity.ea.com (31. 7. 2006)
8. www.gymnasion.tudelft.nl/pagesUK/dubes.html (31. 7. 2006)

Virtual Network Marathon: Fitness-Oriented E-Sports in Distributed Virtual Environment

Zhigeng Pan[1], Gaoqi He[1], Shaoyong Su[2], Xiangchen Li[3], and Jingui Pan[2]

[1] State Key Lab of CAD&CG, Zhejiang University, Hangzhou, 310027, P.R.China
{zgpan, hegaoqi}@cad.zju.edu.cn
[2] State Key Lab for Novel Software Technology, Nanjing University, Nanjing, 210093, P.R.China
susy@mes.nju.edu.cn, panjg@nanjing-fnst.com
[3] China Institute of Sports Science, Beijing, 100061, P.R.China
lxc@3s.org.cn

Abstract. E-Sport is a newly emerging research field, especially in China, which has attracted many people's attention. In this paper, an innovative distributed online game platform is designed for fitness-oriented E-Sports, supporting multi-players or athletes. To provide users with more sense of immersion, technologies of virtual reality and sport simulation have been integrated into such system. Taking prototype system of Virtual Network Marathon as an example, detail designs are focused on the five aspects: story design, network communication, human computer interface, hardware interface and 3D render engine. All these design philosophies gain advantages of scale expandable, functions extendable, an efficient communication protocol and real-time rendering. Users at a distance can deeply immerse into virtual environment and enjoy exercise, competition and entertainment. Implementation of system is also described to validate the feasibility of our method.

Keywords: E-Sport, virtual reality, sport simulation, distributed online game.

1 Introduction

Computer games have turned into a popular form of entertainment, which use the new appeared technologies to make people deeply immersed into the game environment. Essentially rooted in computer games, E-Sports emerged no more than 10 years. E-Sports are competitive and intellectual computer games. In the distributed virtual environment built by information technologies, users take software and hardware devices as interactive tools, and obey the uniform rules [1]. Following this, users of E-Sports are no longer lost in computer games, but will take active part in modern competitive sports and enjoy playing with others all over the world instead. With the great development of information technologies and prevalence of Internet, E-Sports has attracted millions of fans and professional electronic playersand gradually become a remarkable phenomenon

H. Zha et al. (Eds.): VSMM 2006, LNCS 4270, pp. 520–529, 2006.

of sports culture [2]. There are three famous E-Sports competitions, which are WorldCyber Games (WCG) in Korea, Cyber Playing League (CPL) in America and Sports World Cyber(ESWC) in France. In China, E-Sport has been announced as the 99th official competition sports since 2003 and China ESport Games (CEG)[3] has been set up then. E-Sports related industries have formed a chain which makes a full impact on a country's economy. Gradually, this field is very concerned by many researchers coming from different disciplines, such as computer graphics, human computer interface, sports simulation, network communication, and so on.

E-Sports put a higher demand on the players' abilities than common computer games, not only superb coordination capacity between hands and eyes, rapid response capacity and skilful handling capacity of mouse and keyboard, but also complex strategic and tactical thinking ability[2]. However, E-Sports have some critical concerns, including unsuitable content of the games, social isolation of the players and lack of physical activities[4]. So, new E-Sports projects should overcome such limitations. Game contents prefer functions of education and leisure to shooting or killing activities. Through local area network (LAN) or Internet, users in E-Sports play together with more communication and feedback. Apart from typical input devices which bind people staying long statically, such as keyboard, mouse and joystick, an exertion interface is an alternation which requires more users' physical activities [5]. Inspired by the above considerations, fitness-oriented E-Sport is one of the best options. However, no general development patterns were found in previous literatures. Therefore, a distributed development framework will be introduced firstly. Based on it, Virtual Network Marathon (VNM) is designed as a typical application. Main ideas of VNM are that users do physical exercise and competition in a distributed virtual environment. When users run on the elliptical machine, their body motions are captured by sensors. They can observe their actions and current environment real-time rendered through output screen, and control their actions by multimodal interactions or interactive with other users by network.

In virtual space, the most important experience users hanker for is not the competition itself, but the sense of immersion into the computer generated environment. When users enjoy a certain fitness-oriented E-Sports, the optimal feeling is that they are unaware of their presence in physical surroundings but just feel as a part of the game environment. Moreover, actions of the avatar must be the high realistic simulations of body movements. The former is related to virtual reality (VR) research, and the latter touches the technology of sport simulation. VR is the use of computer graphics systems in combination with various display and interface devices to provide the effect of immersion in the interactive 3D environment[6]. While distributed virtual environment (DVE) integrates virtual reality with Internet to enable users' real-time sharing information and performing interaction in network virtual environment [7]. Sport simulation integrates sport exercise and state-of-art science technologies to add interesting into scientific training[8].

This paper focuses on both design and implementation of fitness-oriented E-Sports. A general development framework will be illustrated. Taking VNM as a typical example, five aspects of realization will be discussed with some innovative solutions. DVE and sport simulation related techniques are adopted to enhance system's performance.

The paper is organized as follows. Firstly related work in sports simulation and virtual reality based sports exercise are presented. In section 3, the system development framework is demonstrated. Detail design philosophies will be discussed in section 4. The implementation of VNM is described in section 5. Conclusions are drawn and future works are pointed out finally.

2   Related Works

The higher the living standards are, the more people care for their health. Health club are chosen to relax, get better bodies, improve their health and compensate for sedentary occupation. Correspondingly, some fitness systems are designed [9] and many researches have been done to improve the performance [10][11].

Group of Pan [9] has designed a virtual bowling game machine, called Easy-Bowling Machine, which integrates body exercise into game playing. Players throw a real bowling ball on a 2-meter-long track, and then the EasyBowling system uses a PC Camera to detect the speed and direction of bowl. After the motion parameters are computed, the movement of the bowling ball and its collision with pins are simulated in real-time and the result is displayed on a large display screen. Since it only requires a small space, this real game mode machine can also be a family game machine. However, this good idea has not been extended to internet environment.

Mokka [10] has developed a fitness computer game which aims at making the exercise session more motivating and rich in experiences. The user is exercising while he is exploring new surroundings or playing a fitness game in VE. The Virtual Fitness Centre (Virku) interface is a combination of an exercise bicycle, a computer and a screen. Such design philosophy is suitable for exercising purposes. However the VE is generated from map information which is less realistic.

Recently, bicycle virtual synthesized training simulation system [11] comes up. Such system applies virtual reality technology in sports simulation to promote motion training level. But the main purpose is to help professional athletes and it is used only locally.

3   System Framework

Fitness-oriented E-Sports in distributed virtual environment is a new-born field that lacks development standard or design guides. The framework introduced here is primarily intended to assist and direct the process of developing prototype of multiplayer networked games, and served as a general pattern. See Figure 1.

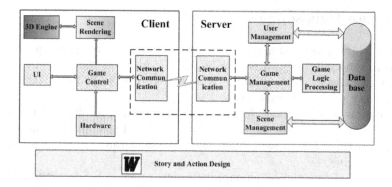

Fig. 1. General development framework

As shown in Figure 1, system framework is made up of four relatively independent parts: (1) client; (2) server; (3) story and action design and (4) network linking client and server.

As for client, users' body motions are captured by sensors. Game control center not only receives information from internet and hardware, but also respond to interactions of player. When user information and scene are updated, 3D engine is called to render real-time. See Figure 2.

As for server, game management center receive data from Internet, forward task and sent required data back. Coming down to the details, user management, scene management and game logic processing are designed to deal with users' login&logout activities, scene updating, and logical computing, respectively.

With regard to fitness-oriented E-Sports, common TCP/IP may not meet the requirments and a specific network protocol is necessary. In order to attract a wide range of participants, a fascinating story and action design are indispensable. Based on all the ideas mentioned above, such pattern is architecture referable, scale expandable and functions able to be enriched.

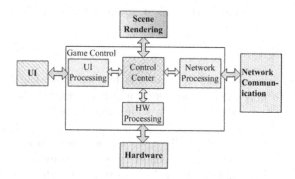

Fig. 2. Game control center at client

4   Design Philosophies

Running is the most commonly mass sport that improves participants' level of health, especially is good for cardiovascular function. Additionally, market capacity of network game in China is evaluated over 8 billion in 2006 [1]. So, VNM owns a promising perspective.

To be more general, main design concepts of system involve: (1) interesting story; (2) efficient network communication model and protocol; (3) natural HCI and Human-Human Interface; (4) instant motion capture and (5) real-time 3D rendering engine.

Taking VNM as a typical example of fitness-oriented E-Sport, the following part describes the detail design philosophies for the five aspects described above. Figure 3 shows the schematic diagram of VNM. There are three major roles: player, spectator and referee. Player exercises on the elliptical machine. Spectator watches the performance of players and vote for his favorite ones. While the referee master the competition rules, control the beginning and ending of the game and announce the final result. Beside the commonly client-server mode, in each client a direct discussion with each other is also feasible using some P2P technologies.

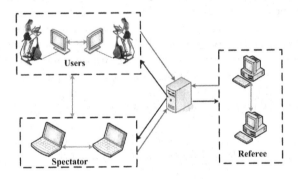

Fig. 3. Schematic diagram of VNM

4.1   Story Design

The most success of one computer game is how to make the users absorbed in it and ready to play again soon. Draw a conclusion, whether your game is interesting enough? In order to catch a wide range of readers, story need to be elaborate designed.

VNM combines fitness, multimedia entertainment with internet training and racing. Several exercise modes and scene choices are available. Fitness or race will be no longer a long and dreary task. Figure 4 shows the outline of story.

As you see in Figure 4, after an introductive animation of Marathon, user tries his login or registers when he is a newcomer. Then he can select a role as a spectator or a player. As a player, various choices of avatar are offered,

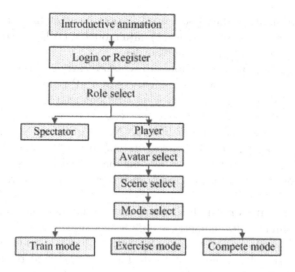

Fig. 4. Outline of story

including shape, clothes and shoes, etc. Some famous Marathon scenes extend users' experience. Then three modes are provided. Detail functions are briefly summarized in Table 1.

Under training mode, sale point lies at independent fitness with professional guidance. While in exercise mode, users can talk with each other, run in the streets of Beijing and walkthrough the scenery near the road. Users enjoy the stunning cityscape and learning some history and culture. Competition mode covers two versions, the mini marathon for irregular participants and the full one for the particular race, respectively.

Table 1. Classification of three modes

Mode		Network	Major function
Training		Offline. User with PC	Professional training guidance.
Exercise		Online.	Walkthrough in the scenery
Compete	Mini Marathon	Online.	Race with others. Piecewise time
	Full Marathon	Online.	Race with others. Complete one time.

4.2   Network Communication

Fitness-oriented E-Sport could be taken part in by internet, also be held in a local region. Consequently, the normal network communication should be adjusted to fit such particular situation. Figure 3 demonstrates that the underlying technical infrastructure for communication is based on a dedicated client-server model architectures, while it combines some peer-2-peer ideas at the same time. Concrete design is focused on three areas: (1) data model of DVE; (2) communication protocol and (3) information transfer burden.

Data model of DVE. VNM adopts the classic centralized structure as a base for its simplicity, and augments its robustness by P2P in local region to remove the high lever of dependence on server. Operations that need store or enquiry database, update scene and judge the users' action use client-server model. Other operations between two users use P2P in LAN, regardless of server.

Communication protocol. Corresponding to data model of DVE, traditional protocol is replaced by a new one, maybe named Fitness E-Sport Protocol (FESP). The structure of package transferred on the network is innovative constructed.

Information transfer burden. To reduce the latency and make full use of limit network bandwidth, geometry compression and progressive transmission technologies are used. Another important rule is that large data is transferred only once (for example, scene) and small data is transferred regularly (for example, user ID).

4.3   Hardware Interface

An inexpensive but multi-functional device is inevitable for fitness-oriented E-Sport. Hardware comprises elliptical machine, a sensor and a displayer. User exercises on the machine, the motions of which are capture by the sensors. Current field of vision and actions representing player himself and other online users are rendered on the displayer.

Elliptical machine was designed to avoid shock to the knees, which provides the same benefits as the treadmill but is a much smoother work-out. The handles are designed so that the user will move their arms in a similar fashion to running. Prototype system now uses a modified machine. In the future a cheap and particular machine will be designed for fitness-oriented E-Sports.

Motion information captured from user now comprises physical information (speed, acceleration, direction) and physiological data (heartbeat, breath). The former are transferred into 6 degree of freedom [12], the latter are used to control exercise time and direct users' training schedule. For generalized application, middleware is imported between hardware and game control module in Figure 1. See Figure 5.

4.4   Human Computer Interface

During the fitness, player watches the screen and interact with the system or other players in the same scene. He executes login or logout activities, selects the mode of scene and sport, and so on. With regard to spectator and referee, a distinct interface is supplied. Collision detections are used to simulate the actions between the player and the other ones or the buildings. See some snapshots during the competition mode from Figure 6.

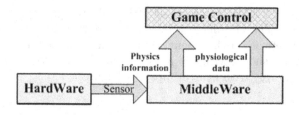

Fig. 5. Hardware abstract layer

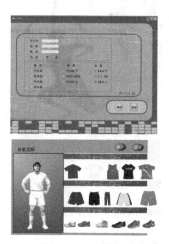 

Fig. 6. From left to right, up to down: Interface of register and mode select; shape select and scene select

4.5   3D Render Engine

What the system outputs is the most users' care. When some locally interactive action or update data from internet/LAN come, rendering occurs. 3D
engine based rendering made developers implement easily and readers understood quickly. Virtual reality and sport simulation can be used here to improve
the performance. For more sense of immersion, a 3D virtual environment is constructed using techniques of IBM&IBR, including road, building, park, trees,
virtual audience with the aid of video clip and sweet background music. User
sees his avatar whose action is realistic simulation of his movement using sports
simulation techniques. Walking, jogging and running of him and online player
in the same scene are perceived by players real-time.

5   Implementations

Prototype under developing uses Lucid engine [13] as the base, realized using
virtual reality and sports simulation in a distributed network. Programming language is VC++.net. Minimum system requirements for the system are Pentium

III or above CPU, 256MB memory, 500MB hard disk space and windows versions XP or 2000. The first demo version supports four users to race with each other in a local network environment. On the panel, finished distance and time, and rank data are shown with the aid of a map located the current position. System runs smoothly with nearly 15fps. See Figure 7.

Fig. 7. Player runs at the Imperial Palace

6   Conclusion and Future Work

E-Sport spreads all over the world in the past ten years, especially in China. More attentions have been paid on this field, not only government and companies, but also research institutes. Fitness-oriented E-Sports have a cheerful prospect. Integrating virtual reality and sport simulation techniques into fitness-oriented E-Sport offers users many functions, not only sport exercise and fun, but also education and meeting other people. This paper touches this area and introduces a general system framework to suit special requirements. Take VNM as example, five key factors are detail analyzed and some solutions are supplied at the same time. Implementation of the prototype system illustrates the feasibility and efficiency of our method.

There are many works should be done to improve the system. Image based modeling provides limited immersion. Maybe it is necessary to exploit the possibility of certain immersive device. Actions of avatar are not fully simulated the movement of users. VNM is expected to be involved into formal E-Sport and the system need validation at a larger scale.

Acknowledgements

All the authors would like to thank all the members of R&D Group of VNM in Beijing for their intelligent efforts. They are Weiwei Chen, Xian Chen, Wei Lu, Guozhen Li and Cuicui Song.

This research was funded by Key NSF Project on Digital Olympic Museum (Grant no: 60533080).

References

1. Zonghao Li, Jian Wang, Bai Li. Study on ConceptionCategory and Development Process of the E-sports. Journal of TJIPE. Vol.19, No.1, 2004, pp:1–3.
2. Peng Jia, Jiaxin Yao. E-sportsa cognitive game based on virtual reality. Journal of Wuhan Institute of Physical Education.Vol.39, No.1, 2005, pp:36–39.
3. http://www.ceg.net.cn/.
4. Wulf, V., Moritz, E. F., Henneke, C., et al. Computer supported collaborative sports: Creating social spaces filled with sports activities. In Proceedings of the Third International Conference on Educational Computing. LNCS, Springer, 2004. pp:80–89.
5. Mueller, F., Agamanolis, S. and Picard, R.. Exertion Interfaces: Sports Over a Distance for Social Bonding and Fun. Proceedings of CHI'03, Conference on Human factors in computing systems.USA, 2003, pp:561–568.
6. Jiaoying Shi, Zhigeng Pan. Virtual Reality:fundamental and practical algorithms. Scientific Publishers, Beijing, 2002.
7. Zhigeng Pan, Xiaohong Jiang, et al. Distributed Virtual Environment: An Overview, Journal of Software.Vol.11, No.4, 2000, pp:461–467.
8. Ji Qingge, Pan Zhigeng, Li Xiangchen. Overview of the Application of Virtual Reality in Sports Simulation. Journal of Computer-aided design & Computer Graphics. Vol.15, No.11, 2003, pp:1333–1338.
9. Zhigeng Pan,Weiwei Xu,et al. Easybowling:a small bowling machine based on virtual simulation.Computers & Graphics 27(2) 2003, pp: 231–238.
10. Mokka, S., Väätänen, A., Heinilä, J., and Välkkynen, P.. Fitness computer game with a bodily user interface. In Proceedings of the Second international Conference on Entertainment Computing. ACM International Conference Proceeding Series, vol.38,2003, pp:1-3.
11. Xia xinhua, Li Xiangchen, Pan Zhigeng. Bicycle Virtual Synthesized Training Simulation.Computer Simulation.Vol.22,No.4,2005, pp:290–293.
12. Liu Yusheng, Wu Zhaotong, et al. Mathematical model of size tolerance for plane based on mathematical definition. Chinese Journal of Mechanical Engineering. Vol.37, No.9, 2001, pp:12–17.
13. Milo Yip, Man Cheung, et al. Lucid3D Programmer Guide. Version 1.0. 2005.

Creating an Authentic Aural Experience in the Digital Songlines Game Engine: Part of a Contextualised Cultural Heritage Knowledge Toolkit

Craig Gibbons[1], Theodor G. Wyeld[2], Brett Leavy[3], and James Hills[4]

[1,2,3,4] Australian CRC for Interactiondesign, ACID, Australia
{Gibbons, Wyeld, Leavy, Hills} craig@acid.net.au
[2] IEP, ITEE, Queensland University, Queensland, Australia
{Wyeld} twyeld@itee.uq.au
[3] Cyberdreaming, Queensland, Australia
{Leavy} brett@cyberdreaming.com.au
[4] Silicon Graphic Incorporated, Queensland, Australia
{Hills} jamesh@sgi.com

Abstract. Digital Songlines is an Australasian CRC for Interaction Design (ACID) project that is developing protocols, methodologies and toolkits to facilitate the collection, education and sharing of indigenous cultural heritage knowledge. The project explores the areas of effective recording, content management and virtual reality delivery capabilities that are culturally sensitive and involve the indigenous custodians, leaders and communities in remote areas of the Australian 'outback'. It investigates how players in a serious gaming sense can experience Indigenous virtual heritage in a high fidelity fashion with culturally appropriate interface tools. This paper describes a 3D ambient audio quilt designed and implemented specifically for the Digital Songlines software, which is built using the Torque Game Engine. The audio quilt developed provides dynamic ambient fauna and flora sound effects to represent the varying audio environment of the landscape. This provides an authentic contextualised interesting aural experience that can be different each time a location is entered. This paper reports on completed and ongoing research in this area.

1 Introduction

The Australasian CRC for Interaction Design (ACID) is a collaborative research organisation formed with a number of universities and industry partners. The Virtual Heritage program is a research program under the auspices of the ACID organisation. The digital Songlines project within the Virtual Heritage program is developing protocols, methodologies and toolkits to facilitate the collection, education and sharing of indigenous cultural heritage knowledge across Australian communities, cultural institutions and commercial businesses [2, 3, 9].

The project objectives are to protect, preserve and promote Australian Indigenous culture, its practices, myths and legends, expanding and re-vitalizing a culture through the visualization of its most prized asset – the land. The project has developed the Digital Songlines software with a virtual landscape encapsulating cultural information, oral histories and mythological stories, based upon the eternal sense of land and

H. Zha et al. (Eds.): VSMM 2006, LNCS 4270, pp. 530–535, 2006.

spirituality understood by the Aboriginal people of Australia, where feeling, knowing and touching the country, kin and spirit can be experienced. Research to-date has focused on investigating how virtual worlds can capture the spirituality, culture and heritage of Indigenous people and impart these in an empathic way so that non-indigenous people throughout the world can understand the significance and cultural heritage of these areas.

Part of the emphasis on providing a simulated contextually accurate experience of indigenous knowledge is the need for an authentic aural experience within the virtual environment. This paper reports on a 3D ambient audio environment designed and implemented in the Torque Game Engine used in the Digital Songlines software. The audio environment attempts to simulate a dynamic aural environment that might be experienced in an Australian 'outback' landscape.

2   The Limitations of Current Ambient Audio Technology

Ambient audio in most current game engines is represented by either a location based looping soundtrack or by placing static 3D audio emitters around specific nodes of interactivity [1, 4, 5, 6, 13]. The design of a looping soundtrack needs to be careful considered so it appears as "dynamic" or randomised.sound, and not a loop [7, 8, 10, 11, 12]. For example, when moving through different terrains the user should notice a change in ambient sound levels; a wooded area should sound more alive with wildlife than a sparse terrain. Careful placement of 3D audio objects can significantly enhance the users experience with aural characteristic unique to each area (see figure 1).

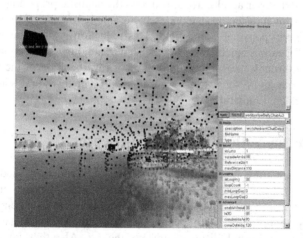

Fig. 1. 3D audio emitter in the Digital Songlines Torque Game Engine environment

3   Collecting Appropriate Audio Assets

By providing the user with multi-sensory awareness information – visual, aural, and tactile (interactive) – a believable landscape simulation experience can be achieved. With the importance of the audio aspect of this virtual landscape experience in mind, the ACID Indigenous Communities project team embarked upon the collection of a variety of authentic audio 'assets' to be used to aurally contextualise a culturally and place-specific 3D virtual environment. A number of locations were identified as suitable. The location reported here is in the remote north-east of Australia. In August of 2005, a field research trip was undertaken to western Carnarvon Gorge in Central Queensland, Australia. The purpose of this trip was to capture the visual and aural environment for incorporation into the Digital Songlines software environment.

3.1 Reflections on the Remote Site Visit: Carnarvon Gorge

As Carnarvon Gorge is a remote area it presented a different aural experience to the urban environment commonly experienced. Most notable was how astoundingly quiet the area is. Such was the extent of this void of sound that quiet sounds, normally obscured through aural masking and filtering, were much more audible. The sound of footsteps on the terrain type being traversed – grasses, leaves, or rocks – could be clearly differentiated with distinct audio differences. These footsteps were capable of dominating the listeners' audio environment during quiet periods of the day, and could be heard from some distance.

Due to the relative quietness, the acoustic horizon appeared to be much closer than in urban settings. Distant sounds could be heard with greater clarity and definition. For example, the human voice, under certain conditions, could be understood at distances of approximately half a kilometre.

This notion of a closer aural horizon is due to the acoustic properties of the aurally thinner air space in rural environments as there are significantly less audio sources within the listeners' personal sound field. This reduction in aural density results in distant sounds appearing much closer to the listener, although a perception of distance is still available through the subsequent density of reverberation of the audio source. This raises the question, "how to capture and represent this aural sensation in the Digital Songlines environment?"

4 Capturing an Authentic Aural Experience

It became apparent, after reviewing the aural landscape and many audio recordings and notes of the Carnarvon Gorge area, that a better audio mechanism was needed than the current looping ambient systems supported by most game engines in order to dynamically represent the aural landscape. We noted how dynamic the aural soundscape changed through different times of the day. Also that, upon returning to an area, even at the same time of day over a number of days, the soundscape seemed to have changed in a number of subtle, yet noticeable, ways – as birds moved, crickets started or stopped, and so on. With this in mind, a new method was developed utilising the existing Digital Songlines Engine (DSE) technology to create this dynamism.

4.1 Implementing a 3D Ambient Audio System in the DSE: Phase 1

To attempt to capture the aural sensations recorded at Carnarvon Gorge a system for dividing the virtual world space into a series of cells was used. This allowed specific actions to be performed in relation to an avatar's movement through the various cells.

The system developed uses a "checkerboard" quilt design methodology with cells monitoring an avatar's movement throughout the virtual landscape. Upon entering, each cell adjusts the surrounding cells' audio arrangements – both density and 3D location within constrained random variables. Audio files are randomly selected from a sound bank and used to aurally populate the surrounding cells. The type of audio assets used to populate surrounding cells is dependant on the time of day and any additional required parameters (see figure 2).

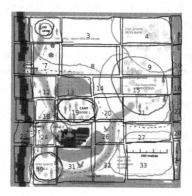

Fig. 2. Checkerboard quilt layout of region-specific audio cells

The first iteration of this system was evaluated within the project team. Not surprisingly, it proved to be better than what was previously used within the DSE (the looping ambient schema). However, once 3D models and characters were added to the scene, the overhead was too great, resulting in poor performance for both sound and graphical components. Also, difficulty with other animated models within the world, such as birds and non-player characters (such as a human or animal bot in the world that runs on AI and not controlled by a user) through the system triggering these squares. A solution needed to be found that would address these issues.

4.2 Implementing a 3D Ambient Audio System in the DSE: Phase 2

With the problem of the unacceptably high overhead caused by the first iteration of this system and the triggering action of other objects in the scene, a revised system was developed which leveraged the capacity of the DSE's bitMap code functionality. BitMap codes are usually used for the population of vegetation, specifically grasses, within the DSE world. For example, a bitMap code is used to analyse a prepared .png overlay on the map to determine what type of grass and level of density is needed to populate a specific region.

We used this semi-random assignment feature of the bitMap code using audio assets in place of models and textures. By implementing the bitMap code for audio, within a controlled radius of the client machine avatar, the ambient audio quilt could be "generated" in real time from a similarly pre-prepared .png overlay. No actual sound generation was taking effect, as every sound was sourced from the prepared sound bank. What was being generated was an algorithmically generated density, placed in a 3-axes coordinated system with a high level control achieved.

For example, we could place a group of frogs around a water source. We could control the density of sounds, yet the computer dealt with where to place the objects, which sound file to use (from the given sound bank), and randomly constrain their placement within the x y z axes.

The use of the bitMap code functionality reduced the overall overhead and made the DSE navigable again. With this implementation, the ambient audio system can be used for dealing with populations of large and small birds, crickets and frogs on the map, among other collections.

Moving around the map gives one the illusion of different aural soundscapes. When returning to a region, the density and placement of subsequent audio emitters may have changed due to the random nature of the algorithmic system, generating the desired different aural soundscapes.

The system is extendable to handle any additional audio materials, with unique density and placement logic for the algorithms to process and deal with. Combined with looping area effects (such as wind), DSE's Ambient Audio Quilt provides a more accurate aural representation of the landscape than existed under the standard TGE technology.

5   Conclusion

The latest iteration of the audio quilt provides for an authentic aural experience in the DSE. This forms a critical part of a highly contextualised cultural heritage knowledge toolkit. The importance of contextualising the stories gathered from the community elders is paramount in addressing the sensitivity of their telling. A key tenet of the project is to protect, preserve and promote Australian Indigenous culture, its practices, myths and legends, expanding and re-vitalizing its culture through visualization in a 3D virtual environment. As such, the audio quilt project helps contextualise the virtual landscape with an authentic soundscape where feeling, knowing, touching, and hearing the country, kin and spirit can be experienced.

Acknowledgements

This work is supported by ACID (the Australasian CRC for Interaction Design) established and supported under the Cooperative Research Centres Program through the Australian Government's Department of Education, Science and Training.

References

1. K.C. Finney, 3D Game Programming All in One, Premier Press, Boston MA, USA, 2004.
2. S. Gard, S. Bucolo, and T. G. Wyeld, "Capturing Australian Indigenous Perceptions of the Landscape: Virtual environments with cultural meanings," in proc. of, ALLC'06, July04-09, Paris, Sorbonne, 2006.
3. B. Leavy, J. Hills, C. Barker, S. Gard, and J. Carrol, "Digital Songlines: Digitising the Arts, Culture and Heritage Landscape of Aboriginal Australia", in proc. of VSMM2004, Ogaki, Japan, Nov 16-22, 2004.
4. G. W. Lecky-Thompson, Infinite Game Universe: Level Design, Terrain and Sound, Charles River Media Inc, Hingam Massachusetts, USA, 2002.
5. A. Marks, The Complete Guide to Game Audio: for Composers, Musicians, Sound Designers and Game Developers, CMP Books, Kansas, USA, 2001.
6. M. McCuskey, Beginning Game Audio Programming, Premier Press, Boston MA, USA, 2003.
7. K. Neil, "Adaptive Audio in Games", Keynote Address and in proc. of ACMC2005, QUT, July12-14, 2005.
8. R. Nordahl, S. Serafin, "Medialogy and Interactive Sound Design", in proc. of ACMC2005, QUT July12-14, 2005.
9. M. Pumpa, and T. G. Wyeld, "Database and Narratological Representation of Australian Aboriginal Knowledge as Information Visualisation using a Game Engine", in proc. of Information Visualisation 06, London, England Jul05 -07, 2006.
10. C. Roads, The Computer Music Tutorial, The MIT Press, Cambridge, Massachusetts, London England, 1996.
11. G.A. Sanger, The Fat Man on Game Audio: Tasty Morsels of Sonic Goodness, New Riders Publishing, USA, 2004.
12. R.M. Schafer, The Soundscape: our Sonic Environment and the Tuning of the World, Destiny Books, USA, 1994.
13. M. Wilde, Audio Programming for Interactive Games, Focal Press, NJ, 2004.

3D Interactive Computer Games as a Pedagogical Tool

In-Cheol Kim

Department of Computer Science, Kyonggi University
Suwon-si, Kyonggi-do, 442-760, South Korea
kic@kyonggi.ac.kr

Abstract. In this paper, we introduce UTBot, a virtual agent platform for teaching agent systems' design. UTBot implements a client for the Unreal Tournament game server and Gamebots system. It provides students with the basic functionality required to start developing their own intelligent virtual agents to play autonomously UT games. UTBot includes a generic agent architecture, CAA (Context-sensitive Agent Architecture), a domain-specific world model, a visualization tool, several basic strategies (represented by internal modes and internal behaviors), and skills (represented by external behaviors). The CAA architecture can support complex long-term behaviors as well as reactive short-term behaviors. It also realizes high context-sensitivity of behaviors. We also discuss our experience using UTBot as a pedagogical tool for teaching agent systems' design in undergraduate Artificial Intelligence course.

1 Introduction

Within the academic setting, pedagogical approaches are needed that provide opportunities for students to perform meaningful experimentation through which they can learn many of guiding principles of agent system development. Interactive computer games are known as one of killer applications for human-level AI [4]. They can provide the environments for research and education on the design of intelligent agent systems. Computer-controlled characters or Non-Player Characters (NPC) in these games are autonomous agents capable of playing without any human intervention. They integrate all the human-level capabilities such as real-time response, interaction with the environment, communication with teammates, planning their activities, learning from experiences, and common sense reasoning. The UTBot was designed to enable a project-based curricular component that facilitates the use of the Unreal Tournament game engine [2] and Gamebots system [1] in undergraduate Artificial Intelligence course. There are several aspects which make it difficult for beginner students to build their own intelligent virtual agent for the UT game and Gamebots system from scratch.

1. There is a large amount of low-level work that needs to be done before starting to develop sophisticated behaviors, for example, parsing the sensor input and creating a world map.

H. Zha et al. (Eds.): VSMM 2006, LNCS 4270, pp. 536–544, 2006.
© Springer-Verlag Berlin Heidelberg 2006

2. It is not easy for beginners to figure out what agent control architecture is appropriate for dynamic virtual environments.
3. Without any templates and sample behaviors, many undergraduate students can not undertake their project promptly.

The UTbot addresses these issues in an effort to provide an effective platform for teaching undergraduate students agent systems' design.

2 Computer Game Environment

Unreal Tournament (UT) is a category of video games known as first-person shooters, where all real time players exist in a 3D virtual world with simulated physics. Every player's senses are limited by their location, bearings, and occlusion within the virtual world. Fig. 1 shows a screenshot of the UT Domination game. The Gamebots [1] is a multi-agent system infrastructure derived from Unreal Tournament. The Gamebots allows UT characters to be controlled over client-server network connections by feeding sensory information to client agents and delivering action commands issued from client agents back to the game server.

Fig. 1. A Screenshot of the Unreal Tournament Game

In a dynamic virtual environment built on the Gamebots system and the UT game engine, agents must display human-level capabilities to play successfully, such as planning paths, learning a map of their 3D environment, using resources available to them, coordinating with takes their adversaries into account. Although the Gamebots system is a great platform for students to build their own intelligent virtual agent, a large amount of low-level work and behavioral complexity make it difficult for a beginner to finish this project in a three-month course.

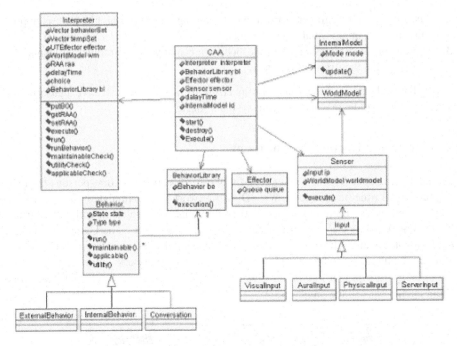

Fig. 2. UML Class Diagram of the CAA

3 Agent Architecture

In order to support students' development of their own agent for the UT and Game-bots environment, we provided them a generic agent architecture called CAA(Context-Sensitive Agent Architecture). Our CAA consists of (1) a world model; (2) an internal model; (3) a behavior library; (4) an interpreter; and (5) a set of sensors and effectors. Fig. 2 shows the UML class diagram of the CAA including these major components. The world model contains a set of objects representing current beliefs or facts about the world. The world model is defined as an abstract class to be implemented as a domain-specific world model for a certain kind of application. The world model is constantly updated upon the sensor information. On the other hand, the internal model contains a set of objects representing internal modes, or intentions. Each internal mode can be viewed as an implicit goal to be pursued. Depending on the changes of the world model, the internal model may be updated accordingly. Transitions between distinct internal modes can be modeled and designed as a finite-state machine. The behavior library contains a set of pre-defined behavior objects. The behavior class has three sub-classes: external behavior, internal behavior and conversational behavior. While external behaviors change the state of the environment through effectors, internal behaviors change the internal state – namely, the internal mode and parameters- without any change of the environment. Conversational behaviors can be used to communicate with other agents in a certain agent communication language or protocol. Conversational behaviors can be also viewed as a special kind of external behaviors.

The behavior class has five main member methods: applicable(), utility(), maintainable(), run(), and failure(). The applicable() method checks if the preconditions of a behavior can be satisfied against the world model and the internal model. The utility() method computes the relative utility of an applicable behavior by considering the current world model and internal model. Whenever multiple behaviors are applicable for a given situation, the highest-utility behavior is automatically selected and executed from them. The maintainable() method continually checks the context of a behavior throughout the execution of the behavior once it starts execution, to make sure that the behavior is still applicable to the intended situation. The run() method is the main body of a behavior. It gets called when the selected behavior starts execution. This method usually generates one or more atomic actions, sets some member variables, and returns. Finally, the failure() method is a procedural specification of what the agent should do when a plan fails. In the CAA, the life cycle of a behavior object consists of seven distinct states: create, waiting, executing, interrupt, fail, resume, and finish.

The interpreter controls the execution of the entire CAA system. Whenever there is new or changed information in the world model or internal model, the interpreter determines a set of applicable behaviors by calling the applicable() method of each behavior. From this set of applicable behaviors, it selects the highest-utility behavior by using the utility() methods. By invoking the run() method of the selected behavior, the interpreter starts the execution of the behavior. Once the selected behavior starts execution, the interpreter continually checks the behavior's context by calling the maintainable() method periodically. If the context of the behavior gets unsatisfied with either the current state of the world model or of the internal model, the interpreter immediately stops the execution of the behavior, and then replaces it with a new behavior appropriate to the changed situation.

Sensors periodically perceive the surrounding environment and update the world model. The input to sensors is divided into several sub-classes: visual input, aural input, physical input, and server input. Effectors execute the atomic actions requested by the run() method of the current external behavior and, as a result, affect the environment. Each sensor and effector has its own thread and work concurrently with the interpreter. An intelligent virtual agent based on the CAA can have multiple domain-specific sensors and effectors.

4 UTBot

The UTBot is a virtual agent platform which provides students with the basic functionality required to start developing their own intelligent virtual agents to play UT games. The UTBot includes the CAA agent architecture, a domain-specific world model, a visualization tool, several basic strategies (represented by internal modes and internal behaviors), and skills (represented by external behaviors).

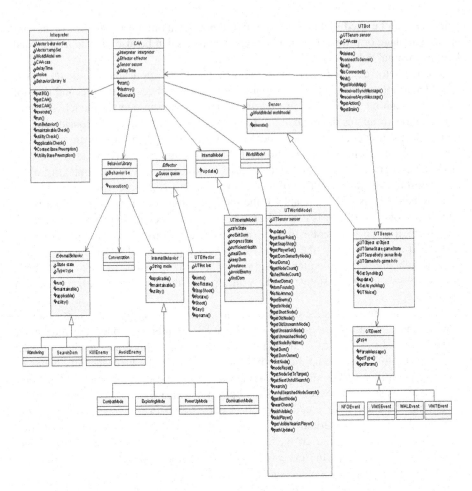

Fig. 3. UML Class Diagram of the UTBot

Fig. 3 shows the UML class diagram of the core components of the UTBot. This world model contains both static and dynamic information. Static information does not change during the course of a game. Static information includes, for example, the agent's name and ID, the team number, the number of team members, the maximum team score, and the address of the game server. In contrast, dynamic information continually changes during the game. Dynamic information includes, for example, the agent's position and direction, the health and skill information, the current weapons and armors, a partial world map, and the discovered domination points. The UT internal model contains an internal mode and the related parameters. There are five distinct internal modes: Explore, Dominate, Collect, Died, and Healed. The internal parameters such as the starting position and the target object may accompany one of the Explore, Dominate, and Collect modes.

Table 1. The Internal Modes and the Associated External Behaviors

Internal Modes	External Behaviors
Explore	MoveTo, Explore, Attack, Chase, Retreat
Dominate	MoveTo, Attack_Point, Defend_Point
Collect	MoveTo, Collect_Powerup, Collect_Weapon, Collect_Armor, Retreat, Attack
Died	No Behaviors
Healed	No Behaviors

The UTBot has several basic external behaviors such as Explore, Attack_Point, Defend_Point, Collect_Powerup, Collect_Weapon, Collect_Armor, Chase, Attack, Retreat, and MoveTo. The applicable() and maintainable() methods of each external behavior may contain conditions against the UT world model, the UT internal model, or both. However, most of applicable external behaviors of the UTBot are primarily categorized depending on the internal mode.

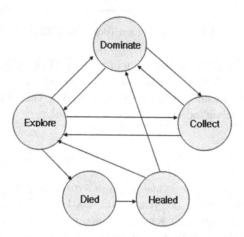

Fig. 4. An Example of Finite-State Automata (FSA) Representing Internal Mode Transitions

During the game, therefore, the set of applicable external behaviors is first restricted by the current internal mode of the agent. Table 1 lists available internal modes and the associated external behaviors. Although more than one external behavior is applicable at a certain internal mode, the utility values may be different among them. To transit from one internal mode to another, the UTBot has a set of internal behaviors such as ExploreToDominate, DominateToCollect, and CollectToDominate. This set of internal behaviors forms a unique strategy for determining the UTBot's external behaviors. Fig. 4 shows an example of Finite-State Automata (FSA) representing a certain set of internal modes and internal behaviors (possible transitions between them).

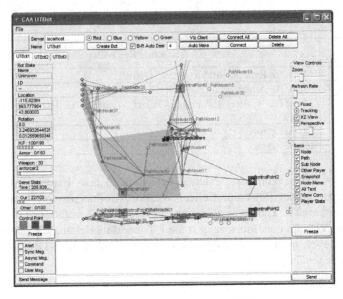

Fig. 5. Visualization Tool of the UTBot

Fig. 5 shows the unique visualization tool of the UTBot. With this tool, users can launch and destroy UTBots. Using this tool, users can also easily keep track of both the current state and executing behavior of each UTBot. Therefore this tool can help users to analyze and debug individual behaviors in detail.

5 Lessons

The author has taught an undergraduate class in Artificial Intelligence at the Kyonggi University three times during the years 2002, 2004-2005. On average, the class is attended by 40-50 students each semester. Since it is junior class in the Computer Science department, the students are assumed to be competent Java programmers and to have some background knowledge on distributed systems. However, there are no formal prerequisites for the class. The class has used as textbook *Artificial Intelligence: A New Synthesis* written by Nilsson. This textbook emphasizes so called agent-oriented approach to AI and deals with how to build intelligent agent systems. We believe that the difficulty in building intelligent agent systems can only be properly understood by actually building fairly complex systems. As such, our class uses a hands-on approach to teaching intelligent agent systems.

Our class has used the UT game engine and Gamebots system as an educational tool since the first time the class was taught. The use of UT and Gamebots has been very successful. The students are made to form teams of four to five students. The teams compete in a UT Domination tournament at the end of the semester. The students are given a month to complete their assignments after some period of practice. The grade for the project is determined by the team's standing in the tournament and the quality of their final report and presentation. The tournament format has proven to be a great motivator. Fig. 6 shows the scene of the final match in the tournament held in this year class.

Fig. 6. The Final Match of Tournament 2005

After the first class we learned that the basic Gamebots client offers so little functionality that students had to spend almost all their time trying to implement basic behaviors such as exploring the unknown environment and constructing a partial world map instead of focusing on the architectural and strategic aspects of agent design. In order to ease this burden we developed the UTBot system. The UTBot provides a generic agent architecture (CAA) and implements a basic player that maintains a world model and executes many useful behaviors such as exploring, attacking and defending a domination point, and collecting power-ups.

Our experience using the UTBot as a learning tool has been overwhelmingly positive. Its use allows students to directly experience the problems inherent in building intelligent agent systems. Even though a short time was given for undergraduate students to build an intelligent virtual agent, all of eleven teams have successfully completed their projects and were satisfied with the result. However, we are not entirely satisfied with our current UTBot implementation. It provides neither mechanism for coordinating team activities nor for self-learning from experiences. We are going to extend the UTBot by building up these additional functionalities for next year class.

6   Conclusions

We introduced UTBot, a virtual agent platform for teaching agent systems' design. The UTBot implements a client for the Unreal Tournament game server and Gamebots system. It provides students with the basic functionality required to start developing their own intelligent virtual agents to play autonomously UT games. Through our experience using the UTBot in undergraduate Artificial Intelligence class, we are sure that it is a very effective tool for teaching principles of agent system development.

References

1. Adobbati, R., Marshall, A.N., Scholer, A., Tejada, S., Kaminka, G.A., Schaffer, S., Sollitto, C.: GameBots: A 3D Virtual World Test Bed for Multiagent Research. Proceedings of the 2nd International Workshop on Infrastructure for Agents, MAS, and Scable MAS (2001)
2. Gertmann, J.: Unreal Tournament: Action game of the year. (1999)
3. José M. Vidal, Paul Buhler, and Hrishikesh Goradia: Tools and Lessons from a Multiagent Systems' Class. Italics, 4(3) (2005)
4. Laird, J.E. and van Lent, M.: Human-level AI's Killer Application: Interactive Games. AAAI Fall Symposium Technical report, North Falmouth, Massachusetts (2000) 80-97

Author Index

Lecture Notes in Computer Science

For information about Vols. 1–4147

please contact your bookseller or Springer

Vol. 4194: V.G. Ganzha, E.W. Mayr, E.V. Vorozhtsov (Eds.), Computer Algebra in Scientific Computing. XI, 313 pages. 2006.

Vol. 4193: T.P. Runarsson, H.-G. Beyer, E. Burke, J.J. Merelo-Guervós, L. D. Whitley, X. Yao (Eds.), Parallel Problem Solving from Nature - PPSN IX. XIX, 1061 pages. 2006.

Vol. 4192: B. Mohr, J.L. Träff, J. Worringen, J. Dongarra (Eds.), Recent Advances in Parallel Virtual Machine and Message Passing Interface. XVI, 414 pages. 2006.

Vol. 4191: R. Larsen, M. Nielsen, J. Sporring (Eds.), Medical Image Computing and Computer-Assisted Intervention – MICCAI 2006, Part II. XXXVIII, 981 pages. 2006.

Vol. 4190: R. Larsen, M. Nielsen, J. Sporring (Eds.), Medical Image Computing and Computer-Assisted Intervention – MICCAI 2006, Part I. XXXVVIII, 949 pages. 2006.

Vol. 4189: D. Gollmann, J. Meier, A. Sabelfeld (Eds.), Computer Security – ESORICS 2006. XI, 548 pages. 2006.

Vol. 4188: P. Sojka, I. Kopeček, K. Pala (Eds.), Text, Speech and Dialogue. XIV, 721 pages. 2006. (Sublibrary LNAI).

Vol. 4187: J.J. Alferes, J. Bailey, W. May, U. Schwertel (Eds.), Principles and Practice of Semantic Web Reasoning. XI, 277 pages. 2006.

Vol. 4186: C. Jesshope, C. Egan (Eds.), Advances in Computer Systems Architecture. XIV, 605 pages. 2006.

Vol. 4185: R. Mizoguchi, Z. Shi, F. Giunchiglia (Eds.), The Semantic Web – ASWC 2006. XX, 778 pages. 2006.

Vol. 4184: M. Bravetti, M. Núñez, G. Zavattaro (Eds.), Web Services and Formal Methods. X, 289 pages. 2006.

Vol. 4183: J. Euzenat, J. Domingue (Eds.), Artificial Intelligence: Methodology, Systems, and Applications. XIII, 291 pages. 2006. (Sublibrary LNAI).

Vol. 4182: H.T. Ng, M.-K. Leong, M.-Y. Kan, D. Ji (Eds.), Information Retrieval Technology. XVI, 684 pages. 2006.

Vol. 4180: M. Kohlhase, OMDoc – An Open Markup Format for Mathematical Documents [version 1.2]. XIX, 428 pages. 2006. (Sublibrary LNAI).

Vol. 4179: J. Blanc-Talon, W. Philips, D. Popescu, P. Scheunders (Eds.), Advanced Concepts for Intelligent Vision Systems. XXIV, 1224 pages. 2006.

Vol. 4178: A. Corradini, H. Ehrig, U. Montanari, L. Ribeiro, G. Rozenberg (Eds.), Graph Transformations. XII, 473 pages. 2006.

Vol. 4177: R. Marín, E. Onaindía, A. Bugarín, J. Santos (Eds.), Current Topics in Artificial Intelligence. XV, 482 pages. 2006. (Sublibrary LNAI).

Vol. 4176: S.K. Katsikas, J. Lopez, M. Backes, S. Gritzalis, B. Preneel (Eds.), Information Security. XIV, 548 pages. 2006.

Vol. 4175: P. Bücher, B.M.E. Moret (Eds.), Algorithms in Bioinformatics. XII, 402 pages. 2006. (Sublibrary LNBI).

Vol. 4174: K. Franke, K.-R. Müller, B. Nickolay, R. Schäfer (Eds.), Pattern Recognition. XX, 773 pages. 2006.

Vol. 4173: S. El Yacoubi, B. Chopard, S. Bandini (Eds.), Cellular Automata. XV, 734 pages. 2006.

Vol. 4172: J. Gonzalo, C. Thanos, M. F. Verdejo, R.C. Carrasco (Eds.), Research and Advanced Technology for Digital Libraries. XVII, 569 pages. 2006.

Vol. 4169: H.L. Bodlaender, M.A. Langston (Eds.), Parameterized and Exact Computation. XI, 279 pages. 2006.

Vol. 4168: Y. Azar, T. Erlebach (Eds.), Algorithms – ESA 2006. XVIII, 843 pages. 2006.

Vol. 4167: S. Dolev (Ed.), Distributed Computing. XV, 576 pages. 2006.

Vol. 4166: J. Górski (Ed.), Computer Safety, Reliability, and Security. XIV, 440 pages. 2006.

Vol. 4165: W. Jonker, M. Petković (Eds.), Secure, Data Management. X, 185 pages. 2006.

Vol. 4163: H. Bersini, J. Carneiro (Eds.), Artificial Immune Systems. XII, 460 pages. 2006.

Vol. 4162: R. Královič, P. Urzyczyn (Eds.), Mathematical Foundations of Computer Science 2006. XV, 814 pages. 2006.

Vol. 4161: R. Harper, M. Rauterberg, M. Combetto (Eds.), Entertainment Computing - ICEC 2006. XXVII, 417 pages. 2006.

Vol. 4160: M. Fisher, W.v.d. Hoek, B. Konev, A. Lisitsa (Eds.), Logics in Artificial Intelligence. XII, 516 pages. 2006. (Sublibrary LNAI).

Vol. 4159: J. Ma, H. Jin, L.T. Yang, J.J.-P. Tsai (Eds.), Ubiquitous Intelligence and Computing. XXII, 1190 pages. 2006.

Vol. 4158: L.T. Yang, H. Jin, J. Ma, T. Ungerer (Eds.), Autonomic and Trusted Computing. XIV, 613 pages. 2006.

Vol. 4156: S. Amer-Yahia, Z. Bellahsène, E. Hunt, R. Unland, J.X. Yu (Eds.), Database and XML Technologies. IX, 123 pages. 2006.

Vol. 4155: O. Stock, M. Schaerf (Eds.), Reasoning, Action and Interaction in AI Theories and Systems. XVIII, 343 pages. 2006. (Sublibrary LNAI).

Vol. 4154: Y.A. Dimitriadis, I. Zigurs, E. Gómez-Sánchez (Eds.), Groupware: Design, Implementation, and Use. XIV, 438 pages. 2006.

Vol. 4153: N. Zheng, X. Jiang, X. Lan (Eds.), Advances in Machine Vision, Image Processing, and Pattern Analysis. XIII, 506 pages. 2006.

Vol. 4152: Y. Manolopoulos, J. Pokorný, T. Sellis (Eds.), Advances in Databases and Information Systems. XV, 448 pages. 2006.

Vol. 4151: A. Iglesias, N. Takayama (Eds.), Mathematical Software - ICMS 2006. XVII, 452 pages. 2006.

Vol. 4150: M. Dorigo, L.M. Gambardella, M. Birattari, A. Martinoli, R. Poli, T. Stützle (Eds.), Ant Colony Optimization and Swarm Intelligence. XVI, 526 pages. 2006.

Vol. 4149: M. Klusch, M. Rovatsos, T.R. Payne (Eds.), Cooperative Information Agents X. XII, 477 pages. 2006. (Sublibrary LNAI).

Vol. 4148: J. Vounckx, N. Azemard, P. Maurine (Eds.), Integrated Circuit and System Design. XVI, 677 pages. 2006.